ECONOMICS OF STRATEGY

6th Edition

International Student Version

David Besanko / *Northwestern University*

David Dranove / *Northwestern University*

Mark Shanley / *University of Illinois at Chicago*

Scott Schaefer / *University of Utah*

PREFACE

A lot has happened to the business landscape in the 20 years since my colleagues and I began teaching business strategy at the Kellogg School of Management. Several years of steady but unspectacular economic growth culminated with the dot-com bubble and a subsequent global recession. A broad-based recovery enabled many firms in both the "old" and "new" economies to enjoy unprecedented profitability, only to see profits dry up in the wake of a credit crunch and rising energy costs. The global economy now seems on hold, as nations deal with long-term structural budget issues.

Through it all, the strategy gurus have been quick to remind us that "the rules of business have changed."[1] The French have an apt rejoinder: Plus ça change, plus c'est la même chose. (The more things change, the more they stay the same.) Consider the fate of managers and investors who followed the latest fads of the last decade without paying attention to tried and true economic concepts. Dot-com businesses sold identical products (pet food, toys, you name it) and discovered the perils of perfect competition. Movie studios followed the mantra of convergence, creating entertainment supergiants that failed to overcome the risks of extensive vertical integration. Banks ignored basic economic principles of asymmetric information and loaned billions of dollars to home buyers who could not repay them.

These catastrophic mistakes confirm an important pedagogical message: there is a set of business principles that apply at all times to all sectors of the economy. Sound strategic management requires mastery of these principles, not blind adherence to the "strategy du jour." Managers who ignore these principles do so at their own peril.

By their nature, principles are enduring. But they are not always well understood and, as a result, managers often fail to adhere to them. Michael Porter's classic treatment of the principles of competition, *Competitive Strategy*, published until 1980, addressed this problem. Porter's book provided an important illustration of how economic reasoning can inform practicing managers, particularly with regard to strategies for dealing with a firm's external environment. But *Competitive Strategy* is not a textbook and does not provide the kind of economic foundation that we believe is required for deep strategic thinking.

David Besanko, Mark Shanley, and I joined Kellogg in 1991, where we were immediately charged by Dean Donald Jacobs with revitalizing the strategy curriculum. (Scott Shaeffer joined Kellogg shortly afterward and joined the *Economics of Strategy* writing team for the third edition.) We searched for a textbook that might provide a broader and deeper economic foundation for strategic analysis. What we found was at first discouraging. Most of the available texts in strategic management lacked disciplinary grounding. Few contained serious discussions of economics principles that are essential to strategy, such as economies of scale, transactions-cost economics, oligopoly theory, entry, commitment, incentives for innovation, and agency. Moreover, most of these books were targeted at more general audiences than what one finds at a business school such as Kellogg. We also learned that we were not the only ones struggling to find an appropriate text for teaching business strategy. Indeed, the choice of a text for the core strategy course appeared to be problematic at many business schools.

Seeking to expand on Porter's contributions to taking an economics-based approach to teaching strategy, we considered possible solutions. One possibility was to use a microeconomics text, which offers many real-world examples to demonstrate the practical importance of economics. But this represents at best a compromise between traditional microeconomics and management strategy.

In the years preceding our work on the first edition of *Economics of Strategy*, two important books appeared. Sharon Oster's *Modern Competitive Analysis* was remarkable for its breadth, covering most of the topics that we had identified as important to teach in a management strategy class. Paul Milgrom and John Roberts's *Economics, Organization, and Management* was remarkable for its depth. Milgrom and Roberts provided a deep theoretical basis for understanding issues involving organization, incentives, and hierarchy. Our objective in writing *Economics of Strategy* was, in part, to capture the breadth of Oster at a level of analysis approaching Milgrom and Roberts, while offering the kinds of illustrative examples that appear in both books.

ORGANIZATION OF THE BOOK

In preparing to write the sixth edition, I heard from many instructors that they preferred the organization of editions one through four. The sixth edition therefore reverts to form. Part One focuses on the boundaries of the firm; Part Two explores competition; Part Three covers positioning and sustaining advantage; and Part Four examines the interface between the theory of the firm, organization design, and business strategy. Despite these surface similarities to earlier editions, the sixth edition represents the most substantial revision to date, with many substantial changes including the following:

- Several chapters have been consolidated. Economies of Scale and Diversification are now combined in a single chapter. This reflects the logical connections between the two topics. Commitment and Dynamics of Competition have been consolidated into a single chapter titled "Dynamics: Competing Across Time." This chapter builds on static oligopoly models to explore the many ways that firms compete across time, including an expanded discussion of how industry structures evolve across time. Finally, I have combined the chapters on Sustaining Advantage and The Origins of Competitive Advantage, again reflecting the strong logical connections between the two.

- The chapter on Positioning has been dramatically streamlined.

- I have added a new chapter on Information and Value Creation. Heretofore, strategy books have emphasized that firms must differentiate themselves to thrive. But there has been little discussion of how firms inform consumers about their points of differentiation. This chapter describes how firms, markets, and certifiers disclose information about product attributes. This material helps explain the success of Google, Facebook, and many Internet businesses.

- I expand on many important theoretical ideas and introduce some new ones. Readers will find detailed treatment of the Property Rights Theory of the Firm, Business Groups, Dynamic Learning Models, Endogenous Sunk Costs, Rent-Seeking Behavior, Disruptive Technologies, and other topics.

As always, the book is liberally interspersed with real-world examples that bring the economic models to life. The examples are drawn from around the world and cover business practice from the eighteenth century to the present day. I have updated examples as needed and added many new examples including several that discuss business in China and India. I am especially grateful to doctoral student Bingyang Li for developing the China examples. The business world is ever changing, and by the time you read this book, some references to organizations and individuals will be obsolete. I hope that the lessons learned from them will endure.

My colleagues and I believe that this book can be used as a text either in a core strategy course or in a business economics course that focuses on the economics of industry and the economics of the firm. In our 10-week strategy course for first-year MBA students at Kellogg, we typically assign the following chapters:

Primer	Basic Principles
Chapter 2	The Horizontal Boundaries of the Firm
Chapter 3	The Vertical Boundaries of the Firm
Chapter 8	Industry Analysis
Chapter 9	Strategic Positioning for Competitive Advantage
Chapter 11	Sustaining Competitive Advantage

If we had an entire semester for our strategy course, we would add Chapter 5 (Competitors and Competition), Chapter 10 (Information and Value Creation), and Chapter 12 (Performance Measurement and Incentives). A more organizations-focused course might replace Chapters 5 and 10 with Chapters 13 (Strategy and Structure) and/or 14 (Environment, Power, and Culture).

The placement of the boundaries of the firm chapters (1–4) before the strategy chapters (9–11) may strike some as atypical. However, it is not at all essential that instructors follow this ordering. As long as students understand the material in the Economics Primer and the material on economies of scale and scope in Chapter 2, the strategy chapters can be taught before the chapters on the boundaries of the firm.

Chapters 6 and 7 are the most "game theoretic" of the chapters in the book and are the most demanding for students with weaker economic backgrounds (though the introduction to game theory in the Economics Primer coupled with material in Chapter 5 should be sufficient for students to understand this material). Because students in our basic strategy course at Kellogg have not yet taken economics, we do not cover these chapters until the advanced class in Competitive Strategy. The material in Chapters 12 and beyond does not depend on the material in Chapters 9–11, so these chapters can be easily skipped without any loss in continuity.

The book can also be used in a managerial economics course that emphasizes competitive strategy and modern industrial organization. For a one-quarter course, we recommend use of these chapters:

Primer	Basic Principles
Chapter 2	The Horizontal Boundaries of the Firm
Chapter 3	The Vertical Boundaries of the Firm
Chapter 5	Competitors and Competition
Chapter 6	Entry and Exit
Chapter 7	Dynamics: Competing Across Time
Chapter 8	Industry Analysis
Chapter 9	Strategic Positioning for Competitive Advantage
Chapter 11	Sustaining Competitive Advantage

For a one-semester course, one could add Chapters 4 and 10.

SUPPLEMENTARY MATERIALS

Companion Web Site

A companion web site specific for this text contains the resources found here and more. www.wiley.com/college/besanko

Extra Case Studies

Designed for instructors teaching outside of the US, there are additional case materials on the website, including short cases on the Danish Mobile Phone Market, Excess Supply in the European Car Market, and Capacity Competition in the Container-Shipping Industry. Longer cases include Easygroup, Amazon and Petrol Retailing in the UK Market.

Instructor's Manual

The Instructor's Manual provides several valuable resources that enhance each chapter of the text, including a list of the chapter contents, a chapter summary, approaches to teaching the chapter, suggested Harvard Business School Case Studies that complement the chapter, Suggested extra related readings, and answers to all of the end-of-chapter questions.

PowerPoint Presentations

PowerPoint Slides including text art and lecture outlines for each chapter are provided on the companion web site and can be viewed or downloaded to a computer.

Test Bank

Sample tests for each chapter contain a mix of multiple-choice questions varying in level of difficulty.

ACKNOWLEDGMENTS

Many individuals helped make the sixth edition of *Economics of Strategy* possible. We are especially grateful to Jennifer Manias and Emily McGee of Wiley for the substantial work they did in coordinating the development of the book. We want to also thank Suzanne Ingrao of Ingrao Associates for so ably keeping the production of this book on track. And a special thanks to Angie Malakhov for preparing the "Businesses in the Book."

Many of the improvements in the sixth edition are the result of comments received by instructors who used previous editions. My thanks to colleagues who so kindly pointed out the problem areas and suggested ways to improve them. I am also grateful for the comments we received from those who reviewed the book, including Jed DeVaro, California State University, East Bay; Stephan F. Gohmann, University of Louisville; Richard R. Hawkins, University of West Florida; Christine P. Ries, Georgia Tech; Matthew Roelofs, Western Washington University; and, Frank C. Schultz II, University of California, Berkeley. I was pleased by the many substantive suggestions they offered for a book that has already been through five editions.

David Dranove
Evanston, Illinois

ENDNOTE

[1] A Google search of "the rules have changed" comes up with hundreds of business-related hits. I conduct a similar search for every edition and always discover a multitude of hits. I wonder how they can be called rules if they are constantly changing.

BRIEF CONTENTS

CONTENTS

PART FOUR: INTERNAL ORGANIZATION 399

INTRODUCTION: STRATEGY AND ECONOMICS

WHY STUDY STRATEGY?

To answer this question, we first have to understand what strategy is. Consider how three leading contributors to the field define the concept of strategy:

> . . . the determination of the basic long-term goals and objectives of an enterprise, and the adoption of courses of action and the allocation of resources necessary for carrying out these goals—Alfred Chandler[1]
> . . . the pattern of objectives, purposes or goals, and the major policies and plans for achieving these goals, stated in such a way as to define what business the company is in or should be in and the kind of company it is or should be—Kenneth Andrews[2]
> . . . what determines the framework of a firm's business activities and provides guidelines for coordinating activities so that the firm can cope with and influence the changing environment. Strategy articulates the firm's preferred environment and the type of organization it is striving to become—Hiroyuki Itami[3]

These definitions have much in common. Phrases such as "long-term goals" and "major policies" suggest that strategy has to do with the "big" decisions a business organization faces, the decisions that ultimately determine its success or failure. The emphasis on "pattern of objectives" and "the framework of a firm's business" suggests that strategy is revealed in terms of consistent behavior, which in turn implies that strategy, once set, is not easy to reverse. Finally, the idea that strategy "defines . . . what kind of company it is or should be" suggests that strategic decisions shape the firm's competitive persona, its collective understanding of how it is going to succeed within its competitive environment.

Strategy is, in short, fundamental to an organization's success, which is why the study of strategy can be both profitable and intellectually engaging. The objective of this book is to study and analyze strategy primarily (though not exclusively) from the perspective of economics. Our central theme is that much can be learned by uncovering durable economic principles that are applicable to many different strategic situations. This value shows up in two fundamental ways: one, by gaining a better understanding of how firms compete and organize themselves, and two, by developing a more secure foundation for making good strategic decisions.

WHY ECONOMICS?

One can approach the study of strategy in many ways. One could study strategy from the perspective of mathematical game theory, seeking to discover the logic of choice in situations that involve rivalry. Strategy could also be studied from the perspective of psychology, focusing on how the motivations and behaviors of individual decision makers shape the direction and the performance of their organizations. One could study strategy-related questions from an organizational perspective, political science, or even anthropology.

There is much to be said for viewing strategy from the perspective of multiple disciplinary lenses. But depth of strategic knowledge is as important as breadth. Deep knowledge of a discipline permits the formulation of subtle and powerful hypotheses that generate rich strategies. An advantage of economics, and one reason for its widespread use for analyzing individual and institutional decision making, is that it requires the analyst to be explicit about the key elements of the process under consideration. Economic models must carefully identify each of the following:

- *Decision makers.* Who are the active players? Whose decisions are "fixed" in the situation at hand?

- *Goals.* What are the decision makers trying to accomplish? Are they profit maximizing, or do they have nonpecuniary interests?

- *Choices.* What actions are under consideration? What are the strategic variables? What is the time horizon over which decisions can be made?

- *Relationship between choices and outcomes.* What is the mechanism by which specific decisions translate into specific outcomes? Is the mechanism complicated by uncertainty regarding such factors as taste, technology, or the choices of other decision makers?

While other social sciences often address the same questions, economic theory is distinctive, we think, in that the answers to these questions are nearly always explicitly obtained as part of the development of the theory. The advantage to this is that there is clear linkage between the conclusions one draws from the application of economic reasoning and the assumptions used to motivate the analysis. This leaves what Garth Saloner has called an "audit trail" that allows one to distinguish between logically derived propositions and unsupported conjectures.[4] We will not provide the detailed audit trails that support our propositions, as this will require countless pages and advanced mathematics. But we will provide the intuition behind each of the propositions that we advance.

Economic modeling, by its very nature, abstracts from the situational complexity that individuals and firms face. Thus, the application of economic insights to specific situations often requires creativity and a deft touch. It also often requires explicit recognition of the constraints imposed on firms by mistakes, history, and organizational and political factors. Nor does economics fully address the *process* by which choices are made and translated into actions and outcomes. The process of managing the implementation of a competitive strategy decision or a change in the nature of internal organization is often fundamental to a firm's success. Our emphasis on economics in this book is not intended to downgrade the importance of process; it is simply beyond the scope of our expertise to say much about it.

The Need for Principles

There is an understandably keen interest among serious observers of business to understand the reasons for profitability and market success. Observers of business often leap uncritically to the conclusion that the keys to success can be identified by watching and imitating the behaviors of successful firms. A host of management prescriptions by consultants and in the popular business press are buttressed by allusions to the practices of high-performing firms and their managers.

A classic example of this type of analysis is provided by the famous 1982 book, *In Search of Excellence*, by Thomas Peters and Robert Waterman.[5] Peters and Waterman studied a group of 43 firms that were identified as long-term superior performers on dimensions such as profitability and growth. The study concluded that successful firms shared common qualities, including "close to the customer," "stick to the knitting," and "bias for action."

Another famous example is provided by *The New Market Leaders*, by Fred Wiersema.[6] Wiersema identified the behaviors of leading firms in the "new economy," with a focus on Internet, technology, and telecom firms. The average annual return for investors in these firms was 48 percent. In explaining their success, Wiersema's findings mirror those of Peters and Waterman. New market leaders are close to their customers and skilled at segmenting markets. They develop new products, advertise intensively, and outsource all but core activities, so as to better concentrate on what they do best.

A final seminal work is *Good to Great*, by Jim Collins.[7] Collins studied the characteristics of firms that broke a long pattern of good (above-average) performance and entered into a 15-year period of great performance (cumulative stock return three times that of the general market). Only 11 firms met this demanding hurdle, including such well-known firms as Walgreens, Wells Fargo, Philip Morris, and Abbott. Collins finds several characteristics that help explain his group's performance. These firms possess leaders who shun the spotlight and work for the firm. Performance shifts at these firms begin with management staffing, so that the "right" people are put in place. The firms use technology to support their strategies, not determine them. Managers at these firms can "confront the brutal facts" of their situation and determine what to do about it.

So What's the Problem?

The traditional approach to strategy, one that is embodied in best-selling strategy trade books including the three classic books cited above, has at least two key features. First, these books derive their recommendations by studying the past performance of successful firms. Second, their recommendations seem to make sense. Who wouldn't strive to "put the right people in the right places," or have a "bias toward action." Let us address the latter feature first; the former will require a bit more time.

Popularizers of business strategy are persuasive arguers, often relying on "proof by assertion." Armed with doctoral degrees and academic titles, they make assertions that carry substantial gravitas. When these assertions also carry the weight of common sense, it would be foolish for the average manager to ignore them. But in the book *Everything Is Obvious*, Duncan Watts warns against basing decisions on common-sense arguments. Watts gives the example of strategy guru Malcolm Gladwell, who claimed that "social epidemics are launched by a few *exceptional* people who possess the ability to make ideas go viral." This argument, which was based on observational studies of a few successful firms, makes so much sense that readers take it as a proven fact. As a result, firms commonly pay a handful of "heavy influencers" substantial fees to push new products through social networks. The problem is that Gladwell's observational studies do not stand up to rigorous scrutiny. Watts's research finds that *unexceptional* people can effectively exert social influence. It might therefore be less costly to pay small amounts to thousands of "ordinary Twitter" users than a small fortune to one or two exceptional influencers.

Watts shows that obvious arguments—for example, "put the right people in the right places"—are not always correct and that "proof by assertion" is no proof at all. While many of the ideas in *Economics of Strategy* may seem obvious upon reflection, they are supported by more than just the assertions of the authors or a few casual observational studies. Our ideas were developed from fundamental principles of economic theory and debated by the profession, often for decades. This provides the arguments with an "audit trail" through which it is possible to explore the exact set of assumptions that lead to the conclusions. Moreover, most of the ideas in this book have been subject to rigorous empirical testing that has survived peer review. (Most trade books do not undergo such scrutiny.)

Most trade strategy books do not provide an audit trail of assumptions and conclusions, but they seem to offer empirical support through extensive case studies. We believe that using a given firm's experiences to understand what would make all firms successful is extremely difficult and not likely to lead to valid conclusions. For one thing, the reasons for success are often unclear and also are likely to be complex. We can think of no better example than Enron. Enron was once held up as an exemplar of how to conduct business in the new economy, but was ultimately revealed to be a company that relied on accounting shell games and lacked any real sustainable advantage. There are many other, less pernicious, examples of this complexity. The internal management systems of a firm may spur product innovation particularly well but may not be apparent to individuals who are unfamiliar with how the firm operates. In addition, the industry and market conditions in which successful firms operate may differ greatly from the conditions faced by would-be imitators. Success may also be due in part to a host of idiosyncratic factors that will be difficult to identify and impossible to imitate.

Finally, there may be a bias resulting from trying to understand success solely by examining the strategies of successful firms. Strategies associated with many successful firms may have been tried by an equally large number of unsuccessful firms. In addition, successful firms may pursue several strategies, only some of which contribute toward their success. Finally, successful firms may possess proprietary assets and know-how that allow them to succeed where imitators would fail. Under any of these conditions, a "monkey see, monkey do" strategy offers no guarantee of success.

To further understand the potential bias, consider that the choices of successful firms always seem correct in *hindsight*. But managers want to determine which strategic choices will work in *advance*. To appreciate the distinction, consider a firm investing in a risky new technology. If it is fortunate enough to select the correct technology, then the firm will succeed and the technology will appear to "support its strategy," a good thing according to strategy gurus. But if it chooses incorrectly, the firm will struggle. The gurus will say that the firm is struggling because it has let technology determine its strategy. But the real mistake was in selecting the wrong technology to begin with, not its ongoing application. In fact, economics teaches us that it may still be optimal to stick with the chosen technology, especially if the costs cannot be recovered and the firm has no better alternative. "Monkey see, monkey do" strategizing ignores these important nuances.

Managers cannot wait until after the fact to determine what technologies to adopt, which employees to hire, or which customers to cultivate. This is what makes managerial work risky. We do believe that it is useful to study the behaviors of firms. The value of this study, however, lies in helping us identify the general principles behind why firms behave as they do, not in trying to develop lists of characteristics that lead to automatic success. *There is no such list.* A strategy textbook can provide the general principles that underlie strategic decisions. Success depends on the manager who must match principles with conditions.

To see this point, consider the variety of strategies employed by some of today's most successful firms: Trek, Usiminas, and Wal-Mart.[8] Each of them has a different organizational structure and corporate strategy. Trek's success is built largely on low-cost outsourcing of bicycle production and careful brand management. Trek performs few of the functions traditionally associated with large industrial firms and instead uses independent contractors for much of its production, distribution, and retailing. Usiminas is a traditional, vertically integrated steel firm best known for its operational excellence in manufacturing. That excellence, coupled with its access to Brazil's low-cost labor and abundant energy supplies, has made Usiminas one of the lowest-cost producers of steel in the world. Unlike the first two, Wal-Mart is a distributor and retailer. It relies on the initiative of its local store managers, combined with sophisticated purchasing and inventory management, to keep its retailing costs below those of its rivals.

Making sense of this variety of strategies can be frustrating, especially because, within most industries, we see poorly performing firms employing the same strategies and management practices as industry exemplars. For every Trek, there is a Raleigh. For every Usiminas, there is a Bethlehem Steel. For every Wal-Mart, there is a Kmart. If we find this variety of management practices bewildering, imagine the reactions of a manager from 1910, or even 1960, who was transported ahead in time. The large hierarchical firm that dominated the corporate landscape throughout most of the twentieth century seems out of place today. General Motors received its share of criticism in the wake of the oil shortages and Japanese invasion of the 1970s, but its structure and strategy were models for manufacturing from the 1920s through the 1960s. United States Steel, the first firm in the world to achieve annual sales of one billion dollars at the time of its inception in 1901, is no longer ranked among the Fortune 100 and has struggled to make money in recent years. The list of once-admired firms that today are struggling to survive is a long one.

There are two ways to interpret this bewildering variety and evolution of management practice. The first is to believe that the development of successful strategies is so complicated as to be essentially a matter of luck. The second interpretation presumes that successful firms succeeded because the strategies best allowed them to exploit the potential profit opportunities that existed at the time or to adapt to changing circumstances. If you are reading this book, then it is likely that you (or your professor) believe in this second interpretation. We certainly do. While there is no doubt that luck, both good and bad, plays a role in determining the success of firms, we believe that success is often no accident. We believe that we can better understand why firms succeed or fail when we analyze decision making in terms of consistent principles of market economics and strategic action. And we believe that the odds of competitive success increase when managers try to apply these principles to the varying conditions and opportunities they face. While these principles do not uniquely explain why firms succeed, they should be the basis for any systematic examination of strategy.

Because this is an *economics* book, we will necessarily gloss over (if not completely ignore) some possible paths to profitability. We will not discuss how firms can improve manufacturing techniques or reduce inventory costs. We will mention advertising only insomuch as it touches other topics that are of direct interest to strategy, such as entry deterrence. We examine accounting mainly to point out that costs and profits reported on accounting statements are often poor measures of economic performance. We give short shrift to leadership and team building, not because these are unimportant, but because economics has little to say about them.

FIRMS OR MARKETS?

Some books, including Porter's *Competitive Strategy*, take the view that firms can prosper if their industries avoid grueling competitive forces. Others, including Gary Hamel and C. K. Prahalad's *Competing for the Future*, pay little regard to market competition and argue instead that successful firms get that way by outperforming their rivals. Our view is that the economics of the firm's market and the firm's position in that market jointly determine the firm's profitability. But how would we determine which is more important?

To answer this question, imagine taking a broad sample of different firms over many years. Would we see persistent variation in profitability of firms *within industries* but little variation in profitability *across industries*? If so, we would conclude that the effect of the market environment on profitability (the market effect) is unimportant, but the effect of a firm's competitive position in the industry (the positioning effect) is important. Or would we see little variation in profitability of firms within industries but persistent variation in profitability of entire industries? If so, the market effect is paramount, and the positioning effect is unimportant.

In fact, research suggests that the profitability varies both within and across industries, and that within-industry variability is a bit bigger than across-industry variability. In other words, firms matter and markets matter, though perhaps firms matter a bit more. Note also that a large component of the variation in profitability across firms is not persistent over time. Turnover of key management personnel, or a failed product launch, new regulations, or just plain luck could cause temporary swings in profitability.

We believe that the successful strategist must master principles associated with both market competition and positioning and that this motivates the framework for strategy that we provide in this book.

A FRAMEWORK FOR STRATEGY

In our opening discussion of what strategy is, we asserted that strategy is concerned with the "big" issues that firms face. But what specifically does this mean? What are these "big" issues? Put another way, to formulate and implement a successful strategy, what does the firm have to pay attention to? We would argue that to successfully formulate and implement strategy, a firm must confront four broad classes of issues:

- *Boundaries of the firm.* What should the firm do, how large should it be, and what businesses should it be in?

- *Market and competitive analysis.* What is the nature of the markets in which the firm competes and the nature of competitive interactions among firms in those markets?

- *Positioning and dynamics.* How should the firm position itself to compete, what should be the basis of its competitive advantage, and how should it adjust over time?

- *Internal organization.* How should the firm organize its structure and systems internally?

Boundaries of the Firm

The firm's boundaries define what the firm does. Boundaries can extend in three different directions: horizontal, vertical, and corporate. The firm's horizontal boundaries refer to how much of the product market the firm serves, or essentially how big it is. The firm's vertical boundaries refer to the set of activities that the firm performs itself and those that it purchases from market specialty firms. The firm's corporate boundaries refer to the set of distinct businesses the firm competes in. All three boundaries have received differing amounts of emphasis at different times in the strategy literature. The Boston Consulting Group's emphasis on the learning curve and market growth in the 1960s gave prominence to the firm's horizontal boundaries. Formal planning models organized around tools, such as growth-share matrices, gave prominence to the firm's corporate boundaries. More recently, such concepts as "network organizations" and the "virtual corporation" have given prominence to the firm's vertical boundaries. Our view is that all are important and can be fruitfully analyzed through the perspectives offered by economics.

Market and Competitive Analysis

To formulate and execute successful strategies, firms must understand the nature of the markets in which they compete. As Michael Porter points out in his classic work *Competitive Strategy*, performance across industries is not a matter of chance or accident.[9] There are reasons why, for example, even mediocre firms in an industry such as pharmaceuticals have, by economywide standards, impressive profitability performance, while the top firms in the airline industry seem to achieve low rates of profitability even in the best of times. The nature of industry structure cannot be ignored either in attempting to understand why firms follow the strategies they do or in attempting to formulate strategies for competing in an industry.

Positioning and Dynamics

Positioning and dynamics are shorthand for how and on what basis a firm competes. Position is a static concept. At a given moment in time, is the firm competing on the basis of low costs or because it is differentiated in key dimensions and can thus charge a premium price? Position, as we discuss it, also concerns the resources and capabilities that underlie any cost or differentiation advantages that a firm might have. Dynamics refers to how the firm accumulates resources and capabilities, as well as to how it adjusts over time to changing circumstances. Fundamentally, dynamics has to do with the process emphasized by the economist Joseph Schumpeter, who argued that "the impulse of alluring profit," even though inherently temporary, will induce firms and entrepreneurs to create new bases of competitive advantage that redefine industries and undermine the ways of achieving advantage.

Internal Organization

Given that the firm has chosen what to do and has figured out the nature of its market, so that it can decide how and on what basis it should compete, it still needs to organize itself internally to carry out its strategies. Organization sets the terms by which resources will be deployed and information will flow through the firm. It will also determine how well aligned the goals of individual actors within the firm are with the overall goals of the firm. How the firm organizes itself—for example, how it structures its organization, the extent to which it relies on formal incentive systems as opposed to informal influences—embodies a key set of strategic decisions in their own right.

THE BOOK

This book is organized along the lines of this framework. Part One explores firm boundaries; Part Two deals with competition; Part Three addresses positioning; and Part Four examines internal organization.

The principles that we present should prove useful to managers across a wide range of business conditions and situations. They will clearly benefit managers trying to improve results that have been below expectations. Managers often can make immediate improvements in performance by better matching their firm's strategy to the demands of the business environment. Learning about principles, however, can also benefit managers of the most successful firms. As most managers should know, conditions change over time and industry contexts evolve. Strategies that are appropriate for today's business environment may evolve into arrangements that are inappropriate and out of touch with competitive conditions. Sometimes conditions that influence the business environment change gradually, as with the growth of suburban areas in the United States after 1950. Sometimes changes come more quickly, such as with the rapid improvements in communications, information processing, and networking technology during the 1990s. Some changes with major business repercussions seem to occur overnight, as with the privatization of businesses in Eastern Europe and the former Soviet Union after 1989 or the credit crisis of 2008. Armed with some general principles, however, the manager will be better prepared to adjust his or her firm's business strategy to the demands of its ever-changing environment and will have less need to rely on good luck.

ENDNOTES

[1]Chandler, A., *Strategy and Structure: Chapters in the History of the American Industrial Enterprise*, Cambridge, MA, MIT Press, 1962, p. 13.

[2]Andrews, K., *The Concept of Corporate Strategy*, Homewood, IL, Irwin, 1971.

[3]Itami, H., *Mobilizing Invisible Assets*, Cambridge, MA, Harvard University Press, 1987.

[4]Saloner, G., "Modeling, Game Theory, and Strategic Management," *Strategic Management Journal*, 12, Winter 1991, pp. 119–136.

[5]Peters, T. J. and R. H. Waterman, *In Search of Excellence*, New York, Harper and Row, 1982.

[6]Wiersema, F., *The New Market Leaders*, New York, Free Press, 2001.

[7]Collins, J. C., *Good to Great*, New York, Harper Business, 2001.

[8]The full name of Usiminas is Usinas Siderurgicas de Minas Gerais.

[9]Porter, M., *Competitive Strategy*, New York, Free Press, 1980.

ECONOMICS PRIMER: BASIC PRINCIPLES

I n 1931 conditions at the Pepsi-Cola Company were desperate.[1] The company had entered bankruptcy for the second time in 12 years and, in the words of a Delaware court, was "a mere shell of a corporation." The president of Pepsi, Charles G. Guth, even attempted to sell Pepsi to its rival Coca-Cola, but Coke wanted no part of a seemingly doomed enterprise. During this period, Pepsi and Coke sold cola in 6-ounce bottles. To reduce costs, Guth purchased a large supply of recycled 12-ounce beer bottles. Initially, Pepsi priced the 12-ounce bottles at 10 cents, twice the price of 6-ounce Cokes. However, this strategy failed to boost sales. But then Guth had an idea: Why not sell 12-ounce Pepsis for the same price as 6-ounce Cokes? In the Depression, this was a brilliant marketing ploy. Pepsi's sales shot upward. By 1934 Pepsi was out of bankruptcy. Its profit rose to $2.1 million by 1936 and to $4.2 million by 1938. Guth's decision to undercut Coca-Cola saved the company.

This example illustrates an important point. Clearly, in 1931 Pepsi's chief objective was to increase profits so it could survive. But merely deciding to pursue this objective could not make it happen. Charles Guth could not just order his subordinates to increase Pepsi's profits. Like any company, Pepsi's management had no direct control over its profit, market share, or any of the other markers of business success. What Pepsi's management did control were marketing, production, and the administrative decisions that determined its competitive position and ultimate profitability.

Pepsi's success in the 1930s can be understood in terms of a few key economic relationships. The most basic of these is the law of demand. The law of demand says that, all other things being the same, the lower the price of a product, the more of it consumers will purchase. Whether the increase in the number of units sold translates into higher sales revenues depends on the strength of the relationship between price and the quantity purchased. This is measured by the price elasticity of demand. As long as Coke did not respond to Pepsi's price cut with one of its own, we would expect that the demand for Pepsi would have been relatively sensitive to price, or in the language of economics, price elastic. As we will see later in this chapter, price-elastic demand implies that a price cut translates not only into higher unit sales, but also into higher sales revenue. Whether Coke is better off responding to Pepsi's price cut depends on another relationship, that between the size of a competitor and the profitability of price matching. Because Coke had such a large share of the market, it was

9

more profitable to keep its price high (letting Pepsi steal some of its market) than to respond with a price cut of its own.[2] Finally, whether Pepsi's higher sales revenue translates into higher profit depends on the economic relationship between the additional sales revenue that Pepsi's price cut generated and the additional cost of producing more Pepsi-Cola. That profits rose rapidly after the price reduction suggests that the additional sales revenue far exceeded the additional costs of production.

This chapter lays out basic microeconomic tools for business strategy. Most of the elements that contributed to Pepsi's successful price-cutting strategy in the 1930s will be on display here. An understanding of the language and concepts in this chapter will, we believe, "level the playing field," so that students with little or no background in microeconomics can navigate most of this book just as well as students with extensive economics training. The chapter has five main parts: (1) costs; (2) demand, prices, and revenues; (3) the theory of price and output determination by a profit-maximizing firm; (4) the theory of perfectly competitive markets; and (5) game theory.[3]

Costs

A firm's profit equals its revenues minus its costs. We begin our economics primer by focusing on the cost side of this equation. We discuss four specific concepts in this section: cost functions; long-run versus short-run costs; sunk costs; and economic versus accounting costs.

Cost Functions

Total Cost Functions

Managers are most familiar with costs when they are presented as in Tables P.1 and P.2, which show, respectively, an income statement and a statement of costs of goods manufactured for a hypothetical producer during the year 2008.[4] The information in these tables is essentially retrospective. It tells managers what happened during the past year. But what if management is interested in determining whether a price

TABLE P.1
INCOME STATEMENT: 2008

(1) Sales Revenue		$35,600
(2) Cost of Goods Sold		
Cost of Goods Manufactured	$13,740	
Add: Finished Goods Inventory 12/31/07	$ 3,300	
Less: Finished Goods Inventory 12/31/08	$ 2,950	
		$14,090
(3) Gross Profit: (1) minus (2)		$21,510
(4) Selling and General Administrative Expenses		$8,540
(5) Income from Operations: (3) minus (4)		$12,970
Interest Expenses		$1,210
Net Income Before Taxes		$11,760
Income Taxes		$4,100
Net Income		$7,660

All amounts in thousands.

TABLE P.2
STATEMENT OF COST OF GOODS MANUFACTURED: 2008

Materials:		
Materials Purchases	$8,700	
Add: Materials Inventory 12/31/07	$1,400	
Less: Materials Inventory 12/31/08	$1,200	
(1) Cost of Materials		$8,900
(2) Direct Labor		$2,300
Manufacturing Overhead		
Indirect Labor	$700	
Heat, Light, and Power	$400	
Repairs and Maintenance	$200	
Depreciation	$1,100	
Insurance	$50	
Property Taxes	$80	
Miscellaneous Factory Expenses	$140	
(3) Total Manufacturing Overhead		$2,670
Total Cost of Manufacturing: (1) + (2) + (3)		$13,870
Add: Work-in-Process Inventory 12/31/07		$2,100
Less: Work-in-Process Inventory 12/31/08		$2,230
Cost of Goods Manufactured		$13,740

All amounts in thousands.

reduction will increase profits, as with Pepsi? The price drop will probably stimulate additional sales, so a firm needs to know how its total costs would change if it increased production above the previous year's level.

This is what a total cost function tells us. It represents the relationship between a firm's total costs, denoted by TC, and the total amount of output it produces in a given time period, denoted by Q. Figure P.1 shows a graph of a total cost function. For each level of output the firm might produce, the graph associates a unique level of total

FIGURE P.1
TOTAL COST FUNCTION

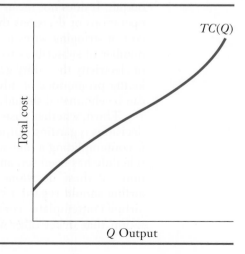

The total cost function $TC(Q)$ shows the total costs that the firm would incur for a level of output Q. The total cost function is an efficiency relationship in that it shows the lowest possible total cost the firm would incur to produce a level of output, given the firm's technological capabilities and the prices of factors of production, such as labor and capital.

cost. Why is the association between output and total cost unique? A firm may currently be producing 100 units of output per year at a total cost of $5,000,000, but if it were to streamline its operations, it might be able to lower costs, so that those 100 units could be produced for only $4,500,000. We resolve this ambiguity by defining the total cost function as an efficiency relationship. It represents the relationship between total cost and output, assuming that the firm produces in the most efficient manner possible given its current technological capabilities. Of course, firms do not always produce as efficiently as they theoretically could. The substantial literature on total quality management and reengineering attests to the attention managers give to improving efficiency. This is why we stress that the total cost function reflects the current capabilities of the firm. If the firm is producing as efficiently as it knows how, then the total cost function must slope upward: the only way to achieve more output is to use more factors of production (labor, machinery, materials), which will raise total costs.[5]

Fixed and Variable Costs

The information contained in the accounting statements in Tables P.1 and P.2 allows us to identify the total cost for one particular level of annual output. To map out the total cost function more completely, we must distinguish between fixed costs and variable costs. Variable costs, such as direct labor and commissions to salespeople, increase as output increases. Fixed costs, such as general and administrative expenses and property taxes, remain constant as output increases.

Three important points should be stressed when discussing fixed and variable costs. First, the line dividing fixed and variable costs is often fuzzy. Some costs, such as maintenance or advertising and promotional expenses, may have both fixed and variable components. Other costs may be *semifixed*: fixed over certain ranges of output but variable over other ranges.[6] For example, a beer distributor may be able to deliver up to 5,000 barrels of beer a week using a single truck. But when it must deliver between 5,000 and 10,000 barrels, it needs two trucks, between 10,000 and 15,000, three trucks, and so forth. The cost of trucks is fixed within the intervals (0, 5,000), (5,000, 10,000), (10,000, 15,000), and so forth, but is variable between these intervals.

Second, when we say that a cost is fixed, we mean that it is invariant to the firm's output. It does not mean that it cannot be affected by other dimensions of the firm's operations or decisions the firm might make. For example, for an electric utility, the cost of stringing wires to hook up houses to the local grid depends primarily on the number of subscribers to the system, and not on the total amount of kilowatt-hours of electricity the utility generates. Other fixed costs, such as the money spent on marketing promotions or advertising campaigns, arise from management decisions and can be eliminated should management so desire.[7]

Third, whether costs are fixed or variable depends on the time period in which decisions regarding output are contemplated. Consider, for example, an airline that is contemplating a one-week-long fare cut. Its workers have already been hired, its schedule has been set, and its fleet has been purchased. Within a one-week period, none of these decisions can be reversed. For this particular decision, then, the airline should regard a significant fraction of its costs as fixed. By contrast, if the airline contemplates committing to a year-long reduction in fares, with the expectation that ticket sales will increase accordingly, schedules can be altered, planes can be leased or purchased, and workers can be hired. In this case, the airline should regard most of its expenses as variable. Whether the firm has the freedom to alter its physical capital or other elements of its operations has important implications for its cost structure and the nature of its decision making. This issue will be covered in more detail below when we analyze the distinction between long-run and short-run costs.

Average and Marginal Cost Functions

Associated with the total cost function are two other cost functions: the average cost function, $AC(Q)$, and the marginal cost function, $MC(Q)$. The average cost function describes how the firm's average or per-unit-of-output costs vary with the amount of output it produces. It is given by the formula

$$AC(Q) = \frac{TC(Q)}{Q}$$

If total costs were directly proportional to output—for example, if they were given by a formula, such as $TC(Q) = 5Q$ or $TC(Q) = 37,000Q$, or more generally, by $TC(Q) = cQ$, where c is a constant—then average cost would be a constant. This is because

$$AC(Q) = \frac{cQ}{Q} = c$$

Often, however, average cost will vary with output. As Figure P.2 shows, average cost may rise, fall, or remain constant as output goes up. When average cost decreases as output increases, there are economies of scale. When average cost increases as output increases, there are diseconomies of scale. When average cost remains unchanged with respect to output, we have constant returns to scale. A production process may exhibit economies of scale over one range of output and diseconomies of scale over another.

FIGURE P.2
AVERAGE COST FUNCTION

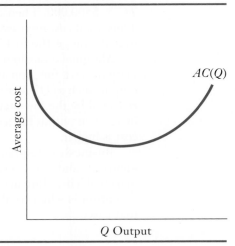

The average cost function $AC(Q)$ shows the firm's average, or per-unit, cost for any level of output Q. Average costs are not necessarily the same at each level of output.

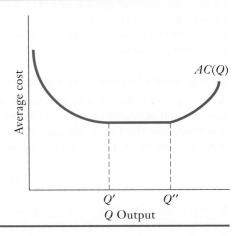

This average cost function exhibits economies of scale at output levels up to Q'. It exhibits constant returns to scale between Q' and Q''. It exhibits diseconomies of scale at output levels above Q''. The smallest output level at which economies of scale are exhausted is Q'. It is thus known as the minimum efficient scale.

Figure P.3 shows an average cost function that exhibits economies of scale, diseconomies of scale, and constant returns to scale. Output level Q' is the smallest level of output at which economies of scale are exhausted and is thus known as the minimum efficient scale. The concepts of economies of scale and minimum efficient scale are extremely important for understanding the size and scope of firms and the structure of industries. We devote all of Chapter 2 to analyzing economies of scale.

Marginal cost refers to the rate of change of total cost with respect to output. Marginal cost may be thought of as the incremental cost of producing exactly one more unit of output. When output is initially Q and changes by ΔQ units and one knows the total cost at each output level, marginal cost may be calculated as follows:

$$MC(Q) = \frac{TC(Q + \Delta Q) - TC(Q)}{\Delta Q}$$

For example, suppose when $Q = 100$ units, $TC = \$400,000$, and when $Q = 150$ units, $TC = \$500,000$. Then $\Delta Q = 50$, and $MC = (\$500,000 - \$400,000)/50 = \$2,000$. Thus, total cost increases at a rate of $\$2,000$ per unit of output when output increases over the range 100 to 150 units.

Marginal cost often depends on the total volume of output. Figure P.4 shows the marginal cost function associated with a particular total cost function. At low levels of output, such as Q', increasing output by one unit does not change total cost much, as reflected by the low marginal cost. At higher levels of output, such as Q', a one-unit increase in output has a greater impact on total cost, and the corresponding marginal cost is higher.

Businesses frequently treat average cost and marginal cost as if they were identical, and use average cost when making decisions that should be based on marginal cost. But average cost is generally different from marginal cost. The exception is when total costs vary in direct proportion to output, $TC(Q) = cQ$. In that case,

$$MC(Q) = \frac{c(Q + \Delta Q) - cQ}{\Delta Q} = c$$

FIGURE P.4
RELATIONSHIP BETWEEN TOTAL COST AND MARGINAL COST

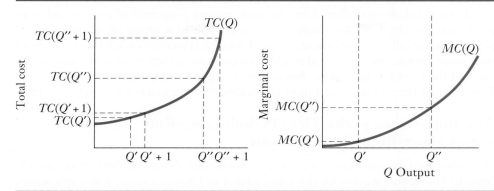

The marginal cost function $MC(Q)$ on the right graph is based on the total cost function $TC(Q)$ shown in the left graph. At output level Q', a one-unit increase in output changes costs by $TC(Q' + 1) - TC(Q')$, which equals the marginal cost at Q', $MC(Q')$. Since this change is not large, the marginal cost is small (i.e., the height of the marginal cost curve from the horizontal axis is small). At output level Q'', a one-unit increase in output changes costs by $TC(Q'' + 1) - TC(Q'')$, which equals the marginal cost at Q''. This change is larger than the one-unit change from Q', so $MC(Q'') > MC(Q')$. Because the total cost function becomes steeper as Q gets larger, the marginal cost curve must increase in output.

which, of course, is also average cost. This result reflects a more general relationship between marginal and average cost (illustrated in Figure P.5):

- When average cost is a decreasing function of output, marginal cost is less than average cost.

- When average cost neither increases nor decreases in output—because it is either constant (independent of output) or at a minimum point—marginal cost is equal to average cost.

FIGURE P.5
RELATIONSHIP BETWEEN MARGINAL COST AND AVERAGE COST

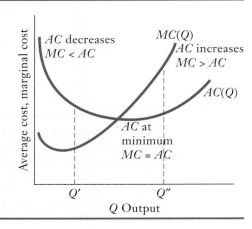

When average cost is decreasing (e.g., at output Q'), $AC > MC$ (i.e., the average cost curve lies above the marginal cost curve). When average cost is increasing (e.g., at output Q''), $AC < MC$ (i.e., the average cost curve lies below the marginal cost curve). When average cost is at a minimum, $AC = MC$, so the two curves must intersect.

- When average cost is an increasing function of output, marginal cost is greater than average cost.

These relationships follow from the mathematical properties of average and marginal cost, but they are also intuitive. If the average of a group of things (costs of manufacturing cellular phones, test scores, or whatever) increases when one more thing (one more phone, one more test) is added to the group, then it must be because the value of the most recently added thing—the "marginal"—is greater than the average. Conversely, if the average falls, it must be because the marginal is less than the average.

The Importance of the Time Period: Long-Run versus Short-Run Cost Functions

We emphasized the importance of the time horizon when discussing fixed versus variable costs. In this section, we develop this point further and consider some of its implications.

Figure P.6 illustrates the case of a firm whose production can take place in a facility that comes in three different sizes: small, medium, and large. Once the firm commits to a production facility of a particular size, it can vary output only by varying the quantities of inputs other than the plant size (e.g., by hiring another shift of workers). The period of time in which the firm cannot adjust the size of its production facilities is known as the short run. For each plant size, there is an associated short-run average cost function, denoted by SAC. These average cost functions include the annual costs of all relevant variable inputs (labor, materials) as well as the fixed cost (appropriately annualized) of the plant itself.

If the firm knows how much output it plans to produce before building a plant, then to minimize its costs, it should choose the plant size that results in the lowest

FIGURE P.6
SHORT-RUN AND LONG-RUN AVERAGE COST FUNCTIONS

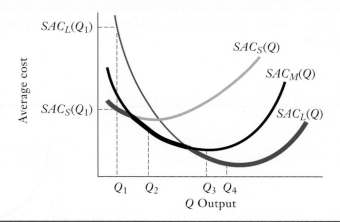

The curves labeled $SAC_S(Q)$, $SAC_M(Q)$, and $SAC_L(Q)$ are the short-run average cost functions associated with small, medium, and large plants, respectively. For any level of output, the optimal plant size is the one with the lowest average cost. For example, at output Q_1, the small plant is best. At output Q_2, the medium plant is best. At output Q_3, the large plant is best. The long-run average cost function is the "lower envelope" of the short-run average cost functions, represented by the bold line. This curve shows the lowest attainable average cost for any output when the firm is free to adjust its plant size optimally.

short-run average cost for that desired output level. For example, for output Q_1, the optimal plant is a small one; for output Q_2, the optimal plant is a medium one; for output Q_3, the optimal plant is a large one. Figure P.6 illustrates that for larger outputs, the larger plant is best; for medium-output levels, the medium plant is best; and for small-output levels, the small plant is best. For example, when output is Q_1, the reduction in average cost that results from switching from a large plant to a small plant is $SAC_L(Q_1) - SAC_S(Q_1)$. This saving not only arises from reductions in the fixed costs of the plant, but also because the firm can more efficiently tailor the rest of its operations to its plant size. When the firm produces Q_1 in the large plant, it may need to utilize more labor to assure steady materials flows within the large facility. The small plant may allow flows to be streamlined, making such labor unnecessary.

The long-run average cost function is the lower envelope of the short-run average cost functions and is depicted by the bold line in Figure P.6. It shows the lowest attainable average cost for any particular level of output when the firm can adjust its plant size optimally. This is the average cost function the firm faces before it has committed to a particular plant size.

In this example, the long-run average cost function exhibits economies of scale. By operating with larger plant sizes, the firm can lower its average costs. This raises a deceptively simple but extremely significant point. To realize the lower average costs, the firm must not only build a large plant but must also achieve sufficient output, so that the large plant is indeed the optimal one. It would be disastrous for the firm to build a large plant if it only achieved an output of, say, Q_1. The firm would be saddled with an expensive underutilized facility. If we were to observe a firm in this situation, we might be tempted to conclude that the scale economies inherent in the production process were limited or nonexistent. This would be incorrect. Scale economies exist, but the firm is not selling enough output needed to exploit them. These concepts are closely tied to the concept of *throughput* that we introduce in Chapter 1. Essentially, firms cannot fully exploit economies of scale unless they have sufficient inputs for production and distribution to get their products to market. Without such throughput, strategies that hinge on scale economies are doomed to fail.

It is often useful to express short-run average costs as the sum of average fixed costs (AFC) and average variable costs (AVC):

$$SAC(Q) = AFC(Q) + AVC(Q)$$

Average fixed costs are the firm's fixed costs (i.e., the annualized cost of the firm's plant plus expenses, such as insurance and property taxes, that do not vary with the volume of output) expressed on a per-unit-of-output basis. Average variable costs are the firm's variable costs (e.g., labor and materials) expressed on a per-unit-of-output basis. For example, suppose the firm's plant has an annualized cost of $9 million and other annual fixed expenses total $1 million. Moreover, suppose the firm's variable costs vary with output according to the formula $4Q^2$. Then we would have

$$AFC(Q) = \frac{10}{Q}$$

$$AFC(Q) = 4Q$$

$$AFC(Q) = \frac{10}{Q} + 4Q$$

Note that as the volume of output increases, average fixed costs become smaller, which tends to pull down SAC. Average fixed costs decline because total fixed costs are being spread over an ever-larger production volume. Offsetting this (in this example) is the fact that average variable costs rise with output, which pulls *SAC* upward. The net effect of these offsetting forces creates the U-shaped *SAC* curves in Figure P.6.

Sunk versus Avoidable Costs

When assessing the costs of a decision, the manager should consider only those costs that the decision actually affects. Some costs must be incurred no matter what the decision is and thus cannot be avoided. These are called *sunk costs*. The opposite of sunk costs is *avoidable costs*. These costs can be avoided if certain choices are made. When weighing the costs of a decision, the decision maker should ignore sunk costs and consider only avoidable costs.

To illustrate the concept of sunk costs, take the case of an online merchandiser of laser printers. The merchandiser traditionally purchased large quantities of printers from the manufacturer, so that it could satisfy rush orders. Increasingly, though, the merchandiser was carrying high inventories, including some lines that the manufacturer no longer produced and would not repurchase. A natural response to this problem would be to put the discontinued lines on sale and reduce inventory. However, the firm's managers were reluctant to do this. They felt that even in the best of times the margins on their products barely covered their overhead, and by cutting the price, they would be unable to cover their cost of the goods they sold.

This argument is wrong. The cost incurred to purchase the laser printers is a sunk cost as far as pricing is concerned. Whether or not the merchandiser cuts price, it cannot avoid these costs. If it believes that a seller should never price below average cost, the merchandiser will end up with large losses. Instead, it should accept that it cannot undo past decisions (and their associated sunk costs) and strive to minimize its losses.

It is important to emphasize that whether a cost is sunk depends on the decision being made and the options at hand. In the example just given, the cost of the discontinued lines of printers is a sunk cost with respect to the pricing decision today. But before the printers were ordered, their cost would not have been sunk. By not ordering them, the merchandiser would have avoided the purchase and storage costs.

Students often confuse sunk costs with fixed costs. The two concepts are not the same. In particular, some fixed costs need not be sunk. For example, a railroad serving Sydney to Adelaide needs a locomotive and a crew whether it hauls 1 carload of freight or 20. The cost of the locomotive is thus a fixed cost. However, it is not necessarily sunk. If the railroad abandons its Sydney to Adelaide line, it can sell the locomotive to another railroad or redeploy it to another route.

Sunk costs are important for the study of strategy, particularly in analyzing rivalry among firms, entry and exit decisions from markets, and decisions to adopt new technologies. For example, the concept of sunk costs helps explain why established American steel firms were unwilling to invest continuous casting technology, even as new Japanese firms building "greenfield" facilities did adopt the new technology. The new technology had higher fixed costs, but lower variable operating costs. Established American firms viewed the fixed cost of their old technologies as sunk. Thus, they compared the savings in operating costs against the fixed cost of the new technology. The Japanese firms, in contrast, compared the savings in operating costs against the *difference* between the fixed costs of the new and old technologies. American firms thus required a larger cost savings than the Japanese firms to induce them to adopt the new technology. Despite criticism in the popular business press, the American firms' decisions to delay adoption of new technology was economically sound, serving to maximize profits even if it did entail higher operating costs. We will return to the concept of sunk costs throughout the text.

ECONOMIC COSTS AND PROFITABILITY

Economic versus Accounting Costs

The costs in Tables P.1 and P.2 reflect the accountant's concept of costs. This concept is grounded in the principles of accrual accounting, which emphasize historical costs. Accounting statements—in particular, income statements and balance sheets—are designed to serve an audience outside the firm—for example, lenders and equity investors. The accounting numbers must thus be objective and verifiable, principles that are well served by historical costs.

However, the costs that appear in accounting statements are not necessarily appropriate for decision making inside a firm. Business decisions require the measurement of economic costs, which are based on the concept of opportunity cost. This concept says that the economic cost of deploying resources in a particular activity is the value of the best foregone alternative use of those resources. Economic cost may not correspond to the historical costs represented in Tables P.1 and P.2. Suppose, for example, that the firm purchased its raw materials at a price below their current market price. Would the costs of goods manufactured in Table P.2 represent the economic cost to the firm of using these resources? The answer is no. When the firm uses them to produce finished goods, it forsakes the alternative of reselling the materials at the market price. The economic cost of the firm's production activities reflects this foregone opportunity.

At a broader level, consider the resources (plant, equipment, land, etc.) that have been purchased with funds that stockholders provide to the firm. To attract these funds, the firm must offer the stockholders a return on their investment that is at least as large as the return that they could have received from investing in activities of comparable risk. To illustrate, suppose that at the beginning of 2012, a firm's assets could have been liquidated for $100 million. By tying their funds up in the firm, investors lose the opportunity to invest the $100 million in an activity providing an 8 percent return. Moreover, suppose because of wear and tear and creeping obsolescence of plant and equipment, the value of the assets declines by 1 percent over the year 2012. The annualized cost of the firm's assets for 2012 is then $(0.08 + 0.01) \times$ $100 million = $9 million per year. This is an economic cost, but it would not appear in the firm's income statement.

In studying strategy, we are interested in analyzing why firms make their decisions and what distinguishes good decisions from poor ones, given the opportunities and the constraints firms face. In our formal theories of firm behavior, we thus emphasize economic costs rather than historical accounting costs. This is not to say that accounting costs have no place in the study of business strategy. Quite the contrary: In assessing the past performance of the firm, in comparing one firm in an industry to another, or in evaluating the financial strength of a firm, the informed use of accounting statements and accounting ratio analysis can be illuminating. However, the concept of opportunity cost provides the best basis for good economic decisions when the firm must choose among competing alternatives. A firm that consistently deviated from this idea of cost would miss opportunities for earning higher profits.

In the end, it might be driven out of business by firms that are better at seizing profit-enhancing opportunities, or it may find itself starved for capital as investors bid down its stock price Whenever we depict a cost function or discuss cost throughout this book, we have in mind the idea of costs as including all relevant opportunity costs.

Economic Profit versus Accounting Profit

Having distinguished between economic cost and accounting cost, we can now distinguish between economic profit and accounting profit:

- Accounting Profit = Sales Revenue − Accounting Cost.
- Economic Profit = Sales Revenue − Economic Cost
    = Accounting Profit − (Economic Cost − Accounting Cost).

To illustrate the distinction between the two concepts, consider a small software development firm that is owner operated. In 2009, the firm earned revenue of $1,000,000 and incurred expenses on supplies and hired labor of $850,000. The owner's best outside employment opportunity would be to earn a salary of $200,000 working for Microsoft. The software firm's accounting profit is $1,000,000 − $850,000 = $150,000. The software firm's economic profit deducts the opportunity cost of the owner's labor services and is thus $1,000,000 − $850,000 − $200,000 = − $50,000. This means that the owner made $50,000 less in income by operating this business than she could have made in her best outside alternative. The software business "destroyed" $50,000 of the owner's wealth in that, by operating the software business, she earned $50,000 less income than she might have otherwise.

DEMAND AND REVENUES

The second component of profit is sales revenue, which is intimately related to the firm's pricing decision. To understand how a firm's sales revenue depends on its pricing decision, we will explore the concept of a demand curve and the price elasticity of demand.

Demand Curve

The demand function describes the relationship between the quantity of product that the firm is able to sell and all the variables that influence that quantity. These variables include the price of the product, the prices of related products, the incomes and tastes of consumers, the quality of the product, advertising, and many other variables commonly thought to make up the firm's marketing mix. With so many variables, it would be difficult to depict the demand function on a graph.

Of special interest is the relationship between quantity and price. To focus on this important relationship, imagine that all the other variables that influence the quantity demanded remain fixed, and consider how the quantity demanded would change as the price changes. We can show this simple relationship on a graph. Figure P.7 depicts a demand curve. We would expect the demand curve to be downward sloping: the lower the price, the greater the quantity demanded; the higher the price, the smaller the quantity demanded. This inverse relationship is called the *law of demand*.

FIGURE P.7
DEMAND CURVE

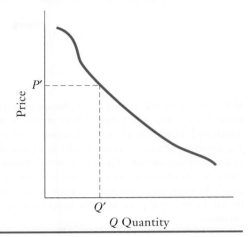

The demand curve shows the quantity of a product that consumers will purchase at different prices. For example, at price P' consumers purchase Q' units of the product. We would expect an inverse relationship between quantity and price, so this curve is downward sloping.

The law of demand may not hold if high prices confer prestige or enhance a product's image, or when consumers cannot objectively assess the potential performance of a product and use price to infer quality. Both prestige and signaling effects could result in demand curves that slope upward for some range of prices. Even so, personal experience and countless studies from economics and marketing confirm that the law of demand applies to most products.

As Figure P.7 shows, the demand curve is typically drawn with price on the vertical axis and quantity on the horizontal axis. This may seem strange because we think that price determines the quantity demanded, not the other way around. However, this representation emphasizes a useful alternative interpretation for a demand curve. Not only does the demand curve tell us the quantity consumers will purchase at any given price, it also tells us the highest possible price that the market will bear for a given quantity or supply of output. Thus, in Figure P.7, if the firm sets a target of selling output level Q' (which might be what it can produce by running at full capacity), the demand curve tells us that the highest price the firm can charge is P'.

The Price Elasticity of Demand

Look at a firm that is considering a price increase. The firm understands that according to the law of demand, the increase in price will result in the loss of some sales. This may be acceptable if the loss in sales is not "too large." If sales do not suffer much, the firm may actually increase its sales revenue when it raises its price. If sales drop substantially, however, sales revenues may decline, and the firm could be worse off.

Figure P.8 illustrates the implications of the firm's pricing decision when its demand curve has one of two alternative shapes, D_A and D_B. Suppose the firm is currently charging P_0 and selling Q_0, and is considering an increase in price to P_1. If the firm's demand curve is D_A, the price increase would cause only a small drop in sales. In this case, the quantity demanded is not very sensitive to price. We would suspect that the increase in price would increase sales revenue because the price increase swamps the quantity decrease. By contrast, if the firm's demand curve is D_B, the increase in price

FIGURE P.8

PRICE SENSITIVITY AND THE SHAPE OF THE DEMAND CURVE

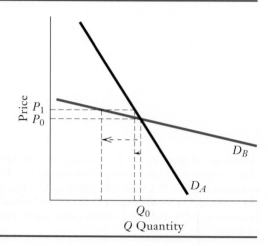

When the demand curve is D_A, a change in price from P_0 to P_1 has only a small effect on the quantity demanded. However, when the demand curve is D_B, the same change in price results in a large drop in quantity demanded. When D_A is the demand curve, we would conjecture that the increase in price would increase sales revenues, but when D_B is the demand curve, the price increase would reduce sales revenues.

would cause a large drop in sales. Here, the quantity demanded is very sensitive to price. We would expect that the price increase would decrease sales revenues.

As this analysis shows, the shape of the demand curve can strongly affect the success of the firm's pricing strategy. The concept of the price elasticity of demand summarizes this effect by measuring the sensitivity of quantity demanded to price. The price elasticity of demand, commonly denoted by η, is the percentage change in quantity brought about by a 1 percent change in price. Letting subscript "0" represent the initial situation and "1" represent the situation after the price changes, the formula for elasticity is

$$\eta = -\frac{\Delta Q/Q_0}{\Delta P/P_0}$$

where $\Delta P = P_1 - P_0$ is the change in price, and $\Delta Q = Q_1 - Q_0$ is the resulting change in quantity.[8] To illustrate this formula, suppose price is initially $5, and the corresponding quantity demanded is 1,000 units. If the price rises to $5.75, though, the quantity demanded would fall to 800 units. Then

$$\eta = -\frac{\dfrac{800 - 1000}{1000}}{\dfrac{5.75 - 5}{5}} = \frac{-0.20}{0.15} = 1.33$$

Thus over the range of prices between $5.00 and $5.75, quantity demanded falls at a rate of 1.33 percent for every 1 percent increase in price. The price elasticity η might be less than 1 or greater than 1.

- If η is less than 1, we say that demand is *inelastic*, which is the situation along demand curve D_A for the price change being considered.

- If η is greater than 1, we say that demand is *elastic*, which is the situation along demand curve D_B for the price change being considered.

Given an estimate of the price elasticity of demand, a manager could calculate the expected percentage change in quantity demanded resulting from a given change in price by multiplying the percentage change in price by the estimated elasticity. To illustrate, suppose management believed $\eta = 0.75$. If it contemplated a 3 percent increase in price, then it should expect a $3 \times 0.75 = 2.25$ percent drop in the quantity demanded as a result of the price increase.[9]

Price elasticities can be estimated using statistical techniques, and economists and marketers have estimated price elasticities for many products. But in most practical situations, managers will not have the benefit of a precise numerical estimate of elasticity based on statistical techniques. Consequently, the manager must rely on his or her knowledge of the product and the nature of the market to estimate price sensitivity. Among the factors that tend to make demand for the firm's product more sensitive to price are the following:

- The product has few unique features that differentiate it from rival products, and buyers are aware of the prices and features of rival products. Airline service is a good example of a product that is hard to differentiate and where consumers can easily inform themselves of the range of prices that exist in a particular market.

- Buyers' expenditures on the product are a large fraction of their total expenditures. In this case, the savings from finding a comparable item at a lower price are large, so consumers tend to shop more than when making small purchases. Refrigerators and washing machines are products whose demand is fairly price sensitive because consumers are motivated to shop around before purchasing.

- The product is an input that buyers use to produce a final good whose demand is itself sensitive to price. In this case, if buyers tried to pass through to their customers even small changes in the price of the input, demand for the finished good could decrease dramatically. The input buyers will thus be very sensitive to price. For example, a personal computer manufacturer's demand for components and materials is likely to be highly price elastic because consumer demand for personal computers is highly price elastic.

Among the factors that tend to make demand less sensitive to price are the following:

- Comparisons among substitute products are difficult. This could be because the product is complex and has many performance dimensions; because consumers have little or no experience with substitute products and thus would face a risk if they purchased them; or because comparison shopping is costly. Items sold door-to-door, such as Avon cosmetics, have traditionally been price inelastic because, at the time of sale, most consumers lack good information about the prices of alternatives.

- Because of tax deductions or insurance, buyers pay only a fraction of the full price of the product. Health care is an excellent example.

- A buyer would incur significant costs if it switched to a substitute product. Switching costs could arise if the use of a product requires specialized training or expertise that is not fully transferable across different varieties of the product. For example, to the extent that a consumer develops expertise in using a particular word processing package that is incompatible with available alternatives, switching costs will be high, and price sensitivity for upgrades will be low.

- The product is used in conjunction with another product that buyers have committed themselves to. For example, an owner of a copying machine is likely to be fairly insensitive to the price of toner, because the toner is an essential input in running the copier.

Brand-Level versus Industry-Level Elasticities

Students often mistakenly suppose that just because the demand for a product is inelastic, the demand facing each seller of that product is also inelastic. Consider, for example, gasoline. Many studies have documented that the demand for gasoline is price inelastic, with elasticities of around 0.10–0.20. This suggests that a general increase in the prices charged at all gas stations would only modestly affect overall gasoline demand. However, if only one gas station increases its price, the demand for that gas station would probably drop substantially because consumers would patronize other stations. Thus, while demand can be inelastic at the industry level, it can be highly elastic at the brand level.

Should a firm use an industry-level elasticity or a firm-level elasticity in assessing the impact of a price change? The answer depends on what the firm expects its rivals to do. If a firm expects that rivals will quickly match its price change, then the industry-level elasticity is appropriate. If, by contrast, a firm expects that rivals will not match its price change (or will do so only after a long lag), then the brand-level elasticity is appropriate. For example, Pepsi's price cut succeeded because Coke did not retaliate. Had Coke cut its price, the outcome of Pepsi's strategy would have been different. Making educated conjectures about how rivals will respond to pricing moves is a fascinating subject. We will encounter this subject again in Chapter 5.

TOTAL REVENUE AND MARGINAL REVENUE FUNCTIONS

A firm's total revenue function, denoted by $TR(Q)$, indicates how the firm's sales revenues vary as a function of how much product it sells. Recalling our interpretation of the demand curve as showing the highest price $P(Q)$ that the firm can charge and sell exactly Q units of output, we can express total revenue as

$$TR(Q) = P(Q)Q$$

Just as a firm is interested in the impact of a change in output on its costs, it is also interested in how a change in output will affect its revenues. A firm's marginal revenue, $MR(Q)$, is analogous to its marginal cost. It represents the rate of change in total revenue that results from the sale of ΔQ additional units of output:

$$MR(Q) = \frac{TR(Q + \Delta Q) - TR(Q)}{\Delta Q}$$

It seems plausible that total revenue would go up as the firm sells more output, and thus MR would always be positive. But with a downward-sloping demand curve, this is not necessarily true. To sell more, the firm must lower its price. Thus, while it generates revenue on the extra units of output it sells at the lower price, it loses revenue on all the units it would have sold at the higher price. Economists call this the *revenue destruction* effect. For example, an online electronics retailer may sell 110 DVDs per day at a price of $11 per disc and 120 DVDs at $9 per disc. It gains additional revenue of $90 per day on the extra 10 DVDs sold at the lower price of $9, but it sacrifices $220 per day on the 110 DVDs that it could have sold for $2 more. The marginal revenue in this case would equal $- \$130/10$ or $- \$13$; the store loses sales revenue of $13 for each additional DVD it sells when it drops its price from $11 to $9.

In general, whether marginal revenue is positive or negative depends on the price elasticity of demand. The formal relationship (whose derivation is not important for our purposes) is

$$MR(Q) = P\left(1 - \frac{1}{\eta}\right)$$

For example, if $\eta = 0.75$, and the current price $P = \$15$, then marginal revenue $MR = 15(1 - 1/0.75) = - \$5$. More generally,

- When demand is elastic, so that $\eta > 1$, it follows that $MR > 0$. In this case, the increase in output brought about by a reduction in price will raise total sales revenues.

- When demand is inelastic, so that $\eta < 1$, it follows that $MR < 0$. Here, the increase in output brought about by a reduction in price will lower total sales revenue.

Note that this formula implies that $MR < P$. This makes sense in light of what we just discussed. The price P is the additional revenue the firm gets from each additional unit it sells, but the overall change in revenues from selling an additional unit must factor in the revenue destruction effect.

Figure P.9 shows the graph of a demand curve and its associated marginal revenue curve. Because $MR < P$, the marginal revenue curve must lie everywhere below the demand curve, except at a quantity of zero. For most demand curves, the marginal revenue curve is everywhere downward sloping and at some point will shift from being positive to negative. (This occurs at output Q' in the figure.)

FIGURE P.9
THE MARGINAL REVENUE CURVE AND THE DEMAND CURVE

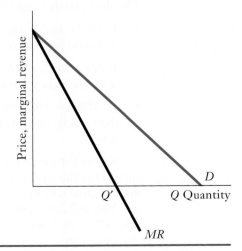

MR represents the marginal revenue curve associated with the demand curve D. Because $MR < P$, the marginal revenue curve must lie everywhere below the demand curve except at a quantity of 0. Marginal revenue is negative for quantities in excess of Q'.

THEORY OF THE FIRM: PRICING AND OUTPUT DECISIONS

Part Two of this book studies the structure of markets and competitive rivalry within industries. To set the stage for this analysis, we need to explore the theory of the firm, a theory of how firms choose their prices and quantities. This theory has both explanatory power and prescriptive usefulness. That is, it sheds light on how prices are established in markets, and it also provides tools to aid managers in making pricing decisions.

The theory of the firm assumes that the firm's ultimate objective is to make as large a profit as possible. The theory is therefore appropriate to managers whose goal is to maximize profits. Some analysts argue that not all managers seek to maximize profits, so that the theory of the firm is less useful for describing actual firm behavior. An extensive discussion of the descriptive validity of the profit-maximization hypothesis would take us beyond this primer. Suffice it to say that a powerful "evolutionary" argument supports the profit-maximization hypothesis: if, over the long haul, a firm's managers did not strive to achieve the largest amount of profit consistent with industry economics and its own particular resources, the firm would either disappear or its management would be replaced by one that better served the owners' interests.

Ideally, for any given amount of output the firm might want to sell, it would prefer to set price as high as it could. As we have seen, though, the firm's demand curve limits what that price can be. How, then, is the optimal output determined? This is where the concepts of marginal revenue and marginal cost become useful. Recalling that "marginals" are rates of change (change in cost or revenue per one-unit change in output), the change in revenue, cost, and profit from changing output by ΔQ units (where ΔQ can either represent an increase in output, in which case it is a positive amount, or a decrease in output, in which case it is a negative amount) is

$$\text{Change in Total Revenue} = MR \times \Delta Q$$
$$\text{Change in Total Cost} = MC \times \Delta Q$$
$$\text{Change in Total Profit} = (MR - MC) \times \Delta Q$$

The firm clearly would like to increase profit. Here's how:

- If $MR > MC$, the firm can increase profit by selling more ($\Delta Q > 0$), and to do so, it should *lower* its price.

- If $MR < MC$, the firm can increase profit by selling less ($\Delta Q < 0$), and to do so, it should *raise* its price.

- If $MR = MC$, the firm cannot increase profits by either increasing or decreasing output. It follows that output and price must be at their optimal levels.

Figure P.10 shows a firm whose output and price are at their optimal levels. The curve D is the firm's demand curve, MR is the marginal revenue curve, and MC is the marginal cost curve. The optimal output occurs where $MR = MC$, that is, where the MR and MC curves intersect. This is output Q^* in the diagram. The optimal price P^* is the associated price on the demand curve.

An alternative and perhaps more managerially relevant way of thinking about these principles is to express MR in terms of the price elasticity of demand. Then the term $MR = MC$ can be written as

$$P\left(1 - \frac{1}{\eta}\right) = MC$$

Let us now suppose, that as a first approximation, the firm's total variable costs are directly proportional to output, so that $MC = c$, where c is the firm's average variable cost. The percentage contribution margin or PCM on additional units sold is the ratio of profit per unit to revenue per unit, or $PCM = (P - c)/P$. Algebra establishes that

$$MR - MC > 0 \text{ as } \eta > 1/PCM$$
$$MR - MC < 0 \text{ as } \eta < 1/PCM$$

which implies that

- A firm should lower its price whenever the price elasticity of demand exceeds the reciprocal of the percentage contribution margin on the additional units it would sell by lowering its price.

- A firm should raise its price when the price elasticity of demand is less than the reciprocal of the percentage contribution margin of the units it would not sell by raising its price.

These principles can guide pricing decisions even though managers do not know the firm's demand curve or marginal cost function. Managers have only to make educated conjectures about the relative magnitude of elasticities and contribution margins.[10] An example may help cement these concepts. Suppose $P = \$10$ and $c = \$5$, so $PCM = 0.50$. Then the firm can increase profits by lowering its price if its price elasticity of demand η exceeds $1/0.5 = 2$. If, instead, $P = \$10$ and $c = \$8$, so that $PCM = 0.2$, the firm should cut its price if $\eta > 5$. As this example shows, the lower a firm's PCM (e.g., because its marginal cost is high), the greater its price elasticity of demand must be for a price-cutting strategy to raise profits.

FIGURE P.10
OPTIMAL QUANTITY AND PRICE FOR A PROFIT-MAXIMIZING FIRM

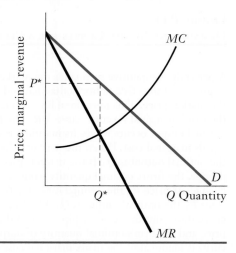

The firm's optimal quantity occurs at Q^*, where $MR = MC$. The optimal price P^* is the price the firm must charge to sell Q^* units. It is found from the demand curve.

PERFECT COMPETITION

A special case of the theory of the firm is the theory of perfect competition. This theory highlights how market forces shape and constrain a firm's behavior and interact with the firm's decisions to determine profitability. The theory deals with a stark competitive environment: an industry with many firms producing identical products (so that consumers choose among firms solely on the basis of price) and where firms can enter or exit the industry at will. This is a caricature of any real market, but it does approximate industries such as aluminum smelting and copper mining in which many firms produce nearly identical products.

Because firms in a perfectly competitive industry produce identical products, each firm must charge the same price. This market price is beyond the control of any individual firm; it must take the market price as given. For a firm to offer to sell at a price above the market price would be folly because it would make no sales. Offering to sell below the market price would also be folly because the firm would needlessly sacrifice revenue. As shown in Figure P.11, then, a perfectly competitive firm's demand curve is perfectly horizontal at the market price, even though the industry demand curve is downward sloping. Put another way, the firm-level price elasticity of demand facing a perfect competitor is infinite, even though the industry-level price elasticity is finite.

Given any particular market price, each firm must decide how much to produce. Applying the insights from the theory of the firm, the firm should produce at the point where marginal revenue equals marginal cost. When the firm's demand curve is horizontal, each additional unit it sells adds sales revenue equal to the market price. Thus, the firm's marginal revenue equals the market price, and the optimal output, shown in Figure P.11, is where marginal cost equals the market price. If we were to graph how a firm's optimal output changed as the market price changed, we would trace out a curve that is identical to the firm's marginal cost function. This is known as the firm's supply curve. It shows the amount of output the perfectly competitive firm would sell at various market prices. Thus, the supply curve of a perfectly competitive firm is identical to its marginal cost function.

If we aggregate over the firm supply curves of all active producers in the industry, we get the industry supply curve, depicted in Figure P.12 as SS. This figure

FIGURE P.11
DEMAND AND SUPPLY CURVES FOR A PERFECTLY COMPETITIVE FIRM

A perfectly competitive firm takes the market price as given and thus faces a horizontal demand curve at the market price. This horizontal line also represents the firm's marginal revenue curve MR. The firm's optimal output occurs where its marginal revenue equals marginal cost. When the market price is P_0, the optimal output is Q_0. If the market price were to change, the firm's optimal quantity would also change. At price P_1, the optimal output is Q_1. At price P_0, the optimal output is Q_0. The firm's supply curve traces out the relationship between the market price and the firm's optimal quantity of output. This curve is identical to the firm's marginal cost curve.

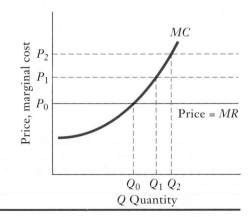

FIGURE P.12
FIRM AND INDUSTRY SUPPLY CURVES UNDER PERFECT COMPETITION

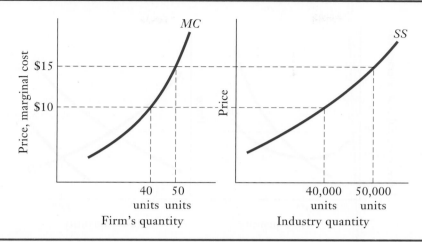

A single firm's supply curve is shown in the graph on the left. The industry's supply curve *SS* is shown in the graph on the right. These graphs depict an industry of 1,000 identical firms. Thus, at any price the industry supply is 1,000 times the amount that a single firm would supply.

shows an industry with 1,000 identical active firms. At any price, the industry supply is 1,000 times the supply of an individual firm. Given the industry supply curve, we can now see how the market price is determined. For the market to be in equilibrium, the market price must be such that the quantity demanded equals the quantity supplied by firms in the industry. This situation is depicted in Figure P.13, where

FIGURE P.13
PERFECTLY COMPETITIVE INDUSTRY PRIOR TO NEW ENTRY

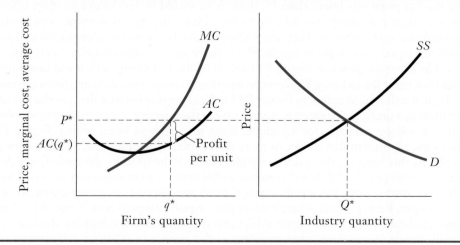

At the price P^*, each firm is producing its optimal amount of output q^*. Moreover, the quantity demanded equals the quantity Q^* supplied by all firms in the industry. However, each firm is earning a positive profit because at q^*, the price P^* exceeds average cost $AC(q^*)$, resulting in a profit on every unit sold. New firms would thus want to enter this industry.

FIGURE P.14

PERFECTLY COMPETITIVE INDUSTRY AT LONG-RUN EQUILIBRIUM

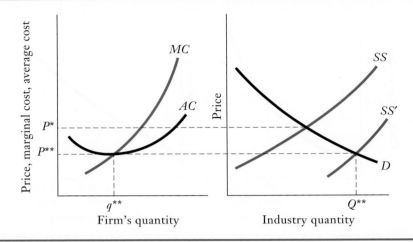

At price P^*, new entrants are attracted to the industry. As they come in, the industry's supply curve shifts to the right, from SS to SS', resulting in a reduction in market price. Entry ceases to occur when firms are earning as much inside the industry as they can earn outside it. Each firm thus earns zero economic profit, or equivalently, price equals average cost. Firms are choosing the optimal output and earning zero economic profit when they produce at the point at which market price equals both marginal cost and average cost. This occurs when the price is P^{**} and firms produce q^{**}. Firms are thus at the minimum point on their average cost function.

P^* denotes the price that "clears" the market. If the market price was higher than P^*, then more of the product would be offered for sale than consumers would like to buy. The excess supply would then place downward pressure on the market price. If the market price was lower than P^*, then there would be less of the product offered for sale than consumers would like to buy. Here, the excess demand would exert upward pressure on the market price. Only when the quantities demanded and supplied are equal—when price equals P^*—is there no pressure on price to change.

The situation shown in Figure P.13 would be the end of the story if additional firms could not enter the industry. However, in a perfectly competitive industry, firms can enter and exit at will. The situation in Figure P.13 is thus unstable because firms in the industry are making a profit (price exceeds average cost at the quantity q^* that each firm supplies). Thus, it will be attractive for additional firms to enter and begin selling. Figure P.14 shows the adjustment that occurs. As more firms enter, the supply curve SS shifts outward to SS'. As this happens, the quantity supplied exceeds the quantity demanded, and there is pressure on price to fall. It will continue to fall until no additional entry occurs. This is when the market price just equals a typical firm's average cost. As we have seen, to optimize output, firms produce where market price equals marginal cost. Thus, in the long-run equilibrium depicted in Figure P.14, firms are producing at minimum efficient scale (recall, this is the quantity corresponding to the minimum point on the average cost curve), and the equilibrium market price P^{**} equals the minimum level of average cost.

Suppose, now, that market demand suddenly falls. Figure P.15 shows what happens. The fall in market demand is represented by a shift from demand curve D_0 to D_1. Initially, market price would fall to P', and firms' revenues would not cover their economic costs. The industry "shakeout" then begins. Firms begin to exit the industry.

FIGURE P.15

EFFECT OF A REDUCTION IN DEMAND ON THE LONG-RUN PERFECTLY
COMPETITIVE EQUILIBRIUM

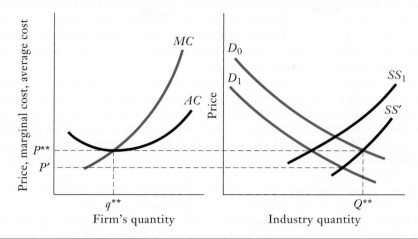

When demand falls, the demand curve shifts from D_0 to D_1, and price would initially fall to P'. Firms would earn less than they could elsewhere and would eventually begin to leave the industry. As this happens, the supply curve shifts to the left from SS' to SS_1. The industry shakeout ends when price is again P^{**}.

As this occurs, the industry supply curve shifts to the left, and price begins to rise. Once the "shakeout" fully unfolds, the industry supply curve will have shifted to SS', and the market price will once again reach P^{**}. Firms are then again optimizing on output and earning zero profit. Thus, no matter what the level of industry demand, the industry will eventually supply output at the price P^{**}.[11]

This theory implies that free entry exhausts all opportunities for making profit. This implication sometimes troubles management students because it seems to suggest that firms in perfectly competitive industries would then earn zero net income. But remember the distinction between economic costs and accounting costs. Economic costs reflect the relevant opportunity costs of the financial capital that the owners have provided to the firm. Zero profits thus means zero economic profit, not zero accounting profit. Zero economic profit simply means that investors are earning returns on their investments that are commensurate with what they could earn from their next best opportunity.

That free entry dissipates economic profit is one of the most powerful insights in economics, and it has profound implications for strategy. Firms that base their strategies on products that can be easily imitated or skills and resources that can be easily acquired put themselves at risk to the forces that are highlighted by the theory of perfect competition. To attain a competitive advantage, a firm must secure a position in the market that protects itself from imitation and entry. How firms might do this is the subject of Chapters 9, 10, and 11.

GAME THEORY

The perfectly competitive firm faces many competitors, but in making its output decision, it does not consider the likely reactions of its rivals. This is because the decisions of any single firm have a negligible impact on market price. The key strategic challenge of a perfectly competitive firm is to anticipate the future path of prices in the industry and maximize against it.

In many strategic situations, however, there are few players. For example, four producers—Asahi, Kirin, Sapporo, and Suntory—account for well over 90 percent of sales in the Japanese beer market. In the market for transoceanic commercial aircraft, there are just two producers: Boeing and Airbus. In these "small numbers" situations, a key part of making strategic decisions—pricing, investment in new facilities, and so forth—is anticipating how rivals may react.

A natural way to incorporate the reactions of rivals into your analysis of strategic options is to assign probabilities to their likely actions or reactions and then choose the decision that maximizes the expected value of your profit, given this probability distribution. But this approach has an important drawback: How do you assign probabilities to the range of choices your rivals might make? You may end up assigning positive probabilities to decisions that, from the perspective of your competitors, would be foolish. If so, then the quality of your "decision analysis" would be seriously compromised.

A more penetrating approach would be to attempt to "get inside the minds" of your competitors, figure out what is in their self-interest, and then maximize accordingly. However, your rivals' optimal choices will often depend on their expectations of what you intend to do, which, in turn, depend on their assessments of your assessments about them. How can one sensibly analyze decision making with this circularity?

Game theory is most valuable in precisely such contexts. It is the branch of economics concerned with the analysis of optimal decision making when all decision makers are presumed to be rational, and each is attempting to anticipate the actions and reactions of its competitors. Much of the material in Part Two on industry analysis and competitive strategy draws on game theory. In this section, we introduce these basic ideas. In particular, we discuss games in matrix and game tree form, and the concepts of a Nash equilibrium and subgame perfection.

Games in Matrix Form and the Concept of Nash Equilibrium

The easiest way to introduce the basic elements of game theory is through a simple example. Consider an industry that consists of two firms, Alpha and Beta, that produce identical products. Each must decide whether to increase its production capacity in the upcoming year. We will assume that each firm always produces at full capacity. Thus, expansion of capacity entails a trade-off. The firm may achieve a larger share of the market, but it may also put downward pressure on the market price. The consequences of each firm's choices are described in Table P.3. The first entry is Alpha's annual economic profit; the second entry is Beta's annual economic profit.

TABLE P.3
CAPACITY GAME BETWEEN ALPHA AND BETA

| | | Beta | |
		Do Not Expand	Expand
Alpha	DO NOT EXPAND	$18, $18	$15, $20
	EXPAND	$20, $15	$16, $16

All amounts are in millions per year. Alpha's payoff is first; Beta's is second.

Each firm will make its capacity decision simultaneously and independently of the other firm. To identify the "likely outcome" of games like the one shown in Table P.3, game theorists use the concept of a Nash equilibrium. At a Nash equilibrium outcome, each player is doing the best it can, given the strategies of the other players. In the context of the capacity expansion game, the Nash equilibrium is that pair of strategies (one for Alpha, one for Beta) such that

- Alpha's strategy maximizes its profit, given Beta's strategy.

- Beta's strategy maximizes its profit, given Alpha's strategy.

In the capacity expansion game, the Nash equilibrium is (EXPAND, EXPAND); that is, each firm expands its capacity. Given that Alpha expands its capacity, Beta's best choice is to expand its capacity (yielding profit of 16 rather than 15). Given that Beta expands its capacity, Alpha's best choice is to expand its capacity.

In this example, the determination of the Nash equilibrium is fairly easy because for each firm, the strategy EXPAND maximizes profit no matter what decision its competitor makes. In this situation, we say that EXPAND is a dominant strategy. When a player has a dominant strategy, it follows (from the definition of the Nash equilibrium) that that strategy must also be the player's Nash equilibrium strategy. However, dominant strategies are not inevitable; in many games players do not possess dominant strategies (e.g., the game in Table P.4).

Why does the Nash equilibrium represent a plausible outcome of a game? Probably its most compelling property is that it is a self-enforcing focal point: if each party expects the other party to choose its Nash equilibrium strategy, then both parties will, in fact, choose their Nash equilibrium strategies. At the Nash equilibrium, then, expectation equals outcome—expected behavior and actual behavior converge. This would not be true at non-Nash equilibrium outcomes, as the game in Table P.4 illustrates. Suppose Alpha (perhaps foolishly) expects Beta not to expand capacity and refrains from expanding its own capacity to prevent a drop in the industry price level. Beta—pursuing its own self-interest—would confound Alpha's expectations, expand its capacity, and make Alpha worse off than it expected to be.

The "capacity expansion" game illustrates a noteworthy aspect of a Nash equilibrium. The Nash equilibrium does not necessarily correspond to the outcome that maximizes the aggregate profit of the players. Alpha and Beta would be collectively better off by refraining from the expansion of their capacities. However, the rational pursuit of self-interest leads each party to take an action that is ultimately detrimental to their collective interest.

TABLE P.4
MODIFIED CAPACITY GAME BETWEEN ALPHA AND BETA

		Beta		
		Do Not Expand	*Small*	*Expand*
Alpha	DO NOT EXPAND	$18, $18	$15, $20	$9, $18
	SMALL	$20, $15	$16, $16	$8, $12
	LARGE	$18, $9	$12, $8	$0, $0

All amounts are in millions per year. Alpha's payoff is first; Beta's is second.

This conflict between the collective interest and self-interest is often referred to as the prisoners' dilemma. The prisoners' dilemma arises because in pursuing its self-interest, each party imposes a cost on the other that it does not take into account. In the capacity expansion game, Alpha's addition of extra capacity hurts Beta because it drives down the market price. As we will see in Part Two of the book, the prisoners' dilemma is a key feature of equilibrium pricing and output decisions in oligopolistic industries.

Game Trees and Subgame Perfection

The matrix form is particularly convenient for representing games in which each party moves simultaneously. In many situations, however, decision making is sequential rather than simultaneous, and it is often more convenient to represent the game with a game tree instead of a game matrix.

To illustrate such a situation, let us modify the capacity expansion game to allow the firm to choose among three options: no expansion of current capacity, a small expansion, or a large expansion. For contrast, let us first examine what happens when both firms decide simultaneously. This game is represented by the 3 by 3 matrix in Table P.4. We leave it to the reader to verify that the Nash equilibrium in this game is (SMALL, SMALL).

But now suppose that Alpha seeks to preempt Beta by making its capacity decision a year before Beta's. Thus, by the time Beta makes its decision, it will have observed Alpha's choice and must adjust its decision making accordingly.[12] We can represent the dynamics of this decision-making process by the game tree in Figure P.16.

FIGURE P.16
GAME TREE FOR SEQUENTIAL CAPACITY EXPANSION GAME

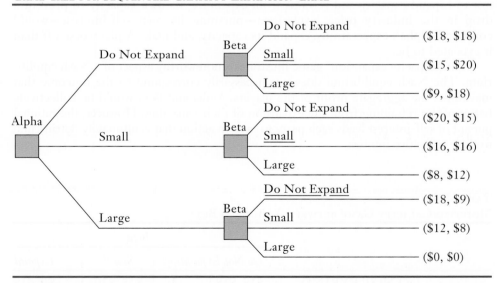

Alpha has three choices: DO NOT EXPAND, SMALL, and LARGE. Given Alpha's choice, Beta must then choose among DO NOT EXPAND, SMALL, and LARGE. For whatever choice Alpha makes, Beta will make the choice that maximizes its profit. (These are underlined.) Given Beta's expected choices, Alpha's optimal choice is LARGE.

In analyzing this game tree, we see what is known as a subgame perfect Nash equilibrium (SPNE). In an SPNE, each player chooses an optimal action at each stage in the game that it might conceivably reach and believes that all other players will behave in the same way.

To derive the SPNE, we use the so-called fold-back method: We start at the end of the tree, and for each decision "node" (represented by squares), we find the optimal decision for the firm situated at that node. In this example, we must find Beta's optimal decision for each of the three choices Alpha might make: DO NOT EXPAND, SMALL, and LARGE. By folding back the tree in this fashion, we assume that Alpha anticipates that Beta will choose a profit-maximizing response to any strategic move Alpha might make. Given these expectations, we can then determine Alpha's optimal strategy. We do so by mapping out the profit that Alpha gets as a result of each option it might choose, given that Beta responds optimally. The fold-back analysis tells us the following:

- If Alpha chooses DO NOT EXPAND, then given Beta's optimal reaction, Alpha's profit will be $15 million.

- If Alpha chooses SMALL, then given Beta's optimal reaction, Alpha's profit will be $16 million.

- If Alpha chooses LARGE, then given Beta's optimal reaction, Alpha's profit will be $18 million.

The SPNE is thus for Alpha to choose LARGE. Beta responds by choosing DO NOT EXPAND.

Note that the outcome of the sequential-move game differs significantly from the outcome of the simultaneous-move game. Indeed, the outcome involves a strategy for Alpha (LARGE) that would be dominated if Alpha and Beta made their capacity choices simultaneously. Why is Alpha's behavior so different when it can move first? Because in the sequential game, the firm's decision problems are linked through time: Beta can see what Alpha has done, and Alpha can thus count on a rational response by Beta to whatever action it chooses. In the sequential-move game, Alpha's capacity choice has commitment value; it forces Beta into a corner. By committing to a large-capacity expansion, Alpha forces Beta into a position where Beta's best response yields the outcome that is most favorable to Alpha. By contrast, in the simultaneous-move game, Beta cannot observe Alpha's decision, so the capacity decision no longer has commitment value for Alpha. Because of this, the choice of LARGE by Alpha is not nearly as compelling as it is in the sequential game. We discuss commitment in detail in Chapter 7.

CHAPTER SUMMARY

- The total cost function represents the relationship between a firm's total costs and the total amount of output it produces in a given time period.
- Total costs consist of fixed costs, which do not vary with output, and variable costs.
- Average costs equal total costs divided by total output. Marginal costs represent the additional cost of producing one more unit of output. Average costs are minimized at the point where average costs equal marginal cost.

- Sunk costs are costs that cannot be recovered if the firm stops producing or otherwise changes its decisions.

- Economic costs and economic profits depend on the costs and profits the firm would have realized had it taken its next best opportunity. These are distinct from costs and profits reported on accounting statements.

- The demand curve traces the amount that consumers are willing to pay for a good at different prices, all else equal. Most demand curves are downward sloping. The price elasticity of demand measures the percentage change in the quantity purchased for a 1 percent change in price, all else equal.

- Firms facing downward-sloping demand curves must reduce price to increase sales. A firm's marginal revenue is the additional revenue generated when the firm sells one more unit.

- Firms maximize profits by producing up to the point where the marginal revenue from an additional sale exactly equals the marginal cost.

- In a perfectly competitive market, there are many firms selling identical products to many consumers. No firm can influence the price it charges.

- The supply curve in a perfectly competitive market is the sum total of each firm's marginal cost curve and represents the total quantity that firms are willing to sell at any given price. The market demand curve represents the total quantity that consumers are willing to purchase at any given price.

- In a competitive equilibrium, the market price and quantity are given by the point where the supply curve intersects the demand curve.

- In the competitive equilibrium, firms produce up to the point where price equals marginal cost. In the long run, entry forces prices to equal the minimum average cost of production.

- Game theoretic models explicitly account for how one firm's decisions may affect the decisions of its rivals. In a Nash equilibrium, all firms are making optimal choices, given the choices of their rivals.

- Matrix forms may be used to analyze games in which firms make simultaneous choices. Extensive forms are more appropriate for analyzing games when choices are sequential.

QUESTIONS

1. What are the distinctions among fixed costs, sunk costs, variable costs, and marginal costs?

2. If the average cost curve is increasing, must the marginal cost curve lie above the average cost curve? Why or why not?

3. Why are long-run average cost curves usually at or below short-run average cost curves?

4. What is the difference between economic profit and accounting profit? Why should managers focus mainly on economic profits? Why do you suppose managers often focus on accounting profits?

5. Explain why we might expect the price elasticity of demand for nursing home care to be more negative than the price elasticity of demand for heart surgery.

6. Why is marginal revenue less than total revenue?

7. Why does the elasticity of demand affect a firm's optimal price?

8. Explain why long-run prices in a perfectly competitive market tend toward the minimum average cost of production.

9. Is the prisoners' dilemma always a Nash equilibrium? Is a Nash equilibrium always a prisoners' dilemma? Explain.

10. Does the equilibrium outcome of a game in extensive form depend on who moves first? Explain.

ENDNOTES

[1]This example is drawn from Richard Tedlow's history of the soft drink industry in his book, *New and Improved: The Story of Mass Marketing in America*, New York, Basic Books, 1990.

[2]We will discuss this relationship in Chapter 9.

[3]The third, fourth, and fifth sections of this chapter are the most "technical." Instructors not planning to cover Chapters 5–7 can skip this material.

[4]The first part of this section closely follows the presentation of cost functions on pp. 42–45 of Dorfman, R., *Prices and Markets*, 2nd ed., Englewood Cliffs, NJ, Prentice-Hall, 1972.

[5]Students sometimes confuse total costs with average (i.e., per unit) costs, and note that for many real-world firms "costs" seem to go down as output goes up. As we will see, average costs could indeed go down as output goes up. The total cost function, however, always increases with output.

[6]This term was coined by Thomas Nagle in *The Strategy and Tactics of Pricing*, Englewood Cliffs, NJ, Prentice-Hall, 1987.

[7]Some authors call these *programmed costs*. See, for example, Rados, D. L., *Pushing the Numbers in Marketing: A Real-World Guide to Essential Financial Analysis*, Westport, CT, Quorum Books, 1992.

[8]It is customary to put the minus sign in front, so that we convert what would ordinarily be a negative number (because ΔQ and ΔP have opposite signs) into a positive one.

[9]One complication should be noted: A given product's price elasticity of demand is not the same at all price levels. This means that an elasticity that is estimated at a price level of, say, $10 would be useful in predicting the impact of an increase in price to $11, but it would not accurately predict the impact of an increase to, say, $50, a price that is far outside the neighborhood of the price at which the elasticity was originally estimated. This is due to the properties of percentages, which require dividing by base amounts. If the price is so high that the quantity demanded is close to zero, even small absolute increases in quantity can translate into huge percentage increases.

[10]The use of this formula is subject to the caveat expressed earlier about the use of elasticities. It is useful for contemplating the effects of "incremental" price changes rather than dramatic price changes.

[11]This result is subject to the following qualification. If certain key inputs are scarce, the entry of additional firms bids up the prices of these inputs The firm's average and marginal cost functions then shift upward, and in the long run, the market price will settle down at a higher level. An industry in which this happens is known as an increasing-cost industry. The case we focus on in the text is known as a constant-cost industry.

[12]To keep the example as simple as possible, we will assume only two stages of decision making: Alpha makes its choice first, and then Beta responds. We do not consider the possibility that Alpha might respond to the capacity decision that Beta makes.

PART ONE
FIRM BOUNDARIES

THE POWER OF PRINCIPLES: AN HISTORICAL PERSPECTIVE

1

T his book identifies general economic principles that underly strategic decisions of firms. We have already encountered several in the Economics Primer—pricing rules, basic concepts in game theory, and the importance of economies of scale. By definition, principles are enduring. The applications change, but only because the environment changes. As the business environment continues to evolve, managers will rely on the same principles to guide their strategic choices.

We illustrate the enduring power of principles by examining how the scale and scope of the firm has evolved over the past two centuries. We focus on three points in time: 1840, 1910, and today; the first two dates represent milestones in the evolution of the business environment. While some aspects of business infrastructure developed prior to 1840, limited transportation and communications constrained firms to operate in small localized markets. Changes in infrastructure and production technology between 1840 and 1910 encouraged the growth of national and international markets and corporate giants such as British Petroleum, U.S. Steel, and Bayer Chemical. Even the largest and best-managed firms, however, were constrained by problems of coordination and control—how to gain sufficient information on a timely basis to manage large-scale operations and adapt to market changes. Since 1910, and particularly in the last 30 years, changes in communications, data processing, and networking have revolutionized firms' abilities to control their operations and interact with suppliers, customers, competitors, and other stakeholders.

Although we have witnessed fundamental changes in nearly all aspects of the business environment, principles for business decision making have not changed. When one applies these principles to the ever changing environment, the remarkable evolution of business practices over the three generations that we discuss makes perfect sense.

DOING BUSINESS IN 1840

Before 1840, businessmen[1] managed their own firms in ways that today's managers might point to as damning evidence against the durability of business principles. The experience of John Burrows was typical.[2] Burrows was an Iowa merchant who bought potatoes from nearby farmers and cleaned and packaged them. Hearing that potatoes were fetching $2 a bushel in New Orleans, he loaded an Illinois River flatboat and floated downstream. On the trip, he was offered 50 cents a bushel for his potatoes but rejected it in hope of getting a better price in New Orleans. While floating south, he was joined by other potato merchants seeking the same high prices. Soon, the New Orleans market was glutted. Supply and demand dictated that potato prices would plummet. After a six-week journey, Burrows sold his potatoes to a Bermuda ship captain for 8 cents a bushel. Viewed from a modern perspective, this way of doing business makes little sense. But in 1840, Burrows's way of doing business represented a very sensible response to the infrastructure and technology of the time.

Burrows was a merchant known as a "factor." Farmers in the United States and Europe sold their output to factors like Burrows, who brought the goods to major markets, such as New Orleans or New York, in search of buyers. Some of these buyers were local merchants, looking to stock their grocery stores. Most buyers, however, were "agents," representing out-of-town merchants, including some from Europe. Factors and agents rarely dealt directly with each other. Instead, they enlisted the help of "brokers" who served as matchmakers between factors and agents. Brokers possessed specialized knowledge of market conditions that individual factors and agents lacked, including the names of factors and agents, the availability of supplies, and the magnitude of demands.

Selling was informal. Transactions were relatively infrequent, the cast of potential transaction partners changed constantly, and timely information about the sales of comparable goods and the prices obtained for them was often unavailable. These problems increased with the geographic distance between buyers and sellers. As a result, factors and agents sought out brokers with whom they had done business before. Terms were rarely set in advance or specified in a contract. Instead, the brokers tried to arrange a price that best balanced supply and demand for a given situation.

This was how most business was transacted in 1840, and it was the best anyone could do under the circumstances. The brokerage arrangement no longer dominates the American business landscape, but it does survive in various forms, in businesses such as real estate. An important modern example of the broker role is the "market maker" in securities transactions. Market makers in the New York Stock Exchange (NYSE) match the buy and sell orders of parties who do not know each other, facilitating transactions that would otherwise be difficult to complete.

Buy and sell orders for shares traded on the NYSE are filled almost immediately, giving both parties to a transaction reasonable certainty about the price. John Burrows's experience shows that this was not the case in 1840. Factors and agents faced considerable price risk—that is, the price that they expected when they began doing business (e.g., when Burrows started floating his potatoes downstream) may have been very different from the price received when the transaction took place (e.g., when Burrows reached New Orleans). This risk obviously increased with the distance between the site of production and its final destination. European merchants trading with the United States ran even larger risks than those Mr. Burrows faced.

The lack of knowledge about prices, buyers and sellers, and the associated risks dramatically shaped the nature of business. Farmers faced the most risk, and they relied on factors like Burrows to assume some of it, by selling different farm products at different times of the year, and by selling specific products at various times on the way to market. Presumably, Burrows was more willing to bear risk than most farmers, which may have been why he became a factor rather than a farmer. Once Burrows reached the market himself, he relied on brokers to find buyers for his potatoes, a task that he could not easily perform himself.

With few exceptions, such as in textiles, clockmaking, and firearms, most "firms" in 1840 were very small, exemplified by the individual and family-run businesses that dominated the potato industry. This stands in stark contrast to today, where a firm employing 50 workers is considered small, and there is often a clear distinction between owners (shareholders), managers, and employees. Given the local nature of markets and the uncertainty about prices, it is not surprising that individuals in 1840 were reluctant to use their own limited resources to expand the size of their businesses. For similar reasons, banks were also unwilling to finance business expansion, leading to underdeveloped capital markets. Because of problems with transportation and communication, which we describe below, firms could not justify investing in the acquisition of raw materials or the distribution of final products, even though this might have allowed them to coordinate the production process more efficiently. As a result, production and distribution required the coordination of many small, local firms. Market conditions at the time made any other system impractical.

Business Conditions in 1840: Life Without a Modern Infrastructure

The dominance of the family-run small business in 1840 was a direct consequence of the *infrastructure* that was then in place. Infrastructure includes those assets that assist in the production or distribution of goods and services that the firm itself cannot easily provide. Infrastructure facilitates transportation, communication, and financing. It includes basic research, which can enable firms to find better production techniques. The government has a key role in a nation's infrastructure because it affects the conditions under which firms do business (e.g., by regulating telecommunications), and often supplies infrastructure investments directly (e.g., national highways). Government investments in infrastructure are especially important for *public goods*, where individual firms are unable to capture more than a fraction of the benefits and are therefore reluctant to bear the costs.

Limitations in transportation, communications, and finance created the business environment with which John Burrows and others of his time had to cope. While we discuss the situation in America in this and subsequent sections, European businessmen faced similar limitations, often made worse by political factors.

Transportation

The harnessing of steam power revolutionized transportation in the first half of the nineteenth century. Although the Romans had made attempts to develop roadbeds by means of rails of different sorts, the modern railroad did not add value to commerce until the introduction of the steam engine and the use of iron and steel rails. By 1840, the railroads began to replace the horse and wagon for the shipment of raw materials and consumer goods. Rails in the United States took time to develop, however. As late as 1836, only 175 miles of railroad track were laid in one year.[4] By 1850, U.S. railway systems were still too fragmented to foster the growth of national markets. Few rails ran west of the Appalachian Mountains, "connecting" lines often had different gauges, and schedules were seldom coordinated. The development of an integrated transportation infrastructure through railroads in the United States would not be complete until after 1870.

Until the railroads developed, manufacturers used the waterways to transport goods over long distances, even though water transportation left much to be desired.

EXAMPLE 1.1   THE EMERGENCE OF CHICAGO[3]

The emergence of Chicago as a major commercial center in the 1800s illustrates the core concepts that we have discussed, albeit for a city rather than a business. In the 1840s, growing cities in the Midwest, including Cincinnati, Toledo, Peoria, St. Louis, and Chicago, were all competing, as vigorously as firms in any other markets might compete, to become the region's center of commerce. Their success would ultimately be decided by the same conditions that determined the horizontal and vertical boundaries of business firms. Significant changes in *infrastructure* and *technology* enabled Chicago's business organizations, and with them the city's financial fortunes, to outstrip other cities. For example, by 1860, the Chicago Board of Trade bought and sold nearly all the grain produced in the Midwest. Similarly, two Chicago meatpackers, Armour and Swift, dominated their industry.

Chicago prospered because it conducted business differently from competing commercial centers. Chicago businesses were the first to take advantage of new technologies that reduced costs and risks. For example, Swift and Armour simultaneously adopted the refrigerated train car, which had first been used by Illinois fruit growers. (Lining a standard freight car with ice from Lake Michigan produced the refrigerator car.) This allowed cattle and hogs to be butchered in Chicago, before they lost weight (and value) on the way to market. Cyrus McCormick and others took advantage of the recently invented grain elevator to inexpensively sort, store, and ship grain bought from midwestern farmers. They reduced the risk of dealing with large quantities of grain by buying and selling grain futures at the newly founded Chicago Board of Trade.

The businesses run by Swift, Armour, McCormick, and other Chicago entrepreneurs required substantial investments in rail lines, icing facilities, grain elevators, the futures market, and so forth. These businessmen recognized that they could not recoup their investments without high volumes of business. This would require *throughput*: the movement of inputs and outputs through a production process. The meatpacking and grain businesses of Chicago required large supplies of ice and large assured movements of grain and livestock from the farmlands and grain and butchered meat to eastern markets. The need for throughput explains why Chicago emerged as the business center of the Midwest. Only Chicago, with its unique location as the terminus of rail and water routes from the East and West, had the transportation infrastructure necessary to assure throughput. Chicago thus emerged during the mid-1800s and remains today the "market leader" among midwestern cities.

For example, while the new steamships plied major American rivers and the Great Lakes as early as 1813, no direct route connected the major Atlantic seaboard cities to the Great Lakes until the completion of the Erie Canal in 1825. Steamships could not unload in Chicago until the 1840s. The trip from New York to Chicago was both lengthy and risky, especially during bad weather. Possible waterway routes were limited, and constructing and maintaining canals was expensive. Nonetheless, the opening of the Erie Canal led to startling growth. For example, between 1830 and 1840, the population of Illinois tripled, from 157,000 to 476,000, and the population of Chicago grew eightfold, from 500 to more than 4,000.[5]

Ocean transport at this time was still dominated by sailing ships, and innovations such as the steam engine and the screw propeller were new to this mode of travel. The White Star line, the famous British steamship firm and eventual owner of the *Titanic*, was founded during this time (1845).

Communications

The primary mode of long-distance communication in 1840 was the public mail. The U.S. Postal Service had developed into the largest postal system in the world by 1828. Even so, as late as 1840, the postal service depended almost exclusively on the horse and stagecoach, and had difficulty adjusting to the volume of communication that followed western U.S. expansion. It was not until the establishment of the Railway Mail Service in 1869 that the postal service shifted to railroads as the principal means for transporting mail nationally. This was hardly the instantaneous communication we have come to associate with a modern infrastructure.

Using the mails for business correspondence proved expensive and unpredictable. For example, correspondence from the Waterbury, Connecticut, headquarters of the Scovill Company in the 1840s took one day to reach New York City and two days to reach Philadelphia in good weather. In bad weather, it could easily take a week. To send a one-sheet letter from Waterbury cost 12.5 cents to New York and 18.5 cents to Philadelphia. The absence of postmarks on some letters from this time suggests that high postage rates encouraged Scovill owners and their agents to hand-carry items. Business mail volume increased after the U.S. Postal Service significantly lowered its rates twice, in 1845 and 1851, in response to the growth of competition from private delivery services.[6]

The first modern form of communication was the telegraph, which required laying wires between points of service. In 1844, Samuel Morse linked Baltimore and Washington by telegraph on a project funded by the U.S. Congress. While Morse's venture quickly proved unprofitable, other telegraph lines soon flourished. By 1848, New York was linked to both Chicago and New Orleans. By 1853, a total of 23,000 miles of line had been strung.

By the 1860s, transatlantic cables connected the United States and Europe. These cables and their descendants remain important infrastructure elements today. After a period of explosive growth, the industry consolidated around a dominant firm—Western Union.

Even when modern communication capabilities became available, firms did not always adopt them, since their potential value was unclear at first while their start-up costs were high. Firms initially used the telegraph for its value in bridging distances with agents over matters such as pricing. Although using the telegraph was expensive, important time-sensitive messages justified the cost. Railroads used the telegraph for these reasons, but were slow to adopt it for regular scheduling. The New York and Erie Railroad was the first to do this in the United States in 1851, following the example of British railroads.[7] In time, however, telegraph lines came to parallel most major train lines and proved indispensable for railroad scheduling and operations. Some modern telecommunications firms, such as Sprint, saw their beginnings in these types of arrangements.

Finance

Few individuals could afford to build and operate a complex firm themselves. Financial markets bring together providers and users of capital, enabling them to smooth out cash flows and reduce the risk of price fluctuation. In the first half of the nineteenth century, however, financial markets were immature at best. Most businesses at the time were sole proprietorships or partnerships that found it difficult to obtain long-term debt. In addition, stocks were neither easily nor widely traded, which diluted their value and increased the cost of equity capital. Investors also found it hard to protect themselves against the increased risks of larger capital projects.

The major role of private banks at this time was the issuance of credit. By 1820, there were more than 300 banks in the United States. By 1837, there were 788. By offering short-term credit, banks smoothed the cash flows of buyers and sellers and facilitated reliable transactions, although considerable risk from speculation and inflation remained throughout the nineteenth century. There was a recurring pattern of boom and bust, with periodic major depressions, such as the Panic of 1837.

Many smaller firms had difficulty getting credit, however, and if it was available at all, credit was often granted informally on the basis of personal relationships. Government or private consortia—groups of private individuals brought together to finance a specific project—funded larger projects. All told, from 1820 until 1838, 18 states advanced credit of $60 million for canals, $43 million for railroads, and $4.5 million for turnpikes.

As the scale of capital projects increased after 1840, government support or larger public debt or equity offerings by investment banks increasingly replaced financing by private individuals and small groups of investors as the principal sources of capital funds for businesses.

In 1840, no institutional mechanisms were available that reduced the risk of price fluctuation. This would require the creation of futures markets. Through futures markets, individuals purchase the right to buy and/or sell goods on a specified date for a predetermined price. Futures markets require verification of the characteristics of the product being transacted. They also require that one party to the transaction is willing to bear the risk that the "spot" (i.e., current) price on the date the futures transaction is completed may differ from the transacted price. The first futures market was created by the Chicago Board of Trade (CBOT) in 1858 and profoundly affected the farming industry, as we discuss in Example 1.1. The CBOT would not have been possible without the telegraph; in this way we see how one form of infrastucture facilitated another.

Production Technology

Production technology was relatively undeveloped in 1840. Where factories existed at all, they produced goods in much the same way they had been produced in the previous century. Textile plants had begun to be mechanized before 1820 and standardization was common in the manufacture of clocks and firearms, but the "American System" of manufacturing through the use of interchangeable parts was only just beginning to be adopted. Many of the scale-intensive industries most associated with industrial growth, such as steel, oil, chemicals, or automobiles, developed volume production only in the late nineteenth or early twentieth century.

Government

The economics underlying public works projects like the Erie Canal are similar to the economics of the prisoners' dilemma, which we described in the Economics Primer. The economy as a whole benefits if all citizens chip in to bear their cost, but no one individual or firm finds it worthwhile taking on the project alone. Thus, the government steps in and provides the public good on behalf of everyone. Aside from such infrastructure investments, the U.S. government was not much involved in the economy prior to 1840. During the Civil War, President Lincoln's administration sponsored the competition between the Union Pacific and Central Pacific Railroads to build the first transcontinental railroad, which was completed in 1869. This project arguably had an equal or a greater effect on the economy of the time than did the creation of the Internet, another government infrastructure project.

By the end of the nineteenth century, the U.S. government was becoming more actively involved in the business environment. The first major industry regulatory agency, the Interstate Commerce Commission, was created in 1887 to regulate the railroads. The Sherman Antitrust Act was enacted in 1890. Another important but less well-known example of government involvement in building commercial infrastructure during this time occurred in 1884, when the U.S. government hosted the Prime

---

EXAMPLE 1.2 BUILDING NATIONAL INFRASTRUCTURE: CHINA AND THE UNITED STATES

In January of 2009, China began one of the largest ever spending programs to build national infrastructure. The context for the enormous amounts (estimated at hundreds of billions of U.S. dollars) was the global economic downtown, as increased government spending would provide a stimulus to China's macroeconomy. However, as with all investment spending, the expectation is that there will be benefits over the longer term as well.

It has long been recognized that improved transportation is key to economic development. Indeed, according to a story in *The New York Times*, the spending plan "promises to carry the modernity of China's coasts deep into the hinterlands," with the effect of "priming China for a new level of global competition."[8]

Included in the spending plan are both passenger railways and freight railways of both (relatively) long and short distances. The highest priority project is $88 billion of spending to construct intercity rail lines, which should encourage decreased use of personal automobiles, thereby reducing China's dependence on oil imports and helping to decrease air pollution. Among the other projects in the plan, the biggest are a $17.6 billion passenger rail across the deserts of northwest China, a $22 billion network of freight rail lines in north-central China, and a $24 billion high-speed passenger rail from Beijing to Guangzhou in southeastern China. However, almost no part of China will be unaffected as projects will be undertaken in "practically every town, city, and county across the country." This will "change the face of China, giving the country a world-class infrastructure for moving goods and people quickly, cheaply and reliably across great distances."[9] According to John Scales, transport coordinator for China at the World Bank, this undertaking by the Chinese is of the same significance as the growth of the U.S. rail network in the early 1900s.

The United States built its transcontinental railroad between 1863 and 1869. It connected the eastern end of the Union Pacific Railroad with the western home of the Central Pacific Railroad. This project reduced the time and expense of moving people, goods, and information from the population centers in the East to California. Before its completion, trips to California took months by sea or over land, cost thousands of dollars, and were fraught with risks. Within months of its completion, a trip from New York to San Francisco took seven days, was much safer, and cost less than $100. Mail to California, which had been priced at dollars per ounce before 1869, cost pennies per ounce shortly afterward.

The railroad fostered the growth of a national and continental perspective, such that a national stock market and national commodity markets developed. It also set the stage for the growth of national retail markets by the early years of the twentieth century. As with China in 2009, the U.S. government heavily subsidized the builders of the railroad with financing and land grants. As is also the case with the Internet today, managers, investors, government officials, and others were very uncertain regarding how to harness the commercial and transformative potential of the transcontinental railroad so that it could become profitable. Problems of overbuilding and financial and political scandals plagued the railroads through the 1870s and the situation was worsened by a major national recession. Many of the major railroads went bankrupt and fell under the control of speculators and it was not until the 1890s that the transcontinental railroad was rationalized, unprofitable operations were closed, and remaining operations were upgraded and standardized. This allowed economies of scale in railroad network operations to be better realized. The result was an efficient and profitable industry that dominated transportation until the advent of the automobile.

Meridian Conference in Washington, D.C. This led to the nearly worldwide adoption of a system of standard time, including the now-familiar 24 standard time zones, the location of the Prime Meridian in Greenwich, England, and the adoption of an International Date Line. This system was necessary to meet the demands for coordination in transportation, communication, and contracting that arose out of the worldwide expansion of markets due to improvements in transportation and communications. It is now commonplace for government to relax antitrust laws to allow erstwhile competitors to meet and establish technology standards.

Summary The lack of a modern infrastructure limited economic activity in 1840. Firms were small and informally organized. There were no professional managers; owners ran their own enterprises. Technology prevented production from expanding much beyond traditional levels in local markets. The limited transportation and communication infrastructure would have made investments in large-scale manufacturing too risky even if production technology permitted. Market demand and technological development were needed before high-speed and high-volume production and distribution could occur. There were forces in play, however, that would change the conditions in which business operated and greatly increase its scale of operations and quality of management.

DOING BUSINESS IN 1910

Business changed greatly from 1840 to 1910, and the business practices and organizations of 1910 would seem much more familiar to the modern businessperson than those of 1840. The evolution of business resulted not from newly developed management principles, but from changes in infrastructure and technology. No change was more important than the development of mass-production technologies, such as the Bessemer process for making steel, or the continuous-process tank furnace that facilitated the mass production of many products, such as plate glass. These new technologies enabled goods to be produced at costs far below what firms using older technologies could achieve. The fixed investments required to develop these outlets were justified only when large volumes of goods flowed through them. In other words, firms needed to assure a sufficiently large *throughput* to make the expansion of productive capacity economical. The needed throughput was assured by developing infrastructure: railroads for shipping inputs and finished goods; telegraph and telephone for communication, control, and coordination of materials over expanded areas; and banking and accounting practices to provide the investment capital needed to finance production and distribution facilities. The combination of scale economies and throughput enabled corporate giants to reach many more customers at lower costs per customer than their smaller competitors.

Product line and volume expansion altered relationships among manufacturers, their suppliers, and their distributors. Manufacturing firms increasingly chose to *vertically integrate*; that is, they chose to produce raw materials and/or distribute finished goods themselves, rather than rely on independent suppliers, factors, and agents for these tasks. Chapter 3 discusses the costs and benefits of vertical integration in depth. In a nutshell, manufacturing firms found it desirable to vertically integrate because the high volume of production made them more vulnerable to gaps in the chain of supply and distribution.

In the years immediately following 1910, many firms, such as DuPont, General Motors, and Alcoa, expanded horizontally by using established production technologies to offer a wider variety of products. Some of these firms found that the increased size and complexity of multiproduct operations necessitated a further reorganization into semiautonomous divisions. For example, the divisions of General Motors made operating decisions for each car line, while corporate management controlled corporate finance, research and development, and new model development. This organizational form, known as the multidivisional or *M-form*, became characteristic of the largest industrial firms until the 1960s.

The expansion of mass production was also associated with the subsequent growth of mass distribution firms in such sectors as groceries, apparel, drugstores, and general variety merchandising. While chain stores dated to the mid-nineteenth century, they greatly expanded in number and market share after World War I. In the United States, the number of A&P food stores tripled, as did J.C. Penney stores, while the number of Walgreens drugstores increased twentyfold. By 1929, the national market share of the top three grocery chains (A&P, Kroger, and Safeway) approached 40 percent. (The growth of national chains came more slowly in Europe, which had been beaten down by the First World War.)

The growth of vertically and horizontally integrated firms often reduced the number of firms in an industry and increased the potential for collusion to restrict competition and increase profits. During the period around 1910, the U.S. government directed antitrust activities toward breaking up firms that appeared to be national monopolies. Among the major cases during this time were those involving Standard Oil (1911), American Tobacco (1911), DuPont (1912), International Harvester (1918), and Eastman Kodak (1920).

Integrated firms employed more individuals in more complex and interrelated tasks than had earlier firms. They responded by standardizing jobs and tasks, monitoring worker compliance with management directives, appraising worker performance, and testing and training employees. These approaches spread widely among large firms, under the influence of a new type of specialist, the management consultant. Perhaps the best known of these approaches was "Scientific Management," developed by Frederick W. Taylor, which sought to identify the most efficient ways of performing tasks through "time-and-motion" studies and then motivate workers to adopt these ways of working through the use of incentives, rewards, and sanctions.[10]

As firms grew larger, the functional areas of business—purchasing, sales, distribution, and finance—grew more important. The owner-manager could no longer perform these tasks alone. Firms created dedicated central offices staffed by professional managers, who ensured that production went smoothly and finished goods made it to market. As Alfred Chandler describes, the resulting hierarchy substituted the *visible* hand of management for the *invisible* hand of the market.[11]

These changes in the nature of the firm and its managers caused problems and conflicts. The development of internal controls needed for coordination and efficiency could easily turn into excessive bureaucracy. Newly expanded workforces resisted the controls on their behavior and the standardization of their work habits that were needed to foster greater and more predictable throughput. This aided the growth of unions, and with them increased labor-related conflicts.

Business Conditions in 1910: A "Modern" Infrastructure

A substantially new infrastructure for business had emerged by 1910, notably in transportation and communications. These developments fostered the growth of national markets by enabling firms to count on the fast and reliable movements of goods, along with instantaneous and accurate communication over vast areas.

Production Technology

Most people did not begin to hear about mass production until after 1913, the year in which Henry Ford began producing the Model T. Mass-production processes permitted high-volume, low-cost manufacturing of many products, including steel, aluminum, chemicals, and automobiles, to name only a few. These products proved to be of more than sufficient quality to compete with the lower-volume custom products they replaced. The technology of producing "management services" also developed. Innovations in document production (typewriters), copying (carbon paper; photocopying), analysis (adding machines; punched-card tabulators), and organization (vertical file systems) enabled managers to coordinate the increased volume of transactions. Supplying these products spurred the growth of such firms as IBM, Burroughs, and Remington Rand.

Transportation

The continued consolidation and rationalization of the railroads after the initial period of growth assured the throughput necessary for economical mass production. By 1910, railroads dominated passenger and freight transportation. Travel by rail became faster, safer, and more reliable. Manufacturers could obtain raw materials from distant sources and swiftly ship their products to customers hundreds or even thousands of miles away. Smaller manufacturers sold to the new mass-distribution firms, such as Sears, which could cheaply distribute via the rails vast arrays of goods to scattered customers. Motorcars were also developing as a fundamental means of transportation, but trucks would not displace the U.S. railroads until the development of an extensive system of interstate highways following World War II.

Communications

The main components of the communications infrastructure in 1840—the postal system and the telegraph—were still important in 1910 and were increasingly becoming part of the management and communications systems of large firms. During this time, however, the telephone grew more important. Phone calls to suppliers and distributors could instantly assure managers that large production runs were feasible and that there were markets for their output.

   The growth of American Telephone and Telegraph (AT&T) illustrates how the development of large firms depended on market and technological conditions. When the telephone was invented in 1876, its technological potential (and hence its profitability) was uncertain because some devices essential for telephone service as we know it, such as the switchboard, were unknown. The market conditions facing the telephone were also uncertain because of patent conflicts. This led to local competition to provide service. By the 1880s, patent conflicts had been resolved, and new technology made consolidation possible. In 1883, under the leadership of Theodore Vail, AT&T adopted a strategy of merging local telephone companies into a national system. The resulting network reduced the costs of interconnecting large numbers of users, and the telephone quickly replaced the telegraph as the communications technology of choice.[12] The telephone also had implications for how the emerging firms of this era were organized. For example, it is hard to imagine the growth of the multistory headquarters office building without the telephone to connect all headquarters employees with each other and with field offices.[13]

EXAMPLE 1.3   EVOLUTION OF THE STEEL INDUSTRY

In the first half of the twentieth century, success in the steel industry required both horizontal and vertical integration. Traditionally, the leading firms, such as U.S. Steel, Bethlehem Steel, and Republic Steel, produced a wide array of high-volume steel products and controlled the production process, from the mining of ore through the production of the finished steel products to marketing and distribution. But in the early 1950s, changes in market demand and technology transformed the industry.

The most significant change in market demand was driven by shifts in the economy. In the 1950s, "lighter" products, such as strips and sheets used to produce appliances, automobiles, and computers, became relatively more important than "heavier" products, such as rails and plates used for railroad and ship building. But the large steel producers, particularly U.S. Steel, were committed to the "heavy" products. Much of the steelmakers' capacity was also poorly located to meet the new demands for lighter products. These factors allowed foreign producers to penetrate American markets.

The most notable technological advances were the basic oxygen furnace, the continuous casting process, and scrap metal processing with the electric arc furnace. The basic oxygen furnace, which was commercialized in 1950 by an Austrian firm, Linz-Donawitz, replaced the open-hearth process as the fastest way to convert iron into raw steel. Continuous casting, a German invention that was perfected in the early 1960s by a small American company, Roanoke Electric, allowed steel producers to bypass the costly process of pouring molten steel into ingots and reheating them for milling and finishing. The electric arc furnace was available before World War II but was little used before 1960.

However, the increasing availability of scrap steel from discarded automobiles changed that, and by 1970, the electric arc furnace had become a viable way of producing nonalloy steel.

These technological advances had two profound effects. First, in postwar Japan and Germany, and later in Brazil and South Korea, start-up steel firms quickly adopted the basic oxygen furnace and continuous casting. By contrast, in the United States, the established integrated mills had made nonrecoverable investments in the older technologies, in terms of both physical capital and expertise. These firms were therefore reluctant to shift to the new technologies. As late as 1988, 93 percent of all Japanese firms and 88 percent of South Korean steel firms had adopted continuous casting, while only 60 percent of American firms had done so, and nearly half of these U.S. firms had made the changes only in the 1980s.[14] This allowed foreign producers to become competitive threats to the large integrated American producers.

Second, the new technology spurred the development of *minimills*, small nonintegrated producers that convert scrap metal into finished steel products. The success of minimill producers, such as Nucor, Chapparal, and North Star, is emblematic of the significance of this new way of producing steel. Minimills have eliminated the advantages of high-volume manufacturing in product lines, such as steel bars, structural shapes, and wire rods, and with Nucor's recent breakthrough in thin-slab casting, they may also take away the advantages of scale in the production of hot- and cold-rolled sheet. Although the large integrated producers have not disappeared, their importance has clearly diminished.

Finance

Since the 1860s, large investment banking houses had been underwriting most stock transactions that were essential for the financing of large firms. In 1910, securities markets publicly traded the shares of the largest industrial firms. The development of a financial infrastructure was further aided by the systematization and circulation of credit information (credit bureaus), the availability of installment financing, and the development of the communications infrastructure.

During this time, owners, managers, and investors realized that the growing scope of business required new ways of keeping track of a firm's activity and reporting its results. For example, the railroads produced major innovations in cost accounting to manage their requirements of operating efficiencies, while mass-marketing firms such as Sears developed new accounting concepts, such as inventory turnover, to link profits to fluctuations in sales volume.

Accounting developments also focused on the idea of public accounting—the public disclosure of details of a firm's operations to ensure that investors were not being cheated by managers and that capital was being maintained. Laws enacted in England between 1844 and 1900 required the presentation of a "full and fair" balance sheet at shareholders' meetings, the payment of dividends out of profits, the maintenance of a firm's capital stock, and the conduct of compulsory and uniform audits of all registered firms. Similar developments occurred in the United States. The first U.S. independent accounting firm was founded in New York in 1883, and the American Association of Public Accountants was formed in 1886.

Government

Government regulation of the conditions under which business was conducted, in such areas as corporate law and governance, antitrust, provisions for disability insurance and worker safety, and insurance for widows and children, increased during this period. (Securities markets and labor relations were not fully regulated until the 1930s.) This increased regulation affected not only how firms behaved toward competitors and employees, but also how they were managed, since government forced managers to collect detailed data on their operations that had not been gathered before and that were useful to professional managers. Nearly universal mandatory secondary school education also became the norm for industrialized nations in the first half of the twentieth century. This produced a workforce able to meet the specialized needs of large bureaucratic firms. Finally, through continued infrastructure investments, along with increasing military and shipbuilding expenditures, government became an important customer and partner of industry. These different roles embodied numerous potential conflicts and did not always fit together well in the new economic terrain.

Summary   The business infrastructure in 1910 made it efficient for firms to expand their markets, product lines, and production quantities. New technologies permitted a higher volume of standardized production, while the growth of the rail system allowed the reliable distribution of manufactured goods to a national market. The telegraph enabled large firms to monitor and control geographically separate suppliers, factories, and distributors. The growth of futures markets, capital markets, insurance companies, investment banks, and other financial institutions enabled business to be transacted on a scale that would have been impossible in 1840. By one estimate, the "transaction-processing sector," which included transportation, communication, and financial institutions, had become one-third of the U.S. economy by 1910.[15] To achieve the cost savings afforded by mass production and distribution, many firms reorganized and became more vertically and horizontally integrated. Increasingly, a new class of professional managers developed during this period and made critical decisions for firms. These managers became expert in functions that had not previously been handled by individual owners and entrepreneurs. The skills of those managers became a source of competitive advantage for firms in industries that could benefit from expansion.

DOING BUSINESS TODAY

Two world wars took their toll on global economic development, and the business world in 1950 had changed only incrementally over the previous 50 years. (An important exception is the automobile industry.) Since then, and particularly in the last 30 years, the ways of doing business have changed profoundly. Again, innovations in infrastructure are at the heart of the revolution in business practices. Computerized production processes allow specialized niche firms to offer tailor-made products at costs previously enjoyed only by larger firms exploiting scale economies. Modern telecommunication facilitates global business ventures, and the so-called BRICS economies (*Brazil, Russia, India, China, South Africa* and other nations at a similar stage of economic development) have taken advantage by offering highly skilled, low-wage workers to Western companies looking to reduce production costs. These forces are encouraging large firms that once dominated the economy to increasingly prefer global alliances and joint ventures to domestic mergers and acquisitions.

Perhaps the most notable change in the business environment has been the decline of the large vertically integrated corporate giants. In helping to explain this decline, Adam Smith's theory of the division of labor (described in Chapter 2) is proof positive of the power of principles. In a small growing economy, a firm must perform all of the tasks in the vertical chain because the market cannot yet support specialists in accounting, marketing, distribution, and such. Specialists emerge as markets grow, and firms no longer need to perform these activities in-house.

The twentieth century also saw firms expand and then shrink their horizontal boundaries. While some firms had begun to diversify beyond traditional product lines as early as 1890, the pace of diversification increased significantly after World War II, as firms like DuPont and General Foods discovered that their capabilities and skills were not exhausted by their historical product mix. Other firms, such as ITT and Textron, acquired portfolios of unrelated businesses. Senior management ran these firms as holding companies and delegated most strategic and operating decisions to the individual business units. While diversification was initially popular during the 1960s, the subsequent performance of conglomerates disappointed investors; the trend of subsequent mergers and acquisitions has been toward "deconglomeration" and a focus on core markets and enhanced linkages among business units.

Even with reduced conglomeration, firms have continued to form linkages across diverse businesses. Nowadays, diversification often takes place by strategic alliances and joint ventures as well as by merger and acquisition, and today's managers must manage global supply chains in much the same way that managers in 1910 coped with domestic supply chains. This has been facilitated by the growth of data processing, telecommunications, and networking capabilities.

Firms have also taken a fresh look at their internal structure and the organization of the vertical chain of production. Until the 1960s, most large diversified firms followed the General Motors model and employed the M-form. But as these firms diversified into less related businesses, they eliminated layers of hierarchy and reduced corporate staffs. Some firms, such as Dow Corning, Amoco, and Citibank, had difficulty coordinating complicated production processes across different customer groups and market areas using traditional multidivisional structures. These firms adopted complex matrix structures, in which two or more overlapping hierarchies are used simultaneously. Other firms, including Benetton, Nike, and Harley-Davidson, simplified their internal hierarchies, controlling product design and brand image but leaving most other functions, including manufacturing, distribution, and retailing, to independent market specialists.

Modern Infrastructure

Infrastructure today is marked by communications, transportation, and computing technologies that ensure coordination of extensive activities on a global scale. This, in turn, increases the interdependence of geographical markets and has magnified the costs of infrastructure failure. The interdependence of contemporary infrastructure was made tragically apparent in the aftermath of the September 11, 2001 terrorist attacks on New York and Washington. These attacks simultaneously halted two critical infrastructure sectors of the world economy—financial markets and air traffic. In addition, the attacks placed huge strains on other sectors whose influence cuts across the world economy, for example, insurance and leisure resorts.

Transportation

Automobile and air travel transformed the transportation infrastructure. Interstate trucking has become a competitor to the railroads in the shipment of freight. Air, rail, and ground travel have become better coordinated. Increasing demands from shippers of large volumes of goods for efficient and reliable transportation over long distances, coupled with more sophisticated communications and data processing technology, have allowed goods to be shipped in containers that move from ships to railroads to trucks. The widespread use of air travel for both freight and passengers has reduced the need for cities and firms to be close to railroads and waterways. What Chicago was to the second half of the nineteenth century, Atlanta was to the second half of the twentieth, despite its relatively poor rail and water connections.

Communications

Although fundamental developments in broadcasting, telecommunications, and computer technology occurred before World War II, many observers argue that the growth of these areas since 1950 has defined the economic infrastructure in the late twentieth century and set the stage for the twenty-first century. Observers struggle with how to characterize this new infrastructure, a recent effort being Thomas Friedman's discussion of a "flat" world that combines globalization, technological change, and post-9/11 world politics.[16] In particular, telecommunications technologies, such as the fax or the modem, have made possible the nearly instantaneous transmission and reception of large amounts of complex information over long distances, creating global markets for a wide range of products and services. This technology, coupled with continuing improvements in data processing, has also drastically increased worker productivity, and has made the paper-based coordination and control of older integrated firms obsolete. The Internet has increased the possibilities for interfirm coordination via contracts, alliances, and joint ventures.

Finance

The failure of financial markets in 1929, followed by worldwide recession in the 1930s, led to the creation of the modern financial infrastructure, through the separation of commercial and investment banking, the enhanced role of central banks, and the increased regulation of securities markets. The result was a stable financial services sector that supplied firms with equity and debt funding that the firms themselves could not provide through their retained earnings.

Deregulation of financial services in the 1970s and 1980s changed the role of the financial sector in the economic infrastructure. Since 1980, capital markets have more actively evaluated firm performance. The ready availability of large investment funds allowed mergers and acquisitions (M&A) to multiply in number and dollar amount per deal. Most recently, venture capitalists and investment banks are enabling entrepreneurs with good ideas to rapidly achieve the scale necessary to compete with larger rivals.

Production Technology

Computerization, the Internet, and other innovations have increased the sophistication of production technology, though with complex economic implications. Changes in production technology, such as the development of computer-aided design and manufacturing (CAD/CAM), have changed traditional ideas of price/quality trade-offs and allowed the production of high-quality, tailor-made goods at low cost. In using new technologies, however, managers in the 2000s must choose between reformulating their strategies and reorganizing around new information and production technologies or using these technologies incrementally to reinforce traditional modes of production and organization.

Government

Government regulation of economic activities increased in the first half of the twentieth century, in response to two world wars and the Great Depression. Since the 1960s, the government has relaxed many of the traditional regulations on some industries while increasing them on others. The breakup of the Bell System, the deregulation of airline, trucking, financial services, and health care industries, and the weakening of banking regulations have been major influences in the economy since 1970. Intergovernmental treaties and agreements on the development of regional free trade zones, such as with the North American Free Trade Agreement (NAFTA) or the European Community, have greatly affected how firms compete in an increasingly global marketplace. Regulation of workplace safety, discrimination, and the environment became common in the 1960s and 1970s.

The government also spent vast sums on the military and public works. One area where the government has influenced infrastructure has been in support of Research and Development (R&D). Throughout the twentieth century, U.S. antitrust policy encouraged firms to develop new capabilities internally, through R&D efforts, rather than through M&As. Since World War II, a complex R&D establishment has developed that involves extensive government funding of basic research priorities in partnership with major research universities and private firms. Government policy has encouraged the diffusion and commercialization of R&D projects as well. The growth of the Internet out of the U.S. Defense Department and National Science Foundations origins is just a recent instance of the importance of government support of infrastructure R&D.

Summary Ever-rising demand in developed nations and globalization of trade flows have increased every firm's potential market size. This has made it possible for specialized firms to achieve the kinds of economies of scale that were once enjoyed only by vertically integrated corporate giants. Rapid improvements in transportation and communication make it easier for independent firms to do business with each other. As a result, modern businesses are more "focused" on a narrower range of activities. At the same time, changes in the financial sector speed the rate at which established firms may grow, but also speed the rate at which new firms can enter and challenge incumbents for market superiority.

Infrastructure in Emerging Markets

The technologies that have revolutionized modern infrastructure are widely accessible, yet infrastructure hinders economic development in many emerging markets. The quality of transportation systems varies from nation to nation. Central Africa, for example, has few highways, and its rails have deteriorated since colonial days. Southeast Asian nations often boast ultramodern rail lines and seaports. But even there, transportation within urban business centers can be excruciatingly difficult.

Developing nations often lack other forms of infrastructure. Their businesses and consumers have limited access to the Internet, particularly through high-speed ISDN or broadband connections. They lack a diligent independent banking sector that

---

EXAMPLE 1.4   THE *GAIZHI* PRIVATIZATION PROCESS IN CHINA

The modern privatization movement in China started in 1992, after President Deng Xiaoping gave a speech encouraging the development of private enterprises and a market economy. By the mid-1990s, most local governments began to privatize their small state-owned enterprises (SOEs), but some cities went further by privatizing almost all their state and collective firms. In 1995, the central Chinese government decided to keep 500 to 1,000 large state firms and allow smaller firms to be leased or sold, mainly through management buyouts. This process came to be known as *gaizhi*, or "restructuring." By the end of the decade, nearly half of China's 87,000 industrial SOEs had been through *gaizhi* or were being prepared for sale.

Managers who acquired their firms through the *gaizhi* process stood to reap substantial profits if their firms improved their performance. And *gaizhi* gave the managers considerable opportunities for such improvements. Managers could more easily hire and fire workers as well as decide how to deploy their staff. Managers also obtained greater control over investments and research and development.

A key feature of *gaizhi* is the purchasing process. Managers could purchase their firms at a price determined by independent accounting firms. By law, the accountants valued assets according to the earnings they can bring in or their current market value. China has poorly developed capital markets, however, so the latter option is usually not available. As a result, accountants often valued firms according to their current profitability.

Feng Susan Lu and David Dranove observed that the valuation process created a perverse incentive for managers.[17] If they could reduce profitability prior to *gaizhi*, say by easing off on workers or purposefully ignoring market opportunities, that would depress the purchase price. Once managers acquired their firms, they could renew their efforts and restore (or even increase) profits to pre-*gaizhi* levels. In this way, managers could obtain profitable firms at bargain prices. Lu and Dranove found evidence consistent with such behavior. They examined profitability trends pre- and post-*gaizhi* while also examining a matched set of firms that were not privatized. The *gaizhi* firms saw profits drop in the year before privatization and then return to pre-*gaizhi* levels immediately afterwards.

provides financial capital and management oversight. Entrepreneurs must rely instead on microlending for seed capital but are hard pressed to obtain substantial loans to facilitate growth. The economies of many developing nations have been crippled by their own governments. Businesses have been reluctant to invest in central and east Africa, for example, because of the lack of established contract law, government corruption, cronyism, and civil war.

THREE DIFFERENT WORLDS: CONSISTENT PRINCIPLES, CHANGING CONDITIONS, AND ADAPTIVE STRATEGIES

Businesses in 1840 focused on one or two activities. By 1910, integration was the name of the game, with many corporate giants extending their reach throughout the vertical chain. Modern businesses are once again narrowing their scope. Business gurus write about current trends as if they have just now discovered the virtues of focus. In doing so, they criticize the business practices of earlier generations of managers. Such criticism is unwarranted. The enormous differences in business practices among the three periods we surveyed illustrate a key premise of this book: *Successful strategy results from applying consistent principles to constantly changing business conditions.* Strategies are—and should be—the adaptive, but principled, responses of firms to their surroundings.

The infrastructure and market conditions of business do not uniquely determine the strategies that firms choose. In all three of our periods, there was considerable experimentation by firms, and various types of firms succeeded and failed. But market conditions and infrastructure do constrain how business can be conducted and the strategic choices that most managers can make. As these conditions change, so too do optimal business strategies. The world of factors, agents, and brokers was undone by the development of the railroad, telegraph, and telephone. Computers and the Internet reduced the need for vertical integration. If the past is prologue, then by 2050 if not sooner, some as yet unimagined innovations will once again transform business infrastructure, and firms will reinvent themselves yet again.

Because circumstances change, one might conclude that an education in business strategy will soon become obsolete. Indeed, the survey in this chapter suggests that specific strategies that purport to work under a given set of market conditions (e.g., "Divest any business that does not have the largest or second-largest share in its market") are bound to fail eventually. Principles, however, are different from recipes. Principles are economic and behavioral relationships that apply to wide classes of circumstances. Because principles are robust, organizing the study of strategy around principles allows us to understand why certain strategies, business practices, and organizational arrangements are appropriate under one set of conditions but not others.

In the remaining chapters, we develop principles that pertain to the boundaries of the firm, the nature of industry structure and competition, the firm's strategic position within an industry, and the internal organization and management of the firm. Through the study of these principles, we believe that students of management can understand why firms and industries are organized the way they are and operate the way they do. We also believe that by judiciously applying these principles, managers can enhance the odds of successfully adapting their firms' strategies to the environments in which they compete.

CHAPTER SUMMARY

- A historical perspective demonstrates that while the nature of business has changed dramatically since 1840, successful businesses have always applied consistent principles to their business conditions.

- In 1840, communications and transportation infrastructures were poor. This increased the risk to businesses of operating in too large a market and mitigated against large-scale production.

- Business in 1840 was dominated by small, family-operated firms that relied on specialists in distribution as well as market makers who matched the needs of buyers and suppliers.

- By 1910, improvements in transportation and communications made large-scale national markets possible and innovations in production technology made it possible to greatly reduce unit costs through large-scale production. Mass distribution firms developed along with the growth in mass production.

- Businesses in 1910 that invested in these new technologies needed to assure a sufficient throughput to keep production levels high. This led them to vertically integrate into raw materials acquisition, distribution, and retailing.

- Manufacturing firms also expanded their product offerings, creating new divisions that were managed within an "M-form" organization.

- These large hierarchical organizations required a professional managerial class. Unlike managers in 1840, professional managers in 1910 generally had little or no ownership interest in their firms.

- Continued improvements in communications and transportation have made the modern marketplace global. New technologies have reduced the advantages of large-scale production and vertical integration and promoted the growth of market specialists.

- In many industries, small manufacturers can meet the changing needs of their clients better than large hierarchical firms. In other industries, market specialists use the Internet and telecommunication to coordinate activities that used to require a single integrated firm.

- Limited infrastructure hinders growth in many developing economies. The growing interconnectedness of firms in developed economies makes them increasingly vulnerable to global events and discontinuities beyond their normal scope of business.

QUESTIONS

1. Why is infrastructure essential to economic development?
2. What was the role of the factor in the mid-nineteenth century economy? Does such a role exist in the modern economy?
3. How would John Burrows's life been different if he had access to the Internet? What if farmers and retailers also had access to the Internet?
4. What is throughput? Is throughput as important today as it was 100 years ago?

5. If nineteenth-century Americans had the benefit of modern technology as they expanded westward, would Chicago, with its close access to the Great Lakes and Mississippi River system, still have emerged as the business center of the Midwest?

6. Two features of developing nations are an absence of strong contract law and limited transportation networks. How might these factors affect the vertical and horizontal boundaries of firms within these nations?

7. Fifteenth-century Florence was the birthplace of the Renaissance, home to artists such as Donatello, Botticelli, and Michelangelo. Why did so many great artists emerge from just this one city-state? Do you believe that a single city could become the Florence of the twenty-first century?

8. The advent of professional managers was accompanied by skepticism regarding their trustworthiness and ethics in controlling large corporate assets on behalf of the shareholders. Today, this skepticism remains and has changed little since the founding of the managerial class a century ago, and new laws concerning appropriate governance, such as Sarbanes-Oxley, continue to be introduced. Why has this skepticism remained so strong?

9. There is considerable disagreement as to whether government regulation has largely positive or negative influences on economic growth. Compare and contrast the ways in which government involvement in particular industries may positively or negatively influence the evolution of those industries.

10. Some firms seem to last forever. (For an extreme example go to www.hbc.com.) In some industries, however, even the most effective firms may expect short lifetimes (lawn crews; Thai restaurants). Size certainly has something to do with longevity, but are there other factors involved? How does size help larger firms or imperil smaller ones? What other factors besides size contribute to longevity?

11. How might a persistent global credit crisis affect the scale and scope of modern firms?

ENDNOTES

[1]We use the term *businessmen* literally. Few, if any, women were involved in business in 1840. This had not changed much by 1910.

[2]This example comes from William Cronon's excellent history of the city of Chicago, *Nature's Metropolis*, New York, Norton, 1991.

[3]This example draws from Cronon, W., *Nature's Metropolis*, New York, Norton, 1991.

[4]Cochran, T. C., and W. Miller, *The Age of Enterprise: A Social History of Industrial America*, New York, Harper & Row, 1961, p. 45.

[5]Cochran and Miller, *The Age of Enterprise*, p. 42.

[6]Yates, J., *Control through Communication: The Rise of System in American Management*, Baltimore, MD, Johns Hopkins University Press, 1989, pp. 160–161.

[7]Yates, *Control through Communication*, pp. 22–23.

[8]"China's Route Forward," by Keith Bradsher, The New York Times, January 22, 2009. Accessed on June 23, 2009 at http://www.nytimes.com/2009/01/23/business/worldbusiness/23yuan.html?_r=1&hp

[9]Ibid.

[10]Kanigel, R., *The One Best Way: Frederick Winslow Taylor and the Enigma of Efficiency*, New York, Viking, 1997.

[11]Chandler, A. D., *Scale and Scope: The Dynamics of Industrial Capitalism*, Cambridge, MA, Belknap, 1990.

[12]For details, see Garnet, R. W., *The Telephone Enterprise: The Evolution of the Bell System's Horizontal Structure, 1876–1909*, Baltimore, MD, Johns Hopkins University Press, 1985. Also see Smith, G. D., *The Anatomy of a Business Strategy: Bell, Western Electric, and the Origins of the American Telephone Industry*, Baltimore, MD, Johns Hopkins University Press, 1985.

[13]John, Richard R., "Recasting the Information Infrastructure for the Industrial Age," in A. D. Chandler Jr. and J. W. Cortada (eds.), *A Nation Transformed by Information: How Information Has Shaped the United States from Colonial Times to the Present*, Oxford, UK, Oxford University Press, 2000, pp. 55–105.

[14]Adams, W., and H. Mueller, "The Steel Industry," in W. Adams (ed.), *The Structure of American Industry*, 8th ed., New York, Macmillan, 1988, p. 90.

[15]Wallis, J. J., and D. C. North, "Measuring the Transaction Sector in the American Economy, 1870–1970," Chap. 3 in Engerman, S. L. and R. E. Gallman (eds.), *Long-Term Factors in American Economic Growth*, Chicago, University of Chicago Press, 1986, pp. 95–161.

[16]Friedman, T. L., *The World Is Flat: A Brief History of the Twenty-First Century*, New York, Farrar, Straus, & Giroux, 2005.

[17]Lu, F., and D. Dranove, 2008, "The Gaizhi Privatization Process in China," Northwestern University, Unpublished Mimeo.

THE HORIZONTAL BOUNDARIES OF THE FIRM

2

Few concepts in microeconomics, if any, are more fundamental to business strategy than the horizontal boundaries of the firm and the closely related topics of economies of scale and economies of scope. Economies of scale allow some firms to achieve a cost advantage over their rivals and are a key determinant of market structure and entry. Even the internal organization of a firm can be affected by the importance of realizing scale economies.

We mostly think about economies of scale as a key determinant of a firm's horizontal boundaries, which identify the quantities and varieties of products and services that it produces. In some industries, such as microprocessors and airframe manufacturing, economies of scale are huge and a few large firms dominate. In other industries, such as web site design and shoe production, scale economies are minimal and small firms are the norm. Some industries, such as beer and computer software, have large market leaders (Anheuser-Busch, Microsoft), yet small firms (Boston Beer Company, Blizzard Entertainment) fill niches where scale economies are less important.

An understanding of the sources of economies of scale and scope is clearly critical for formulating and assessing competitive strategy. This chapter identifies the key sources of economies of scale and scope and provides approaches for assessing their importance.

DEFINITIONS

Informally, when there are economies of scale and scope, "bigger is better." To facilitate identification and measurement, it is useful to define economies of scale and scope more precisely.

Definition of Economies of Scale

The production process for a specific good or service exhibits *economies of scale* over a range of output when average cost (i.e., cost per unit of output) declines over that range. If average cost (AC) declines as output increases, then the marginal cost of

FIGURE 2.1
A U-SHAPED AVERAGE COST CURVE

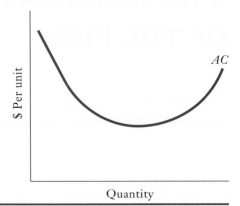

Average costs decline initially as fixed costs are spread over additional units of output. Average costs eventually rise as production runs up against capacity constraints.

the last unit produced (*MC*) must be less than the average cost.[1] If average cost is increasing, then marginal cost must exceed average cost, and we say that production exhibits *diseconomies of scale*.

An *average cost curve* captures the relationship between average costs and output. Economists often depict average cost curves as U-shaped, as shown in Figure 2.1, so that average costs decline over low levels of output, but increase at higher levels of output. A combination of factors may cause a firm to have U-shaped costs. A firm's average costs may decline initially as it spreads *fixed costs* over increasing output. Fixed costs are insensitive to volume; they must be expended regardless of the total output. Examples of such volume-insensitive costs are manufacturing overhead expenses, such as insurance, maintenance, and property taxes. Firms may eventually see an upturn in average costs if they bump up against capacity constraints, or if they encounter coordination or other and agency problems. We will develop most of these ideas in this chapter. Coordination and agency problems are addressed in Chapters 3 and 4.

If average cost curves are U-shaped, then small and large firms would have higher costs than medium-sized firms. In reality, large firms rarely seem to be at a substantial cost disadvantage. The noted econometrician John Johnston once examined production costs for a number of industries and determined that the corresponding cost curves were closer to L-shaped than U-shaped. Figure 2.2 depicts an L-shaped cost curve. When average cost curves are L-shaped, average costs decline up to the *minimum efficient scale* (*MES*) of production and all firms operating at or beyond MES have similar average costs.

Sometimes, production exhibits U-shaped average costs in the short run, as firms that try to expand output run up against capacity constraints. In the long term, however, firms can expand their capacity by building new facilities. If each facility operates efficiently, firms can grow as large as desired without driving up average costs. This would generate the L-shaped cost curves observed by Johnston. A good example is when a cement company builds a plant in a new location. We have more to say about the distinction between short- and long-run costs later in this chapter.

FIGURE 2.2
AN L-SHAPED AVERAGE COST CURVE

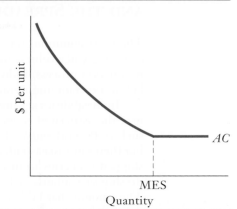

When capacity does not prove to be constraining, average costs may not rise as they do in a U-shaped cost curve. Output equal to or exceeding minimum efficient scale (MES) is efficient from a cost perspective.

Definition of Economies of Scope

Economies of scope exist if the firm achieves savings as it increases the variety of goods and services it produces. Because it is difficult to show scope economies graphically, we will instead introduce a simple mathematical formulation. Formally, let $TC(Q_x, Q_y)$ denote the total cost to a single firm producing Q_x units of good X and Q_y units of good Y. Then a production process exhibits scope economies if

$$TC(Q_x, Q_y) < TC(Q_x, 0) + TC(0, Q_y)$$

This formula captures the idea that it is cheaper for a single firm to produce both goods X and Y than for one firm to produce X and another to produce Y. To provide another interpretation of the definition, note that a firm's total costs are zero if it produces zero quantities of both products, so $TC(0, 0) = 0$. Then, rearrange the preceding formula to read:

$$TC(Q_x, Q_y) - TC(0, Q_y) < TC(Q_x, 0)$$

This says that the incremental cost of producing Q_x units of good X, as opposed to none at all, is lower when the firm is producing a positive quantity Q_y of good Y.

When strategists recommend that firms "leverage core competencies" or "compete on capabilities," they are essentially recommending that firms exploit scope economies. Tesco's capability in warehousing and distribution gives it a cost advantage across many geographic markets. Apple's core competency in engineering allows it to make popular cell phones, laptops, and tablet computers. Ikea's skills in product design extends to an enormous range of home furnishing products. As these examples suggest, economies of scale and scope may arise at any point in the production process, from acquisition and use of raw inputs to distribution and retailing. Although business managers often cite scale and scope economies as justifications for growth activities and mergers, they do not always exist. In some cases, bigger may be worse! Thus, it is important to identify specific sources of scale economies and, if possible, measure their magnitude. The rest of this chapter shows how to do this.

SCALE ECONOMIES, INDIVISIBILITIES, AND THE SPREADING OF FIXED COSTS

The most common source of economies of scale is the spreading of fixed costs over an ever-greater volume of output. Fixed costs arise when there are *indivisibilities* in the production process. Indivisibility simply means that an input cannot be scaled down below a certain minimum size, even when the level of output is very small.

Indivisibilities are present in nearly all production processes, and failure to recognize the associated economies of scale can cripple a firm. Web-based grocery stores such as Peapod and Webvan were once thought to have unlimited growth potential, but their enthusiasts failed to appreciate the challenge of indivisibilities. Webvan once shipped groceries from its Chicago warehouse to suburbs throughout Chicagoland. To ship to a suburb such as Highland Park, Webvan required a truck, driver, and fuel. The amount that Webvan paid for these inputs was largely independent of whether it delivered to one household or 10. Thus, these inputs represented indivisible fixed costs of serving Highland Park. Webvan was unable to generate substantial business in Highland Park (or other Illinois communities, for that matter), so it sent its trucks virtually empty. Unable to recoup warehousing costs, the company went bankrupt. Peapod faces the same problem today, but does enough business in densely populated neighborhoods in downtown Chicago to survive.

Indivisibilities can give rise to fixed costs, and hence scale and scope economies, at several different levels: the product level, the plant level, and the multiplant level. The next few subsections discuss the link between fixed costs and economies of scale at each of these levels.

Economies of Scale Due to Spreading of Product-Specific Fixed Costs

Product-specific fixed costs may include special equipment such as the cost to manufacture a special die used to make an aircraft fuselage. Fixed costs may also include research and development expenses such as the cost of developing graphics software to facilitate development of a new video game. Fixed costs may include training expenses such as the cost of a one-week training program preceding the implementation of a total quality management initiative. Fixed costs may also include setup costs such as the time and expense required to design a retailer web page.

Even a simple production process may require substantial fixed costs. The production of an aluminum can involves only a few steps. Aluminum sheets are cut to size, formed and punched into the familiar cylindrical can shape, then trimmed, cleaned, and decorated. A lid is then attached to a flange around the lip of the can, and a tab is fastened to the lid. Though the process is simple, a single line for producing aluminum cans can cost about $50 million. If the opportunity cost of tying up funds is 10 percent, the fixed costs expressed on an annualized basis amount to about $5 million per year.[2]

The average fixed cost of producing aluminum cans falls as output increases. To quantify this, suppose that the peak capacity of a fully automated aluminum can plant is 500 million cans annually (or about 0.5 percent of the total U.S market). The average fixed cost of operating this plant at full capacity for one year is determined by dividing the annual cost ($5,000,000) by total output (500,000,000). This works out to one cent per can. On the other hand, if the plant only operates at 25 percent of capacity, for total annual production of 125 million cans, then average fixed costs equal four cents per can. The underutilized plant is operating at a three-cent cost differential per can. In a price-competitive industry like aluminum can manufacturing, such a cost differential could make the difference between profit and loss.

Economies of Scale Due to Trade-offs among Alternative Technologies

Suppose that a firm is considering entering the can manufacturing business but does not anticipate being able to sell more than 125 million cans annually. Is it doomed to a three-cent-per-can cost disadvantage? The answer depends on the nature of the alternative production technologies and the planned production output. The fully automated technology described previously may yield the greatest cost savings when used to capacity, but it may not be the best choice at lower production levels. There may be an alternative that requires less initial investment, albeit with a greater reliance on ongoing expenses.

Suppose that the fixed costs of setting up a partially automated plant are $12.5 million, annualized to $1.25 million per year. The shortcoming of this plant is that it requires labor costs of one cent per can that are not needed at the fully automated plant. The cost comparison between the two plants is shown in Table 2.1.

Table 2.1 shows that while the fully automated technology has lower average total costs at high production levels, it is more costly at lower production levels. This is seen in Figure 2.3, which depicts average cost curves for both the fully and partially automated technologies. The curve labeled SAC_1 is the average cost curve for a plant that has adopted the fully automated technology; the curve labeled SAC_2 is the average cost curve for a plant that has adopted the partially automated technology. At output levels above 375 million, the fully automated technology has lower average total costs. At lower output levels, the partially automated technology is cheaper.

The aluminum can example demonstrates the difference between economies of scale that arise from increased capacity utilization with a given production technology and economies of scale that arise as a firm chooses among alternative production technologies. Reductions in average costs due to increases in capacity utilization are *short-run* economies of scale in that they occur within a plant of a given size. Reductions due to adoption of a technology that has high fixed costs but lower variable costs are *long-run* economies of scale. Given time to build a plant from scratch, a firm can

TABLE 2.1
COSTS OF PRODUCING ALUMINUM CANS

	500 Million Cans per Year	*125 Million Cans per Year*
Fully automated	Average fixed costs = .01	Average fixed costs = .04
	Average labor costs = .00	Average labor costs = .00
	Average materials costs = .03	Average materials costs = .03
	Average total costs = .04	Average total costs = .07
Partially automated	Averge fixed costs = .0025	Average fixed costs = .01
	Averge labor costs = .01	Average labor costs = .01
	Averge materials costs = .03	Average materials costs = .03
	Averge total costs = .0425	Average total costs = .05

FIGURE 2.3
AVERAGE COST CURVES FOR CAN PRODUCTION

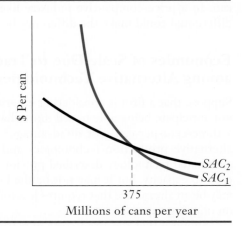

SAC_1 represents a high fixed/low variable cost technology. SAC_2 represents a low fixed cost/high variable cost technology. At low levels of output, it is cheaper to use the latter technology. At high outputs, it is cheaper to use the former.

choose the plant that best meets its production needs, avoiding excessive fixed costs if production is expected to be low, and excessive capacity costs if production is expected to be high.

Figure 2.4 illustrates the distinction between short-run and long-run economies of scale. (The Economics Primer discusses this distinction at length.) SAC_1 and SAC_2, which duplicate the cost curves in Figure 2.3, are the short-run average cost curves for the partially automated and fully automated plants, respectively. If we trace out the lower regions of each curve, we see the long-run average cost curve. The long-run average cost curve is everywhere on or below each short-run average cost curve. This reflects the flexibility that firms have to adopt the technology that is most appropriate for their forecasted output.

Regardless of plant size, firms that plan on exploiting scale economies must achieve the necessary throughput. Recall from Chapter 1 that throughput describes

FIGURE 2.4
SHORT-RUN VERSUS LONG-RUN AVERAGE COST

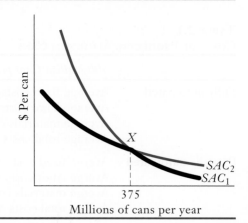

In the long run, firms may choose their production technology as well as their output. Firms planning to produce beyond point X will choose the technology represented by SAC_1. Firms planning to produce less than point X will choose the technology represented by SAC_2. The heavy "lower envelope" of the two cost curves, which represents the lowest possible cost for each level of production, is called the *long-run average cost curve*.

EXAMPLE 2.1 HUB-AND-SPOKE NETWORKS AND ECONOMIES OF SCOPE IN THE AIRLINE INDUSTRY

An important example of multiplant economies of scope arises in a number of industries in which goods and services are routed to and from several markets. In these industries, which include airlines, railroads, and telecommunications, distribution is organized around "hub-and-spoke" networks. In an airline hub-and-spoke network, an airline flies passengers from a set of "spoke" cities through a central "hub," where passengers then change planes and fly from the hub to their outbound destinations. Thus, a passenger flying from, say, Omaha to Boston on United Airlines would board a United flight from Omaha to Chicago, change planes, and then fly from Chicago to Boston.

Recall that economies of scope occur when a firm producing many products has a lower average cost than a firm producing just a few products. In the airline industry, it makes economic sense to think about individual origin–destination pairs (e.g., Omaha to Boston, Chicago to Boston) as distinct products. Viewed in this way, economies of scope exist if an airline's average cost is lower the more origin–destination pairs it serves. To understand how hub-and-spoke networks give rise to economies of *scope*, it is first necessary to explain *economies of density*. Economies of density are essentially economies of scale along a given route, that is, reductions in average cost as traffic volume on the route increases. (In the airline industry, traffic volume is measured as revenue-passenger miles [RPM], which is the number of passengers on the route multiplied by the number of miles, and average cost is the cost per revenue passenger mile.) Economies of density occur because of spreading flight-specific fixed costs (e.g., costs of the flight and cabin crew, fuel, aircraft servicing) and because of the economies of aircraft size. In the airline industry, traffic-sensitive costs (e.g., food, ticket handling) are small in relation to flight-specific fixed costs. Thus, as its traffic volume increases, an airline can fill a larger fraction of its seats on a given type of aircraft (in airline industry lingo, it

increases its *load factor*—the ratio of passengers to available seats), and because the airline's total costs increase only slightly, its cost per RPM falls as it spreads the flight-specific fixed costs over more traffic volume. As traffic volume on the route gets even larger, it becomes worthwhile to substitute larger aircraft (e.g., 300-seat Boeing 767s) for smaller aircraft (e.g., 150-seat Boeing 737s). A key aspect of this substitution is that the 300-seat aircraft flown a given distance at a given load factor is less than twice as costly as the 150-seat aircraft flown the same distance at the same load factor. The reason for this is that doubling the number of seats and passengers on a plane does not require doubling the sizes of flight and cabin crews or the amount of fuel used, and that the 300-seat aircraft is less than twice as costly to build as the 150-seat aircraft, owing to the cube-square rule, which will be discussed below.

Economies of scope emerge from the interplay of economies of density and the properties of a hub-and-spoke network. To see how, consider an origin–destination pair such as Omaha to Boston. This pair has a modest amount of daily traffic. An airline serving only this route would use small planes and operate with a relatively low load factor. But now consider United's traffic on this route. United offers daily flights from Omaha to Chicago. It not only draws passengers who want to travel from Omaha to Chicago, but it would also draw passengers traveling from Omaha to all other points accessible from Chicago in the network, including Boston. By including the Omaha–Chicago route as part of a larger hub-and-spoke network, United can operate a larger airplane at higher load factors than can an airline serving only Omaha–Chicago. United benefits from economies of density to achieve a lower cost per RPM along this route. Moreover, because there will now be passengers traveling between Chicago and other spoke cities in this network, the airline's load factors on these other spokes will increase somewhat, thereby lowering the costs per RPM on these routes as well. This is precisely what is meant by economies of scope.

As more travelers take to the skies, and as smaller and more efficient jet aircraft reach the market, it is becoming possible to fly efficient nonstop flights between what were previously spoke cities. For example, Southwest flies nonstop from Boston to St. Louis. Previously, this trip required flying on another carrier and changing at a hub city. This trend is reducing the economic advantages that were previously enjoyed by the major hub-and-spoke carriers.

the movement of raw materials into the plant and the distribution and sale of finished goods. Throughput requires access to raw materials, transportation infrastructure, warehousing, and adequate market demand, spurred on if necessary by sales and marketing. For example, consider the requirements for a successful web-based grocery store. Webvan had ample access to inputs, transportation, and warehousing. The brand was well known, and the company even received a lot of free publicity during the dot-com boom. Webvan failed to achieve the necessary throughput for the simplest of reasons—there was insufficient demand for the product. In a business where scale economies are essential, the failure to achieve throughput doomed Webvan to high average costs and, eventually, bankruptcy.

Indivisibilities Are More Likely When Production Is Capital Intensive

When the costs of productive capital such as factories and assembly lines represent a significant percentage of total costs, we say that production is *capital intensive*. Much productive capital is indivisible and therefore a source of scale economies. As long as there is spare capacity, output can be expanded at little additional expense. As a result, average costs fall. Conversely, cutbacks in output may not reduce total costs by much, so average costs rise. When most production expenses go to raw materials or labor, we say that production is *materials* or *labor intensive*. Because materials and labor are divisible, they usually change in rough proportion to changes in output, with the result that average costs do not vary much with output. As a first step toward assessing the importance of scale economies, one can follow the following rules of thumb:

- Substantial product-specific economies of scale are likely when production is capital intensive.

- Minimal product-specific economies of scale are likely when production is materials or labor intensive.

The second rule of thumb should not be followed slavishly. There are many instances where labor expenses should be treated as fixed costs. For example, there are substantial fixed travel costs each time a pharmaceutical sales rep visits physicians in a given market area. Drug makers reduce average selling costs whenever their sales reps can promote more drugs per visit. In fact, when drug makers experience a decline in their portfolio of branded drugs, they sometimes offer to co-promote other companies' drugs. As long as the sales reps are making calls on doctors, they may as well have products to promote. To take another example, a large percentage of the costs of video games is associated with development and beta testing. Average cost per game falls as total sales increase.

EXAMPLE 2.2   THE DIVISION OF LABOR IN MEDICAL MARKETS

An interesting application of Smith's theorem involves the specialization of medical care. Physicians may practice general medicine or specialty medicine. Generalists and specialists differ in both the amount of training they receive and the skill with which they practice. Take the case of surgery. To become general surgeons, medical school graduates spend three to four years in a surgical residency. They are then qualified to perform a wide variety of surgical procedures. Because their training is broad, general surgeons do all kinds of surgery with good, but not necessarily great, skill.

Contrast this with the training and skills of a thoracic surgeon. Thoracic surgeons specialize in the thoracic region, between the neck and the abdomen. To become a thoracic surgeon, a medical school graduate must complete a residency in general surgery and then an additional two-year residency in thoracic surgery. Figure 2.5 depicts average "cost" curves for thoracic surgery performed by a general surgeon and a thoracic surgeon. We use "cost" in quotes because it represents the full cost of care, which is lower if the surgery is successful. (Successful surgery usually implies fewer complications, shorter hospital stays, and a shorter period of recuperation.) The average cost curves are downward sloping to reflect the spreading out of the initial investments in training. The cost curve for the thoracic surgeon starts off much higher than the cost curve for the general surgeon because of the greater investment in time. However, the thoracic surgeon's cost curve eventually falls below the cost curve of a general surgeon because the thoracic surgeon will perform thoracic surgery more effectively than most general surgeons.

According to Smith's theorem, when the demand for thoracic surgery in a market is low, then the market will not support a specialized surgeon. Instead, thoracic surgery will be performed by a general surgeon, who may also perform other kinds of surgery. This may be seen in Figure 2.6, which superimposes demand curves over cost curves. For low levels of demand, such as at D_1, the market can support a general surgeon. A general surgeon who charges a price for thoracic surgery above P_1 can more than cover average costs. When demand is D_1, the market cannot support a thoracic surgeon. There is no price high enough to enable thoracic surgeons to recoup their costs.

FIGURE 2.5
COST CURVES FOR GENERAL AND THORACIC SURGEONS

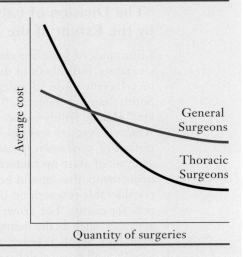

General surgeons incur lower training costs than do thoracic surgeons but are usually less efficient in performing thoracic surgery. Thus, the general surgeon's average cost curve is below the thoracic surgeon's for low volumes (reflecting lower average fixed costs) but above the thoracic surgeon's for high volumes (reflecting higher average variable costs).

FIGURE 2.6
COST AND DEMAND FOR THORACIC SURGERY

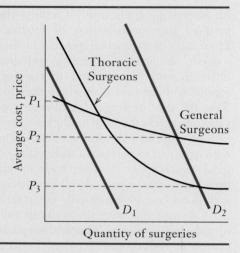

At low demands (D_1), general surgeons may be able to cover their average costs, but thoracic surgeons may not. At high demands (D_2), thoracic surgeons may be able to offer lower effective prices than can general surgeons (where the effective price to the consumer includes the costs associated with ineffective surgery).

When demand increases to D_2, the market can support a thoracic surgeon. A thoracic surgeon who charges a price above P_3 can cover average costs. Moreover, at prices between P_2 and P_3, the thoracic surgeon can make a profit, but the general surgeon cannot. Thus, at this high level of demand, the thoracic surgeon can drive the general surgeon from the market for thoracic surgery.

The same logic should apply to other specialized surgical and medical services. Thus, in large markets, we may expect to see a range of specialists and few or no generalists. Researchers at the RAND Corporation documented this pattern of the division of labor in medical markets.[3] They found that general practitioners are disproportionately located in smaller towns—they do not appear to fare well in larger markets, which have a wider assortment of specialists. James Baumgardner also found that physicians who practice in small towns treat a wider range of illnesses than do their big-city counterparts.[4]

"The Division of Labor Is Limited by the Extent of the Market"

Economies of scale are closely related to the concept of specialization. To become specialists, individuals or firms must often make substantial investments, but they will be reluctant to do so unless demand justifies it. This is the logic underlying Adam Smith's famous theorem, "The division of labor is limited by the extent of the market." (Adam Smith is the father of laissez-faire economics. His best-known work, *Wealth of Nations*, was published in 1776.) The *division of labor* refers to the specialization of productive activities, such as when a financial analyst specializes in the analysis of start-up biotech companies. Such specialization often requires upfront investments that should be treated as fixed costs; for example, the analyst must do considerable research on the biotech industry before having the credibility to compete for clients. The *extent of the market* refers to the magnitude of demand for these activities, such as the demand for financial advice about start-up biotech companies. Although Smith referred mainly to specialization by individuals, his ideas apply equally well to specialization by firms.

Smith's theorem states that individuals or firms will not make specialized invest-ments unless the market is big enough to support them. This is a variant of the rule that realizing scale economies requires throughput. One additional implication of Smith's theorem is that larger markets will support narrower specialization. A small town may have a pet store that caters to owners of all kinds of critters. A big city will have dog groomers, salt-water aquarium boutiques, and exotic bird stores.

SPECIAL SOURCES OF ECONOMIES OF SCALE AND SCOPE

This section describes six specific sources of economies of scale and scope:

1. Economics of density
2. Purchasing
3. Advertising
4. Research and development
5. Physical properties of production
6. Inventories

The first four rely entirely or in part on spreading of fixed costs. Physical properties of production and inventory-based economies do not.

Economics of Density

Economies of density refer to cost savings that arise within a transportation net-work due to a greater geographic density of customers. The savings may result from increasing the number of customers using a given network, such as when an airline's unit costs decline as more passengers are flown over a given route. (See Example 2.1.) Savings can also result from reducing the size of the area, and there-fore reducing the cost of the network, while maintaining the same number of cus-tomers. For example, a beer distributor that operates in a densely populated urban area has lower unit costs than a distributor selling the same amount of beer in more sparsely populated suburbs.

Purchasing

It is conventional wisdom that "purchasing power" through bulk buying invariably leads to discounts. There is no necessary reason for big buyers to obtain bulk discounts. A supplier might not care whether it sells 100 units to a single buyer or 10 units to each of 10 different buyers. There are three possible reasons why a supplier would care:

1. It may be less costly to sell to a single buyer, for example, if each sale requires some fixed cost in writing a contract, setting up a production run, or delivering the product.
2. A bulk purchaser has more to gain from getting the best price, and therefore will be more price sensitive. For example, someone purchasing hundreds of computer printers on behalf of a university is more likely to switch vendors over small price differences than someone else buying one printer for personal use.
3. The supplier may fear a costly disruption to operations, or in the extreme case, bankruptcy, if it fails to do business with a large purchaser. The supplier may offer a discount to the large purchaser so as to assure a steady flow of business.

Small firms can take steps to offset these conditions and nullify purchasing economies. For example, nearly 10,000 independent hardware stores belong to the Ace and True Value purchasing groups. Ace and True Value obtain discounts from suppliers that are comparable to those realized by hardware superstores like Lowe's and Home Depot. Ace and True Value also operate regional warehouses that hold down inventory costs for their independent retailers.

Sometimes, small firms may have purchasing advantages over large firms. U.S. mail order pharmacies often do not stock a full selection of therapeutically equivalent drugs. For example, a mail order pharmacy may stock either Merck's Mevacor or Pfizer's Lipitor but not both (both are statin drugs that can lower LDL cholesterol). This allows the pharmacy to play off Merck against Pfizer to obtain deep discounts. Large pharmacy chains like Walgreens tend to stock a complete line of drugs, which limits their bargaining power and drives up their purchasing costs.

Advertising

The advertising cost per consumer of a product may be expressed by the following formula:

$$\frac{\text{Cost of sending a message}}{\text{Number of potential consumers receiving the message}} \div \frac{\text{Number of actual consumers as a result of message}}{\text{Number of potential consumers receiving the message}}$$

Larger firms may enjoy lower advertising costs per consumer either because they have lower costs of sending messages per potential consumer (the first term) or because they have higher advertising *reach* (the second term).

Costs of Sending Messages per Potential Consumer

There are important fixed costs associated with placing an ad, including preparation of the ad and negotiation with the broadcaster. If ad preparation costs and the costs of negotiating a single national and local advertising "buy" are about the same, the national advertiser will have a lower cost per potential consumer because these fixed costs get spread over a larger base of potential consumers.

To illustrate, suppose that Anheuser-Busch places an ad in *USA Today* and pays Gannett (the publisher of *USA Today*) $10 per thousand papers sold to run this ad. Because *USA Today* has a daily circulation of about 1.75 million, the direct costs of this ad to Anheuser-Busch would be $10 \times (1,750,000/1000)$ or $17,500. The same day, Hudepohl, a local brewery in Cincinnati, Ohio, owned by the Schoenling Brewing Company, places an ad in the *Cincinnati Enquirer* (the local paper) and, let's say, pays the same rate of $10 per thousand papers sold. The *Enquirer* has a daily circulation of about 150,000, so the direct cost to Hudepohl would be $10 \times (150,000/1,000)$ or $1,500. Finally, suppose that for both companies the cost of preparing the ad is $3,500.

Let us now look at the advertising cost per potential consumer for Anheuser-Busch and Hudepohl:

- Anheuser-Busch advertising cost per potential consumer = ($17,500 + $3,500)/ 1,750,000 = $.012 per potential consumer, or $12.00 per 1,000 potential consumers.

- Hudepohl advertising cost per potential consumer = ($1,500 + $3,500)/150,000 = $.033 per potential consumer, or $33.33 per 1,000 potential consumers.

This example illustrates the approximate difference in the cost per potential consumer between national and local advertising.

The logic underlying this example illustrates why national firms, such as McDonald's, enjoy an advertising cost advantage over their local counterparts, such as Gold Coast Dogs (a chain of hot dog restaurants in Chicago).

Advertising Reach and Umbrella Branding

Even when two firms have national presences, the larger one may still enjoy an advantage. Suppose that Harvey's and McDonald's both place advertisements on CSN, Canada's television sports network. Both ads are equally persuasive—10,000 viewers of the Harvey's ad have an urge to purchase a Great Canadian burger; 10,000 viewers of the McDonald's ad are motivated to buy a Big Mac. Despite these similarities, the cost per effective message is much lower for McDonald's. The reason is that there are about five times as many McDonald's in Canada as there are Harvey's. Almost all of the 10,000 viewers craving McDonald's can find one nearby, but many of the 10,000 who crave Harvey's cannot.

The effectiveness of a firm's ad may also be higher if that firm offers a broad product line under a single brand name. For example, an advertisement for a Samsung flat screen plasma television may encourage customers to consider other products made by Samsung, such as DVD players. This is known as *umbrella branding*. Umbrella branding is effective when consumers use the information in an advertisement about one product to make inferences about other products with the same brand name, thereby reducing advertising costs per effective image.

Research and Development

R&D expenditures exceed 10 percent of total sales revenues at many companies, including Nokia, Microsoft, GlaxoSmithKline, and Google. The nature of engineering and scientific research implies that there is a minimum feasible size to an R&D project as well as an R&D department. For example, Toyota spent an estimated $1 billion to develop the Prius hybrid vehicle, while drug companies must spend upwards of $500 million to successfully develop a single new drug.[5]

All firms can lower average costs by amortizing R&D expenses over large sales volumes, but this does not imply that larger firms are more innovative than smaller firms. Smaller firms may have greater incentives to perform R&D and, depending on the nature of the science, small firms taking a variety of research approaches may be more innovative than a large firm aggressively pursuing a narrow research agenda. We elaborate on these ideas in Chapter 11.

Physical Properties of Production

Economies of scale may arise because of the physical properties of processing units. An important example of this is the *cube-square rule*, well-known to engineers.[6] It states that as the volume of the vessel (e.g., a tank or a pipe) increases by a given proportion (e.g., it doubles), the surface area increases by less than this proportion (e.g., it less than doubles).

The cube-square rule is not related to spreading of fixed costs. So what does the cube-square rule have to do with economies of scale? In many production processes, production capacity is proportional to the *volume* of the production vessel, whereas the total cost of producing at capacity is proportional to the *surface area* of the vessel. This implies that as capacity increases, the average cost of producing at capacity decreases because the ratio of surface area to volume decreases. More generally, the physical properties of production often allow firms to expand capacity without comparable increases in costs.

Oil pipelines are an excellent example of this phenomenon. The cost of transporting oil is an increasing function of the friction between the oil and the pipe. Because the friction increases as the pipe's surface area increases, transportation costs are proportional to the pipe's surface area. By contrast, the amount of oil that can be pumped through the pipe depends on its volume. Thus, the average cost of a pipeline declines as desired throughput increases. Other processes that exhibit scale economies owing to the cube-square rule or related properties include warehousing (the cost of making the warehouse is largely determined by its surface area) and brewing beer (the volume of the brewing tanks determines output).

Inventories

Firms carry inventory to minimize the chances of running out of stock. This may include "traditional" inventory, such as parts at an auto repair shop, and nontraditional inventories, such as customer service agents at a call center. For a manufacturer, a stock-out for a single part may delay an entire production process. For a retailer, a stock-out can cause lost business and lead potential customers to seek more reliable suppliers. Of course, there are costs to carrying inventory, including interest on the expenses borne in producing the inventory and the risk that it will depreciate in value while waiting to be used or sold.

Inventory costs drive up the average costs of the goods that are actually sold. Suppose, for example, that a firm needs to hold inventories equal to 10 percent of its sales to maintain a tolerable level of expected stock-outs. This will increase its average cost of goods sold by as much as 10 percent. (The increase will be smaller if, at the end of the selling season, the firm can sell its inventories at some fraction of original cost.)

In general, inventory costs are proportional to the ratio of inventory holdings to sales. The need to carry inventories creates economies of scale because firms doing a high volume of business can usually maintain a lower ratio of inventory to sales while achieving a similar level of stock-outs.[7] Mass merchandisers such as Aldi, Carrefour, and Wal-Mart reduce inventory costs at their retail stores by maintaining regional warehouses and executing just-in-time distribution from warehouses to stores. By centralizing inventories they reduce their overall inventory to sales ratios.

COMPLEMENTARITIES AND STRATEGIC FIT

Economists usually use the concept of scope economies to describe the synergies enjoyed by a firm that produces an array of complementary products and services. Paul Milgrom and John Roberts coined the term *complementarities* to describe synergies among organizational practices.[8] Practices display complementarities when the benefits of introducing one practice are enhanced by the presence of others. For example, Southwest Airlines strives for the fastest turnaround of any airline, often landing a plane and departing within 30 minutes. To do this, Southwest uses several complementary practices. It does not cater its flights. It uses a single type of plane (Boeing 737), thereby simplifying baggage handling, refueling, and maintenance procedures. It does not fly into congested airports. Each of these practices makes the others more effective by eliminating potential bottlenecks. The reduction in maintenance time afforded by the use of a single type of plane would be wasted if Southwest took the time to cater meals.

The concept of complementarities is better known in the strategy literature as *strategic fit*. Harvard Business School Professor Michael Porter has argued that strategic fit among processes is essential to firms seeking a long-term competitive advantage over their rivals. Through strategic fit, the "whole" of a firm's strategy exceeds the "sum of the parts" of its organizational processes. Moreover, it is difficult for other firms to copy the strategy because they would have to successfully copy each individual process. For example, United Airlines could switch to a single type of plane, or stop onboard catering, but unless it moved out of its congested Chicago hub, it could not hope to match Southwest's operational efficiencies.

The power of strategic fit can be seen by a simple mathematical exercise. Suppose that a firm like Southwest has successfully implemented ten different organizational practices. Its rivals observe these practices and try to emulate them. But suppose that the probability of successfully copying any one practice is only .80, either because Southwest possesses unique skills or, what is more likely, the history of the competition restricts what they can do. In this case, the probability of copying all ten practices equals $.80^{10} = .11$, or 11 percent. Not only are Southwest's rivals unlikely to copy all ten practices, but complementarity among the ten practices implies that there is a substantial disadvantage to firms that can copy even eight or nine of them.

SOURCES OF DISECONOMIES OF SCALE

Given the attention we have paid to scale and scope economies, one might expect some colossal "megafirm" to dominate production across all industries. Antitrust laws (discussed in Chapter 5) place some limits to firm growth. Even without government regulation, colossal firms would be few and far between because there are limits to economies of scale. Beyond a certain size, bigger is no longer better and may even be worse. Here are some of the most important sources of diseconomies of scale.

Labor Costs and Firm Size

Larger firms generally pay higher wages and provide greater benefits. For example, a recent survey found that Korean firms with over 1,000 employees paid their workers about 16 percent more than firms with fewer than 300 employees, after controlling for sex and education.[9] Even if one controls for other determinants of wages such as work experience and job type, a wage gap of 10 percent or more is not unusual. Labor economists offer several possible reasons for the wage gap. Large firms are more likely to be unionized than small firms. The wage gap may also represent a *compensating differential*, which is the wage premium that firms must pay to lure workers to less attractive jobs. Workers in smaller firms may enjoy their work more, or large firms may need to draw workers from greater distances; either of these would require large firms to pay a compensating differential. Some economists speculate that the wage premium reflects hard to measure aspects of worker quality, such as skill and experience in capital-intensive production processes. According to this view, size does not handicap larger firms. Instead, large firms are merely paying a premium to workers with unique and highly valued skills.

Two factors work in favor of larger firms. First, worker turnover at larger firms is generally lower, allowing them to minimize the thousands of dollars it often takes to recruit and train new employees. Second, large firms may be more attractive to highly qualified workers who want to move up the corporate ladder without changing employers.

Spreading Specialized Resources Too Thin

Many talented individuals believe that having achieved success in one venue, they can duplicate it elsewhere. Sometimes this is sheer hubris, such as when Donald Trump felt that lending his name, but not his personal attention, to Atlantic City casinos would be enough to ensure their success. (Trump Hotel & Casino Resorts filed for bankruptcy in November 2004.) Others fail because they lack the skills necessary to translate their success to a new situation, such as when investment wiz Edward Lampert purchased and assumed management control of Sears and KMart. Some individuals simply spread themselves too thin. Gordon Ramsay Holdings Ltd. breached its debt covenants in 2008 after its eponymous owner, celebrity chef Gordon Ramsay, overexpanded. Ramsay had opened dozens of restaurants world-wide, wrote cookbooks, and was starring in several television shows about cooking and restaurant management. Unable to devote full attention to all of his endeavors, Ramsay experienced a revenue shortfall, and he had to close or sell all but his best performing restaurants.

The same lessons also apply to specialized capital inputs, such as computers, tools and dies, or assembly lines. If a specialized input is a source of advantage for a firm, and that firm attempts to expand its operations without duplicating the input, the expansion may overburden the specialized input. This is another way of saying that short-run average cost curves are U-shaped and it is possible to push output beyond minimum efficient scale, into the region of increasing average costs.

Bureaucracy

The term *bureaucracy* has a negative connotation of "red tape" and other barriers to getting things done. There are reasons why bureaucracy gets such a bad name. Incentives within large firms can be muted. Information flows can be slow. Departments fighting for scarce corporate resources can work across purposes. We discuss these issues in considerable detail in Chapters 3, 13, and 14.

Economies of Scale: A Summary

Although there are many potential sources of economies of scale, the key word here is *potential*. Table 2.2 provides a comprehensive listing of sources of scale economies as well as sources of diseconomies of scale. Firms that believe they may enjoy economies of scale should carefully consider this list of sources and determine which, if any, apply. In the Appendix, we describe a number of techniques for quantifying the magnitude of scale economies.

TABLE 2.2
SOURCES OF SCALE ECONOMIES AND DISECONOMIES

Sources of Economies	Comment
Product-specific fixed costs	These costs include specialized tools and dies, training, and setup costs; they are usually associated with capital-intensive production.
Trade-offs among alternative production technologies	Larger plants may have lower average costs, provided they operate near capacity.
Cube-square rule	This rule applies whenever output is proportional to the volume of the production vessel but costs are proportional to the surface area of the vessel.
Purchasing	Larger purchasers can get better prices by reducing seller costs or by demonstrating greater willingness to shop around.
Advertising	Fixed costs of producing advertisements generate scale economies; umbrella branding spreads marketing costs over more customers.
Inventories	Consolidating inventories reduces stocking and outage costs.
Ambiguous	
Research and development	Large firms can spread R&D costs. Smaller firms may have more incentive to innovate and pursue a wider range of research ideas.
Sources of Diseconomies	
Labor costs	Larger firms usually pay higher wages, all else equal.
Spreading resources too thin	Firms often rely on a few key personnel whose skills cannot be "replicated."
Bureaucracy	Incentives, information flows, and cooperation can suffer in large organizations.

THE LEARNING CURVE

Medical students are encouraged to learn by the axiom "See one, do one, teach one." This axiom grossly understates the importance of experience in producing skilled physicians—one surgery is not enough! Experience is an important determinant of ability in many professions, and it is just as important for firms. The importance of experience is conveyed by the idea of the learning curve.

The Concept of the Learning Curve

Economies of scale refer to the advantages that flow from producing a larger output at a given point in time. The *learning curve* (or experience curve) refers to advantages that flow from accumulating experience and know-how. It is easy to find examples of learning. A manufacturer can learn the appropriate tolerances for producing a system component. A retailer can learn about its customers' tastes. An accounting firm can learn the idiosyncrasies of its clients' inventory management. The benefits of learning manifest themselves in lower costs, higher quality, and more effective pricing and marketing.

FIGURE 2.7
THE LEARNING CURVE

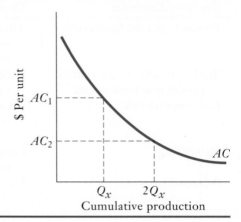

When there is learning, average costs fall with cumulative production. Here, as cumulative production increases from Q_x to $2Q_x$, the average cost of a batch of output falls from AC_1 to AC_2.

The magnitude of learning benefits is often expressed in terms of a *slope*. The slope for a given production process is calculated by examining how far average costs decline as cumulative production output doubles. It is important to use cumulative output rather than output during a given time period to distinguish between learning effects and simple economies of scale. As shown in Figure 2.7, suppose that a firm has cumulative output of Q_x with average cost of production of AC_1. Suppose next that the firm's cumulative output doubles to $2Q_x$ with average cost of AC_2. Then the slope equals AC_2/AC_1.

Slopes have been estimated for hundreds of products.[10] The median slope appears to be about .80, implying that for the typical firm, doubling cumulative output reduces unit costs by about 20 percent. Slopes vary from firm to firm and industry to industry, however, so that the actual slope enjoyed by any one firm for any given production process generally falls between .70 and .90 and may be as low as .6 or as high as 1.0 (e.g., no learning). Note that estimated slopes usually represent averages over a range of outputs and do not indicate whether or when learning economies are fully exploited.

While most studies of the learning curve focus on costs, some studies have documented the effects of learning on quality. Example 2.3 discusses a recent study of learning in medicine, where experience can literally be a matter of life and death.

Expanding Output to Obtain a Cost Advantage

When firms benefit from learning, they may want to ramp up production well past the point where the additional revenues offset the added costs. This strategy makes intuitive sense, because it allows the firm to move down the learning curve and realize lower costs in the future. Though it might seem to violate the cardinal rule of equating marginal revenue to marginal cost (see the Economics Primer), the strategy is in fact completely consistent with this rule if one properly construes the cost of current production in the presence of learning. To see why this is so, consider the following example:

Suppose that a manufacturer of DRAM chips has cumulative production of 10,000 chips. The cost to manufacture one additional chip is $2.50. The firm believes

EXAMPLE 2.3   LEARNING BY DOING IN MEDICINE

Learning curves are usually estimated for costs—as firms accumulate experience, the cost of production usually falls. But learning manifests itself in other ways, perhaps none as vital as in medicine, where learning can literally be a matter of life and death.

Researchers have long noted that high-volume providers seem to obtain better outcomes for their patients. This volume/outcome relationship appears dramatically in the so-called January/July effect. This is the well-documented fact that mortality rates at teaching hospitals spike in early January and July. One might explain the January spike as the after-effect of New Year's Eve revelry, but that won't explain July. The real reason is that medical residents usually change their specialty rotations in January and July. Hospital patients during these time periods are therefore being treated by doctors who may have no experience treating their particular ailments. Many other studies document the problems of newly minted physicians.

But the volume/outcome relationship also applies to established physicians. Back in the 1970s, this was taken as *prima facie* evidence of a learning curve. But there is another plausible explanation for the relationship—perhaps high-quality physicians receive more referrals. If so, then outcomes drive volume, not vice versa. This might not matter to patients who would clearly be served by visiting a high-volume provider regardless of how this chicken/egg question was resolved, but it would matter to policy makers who have often proposed limiting the number of specialists in certain fields on the grounds that entry dilutes learning.

There is a statistical methodology that can be used to sort out causality. The technique is commonly known as instrumental variables regression and requires identifying some phenomenon that affects only one side of the causality puzzle. In this case, the phenomenon would have to affect volume but not outcomes. Statistical analysis could then be used to unambiguously assess if higher volumes really do lead to better outcomes.

In a recent study, Subramaniam Ramanarayanan used instrumental variables regression to study the learning curve.[11] He studied cardiac surgery, where mortality rates for physicians can vary from below 2 percent to above 10 percent. As an instrument, Ramanarayanan chose the retirement of a geographically proximate heart surgeon. When a surgeon retires, volumes of other surgeons can increase by 20 patients or more annually. Retirement is a good instrument because it affects volumes but does not otherwise affect outcomes. Ramanarayanan found that surgeons who treat more patients after the retirement of a colleague enjoy better outcomes. Each additional surgical procedure reduces the probability of patient mortality by 0.14 percent. This reduction is enjoyed by all of the surgeon's patients. Ramanarayanan's study offers compelling evidence that surgeons need to maintain high volumes to be at their best.

that once it has produced 100,000 chips its unit costs will fall to $2.00, with no further learning benefits. The company has orders to produce an additional 200,000 chips when it unexpectedly receives a request to produce 10,000 chips to be filled immediately. Given the current unit cost of $2.50 per chip, it might seem that the firm would be unwilling to accept anything less than $25,000 for this order. This might be a mistake, as the true marginal cost is less than the current unit cost.

To determine the true marginal cost, the chip maker must consider how its accumulated experience will affect future costs. Before it received the new order, the chip maker had planned to produce 200,000 chips. The first 100,000 would cost $2.50 per chip, and the remaining 100,000 would cost $2.00 per chip, for a total of

$450,000 for 200,000 chips. If the firm takes the new order, then the cost of producing the next 200,000 chips is only $445,000 (90,000 chips @ $2.50 + 110,000 chips @ $2.00).

By filling the new order, the DRAM manufacturer reduces its future production costs by $5,000. In effect, the incremental cost of filling the additional order is only $20,000, which is the current costs of $25,000 less the $5,000 future cost savings. Thus, the true marginal cost per chip is $2.00. The firm should be willing to accept any price over this amount, even though a price between $2.00 and $2.50 per chip does not cover current production costs.

In general, when a firm enjoys the benefits of a learning curve, the marginal cost of increasing current production is the expected marginal cost of the last unit of production the firm expects to sell. (This formula is complicated somewhat by discounting future costs.) This implies that learning firms should be willing to price below short-run costs. They may earn negative accounting profits in the short run but will prosper in the long run.

Managers who are rewarded on the basis of short-run profits may be reluctant to exploit the benefits of the learning curve. Firms could solve this problem by directly accounting for learning curve benefits when assessing profits and losses. Few firms that aggressively move down the learning curve have accounting systems that properly measure marginal costs, however, and instead rely on direct growth incentives while placing less emphasis on profits.

Learning and Organization

Firms can take steps to improve learning and the retention of knowledge in the organization. Firms can facilitate the adoption and use of newly learned ideas by encouraging the sharing of information, establishing work rules that include the new ideas, and reducing turnover. Lanier Benkard argues that labor policies at Lockheed prevented the airframe manufacturer from fully exploiting learning opportunities in the production of the L-1011 TriStar.[12] Its union contract required Lockheed to promote experienced line workers to management, while simultaneously upgrading workers at lower levels. This produced a domino effect whereby as many as 10 workers changed jobs when one was moved to a management position. As a result, workers were forced to relearn tasks that their higher-ranking coworkers had already mastered. Benkard estimates that this and related policies reduced labor productivity at Lockheed by as much as 40 to 50 percent annually.

While codifying work rules and reducing job turnover facilitates retention of knowledge, it may stifle creativity. At the same time, there are instances where worker-specific learning is too complex to transmit across the firm. Examples include many professional services, in which individual knowledge of how to combine skills in functional areas with specific and detailed knowledge of particular clients may give individuals advantages that they cannot easily pass along to others. Clearly, an important skill of managers is to find the correct balance between stability and change so as to maximize the benefits of learning.

Managers should also draw a distinction between firm-specific and task-specific learning. If learning is task-specific rather than firm-specific, then workers who acquire skill through learning may be able to shop around their talents and capture the value for themselves in the form of higher wages. When learning is firm-specific, worker knowledge is tied to their current employment, and the firm will not have to raise wages as the workers become more productive. Managers should encourage firm-specific learning, but must usually rely on their judgment to determine if learning is firm or task-specific.

The Learning Curve versus Economies of Scale

Economies of learning differ from economies of scale. Economies of scale refer to the ability to perform an activity at a lower unit cost when it is performed on a larger scale at a particular point in time. Learning economies refer to reductions in unit costs due to accumulating experience over time and can be independent of current scale of the activity. Economies of scale may be substantial even when learning economies are minimal. This is likely to be the case in simple capital-intensive activities, such as two-piece aluminum can manufacturing. Similarly, learning economies may be substantial even when economies of scale are minimal. This is likely to be the case in complex labor-intensive activities, such as the practice of antitrust law.

Figure 2.8 illustrates how one can have learning economies without economies of scale. The left side of the figure shows a typical learning curve, with average costs declining with cumulative experience. The right side shows two average cost curves, for different experience levels. Both average cost curves are perfectly flat, indicating that there are no economies of scale. Suppose that the firm under consideration enters a given year of production with cumulative experience of Q_1. According to the learning curve, this gives it an average cost level of AC_1. This remains constant regardless of current output because of constant returns to scale. Entering the next year of production, the firm has cumulative output of Q_2. Its experiences in the previous year enable the firm to revamp its production techniques. In thus moving down the learning curve, it can enjoy an average cost level of AC_2 in the next year of production.

FIGURE 2.8
LEARNING ECONOMIES WHEN SCALE ECONOMIES ARE ABSENT

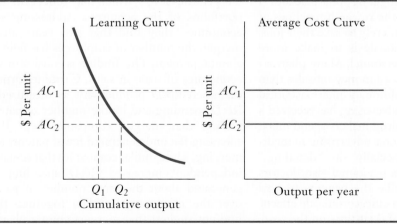

It is not necessary to have economies of scale to realize learning economies. The production process depicted here shows constant returns to scale, as evidenced by the flat average cost curves, which show output *within a given year*. The level of average cost falls with cumulative experience *across several years*, however, as shown by the learning curve.

Managers who do not correctly distinguish between economies of scale and learning may draw incorrect inferences about the benefits of size in a market. For example, if a large firm has lower unit costs because of economies of scale, then any cutbacks in production volume will raise unit costs. If the lower unit costs are the result of learning, the firm may be able to cut current volume without necessarily

---

EXAMPLE 2.4 THE PHARMACEUTICAL MERGER WAVE

Beginning in the 1990s, pharmaceutical companies faced an unprecedented strategic challenge. The growth of managed care in the United States and the tightening of government health care budgets in other nations forced manufacturers to lower prices on many drugs. Traditional research pipelines began to dry up, while the advent of biotechnology promised new avenues for drug discovery coupled with new sources of competition. In response to these pressures, the pharmaceutical industry underwent a remarkable wave of consolidation, with the total value of merger and acquisition activity exceeding $500 billion. As a result, the combined market shares of the 10 largest firms has grown from 20 percent to more than 50 percent. Using almost any yardstick, we can view Glaxo's 2000 acquisition of SmithKline Beecham and Pfizer's 2003 acquisition of Pharmacia as among the largest in business history.

Industry analysts point out three potential rationales for consolidation. One cynical view is that executives at struggling pharmaceutical companies are buying the research pipelines of more successful rivals merely to save their jobs. Another potential rationale is to make more efficient use of sales personnel. Many pharmaceutical firms spend more money on sales than they do on R&D. Although pharmaceutical "direct to consumer" advertising has received a lot of attention lately, drug makers spend much more money on traditional advertising in medical journals and especially on "detailing." Detailing is when sales personnel visit doctors and hospitals to describe the benefits of new drugs and share data on efficacy and side effects. Detailers spend most of their time on the road, creating an obvious opportunity for scale economies. A detailer who can offer several cardiovascular drugs to a cardiologist will have a much higher ratio of selling time to traveling time. Why have two detailers from two companies visiting the same cardiologist when one will do?

Perhaps the most common explanation offered for the merger wave is to exploit economies of scale in R&D. As we discuss in the accompanying text, there are conflicting theories as to whether bigger firms will be more innovative or will innovate at lower cost. The theoretical considerations apply especially well in pharmaceutical R&D, and those in the industry who bank on achieving greater research effectiveness through scale economies in R&D may not have solid footing.

Two recent studies examine some of these potential scale economies.[13] Danzon, Epstein, and Nicholson found that acquirers tended to have older drug portfolios, lending some support to the cynical explanation for acquisitions. In contrast, targets had average-to-possibly-slightly younger portfolios. Combined sales after the merger seem to be slightly below pre-merger sales levels, which may reflect the weak portfolios of the acquirers. Addressing scale economies, they find that two years after a merger, the number of employees has fallen by about 6 percent. This finding is consistent with economies of scale in sales. Carmine Ornaghi examined R&D productivity, as measured by R&D spending and by the number of patents, finding that merged companies kept R&D spending flat and generated fewer patents after merging, while similar companies that remained independent increased R&D spending and generated about the same number of patents over the time period. Taken together, these findings suggest that mergers among pharmaceutical firms may have led to lower sales costs but almost surely did not generate increased research productivity.

raising its unit costs (depending on the rate of forgetting.) To take another example, if a firm enjoys a cost advantage due to a capital-intensive production process and resultant scale economies, then it may be less concerned about labor turnover than a competitor that enjoys low costs due to learning a complex labor-intensive production process.

DIVERSIFICATION

We have thus far considered the importance of size in firms that remain focused on a single activity (economies of scale) or related activities (economies of scope). Many well-known firms operate in seemingly far-flung industries. Sometimes the industries are connected by subtle but important scope economies, such as the product design skills that allow Apple to prosper in computers and cell phones. But in many cases the potential for scope economies is limited, such as when England's EMI diversified in medical-imaging equipment and popular music. These firms are often described as *conglomerates* involved in *unrelated diversification*. Many of the world's largest firms follow this strategy. India's Tata Group operates in a wide range of businesses including information technology, energy, pharmaceuticals, Italian handcrafted furniture, and automobiles (including the Tata, Jaguar, and Land Rover nameplates). South Korea's Hyundai Group is in steel production, elevators, ocean shipping, and, of course, automobiles.

In the remainder of this chapter, we explore a variety of rationales for business conglomerates, as well as examine empirical evidence that casts some doubt on the wisdom of unrelated diversification.

WHY DO FIRMS DIVERSIFY?

Diversification is costly, especially when one firm acquires another. In addition to the costs of financing the deal, the resulting conglomerate may suffer from a variety of costs loosely associated with bureaucracy. We take up these bureaucracy costs in Chapter 3.

If diversification has its costs, there must be some equal or greater benefits. Firms may choose to diversify for either of two reasons. First, diversification may benefit the firm's owners by increasing the efficiency of the firm. Second, if the firm's owners are not directly involved in deciding whether to diversify, diversification decisions may reflect the preferences of the firm's managers.

In this section we explore both possibilities. First we discuss how diversification may affect corporate efficiency and thereby affect the value accruing to the firm's owners. We discuss ways in which diversification can both enhance and reduce efficiency. We then discuss how a firm's manager may benefit from diversifying the firm, why shareholders may be unable to prevent diversification that does not create value, and what forces constrain management's ability to diversify firms.

Efficiency-based Reasons for Diversification

We begin by discussing both the benefits and the costs of corporate diversification to a firm's shareholders.

Scope Economies

One motive for diversification may be to achieve economies of scope. Although there may be little opportunity to spread fixed production costs across businesses like automobiles and pharmaceuticals, scope economies can come from spreading a firm's underutilized organizational resources to new areas.[14] In particular, C. K. Prahalad and Richard Bettis suggest that managers of diversified firms may spread *their own managerial talent* across business areas that do not seem to enjoy economies of scope. They call this a "dominant general management logic," which comprises "the way in which managers conceptualize the business and make critical resource allocations—be it in technologies, product development, distribution, advertising, or in human resource management."[15] The dominant general management logic may seem at odds with the notion of diseconomies of scale, discussed earlier, that result when talent is spread too thin, which is why we emphasize the gains from spreading *underutilized* resources.

EXAMPLE 2.5 APPLE: DIVERSIFYING OUTSIDE OF THE BOX

Over the past decade, Apple has gone from being a focused computer maker given up for dead to the world's most valuable technology company. From the Mac to the iPod, iPhone and iPad, Apple has thrived by leveraging economies of scope to suit changing trends and times. Constant innovation and efficient diversification have helped Apple excite its customers and build remarkable brand loyalty. As a result, Apple dominates its markets and commands a price premium.

Steve Jobs, Steve Wozniak, and Ronald Wayne founded Apple in the 1970s. With Jobs at the helm, the company quickly became known for its personal computers with a user-friendly operating system. Apple garnered rave reviews from loyal users, but most consumers purchased Microsoft-based personal computers because of Microsoft's lower price and greater availability. Apple made a big splash in 1984 when it ran a famous commercial for its McIntosh computer during the Super Bowl. But an industrywide sales slump led to Jobs's dismissal later that same year. Despite constant design innovations and ongoing problems with Microsoft Windows operating systems, Apple could not build its market share of the PC business much above its loyal 10 percent.

In an effort to reverse its fortunes, Apple brought Jobs back in 1996. He immediately terminated several ongoing projects and focused on a question that must have seemed anything but innovative at the time: "What can we do to make more people buy the Mac?" Apple introduced the iMac, with its revolutionary design that integrated the computer into the monitor, doing away with the traditional big black box. With sales of the Mac on the rise, Apple began looking outside of the box for further growth.

Apple saw great opportunities in personal digital devices. Digital cameras and camcorders already had well-established markets, but existing digital music players were either big and clunky or small and useless, with unfriendly user interfaces. Jobs asked veteran engineer Jon Rubinstein to build a better product, one that used the iMac as a programming engine. Robinson had been responsible for many of the company's hardware innovations and saw the potential of a miniature hard drive newly developed by Apple's supplier Toshiba. This little disk became one of the core technologies of the iPod. Apple licensed the SoundJam MP music player from a small company and retooled it into its own media player, iTunes. Apple also relied heavily on its own capabilities. Apple's prestigious design group made prototype after prototype to ensure that iPod would fit Apple's "user friendly" brand image. The design group worked with Apple's hardware engineers, power group, and programmers, leveraging technologies and skills used on the iMac.

Apple introduced the iPod in October 2001. Together with iTunes, it not only turned around Apple's finances, it rewrote the entire digital music landscape. This remarkable success changed the face of Apple overnight from being a rebel computer company to the trendy digital electronics company. And the iPod had a "halo effect" on the iMac; Apple products were trendier than ever.

Apple next turned its attention to cellular phones. Inspired by tablet PCs, Jobs believed that cell phones were going to become important devices for portable information access. Although the headset business was highly competitive, one point of market share was worth $1.4 billion. More importantly, there were no products that integrated all of the functions that one could incorporate into a handheld device. Research in Motion's Blackberry had taken a big step toward convergence, but Apple planned to go further, and expected to command a steep price premium if it succeeded. Once again building on existing strengths, Jobs took the video iPod and stuffed it with a version of the OS X operating system, so that the phone could handle web browsers and e-mail clients. GPS and wireless capabilities were added. Independent programmers found the iPhone to be a perfect vehicle for new applications. Today's iPhones are expensive and highly profitable. By the end of fiscal year 2011, Apple had sold a total of 140 million iPhones, which accounts for a market share of less than 10 percent of all cell phones. More important to Apple, the product generates over half of total industry profits.

With each innovation, from the iPod to the iPhone and the iPad, Apple puts its existing skills in design, engineering, and programming to surprising new uses. Time will tell what new surprises Apple has in store.

The dominant general management logic applies most directly when managers develop specific skills—say, in information systems or finance—that can be applied to seemingly unrelated businesses without stretching management too thin. Managers sometimes mistakenly apply this logic when they develop particular skills but diversify into businesses that do not require them. For example, some observers of the 1995 Disney–ABC merger wondered whether Michael Eisner's ability to develop marketing plans for Disney's animated motion pictures would translate into skill at the scheduling of network television programming. The dominant general management logic is more problematic when managers perceive themselves to possess superior general management skills with which they can justify any diversification. Indeed, the dominant general management logic may be used to justify any and all unjustifiable diversifications.

Internal Capital Markets

Combining unrelated businesses may also lead a firm to make use of an *internal capital market*. The *internal capital market*, which we describe in more detail in Chapter 3, describes the allocation of available working capital within the firm, as opposed to the capital raised outside the firm via debt and equity markets. To understand the role of internal capital markets in diversification, suppose that a cash-rich business and a cash-constrained business operate under a single corporate umbrella. The central office of the firm can use proceeds from the cash-rich business to fund profitable investment opportunities in the cash-constrained business. Thus, the diversified firm can create value in a way that smaller focused firms cannot, provided that diversification allows the cash-constrained business to make profitable investments *that would not otherwise be made*, for example, by issuing debt or equity. This idea forms the basis of the important Boston Consulting Group Growth/Share paradigm.

FIGURE 2.9
THE BCG GROWTH/SHARE MATRIX

The growth/share matrix divides products into four categories according to their potential for growth and relative market share. Some strategists recommended that firms use the profits earned from cash cows to ramp up production of rising stars and problem children. As the latter products move down their learning curves, they become cash cows in the next investment cycle.

		Relative Market Share	
		High	Low
Relative Market Growth	High	Rising star	Problem child
	Low	Cash cow	Dog

Beginning 30 years ago, the Boston Consulting Group (BCG) has preached aggressive growth strategies as a way of exploiting the learning curve. Figure 2.9 depicts a typical BCG *growth/share matrix*. The matrix distinguishes a firm's product lines on two dimensions: growth of the market in which the product is situated, and the product's market share relative to the share of its next-largest competitors. A product line was classified into one of four categories. A *rising star* is a product in a growing market with a high relative share. A *cash cow* is a product in a stable or declining market with a high relative share. A *problem child* is a product in a growing market with a low relative share. A *dog* is a product in a stable or declining market with a low relative share.

The BCG strategy for successfully managing a portfolio of products was based on taking advantage of learning curves and the *product life cycle*.[16] According to this product life-cycle model, firms use profits from established cash cow products to fund increased production of early-stage problem child and rising star products. Learning economies cement the advantages of rising stars, which eventually mature into cash cows and help renew the investment cycle.

BCG deserves credit for recognizing the strategic importance of learning curves. However, it would be a mistake to apply the BCG framework without considering its underlying principles. As we have discussed, learning curves are by no means ubiquitous or uniform where they do occur. At the same time, product life cycles are easier to identify after they have been completed than during the planning process. Many products ranging from nylon to the Segway personal transporter that were forecast to have tremendous potential for growth did not meet expectations.

Perhaps the most controversial element of the BCG framework is the role of the firm as "banker." Recall that diversification allows businesses access to a corporation's working capital. Thus, the central office of the corporation must act like a banker, deciding which businesses to invest in. Given the sophistication of modern financial markets, one wonders if firms must really rely on "cash cows" to find capital to fund their "rising stars." Jeremy Stein argues that the answer to this question may well be yes, for several reasons.[17] First, a firm may find it difficult to find external providers willing to fund new ventures due to *asymmetric information*. Firms seeking to expand usually know more about their prospects for success than potential bond- and equity holders outside the firm. Outsiders may suspect that firms disproportionately seek outside funding for questionable projects, saving their internal working capital for the most promising projects. When firms seek outside funding for projects that they believe are truly worthwhile, they can be met with skepticism and high interest rates.

Second, outsiders will be reluctant to provide capital to firms that have existing debt. This is because new debt and equity are typically junior to the existing debt, which means that existing bondholders have first dibs on any positive cash flows. Third, external finance consumes monitoring resources, for bond- and equity holders must ensure that managers take actions that serve their interests.

If external finance is costly, then firms without adequate internal capital may have to forego profitable projects. Thus, firms may benefit by having their own "cash cows" to fund "rising stars" even if they are in unrelated businesses.

The benefits of using an internal capital market may extend to *human capital*, that is, labor. As John Roberts observes, firms usually have good information about the abilities of their workers, and large diversified firms may have greater opportunities to assign their best workers to the most appropriate and most challenging jobs.[18] This may help explain the success of diversified business groups in developing nations, such as Mexico's Grupo Carso SAB. We say more about these business groups in Chapter 4.

Problematic Justifications for Diversification

Some of the more commonly cited reasons for diversification do not stand up to scrutiny.

Diversifying Shareholders' Portfolios

Shareholders benefit from investing in a diversified portfolio. By purchasing small holdings in a broad range of firms, investors can reduce the chance of incurring a large loss due to the failure of any single firm and thus insulate themselves from risk. A shareholder seeking to avoid large swings in value might wish to invest in a single diversified firm. But shareholders can diversify their own personal portfolios and seldom need corporate managers to do so on their behalf. Nowadays, investors can choose from countless diversified mutual funds, including some that are invested in thousands of different firms. Diversification to reduce shareholder risk is therefore largely unnecessary.

Identifying Undervalued Firms

Many firms diversify by acquiring established firms in unrelated industries. This can be profitable if the acquirer can identify other firms that are undervalued by the stock market. But how likely is this? This justification requires that the market valuation of the target firm (that is, the firm being purchased) is incorrect *and* that no other investors have yet identified this fact. Given that speculators, fund managers, and other investors are constantly scouring the market in search of undervalued stocks, it seems hard to believe that a CEO whose attention is largely consumed by running his or her own firm could easily identify valuation errors that these other market participants have missed, unless the target firm is in a closely related business.

Consider also that announcements of merger proposals frequently encourage other potential acquirers to bid for the target firm. Bidding wars reduce the profits an acquiring firm can hope to earn through a merger. Consider Verizon's February 2005 offer to purchase MCI for $6.75 billion. A rival telecom firm, Qwest, quickly entered the bidding with an even higher offer. After a protracted struggle, with offers and counteroffers going back and forth several times, Verizon purchased MCI for $8.5 billion. It is possible that MCI was a bargain at $6.75 billion, but the $1.75 billion premium Verizon paid may have significantly cut into its profit from the deal.

Finally, note that successful bidders tend to suffer from the "winner's curse." In other words, the firm with the most optimistic assessment of the target's value will win the bidding. Given that all other bidders' estimates of the target's value are below the final purchase price, it is likely that the winner has overpaid. As Max Bazerman and William Samuelson point out in their article "I Won the Auction but Don't Want the Prize," unless the diversifying firm knows much more about the target than other bidders do, it will probably pay too much to "win" the bidding.[19]

Reasons Not to Diversify

When scope economies are not available, there are several reasons to avoid diversification. Within a diversified portfolio of holdings, a conglomerate will have some divisions that outperform others; the profitable ones effectively cross-subsidize the money losers. Not only does this reduce the share value of the conglomerate, it reduces the incentives of the managers of the money-losing divisions, who would be far more concerned for their jobs if theirs were stand-alone businesses.

Other reasons to avoid diversification may be loosely classified as stemming from bureaucracy effects. We take up most of these reasons in Chapter 3 in the context of vertical integration. Here is a brief synopsis. It is difficult to maintain the hard-edged incentives of the market within a diversified firm. The allocation of internal capital may suffer due to influence activities, whereby each division and work unit manager seeks corporate resources to advance their own careers. Finally, diversification imposes a uniform organizational design on business units that may benefit from different organizational structures.

MANAGERIAL REASONS FOR DIVERSIFICATION

A key feature of large corporations in modern economies is the separation of ownership and control. Hence, it is important to know whether managers may undertake diversifying acquisitions that do not generate net benefits for the firm's shareholders.

Benefits to Managers from Acquisitions

One reason managers may diversify is that they enjoy running larger firms. As Michael Jensen puts it:

> Corporate growth enhances the social prominence, public prestige, and political power of senior executives. Rare is the CEO who wants to be remembered as presiding over an enterprise that makes fewer products in fewer plants in fewer countries than when he or she took office.[20]

One might wonder whether this is a bad thing; after all, don't shareholders want their firms to grow and prosper? Of course they do, but it is important to realize that growth can be either profitable or unprofitable. Shareholders want their firms to grow only if such growth leads to increases in profits. Jensen's claim is that managers value growth whether or not it is profitable, especially if the manager's compensation is only loosely tied to overall profitability and the manager personally values firm size, perhaps due to social prominence or prestige.

Although it is difficult to devise precise measures of such abstract notions as social prominence and public prestige, researchers have identified some ways in which

CEOs who undertake acquisitions appear to benefit. Chris Avery, Judy Chevalier, and Scott Schaefer, for example, found that CEOs who undertake acquisitions are more likely to be appointed to *other firms'* boards of directors.[21] If CEOs value such appointments, they may wish to pursue acquisitions in order to secure them.

Managers may pursue unrelated acquisitions in order to increase their compensation. Robert Reich wrote:

> When professional managers plunge their companies deeply into debt in order to acquire totally unrelated businesses, they are apt to be motivated by the fact that their personal salaries and bonuses are tied to the volume of business their newly enlarged enterprise will generate.[22]

Evidence on this point is mixed. It is true that executives of larger firms earn higher compensation, but this does not imply that a given executive can increase compensation through diversification. Moreover, most executive compensation includes substantial stock and options; diversification that reduces firm value will automatically reduce compensation.

Although diversification is not a useful way to reduce investor risk, it may lessen managerial risk. Yakov Amihud and Baruch Lev observe that shareholders are unlikely to replace top management unless the firm performs poorly relative to the overall economy.[23] By diversifying their firm, managers limit the risk of extremely poor overall profitability, which helps protect their jobs. This is not necessarily a bad thing for the owners of the diversified company—managers may be willing to accept lower wages in exchange for job security.

Problems of Corporate Governance

Managerial motives for diversification rely on the existence of some failure of *corporate governance*—that is, the mechanisms through which corporations and their managers are controlled by shareholders. If shareholders could (1) determine which acquisitions will lead to increased profits and which ones will not and (2) direct management to undertake only those that will increase shareholder value, the possibility of managerially driven acquisitions would disappear.

In practice, however, neither condition (1) nor condition (2) is likely to hold. First, it is unlikely that shareholders can easily determine which acquisitions will increase profits and which ones will not. Typically, shareholders have neither the expertise nor the information to make such determinations. Second, even if shareholders do disagree with management's decisions, they may find it difficult to change those decisions. Formally, boards of directors are charged with the responsibility of monitoring management to ensure that actions are taken to increase shareholder value. However, many authors, including Benjamin Hermalin and Michael Weisbach, have suggested that CEOs may exercise considerable control over the selection of new directors.[24]

THE MARKET FOR CORPORATE CONTROL AND RECENT CHANGES IN CORPORATE GOVERNANCE

If diversification is driven in part by managerial objectives, what forces work to keep managers focused on the goals of owners? Henry Manne suggests that the "market for corporate control" serves as an important constraint on the actions of managers.[25]

Manne's argument is as follows. Managers who undertake acquisitions that do not serve the interests of shareholders will find that their firms' share prices fall, for two reasons.

First, if a manager overpays for a diversifying acquisition, the value of his or her firm will fall by the amount of the overpayment. Second, if the stock market expects the firm to overpay for additional acquisitions in the future, the market price of the firm's shares will fall today in expectation of these events. This disparity between the firm's *actual* and *potential* share prices presents an opportunity for another entity (either an individual, another firm, or a specialist investment bank) to try a takeover. A potential acquirer can purchase control of the firm simply by buying its shares on the market. With a sufficiently large block of shares, the acquirer can vote in its own slate of directors and appoint managers who will work to enhance shareholder value. The acquirer profits by purchasing shares at their actual value and then imposing changes that return the shares to their potential value. Note that the market for corporate control can serve to discipline managers even *without* takeovers actually occurring. If an incumbent manager is concerned that he or she may lose his or her job if the firm is taken over, he or she may work to prevent a takeover by keeping the firm's share price at or near its potential value.

Michael Jensen argues that the market for corporate control was in full swing during the wave of leveraged buyout (LBO) transactions observed in the 1980s. Jensen claims that firms in many U.S. industries had free cash flow—that is, cash flow in excess of profitable investment opportunities—during this period. Managers elected to invest this free cash flow to expand the size of the business empires they controlled, both by undertaking unprofitable acquisitions and by overexpanding core businesses. Given that these investments were unprofitable, Jensen reasons that shareholders would have been better served had the free cash flow been paid out to them in the form of dividends. In an LBO, a corporate raider borrows against the firm's future free cash flow and uses these borrowings to purchase the firm's equity. Such a transaction helps the firm realize its potential value in two ways. First, since the number of shares outstanding is greatly reduced, it is possible to give the firm's management a large fraction of its equity. This improves incentives for management to take actions that increase shareholder value. Second, since the debt must be repaid using the firm's future free cash flow, management no longer has discretion over how to invest these funds. Management must pay these funds out to bondholders or risk default. This limits managers' ability to undertake future acquisitions and expand core businesses.

The LBO merger wave ended rather abruptly around 1990. Holmstrom and Kaplan attribute this development to changes in corporate governance practices since the mid-1980s.[26] They point out that firms increased CEO ownership stakes (dramatically, in many cases) and introduced new performance measures that forced an accounting for the cost of capital (such as Economic Value Added). In addition, large shareholders such as pension funds began to take a more active role in monitoring managers. These recent changes in corporate governance practices may serve to constrain managers' actions without relying on corporate takeovers.

PERFORMANCE OF DIVERSIFIED FIRMS

Although we have discussed why diversification may be profitable, many academics and practitioners remain skeptical of the ability of diversification strategies to add value. Michael Goold and Kathleen Luchs, in their review of 40 years of diversification, sum up the skeptics' viewpoint:

Ultimately, diversity can only be worthwhile if corporate management *adds value* (emphasis added) in some way and the test of a corporate strategy must be that the businesses in the portfolio are worth more than they would be under any other ownership.[27]

Studies of the performance of diversified firms, undertaken from a variety of disciplines and using different research methods, have consistently *failed to find significant value added* from diversification. And whereas the BCG model encourages diversified firms to use the profits from cash cows to fuel the growth of rising stars, in reality diversified firms end up underinvesting in their strongest divisions. This may be due to *influence activities*, a central issue in diversified firms that we postpone discussing until Chapter 3. Simply put, the overall performance of diversified firms lags behind more focused companies; that is, diversified firms usually fail the Goold/Luchs test of corporate strategy that we quoted above. This helps explain why it is often quite profitable for corporate "raiders" to purchase a conglomerate and sell off its unrelated business holdings.

Many well-known and respected firms have fallen victim to the inefficiencies of diversification. Consider Beatrice, which once owned Avis Rent-a-Car, Samsonite Luggage, and Dannon yogurt; the Daewoo Group, which once sold eponymous automobiles and consumer electronics, as well as oil tankers and textiles; and Nueva Rumasa, the Spanish business group whose business empire included yogurt and ice cream, hotels, wine and spirits, real estate management, and a soccer team. Beatrice, which ranked 35th on the 1980 Fortune 500, was split up after a hostile takeover by Kohlberg Kravis Roberts in 1986. Daewoo, once the second largest conglomerate in South Korea, went bankrupt in 1999. In 2011, Nueva Rumasa, one of Spain's largest conglomerates, had to sell off several of its businesses to avoid bankruptcy.

Many successful firms have experienced trouble when diversifying from their core businesses. Microsoft has made unsuccessful forays into PDAs, music players, and television (with the MSNBC cable network). The road to bankruptcy for Circuit City, once the largest electronics retailer in the United States, began when it rapidly expanded its CarMax used car subsidiary and accelerated when it launched the DIVX video disc format as an alternative to DVD. Example 2.6 describes the problems that arose at Haier—China's largest consumer electronics firm—when it diversified away from its core portfolio of businesses.

The early evidence on diversification offered by management scholars was fairly conclusive that diversified firms underperformed more focused firms in the 1980s. Other research consistently finds that the overall shareholder value is increased when conglomerates split up. But this does not automatically imply that diversification is unprofitable. From a theoretical perspective, there are genuine benefits of scope economies and the use of internal capital markets. As an empirical matter, we must remember the statistical adage that correlation does not imply causality. The firms that diversify may have been underperformers regardless of diversification. And more recent research finds that the stock market reacted positively to diversifying acquisitions in the 1990s.

It is too simplistic to conclude that "diversification sometimes works and sometimes doesn't." When firms believe they have found a money-making opportunity by diversifying, the market reacts positively. And the market also reacts positively when conglomerates stem losses by shedding business units that are better off as stand-alone firms. In other words, when it comes to the question of whether firms should diversify, the answer is "yes, but only when the economics make sense."

EXAMPLE 2.6 HAIER: THE WORLD'S LARGEST CONSUMER APPLIANCE AND ELECTRONICS FIRM

It may be surprising to learn that the world's top-selling brand of consumer appliances and electronics is not Bosch or Sony or General Electric. That honor goes to the Haier Group, a Chinese firm with 70,000 employees and annual revenues of $20 billion. Those familiar with the Haier Group may be even more surprised that less than two decades ago the firm was in the midst of a disastrous diversification strategy with corporate tentacles reaching into pharmaceuticals, restaurants, and many other unrelated businesses. Haier's success today is due to a corporate decision to narrow its reach, to retrench from diversification.

Haier is headquartered in Shandong where it started life in the 1920s as a refrigerator manufacture. Haier was turned into a state-owned enterprise after the establishment of the People's Republic of China in 1949, and for a long time thereafter the firm suffered from inadequate capital investment, poor management, and a lack of quality control. The company's fortunes changed in 1985 when the local government appointed Zhang Ruimin as the managing director.

Zhang's first step was to implement strict quality control, a notion that seemed foreign to Chinese workers. According to one story, after a customer complained about a faulty refrigerator, Zhang went through the entire inventory and found that 76 out of 400 refrigerators were defective. Zhang lined up the 76 refrigerators, distributed sledgehammers to employees, and ordered them to join him in destroying them. What makes this truly remarkable is that at the time, one refrigerator cost about 2 years' worth of wages for the average Chinese worker. Through this emphasis on quality, Haier became one of the first Chinese brands to establish a reputation for quality; within China, Haier was known for its "zero-defect" refrigerators.

Recognizing the benefits of quality control in related markets and eager to leverage its brand, Haier started diversifying by acquiring other home appliance companies. By the early 1990s, Haier was China's largest seller of washing machines and air conditioners and was ranked third in freezers. By mid-decade, Haier was exporting into the international market. Flush with success, Zhang set his sights on turning Haier into the "GE" of China, and adopted a more aggressive diversification strategy. Beginning in 1995, Haier acquired or launched businesses in such far-flung industries as pharmaceuticals, televisions, personal computers, software, logistics, and financial services. But Haier's magic touch with home appliances did not reach into these new industries. For example, in 1995 the nutritional supplement market of China was booming, and Haier decided to build a "Kingdom of Health Products." Its first step was to introduce Cai Li Oral Solution. But Haier's management knew very little about the health products market and lacked the expertise to do appropriate consumer research. So it chose to mimic the business model and marketing strategy of "San Zhu," one of the most popular nutritional supplement products in the market. Cai Li never bested San Zhu in sales, and when the supplement market proved to be a fad, Haier pulled Cai Li from the market. Haier faced similar problems in the pharmaceutical sector, failing to produce a single blockbuster product. In 2007, Haier sold its pharmaceutical division to a company in Hong Kong.

Haier even ventured into fast food, launching the "Dasaozi" Noodle House in its headquarters city of Qingdao and then spreading nationwide. Haier positioned Dasaozi as a budget fast-food franchise, in stark contrast with its reputation for high quality in appliances. Dasaozi enjoyed limited success in Qingdao, but confusion about the brand kept customers in other cities away. Today, Dasaozi operates only in Qingdao. This story has repeated itself in other industries; today, Haier remains focused on consumer appliances and electronics, having learned some painful lessons about unrelated diversification.

CHAPTER SUMMARY

- A production process exhibits economies of scale if the average cost per unit of output falls as the volume of output increases. A production process exhibits economies of scope if the total cost of producing two different products or services is lower when they are produced by a single firm instead of two separate firms.

- An important source of economies of scale and scope is the spreading of indivisible fixed costs. Fixed costs do not vary as the level of production varies.

- In general, capital-intensive production processes are more likely to display economies of scale and scope than are labor- or materials-intensive processes.

- There are often economies of scale associated with inventory management, marketing expense, and purchasing. Large-scale marketing efforts often have lower costs per message received than do smaller-scale efforts.

- The costs of large research ventures may be spread over greater output, although big size may be inimical to innovation. Small firms may obtain purchasing discounts comparable to those obtained by large firms by forming purchasing groups.

- Sometimes, large size can create inefficiencies. These may result from higher labor costs, agency problems, or dilution of specialized resources.

- Individuals and firms often improve their production processes with experience. This is known as learning. In processes with substantial learning benefits, firms that can accumulate and protect the knowledge gained by experience can achieve superior cost and quality positions in the market.

- A firm is diversified if it produces for numerous markets. Most large and well-known firms are diversified to some extent.

- Economies of scope provide the principal rationale for diversification. These economies can be based on market and technological factors as well as on managerial synergies.

- Firms may diversify in order to make use of an internal capital market. Combining a cash-rich business and a cash-poor business into a single firm allows profitable investments in the cash-poor business to be funded without accessing external sources of capital.

- Diversification may also reflect the preferences of a firm's managers rather than those of its owners. If problems of corporate governance prevent shareholders from stopping value-reducing acquisitions, managers may diversify in order to satisfy their preference for growth, to increase their compensation, or to reduce their risk.

- The market for corporate control limits managers' ability to diversify unprofitably. If the actual price of a firm's shares is far below the potential price, a raider can profit from taking over the firm and instituting changes that increase its value.

- Research on the performance of diversified firms has produced mixed results. Where diversification has been effective, it has been based on economies of scope among businesses that are related in terms of technologies or markets. More broadly diversified firms have not performed well.

QUESTIONS

1. A firm produces two products, X and Y. The production technology displays the following costs, where $C(i, j)$ represents the cost of producing i units of X and j units of Y:

   $C(0, 50) = 100 \quad C(5, 0) = 150$
   $C(0, 100) = 210 \quad C(10, 0) = 320$
   $C(5, 50) = 240 \quad C(10, 100) = 500$

   Does this production technology display economies of scale? Of scope?

2. Economies of scale are usually associated with the spreading of fixed costs, such as when a manufacturer builds a factory. But the spreading of fixed costs is also important for economies of scale associated with marketing, R&D, and purchasing. Explain.

3. How does the globalization of the economy affect the division of labor? Can you give some examples?

4. It is estimated that a firm contemplating entering the breakfast cereal market would need to invest $100 million to build a minimum efficient scale production plant (or about $10 million annually on an amortized basis). Such a plant could produce about 100 million pounds of cereal per year. What would be the average fixed costs of this plant if it ran at capacity? Each year, U.S. breakfast cereal makers sell about 3 billion pounds of cereal. What would be the average fixed costs if the cereal maker captured a 2 percent market share? What would be its cost disadvantage if it only achieved a 1 percent share? If, prior to entering the market, the firm contemplates achieving only a 1 percent share, is it doomed to such a large cost disparity?

5. You are the manager of the "New Products" division of a firm considering a group of investment projects for the upcoming fiscal year. The CEO is interested in maximizing profits and wants to pursue the project or set of projects that return the highest possible expected profits to the firm. Three potential alternatives have been proposed, including the following estimated financial projections:

Alpha Project	Upfront Costs	$60 million
	Expected Revenues	$85 million
Beta Project	Upfront Costs	$20 million
	Expected Revenues	$16 million
Gamma Project	Upfront Costs	$30 million
	Expected Revenues	$60 million

   Which set of projects would you recommend if your firm could only spend $70 million in upfront costs on investments and if the investment in the Alpha project decreased the upfront costs required for each of the remaining projects by half?

6. How does the digitization of books, movies, and music affect inventory economies of scale?

7. American and European bricks-and-mortar retailing is increasingly becoming dominated by "hypermarts," enormous stores that sell groceries, household goods,

hardware, and other products under one roof. What are the possible economies of scale that might be enjoyed by hypermarts? What are the potential diseconomies of scale? How can hypermarts fend off competition from web-based retailing?

8. Explain why learning reduces the effective marginal cost of production. If firms set prices in proportion to their marginal costs, as suggested by the Economics Primer, how can learning firms ever hope to make a profit?

9. What is the dominant general manager logic? How is this consistent with the principles of scale economies? How is it inconsistent with these principles?

10. In rapidly developing economies—such as India and South Korea—conglomerates are far more common than they are in the United States and western Europe. Use the BCG growth/share matrix to explain why this organizational form is more suitable for nations where financial markets are less well developed.

11. The following is a quote from a GE Medical Systems web site: "Growth Through Acquisition—Driving our innovative spirit at GE Medical Systems is the belief that great ideas can come from anyone, anywhere, at any time. Not only from within the company, but from beyond as well. . . . This belief is the force behind our record number of acquisitions." Under what conditions can a "growth-through-acquisition" strategy create value for shareholders?

12. "The theory of the market for corporate control cannot be true because it assumes that every individual shareholder is paying careful attention to the performance of management." Agree or disagree.

13. Many publicly traded companies are still controlled by their founders. Research shows that the share values of these companies often increase if the founder unexpectedly dies. Use the theory of the market for corporate control to explain this phenomenon.

14. Summarize the research evidence on diversification. Is the evidence consistent with economic theory?

APPENDIX: USING REGRESSION ANALYSIS TO ESTIMATE THE SHAPES OF COST CURVES AND LEARNING CURVES

Suppose that you had the following cost and output data for three chainsaw manufacturing plants:

Plant	Annual Output	Average Cost
1	10,000	$50
2	20,000	$47
3	30,000	$45

Average costs apparently fall as output increases. It would be natural to conclude from this pattern that there are economies of scale in chainsaw production. But this conclusion might be premature; the cost differences might result from factors that have nothing to do with scale economies. For example, plant 3 may be located in a region where labor costs are unusually low. To be confident that the cost/output relationship truly reflects scale economies, alternative explanations need to be ruled out.

This is the idea underlying *regression analysis* of *cost functions*. Regression analysis is a statistical technique for estimating how one or more factors affect some variable of interest. For cost functions, the variable of interest is average cost, and the factors may include output, wage rates, and other input prices.

To illustrate, suppose that we suspect that the average cost function is a quadratic function of the volume of output:

$$AC = \beta_0 + \beta_1 Q + \beta_2 Q^2 + \beta_3 w + \textit{noise}$$

where Q denotes production volume (e.g., number of standard-size chainsaws produced per year), w denotes the local wage rate, and *noise* represents all of the other factors that affect the level of cost that cannot be measured and that are not explicitly included in the analysis. We expect β_3 to be positive because higher wages contribute to higher costs. If there are economies of scale, then β_1 will be negative. If the cost curve is L- or U-shaped, then we expect β_2 to be small and positive. Thus, at large levels of output (and therefore at very large levels of output squared), average costs may start to level off or even increase, as the positive effect of $\beta_2 Q^2$ offsets or dominates the negative effect of $\beta_1 Q$.

Regression analysis "fits" the cost function to actual cost/output data. In other words, regression provides estimates of the parameters β_1, β_2, and β_3 as well as the precision of these estimates.

There is a large literature on the estimation of cost functions. Cost functions have been estimated for various industries, including airlines, telecommunications, electric utilities, trucking, railroads, and hospitals. Most of these studies estimate functional forms for the average cost function that are more complicated than simple quadratic functions. Nevertheless, the basic ideas underlying these more sophisticated analyses are those described here.

Regression analysis may also be used to estimate learning curves. To do this, we modify the previous equation as follows:

$$AC = \beta_0 + \beta_1 Q + \beta_2 Q^2 + \beta_3 w + \beta_4 E + \textit{noise}$$

where E denotes cumulative production volume. The parameter β_4 indicates how average costs change with cumulative experience. As with the first equation, actual implementation often involves more complex functional forms, but the basic principles remain the same.

ENDNOTES

[1] If you do not understand why this must be so, consider this numerical example. Suppose that the total cost of producing five bicycles is $500. The *AC* is therefore $100. If the *MC* of the sixth bicycle is $70, then total cost for six bicycles is $570 and *AC* is $95. If the *MC* of the sixth bicycle is $130, then total cost is $630 and *AC* is $105. In this example (and as a general rule), when $MC < AC$, AC falls as production increases, and when $MC > AC$, AC rises as production increases.

[2] The opportunity cost is the best return that the investor could obtain if he or she invested a comparable amount of money in some other similarly risky investment. In this example, we have assumed, for simplicity, that the production line never depreciates and thus lasts forever. See the Economics Primer for further discussion.

[3] Newhouse, J. et al., "Does the Geographic Distribution of Physicians Reflect Market Failure?" *Bell Journal of Economics*, 13(2), 1982, pp. 493–505.

[4] Baumgardner, J., "What Is a Specialist Anyway?" Mimeo, Duke University, 1991.

[5]DiMasi, J. et al., "Cost of Innovation in the Pharmaceutical Industry," *Journal of Health Economics*, 10(2), 1991, pp. 107–142.

[6]The name *cube-square rule* comes from the fact that the volume of a cube is proportional to the cube of the length of its side, whereas the surface area is proportional to the square of that length.

[7]A full justification for this statement requires an extensive foray into the complex topic of queuing theory and is well beyond the scope of this text.

[8]Milgrom, P., and J. Roberts, "The Economics of Modern Manufacturing: Technology, Strategy, and Organization," *American Economic Review*, 80(6), 1990, pp. 511–528.

[9]http://www.eaca.asia/site/etc/press_review.htm?mode=view&num=473&page=4&pPart= &pKeyword=&pGroup=15 Accessed July 7, 2011.

[10]See, for example, *Perspectives on Experience*, Boston, Boston Consulting Group, 1970, for estimates of progress ratios for over 20 industries. See Lieberman, M., "The Learning Curve and Pricing in the Chemical Processing Industries," *RAND Journal of Economics*, 15(2), 1984, pp. 213–228, for learning curve estimates for 37 chemical products.

[11]Ramanarayanan, Subramaniam, 2008, "Does Practice Make Perfect? An Empirical Analysis of Learning-by-Doing in Cardiac Surgery" UCLA, Unpublished Mimeo.

[12]Benkard, C. L., "Learning and Forgetting: The Dynamics of Aircraft Production," mimeo, New Haven, CT, Yale University, 1998.

[13]Danzon, P., A. Epstein, and S. Nicholson, "Mergers and Acquisitions Pharmaceutical and Biotech Industries," *Managerial and Decision Economics* 28, 2008, pp. 307–28; and Ornaghi, C., "Mergers and Innovation in Big Pharma," *International Journal of Industrial Organization*, 27, 2009, pp. 70–9.

[14]Penrose, E., *The Theory of the Growth of the Firm*, 3rd ed., Oxford, Oxford University Press, 1995.

[15]Prahalad, C. K., and R. A. Bettis, "The Dominant Logic: A New Linkage Between Diversity and Performance," *Strategic Management Journal*, 7, 1986, pp. 485–501.

[16]The product life-cycle model has its origins in the marketing literature. See, for example, Levitt, T., "Exploit the Product Life Cycle," *Harvard Business Review*, November–December 1965, pp. 81–94.

[17]Stein, J., "Agency, Information and Corporate Investment," in Constantinides, G., M. Harris, and R. Stulz (eds.), *Handbook of the Economics of Finance*, North-Holland, Amsterdam, 2003.

[18]Roberts, J., *The Modern Firm*, Oxford, Oxford University Press, 2004.

[19]Bazerman, M., and W. Samuelson, "I Won the Auction but Don't Want the Prize," *Journal of Conflict Resolution*, 1983, pp. 618–634.

[20]Jensen, M. C., "The Eclipse of the Public Corporation," *Harvard Business Review*, September–October 1989, pp. 61–74.

[21]Avery, C., J. C. Chevalier, and S. Schaefer, "Why Do Managers Undertake Acquisitions? An Analysis of Internal and External Rewards for Acquisitiveness," *Journal of Law, Economics & Organization*, 14, 1998, pp. 24–43.

[22]Reich, R., *The Next American Frontier*, New York, Times Books, 1983.

[23]Amihud, Y., and B. Lev, "Risk Reduction as a Managerial Motive for Conglomerate Mergers," *Bell Journal of Economics*, 12, 1981, pp. 605–617.

[24]Hermalin, B. E., and M. S. Weisbach, "Endogenously Chosen Boards of Directors and Their Monitoring of the CEO," *American Economic Review*, 88(1), 1998, pp. 96–118.

[25]Manne, H., "Mergers and the Market for Corporate Control," *Journal of Political Economy*, 73, 1965, pp. 110–120.

[26]Holmstrom, B., and S. Kaplan, "Corporate Governance and Merger Activity in the U.S.: Making Sense of the 1980s and 1990s," *Journal of Economic Perspectives*, Spring 2001, pp. 121–144.

[27]Goold, M., and K. Luchs, "Why Diversify? Four Decades of Management Thinking," *Academy of Management Executive*, 7, 1993, pp. 7–25.

3

THE VERTICAL BOUNDARIES OF THE FIRM

In early 2000, Internet service provider AOL stunned the business community by acquiring entertainment giant Time Warner. AOL's president, Stephen Case, boasted of the synergies that the two companies would realize under a single corporate umbrella. A year later, AOL Time Warner sought to exploit these synergies by promoting a new girl band called Eden's Crush.[1] Warner Music produced their debut album, "Popstars," the WB network aired a program documenting the band's tryouts and rehearsals, and the band was heavily promoted by AOL. The album was not a success, however, with sales falling short of gold-record status (under 500,000 copies sold). In contrast, another teen group called O-Town debuted at about the same time as Eden's Crush but worked with several independent companies. They released their eponymous debut record on BMG, Disney broadcast the obligatory documentary, and they received heavy publicity from MTV. This seemingly fragmented strategy paid off—their debut album went platinum, with sales exceeding 1.5 million copies.

The production of any good or service, from pop recordings to cancer treatment, usually requires many activities. The process that begins with the acquisition of raw materials and ends with the distribution and sale of finished goods and services is known as the *vertical chain*. A central issue in business strategy is how to organize the vertical chain. Is it better to organize all of the activities in a single firm, as AOL attempted, or is it better to rely on independent firms in the market? There are many examples of successful vertically integrated firms, such as Mexican conglomerate Cemex, which produces cement for its own concrete. Other successful firms, such as Nike, are vertically "disintegrated": they outsource most of the tasks in the vertical chain to independent contractors. Former Hewlett-Packard CEO John Young described outsourcing by his firm as follows: "We used to bend all the sheet metal, mold every plastic part that went into our products. We don't do those things anymore, but somebody else is doing it for us."[2] The *vertical boundaries* of a firm define the activities that the firm itself performs as opposed to purchases from independent firms in the market. Chapters 3 and 4 examine a firm's choice of its vertical boundaries and how they affect the efficiency of production.

MAKE VERSUS BUY

A firm's decision to perform an activity itself or to purchase it from an independent firm is called a *make-or-buy* decision. "Make" means that the firm performs the activity itself; "buy" means it relies on an independent firm to perform the activity, perhaps under contract. A firm that acquires an input supplier is now "making" the input, because it is performing the activity in-house. Typical make-or-buy decisions for a manufacturer include whether to develop its own source of raw materials, provide its own shipping services, or operate its own retail web site. Some firms are highly integrated. Kimberly Clark's Scott Paper division owns forest land, mills timber, and produces consumer paper products. Italian fashion icon Benetton dyes fabrics, designs and assembles clothing, and operates retail stores. Other firms perform a narrow set of activities. Leo Burnett, which created Tony the Tiger, focuses on creating brand icons for consumer products companies. DHL distributes products to customers of many manufacturers and retailers. Korn/Ferry is a successful corporate "headhunting" firm. When other firms buy the services of these specialists, they can obtain a superior marketing program, secure rapid, low-cost distribution, and identify candidates for senior executive positions without having to perform any of these tasks themselves.

Make and buy are two extremes along a continuum of possibilities for vertical integration. Figure 3.1 fills in some of the intermediate choices. Close to "make," integrated firms can spin off partly or wholly owned subsidiaries. Close to "buy," market firms can enter into a long-term contract, tying their interests for several years. In between are joint ventures and strategic alliances, in which two or more firms establish an independent entity that relies on resources from both parents. To illustrate the key economic trade-offs associated with integration decisions, we will focus on the extreme choices of "make" and "buy." As we will discuss in Chapter 4, intermediate solutions share many of the benefits and costs of both the make-and-buy extremes.

Upstream, Downstream

In general, goods in a production process "flow" along a vertical chain from raw materials and component parts to manufacturing, through distribution and retailing. Economists say that early steps in the vertical chain are *upstream* and later steps are *downstream*, much as lumber used to make wooden furniture flows from upstream timber forests to downstream mills. Thinking about these terms more generally,

FIGURE 3.1
MAKE-OR-BUY CONTINUUM

Arm's-length market transactions	Long-term contracts	Strategic alliances and joint ventures	Parent/ subsidiary relationships	Perform activity internally
Less integrated		→ → →		More integrated

Different ways of organizing production lie on a make/buy continuum.

EXAMPLE 3.1   A GLOBAL PERSPECTIVE ON MERGERS FOR VERTICAL INTEGRATION

John Hagel III and Marc Singer argue that traditional pharmaceutical firms actually comprise three core businesses.[3] These three core businesses consist of a product innovation business, an infrastructure business, and a customer relationship business.

Traditional "big pharma" companies no longer dominate the business of innovation. A few decades ago, large pharmaceutical firms used an uneconomical trial-and-error process to screen new drug leads. However, the landmark sequencing of the human genome allows the genes themselves to become the new targets of disease research, resulting in more focused and economical approaches to drug discovery. Although technological breakthroughs like genomics may expedite the drug discovery process, they have also, paradoxically, increased its complexity. Smaller biotech companies are more adept at understanding and adapting to changes in technology than are larger pharmaceutical companies. Companies like Millennium Pharmaceuticals, Celera, Incyte Genomics, and Human Genome Sciences are examples of small, thriving biotechnology companies.

The infrastructure business builds and manages facilities for high-volume, repetitive operational tasks such as manufacturing and communications. The customer relationship business is responsible for finding customers and building relationships with them. These businesses remain the province of pharmaceutical firms, which have production and sales experience that start-up biotech research companies cannot hope to match. Hagel and Singer might have added a fourth core business— obtaining regulatory approval. This requires a working relationship with regulatory agencies such as the U.S. Food and Drug Administration,

and is also largely the province of big pharma, although a substantial percentage of the actual clinical trials have been outsourced to independent "contract research organizations."

Mergers often provide firms with opportunities to benefit from vertical integration. In the global pharmaceutical industry, this can best be understood by looking at how a pharmaceutical firm can expand one or more of its core businesses by an acquisition. Consider, for example, the 2007 acquisition of U.S. pharmaceutical giant Merck's generic drug division by Mylan Laboratories Inc.

Mylan, also based in the United States, outbid Israel's Teva Pharmaceuticals (the largest generic drug maker in the world) and Iceland's Actavis, ultimately paying $6.7 billion, a price that was almost 3 times the yearly sales of Merck generics. What motivated the acquisition?

Mylan CEO Robert J. Coury said the fit between the two companies was "truly outstanding." According to Coury, "Merck Generics provides [Mylan] with leading positions in many of the world's other key regions. Together, we will form a powerful, diverse, robust and vertically integrated generics platform."[4] As a result of the acquisition Mylan gained generic substitutions for some bestselling drugs, and could also realize significant cost savings, the majority of which would be from vertical integration; Mylan would be able to leveraging Merck's Matrix Laboratories Ltd., its generic drug business based in India, "aligning research and development, and increasing manufacturing."[5] But interestingly, in December of 2008, Merck announced that it was back in the generics business, launching a new division called "BioVentures" to develop substitutes for successful biotech drugs.

Cemex cement production is upstream to its concrete production, and cable sports channel ESPN, which assembles a package of sports entertainment programming, is downstream from the National Football League (a content "producer") but upstream to Comcast and other cable companies (content "retailers").

The specific steps required in a vertical chain do not usually depend on the extent of vertical integration. Making and selling wooden chairs begins with chopping down trees and ends with a customer taking delivery of an order, regardless of the extent of vertical integration. In between, someone has to mill the timber, design the chair, assemble it, distribute it, and sell it. And someone will probably be involved in raising capital to support fixed investments while others handle accounting and marketing. Two identical chairs may well go through the same production steps, but the organization of the firms involved in production might be very different. One chair might be made by a fully integrated firm that performs every step in the vertical chain, while another seemingly identical chair might have passed through a series of independent firms, each of which was responsible for one or two specific steps. The make-or-buy decision is not about trying to eliminate steps from the vertical chain. Instead, it is about deciding which firms should perform which steps.

In order to understand the importance of the make-or-buy decision, it is helpful to think about competition between vertical chains. Consider that when consumers choose one of the two chairs discussed above, they are effectively giving their business to all of the firms involved in the vertical chain that made that chair—the timber mill, the designer, and so forth. Consumers will usually choose the finished good produced by the most efficient vertical chain. Thus, if vertical integration improves the efficiency of production of wooden chairs, then the fully integrated chair producer will prosper while the firms in the "independent" vertical chain will struggle. Conversely, if vertical integration is counterproductive, then the independent firms will prosper and the integrated firm will lose out. It follows that firms will want to be part of most successful vertical chains, and the success of the vertical chain requires the right make-or-buy decisions.

Defining Boundaries

Regardless of a firm's position along the vertical chain, it needs to define its boundaries. To resolve the associated make-or-buy decisions, the firm must compare the benefits and costs of using the market as opposed to performing the activity in-house. Table 3.1 summarizes the key benefits and costs of using market firms. These are discussed in detail in the remainder of this chapter.

Table 3.1
Benefits and Costs of Using the Market

Benefits
- Market firms can achieve economies of scale that in-house departments producing only for their own needs cannot.
- Market firms are subject to the discipline of the market and must be efficient and innovative to survive. Overall corporate success may hide the inefficiencies and lack of innovativeness of in-house departments.

Costs
- Coordination of production flows through the vertical chain may be compromised when an activity is purchased from an independent market firm rather than performed in-house.
- Private information may be leaked when an activity is performed by an independent market firm.
- There may be costs of transacting with independent market firms that can be avoided by performing the activity in-house.

Some Make-or-Buy Fallacies

Before detailing the critical determinants of make-or-buy decisions, we need to dispense with five common, but *incorrect*, arguments:

1. Firms should make an asset, rather than buy it, if that asset is a source of competitive advantage for that firm.
2. Firms should buy, rather than make, to avoid the costs of making the product.
3. Firms should make, rather than buy, to avoid paying a profit margin to independent firms. (This fallacy is often expressed this way: "Our firm should backward integrate to capture the profit of our suppliers for ourselves.")
4. Firms should make, rather than buy, because a vertically integrated producer will be able to avoid paying high market prices for the input during periods of peak demand or scarce supply. (This fallacy is often expressed this way: "By vertically integrating, we obtain the input 'at cost,' thereby insuring ourselves against the risk of high-input prices.")
5. Firms should make, rather than buy, to tie up a distribution channel. They will gain market share at the expense of rivals. This claim has merit on some occasions, but it is used to justify acquisitions on many other occasions when it lacks merit.

Though widely held, the first argument is easy to reject. An asset that is easily obtained from the market cannot be a source of advantage, whether the firm makes it or buys it. If it is cheaper to obtain an asset from the market than to produce it internally, the firm should do the former.

The second argument, which stems from the mistaken belief that the correct make-or-buy decision can eliminate steps from the vertical chain, is also easy to reject. Consider an activity on the vertical chain, say, the distribution of finished goods from a manufacturer to retailers. Choosing to buy, rather than make, does not eliminate the expenses of the associated activity. Either way, someone has to purchase the trucks and hire the drivers. And either way, the firm will pay the cost. Once again, if the firm can perform the activity at a lower cost than it takes to buy it from the market, it should do so. But firms often take a look at market prices and the apparent profitability of market firms and fool themselves into thinking they can make at a lower cost. This is the third fallacy.

There are two potential flaws in the third fallacy. The first flaw stems from the difference between *accounting profit* and *economic profit* discussed in the Economics Primer. Accounting profit is the simple difference between revenues and expenses. Economic profit, by contrast, represents the difference between the accounting profits from a given activity and the accounting profits from investing the same resources in the most lucrative alternative activity. Because economic profit speaks to the relative profitability of different investment decisions, it is more useful than accounting profit when making business decisions. Even if an upstream supplier is making accounting profits, this does not imply that it is making economic profits or that a downstream manufacturing firm could increase its own economic profits by internalizing the activity.

But suppose the upstream supplier is generating substantial positive economic profits. The downstream manufacturer might believe that it could make at a cost below the "exorbitant" supply price. Before doing so, however, the manufacturer should ask a critical question: "If the supplier of the input is so profitable, why don't other firms enter the market and drive the price down?" Perhaps it is difficult to obtain the expertise needed to make the desired input, or maybe the existing supplier is the only one large enough to reap economies of scale. In these circumstances, the manufacturer would likely find it cheaper to pay the supplier's high price rather than make the input itself.

Avoiding Peak Prices

To illustrate the subtle issues raised by the fourth fallacy, consider a fictitious manufacturer of log homes, Honest Abe Log Homes. Honest Abe sells log cabins that it assembles from specially milled lumber. The market price of this lumber varies from year to year, and for this reason, Rustic's managers are contemplating backward integration into the raising and milling of trees. This is a tempting but fallacious reason for vertical integration.

To see why, suppose that Honest Abe sells its log cabins for $30,000 each. Besides the costs of milled lumber, it incurs $12,000 in labor costs for every cabin it assembles. During the next year, Honest Abe has 100 confirmed orders for log cabins. It contemplates two options for its raw materials needs:

1. It can purchase lumber in the open market. Honest Abe believes that there is a chance that the price of the lumber needed to build one cabin will be $21,000, a chance that the price will be $15,000, and a chance that the price will be $9,000.
2. It can backward integrate by purchasing forest land and a lumber mill. To finance the purchase, Honest Abe can obtain a bank loan that entails an annual payment of $1,050,000 (or $10,500 per cabin). In addition, the cost of harvesting timber and milling it to produce the finished lumber for one cabin is $4,500. Thus, the effective cost of timber would be $15,000 per cabin.

Table 3.2 illustrates Honest Abe's annual income under these options. Under the vertical integration option, Honest Abe has an assured annual profit of $300,000. Under the nonintegration option, its net income is uncertain: it could be $900,000, it could be $300,000, or it could be −$300,000. The expected value of this uncertain income is $300,000.[6]

Even though the vertical integration and nonintegration options entail the same expected profit, it is tempting to argue in favor of vertical integration because it eliminates Honest Abe's risk of income fluctuations. This is an especially tempting argument if management is concerned that when lumber prices are high ($21,000), Honest Abe will not have enough cash to cover its loss and thus will go

TABLE 3.2
RUSTIC LOG HOMES

	Vertical Integration	Nonintegration and Lumber Price Is . . .		
		$9,000	$15,000	$21,000
Revenue	$3,000,000	$3,000,000	$3,000,000	$3,000,000
Cost of Goods Sold				
Lumber	$450,000	$900,000	$1,500,000	$2,100,000
Assembly	$1,200,000	$1,200,000	$1,200,000	$1,200,000
Total	$1,650,000	$2,100,000	$2,700,000	$3,300,000
Interest Expense	$1,050,000	—	—	—
Profit	$300,000	$900,000	$300,000	($300,000)

bankrupt. If Honest Abe is committed to being an ongoing business concern, according to this argument it should vertically integrate to eliminate the risk of being unable to pay its bills.

Honest Abe does not, however, need to vertically integrate to eliminate its income risk. It could counteract price fluctuations by entering into long-term (i.e., futures) contracts with lumber suppliers or by purchasing lumber futures contracts on the Chicago Mercantile Exchange (CME). Examples of other inputs hedged on the CME include natural gas, soybeans, copper, and oil. Even if Honest Abe could not hedge, the argument for vertical integration is still flawed. After all, if Honest Abe could raise the capital to purchase the forest land, it could instead create a capital reserve to weather short-term fluctuations in lumber prices (e.g., perhaps through a line of credit from the same bank that was willing to loan it the money to buy the land and the lumber mill).

Tying Up Channels: Vertical Foreclosure

Integration to tie up channels is known as vertical foreclosure. Using our upstream/downstream terminology, we can envision four ways for a firm to foreclose its rivals.

1. A downstream monopolist acquires an upstream firm and refuses to purchase from other upstream suppliers.
2. An upstream monopolist acquires a downstream competitor and refuses to supply other downstream firms.
3. A competitive downstream firm acquires an upstream monopolist and refuses to supply its downstream competitors.
4. A competitive upstream firm acquires a downstream monopolist and refuses to purchase from its upstream competitors.

In each of these scenarios, foreclosure extends monopolization across the vertical chain and therefore seems to increase profits.

Foreclosure can increase profits but not for the seemingly obvious reasons. One danger of this strategy is that competitors may open new channels. A second danger specific to scenarios (3) and (4) is that the competitive firm will have to pay a steep fee to acquire a monopolist. The acquirer could still prosper if the merger increases the total profits available in the vertical chain. But this is impossible according to an argument associated with the Chicago School of Economics, an argument that also sheds doubt on the profitability of scenarios (1) and (2).

Noted French economic theorists Patrick Rey and Jean Tirole sum up the Chicago School argument as follows:

> The motivation for foreclosure cannot be the desire to extend market power, since there is a single final product and thus a single monopoly profit.[7]

In other words, only so much money can be squeezed out of consumers—the monopoly profit. A firm that monopolizes a single stage in the vertical chain, sometimes said to create a *bottleneck* in the vertical chain, can command that monopoly profit in its entirety. Vertical integration cannot increase profits above the monopoly profit, and therefore there is no reason to foreclose. Because integration cannot increase monopoly power, the Chicago School argument concludes that the courts should ignore vertical integration between a monopolist and another firm. (A variant of this argument applies to horizontal integration.)

It turns out that the Chicago School argument is about half right.[8] There is only so much profit to be squeezed from the vertical chain, and foreclosure does not increase the available profit. But in some situations foreclosure may still be profitable, by allowing monopolists to *protect their profits*. The quintessential example goes as follows. Suppose that an upstream monopolist wants to charge a premium price for its input. In principle, this will translate into premium prices for the finished good, high enough to allow downstream firms to pay for the input and remain in business. In order to assure high downstream prices, the upstream firm must limit its sales of the input. But this creates a conundrum. Once the upstream firm has sold the monopoly level of the input, there is nothing to prevent it from selling even more, in the process flooding the market and driving down prices of the finished good. This must be very tempting to the monopolist. But if downstream firms are aware of this possibility, they will be reluctant to pay monopoly prices for the input. And if that happens, the upstream monopolist cannot realize monopoly profits!

The monopolist might solve this problem by establishing some sort of reputation for limiting output, for example, through a long history of resisting temptation. But this creates a chicken/egg problem; how does the monopolist establish that reputation in the first place? Foreclosure provides a way out of the conundrum. By acquiring the downstream firm and refusing to deal with downstream competitors, the upstream monopolist can now easily limit output. This assumes, of course, that the upstream "division" of the integrated firm does not act rashly and sell the input to the competition. But this does seem easier to control within the integrated organization.

The theory that foreclosure "protects" monopoly profits underlies much of the antitrust laws involving vertical integration. As a result, courts take a careful look at deals that exclude competitors from essential inputs. By the same token, other theories suggest that there are opportunities to increase profits through horizontal combinations between monopolists and competitive firms and that these also motivate antitrust activity—for example, when firms tie together the purchase of two goods, one of which is monopolized. In these situations, the courts must weigh the potential for monopoly profits against the potential for lower costs. Managers must do the same thing, of course. In Chapter 2 we discussed the potential efficiencies of horizontal combinations. In the remainder of this chapter, we do the same for vertical mergers.

EXAMPLE 3.2   EMPLOYEE SKILLS: MAKE OR BUY?

In 2001, Adobe Systems CEO Bruce Chizen executed a major change in strategy. Rather than relying on consumer products like Photoshop, Chizen wanted to focus the firm on selling its Portable Document Format (PDF) standard to large corporate clients. With this change in strategy, however, came a change in the skills required of Adobe's sales force. The firm's pre-2001 salespeople were experts in selling to graphic designers. The new strategy would require salespeople who were more comfortable in a boardroom than at a drafting table. But how should these new capabilities be developed? Should the firm "make" the new employee skill set, by retraining its existing sales force? Or would it be better to "buy" the new skills, by hiring an entirely new sales team?

Firms face this make-or-buy decision any time they consider a corporate training program, and many of the lessons of this chapter apply. Scale economies offer one major benefit of using the market. Many of the costs associated with education are fixed; for example, a university's costs do not rise much when an additional student attends classes. Thus, while accounting firms could, in principle, make their own CPAs with in-house training, this would entail considerable inefficiencies as investments in training facilities are duplicated. It is more cost-effective for the firms to buy their accountants after they have completed university training.

When scale economies are less important, firms often offer training in-house. Consider, as an example, the "mini-MBA" program offered by the consulting firm McKinsey and Company. The firm offers this program to employees who have strong analytical backgrounds—often individuals with MDs or PhDs in hard sciences—but lack direct business experience. While most top MBA programs aim to offer both business knowledge and training in analytical skills, the McKinsey "mini-MBA" program focuses only on business knowledge. Peter Attia, an associate who joined the firm in 2006, is a typical participant. Trained as a surgeon, Attia left medicine after determining it wasn't a good fit for him; he described the mini-MBA as a "boot camp covering all the aspects of business that I didn't have coming in."[9] Because the McKinsey program is somewhat more specialized than, say, a bachelor's degree in accounting, the firm is not at a large cost disadvantage relative to outside providers of education.

Using the market for procuring employee skills has several additional advantages. First, education often generates information that is useful in matching the right employee to the right employer. Suppose two firms each need to hire a computer programmer. One firm's programming tasks are quite complex, and so this firm is willing to pay a very high wage to attract a programmer from the top of his or her class. The second firm's tasks are not as complex, and so it has a lower willingness to pay for programming ability. By going to the market to hire programmers, the firms can each make their hiring decisions contingent on how individuals did in their bachelors of computer science coursework. If the firms adopted a "make" strategy where they hired individuals with no programming background and then offered training, it might be difficult for the first firm to identify which of two prospective programmers would turn out to be a star.

Second, potential employees often develop valuable networks with other students when attending college or graduate school. For example, an investment bank that hires a Kellogg School MBA is also importing connections with that MBA's classmates. It would be very difficult for the bank to match this "network effect" if it relied on in-house training.

As the Nobel Prize–winning economist Gary Becker has pointed out, the problem of determining the best way to invest in employees' skills is complicated by the fact that returns to human capital investments are inalienable.[10] That is, unlike physical capital, human capital cannot be separated from the person making the investment. A firm that pays for an employee to gain skills that are valued by other employers—what Becker refers to as "general-purpose" human capital—may find the employee's wage is bid up after the skills are acquired. Thus, while the employee's productivity may rise as he or she gains skills, the firm does not benefit because of the increased wage bill. Firms that offer general-purpose training (such as McKinsey's mini-MBA) need to think about how to earn a return on this investment in the face of labor-market competition.

While firms may thus be hesitant to invest in building employees' general-purpose skills, employees may be similarly concerned about investing in firm-specific skills. Employees' investments in specific human capital are subject to the holdup problem, which we discuss later in this chapter. Adobe's sales force, for example, may worry that investments in learning how to sell the PDF standard will not be rewarded by the firm, because there is no other employer willing to pay for skills that are specific to PDF.

REASONS TO "BUY"

Firms use the market (or "buy") primarily because market firms are often more efficient. Market firms enjoy two distinct types of efficiencies: they exploit economies of scale and the learning curve, and they eliminate "bureaucracy."

Exploiting Scale and Learning Economies

It is conventional wisdom that firms should focus their activities on what they do best and leave everything else to market firms. There are several reasons for this. First, market firms may possess proprietary information or patents that enable them to produce at lower cost. Second, market firms might be able to aggregate the needs of many customers, thereby enjoying economies of scale. Third, market firms might exploit their experience in producing for many customers to obtain learning economies.

The first argument requires no additional analysis; the last two arguments are more subtle. Recall from Chapter 2 that when economies of scale or learning economies are present, firms with low production levels or little experience in production may be at a severe cost disadvantage relative to their larger, more experienced rivals. Market firms can often aggregate the demands of many potential buyers, whereas a vertically integrated firm typically produces only for its own needs. Market firms can therefore often achieve greater scale, and thus lower unit costs, than can the downstream firms that use the input.

To illustrate this point, consider automobile production. An automobile manufacturer requires a vast variety of upstream inputs: steel, tires, antilock brakes, stereos, computer equipment, and so forth. A manufacturer, Audi, for example, could backward integrate and produce inputs such as antilock brakes itself, or it could obtain them from an independent supplier, such as Bosch or Denso. Figure 3.2 illustrates an average cost function for antilock brakes. According to the figure, the production of antilock brakes displays L-shaped average costs, indicating that there are economies of scale in production. In this example, the minimum efficient scale of production—the smallest level of output at which average cost is minimized—is output level A^*, with resulting average cost C^*.

Suppose that Audi expects to sell A' automobiles with antilock brakes, where $A' > A^*$. Thus, Audi expects to sell enough automobiles to achieve minimum efficient scale in the production of antilock brakes by producing for its own needs alone. This is seen in Figure 3.2, where the average cost of output A' roughly equals C^*. From a cost perspective, Audi gets no advantage by using the market.

FIGURE 3.2
PRODUCTION COSTS AND THE MAKE-OR-BUY DECISION

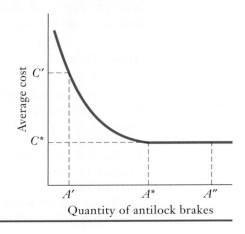

Firms need to produce quantity A^* to reach minimum efficient scale and achieve average costs of C^*. A firm that requires only A' units to meet its own needs will incur average costs of C', well above C^*. A firm that requires output in excess of A^*, such as A'', will have costs equal to C^* and will not be at a competitive disadvantage.

Suppose instead that Audi expects to sell A' automobiles with antilock brakes, where $A' < A^*$. In this case, Audi cannot achieve minimum efficient scale by producing only for its own needs. This is seen in Figure 3.2, where the average cost associated with output A', denoted C', exceeds the minimum average cost C^*. Audi could try to expand antilock brake output to A^*, thereby achieving scale economies. Audi would be producing more brakes than cars, so it would need to sell its excess stock of brakes to other car makers. This is a reminder that, in principle, activities organized through market firms could be organized through vertical integration, and vice versa.

In reality, Audi might have a hard time selling brakes to its rivals. Rivals may fear that Audi will withhold supplies during periods of peak demand or that Audi might gain vital information about planned production levels. Rivals may simply be unwilling to provide financial support to Audi operations. These concerns notwithstanding, competitors sometimes do buy inputs from each other. For example, the Taiwanese firm Giant makes frames for its own bicycles as well as for competitors such as Trek. California-based Oppo Digital makes its own line of Blu-Ray players but also produces for high-end brands such as Theta, Lexicon, and Ayre Acoustics.

Instead of trying to reach minimum efficient scale doing in-house brake production, Audi could purchase antilock brakes from an independent manufacturer such as Bosch. Bosch would reach production of A' in Figure 3.2 just from its sales to Audi. Because there are many more car manufacturers than there are antilock brake makers, Bosch will probably sell its antilock brakes to other car makers. This will allow it to expand output beyond A', thereby exploiting scale economies.

It may be more efficient if Bosch produces the brakes, but Audi benefits only if Bosch passes along some of the cost savings. Under what circumstances will this occur? Recall from the Economics Primer that if markets are competitive, prices will approach average cost. With only four major competitors, the antilock brake market probably falls somewhere between perfect competition and monopoly. Bosch may be able to charge a price in excess of C^*, but it could not charge a price above C'. If it did so, Audi could produce the antilock brakes itself at a lower cost. It is likely that Audi would be able to negotiate a price somewhere between C^* and C', so that Bosch earned positive profits while Audi enjoyed some of the benefits of using an efficient market supplier.

Bureaucracy Effects: Avoiding Agency and Influence Costs

Analysts often state that large firms suffer from "bureaucracy." This catchall term includes a number of specific problems associated with agency and influence costs.

Agency Costs

Managers and workers make many decisions that contribute to the profitability of a firm. Managers and workers who knowingly do not act in the best interests of their firm are *shirking*. *Agency costs* are the costs associated with shirking and the administrative controls to deter it.

It may seem that there is a way to limit agency costs—reward managers and workers for the profit that their efforts contribute to the firm. But as we explain in detail in Chapter 12, this is easier said than done. One problem is that most large firms have common overhead or joint costs that are allocated across divisions. This makes it difficult for top management to measure and reward an individual division's contribution to overall corporate profitability. A second reason is that in-house divisions in many large firms serve as *cost centers* that perform activities solely for their own firms and generate no outside revenue. An example of a cost center would be the laundry service in a hospital or the data processing department in a bank. Cost centers are often insulated from competitive pressures because they have a committed "customer" for their inputs. Moreover, it can be difficult to evaluate the efficiency of cost centers because there is often no obvious market test for judging their performance. The absence of market competition, coupled with difficulties in measuring divisional performance, makes it hard for top management to know just how well a cost center is doing relative to its best achievable performance. This, in turn, gives cost center managers the latitude to shirk.

Even when management is aware of agency costs, it may prefer to ignore them rather than to eliminate them. Many firms are unwilling to endure the ill-will generated by firing a nonproductive worker or ending a costly perk that has pervaded the organization. This is particularly likely if the firm possesses some inherent advantages in the market that insulates it from competition and relieves top management from the pressure of controlling agency costs. Unfortunately, ignoring agency costs can have lasting consequences. As the famous economist Frederick von Hayek pointed out, "How easy it is for an inefficient manager to dissipate the differentials on which profitability rests."[11]

Influence Costs

Another class of costs that arise when transactions are organized internally is what Paul Milgrom and John Roberts have called *influence costs*.[12] To understand influence costs, it is helpful to recall the concept of internal capital markets introduced in Chapter 2. Internal capital markets allocate available working capital within the firm. One of the potential benefits of horizontal integration and diversification is the ability to use internal capital markets to fund investments when access to external funding is limited. The central office of a firm that relies on internal capital faces a conundrum: How does it allocate its scarce capital across many potentially deserving projects?

In order to evaluate competing proposals, the central office must work closely with divisional and department heads, for department heads are best positioned to understand the merits and weaknesses of various projects. But this creates a potential conflict of interest. Lower-level managers will naturally seek to command more of their company's resources so as to advance their own careers and boost their own incomes, possibly at the expense of corporate profits. Milgrom and Roberts describe how lower-level managers may engage in an array of *influence activities* as they seek to move their own projects to the top of the central office's "must fund" list. Lower-level managers may exaggerate the likely success of their pet projects or badmouth proposals from other departments. They may refuse to play ball with other departments, for example by withholding demand forecasts or key personnel. If one department does agree to help another, it might quote a high "transfer price" (a price quote for internal resources that is counted against another department's accounting profits). The end result of these influence activities is that the central office is unable to obtain objective information with which to compare competing projects. The result is an inefficient allocation of internal capital.

When we discussed internal capital markets in Chapter 2, we observed that one reason why firms may find it difficult to attract outside capital is the asymmetry of information between the firm and the bank; banks expect borrowers to exaggerate the profitability of their projects. This same asymmetry exacerbates influence costs within the integrated firm. But it may be more problematic within the integrated firm, where the influence activities of one department manager can hinder the success of others. This is yet another reminder that what goes on among independent market firms also goes on within the vertically integrated firm.

Supply relationships within General Motors nicely illustrate how influence activity can harm a vertically integrated firm. Suppose that the program manager for a new GM product is unhappy with the in-house supplier's bid—it's too high, and in the past the supplier had quality and delivery problems. No sooner does the manager identify an alternative bidder outside the company than the in-house supplier goes to corporate headquarters and explains that the loss of business on his part will require an increase in the costs of similar parts already being supplied by other GM products. Why? Because economies of scale will be lost and the in-house supplier will have excess capacity.

Headquarters, always respectful of scale-economy and capacity-utilization justifications in a mass-production firm such as GM then has a talk with the program manager. The in-house supplier makes solemn (but ultimately empty) promises to try harder to reduce costs while improving quality and delivery reliability—and gets the business. This process explains how, not too long ago, GM managed to have both the world's highest production volume and the world's highest costs in many of its component supply divisions.[13]

One way that firms can limit influence activities is by loosening the connection between a business unit's profitability on the one hand and managerial compensation on the other. Managers are less likely to lobby for resources for their own units when compensation is tied to corporate profits. But this cuts both ways; it may limit influence activities, but it also limits the incentives of managers to take genuine steps to improve their unit's profitability.

EXAMPLE 3.3 DISCONNECTION AT SONY[14]

Sony is one of the most recognizable brand names in the world. Long a leader in home electronics, Sony vertically integrated into "software" (music and movies) with its 1988 acquisition of Columbia/CBS Records, which it rechristened Sony Home Entertainment. The partnership between the Sony hardware and software divisions helped the firm in the late 1990s when Sony joined other hardware makers in launching the DVD technology. While most independent movie studios sat on the fence, Sony Home Entertainment (SHE) released several popular titles from the massive Columbia movie library.

The partnership between hardware and software divisions has not always gone smoothly. In 1998, Sony considered developing digital music technology through the integrated efforts of its hardware and software divisions. From the beginning of this endeavor, conflicts between divisions were the norm. Sony's personal computer and Walkman groups each had their own technologies to push. SHE opposed any effort, fearful that it would encourage illegal downloading that would eat into software sales. Sony allowed each of its groups to take a separate path; the PC and Walkman groups released rival products, while SHE launched an online music portal that was not integrated with either hardware offering.

In the meantime, Apple had launched its iPod. In early 2003, Sony responded by launching the Connect project, to be headed by Howard Stringer and Philip Wiser, two executives from Sony USA. Connect would be a joint effort of Sony's top hardware makers, programmers, and SHE. Unfortunately, Stringer and Wiser did not control the hardware, programming, or SHE groups. The hardware designers were skeptical of Connect, fearing that opposition from SHE would eventually block the entire project. But there were many, more practical problems.

Stringer and Wiser were aware that Sony's software for downloading and playing digital music paled beside Apple's iPod, yet Sony's software division refused to make improvements. Wiser and Stringer wanted Connect to store data on hard drives using the MP3 format. But the hardware folks in Japan's Walkman division opted for the proprietary Atrac format to be stored on minidiscs (a smaller version of the CD that was popular in Japan). The Walkman division eventually gave in on the hard disc, though not the MP3 formatting, but only after the division head complained that hard drives "aren't interesting because anyone can make them." The lack of interest showed in the quality of the finished product. Reviewers of Sony's digital Walkman complained about the Atrac format and the user-unfriendly software interface. To make matters worse, Sony's PC division had launched its own digital music player without any coordination with Connect.

In November 2004, Sony pulled the plug on Connect only to set up Connect 2.0—a new division within Sony that would have its own hardware and software groups. The new Connect turned to a Sony software team in San Jose to revamp the user interface. After some resistance, Connect was also able to recruit a team of flash memory designers from the Walkman group. Sony's PC group even pulled its digital music player from the market. In May 2005, Sony released its new MP3 digital player in Japan and followed up with summer 2005 releases in the United States and Europe. With minimal features and plagued by critical bugs that affected usability, Connect 2.0 met the same fate as its predecessor. In 2006, Sony switched its Connect service to SonicStage, an older in-house product designed to manage portable devices plugged into computers running Windows. This proved to be a case of "too little, too late"; Sony shut down its Connect music store in 2008.

Organizational Design

In Chapter 13, we will describe organizational design, or hierarchy, which defines the lines of reporting and authority within the firm. The organizational design of one firm may not be right for another, and independent firms are free to choose the design that best meets their needs. When firms integrate, they usually unify their organizational design to avoid complexity and limit pay differentials for workers with similar responsibilities in different business units. But a uniform design forces some divisions to give up the lines of reporting and authority that had previously served it best.

To illustrate the pitfalls of organizational design in diversified firms, Oliver Williamson offered the seminal example of Tenneco's acquisition of Houston Oil and Minerals.[15] Houston was an energy exploration company that offered high-powered incentives that allowed key exploration personnel to become very wealthy. Tenneco was a conglomerate with uniform compensation policies across its divisions. After the acquisition, Tenneco imposed its compensation practices on Houston, which prompted Houston's most talented (and best paid) workers to quit.

REASONS TO "MAKE"

Thus far we have provided ample reasons for firms to focus on a narrow set of activities and leave everything else to market firms. But just as markets are not dominated by one or two megafirms, they are not exclusively the province of focused market firms. Sometimes it makes sense for firms to make rather than buy. Transactions among market firms can create serious problems for the profitability of all firms in the vertical chain, however, because owners of market firms have hard-edged incentives to maximize their own profits, without regard to the profits of their trading partners. Firms could write contracts to blunt these incentives, by penalizing market firms that look after their own interests and rewarding those market firms that help their trading partners become more profitable. As we describe below, such contracts would assure efficient production and maximum profits, while rendering meaningless the distinction between integrated firms and market firms. Unfortunately, it is costly to write and enforce such contracts. As a result, the decision to vertically integrate is far from meaningless. Thus, we begin our discussion of "reasons to make" by exploring the limitations of contracts.

The Economic Foundations of Contracts

Contracts define the conditions of exchange. They may take standardized forms, such as the "conditions of contract" on the back of an airline ticket or the terms and conditions of purchase printed on the back of a company's purchase order. Or they may be lengthy and complicated because they are carefully tailored to a specific transaction. For example, the contract for the sale of the Empire State Building in the 1960s involved more than 100 attorneys and was over 400 pages long.[16]

To understand the importance of contracts in the make-or-buy decision, it is useful to ask why firms use contracts. Contracts are valuable, in part, because they list the set of tasks that each contracting party expects the other to perform. But contracts also specify remedies in the event that one party does not fulfill its obligations. If necessary, an injured party may go to court to enforce the contract. It follows that an important reason for contracts is that firms do not completely trust their trading partners. If a firm could be certain that its partners would never shirk, there would be no reason to specify penalties in the event that they do.

Contracts are not equally effective at preventing shirking. Their effectiveness depends on (1) the "completeness" of the contract and (2) the available body of contract law. We discuss each of these factors in turn.

Complete versus Incomplete Contracting

A *complete contract* eliminates opportunities for shirking by stipulating each party's responsibilities and rights for each and every contingency that could conceivably arise during the transaction. A complete contract specifies particular courses of action as the transaction unfolds and makes penalties for breach sufficiently large that neither party shirks. By using a complete contract, a firm can get its trading partners to mimic any and all of the steps that would have been taken by a vertically integrated firm, as well as replicate the profits accruing to each participant in the vertical chain. With complete contracts, the make-or-buy decision becomes moot.

The requirements for complete contracting are severe. Parties to the contract must be able to contemplate all relevant contingencies and agree on a set of actions for every contingency. The parties must also be able to stipulate what constitutes satisfactory performance and must be able to measure performance. Finally, the contract must be enforceable. This implies that an outside party, such as a judge or an arbitrator, must be able to observe which contingencies occurred and whether each party took the required actions. For example, a contract in which the price of an item is tied to the seller's production costs might not be enforceable without an independent auditing mechanism that could verify those costs. Moreover, any specified damages must be within the financial reach of the shirking party. Otherwise it could choose to violate the terms of the contract with impunity.

Virtually all real-world contracts are incomplete: they do not fully specify the "mapping" from every possible contingency to enforceable rights, responsibilities, and actions. Incomplete contracts involve some degree of open-endedness or ambiguity; there are circumstances under which neither party's rights and responsibilities are clearly spelled out. Consider, for example, the case *Cook v. Deltona Corp.*[17] In 1971 Deltona Corporation, a land developer, sold Cook a piece of property in Marco Shores, Florida. The land was under water at the time of the sale. The title to the land was to be delivered in 1980, by which time Deltona was to have dredged and filled the land. However, during the 1970s changes in federal policy toward wetlands made it difficult for developers to obtain dredge-and-fill permits from the Army Corps of Engineers. In 1976, after failing to obtain permits on nearby land, Deltona gave up trying to obtain a permit for Marco Shores. The sales contract did not specify the buyer's rights and the developer's responsibilities under these circumstances, so the contract was incomplete. Because the contract was silent on this unanticipated turn of events, it was not clear whether Deltona had breached the contract by not delivering the land in the condition promised. The outcome was a lawsuit that took nine years to resolve. (Cook won.)

We now consider three factors that prevent complete contracting:

1. Bounded rationality
2. Difficulties specifying or measuring performance
3. Asymmetric information

Bounded Rationality

Bounded rationality refers to limits on the capacity of individuals to process information, deal with complexity, and pursue rational aims. Boundedly rational parties cannot contemplate or enumerate every contingency that might arise during a transaction. As a result, they cannot write complete contracts. In *Cook v. Deltona Corp.*, Deltona offered a defense based on bounded rationality. It argued that changes in regulatory requirements by the Army Corps of Engineers seemed so unlikely when the contract was written as to be unforeseeable. The court acknowledged that, in principle, this could be a valid defense, but it held that evidence that the Army Corps of Engineers had begun to toughen its policy meant that Deltona should have accounted for this risk in the contract.

Difficulties Specifying or Measuring Performance

When performance under a contract is complex or subtle, not even the most accomplished wordsmiths may be able to spell out each party's rights and responsibilities. Language in contracts is thus often left so vague and open-ended that it may not be clear what constitutes fulfillment of the contract. For example, a standard clause in lease contracts for new cars allows the company to bill the lessee for "excess wear and tear." However, the contract does not specify what this means. Some leasing companies have used this clause to charge customers who return the car in less-than-showroom condition.

A related problem is that performance may be ambiguous or hard to measure. For example, public and private health care payers have initiated a "pay for performance" movement intended to improve the quality of care. Primary care physicians can be rewarded if the "process" of care delivery meets established norms—for example, if pediatric patients receive timely vaccinations or if diabetics receive regular eye exams. These metrics are not necessarily the best indicators of quality, but they are easily measured from available patient billing records. Some industry experts want to replace narrow process measures with "patient reported outcomes" that capture the patient's overall quality of life.

Asymmetric Information

Even if the parties can foresee all contingencies and specify and measure relevant performance dimensions, a contract may still be incomplete because the parties do not have equal access to all contract-relevant information. If one party knows something that the other does not, then information is *asymmetric*, and the knowledgeable party may distort or misrepresent that information. For example, suppose that Audi would like to award Bosch a bonus if Bosch maintains stringent quality control in the production of antilock brakes. Because Bosch is responsible for quality control, it is the only one that can verify that appropriate measures have been taken. If the antilock brakes did not perform as expected, Bosch could claim that it took the required steps to assure durability even when it did not. Bosch might even claim that the fault lay in an associated electronics system manufactured by another firm. Understanding Bosch's self-interest, Audi might protest these claims. To enforce this contract, a court would have to look at evidence (e.g., an independent quality audit or testimony from each party) to ascertain whether the contract was fulfilled. But given the complexity of automotive braking systems, this evidence may well be inconclusive, and the court would have little basis on which to resolve the dispute. Under these circumstances, Audi and Bosch may be unable to contract for "quality control."

The Role of Contract Law

A well-developed body of contract law makes it possible for transactions to occur smoothly when contracts are incomplete. In the United States, contract law is embodied in both common law and the *Uniform Commercial Code* (*UCC*), the law governing contracts in all states except Louisiana. (There is no uniform European Civil Code, although many academics have urged European nations to embrace the "Principles of European Contract Law," which is styled after the UCC.) The doctrines of contract law specify a set of "standard" provisions applicable to wide classes of transactions. These doctrines eliminate the need for parties to specify these provisions in every single transaction. However, contract law is not a perfect substitute for complete contracting for two important reasons. First, the doctrines of contract law are phrased in broad language ("reasonable time," "reasonable price") that is open to differing interpretations when applied to specific transactions. Uncertainty about how particular doctrines will be applied raises the costs of transacting the exchange relative to an ideal world in which complete contracting is possible.

Second, litigation can be a costly way of "completing" contracts, both in dollars and time. Litigation can also weaken or destroy business relationships. As Stewart Macauley writes, "A breach of contract suit may settle a particular dispute, but such action often results in 'divorce,' ending the 'marriage' between two businesses, since a contract action is likely to carry charges with at least overtones of bad faith."[18]

By now it should be clear that contracts are an imperfect way to dissuade trading partners from behaving opportunistically at the expense of the entire vertical chain. If the resulting inefficiencies are large enough, it might make sense to limit opportunism by vertically integrating—choosing make over buy. We now describe three situations in which the inefficiencies might prove to be especially large: when it is important to coordinate activities in the vertical chain, when firms must share vital information, and when firms must make crucial investments.

Coordination of Production Flows through the Vertical Chain

Workers at different stages of the vertical chain must often make complementary decisions, that is, decisions that "fit together." Examples include:

- *Timing Fit* The launch of a Heineken marketing campaign must coincide with increased production and distribution by its bottlers.

- *Sequence Fit* The steps in a medical treatment protocol must be properly sequenced.

- *Technical Specification Fit* The sun roof of a car must fit precisely into the roof opening.

- *Color Fit* The tops in Benetton's spring lineup must match the bottoms.

Without good coordination, bottlenecks may arise. The failure of one supplier to deliver parts on schedule can shut down a factory. The failure to coordinate advertising across local markets can undermine a brand's image and dampen sales.

Firms often rely on contracts to ensure coordination. Contracts may specify delivery dates, design tolerances, or other performance targets. A supplier who fails to meet the specified targets might have to pay a penalty; a supplier who exceeds expectations may receive a bonus. For example, penalties and bonuses are commonplace for road construction firms facing completion deadlines. Firms may also assure coordination in the vertical chain by relying on *merchant coordinators*—independent firms that specialize in linking suppliers, manufacturers, and retailers.

The use of contracts and middlemen clauses is widespread, yet in some circumstances the protections afforded by contracts and middlemen may be inadequate. Paul Milgrom and John Roberts explain that coordination is especially important in processes with *design attributes*, which are attributes that need to relate to each other in a precise fashion; otherwise they lose a significant portion of their economic value.[19] Table 3.3 lists activities that are design attributes and those that are not. What the former have in common but the latter lack is that small errors can be exceptionally costly. For example, a slight delay in delivering a critical component can shut down a manufacturing plant. On the other hand, a slight delay in delivering landscaping supplies is unlikely to be critical to completing construction of an office tower.

TABLE 3.3
EXAMPLES OF DESIGN ATTRIBUTES

Are Design Attributes	Are Not Design Attributes
Timely delivery of part necessary for manufacturing process to begin	Timely completion of building construction
Sequencing of courses in MBA curriculum	Sequencing of sports activities in summer camp
Fit of automobile sunroof glass in opening of auto roof	Fit of bicycle handlebar covers on handlebars
Matching colors of sportswear ensembles within narrow tolerances	Matching sizes of sportswear ensembles within narrow tolerances

Because contracts are incomplete, firms cannot rely on them to ensure adequate coordination of design attributes. Whether by accident or design, an upstream supplier may fail to take the steps necessary to ensure a proper fit. If the resulting cost is substantial, then even if the downstream firm seeks compensation in court, it may be unable to recover full economic damages. Confronting such a possibility, the downstream firm may wish to integrate all critical activities and rely on administrative control to achieve the appropriate coordination.

Many firms bring design attributes in-house. Benetton dyes its own fabrics, because slight mismatches of color can ruin a production run. Caremark, which provides home intravenous drug infusion therapy for patients with AIDS, cancer, and other illnesses, writes its own applications software so as to beat its competitors to the market with new drug therapies. Silicon chip makers make both the wiring and the wafers in order to assure a precise fit. In each example, the cost of a small error along the critical design attribute can be catastrophic.

Firms could in principle write contracts to force each trading partner to take precautions to avoid catastrophes. But incomplete contracts may not offer sufficient protection, for all of the reasons we described earlier. When coordination of design attributes is critical to production, the central office of an integrated firm can avoid catastrophes by complementing traditional employment contracts with informal tools associated with governance. For example, top management can promote some managers and fire others without having to abide by precise contractual terms. Or it can promote a culture in which coordination is valued in its own right, regardless of contract. We further explore the important role of governance in the integrated firm in Chapter 4.

EXAMPLE 3.4 NIGHTMARES AT BOEING: THE 787 DREAMLINER

Boeing, the world's leading aerospace company, promised its customers that it would produce a dream of an airliner for twenty-first-century commercial air travel. Boeing designed the 787 Dreamliner to be the most fuel-efficient commercial aircraft ever built and the world's first major airliner to use composite materials for most of its construction. After Boeing announced the 787 project in April 2004, 56 different customers placed orders for over 900 aircraft, making the 787 the most anticipated launch of a new commercial airplane in Boeing's history. Boeing promised to make its first delivery in 2008. As of summer 2011, the next-generation airliner was billions of dollars over budget and Boeing had postponed delivery of the first plane (to All Nippon Airways) until the fall of 2011. Some of these problems could be attributed to the plane's advanced design, engineering, and materials, which made it harder to build. But much of the blame belongs to the company's aggressive strategy of outsourcing the design, manufacture, and assembly of crucial components to subcontractors. It was a costly lesson both for Boeing and the world.

In order to reduce costs and accelerate design and production, Boeing adopted an innovative manufacturing model of being a system integrator and outsourcing most of the design, engineering, manufacturing, and production to external suppliers around the world. Each supplier was fully responsible for detail design and production. Suppliers would complete each section in its entirety before shipping it to Boeing's aircraft hangars in Everett, Washington, for final assembly and inspections. Boeing contracted with over 50 suppliers, some 28 of them outside of the United States. As much as 70 percent of the total value of the 787 was foreign content, compared with 30 percent for the 777 (launched in the 1990s) and just 2 percent for the 727 (launched in the 1960s).

If all went well, Boeing could piece together a 787 from its component parts much the same way that a child assembles a Lego. But all did not go well. Problems emerged as early as the designing stage: instead of providing its subcontractors with detailed blueprints as was done for its previous planes, Boeing gave less detailed specifications about the design and required suppliers to create their own blueprints. However, many of Boeing's first-tier subcontractors did not have the capability to perform this highly uncertain and complex designing and engineering work. Some of them even farmed out their part of designing and engineering to their own subcontractors.

As subcontractors waited on subassembly designs, delays began to mount up. This was just the beginning of Boeing's problems. Boeing required that subcontractors integrate their own sections and send the preassembled sections to Everett for final assembly. But just as some contractors lacked the expertise to do complex design work, so others lacked experience at subassembly integration. They either could not procure the needed parts or perform the subassembly in time, or both. Boeing had to take over the remaining assembly work and complete it as "traveled work." To make matters even worse, some components manufactured by different subcontractors did not fit together, and some sections that were sent to final assembly were missing sufficient documentation of instructions, which almost made Boeing lose control of the process.

Coordination may also involve an *assignment* problem—ensuring that the right people do the right jobs with minimal duplication of effort. As with coordination of design attributes, the assignment problem may be easier to solve by the central office of an integrated firm than by reliance on the market. Again, firms could try to use contracts to solve the assignment problem, but this requires considerable qualitative judgment, which is difficult to specify in a contract.

Coordination can be especially difficult for innovative processes, where there may be no blueprints to facilitate the matching of complementary inputs. The following example, adapted from Qian, Roland, and Xu, combines the coordination and assignment problems in an innovative process:

> Consider the GMC Sierra and Chevrolet Silverado. Suppose a technological innovation in transmission will make a better truck, but requires a change in the technical specification for engines. Unless the development of transmission and engine are coordinated, the trucks will not operate. Because neither the transmission nor engine teams will have each other's final blueprints during the development process, it may be difficult to rely on contracts to assure that the two components are interoperable. In addition, coordination by an integrated General Motors will avoid duplication of efforts required to assure the proper fit. Costs can be further reduced if the Sierra and Silverado can share the same transmission, suggesting that there can be economies of scope in achieving coordination.[20]

Leakage of Private Information

A firm's *private information* is information that no one else knows. Private information may pertain to production know-how, product design, or consumer information. When firms use the market to obtain supplies or distribute products, they risk losing control of valuable private information. Well-defined and well-protected patents afford research-driven organizations the ability to outsource downstream activities from production through marketing without compromising the intellectual property (IP) that is their principal source of competitive advantage.

Patents are not foolproof, however, for many of the same reasons that contracts are incomplete: bounded rationality and difficulties in specifying what is covered by a patent. The urgent need to protect IP can profoundly influence outsourcing decisions. Consider the plight of Peerless Industries, an Illinois manufacturer of flatscreen and projector television mounts. Peerless had outsourced production to a supplier in China, but as its chief operating officer soon discovered, "Knockoffs of our products started showing up in markets here in our own backyard. It wasn't necessarily our supplier doing it; it was our supplier's supplier."[21]

Concerns about IP are not limited to outsourcing in developing nations. Like contracts, patents are often incomplete and rival firms can often "invent around" them. This explains why independent research companies, such as fledgling biotech firms, often bear the considerable expense of bringing their discoveries to market rather than license to larger companies. To convince a big drug maker to pay for a license, a biotech start-up must reveal some technological secrets. Reveal too much and the drug maker will learn enough to invent around the patent.

Firms may find it especially difficult to protect critical information that it must share with employees. Urban legend has it that the secret formula in Coca-Cola is known to only two executives, and each only knows one-half! (The reality is that a small handful of Coke execs know the entire formula.) Professional services firms that jealously guard privileged information and client lists may require employees to sign *noncompete clauses* that bar exiting workers from competing with the firm for several years. But these clauses can be difficult to enforce due to that familiar bugaboo, contractual incompleteness, and some firms remain reluctant to reveal vital information to all but their top employees.

Transactions Costs

The concept of transactions costs was first described by Nobel Prize winner Ronald Coase in his famous paper, "The Nature of the Firm."[22] Coase raised the following question: In light of the efficiencies of the market emphasized in economic theory, why does so much economic activity take place within integrated firms? Coase concluded that there must be costs to using the market that can be eliminated by using the firm. These have come to be known as *transactions costs*. Coordination and protecting information are examples of transactions costs, but the term is usually confined to specific inefficiencies first identified by Nobel Prize–winning economist Oliver Williamson.

In the book, *The Economic Institutions of Capitalism*, Williamson summarizes his pathbreaking work on transactions-costs economics.[23] Williamson notes that transactions costs include the time and expense of negotiating, writing, and enforcing contracts as well as potentially far greater costs that arise when firms exploit incomplete contracts to act opportunistically (i.e., seek private gain at the expense of the greater good). The adverse consequences of opportunistic behavior, as well as the costs of trying to prevent it, are the main focus of Williamson's theory of transactions-costs economics.

Contract law might ameliorate the opportunism that can arise under incomplete contracting, but it is unlikely to eliminate it. Thus, incomplete contracting will inevitably entail some transactions costs. To help explain more precisely the nature of these transactions costs and how they might influence decisions to integrate, this section introduces three important theoretical concepts from transactions-costs economics: *relationship-specific assets*, *quasi-rents*, and the *holdup* problem. The following subsections define these concepts and explain their significance.

Relationship-Specific Assets

A relationship-specific asset supports a given transaction and cannot be redeployed to another transaction without some sacrifice in productivity or some additional cost. Firms that have invested in relationship-specific assets cannot switch trading partners without seeing a decline in the value of these assets. This implies that investments in relationship-specific assets lock the parties into the relationship to some degree.

Forms of Asset Specificity

Asset specificity can take at least four forms:

1. Site specificity
2. Physical asset specificity
3. Dedicated assets
4. Human asset specificity

Site Specificity. Site specificity refers to assets that are located side-by-side to economize on transportation or inventory costs or to take advantage of processing efficiencies. Traditional steel manufacturing offers a good example. Side-by-side location of blast furnaces, steelmaking furnaces, casting units, and mills saves fuel costs, as the pig iron, molten steel, and semifinished steel do not have to be reheated before being moved to the next process in the production chain.

Physical Asset Specificity. Physical asset specificity refers to assets whose physical or engineering properties are specifically tailored to a particular transaction. For example, glass container production requires molds that are custom tailored to particular container shapes and glass-making machines. Physical asset specificity inhibits customers from switching suppliers.

Dedicated Assets. A dedicated asset is an investment in plant and equipment made to satisfy a particular buyer. Without the promise of that particular buyer's business, the investment would not be profitable. The government-run Associated British Ports (ABP) often invests in dedicated facilities to serve the specific needs of import and/or export customers. For example, one facility might be designed with specialized bagging equipment to accommodate construction materials, whereas another may be equipped with concrete batching machines to handle marine aggregates (sand and gravel). ABP usually requires long-term contracts from its customers before making these multimillion pound investments.

Human Asset Specificity. Human asset specificity refers to cases in which a worker, or group of workers, has acquired skills, know-how, and information that are more valuable inside a particular relationship than outside it. Human asset specificity not only includes tangible skills, such as expertise with company-specific software, but it also encompasses intangible assets. Every organization has unwritten "routines" and "standard operating procedures." A manager who has become a skillful administrator within the context of one organization's routines may be less effective in an organization with completely different routines. For example, as hospitals develop new treatment protocols, the training of nurses and other specialized staff will become more firm-specific.

The Fundamental Transformation

The need to create relationship-specific assets transforms the relationship as the transaction unfolds. Before individuals or firms make relationship-specific investments, they may have many alternative trading partners and can choose to partner with those that afford the highest possible profit. But after making relationship-specific investments, they will have few, if any, alternatives. Their profits will be determined by bilateral bargaining. In short, once the parties invest in relationship-specific assets, the relationship changes from a "large numbers" bargaining situation to a "small numbers" bargaining situation. Williamson refers to this change as the *fundamental transformation*.

Rents and Quasi-Rents

The fundamental transformation has significant consequences for the economics of bargaining between buyer and seller, which in turn affects the costs of arm's-length market exchange. To set the stage for our discussion of these costs, we must first define and explain *rent* and *quasi-rent*.

These are hard concepts. To explain them, we will walk through a numerical example about a hypothetical transaction. Suppose your company contemplates building a factory to produce cup holders for Ford automobiles. The factory can make up to 1 million holders per year at an average variable cost of C dollars per unit. You finance the construction of your factory with a mortgage from a bank that requires an annual payment of I dollars. The loan payment of I dollars thus represents your (annualized) cost of investment in this plant. Note that this is an unavoidable cost: You have to make your payment even if you do not do business with Ford.[24] Your total cost of making 1 million cup holders is thus $I + 1,000,000C$ dollars per year.

You will design and build the factory specifically to produce cup holders for Ford. Your *expectation* is that Ford will purchase your holders at a profitable price. But if you build the factory and *do not* end up selling cup holders to Ford, you still have a "bailout" option: You can sell the holders to jobbers who, after suitably modifying them, will resell them to other automobile manufacturers. The "market price" you can expect to get from these jobbers is P_m. If you sell your cup holders to jobbers, you would thus get total revenue of $1,000,000P_m$.

Suppose that $P_m > C$, so the market price covers your variable cost. Thus, *you are more than willing to sell to the jobbers* if you had no other option. Ignoring the investment cost I for a moment, your profit from selling to the jobbers is $1,000,000(P_m - C)$. Suppose also that the annual investment cost $I > 1,000,000(P_m - C)$. This implies that even though you are better off selling to jobbers than not selling at all, *you will not recover your investment cost if you sell only to jobbers*. In this sense, a portion of your investment is specific to your relationship with Ford. In particular, the difference $I - 1,000,000(P_m - C)$ represents your company's *relationship-specific investment (RSI)*.

- The RSI equals the amount of your investment that you cannot recover if your company *does not* do business with Ford.

- For example, if $I = \$8,500,000$, $C = \$3$, and $P_m = \$4$, then the RSI is $\$8,500,000 - 1,000,000(4 - 3) = \$7,500,000$. Of your $\$8,500,000$ investment cost, you lose $\$7,500,000$ if you do not do business with Ford and sell to jobbers instead.

We can now explain rent and quasi-rent. First, let us explain rent.[25] Suppose that before you take out the loan to invest in the cup holder plant, Ford agreed to buy

1 million sets of cup holders per year at a price of P^* per unit, where $P^* > P_m$. Thus, your company expects to receive total revenue of $1,000,000P^*$ from Ford. Suppose that $I < 1,000,000(P^* - C)$, so that given your expectation of the price Ford will pay, you should build the plant. Then,

- Your *rent* is $1,000,000(P^* - C) - I$.

- In words: Your rent is simply the profit you expect to get when you build the plant, assuming all goes as planned.

Let us now explain quasi-rent. Suppose, after the factory is built, your deal with Ford falls apart. You should still sell to the jobbers, because $1,000,000(P_m - C) > 0$; that is, sales to jobbers cover your variable costs.

- Your quasi-rent is the difference between the profit you get from selling to Ford and the profit you get from your next-best option, selling to jobbers. That is, quasi-rent is $[1,000,000(P^* - C) - I] - [1,000,000(P_m - C) - I] = 1,000,000(P^* - P_m)$.

- In words: Your *quasi-rent* is the *extra* profit that you get if the deal goes ahead as planned, versus the profit you would get if you had to turn to your next-best alternative (in our example, selling to jobbers).

It seems clear why the concept of rent is important. Your firm—indeed any firm— must expect positive rents to induce it to invest in an asset. But why is quasi-rent important? It turns out that quasi-rent tells us about the possible magnitude of the holdup problem, a problem that can arise when there are relationship-specific assets.

The Holdup Problem

If an asset was *not* relationship-specific, the profit the firm could get from using the asset in its best alternative and its next-best alternative would be the same. Thus, the associated quasi-rent would be zero. But when a firm invests in a relationship-specific asset, the quasi-rent must be positive—it will always get more from its best alternative than from its second-best alternative. If the quasi-rent is large, a firm stands to lose a lot if it has to turn to its second-best alternative. This opens the possibility that its trading partner could exploit this large quasi-rent, through *holdup*.[26]

- A firm *holds up* its trading partner by attempting to renegotiate the terms of a deal. A firm can profit by holding up its trading partner when contracts are incomplete (thereby permitting breach) and when the deal generates quasi-rents for its trading partner.

To see how this could happen, let's return to our example of Ford and your cup holder company. Ford could reason as follows: You have already sunk your investment in the plant. Even though Ford "promised" to pay you P^* per cup holder, it knows that you would accept any amount greater than P_m per unit and still sell to it. Thus, Ford could break the contract and offer you a price *between* P^* and P_m; if you accept this renegotiation of the deal, Ford would increase its profits.

Could Ford get away with this? After all, didn't Ford sign a contract with you? Well, if the contract is incomplete (and thus potentially ambiguous), Ford could assert that, in one way or another, circumstances have changed and that it is justified breaking the contract. It might, for example, claim that increases in the costs of commodity raw materials will force it to sharply curtail production unless suppliers, such as yourself, renegotiate their contracts. Or it might claim that the quality of your cup holders

---

EXAMPLE 3.5 POWER BARGES

How do you deal with trading partners who are reluctant to make investments that have a high degree of site specificity? This is the problem that many developing nations face in convincing foreign corporations to construct power plants. Power plants are usually highly specialized assets. Once a firm builds a power plant in a developing nation, the associated investment undergoes the "fundamental transformation" and becomes a site-specific asset. If the purchasing government defaults on its payments, the manufacturer has few options for recovering its investment. (The firm could route the power to consumers in other nations, but the defaulting government could easily prevent it.) Even though no manufacturer has had to repossess a plant, the fear of default has scared them off. As a result, growing economies in developing nations may be slowed by power shortages.

The solution to the problem is ingenious. Manufacturers have eliminated the geographic asset specificity associated with power generation! They do this by building power plants on floating barges. Floating power plants are not new. Since the 1930s, U.S. Navy battleships have used their turboelectric motors to provide emergency power to utilities. The idea of installing a power plant on a barge deck originated with General Electric, which manufactured power barges for use by the U.S. military during World War II and have been in use ever since. Recent innovations have reduced the size and increased the reliability of gas turbines, making it possible to house large-capacity generators on a small number of barges. This makes them especially attractive to developing nations that lack the infrastructure to build their own power generation facilities, but have sufficient reserves of natural gas, oil, or geothermal energy to fuel the power barges. A few power barges feature nuclear reactors, requiring minimal on-site fueling.

During the 1990s, power barges became a popular way of providing energy to developing nations. Companies including Raytheon, Westinghouse, Smith Cogeneration, and Amfel built floating power plants for customers such as Bangladesh, Ghana, Haiti, Kenya, and Malaysia, as well intermediaries such as the Power Barge Corporation. There are even a few power barges in developed nations. For example, Consolidated Edison operates a gas-turbine generator that is housed on a barge in the Gowanus Canal in Brooklyn.

Power barges are moored on one or more barges in safe harbors and "plugged into" land-based transformers that send electricity to domestic consumers. If the purchaser defaults, the manufacturer or intermediary can tow the barge(s) away and sell the plant to another customer. Floating power plants can also be assembled off-site and then towed to the purchasing nation. This lowers labor costs because the manufacturers do not have to pay their skilled workers to go to a distant site for a long time. There is one final incentive for floating power plants: an amendment to the 1936 U.S. Merchant Marine Act provides substantial financing advantages for vessels constructed in the United States but documented under the laws of another nation. Floating barges fit this description and enjoy favorable financing.

---

fails to meet promised specifications and that it must be compensated for this lower quality with lower prices.

Unless you want to fight Ford in court for breach of contract (itself a potentially expensive move), you are better off accepting Ford's revised offer than not accepting it. By reneging on the original contract, Ford has "held you up" and has transferred some of your quasi-rent to itself. To illustrate this concretely, suppose $P^* = \$12$ per unit, $P_m = \$4$ per unit, $C = \$3$ per unit, and $I = \$8,500,000$.

- At the original expected price of $12 per unit, your rent is $(12 - 3)1,000,000 - 8,500,000 = \$500,000$ per year.

- Your quasi-rent is $(12 - 4)1,000,000 = \$8,000,000$ per year.

• If Ford renegotiates the contract down to $8 per unit, Ford will increase its profits by $4 million per year and it will have transferred half of your quasi-rents to itself.

Note that after the holdup has occurred, you realize that you are getting a profit of $(8 - 3)1,000,000 - 8,500,000 = -\$3,500,000$. You are losing money on your investment in the factory! This tells us that if, instead of trusting Ford, you had anticipated the prospect of holdup, then you would not have made the investment to begin with. This situation is especially problematic because your rent was small but your quasi-rent was large. When Ford holds you up and extracts a portion of your quasi-rent, you end up with losses that dwarf the expected profits. This example shows why we talk about the holdup problem in the context of vertical integration. If you are afraid of being held up, you might be reluctant to invest in relationship-specific assets in the first place, forcing Ford either to find another supplier of cup holders *or to make them itself.*

Holdup and Ex Post Cooperation

Economist Oliver Hart, whose "property rights theory of the firm" we will encounter in the next chapter, recently offered a theory of holdup that does not require *ex ante* noncontractible investments made at the start of a trading relationship.[27] Suppose instead that a relationship between a buyer and seller is enhanced through *ex post* cooperation as the relationship unfolds. For example, they may share information about quality control, identify potential new markets, or lobby governments. As the trading relationship unfolds, conditions may change in ways that advantages one firm more than another—demand may be higher than expected or costs may drop. Most of the time the buyer and seller will continue to cooperate, but sometimes conditions are so volatile that one firm gains a huge advantage or disadvantage not necessarily at the expense of the other. In these situations, the firm that is relatively worse off may threaten to withhold cooperation unless the contract is renegotiated so as to get a share of the spoils (or pass on some of its losses). In order to force renegotiation, the firms may even withdraw cooperation. This is a form of holdup that as Hart describes, "transforms a friendly relationship into a hostile one." The end result could be the breakdown of cooperation and reduced profitability for both firms.

The Holdup Problem and Transactions Costs

The holdup problem raises the cost of transacting arm's-length market exchanges in four ways. It can lead to:

1. More difficult contract negotiations and more frequent renegotiations
2. Investments to improve *ex post* bargaining positions
3. Distrust
4. Reduced *ex ante* investment in relationship-specific investments and/or reduced *ex post* cooperation.

Contract Negotiation and Renegotiation

When trading partners anticipate the possibility of holdup, initial contract negotiations are likely to be time consuming and costly as each side seeks to put safeguards into the contract. As circumstances change in unanticipated ways, the temptation for a party to hold up its trading partner is likely to lead to frequent renegotiations and additional costs. In addition, renegotiations are likely to be associated with delays or disruptions, raising production costs and impeding delivery of products to customers.

EXAMPLE 3.6 A GAME OF CHICKEN? SPECIFICITY AND UNDERINVESTMENT IN THE BROILER INDUSTRY

Tomislav Vukina and Porametr Leegomonchai have recently studied investments in relationship-specific assets by broiler growers.[28] "Broilers" are chickens grown for their meat. Unlike their commercial-egg-producing cousins, broiler breeds grow fast, mature quickly, and are bred to efficiently turn chicken feed into lean flesh.

Production of broilers in the United States is highly concentrated. Large broiler companies (called processors) contract with independent farmers (growers) to produce chickens. Contracts between processors and growers usually cover one flock at a time and typically stipulate that processors are to provide baby chicks, feed, medication, and some field personnel to the grower. The grower's job is to provide broiler houses (a form of high-tech chicken coop), labor, and management. The processor delivers chicks to the grower, who then raises the chicks into adults, and ships the mature chickens back to the processor for slaughter.

Why does the processor choose to buy rather than make? For broilers, the need for biosecurity provides a strong diseconomy of scale. Placing too many chickens in close proximity increases the likelihood of a devastating outbreak of avian influenza. Processors respond to this threat by distributing their chickens to several growers (and wisely avoid putting all their eggs in one basket). Growers must, however, be close to the processor's plant, since adult chickens cannot be transported far by truck.

Growers must make substantial investments in order to raise broilers successfully. Broiler houses, which usually hold around 25,000 birds, can cost upwards of $250,000 and cannot be easily redeployed for other purposes, such as growing turkeys. Growers must also invest in specialized skills, such as knowledge of biosecurity practices and feed management. The vertical disintegration combined with locational specificity of these investments raises the possibility that processors might try to hold up growers and that growers might underinvest as a result.

Vukina and Leegomonchai test this hypothesis by looking at how growers' levels of investment vary with their degree of locational specificity. They find that the number of houses a grower has under contract is positively related to the number of processors within the grower's local area. Note that while investments in broiler houses—the variable of study here—are contractible, smaller investments in broiler houses probably mean smaller noncontractible investments (in skills and local labor-market knowledge) as well. Vukina and Leegomonchai also show that growers make fewer upgrades to their broiler houses when their assets suffer from locational specificity. Thus, locational specificity does seem to be associated with underinvestment.

Investments to Improve Ex Post Bargaining Positions

Parties that anticipate the possibility of holdup might make investments that improve their postcontractual bargaining positions. This can take several forms. A buyer may acquire a standby production facility for a key input as a hedge against contractual holdup by the input supplier. Alternatively, the buyer might seek a second source for an input. For example, in the early 1980s, Intel's customers (including IBM) pressured it to provide second sources for its 8088 and 80286 microprocessors. Although standby facilities and second sources can reduce the possibility of holdup, they are not without cost. A standby facility that duplicates the production facility of the input supplier may stand idle much of the time, thus representing costly excess capacity that will eventually be borne by the buyer.

Distrust

Oliver Hart emphasizes the breakdown of cooperation that can arise between parties in the relationship.[29] The resulting distrust raises the costs of contracting in two ways. First, it increases the direct costs of contract negotiation as parties insist that more formal safeguards be written into the contract. Second, distrust impedes sharing information or ideas to achieve production efficiencies or quality improvements.

Reduced Investment

Finally, and perhaps worst of all, the possibility of holdup can reduce *ex ante* incentives to invest in specific assets. Firms may reduce investments in relationship-specific assets or substitute general-purpose assets for more specific ones. For example, an alumina producer situated near an aluminum plant might build a small refinery rather than a large one. Or it might build a refinery that can produce many different grades of alumina, instead of the smelter-grade alumina that is used by the neighboring aluminum plant.

The tendency to underinvest in relationship-specific assets causes problems because relationship-specific investments usually allow firms to achieve efficiencies that they cannot achieve with general-purpose investments. An alumina refinery that is set up to produce more than one grade of alumina is generally more costly to operate than one that is designed to produce only smelter-grade. When the holdup problem leads to underinvestment in relationship-specific assets, the result is likely to be lower productivity and higher production costs for the vertical chain as a whole.

Recap: From Relationship-Specific Assets to Transactions Costs

Because the ideas developed in this section are complex and subtle, let's recap the main lines of argument:

- A relationship-specific asset is an asset that supports a particular transaction. Redeploying a relationship-specific asset reduces its productivity or entails extra costs.

- A relationship-specific asset gives rise to quasi-rents. The quasi-rent in a transaction with relationship-specific assets equals the *extra profit* a firm gets when it deploys its relationship-specific assets in their intended use and the transaction goes ahead as planned, as opposed to deploying those assets in their best alternative use.

- When a party has quasi-rents, it can be held up by its trading partner. When this happens, the trading partner transfers some of the quasi-rents to itself. Holdup is especially tempting when contracts are highly incomplete, so that proving breach of contract is difficult.

- The potential for holdup raises the cost of market transaction by making contract negotiations more contentious, by inducing parties to invest in "safeguards" to improve postcontractual bargaining positions, by engendering distrust, and by leading to underinvestment in relationship-specific assets.

In typical economist's fashion, this chapter has identified both costs and benefits to integration. Our analysis raises a host of new questions:

- What exactly does it mean to be integrated?

- How exactly does integration eliminate holdup and coordination problems?

- How should one weigh the benefits and costs of "make" versus "buy?"

- Are there alternatives to the extremes of "make" or "buy?"

The next chapter explores these issues.

SUMMARIZING MAKE-OR-BUY DECISIONS: THE MAKE-OR-BUY DECISION TREE

The make-or-buy decision involves a calculated balancing of several benefits and costs of integration. A manager can easily get lost in the complexity of this balancing act. Figure 3.3 provides a series of questions to guide the manager through the decision-making process. The manager must first assess whether the market provides any alternative to vertical integration. If the answer is no, then the firm must either take on the task itself or prop up a quasi-independent supplier through a joint venture or

FIGURE 3.3
SUMMARIZING THE FRAMEWORKS: AN ISSUE TREE

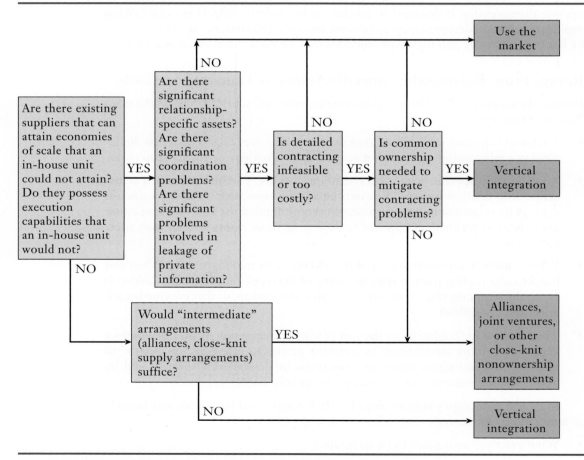

Managers must answer a series of questions before making make-or-buy decisions.

strategic alliance (which are described in the next chapter). If the market does offer alternatives to vertical integration, then the manager must determine whether market relationships will be impeded by information, coordination, or holdup problems. If such problems do not exist, then the firm should use the market. But if they do exist, the manager must finally determine whether these problems can be prevented either through contract (favoring the use of the market) or through internal governance (favoring integration). Though not shown in the decision tree, managers should also consider whether special circumstances of market power are causing double marginalization (taken up in Chapter 4).

CHAPTER SUMMARY

- The production of any good or service usually requires a range of activities organized in a vertical chain. Production activities flow from upstream suppliers of raw inputs to downstream manufacturers, distributors, and retailers.

- The vertical chain includes processing and handling activities associated directly with the processing and distribution of inputs and outputs, and professional support activities, such as accounting and planning.

- A fundamental question is which activities in the vertical chain a firm should perform itself and which it should leave to independent firms in the market. This is known as the "make-or-buy" problem.

- A fallacious make-or-buy argument is that firms should buy to avoid incurring the associated costs. The firm it buys from will have to incur these costs and will charge accordingly.

- A second fallacy is that firms should make, rather than buy, to keep for themselves the profits earned by independent firms. These profits usually represent the returns necessary to attract investment and would be required of the firm that "makes" just as they are required of independent firms.

- A third fallacy is that vertically integrated firms can produce an input at cost and thus have an advantage over nonintegrated firms that must buy inputs at market prices. This argument ignores a hidden opportunity cost to the vertically integrated firm: by using the input to produce its final output, it forgoes outside sales in the open market.

- The solution to the make-or-buy decision depends on which decision leads to the most efficient production. This is determined by assessing the benefits and costs of using the market.

- Market firms can often achieve economies of scale in production of an input that firms choosing to make the input themselves cannot.

- Market firms offer other advantages. While a division within a hierarchical firm may hide its inefficiencies behind complex monitoring and reward systems, independent firms must survive market competition. This encourages efficiency and innovation.

- Vertically integrated firms can try to replicate market incentives but may encounter problems associated with motivation (agency costs) and internal lobbying for resources (influence costs).

- Use of market firms is complicated by incomplete contracts. Contracts may be incomplete because of hidden actions, hidden information, and bounded rationality.

- Use of market firms often presents coordination problems. This is especially problematic for inputs with design attributes that require a careful fit between different components.

- Use of market firms may lead to the holdup problem in which one trading partner exploits contractual incompleteness to renegotiate the terms of a contract. Fearful of losing money on relationship-specific investments, the other trading partner anticipates holdup and refuses to make these valuable investments.

QUESTIONS

1. Describe the vertical chain for the production of motion pictures. Describe the extent of vertical integration of the steps in this chain.

2. A manufacturer of pencils contemplates backward integration into the production of rapeseed oil, a key ingredient in manufacturing the rubberlike material (called factice) that forms the eraser. Rapeseed oil is traded in world commodity markets, and its price fluctuates as supply and demand conditions change. The argument that has been made in favor of vertical integration is this: "Pencil production is very utilization-sensitive (i.e., a plant that operates at full capacity can produce pencils at much lower cost per unit than a plant that operates at less than full capacity). Owning our own source of supply of rapeseed oil insulates us from short-run supply–demand imbalances and therefore will give us a competitive advantage over rival producers." Explain why this argument is wrong.

3. Matilda Bottlers bottles and distributes wines and spirits in Australia. Big Gator is a conglomerate that manufactures, among other things, a popular lager beer. By virtue of a lifetime contract, Matilda has exclusive rights to bottle and distribute Big Gator Beer in New South Wales, the largest state in Australia. Matilda uses its monopsony power to pay a lower price for Big Gator Beer than do bottlers in other states. Is this sufficient justification for Big Gator to buy out Matilda Bottlers?

4. What is the "Chicago School" argument against concerns that vertical integration is anticompetitive? Under what conditions might this argument be wrong?

5. Canon has manufactured high-quality cameras since it was founded in 1933. SLR-cameras (i.e., not point and shoot cameras) are purchased in two parts: the body and the lenses. Photographers who want a Canon product must make the upfront investment in the expensive camera body. Canon earns significant profit from the sale of camera bodies and then earns a stream of profits from camera lenses. An owner of a Canon camera body can also purchase lenses from other companies that produce Canon-compatible products. Would Canon be better off if there were no other firms that made Canon-compatible lenses?

6. In each of the following situations why are firms likely to benefit from vertical integration?
   (a) A *grain elevator* is located at the terminus of a *rail line*.
   (b) A *manufacturer* of a product with a national brand-name reputation uses *distributors* that arrange for advertising and promotional activities in local markets.
   (c) A *biotech firm* develops a new product that will be produced, tested, and distributed by an established *pharmaceutical company*.

7. Consider the following pairs of situations. In each pair, which situation is more likely to be susceptible to *coordination* problems?

(a) Maintenance of *corporate landscaping* by a gardening company versus maintenance of a *football or soccer stadium's grass turf* by a gardening company.

(b) Design of a *toolbox* to hold *tools* versus design of a *wafer* to hold the wires of a microscopic *silicon chip*.

8. Universities tend to be highly integrated—many departments all belong to the same organization. There is no technical reason why a university could not consist of freestanding departments linked together by contracts or other market arrangements. Why do you suppose that universities are not organized in this way?

9. "Influence activities happen in everyday life, in households, schools, and even among close friends." Can you give examples to support this statement?

10. Explain why the make-or-buy decision is moot when contracts are complete.

11. Some contracts, such as those between municipalities and highway construction firms, are extremely long with terms spelled out in minute detail. Others, such as between consulting firms and their clients, are short and fairly vague about the division of responsibilities. What factors might determine such differences in contract length and detail?

12. Production requires coordination of many activities. Why does the make-or-buy decision depend critically on coordination of *design attributes*? What is the connection between your answer and incomplete contracts?

13. Suppose that Arnold Schwarzenegger (AS) pays Besanko, Dranove, Shanley, and Schaefer (BDS^2) an advance of $5 million to write the script to *Incomplete Contract*, a movie version of their immensely popular text on business strategy. The movie contract includes certain script requirements, including one that AS gets to play a strong, silent, business strategist with superhuman analytic powers. BDS^2 spend $100,000 worth of their time to write a script that is tailor-made for the ex-Terminator (AS, that is). When they turn in the script to AS, he claims that it fails to live up to the contractual requirement that he has several passionate love scenes, and so he attempts to renegotiate. Given the ambiguity over what constitutes passion, BDS^2 are forced to agree.

(a) What was BDS^2's rent?

(b) What is their quasi-rent? What assumptions do you have to make to compute this?

(c) Could BDS^2 have held up AS? Explain.

14. In many modern U.S. industries the following patterns seem to hold:

(a) Small firms are more likely to outsource production of inputs than are large firms;

(b) "Standard" inputs (such as a simple transistor that could be used by several electronics manufacturers) are more likely to be outsourced than "tailor-made" inputs (such as a circuit board designed for a single manufacturer's specific needs).

What factors might explain these patterns?

15. Chapter 1 discussed the history of the vertically integrated corporate giants of the early twentieth century. Use the concepts in this chapter to explain why firms facing the following conditions are more likely to vertically integrate: (1) The firm is in a developing economy; (2) the firm uses a capital-intensive production process. Be sure to discuss both reasons to make and reasons to buy.

ENDNOTES

[1]The information is taken from Orwall, B., and M. Peers, "The Message of Media Mergers: So Far, They Haven't Been Hits," *The Wall Street Journal*, May 10, 2002, p. A1.

[2]From *Chicago Tribune*, February 21, 1993, section 1, p. 15.

[3]Hagel, J., and M. Singer, "Unbundling the Corporation," *The McKinsey Quarterly*, 3, 2000, pp. 148–61.

[4]As quoted in "Mylan Buy's Merck Unit for $6.7B," by Daniel Jacobs, *International Business Times*, May 14, 2007. Accessed July 10, 2009 at http://www.ibtimes.com/articles/20070514/merck-mylan-generic-drugs-acquisition.htm

[5]Ibid.

[6]Expected value is found by multiplying the probability of an event by the payoff associated with that event. In this case, the expected value is

$$(1/3) \times (-100,000) + (1/3) \times 100,000 \times (1/3) \times 300,000 = 100,000$$

[7]Rey, P., and J. Tirole, "A Primer on Foreclosure," in Armstrong, M. and R. Porter (eds.), *Handbook of Industrial Organization III*, 2006.

[8]The argument is *about* half right because vertical integration can sometimes lead to more profits in the vertical chain even without foreclosure. One example is when vertical integration eliminates double marginalization, which we discuss in Chapter 4.

[9]"Best Firms to Work For: McKinsey and Company," *Consulting Magazine*, September 28, 2007.

[10]Becker, G., *Human Capital: A Theoretical and Empirical Analysis, with Special Reference to Education*, University of Chicago Press, 1964.

[11]Von Hayek, F., "The Use of Knowledge in Society," *American Economic Review*, 35, September 1945, pp. 519–530.

[12]Milgrom, P., and J. Roberts, "Bargaining Costs, Influence Costs, and the Organization of Economic Activity," in Alt, J., and K. Shepsle (eds.), *Perspectives on Positive Political Economy*, Cambridge, Cambridge University Press, 1990.

[13]Much of the information for this example is taken from Dvorak, P., "Out of Tune: At Sony, Rivalries Were Encouraged; Then Came iPod," *The Wall Street Journal*, June 29, 2005, p. A1.

[14]Hayek, F., "The Use of Knowledge in Society," *American Economic Review*, 35, 1945, pp. 519–530.

[15]Williamson, O., *The Economic Institutions of Capitalism*, New York, Free Press, 1985.

[16]Macauley, S., "Non-Contractual Relations in Business: A Preliminary Study," *American Sociological Review*, 28, 1963, pp. 55–67.

[17]*Cook v. Deltona Corp.*, 753 F2d 1552 (1985), United States Court of Appeals, Eleventh Circuit.

[18]Macauley, "Non-Contractual Relations in Business."

[19]Milgrom, P., and J. Roberts, *Economics, Organization and Management*, Englewood Cliffs, NJ, Prentice-Hall, 1992.

[20]Qian, Y., Roland, G., and C. Xu, "Coordinating Tasks in – Form and U-Form Organisations" LSE STICERD Research Paper No. TE458, 2003.

[21]Koener, B., ' "Made in America' Small Businesses Buck the Offshoring Trend" *Wired*, March 2011, http://www.wired.com/magazine/2011/02/ff_madeinamerica. Searched March 7, 2011.

[22]Coase, R., "The Nature of the Firm," *Economica*, 4, 1937, pp. 386–405.

[23]Williamson, O., *The Economic Institutions of Capitalism*, New York, Free Press, 1985.

[24]We assume that default or declaring "bankruptcy" is not an option. Once you build the factory, you have to make your mortgage payment no matter what. To justify this assumption, imagine that your company has many other profitable business activities that generate enough cash to cover your mortgage payment on this factory under all circumstances. You would thus be legally obligated to pay your mortgage no matter how unprofitable the factory proves to be.

[25]Rent is synonymous with economic profit. To relate this to an important concept from corporate finance, when an investment has a positive rent, it will have a positive net present value. See the Economics Primer for net present value.

[26]The expression "holdup problem" was coined by Victor Goldberg in his article, "Regulation and Administered Contracts," *Bell Journal of Economics*, 7, Autumn 1976, pp. 426–448.

[27]Hart, O. "Hold-Up, Asset Ownership, and Reference Points" *Quarterly Journal of Economics*, February 2009.

[28]Vukina, T., and P. Leegomonchai, "Oligopsony Power, Asset Specificity, and Hold-Up: Evidence from the Broiler Industry," *American Journal of Agricultural Economics*, 88, 2006, pp. 589–605.

[29]Hart, O. *ibid.*

4

INTEGRATION AND ITS ALTERNATIVES

WHAT DOES IT MEAN TO BE "INTEGRATED?"

In Chapter 3, we described why firms contract and how contractual incompleteness affects decisions to vertically integrate. Firms rely on contracts to protect themselves from exploitation by their trading partners. Complete contracts spell out exactly what actions should be taken by which firms; if contracts were complete, integration would be unnecessary. But contracts are invariably incomplete, so that self-interested firms have leeway to take steps to boost their own profits at the expense of other firms in the vertical chain. The resulting coordination, information leakage, and holdup problems may lead to inefficient production. Integration may be necessary to ensure efficient production and successful competition in the finished goods market.

The Property Rights Theory of the Firm

Performance issues associated with coordination, information, and holdup are not just theoretical constructs. They result when people make inefficient decisions about how to use available resources. Technically speaking, integration is merely the transfer of ownership of assets from one group of individuals to another. Vertical integration does not eliminate the people or the resources involved in production (although the new owner could choose to fire or replace workers and sell or replace physical assets). Nor does vertical integration typically change the steps in the production process. How, then, does integration lead to improved performance?

The Property Rights Theory (PRT) of the firm, developed by Sanford Grossman, Oliver Hart, and John Moore, explains how integration affects performance in the vertical chain.[1] The main proposition of PRT is as follows:

> Integration determines the ownership and control of assets, and it is through ownership and control that firms are able to exploit contractual incompleteness.

In other words, integration matters because it determines who gets to control resources, make decisions, and allocate profits when contracts are incomplete and trading partners disagree. When the wrong firm has ownership rights, efficiency suffers.

The PRT begins with a simple but important observation: the resolution of the make-or-buy decision determines the legal right to control assets and disburse revenues obtained from use of the assets. The owner of an asset may grant another party the right to use it or receive revenues from it, but the owner retains all rights of control that are not explicitly stipulated in the contract. These are known as *residual rights of control*. When ownership is transferred, the residual rights of control are transferred as well.

To clarify the concept of residual rights of control, consider the relationship between PepsiCo and its bottlers. PepsiCo has two types of bottlers: independent and company owned. An independent bottler owns the physical assets of the bottling operation and the exclusive rights to the franchise territory. PepsiCo has no direct authority over how the independent bottler manages its operations. If a bottler refuses to stock particular stores or participate in a national campaign like the famous Pepsi Challenge (launched in 1975), PepsiCo can only try to persuade the bottler to cooperate. Suppose, however, that PepsiCo acquires one of its independent bottlers. Unless stated otherwise in a contract, PepsiCo would have the ultimate authority over how the bottling assets are deployed and how the bottler's territory is managed. If the management of the bottling subsidiary refused to participate in the Pepsi Challenge, PepsiCo could replace them with a more cooperative team.

If contracts were complete, it would not matter who owned the assets. Guided by a complete contract, PepsiCo and its bottlers would always know how to resolve disagreements about marketing campaigns, regardless of who owned whom. Taking incomplete contracting as a starting point, the PRT analyzes how ownership affects the willingness of parties to invest in relationship-specific assets. The theory considers a situation in which two firms (or individuals) enter a transaction with each other. To carry out the transaction, the firms must jointly make an array of operating decisions. The theory assumes that they cannot write a contract that specifies these operating decisions in advance. Instead, they must bargain over them once the transaction is underway. Ownership affects the outcome of this bargain, and therefore ownership affects productive efficiency.

Alternative Forms of Organizing Transactions

To better understand PRT, think of two firms, each of which has its own set of managers. For convenience, we will suppose that firm 1 is upstream from firm 2 in the vertical chain. Decisions made by both sets of managers are important to the efficiency of the vertical chain. Moreover, conditions of supply and demand are such that there is no simple contract that would dictate how each set of managers should act. For example, the market environment might be constantly changing, so that a contract one year ago may not give adequate direction to these managers today.

We can imagine three alternative ways to organize the transaction:

1. *Nonintegration*: The two firms are independent; each set of managers has control over its own assets.
2. *Forward Integration*: Firm 1 owns the assets of firm 2 (i.e., firm 1 forward integrates into the function performed by firm 2 by purchasing control over firm 2's assets).
3. *Backward Integration:* Firm 2 owns the assets of firm 1 (i.e., firm 2 backward integrates into the function performed by firm 1 by purchasing control over firm 1's assets).

PRT establishes that the form of integration affects the incentives of both sets of managers to invest in relationship-specific assets. This includes both *ex ante* investments and ongoing investments and other operating decisions that emerge as the relationship evolves. (Chapter 3 describes these investments and operating decisions.) Because these investments and operating decisions may cost one firm more than another, each set of managers may haggle over responsibilities with the result that there is inefficient adaptation to the changing market environment.

PRT suggests that the form of integration can affect the degree of haggling and maladaptation. Suppose, for example, that firm 1 forward integrates and acquires firm 2. By owning firm 2's assets, the managers of firm 1 have a better bargaining position when they negotiate over the operating decisions that could not be contracted. With a better bargaining position, the managers can capture more of the economic value created by the transaction, thus boosting their willingness to make relationship-specific investments. Both sets of managers would welcome this if the investments were valuable to the relationship because these investments would make the vertical chain more efficient. The theory implies that *vertical integration is desirable when one firm's investment in relationship-specific assets has a significantly greater impact on the value created in the vertical chain than does the other firm's investment.* When the investments of both firms are of comparable importance, nonintegration is the best arrangement, as both firms' managers will have sufficient incentives to invest while remaining independent.

This suggests that there are trade-offs in alternative ownership structures. For example, consider the decision of an insurance company to forward integrate into sales—that is, whether the company should use an in-house sales force or sell through independent agents. A key investment involves the time required to develop "client lists"—lists of actual and potential insurance purchasers. According to PRT, the integration decision should turn on the relative importance of investments in developing persistent clients by the agent versus list-building activities by the insurance firm. If customers are loyal to agents, then investments by agents matter. If customers are loyal to the insurance company, then investments by the company matter. It turns out that a purchaser of whole life insurance tends to remain loyal to the company, while a purchaser of term life insurance tends to be loyal to the agent. PRT implies that whole life insurance would typically be sold through an insurance company's in-house sales force. This is consistent with industry practice: most companies that offer whole life insurance have their own sales forces. By contrast, many insurance companies rely on independent agents who own the client list to sell term life coverage.

By emphasizing the importance of asset ownership, PRT helps us understand certain real-world arrangements that fall between vertical integration and arm's-length market contracting. For example, General Motors and Ford often own their own specialized tooling and dies, even though an independent firm produces body parts and components. This is especially likely for components, such as radiators and starters, that require specialized physical assets but do not require much specialized engineering or operational know-how.[2] Similarly, in the glass bottle industry, large buyers will often retain ownership of specialized molds, even though an independent manufacturer produces the jars and bottles. PRT implies that this is a form of vertical integration and is distinct from the situation in which the independent supplier carries out production and owns the physical asset.

EXAMPLE 4.1   VERTICAL INTEGRATION IN A MOUNTAIN PARADISE

Strategy gurus often say that firms should "stick to their knitting," taking on only those activities they know best. But asset specificity often requires firms to perform activities that are far removed from their core competencies. One happy example took place a century ago in isolated, cold, rugged, and beautiful terrain.

The Banff/Lake Louise region of the Canadian Rockies is truly among the natural wonders of the world. The combination of snow-capped peaks, floral-laden mountain valleys, ice fields, and glacier-fed clear blue lakes is breathtaking. Many travelers believe that Lake Louise is the most picturesque spot on earth, and the mountains near Banff have some of the world's best skiing.

Every year, tens of thousands of tourists visit the region from all over the world. Many are fortunate to stay at the Chateau Lake Louise and the Banff Springs Hotel. The two resorts are situated less than an hour apart and have a combined 1,270 beds. They are frequently listed among the finest resorts in the world and for good reason. Not only do they offer spectacular natural scenery, but both resorts have several fine restaurants, spa facilities, horseback riding, hiking trails, and everything else required for a complete vacation. A popular vacation package includes a three-night stay at each resort. Golfers are especially attracted by the prospect of launching 300+ yard drives from the mile-high tees in Banff.

Until the late nineteenth century, the region around Banff/Lake Louise was known only to a few intrepid explorers and naturalists. The area is accessible by the Bow River, which is fed by Lake Louise glacial waters and flows 400 miles past Calgary before feeding the Saskatchewan River (and eventually Hudson Bay). During the 1880s, the Bow River valley proved to be a perfect location for the Canadian Pacific (CP) Railroad as it laid a section of the transcontinental railroad between Calgary (just east of the Canadian Rockies) and Vancouver. In 1883, CP railway workers discovered natural hot springs at the base of Sulphur Mountain, near the conjunction of the Bow and Spray rivers. Shortly thereafter, Canada established Banff National Park—the nation's first—including the hot springs and the surrounding region. Today, Banff National Park stretches for 2,564 square miles and includes all of Banff and Lake Louise.

Despite the new rail line and national park, few tourists came, mainly because there was no place for them to stay. William Van Horne, the general manager of the Canadian Pacific, struck on a novel idea. Fueled by the philosophy, "If we can't export the scenery, we will import the tourists," he ordered the construction of the Banff Springs Hotel at the base of Sulphur Mountain, as well as a series of other resorts on or near the rail line, to include the Chateau Lake Louise. With CP controlling access to the region, it had no choice but to build these hotels itself. No one else would risk such massive investments when the rail line owned the only means of access.

Once Van Horne's vision was realized, the trains and the resorts filled up. Through the mid-twentieth century, CP continued to build new resorts in the Rockies, as well as expand its flagship resorts in Banff and Lake Louise. The Trans-Canada Highway opened in 1962, creating new opportunities for tourists to access the Canadian Rockies. New motels and hotels sprung up in Banff. (The area around Lake Louise is not large enough to support additional development.) As Calgary boomed following the 1988 Olympics (and its airport began handling more flights), tourism to the region skyrocketed. Today, the town of Banff has 7,500 year-round residents and dozens of motels, hotels, and resorts.

Forced to develop its own expertise in operating luxury hotels, Canadian Pacific has become a leading hotelier worldwide. Now a freestanding subsidiary (in accordance with the advice of the gurus!), Canadian Pacific Hotels acquired the CN hotel chain in 1988 and the world-famous Fairmont chain in 1999. Today, the Banff Springs Hotel and the Chateau Lake Louise operate under the Fairmont name.

GOVERNANCE

In our example above, we assumed that after firm 1 acquired firm 2, the managers of firm 1 could dictate what actions the managers of firm 2 should take. But integration does not turn managers into marionettes or eliminate self-interest. The same managers at firm 2 who sought to gain at the expense of firm 1 when transacting at arm's length may also behave selfishly when working in the same firm. It is often taken for granted that contracting inefficiencies disappear when decision makers are joined in the same organization. But this is not necessarily so. Whether integration reduces or eliminates holdup and coordination problems depends on *governance arrangements*. If we think of contracts as delegating decision rights and control of assets *between* firms, then governance arrangements delegate decision rights and the control of assets *within* firms.

An analogy with contracts suggests a useful way to think about governance. When independent trading partners disagree about the proper course of action or division of rewards, they rely on contracts and the courts to sort things out. When individuals within a firm disagree, they rely on the guidance and authority of the central office to sort things out. The central office must be aware that employees, like independent firms, are tempted to act in their own selfish interests. Through the judicious use of carrots and sticks (i.e., bonuses, promotions, and job terminations) the central office can tame that self-interest and get employees to act in the firm's best interests. The success of integration therefore depends on the central office's ability to reward and punish workers in ways that contracts cannot.

Contracts are effective when rewards and punishments can be based on objective criteria. Thus, it is important for the central office to use excellent judgment in implementing subjective criteria. (Otherwise, there would be no benefit from integration.) Moreover, the central office should be sensitive to those aspects of production that are most likely to break down because of selfishness and contractual incompleteness. Thus, the central office should reward workers who sacrifice to assure coordination of design attributes; the central office should not exploit workers who make firm-specific investments (for example, by withholding salary increases relative to workers who have more general human capital); and the central office should punish workers who hold up coworkers (for example, by demanding resources) to extract quasi-rents.

Delegation

Another critical role of the central office is delegation—determining which decisions will be made by the central office and which will be left to workers. PRT helps clarify which decisions should be delegated. Consider two types of decisions that a worker can make—decisions about how to use physical assets (e.g., equipment) and decisions about how to use human capital (e.g., the time and effort devoted to work). The central office may gain control over physical assets, but it can never gain full control over human capital—it is up to each employee to decide how hard to work. As we previously discussed, PRT concludes that the central decision-making rights for an activity should be given to those managers whose decisions will have the greatest impact on the performance of that activity. Bearing this in mind, if a manager's investment in human capital is essential to the productive use of physical assets, then control over the physical assets should be delegated to the manager. Through delegation, the manager is encouraged to make the necessary human capital investments.

We conclude that when human and physical capital are highly complementary within a given application, then delegate authority. When physical capital is complementary across applications, then centralize. For example, consider a hospital with a surgery suite. If all surgeons in the hospital can benefit from upgrades to the surgery suite, then the hospital should maintain control over upgrade decisions. If the surgery suite has specialized equipment so that it is only suitable for heart surgery, then control of the suite could be delegated to the cardiac surgery team.

Recapping PRT

To summarize, PRT says that the central decision-making rights for an activity should be given to those managers whose decisions will have the greatest impact on the performance of that activity. This leads to several possible merger scenarios:

- If the success of a merger between firms A and B depends on the specialized knowledge of the managers of firm B, then decision authority should be given to the managers of firm B. This would typically mean that firm B should acquire firm A, giving B ownership and control of A's assets. The merger could also succeed if A acquired B, provided that A delegated decision rights to B's managers.
- If success depends on synergies associated with the combined assets of firms A and B, such as through the resolution of coordination or holdup problems between a buyer and a supplier, then A and B should merge and the decision-making authority should be centralized.
- If success depends equally on the specialized knowledge of both firms' managers and there are no synergies from combining assets, then A and B should remain independent.

Path Dependence

Of course, governance arrangements are not always optimal. Often, the process by which governance develops exhibits *path dependence*. That is, past circumstances could exclude certain possible governance arrangements in the future. For example, if the period following a merger is marked by conflict, an efficient governance structure requiring cooperation between acquired and acquiring firm managers might not be feasible. These same considerations will also apply to disintegration. One might expect a business unit that was spun off to the market to act as an independent market firm. Initially, however, managers in that unit will not be used to making decisions as an autonomous market actor and may continue to rely on associations with managers in the former parent firm. This would make the relationship between the two firms after a spinoff not a market transaction, but rather a long-term informal association, which is somewhere between being part of an integrated firm and a specialized market actor.

The path-dependent nature of the processes by which firms develop can also affect the firm's capacity to sell the products of a unit to other downstream buyers besides itself. In Chapter 3, we suggested that market specialists could gain economies of scale by selling to multiple downstream buyers. Firms manufacturing for internal use do not typically sell excess output to other firms because this would be both a distraction and an activity for which the firm lacked the requisite skills. If a firm acquired rather than built its supply capacity, however, the situation would be different. The acquired firm would know how to sell to multiple buyers. This marketing capacity would presumably be one of the resources acquired by the parent through the merger. In such a situation, selling product produced primarily for internal uses to outside firms would be neither a distraction nor an activity for which the firm lacked resources. The firm's opportunities for selling to other users of the product could still be limited by competitive conditions, however.

MAKING THE INTEGRATION DECISION

Assuming that firms get governance right, integration can prevent coordination problems and holdup. But even the most diligent central office cannot replicate the hard-edged incentives of the market, or enable the integrated firm to achieve the same scale and learning economies as a market specialist. We have not yet systematically studied how these forces for and against integration trade off against one another in particular circumstances. We must do this to understand why vertical integration differs across industries (e.g., firms in the aluminum industry are generally more vertically integrated than firms in the tin industry), across firms within the same industry (e.g., Hyundai is more vertically integrated than Honda), and across different transactions within the same firm (e.g., U.S. firms tend to outsource transportation services to a much greater degree than warehousing or inventory management).

Technical Efficiency versus Agency Efficiency

The costs and benefits of relying on the market can be classified as relating to either *technical efficiency* or *agency efficiency*. Technical efficiency has several interpretations in economics. A narrow interpretation is that it represents the degree to which a firm produces as much as it can from a given combination of inputs. A broader interpretation—the one used in this chapter—is that technical efficiency indicates whether the firm is using the least-cost production process. For example, if efficient production of a particular good requires specialized engineering skills, but the firm has not invested enough to develop those skills, then the firm has not achieved full technical efficiency. The firm could achieve technical efficiency by purchasing the good in question from a market firm or by investing to develop the skills itself.

Agency efficiency refers to the extent to which the exchange of goods and services in the vertical chain has been organized to minimize the coordination, agency, and transactions costs discussed in Chapter 3. If the exchange does not minimize these costs, then the firm has not achieved full agency efficiency. To the extent that the process of exchange raises the costs of production (e.g., when the threat of holdup leads to reductions in relationship-specific investments and increases in production costs), we would classify this as an agency inefficiency rather than a technical inefficiency.

The make-or-buy decision often has conflicting implications for agency and technical efficiency. For example, when a computer maker obtains memory chips from the market, the firm may improve its technical efficiency by buying from specialized chip manufacturers. But this arrangement may reduce agency efficiency by necessitating detailed contracts that specify performance and rewards. The appropriate vertical organization of production must balance technical and agency efficiencies. Oliver Williamson, whom we encountered in the last chapter in our discussion of transactions costs, uses the term *economizing* to describe this balancing act.[3]

Williamson argues that the optimal vertical organization minimizes the sum of technical and agency inefficiencies. That is, parties undertaking an exchange along the vertical chain arrange their transactions to minimize the sum of production and transactions costs. To the extent that the market is superior for minimizing production costs but vertical integration is superior for minimizing transactions costs, trade-offs between the two costs are inevitable. Even the best organized firms confront the effects of this trade-off, in the form of higher production costs, bureaucracy, breakdowns in exchange, and litigation.

The Technical Efficiency/Agency Efficiency Trade-off

Figure 4.1 provides a useful way to think about the interplay of agency efficiency and technical efficiency.[4] The figure illustrates a situation in which the quantity of the good being exchanged is fixed at a particular level. The vertical axis measures cost *differences* between internal organization and market transactions. Positive values indicate that costs from the internal organization exceed costs from the market transactions. The horizontal axis measures asset specificity, denoted by k. Higher values of k imply greater asset specificity.

The curve ΔT depicts the differences in technical efficiency. It measures the differences in production costs when the item is produced in a vertically integrated firm and when it is exchanged through an arm's-length market transaction. We exclude any differences in production costs that result from differences in incentives to control costs or to invest in cost-reducing process improvements across the two modes of organization. ΔT is positive for any level of asset specificity because outside suppliers can aggregate demands from other buyers and thus can take better advantage of economies of scale and scope to lower production costs than firms that produce those inputs themselves. The cost difference declines with asset specificity because greater asset specificity implies more specialized uses for the input and thus fewer outlets for the outside supplier. As a result, with greater asset specificity, the scale- and scope-based advantages of outside suppliers are likely to be weaker.

FIGURE 4.1
TRADEOFF BETWEEN AGENCY EFFICIENCY AND TECHNICAL EFFICIENCY

The curve ΔT represents the minimum cost of production under vertical integration minus the minimum cost of production under arm's-length market exchange; that is, it reflects differences in technical efficiency. The curve ΔA represents the transactions costs when production is vertically integrated minus the transactions costs when it is organized through an arm's-length market exchange. (This difference includes any increases in production costs over their minimum level that are due to poor incentives or investments that are not made because of the holdup problem.) This curve reflects differences in agency efficiency. The curve ΔC is the vertical sum of ΔT and ΔA and represents the overall cost difference between vertical integration and market exchange.

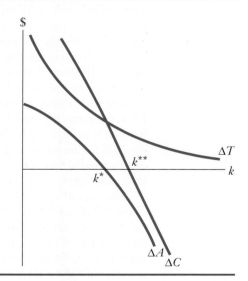

The curve ΔA reflects differences in agency efficiency. It measures differences in exchange costs when the item is produced internally and when it is purchased from an outside supplier in an arm's-length transaction. When the item is purchased from an outside supplier, these costs comprise the direct costs of negotiating the exchange; the costs of writing and enforcing contracts; and the costs associated with holdup and underinvestments in relationship-specific assets that we discussed in Chapter 3. They also include the costs of breakdowns in coordination and leakage of private information, also discussed in Chapter 3. When the item is produced internally, these costs include the agency and influence costs discussed in Chapter 3. In short, the ΔA curve reflects differences in agency efficiency between the two modes of organizing transactions.

The ΔA curve is positive for low levels of asset specificity ($k < k^*$) and negative for high levels of asset specificity. When asset specificity is low, holdup is not a significant problem. In the absence of significant holdup problems, market exchange is likely to be more agency efficient than vertical integration because, as discussed in Chapter 3, independent firms often face stronger incentives to innovate and control production costs than divisions of a vertically integrated firm. As asset specificity increases, the transactions costs of market exchange also increase, and beyond a critical level, k^*, these costs are so large that vertical integration is more agency efficient than market exchange.

The curve ΔC is the vertical summation of the ΔA and ΔT curves. It represents production and exchange costs under vertical integration minus production and exchange costs under market exchange. If this curve is positive, then arm's-length market exchange is preferred to vertical integration. If the curve is negative, the exchange costs of using the market more than offset the production costs savings, and vertical integration is preferred. As shown in Figure 4.1, market exchange is preferred when asset specificity is sufficiently low ($k < k^{**}$). When asset specificity is greater than k^{**}, vertical integration is the preferred mode of organizing the transaction.

Vertical integration becomes increasingly attractive as the economies of scale in production become less pronounced. To see this point, recall that the height of the ΔT curve reflects the ability of an independent producer to achieve scale economies in production by selling to other firms. Weaker economies of scale would correspond to a downward shift in ΔT and ΔC, which in turn results in a wider range in which vertical integration is preferred to arm's-length market contracting. In the extreme case, as economies of scale disappear, the ΔT curve coincides with the horizontal axis, and the choice between vertical integration and market procurement is determined entirely by agency efficiency, that is, the ΔA curve.

Figure 4.2 shows what happens to the choice between market contracting and vertical integration as the scale of the transaction increases. There are two effects. First, the vertically integrated firm could now take fuller advantage of scale economies because it produces a higher output. This reduces the production-cost disadvantage of internal organization and shifts the ΔT curve downward. Second, increasing the scale of the transaction accentuates the advantage of whichever mode of production has lower exchange costs. Thus, the ΔA curve would "twist" clockwise through the point k^*. The overall effect of these two shifts moves the intersection point of the ΔC curve to the left, from k^{**} to k^{***}. (The solid lines are the shifted curves; the dashed lines are the original curves.) This widens the range in which vertical integration is the preferred mode of organization. Put another way, as the scale of the transaction goes up, vertical integration is more likely to be the preferred mode of organizing the transaction for any given level of asset specificity.

FIGURE 4.2

**THE EFFECT OF INCREASED SCALE ON TRADE-OFF BETWEEN
AGENCY EFFICIENCY AND TECHNICAL EFFICIENCY**

As the scale of the transaction increases, the firm's demand for the input goes up, and a vertically integrated firm can better exploit economies of scale and scope in production. As a result, its production-cost disadvantage relative to a market specialist firm will go down, so the curve ΔT will shift downward. (The dashed lines represent the curves at the original scale of the transaction; the solid lines represent the curves when the scale of the transaction increases.) At the same time, increased scale accentuates the advantage of the organizational mode with the lowest exchange costs. Thus, curve ΔA twists clockwise through point k^*. As a result, the intersection of the ΔC curve with the horizontal axis moves leftward, from k^{**} to k^{***}, expanding the range in which vertical integration is the least-cost organizational mode.

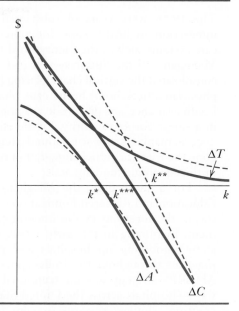

Figures 4.1 and 4.2 yield three powerful conclusions about vertical integration:

1. *Scale and Scope Economies*: We know that a firm gains less from vertical integration when outside market specialists are better able to take advantage of economies of scale and scope. We also know from Chapter 2 that a key source of economies of scale and scope is "indivisible," upfront "setup" costs, such as investments in physical capital or in the development of production know-how. It follows that *if the firm is considering whether to make or buy an input requiring significant upfront setup costs, and there is a large market outside the firm for the input, then the firm should buy the input from outside market specialists*. This will often be the case for routine products and services that are capital intensive or benefit from a steep learning curve.

2. *Product Market Share and Scope*: The more the firm produces, the more its demand for inputs grows. This increases the likelihood that in-house input production can take as much advantage of economies of scale and scope as an outside market specialist. It follows that *a firm with a larger share of the product market will benefit more from vertical integration than a firm with a smaller share of the product market*. It also implies that *a firm with multiple product lines will benefit more from being vertically integrated in the production of shared components*. It will benefit less from being vertically integrated in the production of components for "boutique" or "niche" items that it produces on a small scale.

3. *Asset Specificity*: A firm gains more from vertical integration when production of inputs involves investments in relationship-specific assets If asset specificity is significant enough, vertical integration will be more profitable than arm's-length market purchases, even when production of the input is characterized by strong scale economies or when the firm's product market scale is small.

EXAMPLE 4.2 GONE IN A HEARTBEAT: THE ALLEGHENY HEALTH EDUCATION AND RESEARCH FOUNDATION BANKRUPTCY

The 1990s were years of substantial vertical integration in health care. Integrated health care systems such as the Henry Ford Clinic in Michigan and the Sutter system in California consolidated the vertical chain, placing hospitals, physician offices, home health care, pharmacies, health insurance, and diagnostic imaging facilities in a single corporate entity. By the end of the decade, many systems were foundering, having gone the route of vertical integration regardless of the economic fundamentals.

For a short time, the Allegheny Health Education and Research Foundation (AHERF) was at the forefront of the integration movement. Beginning in the early 1990s, AHERF started gobbling up hospitals and physician practices throughout the Philadephia market. AHERF's strategy was unexceptional in most ways—hospitals across the United States were creating similar systems—except AHERF moved faster than most and piled on loads of debt in the process. The economic motivation was "bigger is better," and few in the industry (except for a few skeptical economists) were arguing otherwise. AHERF even partially integrated into health insurance, following yet another trend that would prove disastrous. AHERF's CEO Sherif Abdelhak was widely admired for riding the integration wave harder and, it seemed, more successfully than anyone else.

But bigger did not prove to be better. AHERF could not achieve economies of scale because it was unable to integrate clinical services across hospitals. The reason should have been anticipated but was not: it was difficult, if not impossible, to convince physicians to move their practices from one hospital to another. (The same problem plagued horizontal integration efforts throughout the nation.) AHERF suffered even more from its vertical strategies. AHERF competed with other hospital systems to acquire physician practices, often paying substantial premiums above the practice earnings. Once they became employees, the acquired physicians slacked off, working shorter hours and not even trying to increase referrals to AHERF hospitals. (Some studies suggest that physician effort declined by as much as 10 percent after acquisition.) And AHERF proved to be a naïve player in the health insurance business. AHERF allowed private insurers to sign up policy holders, but AHERF remained responsible for all the medical costs. As a result, insurers grew lax in medical underwriting (the practice of predicting the medical needs of enrollees), leaving AHERF exposed to an undesirable, unattractive risk pool. Systems like AHERF had margins of −10 percent or worse on their insurance business.

In 1997, AHERF was bankrupt. In a heartbeat, AHERF went from the industry darling to owing creditors $1.5 billion, making this the largest nonprofit bankruptcy in U.S. history. By 2000, the vertical integration wave in health care was over. Hospitals were spinning off their physician practices and getting out of the insurance business. Health care systems are again on the rise, but this time they are built around integration of clinical information technology and disease management systems, both of which require considerable asset specificity and coordination.

REAL-WORLD EVIDENCE

Evidence suggests that many real-world firms behave in accordance with these principles. The evolution of the modern hierarchical firm discussed in Chapter 1 is consistent with the product market scale and the asset-specificity rationales for integration. A key step in the growth of the modern firm was forward integration by manufacturers into marketing and distribution. Between 1875 and 1900, technological breakthroughs allowed for unprecedented economies of scale in manufacturing industries. This, coupled with improvements in transportation and communication that expanded the scope of markets, led to vast increases in the size of firms in capital-intensive industries, such as steel, chemicals, food processing, and light machinery.

As these firms grew, independent wholesaling and marketing agents lost much of their scale- and scope-based cost advantages. As this happened, manufacturers forward integrated into marketing and distribution, a result consistent with the firm-size hypothesis. As predicted by the asset-specificity hypothesis, forward integration was most likely to occur for products that required specialized investments in human capital (e.g., George Eastman's marketing of cameras and film) or in equipment and facilities (e.g., Gustavus Swift's refrigerated warehouses and boxcars). For those industries in which manufacturers remained small (e.g., furniture or textiles) and/or marketing and distribution did not rely on specialized assets (e.g., candy), manufacturers continued to rely on independent commercial intermediaries to distribute and sell their products.

Around the time of the publication of Williamson's *The Economic Institutions of Capitalism*, (which we discussed in Chapter 3), strategy researchers looked for real-world validation of transactions cost theory. Consider these examples:

Automobiles In a classic and oft-cited study, Kirk Monteverde and David Teece examined the choice between vertical integration and market procurement of components by General Motors and Ford.[5] Monteverde and Teece surveyed design engineers to determine the importance of applications engineering effort in the design of 133 different components. Greater applications engineering effort is likely to involve greater human asset specificity, so Monteverde and Teece hypothesized that car makers would be more likely to produce components that required significant amounts of applications engineering effort and more likely to buy components that required small amounts of applications engineering effort. Their analysis of the data confirmed this hypothesis. They also found that GM was more vertically integrated than Ford on components with the same asset specificity. This is consistent with the firm-size hypothesis.

Aerospace Industry Scott Masten studied the make-or-buy decision for nearly 2,000 components in a large aerospace system.[6] He asked procurement managers to rate the design specificity of the components—that is, the extent to which the component was used exclusively by the company or could be easily adapted for use by other aerospace firms or firms in other industries. Consistent with the asset-specificity hypothesis, Masten found that greater design specificity increased the likelihood that production of the component was vertically integrated. He also studied the effect of the complexity of the component, that is, the number of relevant performance dimensions and the difficulty in assessing satisfactory performance. When the item being purchased is complex, parties in an arm's-length market transaction find it hard to protect themselves with contracts. As theory predicts, Masten found that more complex components were more likely to be manufactured internally.

Electric Utility Industry Paul Joskow studied the extent of backward integration by electric utilities into coal mining.[7] Coal-burning electricity-generating plants are sometimes located next to coal mines. Co-location reduces the costs of shipping coal and encourages investments that maximize operating efficiency. The utility in a "mine-mouth" operation will typically design its boilers with tight tolerances to accommodate the quality of coal from that particular mine. The utility may also make large investments in rail lines and transmission capacity, and the mine will often expand its capacity to supply the on-site utilities. The relationship between the utility and the mine thus involves both site and physical-asset specificity. Joskow found that mine-mouth plants are much more likely to be vertically integrated than other plants. Where mine-mouth plants were not vertically integrated, Joskow found that coal suppliers relied on long-term supply contracts containing numerous safeguards to prevent holdup.

Electronic Components   Erin Anderson and David Schmittlein studied vertical integration between electronics manufacturers and sales representatives.[8] Manufacturers' reps operate like the sales department of a firm except that they usually represent more than one manufacturer and work on a commission. Anderson and Schmittlein surveyed territory sales managers in 16 major electronics component manufacturers to determine the extent to which they relied on independent reps or on their own sales forces in a given sales territory for a given product. The survey measured the amount of asset specificity in the selling function and the degree of difficulty in evaluating a salesperson's performance. The measure of asset specificity embraced such factors as the amount of time a salesperson would have to spend learning about the company's product, the extent to which selling the product would necessitate extra training, and the importance of the personal relationship between the salesperson and the customer. Anderson and Schmittlein found that greater asset specificity in the selling function was associated with a greater likelihood that firms rely on their own sales forces rather than manufacturers' reps. They also found that holding asset specificity constant, larger manufacturers were more likely to use a direct sales force than smaller firms. Finally, they found that the more difficult it was to measure performance, the more likely manufacturers were to rely on direct sales forces. All of these findings are consistent with theories of vertical integration.

Automobiles Redux   Although the concepts are so well established that it has become less fashionable to publish research on transactions costs, a recent study by Sharon Novak and Scott Stern explores some of the nuances of the theory.[9] They observe that outsourcing "facilitates access to cutting-edge technology and the use of high-powered performance contracts," while vertical integration allows firms to adapt to unforeseen circumstances and develop firm-specific capabilities over time. Taken together, these factors suggest that firms may achieve higher initial performance by outsourcing but may have greater ability to improve performance by moving production in-house. Evidence from the luxury automobile segment confirms these ideas. More highly integrated manufacturers have poorer initial quality but also enjoy significantly faster quality improvements. The benefits of integration are higher when firms have greater preexisting capabilities and fewer opportunities to access external technology leaders.

Double Marginalization: A Final Integration Consideration

When a firm with market power (e.g., an input supplier) contemplates vertical integration with another firm with market power (e.g., a manufacturer), it needs to consider one additional factor known as *double marginalization*. Recall from the Economics

EXAMPLE 4.3 VERTICAL INTEGRATION OF THE SALES FORCE IN THE INSURANCE INDUSTRY

In the insurance industry, some products (e.g., whole life insurance) are usually sold through in-house sales forces, while other products (e.g., fire and casualty insurance) are mainly sold through independent brokers. The Grossman/Hart/Moore (GHM) theory helps us understand this pattern. Relying on independent agents versus in-house sales employees is essentially a choice by the insurance firm for nonintegration versus forward integration into the selling function. This choice determines the ownership of an extremely important asset in the process of selling insurance: the list of clients. Under nonintegration, the agent controls this key asset; under forward integration, the insurance firm controls it.

If the agent owns the client list, the agent controls access to its clients; clients cannot be solicited without the agent's permission. A key role of an insurance agent is to search out and deliver dependable clients to the insurance company, clients who are likely to renew their insurance policies in the future. To induce an agent to do this, the commission structure must be "backloaded," for example, through a renewal commission that exceeds the costs of servicing and re-signing the client. When the insurance company owns the client list, however, this commission structure creates incentives for the company to hold up the agent. It could threaten to reduce the likelihood of renewal (e.g., by raising premiums or restricting coverage) unless the agent accepts a reduced renewal commission. Faced with the possibility of this holdup problem, the agent would presumably underinvest in searching out and selling insurance to repeat clients. By contrast, if the agent owned the client list, the potential for holdup by the insurance company would be much weaker. If the company did raise premiums or restrict coverage, the agent could invite its client to switch companies. Threats by the company to jeopardize the agent's renewal premium would thus have considerably less force, and underinvestment in the search for persistent clients

would not be a problem. In some circumstances, the holdup problem could work the other way. Suppose the insurance company can engage in list-building activities such as new product development. The agent could threaten not to offer the new product to the customer unless the insurance company paid the agent a higher commission. Faced with the prospect of this holdup, the company is likely to underinvest in developing new products. By contrast, if the insurance company owned the list, this type of holdup could not occur, and the insurance company's incentive to invest in new product development would be much stronger.

This suggests that there are trade-offs in alternative ownership structures that are similar to those discussed above. According to the GHM theory, the choice between an in-house sales force versus independent agents should turn on the relative importance of investments in developing persistent clients by the agent versus list-building activities by the insurance firm. Given the nature of the product, a purchaser of whole life insurance is much less likely to switch insurance companies than, say, a customer of fire and casualty insurance. Thus, the insurance agent's effort in searching out persistent clients is less important for whole life insurance than it is for fire and casualty insurance. For whole life insurance, then, backloading the commission structure is not critical, which diminishes the possibility of contractual holdup when the insurance company owns the client list.

The GHM theory prediction that whole life insurance would typically be sold through an insurance company's in-house sales force is consistent with industry practice: most companies that offer whole life insurance have their own sales forces. By contrast, for term life or standard insurance, the agent's selling and renewal-generation efforts are relatively more important. Consistent with the GHM theory, many insurance companies rely on independent agents who own the client list to sell these products.

Primer that a firm with market power sets its price above marginal costs. Double marginalization results when an upstream supplier exploits its power by marking up prices above marginal costs, and the downstream buyer exploits its own power by applying yet another markup to these already marked-up supply prices. This "double markup" causes the price of the finished good to exceed the price that maximizes the joint profits of the supplier and buyer. (As explained in the Economics Primer, a firm with market power can charge a price that is so high that its profits fall.) Through integration, the downstream firm can base its markup on the actual marginal costs of production, rather than the artificially inflated supply prices set by the independent supplier. In this way, the integrated firm uses just the right amount of market power and maximizes its profits. Although the concept of double marginalization receives considerable attention in microeconomics textbooks, very few mergers appeared to be undertaken to address this problem.

ALTERNATIVES TO VERTICAL INTEGRATION

There are a variety of alternatives between "make" and "buy." In this section we consider four "hybrid" ways of organizing exchange: (1) tapered integration, in which the firm both makes and buys a given input; (2) franchising; (3) strategic alliances and joint ventures; and (4) close-knit semiformal relationships among buyers and suppliers, often based on long-term implicit contracts that are supported by reputations for honesty, cooperation, and trust. Each of these alternatives offers a different way to assign ownership and control of assets and creates distinct governance mechanisms. Thus, each offers a distinct resolution of the various trade-offs in the make-or-buy decision.

Tapered Integration: Make and Buy

Tapered integration represents a mixture of vertical integration and market exchange. A manufacturer might produce some quantity of an input itself and purchase the remaining portion from independent firms. It might sell some of its product through an in-house sales force and rely on an independent manufacturers' representative to sell the rest. Examples of tapered integration include such retailers as Tim Hortons (a Canadian chain known for its coffee and donuts) which owns some of its retail outlets but also awards franchises; Coca-Cola and Pepsi, which have their own bottling subsidiaries, but also rely on independently owned bottlers to produce and distribute their soft drinks in some markets; and BMW, whose Corporate Center Development staff conducts market research but also purchases market research from independent firms.

Tapered integration offers several benefits. First, it expands the firm's input and/or output channels without requiring substantial capital outlays. Second, the firm can use information about the cost and profitability of its internal channels to help negotiate contracts with independent channels. Third, the firm can motivate its internal channels by threatening to expand outsourcing, and at the same time motivate its external channels by threatening to produce more in-house. Finally, the firm can protect itself against holdup by independent input suppliers.

Oil refiners provide a classic example of tapered integration. The refinery capacity of the largest companies, such as Exxon Mobil and Shell, greatly exceeds the amount of oil they recover from their own wells. As a result, they make substantial purchases

EXAMPLE 4.4 FRANCHISE HEAT IN CHINA

Franchising is a relatively new business model. The first Kentucky Fried Chicken franchise opened in 1930. Dunkin' Donuts, McDonald's, and Burger King all started in the 1950s. Franchising was not introduced in China until the late 1980s, and until recently individually owned franchises were not the typical way of doing business there. In early days, franchisers in China often operated substandard businesses, and some may have defrauded franchisees of money. At the same time, franchisees delayed payments to franchisers, and a few infringed on their intellectual property rights. In 1997, the Ministry of Internal Trade established the first Chinese franchise law, leading to a dramatic rise in franchising. By the end of 2010, there were more than 4,500 different franchisers and over 400,000 franchise stores in China, covering 70 industries.

KFC was one of earliest foreign entries and has become the most successful Western fast-food chain in China since it first came to Beijing in 1987. Today there are over 3,300 KFC restaurants in more than 700 cities, with a new KFC opening nearly every day. As a franchiser, KFC sources food from local suppliers and has changed its menu to suit Chinese tastes. In China's KFCs, you can order a typical Kentucky Fried Chicken meal as well as Sichuan spicy sauce and rice, egg soup, or a "dragon twister" (KFC's take on a traditional Beijing duck wrap), all washed down with some soybean milk. The parent company of KFC, Yum! Inc., also introduced Pizza Hut and Taco Bell and its combined 3,900 Chinese franchises earned more revenue than all 19,000 Yum! Brand restaurants in the United States. In April 2011, Yum! made an offer to acquire virtually all the shares of Little Sheep, a very successful domestic hotpot restaurant chain of China, with the intention to further expand its franchise chain in China.

Numerous Chinese restaurants have also found franchising to be a profitable way to expand. A good example is Quanjude, a 147-year-old restaurant famous for its Peking Roast Duck that it has served to many of the world's leading politicians and celebrities. After decades of success under the planned economy, Quanjude started to face fierce competition from both domestic and foreign restaurant brands. In order to expand business and popularize the brand name, it launched a major program of expansion in 1993. Quanjude opened company-owned restaurants in major cities like Beijing and Shanghai, where it could better monitor store operations. In smaller cities, Quanjude relies more on franchisees, who are more familiar with the local market. By scaling, modernizing, and franchising, this century-old company had a boom in business and successfully went public in November 2007. But franchising has not gone smoothly; the company's profits still mostly come from company-owned restaurants in the Beijing area.

Over recent years, franchises in other industries are emerging, with service franchises experiencing the sharpest growth. Dongfangaiyin first introduced the concept of early childhood education into China in 1999 and now has 400 franchise education centers in more than 180 cities. Franchising is especially valuable in this industry due to the highly diversified needs across the Chinese population in different areas. At the same time, foreign leading brands in early childhood education such as Gymboree from the United States and KindyROO from Australia have entered the Chinese market with hundreds of franchises of their own. These companies provide training programs to ensure that the standards of teaching and service quality are in sync with those of the parent company. With advanced education concepts and Western-style education, they are usually more popular in bigger cities. With a burgeoning middle class in midsize and small cities, the early education franchising market is likely to see further growth.

of oil in the open market. This forces their internal production divisions to stay competitive with independent oil producers.

If tapered integration offers the best of both the make-and-buy worlds, it may also offer the worst. Forced to share production, both the internal and external channels might not achieve sufficient scale to produce efficiently. Shared production may lead to coordination problems if the two production units must agree on product specifications and delivery times. Moreover, a firm's monitoring problems may be exacerbated. For example, the firm may mistakenly establish the performance of an inefficient internal supplier as the standard to be met by external suppliers. Finally, managers may maintain inefficient internal capacity rather than close facilities that had formerly been critical to the firm. An example of this approach is the excess capacity for internal productions maintained by major movie studios.

Franchising

Many of the world's best known companies are franchise operations. A typical franchiser, such as McDonald's restaurants and SPAR convenience stores, starts out as a local business. If the business thrives, the owner may wish to expand to new markets. Rather than borrow money and open new stores themselves, the franchiser (e.g., McDonald's Corporation) gives partial ownership rights to franchisees (e.g., owners of local McDonald's restaurants). Franchising allows small-business owners such as Ray Kroc (McDonald's) and Adriaan van Well (SPAR) to grow rapidly. Franchisees put up the capital to build and operate their stores and pay a fee for the right to use the franchiser's name and business model. Franchisers may also require franchisees to purchase from designated suppliers, offer specific products, and conform to architectural and design guidelines.

The economics of vertical integration helps explain the attractiveness of franchising. The franchiser performs tasks that involve substantial scale economies, such as purchasing and branding. Franchisees keep their residual profits, giving them strong incentives to make investments to serve their local markets, such as identifying good locations and tailoring product selections to local tastes. By allocating decision rights in these ways, there is little lost and much gained by dispersing ownership of individual franchises. Franchisers do sometimes face free-riding problems as retailers benefit from the corporate brand reputation. For example, a McDonald's franchise owner can expect a certain amount of business based on brand name alone and may be tempted to cut corners on quality. This would reflect badly on other McDonald's locations, however, and explains why franchisers often maintain tight quality control through frequent surprise inspections, and by dictating certain aspects of production, including choice of suppliers and employee uniforms.

Strategic Alliances and Joint Ventures

Since the 1970s, firms have increasingly turned to strategic alliances as a way to organize complex business transactions collectively without sacrificing autonomy. Alliances may be horizontal, involving collaboration between two firms in the same industry, as when Sina (China's main Internet portal) and Yahoo partnered to offer auction services in China. They may be vertical, such as when Moroccan tile manufacturer Le Mosaiste teamed up with Los Angeles interior designer Vinh Diep to create computer-aided design renderings of Le Mosaiste's mosaic tiles in "real-world" living spaces. Or they may involve firms that are neither in the same industry nor

EXAMPLE 4.5 TOYS "Я" US ENTERS JAPAN

In the 1980s, Toys "Я" Us, the leading toy retailer in the United States, was eager to enter the Japanese market. Japan's Large-Scale Retail Store Law required that Toys "Я" Us be approved by Japan's Ministry of International Trade and Industry (MITI) before building its stores. This law, which protected Japan's politically powerful small merchants, made it difficult even for Japanese retailers, such as supermarket operator Daiei, to open large-scale establishments. Toys "Я" Us concluded that it had to find a local partner. It chose a partner that already had considerable experience bringing an iconic American retailing brand name to Japan: McDonald's.

Toys "Я" Us formed an alliance with McDonald's-Japan to help it navigate the politically charged entry process. McDonald's-Japan's president, Den Fujita, was politically well connected and understood the ordeal Toys "Я" Us faced, having built McDonald's-Japan into the largest fast-food operator in the country. He also had a remarkable knowledge of Japanese real estate. "If you name a city," he bragged, "I can see the post office, train station, everything." In 1990, Toys "Я" Us and McDonald's-Japan formed an alliance in which McDonald's took a 20 percent stake in the Toys "Я" Us Japanese unit, Toys "Я" Us Japan. As part of the alliance, 9 of the 11 Toys "Я" Us stores would have a McDonald's restaurant on the premises.

This transaction was a good candidate for an alliance both because it pertained to a small and specific element of both companies' overall business and because it had elements that strongly argued for both "buying" and "making." Toys "Я" Us needed to obtain McDonald's political know-how, site selection expertise, and business connections to enter the Japanese market. It would have been extremely costly, perhaps even impossible, for Toys "Я" Us to have developed this know-how on its own. These considerations argued for Toys "Я" Us "buying" the political and site selection services from the market rather than "making" them itself.

By taking a stake in the success of Toy's "Я" Us's Japanese venture—through both its 20 percent ownership of the venture and the colocation of the Toys "Я" Us stores and McDonald's restaurants—McDonald's faced hard-edged incentives to carry out its part of the bargain. For example, McDonald's-Japan estimated that a McDonald's restaurant located inside a Toys "Я" Us store would generate three times more customers than a stand-alone restaurant would. The potential payoff from this venture gave McDonald's-Japan a strong incentive to work hard on behalf of Toys "Я" Us. The alliance enabled Toys "Я" Us to obtain the political services and site selection know-how it needed without having to make costly investments of its own. The alliance also avoided the difficult incentive problems that might have arisen had Toys "Я" Us relied on traditional market contracting to obtain the services and know-how it needed.

Today, there are about 170 Toys "Я" Us and Babies "Я" Us stores situated on all three major islands of Japan, as well as two distribution centers. McDonald's also remains strong in Japan, although it recently closed over 400 poorly performing stores (leaving over 3,000 still in operation). But the McDonald's/ Toys "Я" Us affiliation came to an end in 2008 when McDonald's sold its stake in the joint venture to Toys "Я" Us following a legal dispute over business consulting services that McDonald's was supposed to provide to Toys "Я" Us.

related through the vertical chain, as when Toys "Я" Us and McDonald's of Japan allied to build Toys "Я" Us stores in Japan that would include a McDonald's restaurant (see Example 4.5).

A joint venture is a particular type of strategic alliance in which two or more firms create, and jointly own, a new independent organization. The new organization may be staffed and operated by employees of one or more parent firms, or it may be staffed independently of either. Examples of joint ventures include Sony and Samsung's S-LCD, which manufactures LCD panels for televisions; NEC Lenovo Japan Group, which develops low-cost PCs for the Japanese market; and Cemex and Ready Mix, which share cement production and distribution.

Alliances and joint ventures fall somewhere between arm's-length market transactions and full vertical integration. As in arm's-length market transactions, the parties to the alliance remain independent. However, an alliance typically involves more cooperation, coordination, and information sharing than would occur in an arm's-length transaction. Kenichi Ohmae has likened a strategic alliance to a marriage: "There may be no formal contract. . . . There are few, if any, rigidly binding provisions. It is a loose, evolving kind of relationship."[10] Like a marriage, the participants in an alliance rely on norms of trust and reciprocity rather than on contracts to govern their relationship, and they resolve disputes through negotiation rather than through litigation.

What kinds of business transactions should be organized through alliances? The most natural candidates for alliances are transactions for which, using the framework in Chapter 3, there are compelling reasons to both make *and* buy. Specifically, transactions that are natural candidates for alliances have all or most of the following features:

1. The transaction involves impediments to comprehensive contracting. For example, the transacting parties know that as their relationship unfolds, they will need to perform a complex set of activities. But because of uncertainty and the parties' bounded rationality, the parties cannot write a contract that specifies how decisions about these activities are supposed to be made.
2. The transaction is complex, not routine. Standard commercial and contract law could not easily "fill the gaps" of incomplete contracts.
3. The transaction involves the creation of relationship-specific assets by both parties in the relationship, and each party to the transaction could hold up the other.
4. It is excessively costly for one party to develop all of the necessary expertise to carry out all of the activities itself. This might be due to indivisibilities or the presence of an experience curve.
5. The market opportunity that creates the need for the transaction is either transitory, or it is uncertain that it will continue on an ongoing basis. This makes it impractical for the independent parties to merge or even commit themselves to a long-term contract.
6. The transaction or market opportunity occurs in a contracting or regulatory environment with unique features that require a local partner who has access to relationships in that environment. For example, the strong role that the Chinese government plays in regulating foreign investment requires that nearly all foreign ventures in China are joint ventures with Chinese partners.

Although alliances can combine the best features of making and buying, they can also suffer from the drawbacks of both making and buying. For example, just as traditional market transactions involve a risk of leaking private information, independent firms that collaborate through alliances also risk losing control over proprietary information. The risk of information leakage can often be more severe in an alliance than in a traditional market transaction because the conditions that tend to make an alliance desirable (complex, ambiguous transactions that do not lend themselves to comprehensive contracting) often force the parties to exchange a considerable amount of closely held information.

In addition, although the loose, evolving governance structure of an alliance can help the parties adapt to unforeseen events, it may also compromise coordination between the firms. Unlike an "inside-the-firm" transaction, in an alliance there are often no formal mechanisms for making decisions or resolving disputes expeditiously. The "footprints" of this are delay and lack of focus, problems that plagued the highly publicized alliances between IBM and Apple in the early 1990s. These alliances were supposed to develop a new operating system, a multimedia software language, and the PowerPC. Instead, by 1994 IBM's senior management had become so frustrated in its protracted negotiations with Apple over the operating system for the PowerPC that it concluded it would have been better off acquiring Apple rather than dealing with it through an alliance.

Finally, just as agency costs can arise within departments of firms that are not subject to market discipline, alliances can also suffer from agency and influence costs. Agency costs in alliances can arise because the fruits of the alliance's efforts are split between two or more firms. This can give rise to a free-rider problem. Each firm in the alliance is insufficiently vigilant in monitoring the alliance's activities because neither firm captures the full benefit of such vigilance. Firms that repeatedly engage in alliances may be less prone to free ride, lest they establish a reputation that precludes them from finding future partners. Influence costs can arise because the absence of a formal hierarchy and administrative system within an alliance can encourage employees to engage in influence activity, such as lobbying, to augment their resources and enhance their status.

Implicit Contracts and Long-Term Relationships

Strategists pay a lot of attention to organizational structure; corporate executives often agonize over whether to make, buy, or ally. But the pressure to make the right decision is considerably lessened in the presence of *implicit contracts*. An implicit contract is an unstated understanding between independent parties in a business relationship. When implicit contracts are honored, they can substitute for complete contracts, rendering the make-or-buy decision moot. Implicit contracts are generally not enforceable in court, however. Nor is there a central office that can resolve disputes through governance. Parties to an implicit contract must rely on alternative mechanisms to make the understanding viable. A powerful mechanism that makes implicit contracts viable is the threat of losing future business if one party breaks the implicit contract for its own gain.[11]

To see why the threat to withdraw future business can be so powerful, imagine two firms in the vertical chain that routinely transact business with each other. Their longstanding relationship has enabled them to coordinate their activities through formal planning and monitoring of product quality, and as a result, both firms have profited significantly. In particular, suppose that the upstream firm sells inputs to the downstream firm for a $1 million profit every year, and the downstream firm processes the inputs and sells a finished product to consumers for a $1 million profit of its own. Each firm has an alternative trading partner, but each would only reap profits of $900,000 per year if forced to switch.

Although each firm apparently has no reason to switch, the relationship has a potential complication. Each firm could increase its profit at the expense of the other by performing less of the planning and monitoring that make the relationship successful. Specifically, suppose that the upstream firm estimates that by breaking its implied commitments to the downstream firm, it could boost its annual profits to $1.2 million. If it does this, however, the downstream firm will learn that it has broken its commitments, and the relationship will end. Each firm would then be forced to do business with another trading partner.

How much does the upstream firm benefit by honoring its implicit contract indefinitely? In one year, it earns $100,000 more by transacting with the downstream firm than with its alternative trading partner. If the firm's discount rate is 5 percent, the net present value of honoring the implicit contract indefinitely would be $2 million.[12] This far exceeds the short-term (i.e., one-year) increase in profit of $200,000 from breaking the contract. Indeed, to make breaking the implicit contract worthwhile, the discount rate would have to be 50 percent! This high hurdle for switching helps sustain the implicit contract.

Thomas Palay's study of rail freight contracting illustrates the power of long-term relationships in sustaining cooperative behavior.[13] He discusses a railroad that purchased specially designed auto-rack railcars to move a particular make of automobile for a major auto manufacturer. Soon after the railroad made the investment, however, the manufacturer changed the design of the car, making the auto racks obsolete. Even though it was not contractually obligated to do so, the manufacturer compensated the railroad for more than $1 million to cover the unamortized portion of the investment. The director of shipping at the automobile manufacturer alluded to the importance of maintaining a long-term relationship as the basis for this action. "We've got to keep them healthy, viable, and happy to guarantee that we'll get the equipment we need, when we need it."

There are many implicit contracts within firms. Workers often expect raises and promotions later in their job tenure if they work hard early on, even if such rewards are not specified in any contract. Andre Shleifer and Lawrence Summers suggest that hostile corporate takeovers are often motivated by shareholders' desire to renege on implicit contracts with employees who have made relationship-specific investments in the firms they work for.[14] A serious consequence of this—and why, according to Shleifer and Summers, hostile takeovers could hurt the economy—is that in a climate of hostile takeovers, employees will refrain from investing in relationship-specific skills in their firms. This will reduce productivity and raise production costs.

To support their argument, Shleifer and Summers quote from William Owen's book, *Autopsy of a Merger*, about the merger between Trans Union and the Pritzker family's Marmon Group. Most of the employees at Trans Union's corporate head-quarters lost their jobs after the merger, in violation of what many of them felt was Trans Union management's implicit promise of guaranteed employment. Owen asked former employees what they had learned from the experience. One said that in the future he would be much less willing to invest in his relationship with his employer: "I learned that I should cover my butt the next time around . . . and have my foot out the door immediately the next time it happens. . . . All of a sudden, you find the rug pulled out from under you—and there is nothing you can do about it. . . . You've worked hard for many, many years, tried to do the best job you could for the company—I loved that company—but what do you have to show for it? How can you go to another company and give 100% of your effort?"[15]

In response to stories like this, many countries as well as many U.S. states have enacted business combination laws that create barriers to hostile takeovers. For example, in some places the board of a target firm can move to delay an acquisition by as much as five years, even if shareholders have approved the deal. Marianne Bertrand and Sendhil Mullainathan have shown that when manufacturing facilities are protected by business combination laws, they tend to be less productive and are less likely to close.[16] This suggests that, on balance, it is more important to protect the market for corporate control (discussed in Chapter 2) than to preserve implicit contracts within the firm.

EXAMPLE 4.6   INTERFIRM BUSINESS NETWORKS: THE DOWNSIDES OF KEIRETSU

The business system referred to as keiretsu is usually associated with companies in Japan, but as noted elsewhere, similar networks exist in Hong Kong and South Korea. What about on other continents? There has been considerable debate about whether or not the interrelationships involving Germany's Deutsche Bank (along with Dresdner Bank, and Allianz) can be characterized as a European keiretsu (indeed, some would say it's a "super keiretsu"). Is the essence of the keiretsu relationship the key role played by the bank in the network? While Germany permits more extensive bank ownership and oversight of companies than is allowable in other countries that alone may not elevate the network centered on Deutsche Bank to the level of a keiretsu.

The "lost decade" of the 1990s in Japan underscored the role of the banks in the keiretsus. Even the largest of the Japanese banks saw their portfolios battered by bad loans, so much so that some were forced to merge, in effect erasing delineations between separate networks. Moreover, the large keiretsu banks lost their hegemony over corporate acquisitions; they no longer had the funds, and companies outside the system did. Clearly, sources of financing were the lifeblood of the system, a reality that was all too obvious in the global financial crisis of 2008.

Some scholars have suggested that the decline of the keiretsu system might be for the best if Japan is to compete in the post-financial meltdown global economy. Speaking at a symposium at the Keiza Koho Center in May of 2009, Melissa Schilling (a professor of management at New York University's Stern School of Business) assessed the mixed impacts of keiretsu for innovation by Japanese firms.[17] She noted that there might be benefits to "information liquidity" in the network, which means that information could travel between the partners quite readily and quickly, and with a lot of understanding because any particular organization in the keiretsu has multiple points of contact with other organizations in the keiretsu. "This makes it very likely for them to receive information, and makes it easier for them to understand, interpret, assimilate and utilize the information," Schilling added.

However, there is a downside which arises from the system. The resulting outcome of this system is the separated clusters of firms with an inward focus. As Shilling also adds that, "from research, the one thing we know is that if you have a cluster of firms that repeatedly engages only with each other, innovation will decline because the information within that cluster will become homogeneous and redundant . . . there is not enough novelty to stimulate new ideas and new innovations."[18]

Moreover, innovation is often associated with small start-up firms, and the keiretsu system has had the effect of suppressing entrepreneurship in Japan. Small firms may be suppliers to the larger firms in the networks but lack access to sufficient capital. However, as the network ties diminish, such firms may be better able to compete with both domestic firms and foreign firms that the keiretsu system had excluded. Firms will also seek out more opportunities for collaboration as the amount of business they do in the network diminishes.

It seems clear that for Japanese firms to compete in the new global economy, they must catch up with those firms from other developed countries in the way they expand their presence in emerging markets like India and China. They must also learn to do so using different approaches. Song Jingsheng (professor of global operation management at Duke University Fuqua School of Business) pointed out that the Japanese automobile manufacturers operating in China have tended to cluster in one geographic area, along with their "selected parts suppliers."[19] Song notes that this may stem from a desire to ensure product quality, but also suggests that it may have something to do with Japanese management style being translated into a Chinese environment. As she puts it, "promoting Chinese managers in their local operation may open up channels of communication with Chinese employees and other suppliers."[20] The management teams of Japanese firms may have to rethink the implications of closed networks.

Business Groups

For much of the past half century, Japanese and South Korean firms did not organize the vertical chain through arm's-length contracts, vertical integration, or joint ventures. Nor did they rely on the trust that characterizes implicit contracts. Instead, they relied on a labyrinth of long-term, semiformal relationships between firms up and down the vertical chain. These multinational business groups, known in Japan as *keiretsu* and in South Korea as *chaebol*, were often held up as exemplars of organizational design, not just for businesses in developing nations, but for all businesses. Today, the *keiretsu* seem to have withered away while the *chaebol* no longer enjoy enviable rates of growth and profitability. Even so, giant business groups in developing markets are once again getting the attention of business strategists.

Keiretsu

Ever since the 1960s, business strategists have alternately admired and criticized Japanese *keiretsu*. It has always been difficult for outsiders to decipher the exact structure of *keiretsu*. They involved a complex and fluid web of formalized institutional linkages, as depicted in Figure 4.3. Based on data on banking patterns, corporate board memberships, and social affiliations such as executive "lunch clubs," analysts identified six large *keiretsu*—Mitsubishi, Sumitomo, DKB, Mitsui, Fuyo, and Sanwa. At their peak, each had more than 80 member firms. All *keiretsu* had core banks that facilitate relationships among members, and nearly all had members in key industries such as steel, life insurance, and chemicals. Loose accounting standards allowed members to hide assets and liabilities in each other so as to lower taxes. It is generally thought that each member of a *keiretsu* was the first choice of another *keiretsu* member in all business dealings. Research suggested that this was especially true in vertical relationships involving complex and highly specific parts, as supported by Williamsonian economics.[21] This formalization of vertical and horizontal relationships was to be one of the reasons Japanese corporations outperformed U.S. corporations during the crucial period of 1970–1990. It is difficult to overstate the extent to which some U.S. business strategists encouraged American companies to emulate the *keiretsu*.

Not all business strategists were so sanguine. A major concern was that the *keiretsu* benefited poor-performing members at the expense of more profitable partners, in much the same way that successful divisions in Western conglomerates often cross-subsidize struggling divisions. This was usually done informally in the *keiretsu*, for example, by paying inflated fees to inefficient suppliers. During the 1990s, government ministries often intervened by requiring healthier members to pay a "tax" to their struggling *keiretsu* brethren. Regardless of the mechanism, these cross-subsidies served to buttress members against the risk of failure at the expense of promoting efficiency. Moreover, such risk sharing ran counter to the interests of investors, who could avoid risk by diversifying their portfolios. Thus, even though firms in the *keiretsu* remained independent, they did not face the same hard-edged incentives that normally favor arm's-length transactions.

The close ties between banks and manufacturers helped the *keiretsu* respond quickly to growth opportunities after World War II. Sustained growth of the Japanese postwar economy ensured that the *keiretsu* would thrive, and close relationships among trading partners allowed them to develop high-quality products in complex manufacturing environments such as automobiles and electronics. But Western manufacturers eventually caught up, and the economic downturn that resulted from the bursting of the Japanese real estate bubble in the early 1990s meant that *keiretsu*

FIGURE 4.3
DEBT, EQUITY, AND TRADE LINKAGES IN JAPANESE *KEIRETSU*

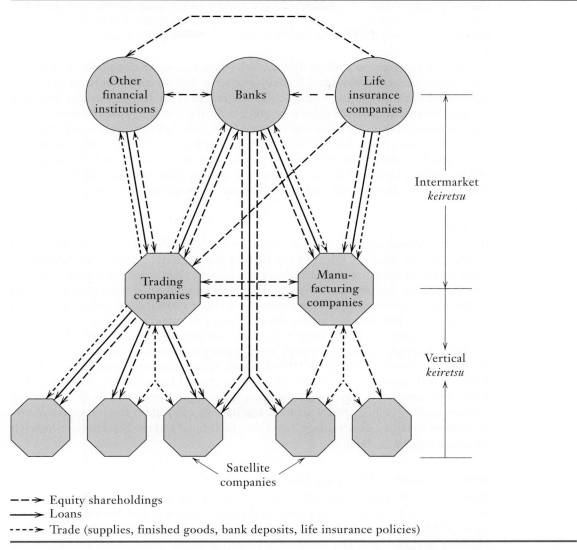

--- ▶ Equity shareholdings
—— ▶ Loans
----▶ Trade (supplies, finished goods, bank deposits, life insurance policies)

The dashed lines show equity holdings within a typical *keiretsu*, the solid lines show loans, and the small dashed lines show the patterns of exchange within the *keiretsu*.
Source: Reprinted by permission of Harvard Business School Press. From Gerlach, M. L., and J. Lincoln, "The Organization of Business Networks in the United States and Japan," in Nohria, N. and R. G. Eccles (eds.), 1994, *Networks and Organizations: Structure, Form, and Action*, Boston, Harvard Business School Press, p. 494.

firms were no longer insulated from macroeconomic conditions. At the same time, the downturn forced the consolidation of banks, followed by consolidation of other industrial members. These unwieldy giants struggled to maintain their close relationships. The last straw may have been changes in accounting rules that had previously favored the *keiretsu*. By the late 1990s, the ties among *keiretsu* members were fraying; even firms that shared the same corporate name, for example, Mitsubishi Automobiles and Mitsubishi Electronics, were no longer closely linked. When Nissan's new CEO Carlos Ghosn dismantled the automaker's supply *keiretsu* in the early 2000s, some Japanese questioned whether this "outsider" understood Japanese culture. But by the end of the decade, Honda and Toyota had also decentralized their supply chains. The traditional *keiretsu* were finished.

Recent research by Yoshior Miwa and J. Mark Ramseyer cast doubt on whether *keiretsu* ever existed.[22] Miwa and Ramseyer observe that executives at firms in a given *keiretsu* belonged to the same lunch clubs and met at other business events, but their business relationships were otherwise quite ordinary. Member firms borrowed substantial amounts from their *keiretsu*'s central bank, but they borrowed nearly as much from other banks. They went outside of the *keiretsu* for other business dealings as well. Miwa and Ramseyer show that *keiretsu* profits were never exceptional. Based on this and other data, Miwa and Ramseyer conclude that the tight-knit and highly profitable structure of the Japanese *keiretsu* is a myth that was perpetuated for 40 years.

Chaebol

Just as the *keiretsu* enjoyed rapid growth in post–World War II Japan, South Korea's *chaebol* enjoyed rapid growth after the Korean War, especially after 1961. *Chaebol* are more varied in structure than *keiretsu*; some feature close relations among independent firms, but the best known—LG, Hyundai, and Samsung—are centralized and controlled by family groups. This assures even closer coordination and investment in specific assets, but also intensifies the drawbacks of integration. The only midsize businesses to thrive in Korea seem to be those that partner with a *chaebol*. *Chaebol* have not been as closely studied as *keiretsu*, and it is not clear whether their success is due to the close ties among members or reflects broader macroeconomic conditions in South Korea, which enjoys a unique mix of a highly trained but relatively low paid labor force. This has always allowed *chaebol* firms to be rapid second movers in technology markets such as cellular phones, but as the pace of innovation has increased, *chaebol* firms seem to be at a disadvantage. Consider the iPhone and the Blackberry, which left Samsung lagging far behind.

Business Groups in Emerging Markets

Widely diversified multinational business groups in emerging markets seem to be taking the world by storm. Along with well-known Japanese and Korean groups like those of Matsushita and Hyundai, strategists are buzzing about Alfa in Mexico, Koc Holding in Turkey, and The Votorantim Group in Brazil. Through his holdings in the Grupo Carso SAB, Mexico's Carlos Slim Helu has become the wealthiest person in the world.

The model for these new business groups may be India's Tata Group. Nearly a century and a half old, Tata businesses have been operating in India since 1868. The family-run group, under the leadership of Ratan Tata since 1991, is India's largest private-sector employer, with 350,000 employees, of which 30 percent work outside of India. It is also India's largest business group, with 2008 revenues of $63 billion. While Tata is the best known group, there are other Indian groups that are very large and possess global capabilities, such as the Aditya Birla group with its Hindalco subsidiary, one of the top five global aluminum firms.

Tata is large and diverse. If it were publicly traded, Tata would be a Global Fortune 500 member. And its penchant for massive horizontal diversification is impressive, even among emerging market business groups. Tata operates 98 companies in seven sectors—engineering, materials, IT, consumer products, energy, chemicals, and services. Tata's two largest businesses are steel and telecommunications. Tata is also big in automobiles, salt, watches, hotels, and artificial limbs and has used its size to finance acquisitions of famous global brands including Jaguar, Daewoo, and Tetley Tea. The favorable financial environment prevailing in India, at least until 2008, has likely contributed to Tata's preference for mergers and acquisitions over alliances. Given that the research evidence (described in Chapter 2) is not kind to unrelated diversification, it is somewhat difficult at first to explain the success of Tata and the rest of these business groups.

Business groups have been evolving as a result of policy and regulatory changes to promote more competitive markets. This has taken place in China since the reforms of Deng Xiao Ping began in 1978 and in India since the regulatory reforms that began 1991. As the growth rate in these countries accelerated to double that of Western economies, business groups have adjusted to these reforms and have innovated their structures and operations in ways that make them much more competitive than their level of horizontal diversification might suggest.

Large groups like Tata have centralized corporate control and enhanced corporate oversight, often supported by efforts to promote a corporate culture and a group code of ethics, with the result that the group is less of a holding company than its business mix might suggest. This control and advisory function is supported by the internal consulting capabilities of Tata Consulting and is complemented by extensive training and exposure to headquarters culture provided in India to the managers of all businesses acquired by the group throughout the world. Groups with such controls can sometimes take advantage of their tight governance in ways that would be predicted by economic principles of value creation. In Tata, for instance, Tata Consulting, Tata Chemicals, and Titan Industries (a Tata subsidiary) worked together to produce the world's cheapest water purifier. Business groups that have not invested in high-powered corporate control can exercise some influence over subsidiaries by instituting corporate board oversight (often involving "interlocks," in which firms' executives serve on each other's boards) and by transferring profits among subsidiaries. However, these activities do not substitute for direct oversight.

These business groups may also take advantage of their close ties to national governments, which provide a favorable regulatory environment. It is not clear whether this reflects government desires to develop prestigious global businesses or whether it merely reflects corruption, as was suggested by some when Tata chairman Ratan Tata was caught on tape conversing with an allegedly corrupt lobbyist. While India has somewhat of a tradition of corruption, as typified in the period of the "License Raj" from the end of British rule until 1980, business group managers today argue that times have changed and economic rules have been reformed. This change is evidenced by the success of Tata and other groups in expanding in overseas and especially Western markets, which would not be possible if their advantage stemmed from corruption.

One of the biggest advantages enjoyed by business groups in India and China is their access to cheap local labor. But this advantage comes at a cost—the same regions that offer a surplus of cheap labor tend to have a scarce supply of well-trained managers. The most successful business groups solve this problem by relying on an internal market for management talent. The groups train their own managers, identify the ones with the most talent, and match them to the toughest and most important management positions—a significant investment for a group. This combination of low-cost labor and in-house management may not be sustainable, however. As economies develop, wages increase. So does the supply of skilled managers available to smaller, independent firms. As the giant business groups lose these advantages, they will succumb to the disadvantages inherent in their organizational structures. Tata has doubled in size over the past two decades, but this expansion has occurred largely through acquisitions, while profits have risen by only a third and Tata's core businesses in steel and telecommunications are struggling.

Chapters 9 and 11 describe how firms can position themselves to outperform their rivals and show why it is difficult for firms to sustain success in the long run. Many of these lessons apply to nations—armed with talented workers willing to work for low wages, we should expect emerging economies in India, China, and elsewhere to enjoy considerable success. It is not clear why this success is often inextricably tied to a handful of diversified multinational business groups. What is clear is that if the advantage conferred by low wages slowly erodes and that advantage is all that these groups possess, then their business models and firm structures will not long endure.

An alternative to this critical perspective on business groups is that the large but low-income consumer markets in countries such as China and India provide large groups with opportunities to innovate and satisfy consumer needs at much lower price levels than are found in Western economies. The intuition is that if a viable product is developed, even at a very low price point, it may be economically feasible because of the large size of the domestic market in India or China and the unwillingness or inability of Western firms to compete in the low-price segment. Moreover, the skills the firm develops in commercializing such products under such constraints will make them more cost competitive against Western firms in their home markets. This innovative side of business groups was first apparent in the aftermath of the Y2K crisis and the rise of such Indian firms as Infosys. It is an important motivation for recent trends toward the offshoring of employees by Western technology firms, who see the need to site their innovation facilities in close proximity to their critical production facilities. For Tata, this can be seen in the Nano Project, in which Tata developed a car that retailed for $2,500 and that had more in common with a scooter than with traditional automobiles. If one only sees groups as pursuing labor cost advantages and neglects this emphasis on innovation, it is hard to understand how Tata could be ranked among the world's most innovative companies by *Business Week* in 2008.

CHAPTER SUMMARY

- According to the Property Rights Theory (PRT) of the firm, the resolution of the integration decision determines the ownership and control of assets. If contracts were complete, asset ownership would not matter. Because of contractual incompleteness, integration changes the pattern of asset ownership and control, and thus alters the bargaining power between parties in a vertical relationship.

- PRT establishes that vertical integration is desirable when one firm's investment in relationship-specific assets has a significantly greater impact on the value chain than does the other firm's investment.

- Integration does not eliminate self-interest. The governance process within an integrated firm must work to ensure that employees work in the interests of the firm. In this way the governance process can improve coordination and avoid holdup.

- PRT suggests that governance of an activity should fall to managers whose decisions have the greatest impact on the performance of that activity.

- The advantages and disadvantages of relying on the market versus relying on internal organization can be expressed in terms of a trade-off between technical efficiency and agency efficiency. Technical efficiency occurs if the firm is using least-cost production techniques. Agency efficiency refers to the extent to which the firm's production and/or administrative costs are raised by the transactions and coordination costs of arm's-length market exchanges or the agency and influence costs of internal organization.

- Vertical integration is preferred to arm's-length market exchange when it is less costly to organize activities internally than it is to organize them through arm's-length market exchange. This cost difference will reflect differences in both technical efficiency and agency efficiency across the two modes of organization.

- Vertical integration is relatively more attractive (a) when the ability of outside market specialists relative to the firm itself to achieve scale or scope economies is limited; (b) the larger the scale of the firm's product market activities; and (c) the greater the extent to which the assets involved in production are relationship-specific.

- Vertical integration and arm's-length market exchange are not the only ways to organize transactions. A firm may pursue tapered integration, in which it supplies part of its input requirement itself and relies on market exchanges for the remainder.

- Firms may franchise when it is important for managers to have local market knowledge.

- Firms may undertake strategic alliances or joint ventures. Although the transacting parties remain legally separate under these modes of organization, they typically entail much closer cooperation and coordination than an arm's-length exchange between two independent firms.

- Implicit contracts can substitute for formal vertical relationships.

- Long-term, arm's-length market relationships can provide strong incentives for cooperative behavior and can thus achieve the advantages of vertical integration (e.g., avoidance of transactions costs, flexibility in governance) without incurring the disadvantages (e.g., softening incentives for innovation). The Japanese *keiretsu* and Korean *chaebol* provide examples of long-lasting business relationships.

- Business groups in developing nations thrive by relying on strong central governance, access to local labor markets, and unique opportunities to innovate.

QUESTIONS

1. What is the Property Rights Theory of the firm? Is this theory consistent with the theories of vertical integration described in Chapter 3?

2. Use Property Rights Theory to explain why stockbrokers are permitted to keep their client lists (i.e., continue to contact and do business with clients) if they are dismissed from their jobs and find employment at another brokerage house.

3. "Integrated firms are more efficient than independent firms if the central office is more efficient than the courts." Explain this statement. To what extent do you agree?

4. How is your ownership of *Economics of Strategy* path dependent? To what extent does this path dependency provide you with a unique opportunity to exploit what you learn from this book?

5. Why is the "technical efficiency" line in Figure 4.1 above the x-axis? Why does the "agency efficiency" line cross the x-axis?

6. How might globalization and advances in information technology affect the trade-offs between technical and agency efficiency?

7. Is the following statement correct? "Double marginalization helps firms because it enables them to raise prices."

8. Analysts often array strategic alliances and joint ventures on a continuum that begins with "using the market" and ends with "full integration." Do you agree that these fall along a natural continuum?

9. How are franchising and tapered integration similar? How do these strategies differ?

10. Most people rely on implicit contracts in their everyday lives. Can you give some examples? What alternatives did you have to achieve the desired outcome?

11. Suppose you observed a hostile takeover and learned that the aftermath of the deal included plant closings, layoffs, and reduced compensation for some remaining workers in the acquired firm. What would you need to know about this acquisition to determine whether it would be best characterized by value creation or value redistribution?

12. What do the *keiretsu* and *chaebol* systems have in common with traditional strategic alliances and joint ventures? What are some of the differences?

13. How are business groups like Tata similar to traditional diversified firms like General Electric? How are they different?

14. The following is an excerpt from an actual strategic plan (the company and product name have been changed to protect the innocent):

> *Acme's primary raw material is pvc sheet that is produced by three major vendors within the United States. Acme, a small consumer products manufacturer, is consolidating down to a single vendor. Continued growth by this vendor assures Acme that it will be able to meet its needs in the future.*

Assume that Acme's chosen vendor will grow as forecast. Offer a scenario to Acme management that might convince them that they should rethink their decision to rely on a single vendor. What do you recommend Acme do to minimize the risk(s) that you have identified? Are there any drawbacks to your recommendation?

ENDNOTES

[1]Grossman, S., and O. Hart, "The Costs and Benefits of Ownership: A Theory of Vertical and Lateral Integration," *Journal of Political Economy*, 94, 1986, pp. 619–719; Hart, O., and J. Moore, "Property Rights and the Nature of the Firm," *Journal of Political Economy*, 98, 1990, pp. 1119–1158.

[2]See Masten, S., J. W. Meehan, and E. A. Snyder, "Vertical Integration in the U.S. Auto Industry: A Note on the Influence of Transactions Specific Assets," *Journal of Economic Behavior and Organization*, 12, 1989, pp. 265–273.

[3]See Williamson, O., "Strategizing, Economizing and Economic Organization," *Strategic Management Journal*, 12, Winter 1991, pp. 75–94, for a complete explanation of this concept along with a brief discussion of its intellectual history.

[4]This figure has been adapted from Oliver Williamson's discussion of vertical integration in *The Economic Institutions of Capitalism*, New York, Free Press, 1985, Chapter 4.

[5]Monteverde, K., and D. Teece, "Supplier Switching Costs and Vertical Integration in the Automobile Industry," *Bell Journal of Economics*, 13, Spring 1982, pp. 206–213.

[6]Masten, S., "The Organization of Production: Evidence from the Aerospace Industry," *Journal of Law and Economics*, 27, October 1984, pp. 403–417.

[7]Joskow, P., "Vertical Integration and Long-Term Contracts: The Case of Coal-Burning Electric Generating Plants," *Journal of Law, Economics, and Organization*, 33, Fall 1985, pp. 32–80.

[8]Anderson, E., and D. C. Schmittlein, "Integration of the Sales Force: An Empirical Examination," *RAND Journal of Economics*, 15, Autumn 1984, pp. 385–395.

[9]Novak, S., and S. Stern, "How Does Outsourcing Affect Performance Dynamics? Evidence from the Automobile Industry," *Management Science*, 12, December 2008, pp. 1963–1979.

[10]Ohmae, K., "The Global Logic of Strategic Alliances," *Harvard Business Review*, March–April 1989, pp. 143–154.

[11]The idea that future flows provide firms with incentives to maintain ongoing relationships was initially developed by Benjamin Klein and Keith Leffler in the article, "The Role of Market Forces in Assuring Contractual Performance," *Journal of Political Economy*, 89, 1981, pp. 615–641.

[12]If the discount rate is i, then an infinite-lived stream of X dollars per year is worth X/i in today's dollars. See the Economics Primer for a fuller discussion of present value.

[13]Palay, T., "Comparative Institutional Economics: The Governance of Rail Freight Contracting," *Journal of Legal Studies*, 13, 1984, pp. 265–287.

[14]Shleifer, A., and L. Summers, "Breach of Trust in Hostile Takeovers," in Auerbach, A. (ed.), *Corporate Takeovers: Causes and Consequences*, Chicago, University of Chicago Press, 1988.

[15]Owen, W., *Autopsy of a Merger*, Deerfield, IL, William Owen, 1986.

[16]Bertrand, M., and S. Mullainathan, "Enjoying the Quiet Life? Corporate Governance and Managerial Preferences," *Journal of Political Economy*, 111(5), 2003, pp. 1043–1075.

[17]As quoted in "Japan Inc. Must Adapt to Survive Post-Crisis Global Competition: Emerging Markets Can Provide the Growth, but Can Developed Economies Meet Their Needs?", by Takashi Kitazume, Japan Times, June 17, 2009. Accessed July 8, 2009 at http://www.americanchronicle.com/articles/yb/131773483

[18]Ibid.

[19]Ibid.

[20]Ibid.

[21]Nagaoka, S., A. Takeishi, and Y. Noro, "Determinants of Firm Boundaries: Empirical Analysis of the Japanese Auto Industry from 1984 to 2002," *Journal of the Japanese and International Economies*, 22(2), 2008, pp. 187–206.

[22]Miwa, Y., and J. M. Ramseyer, "The Fable of the Keiretsu," *Journal of Economics and Management Strategy*, 11(2), 2002, pp. 169–224.

MARKET AND COMPETITIVE ANALYSIS

COMPETITORS AND COMPETITION

5

T he domestic U.S. airline industry has had a bumpy ride over the past two decades. The 1990s began with a mild recession that left carriers with empty seats. Recognizing that the marginal cost of filling an empty seat was negligible, some carriers slashed prices. The result devastated the industry, with aggregate losses exceeding $4 billion in 1992. The economic recovery of the mid-1990s lifted the industry. Flying at or near capacity, carriers raised prices for all passenger classes. When an airline did have empty seats, it utilized computerized pricing algorithms to selectively reduce prices on a short-term basis rather than slash them across the board. By the late 1990s, record losses had given way to record profits, with the industry earning a combined $4 billion in 1999. As the economy softened in 2000 and 2001, airlines once again struggled to fill planes and prices softened. The September 11 attack threatened the solvency of many of the major airlines and necessitated a government bail-out to keep them flying. As the economy revived through the mid-2000s, the airlines filled their planes, raised their prices, and returned to profitability. The Great Recession of the late 2000s triggered yet another decline in demand, but this time the industry was ready for it. Several major carriers had cut capacity, while the Delta/Northwest and United/Continental mergers helped reduce the number of competitors. As a result, airfares did not plummet as they had in previous economic downturns. U.S. airlines managed to turn a healthy profit in 2010, but rising fuel prices ate into those profits in 2011.

This brief history illustrates the interplay among competitors in a concentrated market. The major players in the airline industry understand the need to avoid deep discounting, but they also understand the economics of empty seats and the threat from entry. They have pursued some successful strategies (including reducing capacity in some routes) and have undone some of the damage done by years of cutthroat competition, but they will never be able to undo the economic principles of competition. Chapters 5–8 lay out these principles and explore how firms can craft strategies to cope with market forces.

The present chapter introduces basic concepts in competitive analysis. The first part discusses competitor identification and market definition. The second part considers four different ways in which firms compete: perfect competition, monopoly, monopolistic competition, and oligopoly. Chapters 6–7 present advanced concepts, including entry and industry dynamics. Chapter 8 presents a framework for assimilating and using the material in these chapters.

COMPETITOR IDENTIFICATION AND MARKET DEFINITION

One cannot analyze competition without first identifying the competitors. It is easy to take this for granted. BMW competes with Mercedes and Audi; Tesco competes with Sainsbury; and so forth. Unfortunately, what seems obvious is not always correct or complete. Do the German car makers compete with Jeep and Range Rover? Do Tesco and Sainsbury compete in every town and village, and do they both compete with Pret-a-Manger (a prepared foods carry-out chain)?

Competitor identification begins with the following simple idea: *Competitors are the firms whose strategic choices directly affect one another*. For example, if Mercedes reduced the price on its sports coupe, BMW would have to consider a pricing response. It follows that Mercedes coupes and BMW coupes are direct competitors. Firms also compete indirectly, when the strategic choices of one affect the performance of the other, but only through the strategic choices of a third firm.[1] For example, if Mercedes reduced the price on its sports utility vehicles, Acura might do the same. This might cause Jeep to change price on its Grand Cherokees. In this way Mercedes' pricing decisions affect Jeep; we should at least consider them to be indirect competitors.

Although managers are conversant with these ideas, it is worthwhile to develop methods to systematize competitor identification. These methods force managers to carefully identify the features that define the markets in which they compete, and often reveal aspects of competition that a "quick and dirty" analysis might miss. It is also important to remember that firms compete in both input and output markets and that the competitors and the nature of competition may be quite different in each one. For example, Poland's state-owned Halemba coal mine in Ruda Slaska has little or no competition in the local labor market where the mine is the largest employer, but it faces many competitors in its output market.

The Basics of Competitor Identification

Antitrust agencies, such as the U.S. Department of Justice (DOJ) and the European Commission (EC), are responsible for preventing anticompetitive conduct. They examine whether merging firms will monopolize a market and whether existing monopolists are abusing their power. A necessary first step in identifying monopolists is market definition, also known as competitor identification. The DOJ has developed a simple conceptual guideline for market definition. According to the DOJ, a market is well defined, and all of the competitors within are identified, if a merger among them would lead to a *small but significant nontransitory increase in price*. This is known as the *SSNIP* criterion. "Small" is usually defined to be "more than 5 percent," and "nontransitory" is usually defined to be "at least one year."

To better understand SSNIP, suppose that BMW and Audi proposed a merger. The EC might object on the grounds that the market in which BMW competes consists of "German luxury cars" and that the list of competitors is therefore limited to BMW, Audi, and Mercedes. The proposed merger would thus lead to excessive market concentration; in antitrust parlance, this would be a "3 to 2" merger because it reduces the number of competitors from three to two. BMW might counter that the market in which it competes consists of all luxury cars and should be expanded to include Lexus, Acura, Infiniti, Range Rover, and other luxury brands. The SSNIP test provides a conceptual way to determine whether the EC or BMW is correct. According to the SSNIP criterion, the EC is correct if, in the hypothetical event that all three German car makers merged, they could increase profits by raising their prices for at least one year by 5 percent. If this were the case, then we would conclude that the three German car makers competed among themselves but faced minimal outside competition. BMW would be correct if a single firm consisting of Audi, BMW, and Mercedes would lose money were it to try to raise prices by 5 percent for at least one year. This would imply that the three German car makers faced substantial competition from other brands.

EXAMPLE 5.1   THE SSNIP IN ACTION: DEFINING HOSPITAL MARKETS

The 1990s saw a remarkable degree of consolidation among U.S. hospitals, with the result that many metropolitan areas were dominated by just one or two hospital systems. Antitrust laws are supposed to prevent mergers that lead to monopolization, and many casual observers must have wondered what was going on. In fact, the Federal Trade Commission challenged several hospital mergers during the 1990s but lost every challenge. The decisive factor in nearly every case was market definition.

The merger between Mercy Health Center and Finley Hospital in Dubuque, Iowa, is a case in point. These are the only two hospitals in Dubuque, and it seemed that the merger would create an illegal monopoly. The FTC challenged the deal, but the hospitals argued that they competed in a broad geographic market against hospitals located dozens of miles away. Presenting evidence that Dubuque hospitals treated quite a few out of town patients, the hospitals persuaded the federal court that they faced substantial competition from out of town hospitals. The court allowed the merger.

Decisions such as these did not sit well with economists who had studied hospital pricing data and knew that mergers like the one in Dubuque often led to large price increases. Such price increases could only mean that the court's expansive view of geographic markets was incorrect; if there really was such competition, then prices could not have increased. Cory Capps and colleagues at Northwestern University used the SSNIP criterion as a foundation for a new method of identifying geographic markets.[2] They reasoned that hospitals competed to be part of managed care provider "networks" and that managed care organizations, in turn, offered these networks to local employers and employees. Capps et al. observed that if all of the hospitals in a narrowly defined geographic area were to merge, they could sustain a price increase because the managed care payers could not offer a network that excluded all local providers. Capps et al. developed a statistical model and used it to show that the broad markets affirmed by the courts failed the SSNIP test. Other economists have used different statistical models and reached the same conclusions.

Based on arguments like this, the FTC has pursued hospital consolidation with renewed vigor. It won a court case in which it argued that the northern suburbs of Chicago represented a well-defined geographic market and blocked mergers in Virginia and Ohio on similar grounds. Thanks to SSNIP, U.S. hospital markets may soon be more competitive, with lower hospital prices as a result.

Putting Competitor Identification into Practice

The SSNIP criterion is sensible, but it relies on a hypothetical question that is often difficult to answer in practice: how would firms behave in the event of a hypothetical merger? Even so, the SSNIP criterion points to the kind of evidence needed for market definition and competitor identification. Specifically, the SSNIP criterion suggests that two firms directly compete if a price increase by one firm causes many of its customers to do business with the other. For example, if the German car makers raise prices by 5 percent and, as a result, lose a lot of customers to Lexus and Acura, then these Japanese brands compete with the Germans.

The SSNIP criterion is based on the economic concept of *substitutes*. In general, two products X and Y are substitutes if, when the price of X increases and the price of Y stays the same, purchases of X go down and purchases of Y go up. When asked to identify competitors, most managers would probably name substitutes. For example, a manager at BMW might name Audi, Mercedes, Lexus, and Acura as competitors. In fact, when Lexus and Acura entered the 1980s with relatively low prices, they took considerable business away from BMW. When BMW and other European luxury car makers reduced their prices in the early 1990s, they regained market share from Lexus and Acura. Hyundai is hoping that history will repeat itself with its "budget"-priced Genesis luxury sedan.

At an intuitive level, products tend to be close substitutes when three conditions hold:

1. They have the same or similar *product performance characteristics*.
2. They have the same or similar *occasions for use*.
3. They are sold in the same *geographic market*.

A product's performance characteristics describe what it does for consumers. Though highly subjective, listing product performance characteristics often clarifies whether products are substitutes. BMW and Lexus sedans have the following product performance characteristics in common:

- Ability to seat five comfortably

- High "curb appeal" and prestigious name

- High reliability

- Powerful acceleration and sure handling and braking

- Plenty of features, such as leather seats and excellent audio systems

Based on this short list, we can assume that the products are in the same market. We would probably exclude Subarus from this market, however.

A product's occasion for use describes when, where, and how it is used. Both orange juice and cola quench thirst, but because orange juice is primarily a breakfast drink, they are probably in different markets.

Products with similar characteristics and occasions for use may not be substitutes if they are in different geographic markets. In general, two products are in different geographic markets if (a) they are sold in different locations, (b) it is costly to transport the goods, and (c) it is costly for consumers to travel to buy the goods. For example, a company that mixes and sells cement in Mexico City is not in the same geographic market as a similar company in Oaxaca because the cost of transporting cement 325 miles from one city to the other is prohibitive.

Empirical Approaches to Competitor Identification

Although the intuitive approach to competitor identification is often sufficient for business decision making, it can be subjective. When possible, it is helpful to augment the intuitive approach with data. As pointed out in the Economics Primer, the degree to which products substitute for each other is measured by the cross-price elasticity of demand. If the products in question are X and Y, then the cross-price elasticity measures the percentage change in demand for good Y that results from a 1 percent change in the price of good X. η_{yx} denotes the cross-price elasticity of demand of product Y with respect to product X, Q_y the quantity of Y sold, and P_x the price of product X, then

$$\eta_{yx} = \frac{(\Delta Q_y/Q_y)}{(\Delta P_x/P_x)}$$

When η_{yx} is positive, it indicates that consumers increase their purchases of good Y as the price of good X increases. Goods X and Y would thus be substitutes. Thanks to the growing availability of retail scanner pricing data, it is increasingly possible for the makers of consumer products to directly measure cross-price elasticities of demand. *Regression analysis* uses statistical algorithms to isolate the effects of price changes on purchase patterns, while holding constant other demand-side factors such as product characteristics and advertising spending.

When appropriate data are unavailable, *ad hoc* product market definition may be a necessary alternative to regression analysis. The U.S. Bureau of the Census's Standard Industrial Classification (SIC) system identifies products and services by a seven-digit identifier, with each digit representing a finer degree of classification. For example, within the two-digit category 35 (industrial and commercial machinery and computer equipment) are four-digit categories 3523 (farm machinery and equipment) and 3534 (elevators and moving stairways). Within 3534 are six-digit categories for automobile lifts, dumbwaiters, and so forth. One should use caution when using SIC codes to identify competitors because SIC categories are not always as precise as desired. For example, category 2834 includes all pharmaceuticals, which is overly broad for competitor identification because not all drugs substitute for each other. At the same time, some four-digit categories are too narrow. Firms in the four-digit categories for variety stores (5331), department stores (5311), and general merchandise stores (5399) may all compete against each other.

Geographic Competitor Identification

Though *ad hoc*, government-drawn geographic boundaries provide a good starting point for identifying geographic competitors. City, county, and state lines often provide an adequate first step for delineating the scope of competition. But such boundaries are only a first step. For example, consider trying to define the geographic scope of competition among retail grocers. Is the "city" a reasonable way to delineate markets? The city of Chicago is probably too large to represent a single market; it is unlikely that all the grocery stores in Chicago compete with one another. On the other hand, grocers in the Illinois town of Glencoe surely compete with grocers in the neighboring town of Highland Park.

Rather than rely on *ad hoc* market boundaries, it is preferable to identify competitors by directly examining the flow of goods and services across geographic

EXAMPLE 5.2   DEFINING COCA-COLA'S MARKET

In 1986, the Coca-Cola Company sought to acquire the Dr Pepper Company. At the time, Coca-Cola was the nation's largest seller of carbonated soft drinks, and Dr Pepper was the fourth largest. The Federal Trade Commission (FTC) went before federal judge Gerhard Gesell seeking an injunction to block the merger on the grounds that it violated Section 7 of the Clayton Act, which prohibits any acquisition of stock or assets of a company that may substantially lessen competition. Coca-Cola apparently sought the deal to acquire, and more fully exploit, the Dr Pepper trademark. Coca-Cola's marketing skills and research ability were cited as two factors that would allow it to increase the sales of Dr Pepper. Judge Gesell also noted that Coca-Cola was motivated, in part, by a desire to match the expansion of Pepsi-Cola, which had simultaneously been seeking to acquire 7-Up. Although the threat of FTC action caused Pepsi to abandon the 7-Up acquisition, Coca-Cola pressed on.

Judge Gesell granted the injunction, and the Coca-Cola/Dr Pepper deal was never consummated. In his decision, Judge Gesell addressed the question of market definition. He wrote: "Proper market analysis directs attention to the nature of the products that the acquirer and the acquired company principally sell, the channels of distribution they primarily use, the outlets they employ to distribute their products to the ultimate consumer, and the geographic areas they mutually serve." The judge was concerned not only with the end-user market, but also with intermediate markets for distribution and retailing. Reduction of competition in any of these markets could harm consumers.

Depending on how the market in which Coca-Cola and Dr Pepper competed was defined, one might conclude that the merger would have either no effect on competition or a significant effect. The FTC argued that the appropriate "line of commerce" was carbonated soft drinks. It presented data to show that under this definition, the merger of Coca-Cola and Dr Pepper would increase Coca-Cola's market share by 4.6 percent nationwide and by 10 to 20 percent in many geographic submarkets. (Geographic submarkets were considered because of the special characteristics of soft-drink distribution channels.) Given Coca-Cola's already high market share of 40 to 50 percent in many of these markets, the merger would significantly reduce competition.

In defending the merger, Coca-Cola attempted to define the relevant market as "all . . . beverages including tap water." Under this definition, the proposed merger would have a negligible effect on competition. Judge Gesell ruled: "Although other beverages could be viewed as within 'the outer boundaries' of a product market . . . determined by the reasonable interchangeability of use or the cross-elasticity of demand between carbonated soft drinks and substitutes for them, carbonated soft drinks . . . constitute a product market for antitrust purposes." In reaching this decision, he relied on factors such as the product's distinctive characteristics and uses, distinct consumers, distinct prices, and sensitivity to price changes. Judge Gesell found such indicia to be present in this case, stating that the rival firms "make pricing and marketing decisions based primarily on comparisons with rival carbonated soft drink products, with little if any concern about possible competition from other beverages." In other words, carbonated soft-drink makers constrain each others' pricing decisions, but are unconstrained by other beverages. Thus, carbonated soft drinks constitute a well-defined market.

regions. To illustrate this approach, consider how Lombard Sporting Goods near downtown San Francisco might try to identify its competitors. Lombard might decide that its competitors are the other downtown sporting goods stores. This is mere guesswork and is probably wrong.

Lombard could survey its customers to find out where else they shop. This would certainly identify some competitors, but it might miss others. In particular, Lombard would never hear from customers who live near its store but always shop elsewhere. To identify all of its competitors, Lombard should first ask its customers where they live. The store can identify the contiguous area from which it draws most of its customers, sometimes called the *catchment area*. If most of its customers live near downtown, then Lombard's list of competitors should include other downtown sporting goods stores. But suppose, as seems likely, that some downtown residents shop at sporting goods stores outside of downtown. To identify these competitors, Lombard should perform a second survey of local residents (not just its own customers) to find out where they shop for sporting goods.

This is an example of *flow analysis*—examining data on consumer travel patterns. Although flow analysis is a good starting point for identifying geographic competitors, it is not foolproof. It may turn out that few customers currently shop far from downtown, but they might do so if Lombard and other downtown stores were to raise their prices. Or it may be that many customers who currently shop outside of downtown do so for idiosyncratic reasons—perhaps they are avid hockey players, and downtown stores do not sell hockey gear. With the exception of such exotic merchandise, these distant stores may not be competitors after all.

MEASURING MARKET STRUCTURE

Markets are often characterized according to the degree of seller concentration. This permits a quick and reasonably accurate assessment of the likely nature of competition in a market. These characterizations are aided by measures of *market structure*.

Market structure refers to the number and distribution of firms in a market. A common measure of market structure is the N-firm concentration ratio. This gives the combined market share of the N largest firms in the market. For example, the 5-firm concentration ratio in the UK pesticide industry is about .75, which indicates that the combined market share of the five largest pesticide sellers in the UK is about 75 percent. (Note that the ratio is reported for a specific product within a specific geographic area.) When calculating market share, one usually uses sales revenue, although concentration ratios based on other measures, such as production capacity, may also be used. Table 5.1 shows 4-firm and 20-firm concentration ratios for selected U.S. industries in 2007.

One problem with the N-firm ratio is that it is invariant to changes in the sizes of the largest firms. For example, a 5-firm ratio does not change value if the largest firm gains 10 percent share at the expense of the second largest firm, even though this could make the market less competitive. The Herfindahl index avoids this problem.[3] The Herfindahl index equals the sum of the squared market shares of all the firms in the market; that is, letting S_i represent the market share of firm i, Herfindahl $= \Sigma_i (S_i)^2$. In a market with two firms that each have 50 percent market share, the Herfindahl index equals $.5^2 + .5^2 = .5$. The Herfindahl index in a market with N equal-size firms is $1/N$. Because of this property, the reciprocal of the Herfindahl index is referred to as the *numbers-equivalent of firms*. Thus, a market whose Herfindahl is .20 has a numbers-equivalent of 5. Roughly speaking, such a market is about as competitive as a market with 5 equal-sized firms, whether or not there are exactly 5 firms in the market. When calculating a Herfindahl, it is sufficient to restrict attention to firms with market shares of .01 or larger, since the squared shares of smaller firms are too small to affect the Herfindahl.

TABLE 5.1
CONCENTRATION STATISTICS FOR SELECTED U.S. INDUSTRIES, 2007

Code	Industry	Number of Firms	4-firm CR	20-firm CR
44311	Appliance, television, and other electronics stores	38387	56	67
44312	Computer and software stores	10428	73	79
44711	Gasoline stations with convenience stores	97508	11	32
45311	Florists	19822	2	5
48111	Scheduled passenger air transportation	3129	50	90
48412	General freight trucking, long distance	38769	16	36
49311	General warehousing and storage	10184	25	38
49312	Refrigerated warehousing and storage	1114	39	64
51211	Motion picture and video production	12192	53	75
51213	Motion picture and video exhibition	5133	54	73
51511	Radio broadcasting	7263	38	65
51512	Television broadcasting	2208	43	72
51521	Cable and other subscription programming	717	62	94
52211	Commercial banking	91116	32	56
52393	Investment advice	16708	27	44
61141	Business and secretarial schools	377	20	48
72111	Hotels (except casino hotels) and motels	48108	23	35
72112	Casino hotels	307	41	69
72121	RV parks and recreational camps	7420	7	13
72211	Full service restaurants	220089	9	17

Source: 2007 Economic Census, Various Industry Series Reports; Washington, DC: U.S. Census Bureau.

The Herfindahl conveys more information than the *N*-firm concentration ratio. If one believes that the relative size of the largest firms is an important determinant of conduct and performance, as economic theory suggests, then the Herfindahl is likely to be more informative.

MARKET STRUCTURE AND COMPETITION

The structure of a market can profoundly affect the conduct and financial performance of its firms; the causal connection is known as the *Structure, Conduct, Performance paradigm*. Market structure can range from perfect competition at one extreme to monopoly at the other. In between these extremes are at least two other broad categories of market structure: monopolistic competition and oligopoly. Table 5.2 lists these categories and gives a range of associated Herfindahls. These ranges are *only suggestive*, because there are many factors besides market structure that contribute to conduct and performance. For example, some markets with two firms and a Herfindahl of .5 or higher could experience fierce competition with prices near marginal costs. On the other hand, price competition can be all but nonexistent in some markets that have five competitors or more with Herfindahls below .2. Thus it is essential to assess all the circumstances affecting competition rather than rely solely on measures of market structure.

TABLE 5.2
FOUR CLASSES OF MARKET STRUCTURE AND THE INTENSITY OF PRICE COMPETITION

Nature of Competition	Range of Herfindahls	Intensity of Price Competition
Perfect competition	Usually below .2	Fierce
Monopolistic competition	Usually below .2	May be fierce or light, depending on product differentiation
Oligopoly	.2 to .6	May be fierce or light, depending on interfirm rivalry
Monopoly	.6 and above	Usually light, unless threatened by entry

In the remainder of this section, we describe each of the four market structures. We begin with brief discussions of perfect competition and monopoly. (More detailed discussions may be found in the Economics Primer and in microeconomics textbooks.) We then provide lengthier discussions of monopolistic competition and oligopoly.

Perfect Competition

Recall from the Economics Primer that a firm maximizes profit by producing a volume of output at which marginal revenue equals marginal cost. Recall, too, that the percentage contribution margin (*PCM*) equals $(P - MC)/P$, where P = price and MC = marginal cost. The condition for profit maximization can then be written $PCM = 1/\eta$.[4] In a perfectly competitive market, firms behave as if $\eta = \infty$, so the optimal PCM is 0. In other words, firms expand output until marginal cost of the last unit produced equals the market price.

Market conditions will tend to drive down prices toward marginal costs when at least two of the following conditions are met:

1. There are many sellers.
2. Consumers perceive the product to be homogeneous.
3. There is excess capacity.

We now discuss how each of these features may increase competitive pricing pressures.

Many Sellers

Antitrust agencies vigorously enforce laws designed to promote competition. These agencies are seldom concerned about markets with more than a few sellers. Experience, coupled with economic theory, has taught them that prices tend to fall as the number of sellers increases. This is true for a number of reasons.

First, when there are many sellers, a diversity of pricing preferences is likely. Even if the industry is profitable, a particular seller may prefer a lower price. This is likely to be true for sellers such as Aldi and Wal-Mart that have costs below the industry average. It may also be true for sellers, including many Internet start-ups, that are attempting to boost market share without regard for short-term profitability.

Second, when sellers maintain high prices, consumers make fewer purchases. Some sellers will have to cut production, or prices will fall. When there are many sellers, it can be hard to convince all of them to cut production, even when they are part of an explicit cartel. This point is illustrated by the contrast between the historical success of cartels in the potash and nitrogen industries.[5] The potash cartel that existed before World War II was highly concentrated and generally succeeded in restricting production and keeping prices high. By contrast, the world nitrogen cartel consisted of many firms in the United States, Europe, and South America and was far less successful in its attempts to raise prices above competitive levels.[6]

The third reason is closely related to the second. When sellers do manage to restrict production and increase prices, some may be tempted to "cheat" by lowering price and increasing production. There are many small firms when a market is relatively unconcentrated, and small firms are often the most willing to cheat. A small firm may view the high prices charged by bigger rivals as an opportunity to increase market share and secure learning benefits and economies of scale that will enhance its long-run competitive position. A small firm may also gamble that its larger rivals will not detect or react to its price reductions.

Homogeneous Products

When a firm lowers its price, it expects to increase its sales. The sales increase may come from three different sources:

1. Increased sales to the firm's existing customers
2. Sales to customers of a competing firm who switch to take advantage of the lower price
3. Sales to individuals who were not planning to purchase from any firm at the prevailing price

Customer switching often represents the largest source of sales gain. Korean electronics manufacturers Samsung and LG broke into Western markets by undercutting rivals' prices on comparable-quality televisions and appliances. Customers are more willing to switch from one seller to another when the product is homogeneous, that is, if the characteristics of the product do not vary across sellers. When products are homogeneous, customers tend to be less loyal because any seller's product will meet their needs. This intensifies price competition because firms that lower prices can expect large increases in sales. Samsung and LG benefited when high-definition televisions were sold using standard technologies (e.g., plasma and LCD) at standard screen sizes (e.g., 50-inch diagonal screens with a 16×9 screen aspect). Samsung and LG's small price advantages were enough to offset the lack of brand-name recognition. Other products, such as medical services, are highly differentiated, and most consumers are unwilling to switch just to obtain a lower price.

Excess Capacity

To understand the role of capacity in pricing, recall the distinction between average costs and marginal costs that we made in the Economics Primer. For production processes that entail high fixed costs, marginal cost can be well below average cost over a wide range of output. Only when production nears capacity—the point at which average cost begins to rise sharply—does marginal cost begin to exceed average cost.

The numerical example in Table 5.3 illustrates the implications of excess capacity for a firm's pricing incentives. The table depicts the situation facing a diesel engine manufacturer, such as Deere & Company, whose plant has capacity of 50,000 engines

TABLE 5.3
CAPACITY UTILIZATION AND COSTS

Annual Output	Total Variable Cost ($millions/year)	Total Fixed Cost ($millions/year)	Total Cost ($millions/year)	Average Cost per Engine
10,000	$1	$12	$13	$1,300
20,000	2	12	14	700
30,000	3	12	15	500
40,000	4	12	16	400
50,000	8	12	20	400

EXAMPLE 5.3   THE BOTTOM DROPS OUT ON CUBS TICKETS

For the past 25 years, the Chicago Cubs had been the envy of every professional sports team owner. Rarely a contender and often a doormat, the Cubs still managed to consistently fill venerable Wrigley Field to capacity, selling the vast majority of tickets before the season even began. Tourists from Iowa and beyond visited Wrigley the way that tourists in Paris visit the Eiffel Tower, while locals viewed Wrigley as a gigantic communal beer garden. Demand for seats was so strong that owners of apartment buildings across the street from Wrigley put makeshift stands on their roofs and charged up to $200 per ticket (including food and drinks). Cubs ownership even got a piece of the action.

With such high demand and a fixed supply of seats (even including the rooftops), the Cubs's owners could have set the highest ticket prices in the sport, but chose instead to hold the line on ticket prices. After all, it might be unseemly to charge more for Cubs tickets than for Yankee tickets when the Yankees have won 27 World Series and the Cubs have not won a World Series for over 100 years. Ticket brokers, who buy tickets in bulk at the start of the season and resell them for whatever the market will bear, were major beneficiaries of the Cubs' popularity. Every year, brokers purchased hundreds or even thousands of tickets to every home game and sold them for multiples of their face value. With the growing popularity of the StubHub Internet ticket reselling platform, season ticket holders got into the act, unloading unwanted tickets at prices high enough to more than pay for their entire season ticket packages. Even the Cubs got into the act, holding back some tickets at the start of the year and selling them at their own web site, again at a multiple of face value.

And then 2011 happened. The Cubs had actually played well in the preceding decade, posting a winning record six times and making the playoffs three times. But the team's "success" (they failed to reach the World Series) seemed to change fans' attitudes. For the first time in decades, fans expected to see a winning team. But the team stopped winning. When the team faltered in 2010, a few empty seats could be seen at Wrigley. The Cubs opened the 2011 season alternating wins and losses, but in May the team went into a tailspin and never recovered. Seemingly overnight, everyone noticed that the team was no good and that once quaint Wrigley Field was antiquated, uncomfortable, and occasionally unpleasant. So the fans stopped coming, not in droves, but enough to alter the balance from excess demand to excess supply.

The fundamental economic problem with baseball tickets is that once a game is over, they have zero value. Ticket brokers understand this better than anyone. As much as they would have liked to sell $40 face-value tickets for $200, they found themselves accepting prices well below face value. Prices at StubHub crashed as well. From the Cubs's perspective, the unsold tickets actually had "negative" value, because fans who entered Wrigley could be relied upon to buy food and beer at inflated prices. So Cubs management supposedly gave out free tickets before each game. But even at bargain basement prices, the Cubs are playing to far less than capacity crowds. The other 29 MLB team owners no longer look on in envy.

per year. Because of a recession, suppose that Deere has confirmed orders for only 10,000 engines during the upcoming year. Deere is confident, however, that it can increase sales by another 10,000 engines by stealing a major customer from one of its competitors, Navistar. To do so, Deere has to offer this customer a price of $300 per engine, well below the average cost of $700.[7]

It may seem surprising, but Deere is better off offering this price and stealing the business from Navistar. To see this, note that the increase in Deere's revenue is $3 million, whereas the increase in its total cost is only $1 million. By selling the extra engines at $300, Deere makes a contribution toward fixed costs, and some contribution is better than no contribution. Of course, Navistar may not let Deere steal its business, so the result may be a battle that drives the price for this order below $300. But as long as the order carries a price greater than the average variable cost of $100, Deere would be better off filling the order than not filling it.

In the long run, competition like this can drive price below average cost. If such competition persists, firms may choose to exit rather than sustain long-run economic losses. But if firm capacity is industry specific—that is, it can only be used to produce in this industry—firms will have no choice but to remain in the industry until the plant reaches the end of its useful life or until demand recovers. If demand does not recover, the industry may suffer a protracted period of excess capacity, with prices below average costs.

Monopoly

The noted antitrust economist Frank Fisher describes monopoly power as "the ability to act in an unconstrained way," such as increasing price or reducing quality.[8] Constraints come from competing firms. If a firm lacks monopoly power, then when it raises price or reduces quality its customers take their business to competitors. It follows that a firm is a *monopolist* if it faces little or no competition in its output market. Competition, if it exists at all, comes mainly from fringe firms—small firms that collectively account for no more than about 30 to 40 percent market share and, more importantly, cannot threaten to erode the monopolist's market share by significantly ramping up production and boosting demand for their own products.

A firm is a *monopsonist* if it faces little or no competition in one of its input markets. The analyses of monopoly and monopsony are closely related. Whereas an analysis of monopoly focuses on the ability of the firm to raise output prices, an analysis of monopsony focuses on its ability to reduce input prices. In this chapter we discuss issues concerning monopolists, but all of these issues are equally important to monopsonists.

A monopolist faces downward-sloping demand, implying that as it raises price, it sells fewer units. This is not the same as having a stranglehold on demand. Even monopolists lose customers when they increase price. (If a monopolist raises price without losing customers, then profit maximization behooves it to raise price even further. Eventually, the price will increase to the point where it drives away some customers.) What distinguishes a monopolist is not the fact that it faces downward-sloping demand, but rather that it can set price with little regard to how other firms will respond. This stands in contrast with oligopolists, described below, who also face downward-sloping demand, but must be very mindful of how competitors react to their strategic decisions.

A monopolist selects price so that the marginal revenue from the last unit sold equals the marginal cost of producing it. For example, we shall calculate the profit-maximizing price and quantity for a monopolist that faces demand given by $P = 100 - Q$ and has constant marginal cost of production of 10 per unit. As a benchmark, note that price in a competitive market would equal marginal cost, or 10, and total industry output would be 90.

The monopolist's total revenue is price times quantity, or $100Q - Q^2$. The corresponding marginal revenue is $100 - 2Q$ (see the Economics Primer for further discussion of marginal revenue). The monopolist maximizes profits by producing up to the point where the additional revenue just equals the additional cost, or where marginal revenue equals marginal cost. This occurs here when $100 - 2Q = 10$, or $Q = 45$. It follows that the profit-maximizing price $P = \$55$, and profits (total revenues minus total costs) equal \$2,025. Note that the monopolist's price is well above its marginal cost and its output is well below the competitive level.

This analysis shows that a monopolist's profits may come at the expense of consumers. Policy makers often propose reining in monopolies through taxes or aggressive antitrust enforcement. The economist Harold Demsetz cautions that monopolies often result when firms discover more efficient manufacturing techniques or create new products that fulfill unmet consumer needs.[9] Even at monopoly prices, the benefits that these innovations bring to consumers may be enormous. (Think of blockbuster prescription drugs, the iPad, or Google.) Demsetz argues that policies that limit monopoly profits may discourage all firms from innovating and harm consumers in the long run.

Several firms acting in concert so as to mimic the behavior of a monopolist are known as a *cartel*. Most developed nations have antitrust laws prohibiting private organizations from cartelizing an industry, but there are many international cartels. The Organization of Petroleum Exporting Countries (OPEC) is perhaps the best known cartel even though it accounts for only 40 percent of world oil production. Efforts have been made to cartelize other international commodities industries, including copper, tin, coffee, tea, and cocoa. A few cartels have had short-term success, such as bauxite and uranium, and one or two, such as the DeBeers diamond cartel, appear to have enjoyed long-term success. In general, most international cartels are unable to substantially affect pricing for long.

Monopolistic Competition

The term *monopolistic competition* was introduced by Edward Chamberlin in 1933 to characterize markets with two main features that are important to understanding pricing:[10]

1. There are many sellers. Each seller reasonably supposes that its actions will not materially affect others. For example, there are hundreds of retailers of women's clothing in Chicago. If any one seller were to lower its prices, it is doubtful that other sellers would react. Even if some sellers did notice a small dropoff in sales, they would probably not alter their prices just to respond to a single competitor.
2. Each seller offers a differentiated product. Products A and B are differentiated if there is some price at which some consumers prefer to purchase A and others prefer to purchase B. The notion of product differentiation captures the idea that consumers make choices among competing products on the basis of factors other than just price. Chicago apparel retailing offers a good example. Different women tend to frequent different clothing stores, based on factors such as location and style. Unlike under perfect competition, where products are homogeneous, a differentiated seller that raises its price will not lose all its customers.

Economists distinguish between *vertical differentiation* and *horizontal differentiation*. A product is vertically differentiated when it is unambiguously better or worse than competing products. A clothing manufacturer engages in vertical differentiation when it uses stronger stitching to enhance durability. All consumers will value this enhancement, although they may disagree about how much they are willing to pay for it. A product is horizontally differentiated when only some consumers prefer it to competing products (holding price equal). The popularity of many different brands of blue jeans, at different price points, is a testament to widely diverging consumer tastes for fashion.

Demand for Differentiated Goods

Figure 5.1 illustrates horizontal differentiation based on location. The figure shows the town of Linesville. The only road in Linesville—Straight Street—is exactly 10 miles long. There is a sandwich shop at each end of Straight Street. Jimmy Johns is at the left end of town (denoted by L in the figure); Quiznos is at the right end (denoted by R). There are hungry consumers in Linesville whose homes are equally spaced along Straight Street so that 50 consumers live closer to Jimmy Johns and 50 live closer to Quiznos. For simplicity, we will assume that all 100 consumers buy exactly one sandwich, regardless of price. We also assume that consumers view the two sandwiches to be of identical taste and quality. Thus, we can focus our attention on the role of geographic differentiation as a driver of market share.

Consumers will base their sandwich purchase on two factors: price and transportation costs. Let the cost of traveling one mile equal 50 cents for all consumers (this includes gasoline and time costs). Because travel is costly, some but not all consumers will seek out the lowest price sandwich. For example, suppose that both stores initially charge $5 per sandwich so that the two stores split the market. In this case, each store will have 50 customers. Now suppose that Jimmy Johns lowers its price per sandwich from $5 to $4, while Quiznos keeps its price at $5. To determine how this will affect sales at both stores, we need to identify the location on Straight Street at which a consumer would be indifferent between purchasing from Jimmy Johns and Quiznos. Because travel is costly, all consumers living to the left of that location will visit Jimmy Johns and all living to the right will visit Quiznos.

A consumer will be indifferent between the two shops if total purchase costs (i.e., sandwich plus transportation costs) are identical. Consider a consumer living M miles from Jimmy Johns and $10 - M$ miles from Quiznos. For this consumer, the total cost of visiting Jimmy Johns is $4 + .50M$. The total cost of visiting Quiznos is $5 + .50(10 - M)$.

FIGURE 5.1
SANDWICH RETAILERS IN LINESVILLE

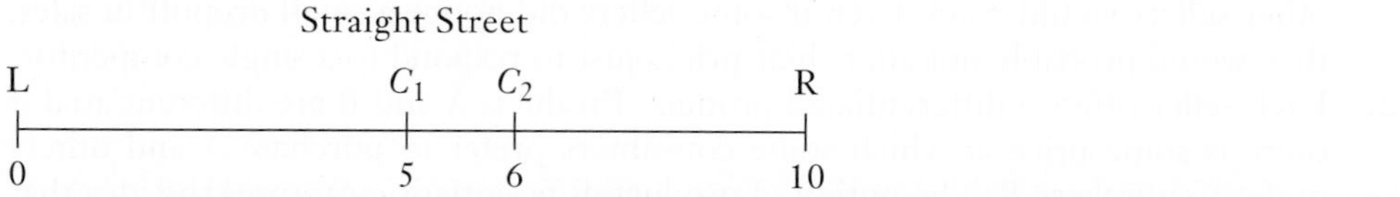

If store L and store R both charge $5 per sandwich, then all consumers living to the left of C_1 shop at store L and all consumers living to the right of C_1 shop at store R. If store L lowers its price to $4 per sandwich, then some customers living to the right of C_1 may wish to travel the extra distance to buy from store L. If travel costs $.50 per mile, then all customers living between C_1 and C_2 will travel the extra distance to save a dollar.

These costs are equal if $M = 6$; a consumer located at $M = 6$ will have total purchase costs of $7 at both shops. It follows that 60 consumers will visit Jimmy Johns and 40 will visit Quiznos.

Jimmy Johns gains 10 customers from Quiznos by charging $1 less per sandwich. One would intuitively expect that as product differentiation declines in importance—in this case, as transportation costs decrease—Jimmy Johns would gain even more customers. The model bears this out. If the transportation costs equal 20 cents per mile, the indifferent consumer would live at $M = 7.5$ and Jimmy Johns would get 75 customers. If the transportation cost is 1 cent, then Jimmy Johns can win all 100 customers by setting a price of $4.90.

This example shows that horizontal differentiation results when consumers have *idiosyncratic preferences*, that is, if tastes differ markedly from one person to the next. Location is not the only source of idiosyncratic preferences. Some consumers prefer conservative business suits, whereas others want Italian styling. Some want the biggest sports utility vehicle they can find, whereas others want good mileage. In these and countless other ways, firms can differentiate their products, raise their prices, and yet find that many of their customers remain loyal.

Of course, consumers may not switch away from a high-priced seller unless they are aware of another seller offering a better value. The degree of horizontal differentiation therefore depends on the magnitude of consumer *search costs*, that is, how easy or hard it is for consumers to learn about alternatives. Retailers like Jimmy Johns often rely on advertising to reduce consumer search costs. Low-price sellers usually want to minimize search costs, for this would likely boost their market shares. But low search costs reduce horizontal differentiation, leading to lower prices and lower profits for all firms. Chapter 10 describes how firms can exploit consumer search to create value and gain competitive advantage.

Entry into Monopolistically Competitive Markets

The theory of optimal pricing implies that firms in differentiated product markets set prices in excess of marginal costs. This creates a powerful competitive dynamic. If prices are high enough to more than cover fixed costs, firms will earn positive economic profits, inviting entry. Entry reduces prices and erodes market shares until economic profits equal zero. If prices are insufficient to cover fixed costs, firms will earn negative economic profits. Exit by some firms will restore the survivors to profitability.

These forces can be understood with a numerical example. Consider a market that currently has 10 firms, called *incumbents*. Each of the 10 incumbents has a constant marginal cost of $10 per unit and a fixed cost of $120. Each incumbent sells a horizontally differentiated product and faces a price elasticity of demand $\eta = 2$, so that the profit-maximizing price for each incumbent firm is $20.[11] Suppose that at this price the total market demand is 240, which is evenly divided among all sellers in the market—each incumbent sells 24 units. This implies that each incumbent has revenues of $480 and total costs of $360, for profits of $120. These facts are summarized in Table 5.4 in the column labeled "Before Entry."

Profits attract entry. Suppose that entrants' and incumbents' costs are identical and that each entrant can differentiate its product, so that all sellers have the same market share. To further streamline the analysis, suppose that after entry the price elasticity of demand facing all sellers remains constant at 2. All firms, entrants and incumbents alike, will continue to set a price of $20. Entry continues until there are no more profits to be earned. This occurs when there are 20 firms in the market, each with sales of 12. The last column of Table 5.4 summarizes these results.

TABLE 5.4
PROFITS AND NUMBER OF FIRMS UNDER MONOPOLISTIC COMPETITION

	Before Entry	After Entry
Number of firms	10	20
Fixed costs per firm	$120	$120
Marginal cost	$10	$10
Price	$20	$20
Market demand	240 units	240 units
Sales per firm	24 units	12 units
Profit per firm	$120	0

This example shows that when product differentiation enables sellers to set prices well above marginal costs, new entrants will steal market share from incumbents and drive down incumbents' profits, *even if price remains unchanged*. If entry intensifies price competition, profits would fall even faster and there would ultimately be fewer than 20 firms in the market.

In Chamberlin's classic model of competition in differentiated goods markets, the amount of entry is thought to be excessive because it drives up fixed costs. But this simple analysis is misleading, for it fails to consider that entrants increase the variety of products and services in the market by staking out new locations, flavors, product styles, and so on. If consumers place a high value on variety, then entry in monopolistically competitive markets will not be excessive. To continue our earlier example, if Subway were to open a shop in the center of Lineville, many consumers would enjoy lower travel costs.

We now turn our attention to what is perhaps the most complex of market structures, oligopoly.

OLIGOPOLY

In perfectly competitive and monopolistically competitive markets, sellers do not believe that their price or output will affect rivals' prices or output. This is a good description of markets with many sellers. In a market with only a few sellers, however, it is more reasonable to expect that the pricing and output choices of any one firm will affect rivals' pricing and output and, as a result, will have a tangible impact on the overall market price and output. A market in which the actions of individual firms materially affect the overall market is called an oligopoly.

Economists have produced many models of oligopolistic markets. A central element of these models is the careful consideration of how firms respond to each other's choices. This is illustrated by considering two of the oldest and most important oligopoly models—Cournot quantity competition and Bertrand price competition.

Cournot Quantity Competition

One of the first models of oligopoly markets was developed by Augustin Cournot in 1835.[12] Cournot initially considered a market in which there were only two firms, firm 1 and firm 2. These might be two producers of DRAM chips, such as Hynix (firm 1) and Micron (firm 2). These firms produce identical goods, so that they are forced to charge

EXAMPLE 5.4   CAPACITY COMPETITION IN THE U.S. BEEF PROCESSING INDUSTRY[13]

The year 2007 was a difficult one for the American cattle slaughter industry. The four industry leaders—Tyson, Cargill, National Beef, and JBS Swift—faced the twin problems of falling demand and rising costs. In the early 2000s, the industry slaughtered 800,000 head annually; today that figure has fallen below 700,000. At the same time, feed prices have increased due to rising demand for corn-based ethanol. By mid-2007, Tyson et al. were losing $10 on every head of cattle. That was before competitive forces stepped in to make things worse.

In May 2007, Latin America's largest beef processor, JBS SA, purchased Swift & Co. to form JBS Swift, the world's largest beef processor. Swift has been a fixture in the U.S. meat industry ever since Gustavus Swift hired Andrew Chase in 1878 to design a ventilated railway car. JBS was a relative newcomer, starting operations in Brazil in 1953. JBS became an industry leader in the 1970s, when it launched an aggressive program to acquire existing slaughterhouses in Brazil and Argentina. JBS's acquisition binge never slowed down. In January 2007, it acquired a slaughterhouse operated by Swift in Buenos Aires. But the acquisition of the entire Swift & Co. was altogether of another magnitude. In explaining its motives for acquiring Swift's North American operations, JBS invoked the usual economies of scale mantra, though the two companies had no geographic overlap and little opportunity to exploit synergies.

It did not take long for JBS to make its presence felt in the U.S. market. In early September 2007, JBS added a second shift to its Greeley, Colorado, processing plant, increasing capacity by 2000 head per day. With the industry now flush with excess capacity, beef packer margins fell to minus $70 per head. Market analysts lowered their forecasts for profits and share prices tumbled. Unless capacity was withdrawn from the industry, the outlook would remain bleak.

Tyson was the first to blink. Having seen its share price cut in half in just less than a year, in January 2008 Tyson closed its Emporia, Kansas, plant, pulling 4000 head of capacity from the market. The Emporia plant seemed like a good candidate for closure, as its location hundreds of miles from major ranches made for some costly logistics. The move was hailed by industry analysts. One of these analysts, from Credit Suisse, observed, "Tyson is demonstrating leadership by doing the right thing for its business and for the industry" but also noted, "Perhaps the biggest winner here is JBS-Swift." Indeed, within a year JBS Swift acquired National Beef Packing and Smithfield, the fourth and fifth largest U.S. beef packers, respectively. In just one year, JBS had become the market share leader and had established a reputation for growth, even if it meant that other beef packers would have to cut back to maintain industry prices.

the same prices. In Cournot's model, the sole strategic choice of each firm is the amount they choose to produce, Q_1 and Q_2. Once the firms are committed to production, they set whatever price is necessary to "clear the market." This is the price at which consumers are willing to buy the total production, $Q_1 + Q_2$. The intuition behind this assumption is that because both firms are committed to production, their incremental costs are zero. Thus, if either one is unable to sell all its output, it will lower price until it is able to do so. The market price is that which enables both firms to sell all their output.

We will analyze the output decisions of Hynix and Micron facing specific demand and cost functions. Suppose that both Hynix and Micron have the following total costs of production:

$$TC_1 = 10Q_1$$
$$TC_2 = 10Q_2$$

In other words, both firms have constant marginal costs of $10 per unit, just as in the case of monopoly discussed earlier. Thus, if $Q_1 = Q_2 = 10$, then $TC_1 = TC_2 = 100$. As in our monopoly example, let market demand be given by $P = 100 - Q$, where Q is the market quantity and equals $Q_1 + Q_2$. With this demand curve, the market price falls if either firm tries to increase the amount that it sells. For example, if Hynix and Micron both produce 10 units (i.e., $Q_1 = Q_2 = 10$), then $P = \$80$. If they both produce 20 units (i.e., $Q_1 = Q_2 = 20$), then $P = \$60$.

How much will each firm produce? Each firm cares about the market price when it selects its production level. Because market price depends on the total production of both firms, the amount that Hynix desires to produce depends on how much it expects Micron to produce (and vice versa). Cournot investigated production under a simple set of expectations. Each firm "guesses" how much the other firm will produce and believes that its rival will stick to this level of output.[14] Each firm's optimal level of production is the *best response* to the level it expects its rival to choose.

A *Cournot equilibrium* is a pair of outputs Q_1^* and Q_2^* and a market price P^* that satisfy three conditions:

(C1) P^* is the price that clears the market given the firms' production levels; that is, $P^* = 100 - Q_1^* - Q_2^*$.

(C2) Q_1^* is Hynix's profit-maximizing output given that it guesses Micron will choose Q_2^*.

(C3) Q_2^* is Micron's profit-maximizing output given that it guesses Hynix will choose Q_1^*.

Conditions C2 and C3 imply that each firm correctly guesses its rival's production level. This may seem like a strong assumption, and we will return to it shortly.

To find the market equilibrium choices of Q_1 and Q_2, consider first Hynix's choice of Q_1. According to condition C2, Hynix's equilibrium choice of Q_1 must maximize its profits, given Micron's choice of Q_2. Suppose that Hynix thinks that Micron is going to produce output Q_{2g}, where the subscript g reminds us that this is a guess rather than the actual value. Then Hynix calculates that if it produces Q_1 units of output, its profits, denoted by Π_1, will be

$$\Pi_1 = \text{Revenue} - \text{Total cost} = P_1 Q_1 - TC_1 = (100 - Q_1 - Q_{2g})Q_1 - 10Q_1$$

Hynix needs to solve for the value of Q_1 that maximizes its profits. We can use calculus to determine that the profit-maximizing value of Q_1 satisfies:[15]

$$\text{Profit-maximizing value of } Q_1 = 45 - .5Q_{2g}$$

Some managers who see the Cournot model for the first time believe that it is all rather abstract and bears little resemblance to how they actually make decisions. Managers may claim that they are more likely to determine the profit-maximizing output through spreadsheet analyses. (The same would apply to computing the optimal price in the Bertrand model that is discussed in the next section.) Yet in this case Hynix would reach the same conclusion if it prepared a spreadsheet as follows:

• Create columns for Hynix's quantity, Micron's quantity, the market price, and Hynix's profits.

• Make a (hopefully) informed guess about Q_2.

- Use the formula $P = 100 - (Q_1 + Q_2)$ to determine how price will vary with different levels of Q_1. Even if Hynix does not have an exact demand formula, it can estimate how market price is likely to change as total output changes.

- Given the values of P computed above, compute profits for different levels of Q_1. This will indicate the profit maximizing value of Q_1 for any estimate of Q_2.

The profit-maximizing value of Q_1 is called Hynix's best response to Micron. According to this equation, Hynix's best response is a decreasing function of Q_{2g}. This implies that if Hynix expects Micron to increase output, it will reduce its own output. This makes sense. If Micron increases output, then condition (C1) states that the market price must decrease. Facing a lower price, Hynix prefers to produce less itself. The line labeled R_1 in Figure 5.2 depicts Hynix's choice of Q_1 as a function of its conjecture about Q_2. Economists call this line Hynix's *reaction function*.

Similarly, we can use condition (C3) to solve for Micron's best response to Hynix's choice of Q_1:

$$\text{Profit-maximizing value of } Q_2 = 45 - .5Q_{1g}$$

Micron's choice of Q_2 as a function of Hynix's choice of Q_1 is shown as reaction function R_2 in Figure 5.2.

Thus far, the Cournot calculations are extremely intuitive. Firms are likely to reach conclusions such as these whether they perform the formal math, rely on spreadsheets, or even just use gut instinct. The remaining Cournot calculations rely on our assumption about equilibrium behavior. Recall that in the Cournot equilibrium, each firm chooses output simultaneously and each correctly guesses its rival's output. In other words, each firm has made the simultaneous best response to the other's output choice. In Chapter 7 we explore other possible equilibria involving sequential choices. A key managerial skill is to understand and even influence how firms are interacting. For now, we will compute the equilibrium choices in the Cournot world.

It turns out that only one pair of outputs is simultaneously the best response to each other. These outputs, which we denote by Q_1^* and Q_2^*, are found by solving both

FIGURE 5.2
COURNOT REACTION FUNCTIONS

The curve R_1 is firm 1's reaction function. It shows firm 1's profit-maximizing output for any level of output Q_2 produced by firm 2. The curve R_2 is firm 2's reaction function. It shows firm 2's profit-maximizing output for any level of output Q_1 produced by firm 1. The Cournot equilibrium outputs, denoted by Q_1^* and Q_2^*, occur at the point where the two reaction functions cross. In this case, the equilibrium output of each firm is 30. At the Cournot equilibrium, each firm is choosing its profit-maximizing output, given the output produced by the other firm.

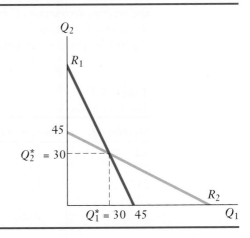

firms' reaction functions simultaneously. In our present example, this solution is $Q_1^* = Q_2^* = 30$. Graphically, this corresponds to the point in Figure 5.2 where the two reaction functions intersect. We can also solve for the equilibrium market price P^* and the profits each firm earns. Recalling that $P = 100 - Q_1 - Q_2$, we find that $P^* = \$40$. Substituting price and quantity into the equation for each firm's profits reveals that each firm makes $900 in profit in equilibrium.

Cournot's assumption that firms will simultaneously select the best response to each other's choices seems rather demanding. How are firms supposed to make such accurate guesses about each other's output? Yet as a focal point for analysis, this assumption may not be too bad. It means that in equilibrium, each firm will be happy with its choice of output, which seems more satisfying than assuming that each firm is consistently unhappy with its choice. Moreover, neither Hynix nor Micron need be omniscient for the Cournot equilibrium quantities to emerge. Suppose that both firms are "out of equilibrium" in the sense that at least one firm has chosen to produce a quantity other than 30. For example, suppose that $Q_1 = Q_2 = 40$. Neither firm will be happy with its choice of quantity—each is producing more than it would like given its rival's production. As a result, we would expect each firm to adjust to the other firm's choices.

Table 5.5 shows an example of the adjustment process. Suppose that Hynix makes the first adjustment. It examines its profit-maximization equation and determines that if $Q_2 = 40$, it should choose $Q_1 = 25$. Suppose now that Hynix reduces its output to 25. Micron will examine its own profit-maximization equation and determine that if Hynix chooses $Q_1 = 25$, then it should choose $Q_2 = 32.5$. Table 5.5 shows that Q_1 and Q_2 continue to converge toward the equilibrium values of $Q_1 = Q_2 = 30$.

The Revenue Destruction Effect

In the Cournot model, equilibrium industry output does not maximize industry profit. Industry profit is maximized at the monopoly quantity and price computed earlier—45 units of output sold at $55 each. By independently maximizing their own profits, firms produce more output than they would if they collusively maximized industry profits. This is characteristic of oligopolistic industries: The pursuit of individual self-interest does not maximize the profits of the group as a whole. This occurs under Cournot competition for the following reason. When one firm, say Hynix, expands its output, it reduces the market price. This reduces revenues from all customers who would have purchased DRAM chips at the higher price. This is known as the *revenue destruction effect*. Unlike a monopolist, which would bear the full burden of the revenue destruction effect, Hynix shares this burden with Micron. Thus, Hynix expands its production volume more aggressively than it would if it were a monopolist,

TABLE 5.5
THE COURNOT ADJUSTMENT PROCESS

Starting Q_1	Starting Q_2	Firm That Is Adjusting	Ending Q_1	Ending Q_2
40	40	Firm 1	25	40
25	40	Firm 2	25	32.5
25	32.5	Firm 1	28.75	32.5
28.75	32.5	Firm 2	28.75	30.63
28.75	30.63	Firm 1	29.69	30.63

TABLE 5.6
COURNOT EQUILIBRIA AS THE NUMBER OF FIRMS INCREASES

Number of Firms	Market Price	Market Quantity	Per-Firm Profits	Total Profits
2	$40	60	$900	$1,800
3	$32.5	67.5	$506.25	$1,518.75
5	$25	75	$225	$1,125
10	$18.2	81.8	$66.94	$669.40
100	$10.9	89.1	$0.79	$79

or if it was trying to maximize industry profit. Micron will do likewise, driving the oligopoly price well below the monopoly price.

The revenue destruction effect helps explain why small firms are often most willing to disrupt pricing stability. Firms of all sizes enjoy the same benefit when they expand output by a given amount, but smaller firms suffer a smaller revenue destruction effect, which is instead borne mainly by their larger rivals. The revenue destruction effect also explains why the Cournot equilibrium price falls as the number of firms in the market increases. Each firm has, on average, a smaller share of the market and so bears a smaller share of the revenue destruction effect. Table 5.6 illustrates this point by showing equilibrium prices, profits, and outputs in a Cournot industry with the same demand curve and cost function as in the preceding example. The equilibrium price and profit per firm decline as the number of firms increases. More generally, it can be shown that the average PCM of a firm in a Cournot equilibrium is given by the formula $PCM = H/\eta$, where H denotes the Herfindahl and η is the price elasticity of market demand. Thus, the less concentrated the industry (the lower the industry's H), the smaller will be PCMs in equilibrium.

Cournot's Model in Practice

Antitrust enforcers often use the Herfindahl index to predict the effects of a merger on pricing. Cournot's model provides a justification for this approach; in markets where firms behave as Cournot describes, one can compute how a merger will affect the Herfindahl index and use the results of the Cournot model to predict the change in price. Because many factors besides market concentration may ultimately affect equilibrium output and price, computation of the Herfindahl is usually just the first step in merger analysis. We will discuss additional factors in the next two chapters.

The Cournot model has another practical use. It is very straightforward to alter one or more parameters of the model—the demand curve and firm costs—and recompute equilibria. This makes it possible to forecast how changes in demand and costs will affect profitability in markets in which firms behave according to the Cournot equilibrium assumption. This makes the Cournot model a valuable tool for planning.

Bertrand Price Competition

In Cournot's model, each firm selects a quantity to produce, and the resulting total output determines the market price. Alternatively, one might imagine a market in which each firm selects a price and stands ready to meet all the demand for its product at that price. This model of competition was first analyzed by Joseph Bertrand

EXAMPLE 5.5 COURNOT EQUILIBRIUM IN THE CORN WET MILLING INDUSTRY

Michael Porter and Michael Spence's case study of the corn wet milling industry is a real-world illustration of the Cournot model.[16] Firms in the corn wet milling industry convert corn into cornstarch and corn syrup. The corn syrup industry was a fairly stable oligopoly until the 1960s, when several firms entered the market, including Archer-Daniels-Midland and Cargill. The new competitors and new capacity disrupted the old equilibrium and drove prices downward. By the early 1970s, however, competitive stability returned to the industry as capacity utilization rates and prices rose. In 1972, a major development hit the industry: the production of high-fructose corn syrup (HFCS) became commercially viable. HFCS can be used instead of sugar to sweeten products, such as soft drinks. With sugar prices expected to rise, a significant market for HFCS beckoned. Firms in the corn wet milling industry had to decide whether and how to add capacity to accommodate the expected demand.

Porter and Spence studied this capacity expansion process. They did so through a detailed simulation of competitive behavior based on an in-depth study of the 11 major competitors in the industry. Porter and Spence postulated that each firm's expansion decision was based on a conjecture about the overall expansion of industry capacity, as well as expectations about demand and sugar prices. Their model also took into account that capacity choices coupled with demand conditions determined industry prices of cornstarch, corn syrup, and HFCS. The notion that a firm's capacity choice is based on conjectures about the capacity choices of other firms is directly analogous to the idea in the Cournot model that each firm bases its output choice on conjectures of the output choices of other firms. The notion that capacity decisions then deter-

mine a market price is also analogous to the Cournot model.

Porter and Spence's simulation of the industry attempted to find an "equilibrium": an industry capacity expansion path that, when each firm made its optimal capacity decision based on the conjecture that this path would prevail, resulted in an actual pattern of capacity expansion that matched the assumed pattern. This is directly analogous to the notion of a Cournot equilibrium, in which each firm's expectations about the behavior of its competitors are confirmed by their actual behavior. Based on their simulation of industry decision making, Porter and Spence determined that an industry equilibrium would result in a moderate amount of additional capacity added to the industry as a result of the commercialization of HFCS. The specific predictions of their model compared with the actual pattern of capacity expansion are shown below.

Though not perfect, Porter and Spence's calculated equilibrium comes quite close to the actual pattern of capacity expansion in the industry, particularly in 1973 and 1974. The discrepancies in 1975 and 1976 mainly reflect timing. Porter and Spence's equilibrium model did not consider capacity additions in the years beyond 1976. In 1976, however, the industry had more than 4 billion pounds of HFCS capacity under construction, and that capacity did not come on line until after 1976. Including this capacity, the total HFCS capacity expansion was 9.2 billion pounds, as compared with the 9.1 billion pounds of predicted equilibrium capacity. Porter and Spence's research suggests that a Cournot-like model, when adapted to the specific conditions of the corn wet milling industry, provided predictions that came remarkably close to the actual pattern of capacity expansion decisions.

	Post-1973	1974	1975	1976	1976	Total
Actual industry capacity	0.6	1.0	1.4	2.2	4	9.2 (billions of lb)
Predicted equilibrium capacity	0.6	1.5	3.5	3.5	0	9.1

in 1883.[17] In Bertrand's model, each firm selects a price to maximize its own profits, given the price that it believes the other firm will select. Each firm also believes that its pricing practices will not affect the pricing of its rival; each firm views its rival's price as fixed.

We can use the cost and demand conditions from the Cournot model to explore the Bertrand market equilibrium, again using the (hypothetical) example of rival DRAM producers Hynix and Micron. (Recall that firm 1 is Hynix and firm 2 is Micron.) We saw earlier that when $MC_1 = MC_2 = \$10$, and demand is given by $P = 100 - Q_1 - Q_2$, the Cournot equilibrium is $Q_1 = Q_2 = 30$ and $P_1 = P_2 = \$40$. This is not, however, a Bertrand equilibrium, because each firm believes it can capture the entire market by slightly undercutting its rival's price. For example, if $P_2 = \$40$ and $P_1 = \$39$, then $Q_1 = 61$ and $Q_2 = 0$. As a result, Hynix earns profits of $1,769$, well above the profits of $900 it would earn if it matched Micron's price of $40.

Of course, $P_1 = \$39$ and $P_2 = \$40$ cannot be an equilibrium either because at these prices, Micron will want to undercut Hynix's price. As long as both firms set prices that exceed marginal costs, one firm will always have an incentive to slightly undercut its competitor. This implies that the only possible equilibrium is $P_1 = P_2 =$ marginal cost $= \$10$. At these prices, neither firm can do better by changing its price. If either firm lowers price, it will lose money on each unit sold. If either firm raises price, it would sell nothing.

In Bertrand's model with firms producing identical products, rivalry between two firms results in the perfectly competitive outcome. When firms' products are differentiated, as in monopolistic competition, price competition is less intense. (Later in this chapter, we will examine Bertrand price competition when firms produce differentiated products.) Bertrand competition can destabilize markets where firms must incur sunk costs to do business, because there is not enough variable profit to cover the sunk costs. If one firm should exit the market, the remaining firm could try to raise its price. But this might simply attract a new entrant that will wrest away some of the remaining firm's business. Price competition may be limited if one or both firms runs up against a capacity constraint and cannot readily steal market share, or if the firms learn to stop competing on the basis of price. These ideas are covered in greater depth in Chapter 7.

Why Are Cournot and Bertrand Different?

The Cournot and Bertrand models make dramatically different predictions about the quantities, prices, and profits that will arise under oligopolistic competition. One way to reconcile the two models is to recognize that Cournot and Bertrand competition may take place over different time frames. Cournot competitors can be thought of as choosing capacities and then competing as capacity-constrained price setters. The result of this "two-stage" competition (first choose capacities and then choose prices) is identical to the Cournot equilibrium in quantities.[18] More cutthroat Bertrand competition results if the competitors are no longer constrained by their capacity choices, either because demand declines or a competitor miscalculates and adds too much capacity.

Another way to reconcile the models is to recognize that they make different assumptions about how firms expect their rivals to react to their own competitive moves. The Cournot model applies most naturally to markets in which firms must make production decisions in advance, are committed to selling all of their output, and are therefore unlikely to react to fluctuations in the rivals' output. This might occur if the majority of production costs are sunk, or because it is costly to hold

EXAMPLE 5.6 GAZPROM

The world's largest producer of natural gas is Russian-based Gazprom. According to the company's website (www.gazprom.com), its mission is "to provide effective and well-balanced gas supply to Russian customers and to safely implement long-term gas export contracts," and its strategy is "to acquire the leading position among the global energy companies by entering new markets, diversifying core business activities, and ensuring reliable supplies." Both its mission and its strategy are supported by the enormous reserves of natural gas that the company holds.

Gazprom was born out of the Soviet Gas Ministry. The state still holds a controlling interest in the firm, just slightly above 50 percent.

Monopolies are often seen as exertion of economic power, and Gazprom is no exception. But the company wields considerable political power as well. Rumors abound regarding how much of the company is owned by former Russian president Vladmir Putin and his cronies, including his (some suggest "hand-picked") successor Dmitri Medvedev, who previously was chairman of Gazprom. As reported by Australia's *The Daily Reckoning*, the *Moscow Times* had an article in November 2007 that suggested that Putin's holdings might be as much as 4.5 percent of Gazprom, estimated at the time to be worth about $13 billion, and described Gazprom as "the world's most politically influential corporation."[19]

Gazprom's political muscle was evident when Russia's State Duma (the lower house of its Parliament) easily passed a bill that gave the company a monopoly on exports of natural gas, including a provision that the gas would have to pass through the pipes, also owned by Gazprom in July 2006. The bill would, of course, be signed into law by President Putin.

The exercise of monopoly power was evident in Russia's 2007 confrontation with Ukraine over the price of gas. According to an article by the Centre for European Policy Studies (CEPS), Gazprom made "deliberate use of monopoly power in stopping supplies to Ukraine and Moldova" and that this revealed to members of the European Union (EU) community that "Russia is showing itself to be all about raw power, with little or no regard for any overarching international legal framework."[20]

The CEPS article details the ways in which Gazprom violated the rules of economic and political conduct set up by the EU in order to rein in monopoly power. Five particular instances of Gazprom's conduct are specified: (1) Gazprom's demand for price increases, and the stop to supplies on January 1st in support of its demand; (2) Gazprom blocked Ukraine's attempt to negotiate directly with Turkmenistan by refusing to grant Turkmenistan the right of way for its gas through the Gazprom pipeline network unless the gas was sold first to Gazprom; (3) this refusal of access to the pipelines is contrary to the EU's competition and internal market policy principles for such networks, adding that, in principle, the EU's jurisdiction extends beyond its frontier where trade with the EU is affected; (4) the refusal of pipeline access to Turkmen gas illustrates the consequences of Russia's refusal at the official policy level to subscribe to basic rules for regulating monopolistic markets, thus leaving room for unconstrained monopolistic behavior by Gazprom; (5) the RosUkrEnergo intermediary between Ukraine and the suppliers is a monumental piece of murky non-transparency for a matter of such strategic economic importance. The CEPS suggests that Russia has two basic options:

It has to either signal credibly that it is willing to enter into and help complete a multilaterally ordered market system for gas that constrains monopolistic behavior by legally binding rules or, by not doing so, provoke gas consuming powers into diversification of investments that will, in due course, create conditions of competition.[21]

Gazprom is planning to extend its sphere of influence, both in terms of searching for gas in other countries and seeking to supply in other markets. In June 2009, the company announced that it had its sights set on supplying 5 to 10 percent of the U.S. market's demand for natural gas. However, its actions resurfaced fears that had been raised decades earlier; that countries dependent on imported gas from Russia might be faced with demands for extreme price increases and refusal of supply when price hikes are not met. Ironically, such actions had never been taken by Gazprom's predecessor, the Soviet Gas Ministry, even in the Cold War period.

inventories—commodities such as natural gas and copper come to mind. In such settings, firms will do what it takes to sell their output and will also believe that its competitors will keep to their planned sales levels. Thus, if a firm lowers its price, it cannot expect to steal customers from its rivals. Because "business stealing" is not an option, Cournot competitors must share in the revenue destruction effect if they expand output. As a result, they set prices less aggressively than Bertrand competitors. Thus, the Cournot equilibrium outcome, while not the monopoly one, nevertheless results in positive profits and a price that exceeds marginal and average cost.

The Bertrand model pertains to markets in which capacity is sufficiently flexible that firms can meet all of the demand that arises at the prices they announce. If firms' products are perfect substitutes, then each Bertrand competitor believes that it can steal massive amounts of business from its competitors through a small cut in price, effectively bearing none of the revenue destruction effect. In equilibrium, price–cost margins are driven to zero.

These distinctions help to explain the pro-cyclicality of airline industry profits. During business downturns, the airlines have substantial excess capacity on many routes. Because many consumers perceive the airlines as selling undifferentiated products, each airline can fill empty seats by undercutting rivals' prices and stealing their customers. The resulting competition resembles Bertrand's model and has led to substantial losses. During boom times, airlines operate near capacity and have little incentive to cut prices. Because they have few empty seats, they are unable to steal business even if they wanted to. Competition resembles Cournot's model and allows the airlines to be profitable. In recent years, domestic U.S. airlines have withdrawn capacity by flying fewer flights and downsizing planes; this has helped stabilize pricing during downturns.

Many other issues may be considered when assessing the likely conduct and performance of firms in an oligopoly. Competition may be based on a variety of product parameters, including quality, availability, and advertising. Firms may not know the strategic choices of their competitors. The timing of decision making can profoundly influence profits. We discuss all of these issues in Chapter 7.

Bertrand Price Competition When Products Are Horizontally Differentiated

In many oligopolistic markets, products are close, but not perfect, substitutes. The Bertrand model of price competition does not fully capture the nature of price competition in these settings. Fortunately, we can adapt the logic of the Bertrand model to deal with horizontally differentiated products.

When products are horizontally differentiated, a firm that lowers its price will only steal some if its rival's customers. This discourages the kind of price cutting that takes place in the Bertrand model with identical products. To illustrate, consider the U.S. cola market. Farid Gasini, J. J. Lafont, and Quang Vuong (GLV) have used statistical methods to estimate demand curves for Coke (denoted by 1) and Pepsi (denoted by 2):[22]

$$Q_1 = 63.42 - 3.98P_1 + 2.25P_2$$
$$Q_2 = 49.52 - 5.48P_2 + 1.40P_1$$

With these demand functions, as Coke lowers its price below that of Pepsi, Coke's demand rises gradually.

We can use the logic of the Cournot model to determine the price we expect each cola maker to charge. Because firms are choosing prices rather than quantities, this is called a *differentiated Bertrand* model. To solve for the differentiated Bertrand equilibrium, we will need information about demand (given above) as well as information about marginal costs. GLV estimated that Coca-Cola had a constant marginal cost equal to $4.96, and Pepsi had a constant marginal cost of $3.96.

Armed with demand and cost data, we follow the same logic that we used to compute the Cournot equilibrium. We start by computing each firm's profit-maximizing price as a function of its guess about its rival's price. Coca-Cola's profit can be written as its price–cost margin times the quantity it sells, which is given by its demand function.

$$\Pi_1 = (P_1 - 4.96)(63.49 - 3.98P_1 + 2.25P_{2g})$$

(We again use the subscript g to emphasize that Coca-Cola is making a guess about Pepsi's price.) Using calculus to solve this maximization problem yields a reaction function[23]

$$P_1 = 10.44 + .2826P_{2g}$$

Pepsi's optimal price is derived similarly. It maximizes

$$\Pi_2 = (P_2 - 3.94)(49.52 - 5.48P_2 + 1.40P_{1g})$$

which yields a reaction function

$$P_2 = 6.49 + .1277P_{1g}$$

As with the Cournot model, Coke and Pepsi could have reached conclusions like these using spreadsheet analysis. Despite what appears to be excessive mathematical formality, there is nothing unrealistic about this approach to modeling pricing decisions.

These reaction functions, displayed in Figure 5.3, are upward sloping. Thus, the lower the price the firm expects its rival to charge, the lower the price it should charge. In this sense, "aggressive" behavior by one firm (price cutting) is met by "aggressive" behavior by rivals. Note the contrast with the Cournot model, where "aggressive" behavior by one firm (output expansion) was met by "passive" behavior by rivals (output reduction).

Solving the two reaction functions simultaneously yields the Bertrand equilibrium in prices:

$$P_1 = \$12.72$$
$$P_2 = \$8.11$$

FIGURE 5.3
BERTRAND EQUILIBRIUM WITH HORIZONTALLY DIFFERENTIATED PRODUCTS

Firm 1's reaction function shows its profit-maximizing price for any price charged by firm 2. Firm 2's reaction function shows its profit-maximizing price for any price charged by firm 1. The Bertrand equilibrium prices occur at the intersection of these reaction functions. In this example, this is at $P_1 = \$12.72$ and $P_2 = \$8.11$. At this point, each firm is choosing a profit-maximizing price, given the price charged by the other firm.

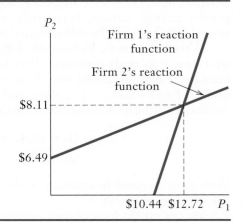

Interestingly, the actual average real prices over the period (1968–1986) to which GLV's analysis pertains were $12.96 for Coca-Cola and $8.16 for Pepsi. The differentiated Bertrand model does an excellent job matching the actual pricing behavior of these two firms in the U.S. market. Note that both Coke and Pepsi's equilibrium prices are well in excess of their marginal production costs. This illustrates that product differentiation softens price competition.

EVIDENCE ON MARKET STRUCTURE AND PERFORMANCE

The theories examined in the previous sections suggest that market structure should be related to the level of prices and profitability that prevail in a market. This is clearly true under Cournot competition, where price is directly related to the Herfindahl. It may also be true under Bertrand competition because each additional firm reduces the opportunities for differentiation. Many economists have tested whether the predicted link between structure and performance actually exists.

Price and Concentration

The relationship between price and concentration could be studied by comparing differences in price–cost margins and concentration levels across different industries. But price–cost margins may vary across industries for many reasons besides concentration, such as accounting practices, regulation, product differentiation, the nature of sales transactions, and the concentration of buyers.

For these reasons, most studies of concentration and price focus on specific industries.[24] In these studies, researchers compare prices for the same products in geographically separate markets that have different numbers of competitors. By comparing the same products across distinct markets, researchers can be more confident that variations in price are due to variations in competition rather than to variations in accounting or other factors.

Leonard Weiss summarizes the results of price and concentration studies in more than 20 industries, including cement, railroad freight, supermarkets, and gasoline retailing. He finds that with few exceptions, prices tend to be higher in concentrated markets. For example, one study found that gasoline prices in local markets in which the top three gasoline retailers had a 60 percent market share were, on average, about 5 percent higher than in markets in which the top three retailers had a 50 percent market share.

Timothy Bresnahan and Peter Reiss used a novel methodology to study the relationship between concentration and prices. They asked, "How many firms must be in a market for price to approach competitive levels?"[25] They examined locally provided services such as doctors, tire dealers, and plumbers. For each service, they calculated "entry thresholds," defined as the minimum population necessary to support a given number of sellers. Let E_n denote the entry threshold for n sellers. For all services, they found that E_2 was about four times E_1. This could make sense only if prices are lower when there are two sellers than when there is one. When this happens, demand must more than double to make up for the intensified competition. They also found that $E_3 - E_2 > E_2 - E_1$, suggesting further intensification of price competition as the number of sellers increases from two to three. Finally, they found that $E_4 - E_3 = E_3 - E_2$, suggesting that once there are three sellers in a market, price competition is as intense as it will get.

CHAPTER SUMMARY

- The first step in analyzing competition is to identify competitors. Competitors in output markets sell products that are substitutes. Competitors in input markets buy inputs that are substitutes.

- Generally, two sellers are competitors in an output market if their products are close substitutes, that is, have similar product-performance characteristics. Price elasticities are useful for determining whether a product has close substitutes.

- Once a market is well defined, its structure may be measured using an N-firm concentration ratio or a Herfindahl index.

- The structure of a market is often related to the conduct of the firms within it. The spectrum of competitive interaction ranges from competition and monopolistic competition to oligopoly and monopoly.

- In competitive markets, consumers are extremely price sensitive, forcing sellers to set prices close to marginal costs. Markets with homogeneous products and many sellers are more likely to feature competitive pricing. Excess capacity exacerbates pricing pressures, often driving prices below average costs.

- Monopolists have such a substantial share of their market that they ignore the pricing and production decisions of fringe firms. They may set prices well above marginal cost without losing much business.

- Monopolistically competitive markets have many sellers, each with some loyal customers. Prices are set according to the willingness of consumers to switch from one seller to another—if consumers are disloyal and have low search costs, sellers may lower prices to steal business from their competitors. Profits may be eroded further by entrants.

- Oligopolies have so few firms that each firm's production and pricing strategy appreciably affects the market price. Market prices can be well above marginal costs, or driven down to marginal costs, depending on the interaction among oligopolists and the degree of product differentiation among them.

- Many markets, including consumer goods markets, feature a small number of large firms that exploit economies of scale in marketing and several niche players.

- Studies confirm that prices are strongly related to industry structure. Price–cost margins tend to be much lower in more competitive markets.

QUESTIONS

1. Why are the concepts of own and cross-price elasticities of demand essential to competitor identification and market definition?

2. In a recent antitrust case, it was necessary to determine whether grocers that specialize in natural and organic foods, such as Whole Foods and Wild Oats, constitute a separate market. How would you go about identifying the market served by these grocers? (The U.S. Federal Trade Commission unsuccessfully attempted to block the Whole Foods/Wild Oats merger.)

3. How would you characterize the nature of competition in the restaurant industry? Are there submarkets with distinct competitive pressures? Are there important

substitutes that constrain pricing? Given these competitive issues, how can a restaurant be profitable?

4. How does industry-level price elasticity of demand shape the opportunities for making profit in an industry? How does the firm-level price elasticity of demand shape the opportunities for making profit in an industry?

5 What is the "revenue destruction effect"? As the number of Cournot competitors in a market increases, the price generally falls. What does this have to do with the revenue destruction effect? Smaller firms often have greater incentive to reduce prices than do larger firms. What does this have to do with the revenue destruction effect?

6. How does the calculation of demand responsiveness in Linesville change if customers rent two videos at a time? What intuition can you draw from this about the magnitude of price competition in various types of markets?

7. Numerous studies have shown that there is usually a systematic relationship between concentration and price. What is this relationship? Offer two brief explanations for this relationship.

8. The relationship described in question 7 does not always appear to hold. What factors, besides the number of firms in the market, might affect margins?

9. The following are the approximate U.S. market shares of different brands of soft drinks: Coke—45% Pepsi—30% Dr. Pepper/7-Up—15% All other brands—10%.

   a. Compute the Herfindahl for the soft-drink market. Suppose that Pepsi acquired Dr. Pepper/7-Up. Compute the post-merger Herfindahl. What assumptions did you make?

   b. Federal antitrust agencies would be concerned to see a Herfindahl increase of the magnitude you computed in (a), and might challenge the merger. Pepsi could respond by defining the market as something other than soft drinks. What market definition might they propose? Why would this change the Herfindahl?

10. "The only way to succeed in a market with homogeneous products is to produce more efficiently than most other firms." Comment. Does this imply that efficiency is less important in oligopoly and monopoly markets?

11. In what ways are monopolistically competitive markets "monopolistic?" In what ways are they "competitive?"

12. Adam and Catherine are choosing between two ice cream shops, Icy and Frosty, located at either end of a 1-mile-long beach. Adam is standing in front of Icy, while Catherine is standing in front of Frosty. Both Adam and Catherine are each willing to pay, at most, $6 for one ice cream cone. It costs them $1 to walk the 1-mile distance between the shops. Icy is government-run, so the price is fixed at exactly $4/cone and will not change. The shops face costs of $0.25/cone. What price should Frosty charge if it is to maximize its total profits from Adam and Catherine?

13. The large turbine generator industry is a duopoly. The two firms, GE and Westinghouse, compete through Cournot quantity setting competition. The demand curve for the industry is $P = 100 - Q$, where P is price (in $millions) and Q is the total quantity produced by GE and Westinghouse. Currently, each firm has marginal cost of $40 and no fixed costs. Show that the equilibrium price is $60, with each firm producing 20 machines and earning profits of $400.

14. The dancing machine industry is a duopoly. The two firms, Chuckie B Corp. and Gene Gene Dancing Machines, compete through Cournot quantity-setting competition. The demand curve for the industry is $P = 120 - Q$, where Q is the total quantity produced by Chuckie B and Gene Gene. Currently, each firm has marginal cost of $60 and no fixed costs.

   a. What is the equilibrium price, quantity, and profit for each firm?

   b. Chuckie B Corp. is considering implementing a proprietary technology with a one-time sunk cost of $200. Once this investment is made, marginal cost will be reduced to $40. Gene Gene has no access to this or any other cost-saving technology, and its marginal cost will remain at $60. Should Chuckie B invest in the new technology? (*Hint*: You must compute another Cournot equilibrium.)

15. Consider a market with two horizontally differentiated firms, X and Y. Each has a constant marginal cost of $20. Demand functions are

$$Q_x = 100 - 2P_x + 1P_y$$
$$Q_y = 100 - 2P_y + 1P_x$$

   Calculate the Bertrand equilibrium in prices in this market.

16. How do you think the equilibrium in question 15 will change if cross-price elasticities of demand increase? How would you alter the equations to show such an increase? Can you compute the new equilibrium?

ENDNOTES

[1] Indirect competitors may also include firms that are not currently direct competitors but might become so. This definition forces managers to go beyond current sales data to identify potential competitors.

[2] Capps, C., D., Dranove, and M. Satterthwaite, "Competition and Market Power in Option Demand Markets," *RAND Journal of Economics*, 2003, 34(4), pp. 737–763.

[3] The index is named for Orris Herfindahl, who developed it while writing a Ph.D dissertation at Columbia University on concentration in the steel industry. The index is sometimes referred to as the Herfindahl-Hirschman index and is often abbreviated HHI.

[4] This was shown in the Economics Primer.

[5] Potash (potassium oxide) is a compound used to produce products such as fertilizer and soap.

[6] Chapters 5 and 6 of Markham, J., *The Fertilizer Industry*, Nashville, TN, Vanderbilt University Press, 1958.

[7] We will assume that this offer does not require Deere to adjust the price at which it sells engines to its other customers.

[8] Fisher, F., *Industrial Organization, Antitrust, and the Law*, Cambridge, MA, MIT Press, 1991.

[9] Demsetz, H., "Two Systems of Belief about Monopoly," in Goldschmidt, H. et al. (eds.), *Industrial Concentration: The New Learning*, Boston, Little, Brown, 1974.

[10] Chamberlin, E. H., *The Theory of Monopolistic Competition*, Cambridge, MA, Harvard University Press, 1933.

[11] Recall that the optimal $PCM = 1/\eta$. Thus, in this case, $PCM = (P - 10)/P = .5$. Solving for P yields $P = \$20$.

[12] Cournot, A., "On the Competition of Producers," Chapter 7 in *Research into the Mathematical Principles of the Theory of Wealth*, translated by N. T. Bacon, New York, Macmillan,

1897. For an excellent review of the Cournot model and other theories of oligopoly behavior, see Shapiro, C., "Theories of Oligopoly Behavior," Chapter 6 in Willig, R., and R. Schmalensee (eds.), *Handbook of Industrial Organization*, Amsterdam, North Holland, 1989.

[13]Aldrich, L., 2008, "Cattle-Market Psychology Shaken by Plant Closure," *The Wall Street Journal*, 1/30/2008, p. B5A.

[14]Cournot's assumption is actually a special case of a modeling assumption known as the Nash equilibrium, which is used to identify likely strategies in a variety of contexts. The Nash equilibrium is discussed in the Economics Primer.

[15]Profit π_1 can be written as: $90Q_1 - Q_1^2 - Q_{2g}Q_1$. If we treat Q_{2g} as a constant and take the derivative of p_1 with respect to Q_1, we get $\delta\pi_1/\delta Q_1 = 90 - 2Q_1 - Q_{2g}$. Setting this derivative equal to 0 and solving for Q_1 yields the profit-maximizing value of Q_1.

[16]Porter, M., and A. M. Spence, "The Capacity Expansion Decision in a Growing Oligopoly: The Case of Corn Wet Milling," in McCall, J. J. (ed.), *The Economics of Information Uncertainty*, Chicago, University of Chicago Press, 1982, pp. 259–316.

[17]Bertrand, J., "Book Review of Recherche sur Les Principes Mathematiques de la Theorie des Richesses," *Journal des Savants*, 67, 1883, pp. 499–508.

[18]The idea that the Cournot equilibrium can (under some circumstances) emerge as the outcome of a "two-stage game" in which firms first choose capacities and then choose prices is due to Kreps, D. and J. Scheinkman, "Quantity Precommitment and Bertrand Competition Yield Cournot Outcomes," *Bell Journal of Economics*, 14, 1983, pp. 326–337.

[19]"Gazprom, the State-Controlled Natural Gas Monopoly," by Dan Amoss, The Daily Reckoning, February 27, 2008. Accessed June 23, 2009 at http://www.dailyreckoning.com.au/gazprom-monopoly/2008/02/27/

[20]"What to do about Gazprom's monopoly power?" Centre for European Policy Studies, February 19, 2007, accessed June 23, 2009 at http://www.ceps.eu/Article.php?article_id=509

[21]Ibid.

[22]Gasini, F., J. J. Lafont, and Q. Vuong, "Econometric Analysis of Collusive Behavior in a Soft-Drink Market," *Journal of Economics and Management Strategy*, Summer 1992, pp. 277–311.

[23]Differentiating total profits Π_1 with respect to P_1 (treating P_{2g} as a constant), setting this expression equal to 0, and solving the resulting equation for P_1 yields firm 1's reaction function.

[24]Two excellent surveys are provided by Weiss, L. (ed.), *Concentration and Price*, Cambridge, MA, MIT Press, 1989, and Schmalensee, R., "Interindustry Studies of Structure and Performance," in Schmalensee, R., and R. Willig (eds.), *The Handbook of Industrial Organization*, Amsterdam, Elsevier, 1989, pp. 951–1010.

[25]Bresnahan, T., and P. Reiss, "Entry and Competition in Concentrated Markets," *Journal of Political Economy*, 99, 1991, pp. 997–1009.

6   ENTRY AND EXIT

Long before the film *The Social Network* made Facebook founder Mark Zuckerberg a household name, another social networking web site was taking the Internet by storm. Founded in 2003 by ex-employees of Friendster (a very early social networking site), MySpace allowed members to create user communities, post content to community boards, publicize parties, and send instant messages to fellow community members. Perhaps the most exciting feature in the early days was the ability of MySpace members to create their own web pages. MySpace and its parent company were purchased in 2005 by Rupert Murdoch for $580 million, and by 2008, MySpace had over 100 million unique visitors each month, making it the most popular social networking Internet site.

Few people realized it at the time, but the decline of MySpace began in 2004, when Zuckerberg launched Facebook. Facebook differed from MySpace in several critical ways. Facebook required that members use their actual names and that their web pages conform to a standard format. In contrast, MySpace members routinely used online pseudonyms, and their web pages were bastions of creative design. Facebook developed an iPhone app in 2007; MySpace did not respond until a year and 12 million iPhones later. Facebook made an explicit effort to be business friendly, for example, by restricting search results. MySpace, with its roots in the Southern California music scene, was much slower to reach out to business. The rest, as they say, is history. By 2009, Facebook had over 250 million unique visitors monthly, while MySpace was on the decline. Today, MySpace hangs on by a thread, largely because there are few ongoing costs associated with maintaining the site.

The world of Chapter 5 was *static;* that is, firms existed at a single point in time and made decisions simultaneously. There was no before or after in the Cournot and Bertrand worlds. There was only that one moment when quantities and prices were chosen. If we are to fully understand competition, we must understand how business decisions evolve over time, or what we might call the *dynamics* of competition. We start examining dynamics in this chapter by considering entry and exit. In the next chapter we consider a range of other issues associated with competitive dynamics. In analogous manner, Chapter 9 will examine how firms can outposition their rivals at a given point in time while Chapter 11 explores how firms attempt to sustain their success over time.

Entry is the beginning of production and sales by a new firm in a market, and exit occurs when a firm ceases to produce in a market. Entrants threaten *incumbents*, that is, the firms that were already in the market, in two ways. First, they take market share away from incumbents. This is the primary way that Facebook harmed MySpace. Second, entry often intensifies competition, leading to lower prices. This is a natural consequence of the Cournot and differentiated Bertrand models discussed in the previous chapter, in which more firms imply lower prices. Moving beyond these models, note that entrants often reduce prices to establish a foothold in the market. There was some element of this in the social networking market, for example, when Facebook allowed small businesses to post banner ads at prices well below the minimum charged by MySpace. In some cases, the mere threat of entry can limit the incumbent firm's ability to raise prices. In such cases we say that the market is *contestable*. We discuss contestability near the end of this chapter. Exit has the opposite effect on competitors: surviving firms increase their share and competition diminishes.

We begin this chapter by documenting the importance of entry and exit. We then describe structural factors (i.e., factors beyond the control of the firms in the market) that affect entry and exit decisions. We also address strategies that incumbents may employ to reduce the threat of entry and/or encourage exit by rivals.

SOME FACTS ABOUT ENTRY AND EXIT

Entry is pervasive in many industries and may take many forms. An entrant may be a new firm, that is, one that did not exist before it entered a market. An entrant may also be a firm that is active in a product or geographic market but has chosen to diversify into others. The distinction between new and diversifying firms is often important, as it may affect the costs of entry and the appropriate strategic response. Recent new entrants in various markets include Cards Against Humanity (a raunchy parlor game), Five Guys (an "upscale" hamburger chain), British Midlands (which provides airline service to the British Isles and several European destinations), and AcousticSounds. com (which sells audiophile recordings over the Internet). Recent diversifying entrants include the Chicago Symphony Resound (which records and distributes its own orchestral performances), Barnes and Noble Booksellers (which sells the Nook eReader), and Netflix (a video-by-mail rental service and online video server, which has entered new geographic markets in Canada, Mexico, and South America).

Exit is the reverse of entry—the withdrawal of a product from a market, either by a firm that shuts down completely or by a firm that continues to operate in other markets. In the last two decades, Rhino Records exited the music recording industry, Renault and Peugeot exited the U.S. automobile market, and Sega exited the video game hardware market.

Timothy Dunne, Marc Roberts, and Larry Samuelson offer important, if dated, evidence on entry and exit patterns for over 250,000 U.S manufacturing firms.[1] Their data span two decades ending in 1982. To summarize the main findings, imagine an average industry in 2012. This industry has 100 firms, with combined annual sales of $100 million. If past patterns of entry and exit still hold, here is what that industry can expect in the next 5 to 10 years:

1. *Entry and exit will be pervasive.* By 2017, between 30 and 40 new firms will enter, with combined annual sales of $12 to $20 million. At the same time, a similar number of firms will exit.
2. *Entrants and exiters tend to be smaller than established firms.* A typical greenfield entrant will be only one-third the size of a typical incumbent. Entrants diversifying from another industry tend to be about the same size as the average incumbent.

In 2012, firms that will leave the industry by 2017 are only about one-third the size of the average firm.

3. *Most entrants do not survive 10 years, but those that do grow precipitously.* Of the 30 to 40 firms that enter the market between 2012 and 2017, roughly 60 percent will exit by 2022. The survivors will nearly double their size by 2022.

4. *Entry and exit rates vary by industry.* Many industries have high entry rates including apparel, lumber, and fabricated metals. Industries with high exit rates included apparel, lumber, and leather. Industries with little entry included tobacco, paper, and primary metals. Industries with little exit included tobacco, paper, and coal. Entry and exit are highly related: Conditions that encourage entry also foster exit.

A more recent study of manufacturing firms in the United Kingdom by Disney, Haskel, and Heden confirms that entry and exit are pervasive.[2] Their study finds two-year entry and exit rates of 16 percent. After five years, 65 percent of firms have exited. Entry and exit is more common in leather goods, footwear, and office machinery, but uncommon in metal manufacturing, synthetic fibers, and plastics processing.

These facts have three important implications for strategy:

1. When planning for the future, the manager must account for entry. While the exact identity of an entrant is hard to predict, the incumbent should expect the entrant to be either a small greenfield enterprise or a large diversifying firm.

2. Managers should expect most new ventures to fail quickly. However, survival and growth usually go hand in hand, so managers of new firms will have to find the capital to support expansion.

3. Managers should know the entry and exit conditions of their industry. Entry and exit are powerful forces in some industries but relatively unimportant in others.

ENTRY AND EXIT DECISIONS: BASIC CONCEPTS

In this chapter we present economic concepts that will help managers who are deciding whether to enter or exit a market, as well as managers attempting to cope with potential new entrants. We begin with some basic terminology. It helps to think of entry as an investment. The entrant must sink some capital that cannot be fully recovered upon exit—it is this element of risk that makes the entry decision difficult. The entrant hopes that *postentry profits* (i.e., the excess of revenues over ongoing operating expenses) exceed the *sunk entry costs*.[3] There are many potential sunk costs to enter a market, ranging from the costs of specialized capital equipment to government licenses. Many sunk entry costs are associated with the fixed costs that give rise to economies of scale, which we discussed in Chapter 2, such as the cost of building a factory or performing R&D. But the factors that give rise to entry costs and economies of scale are not identical. Recall that fixed costs are sunk costs only if the fixed costs are not recoverable. And some sources of scale economies are not fixed costs, such as inventory management.

Postentry profits will vary according to demand and cost conditions, as well as the nature of *postentry competition*. Postentry competition represents the conduct and performance of firms in the market after entry has occurred. For example, the entrant might anticipate that firms will behave like Cournot quantity setters or Bertrand price setters, as described in the previous chapter, with corresponding implications for postentry profits. The potential entrant may use many different types of information about incumbents, including historical pricing practices, costs, and capacity, to assess what postentry competition may be like. The sum total of this analysis of sunk costs and postentry competition determines whether there are *barriers to entry*.

Barriers to Entry

Because the potential for profits is a siren call to investors, a profitable industry invites entry. *Barriers to entry* allow incumbent firms to earn positive economic profits while making it unprofitable for newcomers to enter the industry.[4] Barriers to entry may be *structural* or *strategic*. Structural entry barriers exist when the incumbent has natural cost or marketing advantages, or when the incumbent benefits from favorable regulations. Strategic entry barriers result when the incumbent takes aggressive actions to deter entry. Whether structural or strategic, these entry barriers either raise sunk entry costs or reduce postentry profitability.

Bain's Typology of Entry Conditions

In his seminal work on entry, economist Joseph Bain argued that markets may be characterized according to whether entry barriers are structural or strategic, and whether incumbents can profit from using entry-deterring strategies.[5] Bain described three entry conditions:

Blockaded Entry   Entry is blockaded if structural barriers are so high that the incumbent need do nothing to deter entry. For example, production may require large fixed investments relative to the size of the market (high sunk entry costs), or the entrant may sell an undifferentiated product for which it cannot raise price above marginal cost (low postentry profitability).

Accommodated Entry   Entry is accommodated if structural entry barriers are low, and either (a) entry-deterring strategies will be ineffective or (b) the cost to the incumbent of trying to deter entry exceeds the benefits it could gain from keeping the entrant out. Accommodated entry is typical in markets with growing demand or rapid technological improvements. Entry is so attractive in such markets that the incumbent(s) should not waste resources trying to prevent it.

Deterred Entry   Entry is deterred (a) if the incumbent can keep the entrant out by employing an entry-deterring strategy and (b) if employing the entry-deterring strategy boosts the incumbent's profits. Frank Fisher calls such entry-deterring strategies *predatory acts*.[6] Predatory acts may either raise entry costs or reduce postentry profits. We describe several predatory acts later in this chapter.

Bain argued that an incumbent firm's approach to potential entry should depend on market conditions. If entry is blockaded or accommodated, the firm should not make any effort to deter entry. If blockaded, the effort is superfluous; if accommodated, the effort is wasted. If entry is deterred, the firm should consider engaging in a predatory act.

Analyzing Entry Conditions: The Asymmetry Requirement

Bain's typology has great intuitive appeal but does not address an important question: What is the strategic distinction between entrants and incumbents? As we will see, most of the predatory strategies available to incumbents are also available to entrants.

EXAMPLE 6.1 HYUNDAI'S ENTRY INTO THE STEEL INDUSTRY

Hyundai, Korea's largest firm, started as a construction business and expanded into engineering, automobile, shipbuilding, and other heavy equipment manufacturing. Although most of the Korean conglomerates overlap in many industries, Hyundai has had a greater focus on heavy industrial sectors. (Samsung, the next largest Korean conglomerate, is regarded as more of a consumer products company.) Even so, Hyundai in the 1990s was a bit player in the steel market, with a few small specialty mills. But when Hyundai announced in 1997 that it would build a huge fully integrated blast furnace-type steel mill with a capacity of 6 million tons a year, many in the nation were surprised. The government had opposed Hyundai's entry into the steel market, and this decision became one of the nation's hottest economic issues.

Hyundai had long been eager to expand its presence in steel production. The dominant firm, POSCO, which until 1998 was majority-owned by the government, had two big steel mills with combined production capacity of about 26 million tons. No other company in Korea has a mill approaching even 6 million tons, which is generally regarded to be the minimum efficient scale. Given its cost advantage, POSCO was and remains one of the most profitable companies in Korea. Experts in the Korean steel business noted that POSCO's supply was critical; without POSCO, its customers would have to turn to imports. Hyundai felt that demand for steel would continue to grow, far outstripping POSCO's production capabilities.

With demand forecast to grow, Hyundai felt that the market was ripe for entry. Hyundai felt it could be more efficient than POSCO, which was thought to have much redundancy and bureaucracy. Moreover, Hyundai consumes so much steel itself that it could achieve minimum efficient scale without selling to the market. By ensuring capacity, Hyundai might also be better able to plan its other operations (such as car or ship production) more flexibly and easily. Finally, Hyundai felt that the steel mill would be the most cost-effective way to pull far ahead of Samsung in the battle to be Korea's top firm.

The Korean government discouraged Hyundai from building the plant, claiming that demand was likely to slacken. The real motive may have been the government's decision (not yet publicized) to privatize POSCO. In any event, the government stalled but eventually failed to dissuade Hyundai from building the plant. Hyundai broke ground for the plant in 2006 and began operations in 2010. In the interim, Hyundai acquired several smaller Korean steel companies, including Sammi Steel and Dangjin Steelworks.

As it turned out, Hyundai's forecasts for steel demand were partially correct. Economic growth since the late 1990s has been uneven. Hyundai has also enjoyed mixed fortunes. The *chaebol* (see Chapter 4) has been partially dismantled, but some of the remaining companies, including Hyundai engineering, have enjoyed remarkable growth.

For example, in a strategy known as predatory pricing, the incumbent firm slashes prices in an effort to drive out a new entrant. It is possible that the new entrant could slash prices in an effort to drive out the incumbent (something Wal-Mart allegedly does on occasion when it enters new markets). Incumbents and entrants will naturally differ in financial resources and productive capabilities, but the incumbent does not necessarily have the advantage.

There must be other asymmetries that usually work in favor of the incumbent. Incumbents usually have incurred sunk entry costs while entrants have not. Consider Boeing and Airbus, which are protected from entry by other potential manufacturers of large commercial aviation airframes because they have already made hundreds of millions of dollars of sunk investments in construction facilities, tools, and training. To a newcomer, these would represent incremental costs rather than sunk costs.

Asymmetries also arise from relationships with customers and suppliers that can take years to build. United Airlines spent many years establishing good relationships with its Mileage Plus travelers, employees, government agencies, and Star Alliance partners. These relationships are somewhat specific to Chicago, Denver, and United's other hub cities. An upstart carrier could establish the same relationships, but this would take time, during which it could suffer significant losses. From United's point of view, these costs are sunk. But a new carrier has yet to incur them, creating an asymmetry that deters entry. Of course, United can destroy these relationships, for example, by making dramatic changes to its Mileage Plus program, and if it does, it will lose any advantage it may have over upstart firms and might be better off selling its assets to another carrier, even a newcomer.

As we discuss entry barriers, bear in mind that entrants may enjoy many of the attributes that we normally associate with the incumbent firm. Diversifying entrants are particularly likely to have sunk investments in facilities, tools and training, and have established relationships in the vertical chain of production. If so, entrants can turn these attributes to their own advantage, turning entry-deterring strategies into "incumbent-removing" strategies.

Structural Entry Barriers

To assess entry conditions, the incumbent firm must understand the magnitude of structural entry barriers and consider the likely consequences of strategic entry barriers. We discuss structural entry barriers in this section and strategic entry barriers in the next section.

The three main types of structural entry barriers are:

- Control of essential resources

- Economies of scale and scope

- Marketing advantages of incumbency

Control of Essential Resources

An incumbent is protected from entry if it controls a resource or channel in the vertical chain and can use that resource more effectively than newcomers. One reason why Nintendo dominated the video gaming market in the early 1990s is that its Nintendo Entertainment System (NES) was a superior platform for gaming programmers, who naturally devoted most of their energies to developing games for the NES. This stranglehold was broken when Sony introduced the Playstation system, which proved to be an especially attractive platform for sports games.

Some firms attempt to purchase the resources and channels in the vertical chain, preventing potential entrants from acquiring raw materials and/or getting final goods to market. The International Tin Council, DeBeers diamonds, and Ocean Spray cranberries all maintained or continue to maintain monopolies by controlling the raw materials at their source. Firms that attempt to secure their incumbency by tying up the vertical chain face several risks. First, substitutes can emerge. For example, International Tin succumbed to technological advances in aluminum packaging. Second, new channels can open. For example, several diamond finds in northwest Canada loosened DeBeers's grip on the worldwide diamond market. Third, the price to acquire other firms in the vertical chain can be excessive. DeBeers has tried to buy much of the Canadian diamonds, but the high price cut into the cartel's profits. Finally, firms that attempt to tie up channels via acquisition may face antitrust challenges. In 2002, Northland Cranberries filed an antitrust lawsuit against Ocean Spray, alleging that Ocean Spray had used its dominant position to prevent rivals from having access to retailers. (This is an allegation of vertical foreclosure, which was discussed in Chapter 3.) The private litigation ended in 2004, when Ocean Spray acquired Northland Cranberries' production facilities.

Incumbents can legally erect entry barriers by obtaining patents to novel and nonobvious products or production processes. An individual or firm that develops a marketable new product or process usually applies for a patent in its home country. In Europe, Japan, and India, the patent rights go to the first person to apply for the patent. In the United States the first person to invent the idea gets the patent (although this rule is currently up for debate). As might be expected, firms seeking U.S. patents often go to considerable expense to document precedence of discovery. Once the patent is approved (which usually takes one to two years, during which time the invention is protected from imitation), anyone who wishes to use the process or make the product must obtain permission from the patent holder, at a price determined by the patent holder. Patent lives are currently 20 years in most developed nations. Patent laws in some countries, such as China, are very weak.

Entrants can try to "invent around" existing patents. This strategy can succeed because a government patent office sometimes cannot fully distinguish between a new product and an imitation of a protected product and also because courts may be reluctant to limit competition. As a result, some innovations, such as rollerblades and the personal computer, seem to have had no patent protection whatsoever. Conversely, incumbents may file patent-infringement lawsuits against entrants whose products are seemingly different from the incumbent's. Some observers claim that Intel used this strategy to protect its microprocessors from entry by Advanced Micro Devices. It took a pair of U.S. Supreme Court decisions in the late 1990s to loosen Intel's grip on this market. Firms often stockpile patents so that they can countersue in patent infringement cases. Considering that mobile phone networks involve tens of thousands of patents, it is easy to believe that a lawsuit between Google and Apple could last longer than *Jarndyce v. Jarndyce*, the inheritance case in Dickens's *Bleak House* that takes several decades to wind its way through Chancery court.

Incumbents may not require patents to protect specialized know-how. Coca-Cola has zealously guarded its cola syrup formula for more than a century, and no one has learned how to duplicate the sound of a Steinway piano or the beauty of Daum crystal. Rivals may turn to the legally and ethically questionable practice of industrial espionage to steal such information. In 2006, Korean manufacturer Kolon Industries hired a disgruntled former DuPont employee Michael Mitchell, who allegedly provided his new employer with confidential information about DuPont's Kevlar products. When Mitchell started asking his former colleagues at DuPont for more information, his former employer got suspicious and notified the FBI. Mitchell was sentenced to 18 months in prison. DuPont subsequently sued Kolon for allegedly stealing trade secrets; the trial in U.S. district court began in the summer of 2011.

Economies of Scale and Scope

When economies of scale are significant, established firms operating at or beyond the minimum efficient scale (MES) will have a substantial cost advantage over smaller entrants. The average cost curve in Figure 6.1 illustrates the problem facing a potential

FIGURE 6.1
ECONOMIES OF SCALE MAY BE A BARRIER TO ENTRY

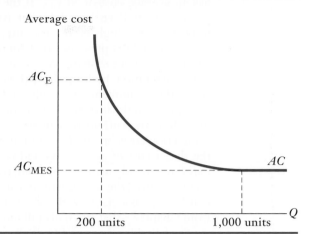

The incumbent firm producing at minimum efficient scale of 1,000 units per year has average costs AC_{MES}. If the potential entrant can only hope to produce a volume of output equal to 200 units per year, its average costs will equal AC_E. Market price must be at least this high for the potential entrant to realize profits from entry.

EXAMPLE 6.2 EMIRATES AIR[7]

Most major airlines earn a disproportionate share of their profits on international routes, where competition is limited and fares are high. Even frequent price wars on domestic routes have failed to put much of a dent in the profits of transoceanic travel. A recent upheaval in a relatively small corner of the industry may subvert this status quo. Emirates Group is a government-owned enterprise that operates international flights out of its hub in Dubai. Emirates has grown rapidly in recent years, with low prices that remind analysts of the no-frills carriers that shook up the U.S. airline industry in the 1980s. Smaller state-owned carriers in Abu Dhabi and Qatar are also slashing prices by as much as a third while expanding capacity by buying dozens of brand-new superjumbo jets including the Airbus A380.

The growth of these Arab-flag carriers is taking a toll on established carriers to the Middle East such as Air France and Qantas, which rely on high margins from international travel for the bulk of their profits. The incumbents have complained that carriers like Emirates are taking advantage of an unfair "home-field advantage" whereby the United Arab Emirates (UAE) not only subsidizes Emirates but also owns and subsidizes the hub in Dubai. Among other benefits, the UAE does not ban late-

night flights, as is customary at other hubs where there is concern about noise pollution. This has allowed Emirates to make fuller use of its planes as well as to offer flight schedules that are especially attractive to travelers from the Pacific Rim. Emirates and other Arab-flag carriers point out that British Airways, Qantas, and other carriers that are complaining are themselves subsidized by their governments and enjoy similar home-field advantages in their own nations. The Arab-flag carriers also benefit from being able to pay lower wages.

Thus far, none of the Arab carriers competes directly with U.S. carriers—there are no overlapping origin/destination pairs. But the U.S. carriers are feeling the impact nonetheless. As Emirates and others expand, there is less room in the market for incumbents. The result is that incumbents are reducing flights to the area and shifting planes to other routes, including transoceanic flights to the United States. Such mobility is commonplace in the airline industry because there are few sunk costs associated with expanding capacity on established routes. Unless global demand along traditional transoceanic routes keeps pace, there could be a glut of capacity, triggering a global price war and killing the goose that has laid the airline's golden egg.

entrant in an industry where the MES is 1,000 units and total industry sales are 10,000 units. An incumbent with a market share of 10 percent or higher reaches the MES and has an average cost of AC_{MES}. If the entrant only achieves a market share of, say, 2 percent, it will have a much higher average cost of AC_E. The market price would have to be at least as high as AC_E for entry to be profitable.

This analysis presumes that there is some asymmetry giving the incumbent the advantage in market share. We can easily imagine this advantage to be the incumbent's brand reputation, built up through years of operation. The entrant might try to overcome the incumbent's cost advantage by spending to boost its market share. For example, it could advertise heavily or recruit a large sales force. Although this strategy may allow the entrant to achieve a market share greater than 2 percent and average production costs below AC_E in Figure 6.1, it involves two important costs. The first is the direct cost of advertising and creating the sales force, costs that the incumbent may have already incurred. Second, the entrant must also be concerned that if it ramps up production, the incumbent may not cut back its own output, as many of the incumbent's costs associated with procuring inputs and paying for labor are sunk. Recall from Chapter 5 that when overall industry output increases, prices and individual firm profits fall. The entrant thus faces a dilemma: to overcome its cost disadvantage, it must increase its market share. But if its share increases, prices will fall.

Fierce price competition frequently results from large-scale entry into capital-intensive industries where capital costs are largely sunk. The U.S. gunpowder industry in the nineteenth century offers an interesting example. In 1889, eight firms, including the industry leader DuPont, formed a "gunpowder pool" to fix price and output. In the early 1890s, three new firms entered the industry. Their growth challenged the continued success of the pool. DuPont's response to one entrant was to "put the Chattanooga Powder Company out of business by selling at lower prices."[8] In this way, the gunpowder pool survived until antitrust enforcers broke it up. In an infamous recent example, rapid entry by fiber-optic telecom providers intensified price competition, saddling market leader WorldCom with over $20 billion in debt and driving it into bankruptcy.

Incumbents may also derive a cost advantage from economies of scope. The U.S. ready-to-eat breakfast cereal industry provides a good example.[9] For several decades, the industry has been dominated by a few firms, including Kellogg, General Mills, General Foods, and Quaker Oats. Although dozens of new cereals have been launched over the years, nearly all are products of the big incumbents, who increased the number of cereals offered for sale from 88 in 1980 to over 200 in 2005. New entrants have had a difficult time gaining even a toehold in the market.

Diversified incumbents may also enjoy scope economies. For example, there are significant economies of scope in producing cereal, stemming from the flexibility in materials handling and scheduling that arises from having multiple production lines within the same plant. These economies make it relatively inexpensive for an incumbent to devote part of an existing production line to a new formulation. A newcomer might have to build an entire new production line, putting much more capital at risk.

Incumbents have established brand names that give them marketing economies (such as Kellogg's Bite-Size Mini-Wheats, a spinoff of Original Frosted Mini-Wheats). Entrants would have to build brand awareness from scratch, and it has been estimated that for entry to be worthwhile, a newcomer would need to introduce 6 to 12 successful brands.[10] Even when incumbents enjoy advantages, the principle that profits attract entrants remains in effect. By the mid-1990s, gross profit margins on brand-name cereals had reached 40 percent or higher. This invited limited entry by private-label manufacturers Malt-O-Meal and Ralston Purina. Even so, most of the successful newcomers have chosen niche markets, such as granola-based cereals, in which they may try to offset their cost disadvantage by charging premium prices.

Marketing Advantages of Incumbency

Chapter 2 discussed umbrella branding, whereby a firm sells different products under the same brand name. This is a special case of economies of scope but an extremely important one in many consumer product markets. An incumbent can exploit the umbrella effect to offset uncertainty about the quality of a new product that it is introducing. The brand umbrella makes the incumbent's sunk cost of introducing a new product less than that of a new entrant because the entrant must spend additional amounts of money on advertising and product promotion to develop credibility in the eyes of consumers, retailers, and distributors.

The umbrella effect may also help the incumbent negotiate the vertical chain. If an incumbent's other products have sold well in the past, distributors and retailers are more likely to devote scarce warehousing and shelf space to its new products. When Coke or Pepsi launches a new product, for example, grocery retailers are confident that there is solid market research behind the launch and are willing to allocate scarce shelf space to them. At the same time, suppliers and distributors may be more willing to make relationship-specific investments in or sell on credit to successful incumbents.

A brand umbrella may increase the expected profits of an incumbent's new product launch, but it might also increase the risk. If the new product fails, consumers may become disenchanted with the entire brand and competitors may view the incumbent as less formidable. Thus, although the brand umbrella can give incumbents an advantage over entrants, the exploitation of brand name credibility or reputation is not risk free.

Barriers to Exit

To exit a market, a firm stops production and either redeploys or sells off its assets. (A change in ownership that does not entail stopping production is not considered an exit.) When deciding whether to exit a market, the firm must compare the value of its assets if deployed in their best alternative use against the present value from remaining in the market. There are *exit barriers* when the firm chooses to remain in the market but, given the opportunity to revisit its entry decision, would not have entered in the first place. Figure 6.2 illustrates how this can happen. The price P_{entry} is the *entry price*—the price at which the firm is indifferent between entering the industry and staying out. The price P_{exit} is the price below which the firm would either liquidate its assets or redeploy them to another market. Exit barriers drive a wedge between P_{exit} and P_{entry}. Because $P_{exit} < P_{entry}$, firms may remain in a market even though price is below long-run average cost. For this reason, high exit barriers are viewed negatively in an analysis of industry rivalry.

Exit barriers often stem from sunk costs, such as when firms have obligations that they must meet whether or not they cease operations. Examples of such obligations include labor agreements and commitments to purchase raw materials. Because these costs are effectively sunk, the marginal cost of remaining in operation is low

FIGURE 6.2
THE PRICES THAT INDUCE ENTRY AND EXIT MAY DIFFER

Firms will enter the industry as long as the market price exceeds P_{entry}, the minimum level of average total costs. Firms will exit the industry only if price falls below P_{exit}, the minimum level of average variable costs.

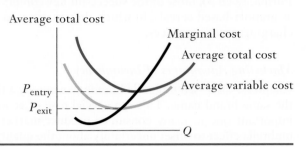

and the firm can recover its incremental costs even if operating revenues fall short of expectations. Hence, the firm is better off remaining in the market. If the firm were revisiting the decision to enter, it would have to cover both sunk entry costs and incremental operating costs, and with the benefit of hindsight it might have chosen to stay out.

Exiting firms can often avoid debt obligations by declaring bankruptcy. Diversified firms contemplating exiting a single market do not enjoy this "luxury," however, because suppliers to a faltering division are assured payment out of the resources of the rest of the firm.

Governments can also pose barriers to exit. For example, most countries forbid owners of nuclear power plants from terminating operation without government approval. Similarly, most states do not allow privately run hospitals to shut down without regulatory approval.

ENTRY-DETERRING STRATEGIES

In the absence of structural entry barriers, incumbents may wish to engage strategically in predatory acts to actively deter entry. In general, entry-deterring strategies are worth considering if two conditions are met:

1. The incumbent earns higher profits as a monopolist than it does as a duopolist.
2. The strategy changes entrants' expectations about the nature of postentry competition.

The reason for the first condition should be obvious; oligopoly theory (see Chapter 5) suggests that this condition is nearly always true. The second condition is usually necessary because any strategy that the incumbent engages in prior to entry can be effective only if it changes the entrant's expectations about postentry competition. Otherwise, the entrant will pay no attention to the entry-deterring strategy, and it will prove futile.

An incumbent may expect to reap additional profits if it can keep out entrants. We now discuss three ways in which it might do so:

1. Limit pricing
2. Predatory pricing
3. Strategic bundling

TABLE 6.1
PRICE AND PROFITS UNDER DIFFERENT COMPETITIVE CONDITIONS

Market Structure	Price	Annual Profit per Firm
Monopoly	$55	$1,225
Cournot duopoly	$40	$ 100

Limit Pricing

Limit pricing refers to the practice whereby an incumbent firm charges a low price to discourage new firms from entering.[11] The intuitive idea behind limit pricing is straightforward. The entrant sees the low price and, being a good student of oligopoly theory, assumes that the price will be even lower after entry. If the incumbent sets the limit price low enough, the entrant will conclude that there is no way that postentry profits will cover the sunk costs of entry; it therefore stays out. At the same time, the incumbent believes that it is better to be a monopolist at the limit price than to share the market at a duopoly price. The following example explains the incumbent's and entrant's reasoning in more detail.

Consider a market that will last two years. Demand in each year is given by $P = 100 - Q$, where P denotes price and Q denotes quantity. Production requires nonrecoverable fixed costs of $800 per year and constant marginal costs of $10. (We ignore discounting.) In the first year, there is a single firm with the technological know-how to compete in this market. We call this firm N. Another firm that we call E has developed the technology to enter the market in year 2. Table 6.1 summarizes useful pricing and profit information about this market. This information can be confirmed by solving for the appropriate profit-maximizing prices and quantities.

If there were no danger of entry, N would select the monopoly price of $55 in each year, earning two-year total profits of $2,450. Unfortunately for firm N, firm E might enter in year 2. To determine if it should enter, E must anticipate the nature of postentry competition. Suppose that when E observes N charging $55 in the first year, it concludes that N will not be an aggressive competitor. Specifically, it expects the Cournot equilibrium to prevail in the second year, with both firms sharing the market equally. Based on this expectation, E calculates that it will earn profits of $100 if it enters. If N shares E's belief that competition will be Cournot, then conditional on entry, firm N would also expect to earn $100 in the second year. This would give it a combined two-year profit of $1,325, which is far below its two-year monopoly profit of $2,450.

Firm N may wonder if it can do better by deterring entry. It might reason as follows:

> If we set a first-year price of, say, $30, then E will surely expect the postentry price to be as low or lower. This will keep E out of the market, allowing us to earn monopoly profits in the second year.

From firm E's point of view, the thought process might go as follows:

> If firm N charges a price of $30 when it is a monopolist, then surely its price in the face of competition will be even lower. Suppose we enter and, optimistically, the price remains at $30, so that total market demand is 70. If we can achieve a 50 percent market share, we will sell 35 units and realize profits of $\{(30 - 10) \times 35\} - 800 = -\$100$. If the price is below $30, we will fare even worse. We should not enter.

EXAMPLE 6.3   LIMIT PRICING BY BRAZILIAN CEMENT MANUFACTURERS

Like many developing nations, Brazil produces and uses a lot of cement. The 57 plants operated by Brazil's 12 cement-producing firms output over 40 million tons per annum, making Brazil the world's sixth leading cement maker. Each of the 57 plants dominates its local market and makes virtually no shipments to adjacent markets. This could be explained by a combination of competitive pricing and high shipping costs. After all, if cement was priced near cost, then only local producers could afford to sell it. But Brazilian cement is priced well above costs—price–cost margins often exceed 50 percent. This is more than enough to cover transportation costs.

Despite the lure of high profit margins, few firms attempt to ship cement across regions. The main exception is when a firm ships cement from a plant in one region into another region dominated by one of its own plants. This provides compelling evidence that it is economically feasible to transport cement across regions. Yet aside from these "friendly" shipments, cross-region shipping almost never occurs. The absence of substantial cross-region shipping is strong evidence that the Brazilian cement makers are tacitly dividing the market.

There is one group of cement makers that may not be willing to go along with this tacit agreement—foreign producers. Thanks to reductions in shipping costs, cement makers in Asia have successfully increased their exports to the Americas—the foreign share of cement in the United States is nearly 20 percent. But in Brazil, that share is at most 2 percent. Part of the difference between the United States and Brazil may be due to shipping costs—shipments to Brazil must pass through the Panama Canal. But economist Alberto Salvo believes that the main reason for the near complete absence of exports to Brazil is that the Brazilian cement makers are limit pricing.[12]

Salvo argues that Brazil's firms have successfully colluded in two ways. The first is by dividing the market. The second is by setting a monopoly price that deters entry by firms with higher costs. This argument is consistent with the facts about market shares. Salvo offers even more confirming evidence. He observes that during periods of high demand for cement in Brazil the price does not rise. A cartel that is not worried about entry would normally increase price during such boom times. But a cartel determined to deter entry by higher cost rivals would hold the line on price. This is exactly what Brazilian firms have been doing.

If both firms follow this logic, then N should set a limit price of $30. By doing so, it will earn $\{(30 - 10) \times 70\} - 800 = \$600$ in the first year and full monopoly profits of $1,225 in the second year, for total profits of $1,825. This exceeds the profits it would have earned had it set the monopoly price of $55 in the first period and then shared the market in the second year.

Is Strategic Limit Pricing Rational?

The preceding arguments hew close to the intuitive explanation of limit pricing: the entrant sees the low incumbent price and reasons that it cannot prosper by entering. A closer look reveals some potential problems with this intuition. For one thing, the analysis assumes that the market lasts only two periods, after which the incumbent and entrant effectively disappear. In the real world, the potential entrant may hang around indefinitely, forcing the incumbent to set the limit price indefinitely. Depending on costs and demand, the incumbent might be better off as a Cournot duopolist than as a perpetual monopoly limit-pricer.

We may also question the assumption that by setting a limit price, the incumbent is able to influence the entrant's expectations about the nature of postentry competition. Let us explore how limit pricing plays itself out when the entrant is less easily manipulated. This analysis is based on the discussion of sequential games in the Economics Primer.

We depict the limit-pricing game in Figure 6.3. The payoffs to N and E are calculated by using the demand and cost data from the previous example. Figure 6.3 shows that in year 1, the incumbent's strategic choices are $\{P_m, P_l\}$, where P_m refers to the monopoly price of $55 and P_l refers to the limit price of $30. The entrant observes N's selection and then chooses from $\{In, Out\}$. If E selects "Out," then N selects P_m in year 2. If E selects "In," then competition is played out in year 2. We suppose that N can control the nature of year 2 competition. In particular, N can maintain the price at $P_l = 30$, or it can "acquiesce" and permit Cournot competition, in which case the price will be $P_c = 40$. Two-year payoffs are reported at the end node for each branch of the game tree.

The limit-pricing outcome is shown by the dashed line in Figure 6.3. Under this outcome, firm N earns total profits of $1,825 and firm E earns $0. Now comes the key point of this analysis: *firm behavior in the limit-pricing outcome is not rational*. (In the parlance of game theory developed in the Primer, the outcome is not a "subgame perfect Nash equilibrium.") To see why not, we must analyze the game using the "fold-back" method.[13] First consider the branch of the game tree in which E ignores the limit price and chooses to enter. According to the limit-pricing argument, E stays out because it expects that *after entry has occurred*, N will select P_l. But examination of the game tree shows that it is not rational for N to select P_l. Conditional on entry having already occurred, N should select P_c. N would earn total profits of $700, which exceeds the profits of $500 it earns if it selects P_l. Thus, E's expectation of N's postentry behavior is flawed.

E should anticipate that if it enters, N will select P_c. E should calculate its profits from entry to be $100, which exceeds the profits of 0 that it earns if it stays out.

FIGURE 6.3
LIMIT PRICING: EXTENSIVE FORM GAME

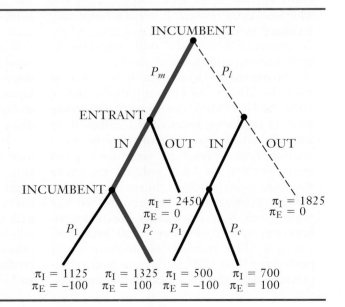

The limit-pricing equilibrium is shown by the dashed line. The incumbent selects P_l, and the potential entrant stays out. This is not a subgame perfect Nash equilibrium because if the potential entrant goes in, the incumbent will select the accommodating price P_c in the second period. The subgame perfect Nash equilibrium is depicted by the heavy line. The incumbent knows that it cannot credibly prevent entry, so it sets P_m in the first period.

INCUMBENT

P_m P_l

ENTRANT

IN   OUT   IN   OUT

INCUMBENT

$\pi_I = 2450$
$\pi_E = 0$

$\pi_I = 1825$
$\pi_E = 0$

P_1 P_c P_1 P_c

$\pi_I = 1125$
$\pi_E = -100$

$\pi_I = 1325$
$\pi_E = 100$

$\pi_I = 500$
$\pi_E = -100$

$\pi_I = 700$
$\pi_E = 100$

Thus, E will choose to enter, even if N has selected P_l in the first stage of the game. Continuing to work backwards, N should anticipate that it cannot prevent entry even if it selects P_l. It should calculate that if it does select P_l, it will earn profits of $700. By selecting P_m in the first stage and P_c in the second stage, N could earn $1,325.

EXAMPLE 6.4 ENTRY BARRIERS AND PROFITABILITY IN THE JAPANESE BREWING INDUSTRY

The Japanese market for beer is enormous, with per-capita consumption of around 60 liters per year. Four firms—Kirin, Asahi, Sapporo, and Suntory—dominate the market. The leaders, Asahi and Kirin, each have nearly 40 percent market share, and their annual sales rival those of Anheuser-Busch, the leading U.S. brewery. All four firms have been profitable for decades.

A profitable industry normally attracts entrants. Even so, Suntory is the only brewery to gain significant market share in Japan in the last 20 years, and its market share is only about 10 percent. (The fifth largest seller, Orion, has a market share below 1 percent.) Profitable incumbents combined with minimal entry usually indicate the presence of entry barriers. Japanese brewers are protected by the high costs of establishing a brand identity, and brands like Kirin's Ichibanshibori and Asahi's Super Dry have loyal followings. But Japanese brewers also enjoy two additional entry barriers. Entry was historically restricted by the Japanese government, and the dominance of "Ma-and-Pa" retail stores complicates access to distribution channels.

Breweries in Japan must have a license from the Ministry of Finance (MOF). Before 1994, the MOF would not issue a license to any brewery producing fewer than 2 million liters annually, creating an imposing hurdle for a start-up firm without an established brand name. In 1994, the MOF reduced the license threshold to 60,000 liters. In the wake of this change, existing small brewers formed the Japan Craft Beer Association. Many microbreweries opened, and new "craft beer bars" emerged. The number of microbreweries peaked at 310 in 1999, but dozens have subsequently closed due to a lack of differentiation (most were poor imitations of German-style beers, though Taisetsu is an award-winning brew), entry by overseas microbreweries, the growing popularity of low-malt (and low-tax) Happoshu beer, and vigorous competition from the big four breweries. The four incumbents responded to the microbrewery movement by offering their own "gourmet" brews (e.g., Kirin's Heartland) and seasonal beers (e.g., Kirin's "Aki Aji" or Fall Taste) and by opening "brew pubs" (e.g., Kirin City). Restaurant owners and bar owners appreciated being able to sell gourmet beers that patrons could not find in retail stores but naturally objected to the direct competition from the breweries. Today, microbreweries still command less than 1 percent of the market.

Japanese brewers have also enjoyed protection from foreign imports, which represent less than 2 percent of the market. Nearby Korea's local brews have failed to catch on in Japan due to an allegedly watery taste, while U.S. and European breweries must pay modest import duties and somewhat more substantial shipping costs. Most critically, distribution in Japan is difficult due to the lack of large-scale storage facilities, requiring exporters to make many small-scale shipments.

Ironically, though protected from entry in their home country, the big Japanese breweries have aggressively expanded overseas. Asahi began producing beer in China in 1994 and now has at least six plants. It also has a joint venture with Chinese brewer Tsingtao to produce and sell beer in Third World nations. Kirin is produced in the UK, Sapporo and Asahi are produced in Canada, and Suntory is produced at an Anheuser-Busch facility in Los Angeles.

Our analysis of the game tree is now complete. N will select P_m in the first stage. E will select "In." Second-year competition will be Cournot. This outcome is shown by the heavy solid line in Figure 6.3.

According to this analysis, limit pricing fails because the incumbent's pre-entry pricing does not influence the entrant's expectations about postentry competition. It seems that the intuitive appeal of limit pricing has run up against the cold hard logic of the game tree. It turns out that there is one additional ingredient that bolsters the intuitive justification but is not captured by the game tree. That ingredient is asymmetric knowledge about industry conditions. To understand the importance of such asymmetries, it is helpful to first discuss another entry-deterring strategy for which simplified economic models and intuition sometimes diverge.

Predatory Pricing

Predatory pricing occurs when a large incumbent sets a low price to drive smaller rivals from the market. The purpose of predatory pricing is twofold: to drive out current rivals and to make future rivals think twice about entry. The second purpose is reminiscent of the goal of limit pricing. Predatory pricing causes rivals to rethink the potential for postentry profits, while the predatory incumbent expects that whatever losses it incurs while driving competitors from the market can be made up later through future monopoly profits.[14]

The Chain-Store Paradox

The idea that an incumbent should slash prices to drive out rivals and deter entry is highly intuitive. Yet a relatively simple example reveals a potential flaw in the argument. Imagine that a rational incumbent firm operates in 12 markets and faces entry in each. In January, it faces entry in market 1; in February, it faces entry in market 2; and so on. Should the incumbent slash prices in January so as to deter entry later in the year?

We can answer this question by working backwards from December to see how earlier pricing decisions affect later entry. The most important thing to note is that regardless of what has occurred in prior months, the incumbent will not benefit from predatory pricing in December. By this time, there is no further entry to deter and therefore no reason for the incumbent to continue slashing prices. *The entrant in the twelfth market knows this* and should enter regardless of previous price cuts. Now let us back up to November. The forward-looking incumbent knows that it cannot deter entry in December and therefore concludes that it cannot benefit from slashing prices in November. The potential November entrant can figure this out too and so enters without fear of retaliation. In this way, the problem completely unravels, so that the incumbent realizes that it has nothing to gain from predatory pricing in January! The striking conclusion: in a world with a finite time horizon in which entrants can accurately predict the future course of pricing, we should not observe predatory pricing. Just like limit pricing, predation seems to be an irrational strategy. This idea is astonishing but does have some empirical support, as we describe in Example 6.5.

The apparent failure of the intuition supporting predatory pricing strategies has given rise to a puzzle in economics known as the *chain-store paradox*.[15] The paradox is that many firms appear to engage in predatory pricing, despite the theoretical conclusion that the strategy is irrational. Standard Oil, whose pricing policies in the nineteenth century drove rivals into bankruptcy, is a quintessential example. Rivals of Wal-Mart have occasionally accused it of predatory pricing. In 2003, the German

Supreme Court agreed with a lower court ruling that Wal-Mart's low prices undermined competition and ordered Wal-Mart to raise its prices; the retailer subsequently sold its German stores and stopped doing business there. Wal-Mart has never lost such a predatory pricing challenge in the United States but has settled at least two cases out of court.

Rescuing Limit Pricing and Predation: The Importance of Uncertainty and Reputation

The economic theories presented above suggest that limit pricing and predatory pricing are irrational strategies, yet firms continue to pursue them. One possible explanation is that firms set prices irrationally. If this explanation is correct, then this analysis should warn firms that set low prices to deter entry: Don't do it! We doubt that many firms will consistently pursue irrational strategies, especially firms like Wal-Mart that have ample opportunity to correct their "mistakes." This leaves two other possible explanations: the theories are wrong, or they are incomplete. We don't believe the theories are wrong—the internal logic is undeniable. But they are almost certainly incomplete, as they require many simplifying assumptions that can artificially drive the results. By lending richness to the chain-store paradox and other models, game theorists have added important nuances to the theories, helping to reconcile the apparent inconsistencies between theory and fact.

Game theorists have shown that predatory actions may be profitable if entrants are uncertain about market conditions. To illustrate the importance of uncertainty, we will revisit the limit-pricing game. The argument against the incumbent's limit-pricing strategy goes something like this:

> If the entrant is *certain* that the low pre-entry price is due to a limit-pricing strategy, then it has every reason to believe that the incumbent will come to its senses after entry and allow prices to increase. As far as the entrant is concerned, limit pricing is like a sunk cost and can have no bearing on future pricing. If the incumbent wants to sacrifice profits prior to entry, that is the incumbent's problem.

This argument presumes that the entrant knows with certainty why the incumbent has set a low pre-entry price. But suppose that the entrant is uncertain about the reasons behind the incumbent's pricing strategy. For example, the entrant might not be certain whether market demand is "meeting expectations" or is "below expectations." Or it might be uncertain whether the incumbent has "typical costs" or "low costs." If market demand is low, or the incumbent has low costs, then it might be sensible for the incumbent to set a low price without regard to strategic considerations. And if the incumbent has low cost or if demand is below expectations, the entrant might prefer staying out of the market. It may even be possible that the incumbent is trying to maximize sales rather than profits. This would again cause the incumbent to set a low price.

All of this uncertainty allows us to rescue limit pricing. Suppose that market demand meets expectations and that the incumbent has a typical cost structure and is trying to maximize profits, *but the entrant does not know this*. By setting a low price, the incumbent may persuade the entrant that demand is low, that its costs are low, or even that it does not care about profits. This might be enough to keep the entrant out of the market. Remember, this approach only works if the entrant is uncertain about the market demand, the incumbent's costs, or the incumbent's motivations. Without such uncertainty, limit pricing falls victim to the theoretical arguments discussed previously.

EXAMPLE 6.5   PREDATORY PRICING IN THE LABORATORY

Predatory pricing is a violation of antitrust laws in most developed nations. Yet there have been very few successful prosecutions for predatory pricing, and most antitrust economists doubt that it happens very often in practice. One reason is that it is difficult, in practice, to distinguish between low prices designed to boost the market shares of efficient firms from abnormally low prices designed to drive rivals from the market. The former is an acceptable business practice that no court would want to outlaw. The rival seems unacceptable but may have no practical impact on consumers if new rivals emerge. Thus, the courts may be hesitant to block any price reductions, regardless of apparent intent.

Economists have wondered whether it is possible to generate true predatory pricing even under laboratory conditions. The relatively new field of experimental economics provides an opportunity to find out. Experimental economists conduct small-scale simulations of business situations, frequently enlisting the participation of undergraduate and graduate students. One of the first important simulations involves participants who "play" a repeated prisoners' dilemma, with cash awards determined by which game cell is played. In the past two decades, the experiments have become more sophisticated, with several experiments exploring predatory pricing.

Mark Isaac and Vernon Smith published the results of the first predatory pricing experiment in 1985.[16] Here was the setup. Two participants competed in a market where they would sell up to a total of 10 units. Each player was "endowed" by Isaac and Smith with a cost function displaying increasing marginal costs. The players named their own prices and the maximum amount they were willing to sell at that price. A player who sold one or more units at a price that exceeded the cost got to keep the profits. Lastly, players had to sell at least one unit in a period to earn the right to play the game again.

Isaac and Smith made sure that one player had lower costs than the other. The low-cost player could drive the rival from the market by offering to sell all 10 units at a price that was below its own marginal cost of selling its last unit, but also below the rival's cost of selling its first unit. This would be a prime example of predatory pricing. Isaac and Smith repeated this experiment with dozens of participants. The lower-cost player never set a predatory price. This explains the title of Isaac and Smith's paper, "In Search of Predatory Pricing."

Other experimental economists pointed out that the high-cost rival in Isaac and Smith's experiment had no opportunity to make money if it exited the market. This might give the rival a strong incentive to match the low-cost player's predatory pricing, even if it meant losing money in the short run. This, in turn, might have discouraged the low-cost player from preying. Economists modified Isaac and Smith's setup to allow high-cost rivals to make money in other markets. In these experiments, low-cost players often did set predatory prices. Other economists have modified Isaac and Smith's experiment by allowing for a series of potential entrants, so that even if the low-cost player drives one rival from the market, it will face future potential rivals. Once again, this seems to encourage low-cost players to set predatory prices.

It is now commonly accepted that predatory pricing occurs in laboratory settings. Does this imply that predation occurs in the real world? It certainly suggests that relative novices can figure out the potential benefits of predation and are willing to take short-run losses provided they are playing with someone else's money. As with the entire field of experimental economics and similar studies of tit-for-tat strategies, price discrimination, commitment, and other game theoretic situations, there is considerable debate as to what this implies for experienced strategists making real-world decisions that involve millions of their own dollars.

A little bit of uncertainty can also increase the effectiveness of predatory pricing. Predatory pricing appears to be irrational because all of the entrants can *perfectly* predict incumbent behavior. But suppose that the last entrant is uncertain about whether the incumbent would actually maintain low prices after entry. As with limit pricing, this could stem from uncertainty about market demand, the incumbent's costs, or the incumbent's objectives. Incumbents can exploit this uncertainty by slashing prices, thereby establishing a *reputation for toughness*. In an experiment, Yun Joo Jung, John Kagel, and Dan Levin found that when students playing a predation game were unsure about the incumbent's tendencies, incumbents did slash prices to deter entry.[17]

The chain-store paradox not only sheds light on the role of uncertainty; it also reminds us of the importance of asymmetry. In our analysis, it is reputation, not incumbency per se, that matters. An entrant might come into the market and slash prices. An incumbent that is uncertain about the entrant's costs or motives may elect to exit, rather than try to ride out the price war.

Wars of Attrition

Price wars harm all firms in the market regardless of who starts them, and are quintessential examples of *wars of attrition*. In a war of attrition, two or more parties expend resources battling with each other. Eventually, the survivor claims its reward, while the loser gets nothing and regrets ever participating in the war. If the war lasts long enough, even the winner may be worse off than when the war began because the resources it expended to win the war may exceed its ultimate reward. An interesting example of price wars is provided by online penny auctions. In these auctions, bidders bid for items such as consumer electronics, clothing, and even cash awards. The high bidder claims the item, but all bidders must pay their bid. Under these rules, every bidder has an incentive to raise his or her bid above the prevailing high bid, even if the high bid exceeds the value of the item being auctioned. (For example, suppose that the item being auctioned is worth $200. It is better to win the item at a bid of, say, $220, than to submit a losing bid of $180.)

Besides price wars, many other types of interactions are wars of attrition. The U.S./Soviet nuclear arms buildup between 1945 and the late 1980s is a classic example. Both countries spent huge sums to increase their nuclear arsenals, each hoping that the other country would be the first to make concessions. Eventually, the Soviet Union fell apart, and Russia acknowledged that it could not afford to carry on the buildup.

Firms that are engaged in a price war should do all they can to convince their rivals that they have no intention of dropping out, so as to hasten their rivals' exit. Firms might even claim that they are making money during the price war, or that they care more about winning the war than they do about profits. (An analogy in the arms race is Ronald Reagan's pronouncement that the United States could survive and win a nuclear war.)

Asymmetries can profoundly influence the outcome of a price war. Suppose that two firms are engaged in a price war and one of the firms has made sunk commitments to workers and other input suppliers. The other firm may as well give up. A firm that has made sunk commitments has low incremental costs of remaining in the market. Any rival who persists in fighting the price war should expect a long battle that is probably not worth fighting.

EXAMPLE 6.6   WAL-MART ENTERS GERMANY . . . AND EXITS

Having conquered nearly every nook and cranny of U.S. retailing, Wal-Mart in the 1990s looked to expand overseas. By 1998, Wal-Mart had over 500 stores in six foreign countries when it set its sights on Europe. Wal-Mart's European strategy began in Germany when it purchased the 21-store Wertkauf chain and acquired 74 warehouse Interspar stores from Spars Handels AG. Wal-Mart immediately instituted the policies that had helped make it so successful in the United States, including door greeters, an ever-smiling staff, and the willingness to forgive shoppers who had more than the five-item express check-out limit. Many analysts forecast the inevitable Wal-Martization of Europe. It was a matter of "when," not "if." They could not have been more mistaken. On July 28, 2006, Wal-Mart announced it was closing up shop in Germany, shuttering the 85 remaining Wal-Mart super-centers.

Wal-Mart found entry to be deceptively easy, requiring little more than an (undisclosed) cash payment to Wertkauf and Interspar and the continuing use of their warehouse facilities. Wal-Mart also had little difficulty hiring workers in a German economy suffering from chronic unemployment. All that was left to do was to change the signs on the stores so as to announce the arrival of the "Big W."

Success proved more elusive. Wal-Mart was surprised by customer resistance to some of its staple marketing strategies. Germans did not want retail clerks to bag their groceries, were put off by door greeters and smiling staff, and objected when shoppers abused their express lane "privileges" by having too many items. Wal-Mart struggled just as hard to maintain employee relations. The company's prohibition against workers flirting with one another met with resentment, and employees mounted a successful legal challenge against Wal-Mart's telephone hotline used by workers to inform on each other. Workers also refused to work overtime or permit video surveillance. Perhaps most significantly, Wal-Mart was unable to drive down labor costs, paying wages comparable to those paid by the competition.

The competition, mainly from Metro, ultimately proved too tough for Wal-Mart. When Wal-Mart entered Germany, Metro was already operating over 1,000 warehouse-style and mass merchandise stores under a variety of names, and Aldi and Lidl were established power-houses in the discount grocery sector, each with thousands of stores. With only 95 stores, Wal-Mart could not hope to match the warehousing and distribution capabilities of these rivals. Considering that its warehousing expertise was a key source of competitive advantage in the United States, it was surely short-sighted for Wal-Mart to compete overseas. Indeed, Metro immediately responded to Wal-Mart's entry by launching a price war. At a disadvantage in customer relations, employee relations, and distribution costs, it was only a matter of time—less than 8 years to be exact—before Wal-Mart exited Germany.

Wal-Mart was fortunate to sell its retail stores and cut its losses. The buyer? Metro.

Predation and Capacity Expansion

Predatory pricing will not deter entry if the predator lacks the capacity to meet the increase in customer demand. Disappointed customers will simply turn to the entrant. Excess capacity makes the threat of predation credible. Marvin Lieberman has detailed the conditions under which an incumbent firm can successfully deter entry by holding excess capacity:[18]

- The incumbent should have a sustainable cost advantage. This gives it an advantage in the event of entry and a subsequent price war.

- Market demand growth is slow. Otherwise, demand will quickly outstrip capacity.

- The investment in excess capacity must be sunk prior to entry. Otherwise, the entrant might force the incumbent to back off in the event of a price war.

- The potential entrant should not itself be attempting to establish a reputation for toughness.

Strategic Bundling

An incumbent firm that dominates one market can use its power to block entry into related markets through a practice known as *strategic bundling*. Bundling occurs when a combination of goods or services are sold at a price that is less than what it would cost to buy the same items separately. Examples abound:

- McDonald's Happy Meals bundle sandwiches, French fries, and soft drinks.

- Vacation packages bundle transportation and lodging.

- Netflix bundles DVD rentals with Internet streaming.

Firms often bundle goods or services for convenience or marketing purposes. Shoe vendors could sell lefts and rights separately but nearly all consumers would rather buy the bundle. Bundling can also help sellers extract higher profits when consumers have imperfectly correlated preferences for related goods. For example, cable television services usually offer a wide range of programming, including channels that specialize in sports, food, drama, and news. Cable services could allow their customers to purchase channels "a la carte," sports fans could purchase just the sports channels, and so forth. But cable services instead set a single bundled price that is not too much more than individual a la carte prices. (For example, the price for the "sports + food + drama + news" bundle is not much more than the price the service would charge for the sports package alone.) Since the cable service has essentially zero marginal cost of selling the bundle, this practice helps increase its profits.

In some cases, bundling can be used strategically to deter entry. An incumbent may consider strategic bundling if it is a monopoly in one market but is threatened in a second market. Strategic bundling works by giving consumers little choice but to buy the entire bundle from the incumbent rather than buy the monopolized good from the incumbent and the second good from competing firms.

To illustrate strategic bundling, consider a manufacturer of office supplies that is a monopoly seller of both sticky note paper and plain note paper. The firm's customers are office supply retailers that purchase note paper by the box. The manufacturer currently charges $30 for a box of sticky note paper and $10 for a box of plain note paper. These are highly profitable prices, as marginal costs are $15 and $5, respectively. The manufacturer currently sells about 1 million boxes of each type of paper monthly, giving it total monthly profits of $20 million.

Several firms are considering entering the plain note paper market. (The technology for sticky note paper is protected by patent.) Should entry occur, prices in this segment would likely drop to $7.50 per box, which is just enough to cover the long-run average costs of an efficient entrant. In addition to experiencing this sharp price decline, the incumbent would also see its share of the plain paper market shrink, and its total monthly profits would fall to $15.5 million.

After crunching some numbers, the manufacturer announces the following pricing strategy to its retailers: continue to pay existing *a la carte* prices or buy *a bundle* *consisting of one box of sticky and one box of plain note paper for $37*. Here is why the manufacturer is confident that this will deter entry: the manufacturer knows that the price of plain note paper will not drop below $7.50. Thus, any retailer wishing to purchase note paper a la carte will have to pay $37.50, which is more than the $37 price of the bundle. Entrants can perform this calculation too and realize that they have no chance of making money selling plain note paper, so they stay out. Having deterred entry, the manufacturer enjoys monthly profits of $17.5 million, which exceeds the $15.5 million in profits it would have made had it not bundled the note papers and allowed entry to occur.

The U.S. Antitrust Modernization Commission recently proposed a test of whether bundled prices are anticompetitive and therefore violated antitrust laws against illegal monopolization.[19] Here are the steps in the test:

- Compute the amount of the discount afforded by the bundle. In this example, the discount is $3.

- Apply the discount to the nonmonopolized, or "bundled" good. The idea is that the firm need not discount a product it monopolizes, so the purpose of the discount is to distort competition for the bundled good. In this example, we subtract $3 from $10 to get an "effective price" of plain note paper of $7.

- Assess whether the "effective price" is less than the cost of efficiently producing the bundled good. If the effective price is below the cost, then the manufacturer of the monopolized good cannot be making any money from the bundled good, unless the purpose of the bundle is to deter entry. In our example, the effective price of $7 is below the cost of efficiently producing a box of note paper, which is $7.50.

In 2007, a version of this test was implemented by a U.S. federal court in a case involving hospital services sold by the PeaceHealth system. The test is sometimes called the PeaceHealth test.

"Judo Economics"

We have argued that an incumbent firm can use its size and reputation to put smaller rivals at a disadvantage. Sometimes, however, smaller firms and potential entrants can use the incumbent's size to their own advantage. This is known as "judo economics."[20] We have already given one theoretical rationale for judo economics—the revenue destruction effect. When an incumbent slashes prices to drive an entrant from the market, it stands to lose more revenue than its smaller rivals.

Incumbents may also be hamstrung by their own sunk costs. The rise of Netflix offers a prime example. At the turn of the twenty-first century, Blockbuster Video was the 800-pound gorilla in the video rental business. Its brick and mortar stores were stocked with vast inventories of new releases and classic films on video. Blockbuster enjoyed inventory economies of scale and purchasing economies that no one could touch. The release of movies on DVD posed a big threat to Blockbuster. DVDs retailed at a price point that minimized Blockbuster's purchasing advantage. And DVDs were much smaller, lighter, and more durable than video tapes, which made them inexpensive to ship through the mail. It should have come as no surprise when Netflix launched its DVD rent-by-mail business in 1997 (the same year that the DVD was introduced).

Blockbuster could have matched Netflix's business model, and with its purchasing clout it might have driven Netflix from the market. But in doing so, Blockbuster would have cannibalized its bricks and mortar operations, while hastening the devaluation of its vast video tape holdings. Blockbuster chose instead to take a wait-and-see attitude toward DVD rental. This may have been the best decision at the time, as it was difficult to forecast the extent of DVD growth and the success of the Netflix business model. Once Blockbuster realized that DVD rental was going to be a huge success, it was too late to copy Netflix. Netflix had a large installed base of customers, its own vast inventories and purchasing clout, and had developed a personalized video rating system that assured customer loyalty (about which we say more in Chapter 10). Netflix used its customer relationships to establish a beachhead in video streaming, which is gradually replacing video-by-mail. The rest is history. Blockbuster filed for bankruptcy in 2011, and Netflix rentals have led to a sharp decline in home video purchasing, threatening the profitability of the biggest Hollywood movie studios.

EVIDENCE ON ENTRY-DETERRING BEHAVIOR

Although theorists have devoted considerable attention to entry deterrence, there is little systematic evidence regarding whether firms pursue entry-deterring strategies and, if they do, whether those strategies are successful. Most of our evidence comes from antitrust cases, where discovery requirements often provide researchers with detailed cost, market, and strategic information.

There may be little evidence on entry deterrence from sources other than antitrust cases for several reasons. First, firms are naturally reluctant to report that they deter entry because this may be sensitive, competitive information and might also violate antitrust statutes. Second, many entry-deterring strategies involve pricing below the short-term monopoly price. To assess whether a firm was engaging in such a practice, the researcher would need to know the firm's marginal costs, its demand curve, the degree of industry competition, and the availability of substitutes. Outside of antitrust cases, such information is difficult for researchers to obtain. Finally, to measure the success of an entry-deterring strategy, a researcher would need to determine what the rate of entry would have been without the predatory act. This, too, is a difficult question to answer.

Despite concerns about the willingness of firms to provide frank responses, Robert Smiley asked major consumer product makers if they pursued a variety of entry-deterring strategies.[21] Smiley surveyed product managers at nearly 300 firms. He asked them whether they used several strategies discussed in this chapter, including:

1. Aggressive price reductions to move down the learning curve, giving the firm a cost advantage that later entrants could only match by investing in learning themselves
2. Intensive advertising to create brand loyalty
3. Acquisition of patents for all variants of a product
4. Enhancement of firm's reputation for predation through announcements or some other vehicle
5. Limit pricing
6. Holding of excess capacity

The first three strategies create high entry costs; the last three change the entrant's expectations of postentry competition.

Table 6.2 reveals the percentage of product managers who report that their firms frequently, occasionally, or seldom use each of the preceding strategies for new products and existing products. Note that managers were asked about exploiting the learning curve for new products only. More than half of all product managers

TABLE 6.2
REPORTED USE OF ENTRY-DETERRING STRATEGIES

	Learning Curve	Advertising	R&D Patents	Reputation	Limit Pricing	Excess Capacity
New Products						
Frequently	26%	62%	56%	27%	8%	22%
Occasionally	29	16	15	27	19	20
Seldom	45	22	29	47	73	48
Existing Products						
Frequently		52%	31%	27%	21%	21%
Occasionally		26	16	22	21	17
Seldom		21	54	52	58	62

surveyed report frequent use of at least one entry-deterring strategy, and virtually all report occasional use of one or more entry-deterring strategies. Product managers report that they rely much more extensively on strategies that increase entry costs than on strategies that affect the entrant's perception about postentry competition.

CONTESTABLE MARKETS

Throughout this chapter we have argued that entry poses two problems for incumbents: entrants steal market share and they drive down prices. The theory of contestable markets, developed by William Baumol, John Panzar, and Robert Willig, states that the mere threat of entry can force the incumbent to lower prices.[22] The key requirement for contestability is "hit-and-run entry." When a monopolist raises price in a contestable market, a hit-and-run entrant rapidly enters the market, undercuts the price, reaps short-term profits, and exits the market just as rapidly if the incumbent retaliates. The hit-and-run entrant prospers if it can set a high enough price for a long enough time to recover its sunk entry costs. If sunk entry costs are zero, then hit-and-run entry is profitable whenever the incumbent's price exceeds the entrant's average variable costs. If the incumbent raised price above the entrant's average cost, there would be immediate entry and price would fall. As a result, the incumbent monopolist has to charge a price no higher than the entrant's average cost, a result that approximates what one would expect to see in a competitive market.

It has proven difficult to find examples of contestable markets, perhaps because the sunk costs of entry into most markets are not trivial. The airline industry has been held up as a possible example. Entry is fairly easy, especially by established carriers entering new routes. A carrier can redeploy aircraft almost overnight, and can secure gates and ground personnel almost as quickly (provided the airports involved are not at capacity). To test contestability theory, Severin Borenstein examined airline pricing.[23] Borenstein found that monopoly routes have higher fares than duopoly routes of comparable lengths, a result consistent with standard oligopoly theory and proof that airline markets are not perfectly contestable; otherwise, fares would be independent of market concentration. But he also found that fares on monopoly routes are lower when another carrier is already operating at one or both ends of the route and therefore had relatively low entry costs. Borenstein concluded that the threat of potential competition causes the monopolist carrier to moderate its prices but not to competitive levels.

An Entry Deterrence Checklist

Table 6.3 lists the variety of entry-deterring tactics that incumbents may consider, when they are most effective, and relevant economic concepts.

TABLE 6.3
ENTRY-DETERRENCE CHECKLIST

Entry Barrier	Most Effective When . . .	Comment
Sunk costs	Incumbent has incurred them and entrant has not.	Costs must truly be sunk. If the incumbent can sell its fixed assets, then so, too, could an entrant. This implies that failure is not very costly, and entry is harder to deter.
Production barriers	Economies of scale or scope, superior access to critical inputs or superior location, process or product patents, or government subsidies exist.	Must be asymmetric (see sunk costs). Technological innovation can cause an abrupt change to the well-being of an incumbent. Patents are not all equally defensible, and the cost of defending a patent can be prohibitive.
Reputation	Incumbents have longstanding relationships with suppliers and customers.	Reputation reflects hard-to-measure factors, such as quality or reliability, that entrants may not be able to promise.
Switching costs	There are few supply-side barriers to entry.	Can the firm prevent imitation? Do consumers really perceive entrants as different from incumbents?
Tie up access	Channels are few and hard to replicate.	Must share spoils with channel. May arouse antitrust scrutiny.
Limit pricing	Entrants are unsure about demand and/or costs.	May require permanent reduction in profit margins to sustain entry deterrence.
Predatory pricing	Firm has reputation for toughness or competes in multiple markets.	Incumbent firm may lose more than entrant; deep pockets and conviction that there are many potential entrants are a must. May arouse antitrust scrutiny.
Holding excess capacity	Marginal costs are low, and flooding the market causes large price reductions.	Capacity investments must be sunk. Demand must not be growing.

ENTERING A NEW MARKET

Thus far we have described entry as a battle between an incumbent firm and the new-comers it would like to keep out. We now consider entry into a new market. As always, a potential entrant into this market must weigh postentry profits against sunk entry costs. When thinking about entry into a new market, however, several scenarios must be considered. In one scenario, any firm can access the production technology and market demand is large enough that many firms can profitably coexist. The result is a competitive market in which the exact number of firms depends on the size of market demand and the extent to which the technology involves scale economies. We explore this situation in greater detail in Chapter 7.

At the other extreme, a single firm has access to the production technology, perhaps because it has a patent and chooses not to license to competitors. In a static (i.e., single period) world, the monopolist should enter if postentry profits exceed sunk entry costs, excluding those costs already sunk into creating the technology. In reality, the monopolist faces a future of changing demand and costs. For example, suppose that the market is small but growing, as is common for new technologies, and current demand is so low that current operating revenues are below current operating costs. In this case, the monopolist should delay entry until demand has increased and operating revenues exceed operating costs.

Preemptive Entry and Rent Seeking Behavior

Things get more interesting when a small number of firms have access to the technology, but the market will never be large enough to support them all. To make this example concrete, consider a small, growing community, Blueville, that is large enough to support a single cement maker but will never be large enough to support two firms. A cement plant requires sunk costs of $10 million; net lifetime profits therefore equal net discounted future profits minus the $10 million entry cost. Big D Cement and Giant E Cement are the only two potential entrants in Blueville. If either firm enters today and faces no competition in the future, the discounted present value of future monopoly profits would be $16 million, giving it net lifetime profits of $6 million. But if both firms enter today, the duopolists will generate postentry future profits of $6 million, incurring net lifetime *losses* of $4 million apiece. These payoffs are depicted in Figure 6.4.

We can use the concept of the Nash equilibrium to determine the earliest point at which entry is likely to occur. (We discussed the Nash equilibrium in the Economics Primer and in Chapter 5.) Remember, Big D and Giant E's entry decisions to enter the market are a Nash equilibrium if each is happy with its choice, given what the

FIGURE 6.4
ENTRY GAME (ALL FIGURES IN $MILLIONS)

	Giant E Enters	Giant E Stays Out
Big D enters	−4, −4	**6, 0**
Big D stays out	**0, 6**	0, 0

The first figure in each cell is the payout to Big D. The two Nash equilibria are "Big D enters/Giant E stays out" and "Big D stays out/Giant E enters."

other firm has chosen. In a static world in which both firms make simultaneous entry decisions, there are two equally plausible Nash equilibria: Big D enters and Giant E stays out, and vice versa. These equilibria are highlighted in Figure 6.4. Economic theory has little to say about which firm will actually enter, and this issue might be determined by idiosyncratic factors not captured by the model.

In both equilibria, the firm that enters earns $6 million and the firm that stays out earns $0, so the firm that stays out will surely feel that it should have done something differently, even if it knows that it would be futile to enter now and lose $4 million. For example, it might have lobbied the local Blueville government for legislation giving it exclusive local rights to mix cement, transferring some of the profits to the legislators who have the power to erect entry barriers. This is known as *rent-seeking behavior*—costly activities intended to increase the chances of landing available profits. (The term *rent* refers to excess returns above and beyond opportunity costs and is often used interchangeably with *economic profit*.)

By leaving the static model and adding a time dimension, we can explore other, less sinister ways for our cement firms to assure themselves of a better shot at the monopoly profits. Remember that Blueville is growing and was not always the bustling metropolis it is today. Rather than entering today, when Blueville is so big that the monopolist's net lifetime profits are $6 million, one of the firms could have entered earlier, when Blueville was much smaller. The discounted lifetime profits would be something less than $6 million, but this would still preempt entry by the other firm, and it is better to earn somewhat less than $6 million than earn nothing at all.

We can again use the concept of the Nash equilibrium to study the timing of entry. Consider the situation if Big D enters the Blueville market today and makes $6 million in net lifetime profits, while Giant E stays out and earns $0. Once we leave the static world, this is not a Nash equilibrium because Giant E could do better by entering the market before Big D. Giant E's net lifetime profits would be somewhat less than $6 million because it would have entered when Blueville was a smaller community, while Big D would earn $0. Provided that Giant E is earning *any* positive profits, this is still not a Nash equilibrium because Big D could do better than earn $0 by entering earlier still. By this logic, the only Nash equilibrium is when either Big D or Giant E enters when the market is very small, so that its net lifetime profits are $0, and the other firm never enters and also earns $0. In this way, early entry dissipates all the monopoly rents.

This example illustrates a broader point. By engaging in rent-seeking behavior, firms that would appear to be in an enviable competitive position, even firms with established monopolies, may have dissipated some or all of the available profits. This may take the form of preemptive entry, lobbying the government, or spending money to develop supplier or customer relationships. And if several firms are competing for the monopoly rents, the "winner" must have some unique assets or abilities—what we have dubbed "asymmetries" in this chapter—if it hopes to end up earning positive profits.

CHAPTER SUMMARY

- Entry and exit are pervasive. In a typical industry, one-third of the firms are less than five years old, and one-third of the firms will exit within the next five years.

- A firm will enter a market if it expects postentry profits to exceed the sunk costs of entry. Factors that reduce the likelihood of entry are called entry barriers.

- A firm will exit a market if it expects future losses to exceed the sunk costs of exit.

- Entry barriers result from asymmetries between incumbent firms and entrants.

- Exogenous market forces can create structural entry barriers. Low demand, high capital requirements, and limited access to resources are all examples of structural entry barriers. Exit barriers arise when firms must meet obligations whether or not they produce.

- An incumbent firm can use predatory acts to deter entry or hasten exit by competitors. Limit pricing, predatory pricing, and capacity expansion change entrants' forecasts of the profitability of postentry competition.

- Limit pricing and predatory pricing can succeed only if the entrant is uncertain about the nature of postentry competition.

- Firms may hold excess capacity to credibly signal their intent to lower prices in the event of entry.

- Firms can engage in predatory practices to promote exit by rivals. Once a firm realizes that it cannot survive a price war, it exits, permitting the survivors to raise price and increase share. A firm may try to convince its rivals that it is more likely to survive a price war to hasten the rival's exit.

- Managers report that they frequently engage in entry-deterring strategies, especially to protect new products.

- Firms competing to enter new markets may engage in rent-seeking behaviors, such as preemptive entry, that dissipate some or all of the available profits.

QUESTIONS

1. Researchers have found that industries with high entry rates tended to also have high exit rates. Can you explain this finding? What does this imply for the pricing strategies of incumbent firms?

2. Dunne, Roberts, and Samuelson examined manufacturing industries in the 1960s to 1980s. Do you think that technological changes since that time will have affected entry and exit patterns? What industries are most likely to have been affected?

3. "All else equal, an incumbent would prefer blockaded entry to deterrable entry." Comment.

4. Under what conditions do economies of scale serve as an entry barrier? Do the same conditions apply to learning curves?

5. Under what conditions can a firm prosper by gaining control of essential resources?

6. Industries with high barriers to entry often have high barriers to exit. Explain.

7. How a firm behaves toward existing competitors is a major determinant of whether it will face entry by new competitors. Explain.

8. Why is uncertainty a key to the success of entry deterrence?

9. An incumbent firm is considering expanding its capacity. It can do so in one of two ways. It can purchase fungible, general-purpose equipment and machinery that can be resold at close to its original value. Or it can invest in highly specialized machinery which, once it is put in place, has virtually no salvage value.

Assuming that each choice results in the same production costs once installed, under which choice is the incumbent likely to encounter a greater likelihood of entry and why?

10. In most models of entry deterrence, the incumbent engages in predatory practices that harm a potential entrant. Can these models be reversed, so that the entrant engages in predatory practices? Why do you think incumbents are more likely to set predatory pricing than are entrants?

11. Suppose that a hospital monopolizes the local market for heart surgery, charging $10,000 per procedure. The hospital does 1,000 heart surgeries annually, and the cost of heart surgery is $5,000 per procedure. The hospital is a duopolist in the market for cataract surgery. The hospital and its competitor both perform 2,000 cataract procedures annually, charge $2,000 per procedure, and have costs of $1,000 per procedure. The hospital plans to go to insurers and offer a bundled price. It will discount the price of heart surgery below $10,000 and hold the price of cataracts at $2,000, provided that it is given exclusivity in the cataract market. What price for heart surgery must the hospital charge to insure that its competitor cannot profitably compete in the cataract market? (Assume that the hospital would match its rival's price in the cataract market if the rival were to respond to this bundling arrangement by cutting its cataract price.)

12. "Judo economics suggests that economies of scale are useless at best." Do you agree or disagree?

13. Recall the discussion of monopolistic competition in Chapter 5. Suppose that an entrepreneur considered opening a video store along Straight Street in Linesville. Where should the entrepreneur position the store? Does your answer depend on whether further entry is expected?

14. Consider a firm selling two products, A and B, that substitute for each other. Suppose that an entrant introduces a product that is identical to product A. What factors do you think will affect (a) whether a price war is initiated, and (b) who wins the price war?

ENDNOTES

[1] Dunne, T., M. J. Roberts, and L. Samuelson, "Patterns of Firm Entry and Exit in U.S. Manufacturing Industries," *RAND Journal of Economics*, Winter 1988, pp. 495–515.

[2] Disney, R., J. Haskel, and Y. Heden, 2003, "Entry, Exit and Establishment Survival in UK Manufacturing," *Journal of Industrial Economics*, 51(1), pp. 91–112.

[3] The theory of real options described in Chapter 7 discusses many of the issues affecting the timing of entry and exit decisions.

[4] This definition is a synthesis of the definitions of entry barriers of Joe Bain in *Barriers to New Competition: Their Character and Consequences in Manufacturing Industries*, Cambridge, MA, Harvard University Press, 1956, and C. C. Von Weizsäcker in *Barriers to Entry: A Theoretical Treatment*, Berlin, Springer-Verlag, 1980.

[5] Bain, *Barriers to New Competition*.

[6] Fisher, F., *Industrial Organization, Economics, and the Law*, Cambridge, MA, MIT Press, 1991.

[7] Much of the information for this example was taken from Michaels, D., "From Tiny Dubai, an Airline with Global Ambition Takes Off," *The Wall Street Journal*, January 11, 2005, p. 1.

[8]Fligstein, N., *The Transformation of Corporate Control*, Cambridge, MA, Harvard University Press, 1990.

[9]For a detailed discussion see Schmalensee, R., "Entry Deterrence in the Ready-to-Eat Breakfast Cereal Industry," *Bell Journal of Economics*, 9(2), 1978, pp. 305–327.

[10]Scherer, F. M., "The Breakfast Cereal Industry," in Adams, W. (ed.), *The Structure of American Industry*, 7th ed., New York, Macmillan, 1986.

[11]Bain, J. S., "A Note on Pricing in Monopoly and Oligopoly," *American Economic Review*, 39, March 1949, pp. 448–464.

[12]Salvo, A., "Inferring Conduct under the Threat of Entry: The Case of the Brazilian Cement Industry," London School of Economics, 2005, Mimeo.

[13]See Chapter 1 for a discussion of the use of the fold-back method to determine subgame perfect equilibria.

[14]See Martin, S., *Industrial Economics*, New York, Macmillan, 1988, for a good review of the various legal tests for predatory pricing that have been proposed.

[15]This term was coined by the game theorist Reinhard Selten in his article, "The Chain Store Paradox," *Theory and Decision*, 9, 1978, pp. 127–159.

[16]Isaac, R., and V. Smith, "In Search of Predatory Pricing," *Journal of Political Economy*, 93, 1985, pp. 320–345.

[17]Jung, Y. J., J. Kagel, and D. Levin, "On the Existence of Predatory Pricing: An Experimental Study of Reputation and Entry Deterrence in the Chain-store Game," *Rand Journal of Economics*, 25(1), 1994, pp. 72–93.

[18]Based on Lieberman, Marvin B., "Strategies for Capacity Expansion," *Sloan Management Review*, Summer 1987, pp. 19–25.

[19]Antitrust Modernization Commission, Report and Recommendation 99 (April 2007), available in full text at http://govinfo.library.unt.edu/amc.

[20]Gelman, J., and S. Salop, "Judo Economics: Capacity Limitation and Coupon Competition," *Bell Journal of Economics*, 14, 1983, pp. 315–325.

[21]Smiley, R., "Empirical Evidence on Strategic Entry Deterrence," *International Journal of Industrial Organization*, 6, 1988, pp. 167–180.

[22]Baumol, W., J. Panzar, and R. Willig, *Contestable Markets and the Theory of Industrial Structure*, New York, Harcourt Brace Jovanovich, 1982.

[23]Borenstein, S., "Hubs and High Fares: Dominance and Market Power in the U.S. Airline Industry," *RAND Journal of Economics*, 20, 1989, pp. 344–365.

7

DYNAMICS: COMPETING ACROSS TIME

Former American Airlines CEO Robert Crandall once famously said, "This industry is always in the grip of its dumbest competitors." Crandall was frustrated by a resumption of price wars in an industry that struggled to turn a profit even in the best of times. In the early 1990s, several U.S. carriers had been in and out of bankruptcy, sometimes more than once. Crandall lectured the competition on the need for higher fares, and in late 1991 American launched "Value Pricing" with just four fare classes on any flight (first class, coach, 7-day and 14-day advanced purchase). American promoted value pricing as a money saver, but many strategists believed instead that the four fare classes could become "focal points" around which the major carriers could fix prices and avoid further price wars. Facing excess capacity during an economic downturn, some carriers apparently did not get the message or refused to go along, and they undercut American's fares. By spring of 1992, Crandall was once again fed up with his "dumbest competitors" and American took airfares even lower. Crandall's attempt to end the price wars ended in failure.

A decade after the Value Pricing fiasco, Crandall had come to understand that with excess capacity throughout the system, airlines would always be tempted to slash prices. Rather than try to coordinate pricing directly, he led an effort to remove capacity. Always thinking of public relations, Crandall and American launched the "Extra Legroom in Coach" promotion in February 2000. Extra legroom meant fewer seats. If other carriers followed suit, then empty seats would be a thing of the past and prices would stabilize. United Airlines took baby steps in the same direction, introducing its Economy Plus seating in 2001. But the remaining domestic carriers saw the Extra Legroom promotion not as an opportunity to change the industry equilibrium in the long term, but as a chance to steal market share in the near term. In October 2004, with the economy soaring and its market share declining, American put the seats back in its planes.

Amid the economic boom of the mid-2000s, when planes were full and fares were high, the industry did something strange. One carrier after another began pulling capacity out of the system. They eliminated routes and switched to smaller commuter jets. Some carriers merged. When the great recession hit in 2008, the industry was ready and airfares remained high. Only the recent rapid increase in fuel prices has kept the industry from sustained profitability.

The airline industry makes for a remarkable case study of competitive dynamics. In this chapter we consider the many facets of dynamics. We will examine the timing of decisions and the importance of commitment. We will explore the concept of a focal point and whether firms can use that concept to avoid the ravages of cutthroat competition. Finally, we consider how the structure of an industry emerges from the competitive interplay of its member firms.

MICRODYNAMICS

We use the term *microdynamics* to refer to the unfolding of competition, over time, among a small number of firms. This contrasts with *macrodynamics*, a term we use to describe the evolution of overall market structure. Chapter 5 discussed two important models of competition among small numbers of firms—the Cournot model of quantity competition and the Bertrand model of price competition. Both of these models were *static*; firms made decisions simultaneously. Though unrealistic, the models did provide insights into important strategic concepts such as the revenue destruction effect, and the impact of capacity constraints and consumer loyalty on competition. But the static nature of the models clearly limits their ability to help us understand strategic decision making in the real world, where strategies unfold over time. In the first part of this chapter we explore how adding a time dimension affects strategic options, by focusing on the following aspects of microdynamics:

- The Strategic Benefits of Commitment

- The Informational Benefits of Flexibility

- Competitive Discipline

Strategic Commitment

A *strategic commitment* alters the strategic decisions of rivals.[1] As such, it must involve an *irreversible* decision that is *visible*, *understandable*, and *credible*. The commitment must be irreversible or it carries no commitment weight: the firm can back down if the commitment does not have the desired strategic effect. It must be visible and understandable or rivals will have nothing to react to. It must be credible so that rivals believe the firm will actually carry out the commitment.[2]

The famous example of Hernán Cortés's conquest of the Aztec Empire in Mexico illustrates these concepts. When he landed in Mexico in 1518, Cortés ordered his men to burn all but one of his ships. What appeared to be a suicidal act was in fact a move that was purposeful and calculated: by eliminating their only method of retreat, Cortés committed his men to the battle. According to Bernal Diaz del Castillo, who chronicled Cortés's conquest of the Aztecs, "Cortés said that we could look for no help or assistance except from God for we now had no ships in which to return to Cuba. Therefore we must rely on our own good swords and stout hearts."[3]

To explore commitment in the context of models of competition, we shall revisit the Cournot model of quantity competition described in Chapter 5. Recall that the basic facts in that model are as follows: there are two firms (1 and 2) with identical cost functions: $TC_1 = 10Q_1$ and $TC_2 = 10Q_2$. Market demand is given by $P = 100 - (Q_1 + Q_2)$. Each firm chooses its output simultaneously and treats its rival's output choice as fixed. We calculated that the resulting equilibrium quantities, prices, and profits are $Q_1 = Q_2 = 30$; $P_1 = P_2 = 40$; and $\pi_1 = \pi_2 = \$900$.

Suppose that instead of choosing quantities simultaneously, firm 1 can commit to Q_1 before firm 2 selects Q_2. This could occur if firm 1 builds a new factory or signs contracts with workers and suppliers prior to firm 2 taking similar actions. In this situation, known as a *Stackelberg* model, firm 1's choice of Q_1 can influence firm 2's choice of Q_2. To see why, recall that firm 2 chooses Q_2 according to the reaction function: $Q_2 = 45 - 0.5Q_1$. (See Chapter 5 for the derivation of the reaction function.) The important difference between the Stackelberg model and the Cournot model is that firm 2 does not have to guess the value of Q_1. By building its factory first, firm 1 has committed to Q_1 and firm 2 knows it.

Because firm 1 can compute firm 2's reaction function, it knows exactly how much firm 2 will produce in response to any choice of Q_1. In other words, firm 1's initial choice of Q_1 completely determines total quantity and the market price. This is enough to allow firm 1 to compute its profits for any choice of Q_1. In particular, firm 1 knows that the market price and profits will be:

$$\text{Price: } P = 100 - (Q_1 + Q_2) = 100 - (Q_1 + (45 - 0.5Q_1)) = 55 - 0.5Q_1$$
$$\text{Profits: } \pi_1 = \text{Revenue} - \text{Cost} = PQ_1 - 10Q_1 = (55 - 0.5Q_1) \cdot Q_1 - 10Q_1$$

Some calculus reveals that the profit-maximizing value of $Q_1 = 45$.[4] In response, firm 2 chooses $Q_2 = 22.5$ and the market price is 32.5. Profits are $\pi_1 = \$1,012.5$ and $\pi_2 = \$506.25$. Firm 1 is doing much better than in the Cournot simultaneous choice model, while firm 2 is doing much, much worse.

By committing to produce 45 units of output instead of 30, firm 1 has forced its rival to cut back production to 22.5; this prevents price from falling too rapidly and makes expansion more profitable for firm 1 than it was in the Cournot model, where firm 2's output was fixed.

As with the Cournot model, it is unrealistic to expect firms to compute such detailed equations and perform the required calculus. But it is completely believable that firm 1 would anticipate that its commitment to expand output would lead firm 2 to cut back production, providing exactly the incentive for expansion that the formal model demonstrates.

Strategic Substitutes and Strategic Complements

In the Stackelberg game, firm 1's decision to expand output caused firm 2 to contract output. When one firm chooses more of some action, such as an output decision, and its rival firm cuts back on the same action, we say that the actions are *strategic substitutes*.[5] Quantities in the Stackelberg game are strategic substitutes. When one firm chooses more of an action and its rival chooses more as well, the actions are *strategic complements*. Prices are usually strategic complements; when one firm raises its price, its rivals may respond by raising theirs. Certainly when one firm lowers its price, we expect its rivals to do so as well. The concepts do not just apply to prices and quantities. If Burger King launches an ad campaign and McDonald's responds in kind, then advertising is a strategic complement. If Glaxo increases R&D investments in cardiovascular products and Merck scales back its cardio R&D spending in response, then R&D is a strategic substitute.

To formalize the concepts of strategic complements and substitutes, we return to the Cournot model of quantity setting and the Bertrand model of price setting. Recall that in the Cournot model it was convenient to represent the equilibrium using reaction functions. In a two-firm Cournot industry, a firm's reaction function shows its profit-maximizing quantity as a function of the quantity chosen by its competitor. In the Cournot model, reaction functions are downward sloping, as Figure 7.1a shows. Reaction functions in the Bertrand model with horizontally differentiated products are defined analogously.[6] In this case, however, the reaction functions are upward sloping, as in Figure 7.1b.

FIGURE 7.1
STRATEGIC SUBSTITUTES AND COMPLEMENTS

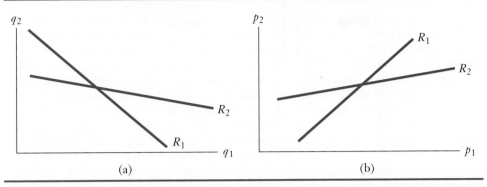

Panel (a) shows the relation functions in a Cournot market. The reaction functions R_1 and R_2 slope downward, indicating that quantities are strategic substitutes. Panel (b) shows the reaction functions in a Bertrand market with differentiated products. The reaction functions slope upward, indicating that prices are strategic complements.

In general, when reaction functions are upward sloping, the firm's actions (e.g., prices) are strategic complements. When actions are strategic complements, the more of the action one firm chooses, the more of the action the other firm will also optimally choose. In the Bertrand model, prices are strategic complements because when one firm reduces prices, the other firm finds it profitable to reduce prices as well. When reaction functions are downward sloping, the actions are strategic substitutes. When actions are strategic substitutes, the more of the action one firm takes, the less of the action the other firm optimally chooses. In the Cournot model, quantities are strategic substitutes because when one firm increases its quantity, the other firm finds it profitable to also increase quantity.

The Strategic Effect of Commitments

Commitments have both a direct and a strategic effect on a firm's profitability. The direct effect of the commitment is its impact on the present value of the firm's profits if the competitor's behavior does not change. This is analogous to thinking about quantity and price choices in the static Cournot and Bertrand models. For example, if Nucor invests in a process that reduces the average variable cost of producing sheet steel, the direct effect of the investment is the present value of the increase in Nucor's profit due to the reduction in its average variable costs, less the upfront cost of the investment. The increase in profit would come not only from cost savings on existing units produced, but also from any benefits Nucor gets from lowering its price or increasing its output.

The strategic effect takes into account the competitive side effects of the commitment. How does the commitment alter the tactical decisions of rivals and, ultimately, the market equilibrium? In the Stackelberg game, the increase in production by firm 1 caused its rival to scale back production, which helped support pricing and increase firm 1's profits. Nucor's investment would have a strategic effect if it caused rivals to adjust their investment plans (or any other business decisions, for that matter). If a firm takes the long view when making its commitment decision, as we believe it should, then it must take into account how the commitment alters the nature of the equilibrium.

EXAMPLE 7.1   LOBLAW VERSUS WAL-MART CANADA[7]

If you have ever gone grocery shopping in Canada, chances are that you have encountered a store owned by Loblaw. With more than 1,050 stores, Loblaw Companies Limited is the largest grocery chain in Canada. Among the stores in its stable of properties are Loblaws, Fortinos, Zehrs Markets, and Your Independent Grocer. In total, Loblaw's various stores account for about 33 percent of Canada's grocery market.

Loblaw's most recent strategic initiative is to construct large superstores that bear the name "The Real Canadian Superstore" or RCSS. These stores, which have 135,000 square feet of selling area, contain a pharmacy–drugstore, a home electronics department, an optical department, a dry cleaner store, apparel and shoe departments, a photo studio, a financial services counter, and, of course, groceries, including the 5,000-plus private label items sold under Loblaw's "President's Choice" brand.

The commitment to build RCSS stores was launched in late 2002. Loblaw's management announced that it would cease building large grocery stores under the names Loblaws, Fortinos, and Zehrs, and would instead embark on a plan to build RCSS stores throughout Canada. Loblaw was very clear about its intentions: it wanted to preempt Wal-Mart Canada from building its own megastores, Wal-Mart Supercenters. Wal-Mart had already built five Sam's Clubs stores in Ontario, but as of 2002, it had yet to build any Wal-Mart Supercenters.

Loblaw took a number of steps to enhance the credibility of its strategic commitment. First, starting in early 2003, Loblaw opened talks with the United Food and Commercial Workers (UFCW) union in an attempt to negotiate wage rollbacks for employees transferring to newly opened RCSS stores. The resulting deal was complex, but Loblaw was ultimately successful in achieving a deal for lower wages in RCCS stores. In addition, Loblaw's management was very public about its ambitions to open RCSS stores throughout Canada. For example, at its annual meeting in May 2004, Loblaw's president, John Lederer, announced that the company had set aside a $1.4 billion capital budget to construct new RCSS stores during 2004.

A case can be made that Loblaw's commitment to build multiple RCSS stores has successfully preempted Wal-Mart. The first RCSS store was opened in late 2003; 13 stores were added in 2004, and 7 were slated to be opened in 2005. By contrast, as of mid-2005, Wal-Mart Canada had yet to open any Supercenters and reputedly had no immediate plans to do so. But even if Loblaw ends up merely delaying Wal-Mart's entry into the megastore segment in Canada, Loblaw's preemptive commitment might still be considered a success. For one thing, by moving first, Loblaw may be able to lock up the best locations in high-population areas, such as Toronto. For another thing, the high publicity surrounding the opening of RCSS stores, coupled with the enormous selection of grocery and nongrocery items, and an ambience that is reportedly "appealing to all the senses," may make an RCSS a destination store that shoppers go out of their way to visit despite the presence of lower-priced stores nearby.

Tough and Soft Commitments

Firms do not always benefit from the strategic effects of their commitments. Whether a commitment has a profitable strategic effect depends on whether the commitment is *tough* or *soft* and whether the choices involve strategic complements or strategic substitutes.[8] Conceptually, a firm's tough commitment is bad for competitors, whereas a soft commitment is good for its competitors. Capacity expansion usually represents a tough commitment, whereas the elimination of production facilities usually represents a soft commitment. In Bertrand competition, a commitment to reduce prices, perhaps through a well-publicized advertising campaign (so that the firm could not back down), is a tough commitment.

Tough commitments conform to the conventional view of competition as an effort to outdo one's rivals. For example, we "understand" why firms may commit to be the largest volume producer or lowest price seller in a market. Tough commitments have a profitable strategic effect if they involve strategic substitutes and a negative strategic effect if they involve strategic complements. If Nucor's rivals reduce investments after Nucor's commitment to expand, then the strategic effect leads to higher prices and raises Nucor's profits. If McDonald's reduces advertising in the wake of Burger King's campaign, that serves to further increase Burger King's market share.

Managers need to be aware of whether the tactical weapons at their disposal are strategic complements or substitutes. This requires some economic insight (would ads be more or less valuable to McDonald's when Burger King is heavily advertising?) and some experience (how has McDonald's reacted in the past when Burger King launched an ad campaign?). The facts on the ground should probably trump the theoretical insights; if McDonald's previously matched ad campaign for ad campaign, then advertising is a strategic complement and the tough commitment by Burger King will have a negative strategic effect.

Firms should not automatically refrain from making soft commitments. In fact, a soft commitment will have a profitable strategic effect when it involves strategic complements. If Burger King finds that McDonald's stubbornly matches its ad dollars, it might benefit by reducing its own ad spending. Of course, Burger King must commit to this reduction or McDonald's may not believe that ad spending will really be restrained. Sometimes it is easier to talk about a commitment than to credibly make that commitment.

A Taxonomy of Commitment Strategies

Drew Fudenberg and Jean Tirole developed a taxonomy of commitment strategies based on the two important dimensions that we have discussed—whether commitments are tough or soft and whether the tactical variables (e.g., quantity and price) are strategic substitutes or strategic complements.[9] There are four ways of combining these dimensions to generate profitable strategic effects, and depending on the combination, the commitment can generate a profitable or unprofitable strategic effect. For example, if the tactical variables are strategic complements (e.g., prices) and the commitment makes the firm tough (e.g., the firm commits to lowering prices), then the commitment causes rival firms to behave more aggressively (e.g., they lower prices in response). In this case, the commitment has a harmful strategic effect, and the firm has an incentive either to forsake the commitment altogether or to underinvest in it—to make the commitment at a lower level. Fudenberg and Tirole call this the "puppy-dog ploy."

The puppy-dog ploy as well as the three other profitable commitment strategies are shown in Table 7.1 and are marked by the superscript *FT*. The profitable alternative to the puppy-dog ploy is the "fat-cat effect," in which the firm makes a soft commitment on tactical variables that are strategic complements. Robert Crandall tried this ploy in 1991 when American Airlines increased its prices through Value Pricing, although the subsequent price cuts suggests that there was little commitment involved in the Value Pricing promotion. When tactical variables are strategic substitutes (e.g.,

TABLE 7.1

Nature of Stage 2 Tactical Variable	Commitment Posture	Commitment Action	Strategy	Comments/Role of Actor in Competitive Arena
Strategic substitutes	Tough	Make	Top Dog[FT]	Assert dominance; force rivals to back off
Strategic substitutes	Tough	Refrain	Submissive Underdog	Accept follower role; avoid fighting
Strategic substitutes	Soft	Make	Suicidal Siberian	Invite rivals to exploit you; may indicate exit strategy
Strategic substitutes	Soft	Refrain	Lean and Hungry Look[FT]	Actively submissive; posturing to avoid conflict
Strategic complements	Tough	Make	Mad Dog	Attack to become top dog; invite battle heedless of costs
Strategic complements	Tough	Refrain	Puppy-Dog Ploy[FT]	Placate top dog; enjoy available scraps
Strategic complements	Soft	Make	Fat-Cat Effect[FT]	Confidently take care of self; share the wealth with rivals
Strategic complements	Soft	Refrain	Weak Kitten	Accept status quo out of fear; wait to follow the leader

quantities), the firm should go ahead with tough commitments (the "top-dog" strategy) and refrain from soft commitments (the "lean and hungry look"). For completeness, we include and name in Table 7.1 those commitment actions that generate harmful strategic effects.

One may occasionally see a firm pursue one of the seemingly harmful strategies. For example, a firm may pursue the "mad-dog" strategy of making a tough commitment when the tactical variables are strategic complements. Robert Crandall appeared to do this when he slashed American Airlines' prices in 1992, though again it is not clear how committed he was to the price cuts. Such strategies, though seemingly counterintuitive, can make sense if the firm views price competition as a dynamic competitive process. If so, short-term strategic losses might be offset by long-term gains. We discuss the long-run dynamics of competition in the next section.

The Informational Benefits of Flexibility

The strategic effects of commitment are rooted in inflexibility. For example, in the Stackelberg model where marginal production costs are low, a firm that preemptively invests in capacity expansion is certain to increase output and drive down prices. In doing so, it may force rival firms to scale back their plans to expand capacity. In this way, the first firm to commit to a capacity expansion can increase its profits at the expense of its rivals. Likewise, a firm that sinks costs to enter a growing market will likely stay rooted in the face of entry, thereby deterring other firms from entering. As in the Stackelberg situation, making an early commitment has a strategic benefit.

EXAMPLE 7.2   COMMITMENT AT NUCOR AND USX: THE CASE OF THIN-SLAB CASTING[10]

Pankaj Ghemawat's case study of the adoption of thin-slab casting by Nucor and the non-adoption by USX (now renamed U.S. Steel) illustrates the relationship between commitment and product market competition, and how previous commitments can limit a firm's ability to take advantage of new commitment opportunities.

In 1987, Nucor Corporation became the first American steel firm to adopt thin-slab casting, a significant improvement over the standard technology of the day, continuous casting. At that time, Nucor was looking to enter the flat-rolled sheet segment of the steel business, a segment that had been unavailable to the minimills, of which Nucor was the largest. Adoption of this thin-slab casting was a major commitment for Nucor. All told, the upfront investment in developing the process and building a facility to use it was expected to be $340 million, close to 90 percent of Nucor's net worth at the time. Nucor's commitment was successful. By 1992, Nucor's thin-slab casting mill in Crawfordsville, Indiana, had become profitable, and Nucor built a second thin-slab casting plant in Arkansas.

USX, the largest American integrated steel producer, which was 60 times larger than Nucor, also showed an early interest in thin-slab casting, spending over $30 million to perfect a thin-slab casting technology known as the Hazelett process. Yet USX eventually decided not to adopt thin-slab casting. Ghemawat argued that this decision was anomalous in light of extant economic theory on process innovations. So why did USX not adopt thin-slab casting? Ghemawat argues that

the decision stemmed from prior organizational and strategic commitments that constrained USX's opportunity to profit from thin-slab casting. For example, in the mid-1980s, USX had already modernized four of its five integrated steel mills. The fifth plant, located in the Monongahela River Valley in Pennsylvania, was a vast complex in which the steelmaking facility and the rolling mill were 10 miles apart. Moreover, the labor cost savings that would accrue to a nonunionized firm like Nucor would not be nearly as significant to unionized USX, which was bound by restrictive work rules. Finally, there was doubt as to whether appliance manufacturers, which were major customers of the sheet steel produced in the Monongahela Valley plant, would purchase sheet steel produced via continuous casting due to the adulteration in the surface quality of the steel that the new process might cause.

Ghemawat argues that USX's prior commitment to modernize existing facilities—in particular the one at Monongahela Valley—as opposed to building "greenfield" plants, locked USX into a posture in which nonadoption of thin-slab casting was a natural outcome. This conclusion highlights an important strategic point: In forecasting the likely reactions of competitors to major strategic commitments, a firm should recognize that prior commitments made by its competitors can constrain those firms' potential responses. In this case, Nucor's management anticipated USX's behavior. Nucor decided to enter the flat-rolled sheet steel business because it expected that integrated producers, such as USX, would not adopt thin-slab casting.

In the strategic situations described above, firms are fully informed about market conditions and costs, they know their rivals' goals and capabilities, and they can observe each other's actions. In reality, strategic commitments are almost always made under conditions of uncertainty. For example, in deciding whether to sink money into building the first CD plant in the United States, Philips had no idea whether CDs would appeal to a mass audience or only to the most dedicated audiophiles. When competitive moves are hard to reverse and their outcomes are shrouded in uncertainty, the value of preserving flexibility by keeping one's future options open must be considered when evaluating the benefits of the commitment.

A firm can preserve its flexibility in a number of ways when making a strategic commitment. A firm can separate a single large commitment into smaller components. For example, Wal-Mart brought its hypermarts to Mexico by opening a few stores in select metropolitan areas. This partly reflected the limited resources available to Wal-Mart (e.g., individuals capable of managing the stores were in short supply), but it also allowed Wal-Mart to learn about market conditions before proceeding with its store rollout. Of course, a smaller commitment will have a smaller strategic effect. If Wal-Mart had thought that by entering Mexico domestic rivals would scale back their own expansion plans, it would have been disappointed.

Real Options

By delaying important decisions, firms can always learn more about market conditions. But this is not an excuse to postpone key decisions indefinitely. By the time the firm acts, it may have lost considerable profits that it might never recapture. And by the inexorable properties of discounting, the future profits that it eventually realizes will be worth less than comparable profits it might have earned earlier on. This raises the question: What is the best time to make a strategic investment when faced with uncertain conditions? The answer is given by the study of *real*[11] *options.*[12]

A real option exists when a decision maker has the opportunity to tailor a decision to information that is unknown today but will be revealed in the future. Real options analysis can be mathematically complex because the formula for valuing an option often involves differential equations. But the underlying intuition is straightforward and can dramatically improve strategic decision making.

To illustrate real options analysis, consider the value of delaying a commitment. Specifically, suppose that a firm can invest $100 million in a plant to enter a new market but is uncertain whether the product will gain widespread acceptance. The firm forecasts two scenarios: with wide product acceptance, net cash flows from the investment will have a present value of $300 million; with low market acceptance, the present value of the net flows will be $50 million. The firm believes that each scenario is equally likely. If the firm invests today, the expected net present value (NPV) of the investment is $0.5(300) + 0.5(50) - 100 = \$75$ million. Using traditional rules for investments—invest in all positive NPV projects—the firm should go ahead with the investment.

But suppose, by waiting a year, the firm can learn for certain which scenario will arise (perhaps by observing the demand for the product in another geographically distinct market). If the product turns out to have a high level of market acceptance, the firm can still invest and obtain a net present value of $200 million. But if the product has low acceptance, the firm is better off putting its money in the next best alternative, which we will assume is a zero NPV investment. Assuming a 10 percent annual discount rate, if the firm waits, its expected NPV is $[0.5(200) + 0.5(0)]/(1.10) = \$91$ million, which exceeds the $75 million NPV from immediate investment. In other words, an investment project that embodies an option to delay is more valuable than one for which the firm faces a "now-or-never" choice of investing or not investing in the project. Delay is valuable because it allows the firm to avoid the money-losing outcome of investing when market acceptance is low.

Real options arise in a variety of business settings.[13] In the mid-1990s, Anheuser-Busch purchased minority interests in brewers in several developing nations, including Mexico's Grupo Modelo and Asia Brewery in the Philippines. By taking small stakes in these companies, Anheuser-Busch was able to learn about different markets and identify those that merited larger investments. This was a more profitable strategy than immediate, large-scale investment. Economists Tom Arnold and Richard Shockley estimated that modest investments of a few million dollars in each brewery had real options value of hundreds of millions of dollars.

Also taking advantage of real options, Airbus and Boeing offer airlines the option of canceling or downsizing orders. Airlines exercise these options when the demand for air travel falls, as it typically does during economic downturns. Airbus and Boeing use the option valuation formula to determine the extra benefit that this flexibility provides to their customers and adjusts the pricing accordingly. As a final example, Hewlett-Packard (HP) customizes some of its products (e.g., ink-jet printers) to particular foreign markets. Traditionally, it would customize the product at the factory and ship it in finished form to individual foreign markets. This was a risky strategy because demand in foreign markets was difficult to predict, and HP often guessed wrong and ended up shipping too many or too few printers. HP now ships partially assembled printers to large overseas warehouses and then customizes the printers for different markets once it has definite orders for them. This increases HP's production costs, but it allows the company to tailor the quantities of different printer models to demand conditions in different markets.

The HP example illustrates two important points. First, firms can often create real options by altering the way in which they configure their internal processes. This implies that a key managerial skill is spotting the potential to create value-enhancing real options. Second, real options often do not come for free; they typically involve trade-offs. In the case of HP, the company traded higher production costs for the added flexibility that came from delaying the customization of printers until it gained more definitive demand information in its individual markets.

Another implication of real options is that the timing of a firm's investments should depend on the degree of uncertainty about future business conditions. By delaying investment decisions, firms postpone any of the benefits of the investment, but they also learn valuable information that can be used to modify the investment. When conditions are volatile, there is more to learn, suggesting that firms should postpone investments when business conditions become more uncertain. Economists have developed formulas for the optimal timing of investments under dynamic uncertainty.[14] Ryan Kellogg studied investment decisions by oil companies and found that these formulas do an excellent job of predicting the timing of drilling of new oil wells.[15]

Competitive Discipline

The Cournot, Bertrand, and Stackelberg models characterize different situations with regard to the competitive variables (e.g., quantity versus price) and the timing of competitive choices. Despite these differences, the models have one thing in common: total industry profits are less than what could be achieved if the firms acted like a cartel, choosing the monopoly price and output. Few if any industries act like cartels, either explicitly or implicitly. This raises two fundamental questions:

1. Why do firms seemingly act against their mutual best interests?
2. Under what circumstances can firms minimize the harmful effects of competition?

Dynamic Pricing Rivalry and Tit-for-Tat Pricing

The starting point for our analysis is the premise that, all else being equal, firms would prefer prices to be as close as possible to monopoly levels. Antitrust laws prohibit open coordination of market prices and quantities, and the penalties for collusion are severe. This means that if managers are to maintain high prices, they must do so *unilaterally*. In this section we explore conditions under which firms might unilaterally arrive at prices that approach collusive levels. (Alternatively, we explore the reasons why it is difficult for unilateral actors to achieve collusive pricing.)

We learned from the Bertrand model that if prices exceed marginal costs there is a strong temptation for each firm to "cheat" by lowering price and grabbing market share. But remember that the Bertrand model is static: firms do not believe that their rivals will respond to price reductions. This is not a very realistic assumption. The economist Edward Chamberlin argued that sellers recognize that the profit they gain from cutting price below the monopoly level is likely to be fleeting:

> *If each seeks his maximum profit rationally and intelligently, he will realize that when there are two or only a few sellers his own move has a considerable effect upon his competitors, and that this makes it idle to suppose that they will accept without retaliation the losses he forces upon them. Since the result of a cut by any one is inevitably to decrease his own profits, no one will cut, and although the sellers are entirely independent, the equilibrium result is the same as though there were a monopolistic agreement between them.[16]*

To better understand Chamberlin's argument, suppose that Shell and Exxon Mobil are the only two sellers of a commodity chemical. They currently charge a price somewhere between the Bertrand price of $20 and the monopoly price of $60, say $40 per hundred pounds. Suppose that Shell is under pressure from shareholders to boost profits and is considering raising its price to the monopoly level of $60. You might think that it would be foolish for Shell to raise its price to $60. After all, if Exxon Mobil keeps its price at $40 it will capture 100 percent of the market and earn $12 million per year, which exceeds the $8 million annual profit it would get by following Shell's lead and charging $60.

But suppose that prices can be changed every week, so that Shell can rescind its price increase without suffering too much loss in profits. In this case, Shell's decision to raise price carries little risk. If Exxon Mobil refuses to follow, Shell can drop its price back to $40 after one week. At most, Shell sacrifices one week's profit at current prices (roughly $115,400 or $0.1154 million). Not only is the risk to Shell low from raising its price, but if Shell puts itself in Exxon Mobil's position, it would see that Exxon Mobil has a compelling motive to follow Shell's price increase.

To see why, suppose that both firms use a 10 percent annual rate to discount future profits. On a weekly basis, this corresponds roughly to a discount rate of 0.2 percent (i.e., 0.002).[17] Shell reasons as follows:

- *Exxon Mobil should anticipate that we will drop our price back down to $40 after the first week if it does not match our price increase. By keeping its price at $40, Exxon Mobil will get a one-week "bump" in profit from $0.1154 million to $0.2307 million per week ($0.2307 = 12/52). However, after we rescind our price increase, Exxon Mobil's weekly profit would go back to $0.1154 million. The discounted present value of Exxon Mobil's weekly profit (expressed in millions of dollars) under this scenario would be $0.2308 + 0.1154/(1.002) + 0.1154/(1.002)^2 + 0.1154/(1.002)^3 + \ldots$, which equals $57.93 million.[18]*

EXAMPLE 7.3   WHAT HAPPENS WHEN A FIRM RETALIATES QUICKLY TO A PRICE CUT: PHILIP MORRIS VERSUS B.A.T. IN COSTA RICA[19]

An excellent illustration of what can happen when one firm cuts its price and its competitor immediately matches the cut occurred in the cigarette industry in Costa Rica in 1993. The most famous cigarette price war of 1993 occurred in the United States, when Philip Morris initiated its "Marlboro Friday" price cuts. The lesser-known Costa Rican price war, also initiated by Philip Morris, began several months before and lasted one year longer than the Marlboro Friday price war.

At the beginning of the 1990s, two firms dominated the Costa Rican cigarette market: Philip Morris, with 30 percent of the market, and B.A.T., with 70 percent of the market. The market consisted of three segments: premium, midpriced, and value-for-money (VFM). Philip Morris had the leading brands in the premium and midpriced segments (Marlboro and Derby, respectively). B.A.T., by contrast, dominated the VFM segment with its Delta brand.

Throughout the 1980s, a prosperous Costa Rican economy fueled steady growth in the demand for cigarettes. As a result, both B.A.T. and Philip Morris were able to sustain price increases that exceeded the rate of inflation. By 1989, industry price–cost margins exceeded 50 percent. However, in the late 1980s, the market began to change. Health concerns slowed the demand for cigarettes in Costa Rica, a trend that hit the premium and midpriced segments much harder than it did the VFM segment. In 1992, B.A.T. gained market share from Philip Morris for the first time since the early 1980s. Philip Morris faced the prospect of slow demand growth and a declining market share.

On Saturday, January 16, 1993, Philip Morris reduced the prices of Marlboro and Derby cigarettes by 40 percent. The timing of the price reduction was not by chance. Philip Morris reasoned that B.A.T.'s inventories would be low following the year-end holidays and that B.A.T. would not have sufficient product to satisfy an immediate increase in demand should it match or undercut Philip Morris's price cut. Philip Morris also initiated its price cut on a Saturday morning, expecting that B.A.T.'s local management would be unable to respond without first undertaking lengthy consultations with the home office in London.

But B.A.T. surprised Philip Morris with the speed of its response. B.A.T. cut the price of its Delta brand by 50 percent, a price that industry observers estimated barely exceeded Delta's marginal cost. Having been alerted to Morris's move on Saturday morning, B.A.T. had salespeople out selling at the new price by Saturday afternoon. The ensuing price war lasted two years. Cigarette sales increased 17 percent as a result of the lower prices, but market shares did not change much. By the time the war ended in 1994, Philip Morris's share of the Costa Rican market was unchanged, and it was U.S. $8 million worse off than it was before the war had started. B.A.T. lost even more—U.S. $20 million—but it had preserved the market share of its Delta brand and was able to maintain the same price gaps that had prevailed across segments before the war.

Why did Philip Morris act as it did? In the early 1990s, Philip Morris had increased Marlboro's market share at B.A.T.'s expense in other Central American countries, such as Guatemala. Perhaps it expected that it could replicate that success in Costa Rica. Still, had it anticipated B.A.T.'s quick response, Philip Morris should have realized that its price cut would not gain it market share. Whatever the motivation for Philip Morris's actions, this example highlights how quick retaliation by competitors can nullify the advantages of a price cut. If firms understand that and take the long view, the anticipated punishment meted out by a tit-for-tat pricing strategy can deter using price as a competitive weapon.

- *If Exxon Mobil follows us and raises its price to $60, we each will earn annual profits of $8 million, which translates into a weekly profit of $153,846 or $0.1538 million. By following our price increase, the discounted value of Exxon Mobil's weekly profit is $0.1538 + 0.1538/(1.002) + 0.1538/(1.002)^2 + 0.1538/(1.002)^3 + \ldots$, which equals $77.05 million. Clearly, Exxon Mobil is better off following our lead, even though for the first week it would be better off if it refused to raise its price to $60.*

Because Exxon Mobil has much to gain by matching Shell's price and Shell loses little if Exxon Mobil does not match, it makes sense for Shell to raise its price to $60. If Exxon Mobil behaves rationally, then it will behave the way Shell expects it to behave (as described by the preceding reasoning), and Exxon Mobil will match Shell's price increase. A simple calculation reveals that the monopoly price is sustainable as long as Exxon Mobil's weekly discount rate is less than 50 percent, which corresponds to an annual discount rate of 2,600 percent! The same logic can be extended to an arbitrary number of firms and to pricing periods of arbitrary lengths (e.g., one month, one quarter, or one year). As long as the number of firms is not too large and the length of time it takes for firms to respond to each other's prices is not too long, it makes sense for firms to adopt a strategy of always matching each other's prices. Once a market "leader" sets the collusive price, the others will follow. But if a firm tries to lower its price, others must match it in order to deter such disruptive business stealing. This is known as *tit-for-tat* pricing.

Why Is Tit-for-Tat So Compelling?

Tit-for-tat is not the only strategy that allows firms to sustain monopoly pricing as a noncooperative equilibrium. Another strategy that, like tit-for-tat, results in the monopoly price for sufficiently low discount rates is the "grim trigger" strategy:

> *Starting this period, we will charge the monopoly price P_M. In each subsequent period, if any firm deviates from P_M, we will drop our price to marginal cost in the next period and keep it there forever.*

The grim trigger strategy relies on the threat of an infinite price war to keep firms from undercutting their competitors' prices. In light of other potentially effective strategies, such as grim trigger, why would we necessarily expect firms to adopt a tit-for-tat strategy? One reason is that tit-for-tat is a simple, easy to describe, and easy to understand strategy. Through announcements such as "We will not be undersold" or "We will match our competitors' prices, no matter how low," a firm can easily signal to its rivals that it is following tit-for-tat.

Another reason for firms to choose a tit-for-tat strategy is that they probably do well over the long run against a variety of different strategies. A compelling illustration of this is discussed by Robert Axelrod in his book *The Evolution of Cooperation*.[20] Axelrod conducted a computer tournament in which entrants were invited to submit strategies for playing a (finitely) repeated prisoners' dilemma game. Each of the submitted strategies was pitted against every other, and the winner was the strategy that accumulated the highest overall score in all of its "matches." Even though tit-for-tat can never beat another strategy in one-on-one competition (at best it can tie another strategy), it accumulated the highest overall score. It was able to do so, according to Axelrod, because it combines the properties of "niceness," "provocability," and "forgiveness." It is nice in that it is never the first to defect from the cooperative outcome. It is provocable in that it immediately punishes a rival that defects from the cooperative outcome by matching the rival's defection in the next period. It is forgiving in that if the rival returns to the cooperative strategy, tit-for-tat will too.

Coordinating on the Right Price

Within the academic community of game theorists, there is a well-known property of dynamic games called the *folk theorem:* if firms expect to interact indefinitely and have sufficiently low discount rates, then any price between the monopoly price and marginal cost can be sustained as an equilibrium.[21] Of course, strategies other than tit-for-tat would be necessary to generate these other equilibria. For example, one equilibrium would be for each firm to set a price equal to marginal cost in each period. Given that it expects its competitors to behave this way, a firm can do no better than to behave this way as well.

The folk theorem implies that cooperative pricing behavior is a possible outcome in an oligopolistic industry, even if all firms act unilaterally. There can be many other outcomes, however, and thus there is no guarantee that cooperative pricing will emerge. Somehow, each firm in the industry must adopt the tit-for-tat strategy without explicit communication that they intend to do so. To succeed, this cooperation-inducing strategy must be a *focal point*—a strategy so compelling that a firm would expect all other firms to adopt it.

Theories of how focal points emerge in economic or social interactions are not well developed.[22] Focal points are highly context- or situation-specific. For example, consider a game called "Divide the Cities" concocted by David Kreps, a professor at the Stanford Graduate School of Business.[23]

> *The following is a list of eleven cities in the United States: Atlanta, Boston, Chicago, Dallas, Denver, Houston, Los Angeles, New York, Philadelphia, San Francisco, and Seattle. I have assigned to each city a point value from 1 to 100 according to the city's importance and its "quality of life." You will not be told this scale until the game is over, except that I tell you now that New York has the highest score, 100, and Seattle has the least, 1. I do think you will find my scale fair. I am going to have you play the following game against a randomly selected student of the Harvard Graduate School of Business. Each of you will be asked to list, simultaneously and without consultation, some subset of these eleven cities. Your list must contain San Francisco and your opponent's must contain Boston. Then, I will give you $100 simply for playing the game. And I will add to/subtract from that amount as follows: For every city that appears on one list but not the other, the person who lists the city will get as many dollars as that city has points on my scale. For every city that appears on both lists, I will take from each of you twice as many dollars as the city has points. Finally, if the two of you manage to partition the cities, I will triple your winnings. Which cities will you list?*

There are hundreds of possible outcomes to this game. Yet, when the game is played by American students, the outcome is nearly always the same: the Stanford student's list is Dallas, Denver, Houston, Los Angeles, Seattle, and San Francisco. The focal point is an East–West division of the United States, coupled with some elementary equity considerations to deal with the fact that there is an odd number (11) of cities to be divided. (Since Seattle is the lowest-valued city, students generally let the western list contain the extra city.) Kreps notes that the focal point of East–West geography becomes less focal when one of the students playing the game is from outside the United States. The U.S. student then often has concerns about the non-U.S. student's knowledge of geography. The game also loses its focal point when the list of cities has a less natural division, for example, if it contains eight western cities and only three eastern ones.

These and similar examples offer several insights for firms attempting to coordinate on price or other decisions. Firms are likely to settle on round number price points (e.g., $300 for digital music players, or perhaps cost plus $100) and round number price increases (e.g., 10 percent annual increases, or perhaps cost plus 5 percent). Even splits of market share are likely to outlast other, less obvious divisions. Status quo market shares are also sustainable. Coordination is likely to be easier when competitors sell products that are nearly identical. Coordination is likely to be difficult in competitive environments that are turbulent and rapidly changing.

IMPEDIMENTS TO COORDINATION

Even if firms coordinate on tit-for-tat pricing, harmony may not ensue. There are many other impediments to implementing a successful tit-for-tat strategy.

The Misread Problem

Tit-for-tat strategy assumes that firms can perfectly observe each other's actions. But rivals will sometimes *misread* their rivals. By "misread," we mean that either (1) a firm mistakenly believes a competitor is charging one price when it is really charging another or (2) a firm misunderstands the reasons for a competitor's pricing decision or their own change in market share. In these situations, a firm might mistakenly believe that its competitor has lowered prices in an attempt to break the "collusive agreement." If the firms are playing tit-for-tat, then rounds of price cutting may ensue, merely because of a misunderstanding.

McKinsey consultants Robert Garda and Michael Marn suggest that some real-world price wars are not prompted by deliberate attempts by one firm to steal business from its competitors.[24] Instead, the wars stem from misreads. To illustrate their point, Garda and Marn cite the example of a tire manufacturer that sold a particular tire at an invoice price of $35, but with an end-of-year volume bonus of $2 and a marketing allowance of $1.50, the manufacturer's net price was really $31.50.[25] This company received reports from its regional sales personnel that a rival firm was selling a competing tire at an invoice price of $32.00. In response, the manufacturer lowered its invoice price by $3.00, reducing its net price to $28.50. The manufacturer later learned that its competitor was not offering marketing allowances or volume discounts. By misreading its competitor's price and reacting immediately, the tire manufacturer precipitated a vicious price war that hurt both firms.

Garda and Marn emphasize that to avoid overreacting to apparent price cuts by competitors, companies should carefully ascertain the details of the competitive initiative and figure out what is driving it before responding. In the same vein, Avinash Dixit and Barry Nalebuff have argued that when misreads are possible, pricing strategies that are less provocable and more forgiving than tit-for-tat are desirable.[26] It may be desirable to ignore what appears to be an uncooperative move by one's competitor if the competitor might revert to cooperative behavior in the next period.

Lumpiness of Orders

Orders are lumpy when sales occur relatively infrequently in large batches as opposed to being smoothly distributed over the year. Lumpy orders are an important characteristic of such industries as airframe manufacturing, shipbuilding, and supercomputers.

EXAMPLE 7.4   FORGIVENESS AND PROVOCABILITY: DOW CHEMICALS AND THE MARKET FOR REVERSE OSMOSIS MEMBRANES

Achieving the right balance between provocability and forgiveness is important, but it can be difficult to do. Dow Chemicals learned this lesson in the mid-1990s in the market for reverse osmosis membranes, an expensive component used in environmental systems for wastewater treatment and water purification. Dow sells this product to large industrial distributors that, in turn, resell it to end users.

Until 1989, Dow held a patent on its Film-Tec membrane and had the U.S. market entirely to itself. In 1989, however, the U.S. government made Dow's patent public property on the grounds that the government had co-funded the development of the technology. Shortly thereafter, a Japanese firm entered the market with a "clone" of Dow's FilmTec membrane.

In 1989, Dow's price was $1,400 per membrane. Over the next seven years, the Japanese competitor reduced its price to about $385 per unit. Over this period, Dow also reduced its price. With slight differentiation based on superior service support and perceived quality, Dow's price bottomed out at about $405 per unit.

During the downward price spiral, Dow alternated back and forth between forgiving and aggressive responses to its competitor's pricing moves as Dow sought to ascertain its rival's motives and persuade it to keep industry prices high. On three different occasions, Dow raised the price of its membrane. Its competitor never followed Dow's increases, and (consistent with tit-for-tat pricing) Dow ultimately rescinded its price increase each time.

During this period, Dow also attempted several strategic moves to insulate itself from price competition and soften the pricing behavior of its competitor. For example, Dow invested in product quality to improve the performance of its membranes. It also tried to remove distributors' focus on price by heavily advertising its membrane's superior performance features. These moves were only moderately successful, however, and Dow was unable to gain a price premium greater than 13 percent.

Eventually, Dow learned that its competitor manufactured its product in Mexico, giving it a cost advantage based on low-cost labor. It also learned that in 1991 the competitor had built a large plant and that its aggressive pricing moves were, in part, prompted by a desire to keep that plant operating at full capacity. Based on this information, Dow abandoned its efforts to soften price competition, either through forgiving pricing moves or strategic commitments aimed at changing the equilibrium in the pricing game. Dow's current strategy is to bypass industrial distributors and sell its product directly to end users. This move was motivated by Dow's discovery that, despite the decreases in manufacturers' prices, distributors' prices to end users remained fairly constant. It is not clear that this strategy would help insulate Dow from price competition. Dow's competitor can presumably imitate this strategy and deal directly with end users as well. It is hard to imagine pricing rivalry in this industry becoming less aggressive.

Lumpy orders reduce the frequency of competitive interactions between firms, lengthen the time required for competitors to react to price reductions, and thereby make price cutting more attractive.

Information about the Sales Transaction

When sales transactions are "public," deviations from cooperative pricing are easier to detect than when prices are secret. For example, all airlines closely monitor each other's prices using computerized reservation systems and immediately know when a carrier has cut fares. By contrast, prices in many industrial goods markets are privately negotiated between buyers and sellers, so it may be difficult for a firm to learn whether a competitor has cut its price. Because retaliation can occur more quickly when prices are public than when they are secret, price cutting to steal market share from competitors is likely to be less attractive, enhancing the chances that cooperative pricing can be sustained.

Secrecy is a significant problem when transactions involve other dimensions besides a list or an invoice price, as they often do in business-to-business marketing settings. For example, a manufacturer of cookies, such as Keebler, that wants to steal business from a competitor, say Nabisco, can cut its "net price" by increasing trade allowances to retailers or by extending more favorable trade credit terms. Because it is often more difficult to monitor trade allowance deals or credit terms than list prices, competitors may find it difficult to detect business-stealing behavior, hindering their ability to retaliate. Business practices that facilitate secret price cutting create a prisoners' dilemma. Each firm individually prefers to use them, but the industry is collectively worse off when all firms do so.

Deviations from cooperative pricing are also difficult to detect when product attributes are customized to individual buyers, as in airframe manufacturing or the production of diesel locomotives. When products are tailor-made to individual buyers, a seller may be able to increase its market share by altering the design of the product or by throwing in "extras," such as spare parts or a service agreement. These are typically more difficult to observe than the list price, complicating the ability of firms to monitor competitors' behavior.

Secret or complex transaction terms can intensify price competition not only because price matching becomes a less effective deterrent to price-cutting behavior, but also because misreads become more likely. Firms are more likely to misinterpret a competitive move, such as a reduction in list prices, as an aggressive attempt to steal business, when they cannot fully observe all the other terms competitors are offering. When this happens, the odds of accidental price wars breaking out rise. To the extent that a firm's pricing behavior is forgiving, the effects of misreads may be containable.

Volatility of Demand Conditions

Price cutting is harder to verify when market demand conditions are volatile and a firm can observe only its own volume and not that of its rival. If a firm's sales unexpectedly fall, it will naturally suspect that one of its competitors has cut price and is taking business from it. Demand volatility is an especially serious problem when production involves substantial fixed costs. Then, marginal costs decline rapidly at output levels below capacity. During times of excess capacity, the temptation to cut price to steal business can be high. Moreover, coordination becomes inordinately difficult, because firms will be chasing a moving target. Finally, suppose one firm does cut price in response to a decline in demand. If other firms see the price cut but cannot detect their rival's volume reduction, they may misread the situation as an effort to steal business.

ASYMMETRIES AMONG FIRMS AND THE SUSTAINABILITY OF COOPERATIVE PRICES

When firms are not identical, either because they have different costs or are vertically differentiated, achieving cooperative pricing becomes more difficult. When firms are identical, a single monopoly price can be a focal point. However, when firms differ,

FIGURE 7.2
MONOPOLY PRICES WITH ASYMMETRICAL FIRMS

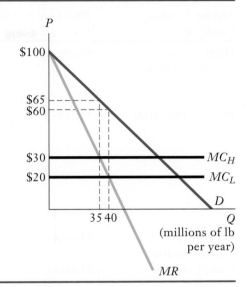

The low-cost firm's marginal cost curve is MC_L, while the high-cost firm's marginal cost curve is MC_H. If the low-cost firm was a monopolist, it would set a price of $60. If the high-cost firm was a monopolist, it would set a price of $65.

there is no single focal price, and it thus becomes more difficult for firms to coordinate their pricing strategies toward common objectives. Figure 7.2 depicts two firms with different marginal costs and shows that the firm with the lower marginal cost prefers a monopoly price lower than the one with the higher marginal cost.

Even when all firms can agree on the cooperative price, differences in costs, capacities, or product qualities may affect their incentives to abide by the agreement. For example, small firms within a given industry often have more incentive to defect from cooperative pricing than larger firms. One reason is that small firms gain more in new business relative to the loss due to the revenue destruction effect. Another reason, also related to the revenue destruction effect, is that large firms often have weak incentives to punish a smaller price cutter and will instead offer a *price umbrella* under which the smaller firm can sustain its lower price.

Smaller firms have an additional incentive to lower price on products, including most consumer goods, for which buyers make repeat purchases. A small firm might lower price to induce some consumers to try its product. Once prices are restored to their initial levels, the small firm hopes that some of the consumers who sampled its product will become permanent customers. This strategy will succeed only if there is a lag between the small firm's price reduction and any response by its larger rivals. Otherwise, few if any new consumers will sample the small firm's product, and its market share will not increase.

Price Sensitivity of Buyers and the Sustainability of Cooperative Pricing

A final factor affecting the sustainability of cooperative pricing is the price sensitivity of buyers. When buyers are price sensitive, a firm that undercuts its rivals' prices by even a small amount may be able to achieve a significant boost in its volume. Under these circumstances, a firm may be tempted to cut price even if it expects that

TABLE 7.2
MARKET STRUCTURE CONDITIONS AFFECTING THE SUSTAINABILITY OF COOPERATIVE PRICING

Market Structure Condition	How Does It Affect Cooperative Pricing	Reasons
High market concentration	Facilitates	• Coordinating on the cooperative equilibrium is easier with few firms • Increases the benefit-cost ratio from adhering to cooperative pricing
Firm asymmetries	Harms	• Disagreement over cooperative price • Coordinating on cooperative price is more difficult • Possible incentive of large firms to extend price umbrella to small firms increases small firms' incentives to cut price • Small firms may prefer to deviate from monopoly prices even if larger firms match
High buyer concentration	Harms	• Reduces probability that a defector will be discovered
Lumpy orders	Harms	• Decreases the frequency of interaction between competitors, increasing the lag between defection and retaliation
Secret price terms	Harms	• Increases detection lags because prices of competitors are more difficult to monitor • Increases the probability of misreads
Volatility of demand and cost conditions	Harms	• Increases the lag between defection and retaliation (perhaps even precluding retaliation) by increasing uncertainty about whether defections have occurred and about identity of defectors
Price-sensitive buyers	Harms	• Increases the temptation to cut price, even if competitors are expected to match

competitors will eventually match the price cut. This is because even a temporary price cut may result in a significant and profitable boost in market share.

Market Structure and the Sustainability of Cooperative Pricing: Summary

This section has discussed how market structure affects the sustainability of cooperative pricing. Table 7.2 summarizes the impact of the market structure characteristics discussed in this section.

FACILITATING PRACTICES

Firms can facilitate cooperative pricing through a number of practices, including

• Price leadership

• Advance announcement of price changes

- Most favored customer clauses
- Uniform delivered prices

Price Leadership

Price leadership is a way to overcome the problem of coordinating on a focal equilibrium. In price leadership, each firm gives up its pricing autonomy and cedes control over industry pricing to a single firm. Examples of well-known price leaders include Kellogg in breakfast cereals, Philip Morris in tobacco, and (until the mid-1960s) U.S. Steel in steel. Firms thus need not worry that rivals will secretly shade price to steal market share.

The kind of oligopolistic price leadership we discuss here should be distinguished from the barometric price leadership that sometimes occurs in competitive markets, such as that for prime rate loans. Under barometric price leadership, the price leader merely acts as a barometer of changes in market conditions by adjusting prices to shifts in demand or input prices. Under barometric leadership, different firms are often price leaders, while under oligopolistic leadership the same firm is the leader for years.

Advance Announcement of Price Changes

In some markets, firms will publicly announce the prices they intend to charge in the future. For example, in chemicals markets firms often announce their intention to raise prices 30 or 60 days before the price change is to take effect. These preannouncements can benefit consumers, such as when cement makers announce prices weeks ahead of the spring construction season, enabling contractors to bid on projects more intelligently. But advance announcements can also facilitate price increases, much to the harm of consumers. Advance announcements of price changes reduce the uncertainty that firms' rivals will undercut them. The practice also allows firms to harmlessly rescind or roll back proposed price increases that competitors refuse to follow. In the early 1990s, the U.S. Department of Justice challenged the airline industry's common practice of announcing fare increases well in advance of the date on which the increases took effect. The DOJ argued that these preannouncements could not possibly benefit consumers and therefore served only the purpose of facilitating price increases. The airlines consented to abandon the practice; nowadays, they often announce price hikes at the close of business on Friday. If competitors do not match over the weekend, they can rescind the hikes on Monday morning without too much damage being done.

Most Favored Customer Clauses

A most favored customer clause is a provision in a sales contract that promises a buyer that it will pay the lowest price the seller charges. There are two basic types of most favored customer clauses: contemporaneous and retroactive.

To illustrate these two types, consider a simple example. Xerxes Chemical manufactures a chemical additive used to enhance the performance of jet fuel. Star Petroleum Refining Company, a manufacturer of jet fuel, signs a contract with Xerxes calling for delivery of 100,000 tons of the chemical over the next three months at the "open order" price of $0.50 per ton.[27] Under a contemporaneous most favored customer policy, Xerxes agrees that while this contract is in effect, if it sells the chemical at a lower price to any other buyer (perhaps to undercut a competitor), it will also

EXAMPLE 7.5   ARE MOST FAVORED NATION AGREEMENTS ANTICOMPETITIVE?

On October 18, 2010, the U.S. Department of Justice and the state of Michigan filed an antitrust suit against Blue Cross Blue Shield of Michigan (BCBSM). Blue Cross Blue Shield is a national federation of 39 health insurance organizations and companies in the United States, and BCBSM is one of its largest independent licensees with 4.3 million members—well over 60 percent of the commercially insured population of the state of Michigan. BCBSM has most favored nation (MFN) contracts with nearly 60 percent of Michigan's 131 general acute care hospitals, including many major hospitals. The lawsuit alleges that BCBSM's use of MFN clauses violated antitrust laws. This is the first time DOJ brought an action against a health insurer challenging the use of MFN clauses since the 1990s.

MFN clauses effectively ensure that all buyers are treated equally. This would seem to be procompetitive, and courts in the United States have usually dismissed antitrust challenges against MFN clauses without conducting a "rule of reason" analysis in which experts present and analyze evidence to determine whether the conduct in question was anticompetitive. Yet economic theory suggests that MFN clauses can have two harmful consequences. Consider BCBSM's situation. Its MNF clauses limit the ability of other insurers to compete effectively by guaranteeing that they never have lower input costs than BCBSM. This can be especially problematic in health care, where one way that insurers have found to lower costs is by contracting with a small subset of providers, guaranteeing them an increase in volume in exchange for deep discounts. The MFN obliges those providers to offer the same deep discounts to BCBSM, even though BCBSM will not guarantee them an increase in volume. This makes it impossible for these low-cost alternatives to compete with BCBSM, so they never appear in the market.

Even if MFNs do not affect market structure, they can directly affect pricing. Providers who grant MFN protection to BCBSM have a disincentive to offer discounts to other insurers, for they would be obligated to pass this discount along to BCBSM. The result can be higher prices for all purchasers, including BCBSM. BCBSM might not mind, however, as it knows that it will pay no more than other insurers. Indeed, research by Fiona Scott Morton showed that when Medicaid (a public insurance program for low-income Americans) obtained MFN status for prescription drugs, the prices paid by private insurers for the same drugs increased.[28] The same may well occur when insurers like BCBSM secure MFN status with hospitals and other providers.

Antitrust economists have raised these objections for several decades. So why did the Department of Justice choose this time to sue BCBSM? The government alleges that BCBSM's MFN agreements go beyond the typical MFN. These MFN contracts allegedly require that participating hospitals charge other insurers an agreed percentage *more* than they charge BCBSM, sometimes as high as 40 percent more than the hospital was charging BCBSM. BCBSM was even willing to increase its payments to large hospitals if they agreed to this add-on fee for competing health plans.

BCBSM has defended itself vigorously, arguing that it uses MFNs as a tool to secure the lowest health service costs and the deepest possible discounts for the large population of Michigan residents it served. It stated in a press release: "Our hospital discounts are a vital part of our statutory mission to provide Michigan residents with statewide access to health care at a reasonable cost. [. . .] Because Blue Cross is the only nonprofit healthcare corporation that is regulated by Michigan Public Act 350, it is the only Michigan insurer that is required to meet the cost, quality, and access goals required by statute."[29]

The outcome of this case could profoundly affect health care markets across the United States. Many other Blue Cross plans have large market shares and use their clout to obtain MFN clauses. It is not known if other plans have the "MFN plus" clause in BCBSM's contracts. But the current lawsuit might clarify the court's position on whether MFN clauses should be examined under the rule of reason.

lower the price to this level for Star Petroleum. Under a retroactive most favored customer clause, Xerxes agrees to pay a rebate to Star Petroleum if during a certain period after the contract has expired (e.g., two years) it sells the chemical additive for a lower price than Star Petroleum paid.

Most favored customer clauses appear to benefit buyers. For Star Petroleum, the "price protection" offered by the most favored customer clause may help keep its production costs in line with those of competitors. However, most favored customer clauses can inhibit price competition by discouraging firms from cutting prices to other customers who do not have these clauses. This theory has motivated a recent U.S. Department of Justice investigation into the use of most favored clauses in contracts between hospitals and Blue Cross health insurance plans, as described in Example 7.5.

Uniform Delivered Prices

In many industries, such as cement, steel, or soybean products, buyers and sellers are geographically separated, and transportation costs are significant. In such contexts, the pricing method can affect competitive interactions. Broadly speaking, two different kinds of pricing policies can be identified. Under uniform FOB pricing, the seller quotes a price for pickup at the seller's loading dock, and the buyer absorbs the freight charges for shipping from the seller's plant to the buyer's plant.[30] Under uniform delivered pricing, the firm quotes a single delivered price for all buyers and absorbs any freight charges itself.[31]

Uniform delivered pricing facilitates cooperative pricing by allowing firms to make a more "surgical" response to price cutting by rivals. Consider, for example, two brick producers, one located in Mumbai and the other in Ahmadabad, India. These firms have been trying to maintain prices at the monopoly level, but the Mumbai producer cuts its price to increase its share of the market in Surat, a city between Mumbai and Ahmadabad. Under FOB pricing, the Ahmadabad producer must retaliate by cutting its mill price, which effectively reduces its price to all its customers (see Figure 7.3). On the other hand, if the firms were using uniform delivered pricing, the Ahmadabad firm could cut its price selectively; it could cut the delivered price to its customers in Surat, keeping delivered prices of other customers at their original level (see Figure 7.4). Like targeted couponing, uniform delivered pricing reduces the "cost" that the "victim" incurs by retaliating. This makes retaliation more likely and enhances the credibility of policies, such as tit-for-tat, that can sustain cooperative pricing.

FIGURE 7.3
FOB PRICING

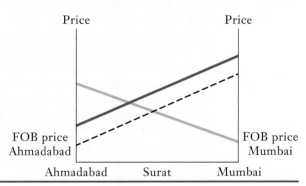

When both firms use FOB pricing, the delivered price that a customer actually pays depends on its location. The delivered price schedules are shown by the solid lines in the figure. If the brick producer in Ahmadabad lowers its FOB price to match that of the Mumbai producer, then it effectively shifts its delivered price schedule downward. (It now becomes the dashed line.) Even though the Ahmadabad firm is retaliating against the Mumbai firm's stealing business in Surat, the Ahmadabad firm ends up reducing its delivered prices to all of its customers.

FIGURE 7.4
DELIVERED PRICING

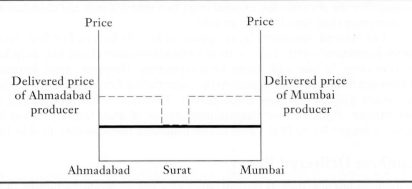

When both firms use delivered pricing, a firm's customer pays the same delivered price, no matter what its location. If the Mumbai firm cuts its delivered price to steal business in Surat, the Ahmadabad producer need only cut its delivered price in Surat to retaliate.

WHERE DOES MARKET STRUCTURE COME FROM?

With the exception of discussion of entry in Chapter 6, our exploration of competition has largely taken market structure as given. But there are reasons why different markets have different structures. Understanding these reasons helps managers anticipate how markets may evolve, or what we call the *macrodynamics* of the market. In this section, we explore the reasons why markets look the way they do.

Simple microeconomic theory provides a good starting point for explaining differences in market structure. Recall from the Economics Primer and Chapter 2 that production processes often display U-shaped average total costs. In other words, there is a specific level of output for each firm that minimizes costs. This level of output is called the minimum efficient scale (MES), which we denoted in the Primer by q^{**}. Recall that the MES is larger when the sunk upfront costs of establishing the production facility are large relative to ongoing variable costs of production. Let the average total cost at the MES be $AC(q^{**})$. Finally, suppose that the level of industry demand when price equals $AC(q^{**})$ is Q^{**}.

Microeconomic theory predicts that if the firms in this example behave competitively, there will be $N^* = Q^{**}/q^{**}$ equal-sized firms in the market, each selling q^{**} units. Simply put, the number of firms depends on the total size of the market relative to the MES of production. The basic theory goes a long way toward explaining variation in market structure over time, across industries, and across geographic areas. In a famous study, John Blair argued that technological change in the industrial revolution increased the MES of production and that this was largely responsible for the long-term trend of increasing concentration in many sectors of the economy.[32]

Looking at the cross section of industries today, we see that high sunk costs associated with research and manufacturing have led to high concentration in commercial airframe manufacturing, while large purchasing and distribution economies limit the number of mass merchandiser chains in any given metropolitan area. By examining different geographic markets within the same industry, we can also confirm that concentration is linked to market size. For example, there are at least five different hypermart chains in Mexico City (including Carrefours and Wal-Mart) but only one or two in smaller Mexican cities.

Microdynamic competitive forces also influence market structure. As we discussed in Chapter 5 and in this chapter, some industries are predisposed to intensive price competition, perhaps because the industry is not amenable to facilitating practices or because there is high potential for misreads. For any given number of firms, prices will be lower in these more competitive industries. As a result, it is more difficult for firms to recover sunk production costs, fewer firms survive, and the market is more concentrated. A particularly good example is provided by Chamberlin's model of monopolistic competition, which we developed in Chapter 5. When goods are highly differentiated, firms can raise prices and increase profits. This attracts additional differentiated entry. We used the market for take-out sandwiches as an example. If sandwich buyers have strongly idiosyncratic preferences so that some greatly prefer Quiznos while others are highly partial to Jimmy Johns, both stores will be able to raise prices. But these high prices will attract other entrants such as Subway and Togos.

The basic theory relating market structure and concentration masks two important empirical regularities: firm sizes vary and are highly skewed. That is, most markets tend to feature a small number of large firms and a great many smaller competitors. In his seminal book *Sunk Costs and Market Structure*, John Sutton offers a powerful explanation for these facts based on the macrodynamics of competition and, in doing so, challenges the notion that the number of competitors in a market is solely a function of market size and production technology.[33]

SUTTON'S ENDOGENOUS SUNK COSTS

Sutton's explanation for market structure is rooted in the facts about consumer products markets. Most consumer goods markets seem to have two or three large firms with national or international brand reputations that serve the whole market, as well as a great many fringe manufacturers that seem to serve market niches. Sutton gives as examples soft drinks, canned food, and breakfast cereals, but we might add countless other industries where production costs are low and brand reputation is important.

If we consider sunk production costs alone, there is no particular reason why the U.S. canned vegetable market should be dominated by Green Giant and Del Monte or why Coke and Pepsi should sell most of the world's soft drinks. And a theory of market structure based solely on the ratio of total market size to minimum efficient scale of production cannot explain why these markets are far more concentrated today than they were a hundred years ago. Consider that at the end of the nineteenth century, Americans were consuming 227 million servings of soft drinks annually, prepared by thousands of independent local "soda fountains." Even after the arrival of mass-production bottling, local sellers dominated the market using their own unique syrups. Ginger ale, sarsaparilla, and root beer were early favorites, though by the 1920s cola drinks had risen to the top in popularity, spurred in part by aggressive marketing by Coke. (Pepsi did not grow rapidly until the 1930s, when it increased the size of its bottle from 6 to 12 ounces and ran a successful ad campaign promoting the added value.) Similar patterns arise in virtually all consumer product markets worldwide.

In explaining these facts, Sutton does not reject the importance of sunk costs and scale economies. Instead, he explains that consumers often gravitate to brand-name products, and that the creation and maintenance of brands requires substantial sunk investments. In other words, the MES for branded products can be very large.

EXAMPLE 7.6   THE EVOLUTION OF THE CHINESE DOWN APPAREL INDUSTRY

Bosideng is undisputedly the brightest star in the Chinese down apparel industry. Starting out as a small garment factory with 11 workers and 8 sewing machines in 1976, its pioneering brand-building and image-conscious approach has made it the national market share leader every year since 1995. In the process, Bosideng has become one of the most prestigious brand names in China. What makes this rise even more remarkable is that just a quarter century ago, the down apparel industry in China was highly fragmented with no well-known brands.

The Chinese down apparel industry began in earnest in late 1970s as increasingly affluent consumers showed their preference for the warmth, light weight, and softness of down jackets over their old, heavy cotton coats. Spurred by demand, over 3,000 manufacturers entered the industry. Their products were barely differentiated, rarely updated, and of marginal quality. Intense price competition inevitably resulted. A series of warm winters followed, and by the early 1990s, less than 20 percent of the down manufacturers were covering their costs.

Bosideng was one of the early entrants, preferring to manufacture down apparel under contract to other firms. Having earned a reputation for quality, Bosideng introduced its own branded line in 1994. Bosideng enjoyed immediate success among the cognoscenti, and within a year it became the market leader with a share of 15 percent. Even so, Bosideng struggled to distinguish itself from the undifferentiated horde of competitors.

Bosideng set about brand-building. In 1998, it became the primary sponsor for the Chinese National Mountain Climbing Team just before a televised mission to Mount Everest. Images of scruffy hard men and women surmounting the highest peak on earth clad in Bosideng were beamed to the nation. Bosideng invited renowned fashion designers to overhaul its styling, and hired pop stars and media celebrities from China and Korea to be celebrity endorsers. Bosideng has recently extended its reach to overseas. In 2005 and 2006, it sponsored the ISU Short Track Speed Skating World Cup, the World Figure Skating Championships, and all Chinese skiing and skating athletes at the Winter Olympics in Torino, all of which helped it expand in the international market.

Bosideng was the first down apparel maker in China to build multiple brands targeting different consumer sectors. Its top-tier brand "Bosideng" targets high-end consumers while "Snow Flying" is sportier in style, "Bengen" focuses on the young, more hip consumer group, and "Kangbo" provides budget choices. This product combination also gives the company flexibility to deal with competitive challenges. In 2000, when a major national competitor started significant price-cutting, Bosideng cut the price of its "Snow Flying" brand while keeping prices for other brands relatively stable, preserving its market share and minimizing revenue loss.

Inspired by Bosideng, other major down apparel manufacturers started paying more attention to branding and fashion. The No. 2 brand of down apparel, Yalu, has also secured celebrity endorsements and introduced several sub-brands. Long-time industry participant Yaya has targeted lower income consumers with products that it bills as the "affordable and budget-friendly choice." Driven by the media savvy of Bosideng, the down apparel industry has become an advertising-intensive industry. In 2000, the entire industry spent RMB 220 million in television advertisements. But in 2008, the spending of one company, Bosideng, on one TV channel, China Central Television (CCTV), amounted to as much as RMB 220 million!

Led by Bosideng, the down apparel market in China underwent a consolidation. There are now about 100 manufacturers, but the top three brands account for 55 percent of the market, led by Bosideng's 37 percent share. Through its massive investments in brand building, Bosideng transformed the market along the line suggested by Sutton—from one with thousands of undifferentiated competitors to one with a small number of branded market leaders and a competitive fringe.

Moreover, the size of the branding investment is not determined by some technology, as is the case for production, but is instead chosen by the firms themselves. For this reason, Sutton describes these investments as *endogenous sunk costs*.

With this key idea, Sutton can explain how market structures evolve. Early in an industry's life cycle, many small firms compete on a level playing field. Whether through superior quality, customer service, brand promotion, or the luck of the draw, some firms grow larger than others. Some firms, usually those that already have an edge in the market, invest in strengthening their brand-name capital, thereby growing their market shares. But branding is very costly, and as a few firms establish strong brands, there may not be enough room in the market for others to match them. As the market keeps growing, the brand leaders may keep investing in their brands, upping the ante for any challengers to their elite brand status. In this way, the number of leading brands may remain fixed even as the market grows. The only option left to would-be challengers is to differentiate and fill niches not exploited by the leaders. At best these challengers become Dr Pepper or 7-Up. Eventually, niches may emerge that are large enough to command new brand investments; thus we get Gatorade and Arizona Iced Tea. But the overall story is the same: a market filled with small, seemingly similar, firms evolves into a split between a handful of leading brands and a larger number of niche competitors. The big winners are those that enjoy some initial advantage and are quick to successfully market their brand.

Sutton's theory also explains why consumer goods markets tend to be more concentrated today than they were a century ago, despite dramatic increases in demand. One hundred years ago, firms relied on their sales force to promote their products. This labor-intensive process displayed few scale economies—the minimum efficient scale was within reach of even small firms. Thanks to the development of broadcast media, mainly television, firms could now invest in developing a brand image and create an ad campaign that reached millions of potential customers. But this requires substantial sunk costs and has big-scale economies. Thus, only a few firms in an industry need apply. Thanks to the Internet, social media, and other transformative technologies, firms today have unprecedented opportunities to identify niches and target niche customers. In Chapter 10, we discuss how these recent developments allow new firms to enter and draw business away from firms that had seemingly dominant brand positions.

Innovation and Market Evolution

While brand creation seems to lead to market concentration in consumer goods industries, other investments by firms in other industries may lead to different results. Sutton considers research and development spending to be another potential endogenous sunk cost. That is, market leaders may aggressively spend on R&D to force other firms to do likewise if they are to effectively compete. Because R&D is a sunk cost, this raises the minimum efficient scale of entry.

Although market leaders may make innovative investments to secure their positions, newcomers often find that innovations allow them to produce better products at lower costs. Clay Christensen describes *disruptive technologies* as unexpected innovations that dramatically transform a product's benefits and/or its costs of production.[34] Digital photography, plastics, and cellular phones are good examples. As described by Clay Christensen, incumbent firms must confront the *innovator's dilemma*. Disruptive technologies may destroy the business of the technology they replace. Incumbents may accelerate the cannibalization of their successful business model by innovating; but failure to innovate will open the door to new-comers, leaving the incumbent without any business.

Economists have long debated whether opportunities for innovation reinforce or undo market concentration. Even disruptive technologies do not necessarily spell doom for incumbents. Digital phones by Sony, Canon, and others may have crippled Kodak and Polaroid, but former landline communications companies like Verizon and France Telecom (under the Orange brand name) have remained highly successful mobile service providers. In a systematic study of 73 industries in the United Kingdom, Paul Geroski and R. Pomroy found that innovation was usually deconcentrating, although the effect was slow and inconsistent.[35] We will return to the topics of innovation and disruption in Chapter 11.

Learning and Industry Dynamics

The BCG growth/share matrix described in Chapter 2 suggests that firms can use the learning curve to secure and maintain market leadership. But in new work on the learning curve, David Besanko and his coauthors point out that learning is not enough for a firm to maintain its dominant position. The reason is that trailing firms also move down the learning curve, and as all firms learn, the gap in knowledge, and the associated gap in production costs, shrinks. Yet many firms in knowledge-intensive industries remain market leaders for a long time. Intel is a good example; AMD has produced enough microprocessor chips over the years that it should have moved far down the learning curve, yet it continues to lag behind Intel.

How do these leaders stay in front? David Besanko and colleagues suggest that the answer lies in a combination of learning and forgetting.[36] When a market leader expands its output, it does move down the learning curve. Perhaps more importantly, it can steal business from its smaller rivals, limiting the extent of their learning. If their rivals lose business, then they may actually forget some of the skills they had already accumulated, so that their production costs increase. In other words, firms may pursue aggressive growth strategies not so much to move down their own cost curves through learning, but rather to drive up rivals' costs through forgetting. Using simulations to model how firms might respond to one another in the presence of these dynamics, Besanko et al. show that many markets can experience sustained periods of concentration as the dominant firm exploits this learning/forgetting strategy.

CHAPTER SUMMARY

- Competitive dynamics evolve over time. Microdynamics refers to the unfolding of competition among a small number of firms. Macrodynamics refers to the evolution of overall market structure.

- Firms can gain an advantage over rivals by making strategic commitments, which are are hard-to-reverse decisions that alter the strategic decisions of rivals.

- A firm's commitments can lead competitors to make decisions that are advantageous for the firm making the commitment.

- The impact of strategic commitments depends on the nature of product market competition. The concepts of strategic complements and strategic substitutes are useful for characterizing how commitment affects competition. When reaction functions are upward sloping, actions are strategic complements. When reaction functions are downward sloping, actions are strategic substitutes.

● In a two-stage setting, in which a firm makes a commitment and then the firm and its competitors choose tactical actions, the desirability of the commitment depends on whether the actions are strategic substitutes or complements and whether the commitment makes the firm tough or soft.

● Flexibility gives the firm option value. A simple example of option value occurs when the firm can delay an investment and await new information that bears on the investment's profitability.

● Firms engaged in oligopolistic competition can increase profits through competitive discipline. Strategies such as "tit-for-tat" pricing can facilitate coordination but are difficult to implement.

● Coordinating on the "right price" is difficult for several reasons. Coordination must be tacit. Firms may disagree as to what constitutes the "right price" and how to "divide the market." Misreads and misjudgments can trigger price wars.

● Market structure affects the sustainability of cooperative pricing. High market concentration facilitates cooperative pricing. Asymmetries among firms, lumpy orders, high buyer concentration, secret sales transactions, volatile demand, and price-sensitive buyers make pricing cooperation more difficult.

● Practices that can facilitate cooperative pricing include price leadership, advance announcements of price changes, most favored customer clauses, and uniform delivered pricing.

● A market's macrodynamics determine its long-run structure. The number of firms is positively correlated with demand and negatively correlated with the minimum efficient scale.

● Firms in consumer goods-intensive markets can endogenously increase the minimum efficient scale through branding. Many consumer goods markets feature two or three dominant branded companies and many smaller niche players.

● Disruptive technologies are unexpected innovations that transform a product's benefits or costs of production. Large incumbents may be reluctant or unable to meet the challenges of disruptive technologies.

● Firms pursuing a learning strategy can steal business from smaller rivals, limiting the extent to which those rivals also learn. This can give learning firms a permanent market advantage.

QUESTIONS

1. Why are the Cournot and Bertrand models considered static? What aspects of real world behavior might be missing in static models?

2. What is the difference between a soft commitment and no commitment?

3. Zellers and Wal-Mart are two of Canada's largest retailers. To reflect the strong position of the Canadian dollar, each firm is considering lowering prices on *some* goods in Canadian stores. The following table displays the payoffs for each firm associated with lowering prices (or not), given the other firm's decision:

If Zellers decides to . . .	And Wal-Mart decides to . . .	Then, Zellers's profits are . . .	And Wal-Mart's profits are . . .
Keep prices the same	Keep prices the same	$200MM	$250MM
Keep prices the same	Drop prices	$150MM	$280MM
Drop prices	Keep prices the same	$230MM	$190MM
Drop prices	Drop prices	$180MM	$220MM

If given the opportunity, how much would Zellers be willing to spend for the right to move first?

4. Explain why prices are usually strategic complements and capacities are usually strategic substitutes.

5. Use the logic of the Cournot equilibrium to explain why it is more effective for a firm to build capacity ahead of its rival than it is for that firm to merely announce that it is going to build capacity.

6. Consider a monopoly producer of a durable good, such as a supercomputer. The good does not depreciate. Once consumers purchase the good from the monopolist, they are free to sell it in the "secondhand" market. Often in markets for new durable goods, one sees the following pricing pattern: The seller starts off charging a high price but then lowers the price over time. Explain why, with a durable good, the monopolist might prefer to commit to keep its selling price constant over time. Can you think of a way that the monopolist might be able to make a credible commitment to do this?

7. Indicate whether the *strategic effects* of the following competitive moves are likely to be positive (beneficial to the firm making them) or negative (harmful to the firm making them).

    (a) Two horizontally differentiated producers of diesel railroad engines— one located in the United States and the other in Europe—compete in the European market as Bertrand price competitors. The U.S. manufacturer lobbies the U.S. government to give it an export subsidy, the amount of which is directly proportional to the amount of output the firm sells in the European market.

    (b) A Cournot duopolist issues new debt to repurchase shares of its stock. The new debt issue will preclude the firm raising additional debt in the foreseeable future, and is expected to constrain the firm from modernizing existing production facilities.

8. Which of the following are examples of real options?

    (a) A basketball team owner delays signing a star free agent to a one-year contract, preferring to wait and see if his team is in contention for a championship.

    (b) A hockey team owner delays building a new stadium because interest rates are high and may soon come down.

    (c) A student delays studying for a final exam because she expects to soon receive a job offer that would make her grade point average moot.

    (d) Blockbuster Video delays entering the DVD rental market (see Chapter 6 for more details on the DVD rental market).

9. *Love Never Dies* is a musical playing in London's West End. The producers are planning a limited run of the musical in Sydney next year. The producers expect that it will cost $1.7 million to mount the play in Sydney. They know that the show could be a hit or a flop. If the show is a hit in Sydney, the producers expect that the resulting revenue (from tickets, merchandise, etc.) will be $3.1 million. If the play is not a hit in Sydney, the producers expect $2.2 million in revenues. In either case, the producers would wish to go ahead with the show. What is the most the producers should be willing to pay a market research firm to help them figure out whether or not the show will be a hit?

10. An article on price wars by two McKinsey consultants makes the following argument.[37]

   That the [tit-for tat] strategy is fraught with risk cannot be overemphasized. Your competitor may take an inordinately long time to realize that its actions can do it nothing but harm; rivalry across the entire industry may escalate precipitously; and as the "tit-for-tat" game plays itself out, all of a price war's detrimental effects on customers will make themselves felt.

   How would you reconcile the views expressed in this quote with the advantages of tit-for-tat claimed in this chapter?

11. How does the revenue destruction effect (see Chapter 5) affect the ability of firms to coordinate on a pricing equilibrium?

12. Firms operating at or near capacity are unlikely to instigate price wars. Briefly explain.

13. Suppose that you were trying to determine whether the leading firms in the automobile manufacturing industry are playing a tit-for-tat pricing game. What real-world data would you want to examine? What would you consider to be evidence of tit-for-tat pricing? How can you distinguish tit-for-tat pricing designed to sustain "collusive" pricing from competitive pricing?

14. It is often argued that price wars may be more likely to occur during low-demand periods than high-demand periods. Are there factors that might reverse this implication? That is, can you think of reasons why the attractiveness of deviating from cooperative pricing might actually be greater during booms (high demand) than during busts (low demand)?

15. Why does Sutton draw a distinction between endogenous sunk costs such as advertising and other sunk costs such as capital investments?

16. Why does Sutton's model apply so well to consumer goods markets? Does Sutton's model describe the structure of other markets?

ENDNOTES

[1]Strategic commitments should be distinguished from tactical decisions—including pricing and short-term production decisions—that are easily reversed and whose impact persists only in the short run.

[2]Avinash Dixit and Barry Nalebuff's excellent book, *Thinking Strategically: The Competitive Edge in Business, Politics and Everyday Life*, New York, Norton, 1991, contains a thorough discussion of credibility and the commitment value of various competitive moves.

[3]This quote comes from Luecke, R., *Scuttle Your Ships Before Advancing and Other Lessons from History on Leadership and Change for Today's Managers*, Oxford, Oxford University Press, 1994, p. 23.

[4]Differentiating the equation for π_1 with respect to Q_1 and equating to zero yields $55 - Q_1 - 10 = 0$, or $Q_1 = 45$.

[5]The terms *strategic complements* and *strategic substitutes* were introduced by Bulow, J., J. Geanakopolos, and P. Klemperer, "Multimarket Oligopoly: Strategic Substitutes and Complements," *Journal of Political Economy*, 93, 1985, pp. 488–511.

[6]Reaction functions in the Bertrand model with undifferentiated products do not concern us because a firm always wants to slightly undercut its rival's price. Hence, throughout this section, we confine our attention to Bertrand industries where firms' products exhibit some degree of horizontal differentiation.

[7]This example draws from "Loblaw's Store of the Future Ready," *Business and Industry*, 21(15), September 20, 2004, p. 11; "Loblaw Companies Limited," *Hoovers Guide*, http://premium.hoovers.com.

[8]The concepts of tough and soft commitments were introduced by Bulow, J., J. Geanakopolos, and P. Klemperer, "Multimarket Oligopoly: Strategic Substitutes and Complements," *Journal of Political Economy*, 93, 1985, pp. 488–511.

[9]Fudenberg, D., and J. Tirole, "The Fat-Cat Effect, the Puppy-Dog Ploy, and the Lean and Hungry Look," *American Economic Review*, 74(2), 1984, pp. 361–366.

[10]This example is based on Ghemawat, P., "Commitment to a Process Innovation: Nucor, USX, and Thin Slab Casting," *Journal of Economics and Management Strategy*, 2, Spring 1993, pp. 133–161.

[11]The term *real* is used in order to distinguish this general concept of an option from the narrower notion of a financial option. There are many kinds of financial options. An example is a call option on a share of stock. The owner of a call option has the right, but not the obligation, to buy a share of stock at a prespecified price.

[12]See Dixit, A. K., and R. S. Pindyck, *Investment under Uncertainty*, Princeton, NJ, Princeton University Press, 1994, for pioneering work on real options. M. Amaran and N. Kulatilaka, *Real Options: Managing Strategic Investments in an Uncertain World*, Boston, Harvard Business School Press, 1999, present a very accessible applied introduction to the analysis of real options.

[13]The following examples draw from "Exploiting Uncertainty: The Real-Options Revolution in Decision Making," *Business Week*, June 7, 1999, p. 118.

[14]Basic derivations may be found in Dixit and Pindyck, *Investment under Uncertainty*.

[15]Kellogg, R., "The Effect of Uncertainty on Investment: Evidence from Texas Oil Drilling," NBER Working Paper No. 16541, November 2010.

[16]Chamberlin, E. H., *Monopolistic Competition*, Cambridge, MA, Harvard University Press, 1933, p. 48.

[17]The weekly discount rate is the annual discount rate divided by 52. Thus, $0.10/52 = 0.002$.

[18]This calculation easily follows by using the formula for the present value of an annuity, which is discussed in the appendix to the Economics Primer. Specifically, for any amount C and discount rate i, $C/(1 + i) + C/(1 + i)^2 + \ldots = C/i$. Thus, the preceding calculation simplifies to $0.2308 + 0.1154/0.002 = 57.93$.

[19]Former Kellogg student Andrew Cherry developed this example.

[20]Axelrod, R., *The Evolution of Cooperation*, New York, Basic Books, 1984.

[21]The term *folk theorem* is used because, like a folk song, it existed in the oral tradition of economics long before anyone got credit for proving it formally.

[22]Perhaps the best work on this subject remains Thomas Schelling's *The Strategy of Conflict*, Cambridge, MA, Harvard University Press, 1960.

[23]Kreps, D. M., *A Course in Microeconomic Theory*, Princeton, NJ, Princeton University Press, 1990, pp. 392–393.

[24]Garda, R. A., and M. V. Marn, "Price Wars," *McKinsey Quarterly*, 3, 1993, pp. 87–100.

[25]A marketing allowance is a discount offered by a manufacturer in return for the retailer's agreement to feature the manufacturer's product in some way.

[26]Dixit, A., and B. Nalebuff, *Thinking Strategically: The Competitive Edge in Business, Politics, and Everyday Life*, New York, Norton, 1991.

[27]An open order price is the price the manufacturer charges any buyer who orders the additive.

[28]Morton, F.S., "The Strategic Response by Pharmaceutical Firms to the Medicaid MFC Rules," *RAND Journal of Economics*, 28(2), 1997, pp. 269–290.

[29]Wolfram, R., and R. Wolfram, "Most Favored Nations Clauses under the Spotlight," Wolters Kluwers Antitrust Connect Blog, January 6, 1011. http://antitrustconnect. com/2011/01/06/%E2%80%98most-favored-nations%E2%80%99-mfn-clauses-under-the-spotlight-u-s-v-blue-cross-blue-shield-of-michigan-%E2%80%94-when-might-otherwise-competitively-neutral-or-procompetitive-mfn-clauses/Accessed August 2, 2011.

[30]FOB stands for "free on board," so the FOB price is the seller quotes for loading the product on the delivery vehicle. If the seller pays the transport charges, they are added to the buyer's bill, and the net price the seller receives is known as the uniform net mill price.

[31]A third type of pricing is basing point pricing in which the seller designates one or more base locations and quotes FOB prices from them. The customer chooses a basing point and absorbs the freight costs between the basing point and its plant.

[32]Blair, J., *Economic Concentration: Structure, Behavior, and Public Policy*, New York, Harcourt Brace Jovanovich, 1972.

[33]Sutton, J., *Sunk Costs and Market Structure*, Cambridge, MA, MIT Press, 1991.

[34]Christensen, Clayton M., *The Innovator's Dilemma: When New Technologies Cause Great Firms to Fail*, Boston, Harvard Business School Press, 1997.

[35]Geroski, P., and R. Pomroy, "Innovation and the Evolution of Market Structure," *Journal of Industrial Economics*, 38(3), 1990, pp. 299–314.

[36]Besanko, D., Doraszelski, U., Kryukov, Y., and M. Satterthwaite, "Learning-by-Doing, Organizational Forgetting, and Industry Dynamics," *Econometrica*, 78(2), 2010, pp. 453–508.

[37]Garda, R. A., and M. V. Marn, "Price Wars," *McKinsey Quarterly*, 3, 1993, pp. 87–100. Quote from pp. 98–99.

8   INDUSTRY ANALYSIS

Part One of this text examines a firm's relationships with its upstream and downstream trading partners. Part Two explores the economics of competition. Given the breadth of material that we have covered, it would be easy for students to lose track of the key insights that we have developed thus far. *Industry analysis* frameworks, such as Michael Porter's *five forces* and Adam Brandenberger and Barry Nalebuff's *Value Net*, provide a structure that enables us to systematically work through these wide-ranging and often complex economic issues.

An industry analysis based on such frameworks facilitates the following important tasks:

- Assessment of industry and firm performance.

- Identification of key factors affecting performance in vertical trading relationships and horizontal competitive relationships.

- Determination of how changes in the business environment may affect performance.

- Identification of opportunities and threats in the business landscape. In this regard, industry analysis is essential to performing "SWOT" analysis, a "bread-and-butter" tool in strategic planning. SWOT stands for strengths, weaknesses, opportunities, and threats. Industry analysis provides insights into "OT," while Part Three of the text provides guidance for identifying "SW." Industry analysis is also invaluable for assessing the generic business strategies that we introduce in Chapter 9.

The concepts that we develop throughout the text are grounded in microeconomics, particularly the economics of the firm and the economics of industrial organization. Although the roots of these fields can be traced back a century or more, they had little impact on business strategy until Michael Porter published a series of articles in the 1970s that culminated in his pathbreaking book *Competitive Strategy*. The book presents a convenient framework for exploring the economic factors that affect the profits of an industry. Porter's main innovation is to classify these factors into five major forces that encompass the vertical chain and market competition.

In their book *Coopetition*, Brandenberger and Nalebuff make a significant addition to the five-forces framework. They describe the firm's "Value Net," which includes suppliers, distributors, and competitors. Whereas Porter describes how suppliers, distributors, and competitors might destroy a firm's profits, Brandenberger and Nalebuff's key insight is that these firms often *enhance* firm profits. In other words, strategic analysis must account for both *coop*eration and com*petition*.

This chapter shows how to perform a five-forces industry analysis that accounts for the economic principles in Parts One and Two. It also shows how to accommodate the Value Net principles introduced by Brandenberger and Nalebuff. We illustrate these ideas by examining four very different markets: hospitals, professional sports, airframe manufacturing, and executive search services. We selected these markets both because they present a diversity of competitive forces and because we have a strong institutional understanding of each. Indeed, solid industry analysis is not possible without such understanding.

Before presenting the five-forces framework, it is important to note its limitations. First, it pays limited attention to factors that might affect demand. It accounts for the availability and prices of substitute and complementary products but ignores changes in consumer income, tastes, and firm strategies for boosting demand, such as advertising. Second, it focuses on a whole industry rather than on individual firms that may occupy unique positions that insulate them from some competitive forces. Third, the framework does not explicitly account for the role of the government, except when the government is a supplier or buyer. The government as a regulator can profoundly affect industry profitability and could be considered a sixth force. Fourth, five-forces analysis is qualitative. For example, an analysis of industry structure may suggest that the threat of entry is high, but the framework does not show how to estimate the cost of entry or the likelihood that entry will occur.

PERFORMING A FIVE-FORCES ANALYSIS

The five forces, as represented in Figure 8.1, are:

- Internal rivalry

- Entry

- Substitute and complementary products

- Supplier power

- Buyer power

Internal rivalry is in the center because it may be affected by each of the other forces.

One assesses each force by asking "Is it sufficiently strong to reduce or eliminate industry profits?" The answer to this question can be found by applying the economic principles that we have presented in this text. For example, when assessing the power of suppliers to affect industry and firm performance, you should determine whether firms in the industry have made relationship-specific investments with their suppliers (or vice versa) and whether they are protected from potential holdup either by contracts or market forces. In the following discussion, we will identify those principles that are most relevant to each force. For the student who has carefully read the preceding chapters, this will serve as a review.

The appendix offers a "five-forces scorecard" for doing industry analysis. The scorecard template includes specific questions about each force. Your responses should indicate whether this force poses a major threat to profits today, as well as identify trends.

FIGURE 8.1
THE FIVE-FORCES FRAMEWORK

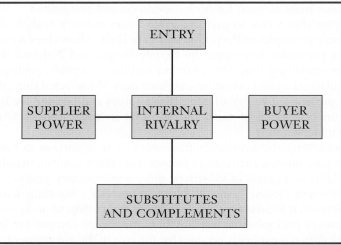

Internal Rivalry

Internal rivalry refers to the jockeying for share by firms within a market. Thus, an analysis of internal rivalry must begin by defining the market. Be sure to include all firms that constrain each other's strategic decision making, as described in Chapter 5, and pay attention to both product market and geographic market definitions. For example, if you are analyzing internal rivalry among hotels, you should consider that most consumers have specific geographic preferences when selecting a hotel. Consumers may also have strong preferences for particular categories of hotels, such as business hotels or family-style resorts. This implies that competition is local and may differ by hotel category. If you are unsure whether to include a firm in the relevant market, remember that you can always exclude it from your consideration of internal rivalry and still consider it when you assess substitutes and complements.

Recall that firms may compete on both price and nonprice dimensions. Nonprice competition erodes profits by driving up fixed costs (e.g., new product development) and marginal costs (e.g., adding product features). To the extent that firms can pass cost increases along to consumers in the form of higher prices (i.e., the industry price elasticity of demand is not too large), nonprice competition is less likely to erode profits than is price competition. In fact, many firms engaged in vigorous nonprice competition enjoy solid profits over an extended period of time. Good examples include couture fashion, where competition is based on style and image; cola, where advertising and new product varieties drive market share; and pharmaceuticals, driven by R&D "patent races."

Price competition is far more likely to erode industry profits, in part because it is difficult to reduce costs by enough to maintain price–cost margins. But industry prices do not fall by themselves—one or more firms must reduce prices. This raises a question that serves as a natural starting point for an analysis of price competition: Why would any firm reduce its prices? The simple answer is that a firm reduces prices if it believes it can gain increased market share by doing so. The gain in share depends on the elasticity of demand facing the firm and on whether rivals reduce their prices in response. Drawing on the analyses from Chapters 5–7, we conclude that each of the following conditions tends to heat up price competition:

- *There Are Many Sellers in the Market.* The theory of oligopoly predicts that prices are lower when there are more firms in the market. There are several reasons for this prediction. When many competitors exist, there is a good chance that at least one is dissatisfied with the status quo and will want to lower price to improve its market position. At the same time, it will shoulder a smaller portion of the revenue-destruction effect. Thinking long term, a firm with a low market share might conclude that its rivals will not respond if it lowers price.

- *The Industry Is Stagnant or Declining.* Firms cannot easily expand their own output without stealing from competitors. This often elicits a competitive response that tends to intensify competition.

- *Firms Have Different Costs.* Firms with lower costs usually have lower profit-maximizing prices. Low-cost firms may also reason that if they cut prices, their high-cost rivals may exit.

- *Some Firms Have Excess Capacity.* Firms with excess capacity may be under pressure to boost sales and often can rapidly expand output to steal business from rivals.

- *Products Are Undifferentiated/Buyers Have Low Switching Costs.* When products are undifferentiated and switching costs are low, firms believe that price reductions will generate substantial increases in market share.

- *Prices and Terms of Sales Are Unobservable/Prices Cannot Be Adjusted Quickly.* This condition increases the response time of rivals, enabling the price cutter to potentially gain substantial market share before its rivals match the price cut. This also increases the potential for misreads and misjudgments and makes it more difficult for firms to develop facilitating practices.

- *There Are Large/Infrequent Sales Orders.* A firm may be tempted to undercut its rivals to secure a particularly large order, believing that the substantial gains may more than offset any losses from future rounds of price cutting. This is especially true if different managers are responsible for different bids, and each is rewarded on the basis of his or her own sales.

- *Industry Does Not Use Facilitating Practices or Have a History of Cooperative Pricing.* In the absence of price leadership, price announcements, or other facilitating practices, firms may be unable to "agree" on a suitable industry price, and some may lower price to gain an advantage. A history of cooperative pricing may assure industry participants that each is striving to find a price that works to everyone's collective benefit.

- *There Are Strong Exit Barriers.* This condition can prolong price wars as firms struggle to survive instead of exiting.

- *There Is High Industry Price Elasticity of Demand.* If industry demand is very price sensitive, then price cutting does not harm the industry nearly as much as when consumers have inelastic industry demand. But remember that when industry demand is price sensitive, nonprice competition can threaten industry profits.

Entry

Entry erodes incumbents' profits in two ways. First, entrants divide market demand among more sellers. (Entrants rarely grow the market by enough to make the incumbents better off.) Second, entrants decrease market concentration and heat up internal rivalry. Some entry barriers are exogenous (i.e., they result from the technological requirements for successful competition), whereas others are endogenous (i.e., they result from strategic choices made by incumbents). Each of the following tends to affect the threat of entry:

- *Production Entails Significant Economies of Sales—Minimum Efficient Scale Is Large Relative to the Size of the Market.* The entrant must achieve a substantial market share to reach minimum efficient scale, and if it does not, it may be at a significant cost disadvantage.

- *Government Protection of Incumbents.* Laws may favor some firms over others.

- *Consumers Highly Value Reputation/Consumers Are Brand Loyal.* Entrants must invest heavily to establish a strong reputation and brand awareness. Diversifying entrants using a brand umbrella may be more successful than entirely new entrants.

- *Access of Entrants to Key Inputs, Including Technological Know-How, Raw Materials, Distribution, and Locations.* Patents, unique locations, and so forth can all be barriers to entry. Incumbent must avoid overpaying to tie up unique inputs and may find it more profitable to sell its patent, location, and the like to a would-be entrant.

- *Experience Curve.* A steep experience curve puts entrants at a cost disadvantage.

- *Network Externalities.* This gives an advantage to incumbents with a large installed base. If incumbents are slow to establish an installed base, an entrant may do so through a large-scale product launch. (See Chapter 11 for details.)

- *Expectations about Postentry Competition.* Do incumbents have a reputation for predatory pricing in the face of entry? Do incumbents have a history of persevering through price wars? Do incumbents have sufficient excess capacity to flood the market, and if necessary, to drive out the entrant?

Substitutes and Complements

Although the five-forces analysis does not directly consider demand, it does consider two important factors that influence demand—substitutes and complements. Substitutes erode profits in the same way as entrants by stealing business and intensifying internal rivalry. (Think of Voice Over Internet Protocol computer-based telecommunications, such as Skype, competing with cellular and landline phones.) Complements boost the demand for the product in question, thereby enhancing profit opportunities for the industry. (Think of games like Angry Birds and Tiny Wings boosting the demand for smart phones, and vice versa.) Bear in mind that changes in demand can also affect internal rivalry, entry, and exit.

Factors to consider when assessing substitutes and complements include:

- *Availability of Close Substitutes and/or Complements.* Consider product performance characteristics when identifying substitutes and complements.

- *Price-Value Characteristics of Substitutes/Complements.* Seemingly close substitutes may pose little threat if they are priced too high. Similarly, complements may fail to boost demand if priced too high. Many new products may be weak substitutes or complements, but may gain strength as manufacturers move down the learning curve and prices fall.

- *Price Elasticity of Industry Demand.* This is a useful measure of the pressure substitutes place on an industry. When the industry-level price elasticity is large, rising industry prices tend to drive consumers to purchase substitute products.

Supplier Power and Buyer Power

An assessment of supplier power takes the point of view of a downstream industry and examines whether that industry's upstream input suppliers can negotiate prices that extract industry profits. Sometimes, the upstream market is competitive. We say that suppliers in a competitive upstream market have "indirect power" because they can sell their services to the highest bidder. The price they charge depends on supply and demand in the upstream market. For example, fuel suppliers have indirect power relative to the airline industry. When supply and demand conditions cause fuel prices to increase, airline profits suffer.

Recall from Chapters 3 and 5 that upstream suppliers can also erode industry profits if (a) they are concentrated or (b) their customers are locked into relationships with them because of relationship-specific investments. In these situations, we say that suppliers have "direct power." An input supplier with direct power can raise prices when its target market is thriving, thereby extracting a share of its customers' profits. The converse also applies—a powerful supplier may lower prices when its target market is struggling. Consistent application of both pricing strategies will permit the supplier to extract much of its target market's profits without destroying that market. Historically, unions have used this strategy to increase workers' wages in good times while granting concessions during down times.

Buyer power is analogous to supplier power. It refers to the ability of individual customers to negotiate purchase prices that extract profits from sellers. Buyers have indirect power in competitive markets, and the price they pay will depend on the forces of supply and demand. The willingness of consumers to shop for the best price could instead be considered a source of internal rivalry, not indirect buyer power. When buyers are concentrated, or suppliers have made relationship-specific investments, buyers may wield direct power, demanding lower prices when suppliers are thriving and accepting higher prices when suppliers are struggling.

The following factors must be considered when assessing supplier power and buyer power. We state each in terms of supplier power relative to the downstream industry that it sells to. An analogous factor must be assessed when considering buyer power:

- *Competitiveness of the Input Market.* If inputs are purchased in competitive markets, then input prices will be determined by the forces of supply and demand.

- *The Relative Concentration of the Industry in Question, Its Upstream, and Its Downstream Industries.* Firms in the more concentrated industry may have greater bargaining power and may be able to achieve a cooperative price that puts firms in the less concentrated industry (due to internal rivalry in that industry) at a disadvantage.

- *Purchase Volume of Downstream Firms.* Suppliers may give better service and lower prices to larger purchasers.

- *Availability of Substitute Inputs.* The availability of substitutes limits the price that suppliers can charge.

- *Relationship-Specific Investments by the Industry and Its Suppliers.* The threat of holdup may determine the allocation of rents between the industry and its suppliers.

- *Threat of Forward Integration by Suppliers.* If credible, firms in an industry may be forced to accept the high supply price or risk direct competition from suppliers.

- *Ability of Suppliers to Price Discriminate.* If suppliers can price discriminate, they can raise the prices they charge more profitable firms.

Strategies for Coping with the Five Forces

A five-forces analysis identifies the threats to the profits of all firms in an industry. Firms may pursue several strategies to cope with these threats. They may position themselves to outperform their rivals by developing a cost or differentiation advantage that somewhat insulates them from the five forces. Chapter 9 discusses positioning strategies in detail. Firms may identify an industry segment in which the five forces are less severe. For example, in the 1970s, Crown, Cork and Seal served manufacturers of "hard-to-hold" liquids, a niche market that was far less competitive than the metal-can segments served by industry leaders American Can and Continental Can. Through this and similar strategies, Crown earned significantly higher rates of return. Firms might even try to change the five forces, although this is difficult to do. They may try to reduce internal rivalry by establishing facilitating practices or creating switching costs. They may reduce the threat of entry by pursuing entry-deterring strategies. They may try to reduce buyer or supplier power by tapered integration. In the extended examples presented later in this chapter, we will see how firms in a variety of industries have attempted to cope, with varying degrees of success, with the five forces.

COOPETITION AND THE VALUE NET

Porter's five forces is an enduring framework that remains widely used for industry analysis. In their book *Coopetition*, Adam Brandenberger and Barry Nalebuff identify an important weakness of the framework. From the viewpoint of any one firm, Porter tends to view all other firms, be they competitors, suppliers, or buyers, as threats to profitability, as if business is a zero or even negative sum game. Brandenberger and Nalebuff observe that interactions among firms can sometimes enhance profits and emphasize the many positive interactions that Porter generally ignores. Examples of positive interactions include the following.

- Efforts by competitors to set technology standards that facilitate industry growth, such as when consumer electronics firms cooperated to establish a single format for high-definition television.

- Efforts by competitors to promote favorable regulations or legislation, such as when domestic U.S. automakers worked together to get the U.S. Department of Energy to endorse a proposal to develop fuel cells rather than tighten gasoline fuel economy standards.

- Cooperation among firms and their suppliers to improve product quality to boost demand, such as when Nintendo offered software developers a substantial share of the profits from games sold for the Nintendo Entertainment System (NES). This encouraged developers to invest heavily in developing high-quality games, which in turn boosted overall demand for the NES system.

- Cooperation among firms and their suppliers to improve productive efficiency, such as when Edward Hospital in Naperville, Illinois, worked closely with its cardiovascular surgeons to develop a handheld computer system to allow the two to rapidly exchange clinical information.

In support of these ideas, Brandenberger and Nalebuff introduce the concept of the *Value Net* as a counterpart to Porter's five forces. The Value Net, which consists of suppliers, customers, competitors, and complementors (firms producing complementary goods and services), is similar to the five forces. Brandenberger and Nalebuff's admonition to perform a comprehensive analysis of the Value Net to prevent blind spots is also reminiscent of Porter. But whereas a five-forces analysis mainly assesses threats to profits, a Value Net analysis assesses opportunities. This important change does not nullify the five-forces approach so much as complement it. A complete five-forces analysis should, therefore, consider both the threats and opportunities each force poses.

To illustrate this point, contrast a traditional five-forces industry analysis of the DVD hardware market in 1997–1998 (the first two years of introduction) with an analysis that accounts for the Value Net. Here are some conclusions that might have emerged from a traditional analysis.

- *Internal Rivalry.* The main source of differentiation was brand—the players were otherwise fairly homogeneous. Unless firms could establish loyalty based on brand, intense price competition could result.

- *Entry.* There were modest technological and physical capital requirements limiting entry. A dozen or more consumer electronics firms had the know-how and access to channels to successfully enter the market.

- *Substitutes and Complements.* Satellite TV posed a clear threat as a substitute. Digital video streaming over the Internet was another potential threat.

- *Supplier Power and Buyer Power.* Powerful studios such as Disney and producers such as George Lucas and Stephen Spielberg could have demanded substantial payments to supply their movies in DVD format, especially given the threat from the alternative DIVX format that Circuit City was poised to launch. Powerful distributors such as Best Buy and Circuit City might demand high margins in exchange for clearing the shelf space needed to promote the new format.

Given this five-forces analysis, DVD hardware makers would have had every reason to be pessimistic about the format.

But this analysis fails to account for the Value Net and, as a result, fails to identify opportunities for industry growth and profitability. The participants in the Value Net—manufacturers, studios, and retailers—recognized that their fortunes were intertwined. If they could generate sufficient interest in DVD, then demand would grow fast enough to make everyone profitable while thwarting DIVX.

Manufacturers had many options for boosting demand. The most obvious would be to set low prices for DVD hardware. This would start a "virtuous cycle" in which solid hardware sales would encourage studios to release more movies in DVD, thereby further boosting demand for hardware. Manufacturers could also heavily promote DVD so as to boost product awareness while blunting the threat from DIVX. In the first year, hardware makers did none of this. They kept prices high so as to profit from early adopters (players sold for $500 to $1,000) rather than to stimulate mass-market acceptance. They ran few advertisements or promotions. As a result, manufacturers sold only about 300,000 players in the United States and a comparable number in Europe and Japan, well within expectations, but hardly enough to guarantee the success of the format. In the second year, manufacturers lowered prices on some players to less than $300 and spent heavily on advertising and promotions. Other participants in the Value Net also pitched in. MGM released special editions of classic films such as *Gone With the Wind*. Warner slashed prices on dozens of popular titles. Columbia and Universal studios accelerated the release of popular action titles such as *Godzilla*. Meanwhile, electronics retailers, especially Best Buy, heavily promoted DVD hardware and software, including a much publicized half-price software sale for Internet purchases. By Christmas 1998, the success of the new DVD format was guaranteed.

DVD succeeded when all the players in the Value Net did their part to promote the overall success of the product, working to increase the size of the DVD "pie" rather than fight for their share of a fixed pie. Some members of the Value Net, such as Warner and Best Buy, even took a temporary loss (by setting prices below costs) so as to contribute to the future success of the format. Through their complementary actions, the participants in the DVD Value Net secured its future and reaped the benefits.

Brandenberger and Nalebuff go beyond encouraging firms to work toward common goals by showing how each firm can prosper even while cooperating with erstwhile competitors. The amount that a firm can expect to reap from participating in the value net can be approximated by this simple formula:

Firm X's profit from the value net = Overall value of the net when firm X participates minus overall value of net when it does not participate

This formula is closely tied to many of the concepts that we will introduce in the next chapter when we discuss how firms can position themselves for profitability. For now, it is sufficient to observe that firms can prosper if they *uniquely* bring value to the net.

APPLYING THE FIVE FORCES: SOME INDUSTRY ANALYSES

The best way to illustrate the five-forces framework is by example. In this section we perform four detailed industry analyses. For each industry, we present background information, proceed with market definition, and identify the most salient economic principles from each of the five forces.

Chicago Hospital Markets Then and Now

For 30 years up until the mid-1980s, hospitals thrived. Then, between 1985 and 2000, an average of 75 U.S. hospitals went bankrupt annually (about 1.5 percent of the nation's total each year), and many others struggled to stay solvent. In the last few years, most hospitals have enjoyed a measure of prosperity, with returns on sales now nearing historically high levels. This dynamic has been experienced throughout the nation, including the Chicago market, which is the focus of this analysis.

Market Definition

Market definition requires identifying both product and geographic markets. We consider the product market to be acute medical services such as maternity care, surgery, and complex diagnostic services. While other providers besides hospitals offer many of these services—outpatient surgery centers are a good example—we will treat their offerings as substitutes. This decision is not essential to our conclusions and illustrates the flexibility of the five-forces framework. (We would be remiss, of course, if we did not consider outpatient surgery at all.)

The geographic scope of hospital competition is subject to considerable debate; federal courts are grappling with this issue as they review the antitrust implications of recent hospital mergers. Research shows that patients strongly prefer to visit nearby hospitals. The geographic market in which Chicago hospitals compete is certainly no larger than the metropolitan area, and in one recently decided antitrust case, a judge ruled that there are distinct submarkets (e.g., suburban regions) that have their own unique competitive dynamics. We will assess internal rivalry in the Chicago metropolitan area and, when appropriate, discuss the importance of submarkets.

Internal Rivalry

There were almost 100 community hospitals in the Chicago market in 1980.[1] Even with dozens of closures, about 70 hospitals survive. Most hospitals were independent in 1980, when the Herfindahl index for the entire metropolitan area was below 0.05. Today, many hospitals belong to systems. There is no dominant system, however, and if we treat each system as a single entity, the regional Herfindahl index is roughly 0.20. If we examine geographic submarkets, however, the Herfindahl increases to 0.25 or higher.

The relatively large number of hospitals is just one factor that could intensify internal rivalry. Another factor is the considerable variation in production costs, which stems from differences in productive efficiency and the fact that Chicago has several large teaching hospitals that must bear the expense of training young, inefficient doctors. There is also some excess capacity, though not so much as in years past; occupancy rates at many hospitals remain below 70 percent, though some suburban hospitals operate at 85 percent or higher. Finally, demand for admissions had been stagnant or declining for a long time. This trend has now reversed itself, thanks to aging baby boomers and their many ailments.

Despite these factors, internal rivalry in 1980 was benign, largely because patients were passive shoppers. When choosing a hospital, patients deferred to their physicians, who tended to concentrate their practices at one or two hospitals. This created a kind of loyalty that greatly lessened the importance of hospital prices. Patients also preferred staying close to home, creating additional differentiation based on location, especially in suburban markets. (Downtown Chicago was home to over a dozen hospitals within a few miles of each other.) Another important factor was that most patients had insurance that paid most of their bills no matter which hospital they chose. For patients with the most generous insurance, price was a complete nonissue. The combination of price-insensitive patients and physician-dominated admission decisions limited the incentives of hospitals to use price as a strategic weapon. As a result, internal rivalry in 1980 was low, and most hospitals in Chicago enjoyed healthy price–cost margins from their privately insured patients. If anything constrained hospital pricing, it was the fear that nonprofit hospitals would lose their tax-exempt status if they made too much money.

During the 1980s, managed-care organizations (MCOs) entered the Chicago market and began selectively contracting with hospitals that offered the best value. MCOs gave enrollees financial inducements (in the form of lower copayments) to encourage them to select the contracting hospitals. By steering patients to the "preferred" hospitals, insurers effectively increased price elasticities of demand.

Three additional features of selective contracting intensified internal rivalry. First, MCOs treated all hospitals as nearly identical, seemingly ignoring patient loyalties. Second, price negotiations between insurers and hospitals were secret, encouraging hospitals to lower prices to win contracts. Finally, sales were infrequent (i.e., a contract lasts two to three years) and lumpy (one insurer may represent over 10 percent of a hospital's business). Hospitals were under intense pressure to win each individual contract without concern for future price rivalry. These factors also limited opportunities for hospitals to develop facilitating practices.

Price rivalry intensified. Hospitals lowered prices by 20 percent or more to stay competitive, profit margins declined, and many Chicago-area hospitals closed. By the late 1990s, hospitals were fighting back. Some, like Northwestern Memorial Hospital, established a strong brand identity. Others diversified into related products, such as skilled nursing services (for which insurers provided generous reimbursements). Some differentiated their services by developing "centers of excellence" in clinical areas such as cancer care and heart surgery. These strategies had varying degrees of success. Diversification helped boost revenues but did nothing to soften competition in the inpatient market. Branding helped those hospitals that already enjoyed strong reputations, but it did little for the average community hospital. And patients saw centers of excellence for what they often were—new labels for already existing facilities.

Two recent trends have done much more to soften competition. First, patients rejected MCOs with "narrow" networks. Today's MCOs must include nearly all hospitals in their networks if they are to attract enrollees. Hospitals know this and hold out for higher prices. Second, there has been considerable consolidation in regional submarkets, including the city of Chicago and the important North Shore suburbs. Mergers among hospitals in these submarkets have further strengthened the hands of hospitals in their contract negotiations with MCOs. Several merging hospitals raised their prices by 10 percent or more.

Entry

Due to regulation, only one entirely new hospital has been built in Chicago in decades. A state board must approve any new hospital. The applicant must demonstrate that the projected utilization at the new hospital could not be met by existing hospitals. (This would be like requiring Microsoft's tablet computer division to show that Apple could not meet demand before allowing Microsoft to enter.) So instead of new hospital construction, existing hospital facilities have undergone repeated remodeling and expansion. Due in part to a recent bribery scandal, the future of the hospital regulatory board is in limbo.

Incumbents may be protected by other entry barriers. Hospitals are capital intensive. A new modest-sized 150-bed hospital can cost $200 million to build. A *de novo* entrant (i.e., an entrant with no current hospital in Chicago) would also have to establish a brand identity, since patients may be reluctant to trust their health to an unknown entity. By the same token, a *de novo* entrant would also need access to distribution "channels"—the medical staff that admits patients. These factors may help explain why nearly all proposals to build new hospitals in Chicago have been floated by existing hospitals.

The barriers to entry are large but not overwhelming. The Chicago area continues to grow, with suburbs stretching 50 miles from downtown. "Outsider" hospital corporations such as Tenet have considerable experience entering new markets and could view Chicago's "exurbs" as fertile ground for growth. Technological change may further lower entry barriers. Innovations in medicine might make it possible to open smaller, cost-competitive inpatient facilities that focus on specific treatments, such as heart surgery. This will reduce the capital and number of physicians required for successful entry. If the regulatory entry barrier breaks down and Chicago hospitals remain profitable, *de novo* entry is sure to follow.

Substitutes and Complements

In 1980, a patient who needed surgery or a complex diagnostic procedure went to the hospital. Since then, there have been dramatic improvements in surgical technique, anesthetics, and antibiotics, so that many types of surgeries can now be safely performed outside the hospital. Home health care has also boomed, allowing providers to monitor the recovery of surgical patients and care for chronically ill patients in patients' homes.

Hospitals have turned out to be major sellers of outpatient services in many markets, including Chicago. They already possessed the technology, personnel, and brand appeal to offer outpatient care. Many viewed outpatient care as a major growth opportunity, while others may have entered the outpatient market to preempt competition from greenfield competitors.

New medical technologies continue to emerge. Some, such as laparoscopic surgery, facilitate even more outpatient treatment. But some technologies, such as implantable cardiac defibrillators and artificial skin, boost the demand for inpatient care. An important generation of new technologies will emerge from genetic research, and it is difficult to predict whether these will be substitutes or complements to inpatient care.

Supplier Power

The main suppliers to hospitals include labor (nurses, technicians, etc.), medical equipment companies, and drug houses. Hospital-based physicians, such as radiologists, anesthesiologists, and pathologists (RAP physicians), are also suppliers. (We consider admitting physicians to be buyers because they can influence patients' choices of hospitals.) These suppliers offer their services in relatively competitive markets, giving them indirect power. Supply and demand forces in the market for nurses have been especially tight in recent years, forcing up wages. The prices of drugs and other medical supplies have also risen precipitously.

Hospitals and their suppliers make few relationship-specific investments. Personnel learn to work in teams but seem to adjust rapidly to new settings. Hospitals can usually replace them at the market wage, and some hospitals routinely use "nursing pools" to handle short-term needs. A national recruiting market usually makes RAP physicians easy to replace, although hospital bylaws and staffing policies can pose obstacles. Medical suppliers without monopoly power cannot credibly threaten to hold up hospitals to obtain higher prices. Suppliers whose innovations are protected by patents can command very high prices if their products make the difference between life and death.

Buyer Power

Buyers include patients, physicians, and insurers who decide which hospitals will get business and how they will be paid. Patients and their physicians in 1980 did little to punish high-price hospitals. Insurers in 1980 were also passive, reimbursing hospitals for whatever they charged rather than shopping around for the best value. The two major government insurers, Medicaid and Medicare, also paid generously. Buyer power in 1980 was low.

Selective contracting has enabled insurers to wield buyer power. The largest buyer, Blue Cross of Illinois, has roughly 60 percent share of the private insurance market and can command significant discounts. At the same time, government payers have used their regulatory powers to set prices well below the levels negotiated by private insurers. Medicare, which insures the elderly and disabled, pays a fixed price per hospital stay—adjusted for the diagnosis—forcing hospitals to swallow excessive treatment costs. Owing to federal budget cuts, Medicare payments are declining relative to past trends. Medicaid, the joint federal/state program that covers treatments for the medically indigent, may be the toughest payer of all. Medicaid in Illinois pays hospitals 25 to 50 percent less than the amount paid by other insurers for comparable services. Medicaid knows each hospital's cost position and can use this information to minimize what it offers to pay.

Physicians may also wield significant power, especially those charismatic and highly skilled physicians who can attract patients regardless of where they practice. Hospitals have been engaged in a wide-ranging and long-run battle to tie up the physician market. During the 1990s, hospitals paid as much as $500,000 to purchase the practices of "run of the mill" physician practices, anticipating an increase in referrals. The strategy has largely failed, however, with many hospitals reporting massive losses. The careful student should be able to use the lessons from Chapters 3 and 4 to diagnose the risks of such an integration strategy.

Table 8.1 summarizes the five-forces analysis of the Chicago hospital market in 1980, 2000, and today. Virtually every factor that affects industry profitability changed for the worse between 1980 and 2000, but many have since softened. As hospitals look to the future, they should be concerned about a few possible trends:

- The Federal Trade Commission has recently had success in blocking hospital mergers in suburban markets.

- Concerned about rising health insurance premiums, employers are asking employees to bear more of their health care costs. This could make patients more price sensitive. At the same time, some employers are reconsidering the decision to opt for wide, but costly, MCO networks.

- If regulatory barriers fall, entry by specialty hospitals in wealthier communities could skim off some of the areas' most profitable patients.

TABLE 8.1
FIVE-FORCES ANALYSIS OF THE CHICAGO HOSPITAL MARKET

	Threat to Profits		
Force	1980	2000	Today
Internal rivalry	Low	Medium	Medium but declining
Entry	Low	Low	Low but growing
Substitutes and complements	Medium	High	High
Supplier power	Medium	Medium	Medium
Buyer power	Low	Medium	Medium but declining

- Employers, payers, regulators, and patients are demanding and getting more information about hospital quality. This could allow the best hospitals to command premium prices but could also increase the willingness of patients and their doctors to switch from hospitals whose quality is merely satisfactory.

Commercial Airframe Manufacturing

The firms that build airplanes are called airframe manufacturers. Airbus Industries and the Boeing Company have been in an effective duopoly since Lockheed pulled out in 1986 and Boeing acquired McDonnell Douglas in 1997. Despite limited competition, Airbus and Boeing still face threats from each other, as well as from some key fringe players.

Market Definition

We confine our analysis to companies that make airplanes for commercial aviation. Business jets, such as Citations and Gulfstreams, are not considered relevant since their prices have no bearing on the market for big jet airplanes. Three other companies, Montreal-based Bombardier and Brazil-based Embraer, and European joint venture ATR manufacture small-capacity (50 seats) and medium-capacity (50 to 100 seats) turboprop and jet aircraft for commercial use. Taken together, these fringe players have a combined market share of about 20–30 percent by aircraft and a much lower share by revenue. If we restrict attention to planes with more than 125 seats, then Boeing and Airbus have the entire market to themselves. Thus, we will largely pay attention to the competitive battle between Boeing and Airbus. These two firms compete globally; there are no meaningful geographic submarkets in which other companies compete.

Internal Rivalry

Boeing was established in 1917 and built military aircraft for the better part of 40 years. It delivered its first commercial aircraft in 1958. Airbus was established in 1967 by a consortium representing the governments of Great Britain, France, and Germany. Airbus did not deliver its first plane until 1974. In part because it is an older company, Boeing has produced many more airplanes than has Airbus—15,000 compared to 7,000. Airplanes are built to last—25 years or longer—and most of the planes that Boeing has built are still flying. Boeing's market dominance seems to be waning, however. In the past few years, both Boeing and Airbus have each delivered about 400 new planes annually. (New aircraft deliveries are much more stable than orders, which can range from under 200 to over 1,000 airplanes per manufacturer per year.)

European governments heavily subsidized Airbus during its early years. These subsidies enabled Airbus to undercut Boeing's prices and build market share. Boeing remained price competitive, in part, because it enjoys scope economies from its military aircraft division. Several factors tempered Airbus's incentives to reduce prices. Demand for air travel grew steadily throughout the 1990s. Although air travel declined during the 2001 recession (and particularly after the September 11 attacks), it quickly recovered. Many airlines are investing to renew their fleets, which has spiked demand for new generations of the Boeing 737 and Airbus 320. At the same time, the emergence of new carriers in the Middle East and Asia, and ever-increasing demand by business for comfortable transoceanic travel, has fueled demand for the new Airbus 380 and Boeing 787. But nothing is guaranteed. Following the financial collapse in 2008, Boeing saw new orders plummet by over 80 percent.

Airbus and Boeing cope with demand volatility by limiting production capacity. During good times, Airbus and Boeing run at capacity, maintaining order backlogs that can take years to fulfill. This helps reduce rivalry to some extent, as neither firm can rapidly expand market share at the other's expense. However, backlogs decline or even disappear during downturns. Neither Boeing nor Airbus has seemed willing to shed productive capacity (through large-scale layoffs and plant closings), with the result that marginal costs decline dramatically during downturns. Not surprisingly, Boeing and Airbus are both willing to renegotiate deals at these times. The fact that a single deal with a major carrier can account for nearly 15 percent of Boeing or Airbus's business intensifies the willingness to shave prices when times are bad.

Historically, Boeing and Airbus enjoyed little product differentiation. Flag carriers British Airways and Air France preferred Airbus, for obvious reasons. Otherwise, the airlines feel that the two manufacturers offer virtually identical products. For example, the Boeing 737 and Airbus A320 have similar seating capacities, performance, fuel economy, and flying range. Even so, airlines have developed loyalties. Southwest and Ryan Air exclusively fly Boeing 737s, allowing the carriers to economize on parts and maintenance. Boeing and Airbus have exploited this trend by making parts interchangeable across different models. The result is that a few carriers buy exclusively from Airbus while others rely on Boeing. This may limit incentives to reduce prices on airplanes in the future, for it will be increasingly difficult for Airbus and Boeing to steal each other's customers.

There is even some differentiation in the products themselves. The Airbus A380 is a double-decker plane capable of seating over 550 passengers (but usually configured for fewer passengers with more amenities). Sales thus far are sluggish, in part because airports need to reconfigure arrival gates to accommodate the jumbo planes. Boeing's 787 Dreamliner is smaller but more fuel efficient than the A380. Orders for the 787 double those for the A380, but Boeing has delivered just a handful of planes due to major production delays that we described in Example 3.4.

Barriers to Entry

High development costs and the experience-based advantages of the incumbents combine to make entry into the commercial airframe manufacturing industry extremely difficult. It cost Airbus an estimated $13 billion to develop the A380. Airbus hopes to make about $50 million in profit per aircraft. With discounting, Airbus will need to sell over 350 planes to break even; thus far, only about 250 have been ordered. A startup manufacturer would likely face higher development costs owing to experience effects. It could also expect smaller margins, both because airlines are reluctant to purchase from start-ups (Airbus discovered this 30 years ago) and because entry would likely engender a price response by Airbus and Boeing. Entry by a newcomer in the jumbo segment would therefore be very risky.

Incumbents are also protected by the learning curve in production. Stanford University economist Lanier Benkard used detailed data on the production of the Lockheed L1011 to estimate the learning curve for producing that plane.[2] He found that with a doubling of experience, the number of personnel required to produce a plane would fall by 35 to 40 percent. However, this effect is mitigated by "forgetting" (i.e., past experience is less valuable as time goes by). In fact, the economic downturn of the early 1970s, which caused a decline in demand for the L1011, helps explain why Lockheed failed to achieve the anticipated learning benefits. Even so, learning effects are usually substantial and help further insulate incumbents from competition by newcomers.

We have already noted that some airlines prefer to purchase from the same manufacturer. This poses yet another barrier to entry. One positive note for entrants—access to raw materials and labor is not a significant barrier.

Substitutes and Complements

From the perspective of the airlines, the only substitute for an airplane made by Boeing or Airbus would be an airplane made by someone else. Historically, Boeing and Airbus made the only planes that met airlines' needs for medium- and large-capacity planes capable of flying thousands of miles. But this is no longer the case.

Passengers are weary of hub-and-spoke travel and the associated delays and lost baggage. Even so, it has not always been economically viable for airlines to replace medium- to long-haul hub-and-spoke flights with nonstop point-to-point travel. Simply put, demand for these routes has been too small to fill the smaller Boeing and Airbus jets. Around 1990, Canadian manufacturer Bombardier and Brazilian manufacturer Embraer filled this important void. The Bombardier CRJ series and Embraer ERJ series "regional jets" seat 50 to 90 passengers and are capable of flying over 2,000 miles. Both companies now offer newer and larger planes capable of seating up to 125 passengers. European joint venture ATR offers smaller turboprops to carriers looking for low-cost short-haul aircraft. Regional jets and turboprops increase the number of economically viable point-to-point routes and allow airlines to increase the frequency of flights on existing routes, for example, flying four round trips daily from Chicago to Syracuse on a small jet, instead of just twice daily on a larger plane. This is especially appealing to airlines courting the lucrative business segment.

The market response has been overwhelming, with about 3,000 regional jets sold to date and about 200–300 new deliveries annually. There is no doubt that much of this has come at the expense of Boeing 737s and Airbus 320s, the traditional workhorses of the major carriers. As demand for air travel rises, some carriers are finding it profitable to switch back to 737s and 320s; the cost per passenger mile is lower on a full 120-seat plane than on a full 50-seater.

Substitution also comes indirectly from other forms of transportation. High-speed rail may be a particularly important substitute, for it matches or exceeds the airlines' "product performance characteristic" of high-speed transport. High-speed rail is currently operational in Japan. The Maglev (a high-speed train) is a levitating train able to reach speeds of up to 500 kilometers per hour. Although this may affect regional aircraft in certain routes, it is unlikely to affect commercial aircraft owing to the high development costs, the long time horizon for development, and their physical constraints.

Teleconferencing and other modes of business communication are probably substitutes for air travel and therefore affect the demand for airplanes.

Supplier Power

Boeing and Airbus can obtain raw materials and components from competitive supplier markets. However, most parts suppliers do more business selling replacement parts to airlines than selling original equipment to Boeing and Airbus, so the airframe makers do not have an iron grip on their suppliers. There are a few suppliers that may be in a position of strength when bargaining with Boeing and Airbus. For example, General Electric competes primarily with Pratt & Whitney and Rolls Royce in the manufacturing of jet engines. When Boeing and Airbus do well, these three firms can negotiate more favorable supplier contracts for themselves.

Unionized labor has substantial supplier power. Currently, nearly half of Boeing's workforce is unionized. The unions have cooperated in developing work rules to encourage and protect specific investments by workers. But unions have threatened to strike (and have gone on strike) over wages and can extract a substantial fraction of Boeing profits. Boeing's decision to outsource much of the production of the 787, as well as to open a new assembly plant in South Carolina (a state without a strong union presence), may have been responses to such threats. It is unclear what percentage of Airbus's workforce is unionized. European labor regulations are stricter than U.S. regulations, providing greater protection of unionized employees. However, a significant percentage of work on Airbus planes is done by subcontractors, serving to mitigate the effects of regulations.

Buyer Power

There are two categories of buyers, each of which has limited power. Some airlines own their own fleets, but many also lease aircraft from aircraft-leasing companies. These companies purchase airframes directly from the manufacturer and then lease the planes to the airlines, keeping the assets off the airlines' books. The major airlines and the largest leasing companies often place orders for dozens of planes at a time. One company's order can make up approximately 15 percent of all of Boeing's or Airbus's commercial airframe orders in a single year.

The fact that there are few substitutes works to the advantage of the manufacturers, but only to the point where it begins to compete with its rival manufacturer to maintain a minimum level of backlog orders. In addition, in times of economic downturns, buyers have the ability to cancel deliveries of aircraft, directly affecting the profitability of manufacturers.

Table 8.2 summarizes the five forces of the commercial aviation industry. As long as market conditions are favorable, Airbus and Boeing will prosper, threatened only by Bombardier and Embraer, and then only in a segment of their market.

Professional Sports

Our next example of industry analysis explores the popular world of professional sports. We focus on the four major U.S. sports leagues—Major League Baseball (MLB), the National Basketball Association (NBA), the National Football League (NFL), and the National Hockey League (NHL). Most of this analysis would apply equally well to sports leagues in other nations, such as European club football (i.e., soccer). For the most part, we will perform our analysis by assuming that team owners are trying to maximize profits. In reality, many team owners would gladly

TABLE 8.2
FIVE-FORCES ANALYSIS OF THE COMMERCIAL AVIATION INDUSTRY

Force	Threat to Profits
Internal rivalry	Low to medium
Entry	Low
Substitutes/complements	Medium
Supplier power	Medium
Buyer power	Medium

sacrifice some profits in exchange for a title; owning a sports team is the ultimate billionaire's "hobby."

Market Definition

It is difficult to define the markets in which professional sports teams compete. Each league competes for labor in a single national (or international) labor market, yet individual teams may be monopolists in the output of, say, "professional football entertainment" in their home cities. We will bear these distinctions in mind as we address how each of the five forces affects firm and industry profits in the major professional sports.

Internal Rivalry

Competition on the playing field does not equate to competition in the business world. Exciting athletic competition that will attract fans requires considerable coordination (some would say collusion) among the teams. Teams must agree on rules and schedules and employ the same pool of referees. They share national broadcast revenues. A sports league also requires some degree of competitive balance to attract fan interest. This has given rise to rules and other arrangements that are jointly designed and agreed-upon by all teams in the league. Teams *do not* coordinate on ticket prices, but they do not have to. When it comes to competition in output markets, most sports teams have substantial market power.

Most sports teams generate the lion's share of revenues from ticket sales. (The exception is the NFL, whose 32 teams split over $3 billion in annual payments from a consortium of television networks.) One might argue that sports teams attempting to maximize their ticket revenues are competing against other local entertainment options. For example, the Chicago Bulls professional basketball team vies for customers who might instead consider attending local blues, jazz, and classical music concerts, theaters, movies, restaurants, the DePaul Blue Demons college basketball games, and the Chicago Blackhawks professional hockey games. But the Bulls are monopolists in the market for Chicago professional basketball, and the elasticity of substitution between Bulls tickets and other entertainment events is modest.[3] Even teams that face direct competition in their local markets—for example, the Chicago White Sox and Chicago Cubs in major league baseball—have fiercely loyal fans who would hardly think of buying tickets to their cross-town rivals' games just to save a few dollars. When it comes to selling tickets to see a major sport, nearly every team in the NFL, NBA, MLB, and NHL has considerable market power.

When sports teams do compete against each other in the traditional business sense, the "playing field" is the market for labor. The market to employ athletes hardly fits the "textbook" model of competition. Athletes in all four major sports are unionized, so the market for their labor is subject to labor laws. These laws are particularly important when it comes to employment of new ballplayers (i.e., rookies). Labor laws permit managers and unionized workers in any U.S. industry, including professional sports, to set conditions for employment of new workers through their collective bargaining agreements. One of the conditions in sports collective bargaining agreements is that new players are assigned to teams though rookie drafts.

All sports fans know how the rookie market works. Each major sports league conducts a rookie draft at the conclusion of its season. Only players meeting certain criteria based on age and/or educational attainment are eligible to be drafted. Teams pick in reverse order of their past performance, so that the worst teams get to choose the best players, and all teams have one-year exclusive rights to contract with their chosen players.[4] Depending on the league, rookies are afforded some latitude in negotiating their initial contract terms, including length and salary. Rookies have few alternatives if they do not wish to sign with the team that drafted them; mainly, they can refuse to play for one year (and lose one year's compensation), or they can sign with another league. Because these alternatives are generally very unattractive, sports teams have tremendous bargaining power over rookies. Some baseball teams, such as the Pittsburgh Pirates and Washington Nationals, have managed to remain reasonably prosperous by relying on low-priced young players. (On occasion, these low-payroll teams have great on-field success.) By contrast, some basketball teams, such as the Indiana Pacers, have shied away from drafting very young rookies, feeling that by the time these athletes develop into stars, their contracts will have expired and they will be free agents, able to sell themselves to the highest bidders.

At one time, all the major sports leagues had rules limiting the mobility of veterans. The NFL had the "Rozelle Rule," named for its famous commissioner Pete Rozelle, which required any team that signed a player from another team to pay compensation, often in the form of a future draft pick. The NBA and NHL had similar rules. By the early 1980s, these rules had been eliminated as part of collective bargaining agreements.

Baseball's route toward a free labor market was more circuitous. For years, professional baseball contracts contained a provision known as the reserve clause. If a player refused to sign the contract offered by his team, the reserve clause gave the team the right to automatically renew his expiring contract for the next year. The traditional interpretation of the reserve clause was that if a player continued to remain unsigned, a team could renew the old contract year after year in perpetuity. As a result, baseball players had virtually no bargaining power vis-à-vis their teams. The reserve clause explains why the immortal Babe Ruth never earned more than $100,000 per season—roughly $1 million today in inflation-adjusted dollars—far less than major league stars earn today.

In 1970, St. Louis Cardinals outfielder Curt Flood (who balked at being traded to the Philadelphia Phillies) filed an antitrust challenge to the reserve clause. In a confusing 1972 ruling, the Supreme Court cited Justice Learned Hand's old ruling that baseball was the "national pastime" and was therefore exempt from antitrust laws. For a time it appeared as if the reserve clause had dodged a bullet and would remain intact. However, in 1975, two major league baseball pitchers, Andy Messersmith and Dave McNally, challenged the interpretation of the reserve clause, contending that the right to re-sign a player who refuses to sign a contract extended, not indefinitely as baseball owners had always contended, but for just one year. Arbitrator Peter Seitz agreed with the Messersmith–McNally interpretation, ruling that a ball club could renew an unsigned player's contract for just one year, after which the player would become a "free agent" who would be able to sell his services to the highest bidder. Seitz, who had been retained by Major League Baseball, was promptly fired, and baseball owners went to court to challenge his decision. In February 1976, a federal judge upheld Seitz's ruling, ushering in baseball's free agency era.

For many reasons, competition in the input market for free agents can be intense. There are numerous competitors—in principle, every team in the league is a potential buyer. There is little differentiation—most players can be equally productive on any team and have little hometown loyalty, though some may take a small pay cut in order to play in a big market like New York or a warm-weather market like Miami.

A few factors soften wage competition, however. Very few athletes can make a major impact on a team's chances of winning a championship; as a result, salaries for midlevel athletes fall well short of the salaries of superstars. Moreover, the number of serious competitors for a star athlete is limited. When superstar pitcher Cliff Lee became a free agent after the 2010 season, only two or three teams entered the bidding war. He signed with the Philadelphia Phillies for $120 million over five years. Despite paying huge salaries to Lee and other stars, the Phillies' owners reportedly earned more than $15 million on total expenses of about $250 million, a tidy return on sales. (The Phillies' owners also enjoyed all the perks of ownership, which should be considered part of their "profit" from owning the team.)

Most professional sports team owners will say that unchecked competition in the labor market makes it almost impossible to make a profit. This is why owners have been so adamant in seeking "salary caps" that limit the total amount teams can pay their players. The NHL owners went so far as to cancel the entire 2004–2005 season to force players to accept a salary cap, and the NBA owners threatened to do the same in 2011. Through the salary cap, teams and players share the profits they enjoy from their monopoly status in the output market. The most important issue in contract negotiations is the magnitude of the cap; this is what determines who gets the largest piece of the monopoly pie. Instead of a salary cap, baseball has a "luxury tax" that kicks in when a team's aggregate salaries exceed roughly $180 million. Thus far, only a handful of teams have ever paid the tax.

Entry

Sports team owners are a motley group—they include media companies like Cablevision (owner of the NBA New York Knicks and NHL New York Rangers) and Time Warner (MLB's Atlanta Braves), and the 100,000 local fans who own stock in the Green Bay Packers. (Don't bother trying to become a part owner—the Packers are not issuing new shares, and existing shares may not be resold.) Many owners are wealthy businessmen for whom owning a sports team is the ultimate high-priced hobby. They include Micky Aronson (heir to the Carnival Cruise empire and owner of the Miami Heat basketball team); real estate tycoon Malcolm Glazer (owner of the NFL Tampa Bay Buccaneers and, much to the chagrin of their fans, English Soccer League powerhouse Manchester United); Mark Cuban (who sits on the bench and prowls the locker room of his Dallas Mavericks); and Mikhail Prokhorov (a Russian billionaire who recently purchased the Brooklyn Nets).

There is no shortage of rich men (and the occasional rich woman) who want to enjoy the limelight of sports team ownership. But it is not so easy—the barriers to entry are very high. Each league has rules governing the addition of new franchises. Potential new owners must pay current owners hundreds of millions of dollars. Most potential owners also offer to build new stadiums, knowing that visiting team owners will share ticket revenues (and therefore might be more inclined to vote in favor of league expansion). Incumbent team owners usually have the right to veto new franchises in their own geographic markets, further hindering entry. Unable to start sports teams from scratch, billionaires looking to join a league are usually forced to purchase an existing team. During the early to mid-2000s, the number of billionaires increased faster than the supply of teams, resulting in dramatic increases in purchase prices. A few teams like the NFL Dallas Cowboys and MLB New York Yankees would reportedly sell for over $1 billion, and Prokhorov paid $200 million for an 80 percent stake in the Nets, a perennial doormat in the NBA. So even though some sports teams post operating losses, their owners may be enjoying huge capital gains.

Short of buying an existing team, the only other way for a would-be sports entrepreneur to enter the professional sports market is to form an entire new league. This raises the stakes for entry considerably—most of the new teams must succeed or the entire league is likely to fail. Though the risks are high, the rewards can be even higher, and a number of leagues have come and gone over the years, including the World Football League, the United States Football League (USFL), the XFL, and the Arena Football League (the NFL is *very* profitable), the American Basketball Association (ABA), and the World Hockey League.

Entry barriers are so severe that new leagues feel the need to differentiate their product in order to survive: The ABA introduced the 3-point shot; the USFL played its games in late winter and spring; the XFL offered a more violent game that shared ownership and marketing savvy with the World Wrestling Federation. The Arena Football League plays indoors on a field the size of a hockey rink.

Not every new league fails. The Arena Football League is 25 years old, though few fans feel it is an adequate substitute for the NFL. The older American Football League (AFL) and, to a lesser extent, the ABA, can be considered success stories, and the paths to their success were very similar. The AFL began in 1960, just as the NFL's popularity was on the rise. The AFL took advantage of three of the NFL's shortcomings: the NFL had teams in just 13 cities, the NFL style downplayed the exciting passing game, and NFL players had yet to earn the rights to free agency and the high salaries that would result. The AFL began with eight teams, six of which were located in cities that did not have NFL franchises.[5] AFL teams emphasized passing, and the resulting high scoring games proved appealing to many fans. Even so, AFL teams lost money year after year. Following the dictum that you have to spend money to make money, in 1965 the AFL launched its most brazen attack on the NFL.

In the previous year, 1964, the AFL signed a $34 million television contract with NBC. (CBS had exclusive rights to NFL games.) AFL teams used the money to outbid the NFL for superstar players. New York Jets owner Sonny Werblin moved first by signing University of Alabama star quarterback Joe Namath to a deal paying an unprecedented $427,000 for the first year. When the AFL's Denver Broncos made a big offer to University of Illinois star Dick Butkus, the NFL assured the future Hall-of-Famer that he would receive "wheelbarrows" full of money if he signed with them. (He chose the NFL's Chicago Bears.) Soon, both leagues were giving wheelbarrows of money to stars like Roman Gabriel, John Brodie, and Pete Gogolak. After Oakland Raiders head coach Al Davis became the AFL's commissioner in April 1966, the bidding wars intensified. The AFL, which was never profitable, took big losses, but it did not matter. The NFL was losing money for the first time in over a decade and sued for peace. In June 1966, the two leagues merged. The owners of AFL teams got what they wanted—the same fan base enjoyed by the NFL. In today's NFL, the American Football Conference still consists largely of former AFL teams.

The American Basketball Association (ABA) started in 1967. Like the AFL, most of the original 11 teams were located in non-NBA cities. Like the AFL, the ABA emphasized scoring, with a wide-open "up and down the court game" and the innovative 3-point shot. Like the AFL, the ABA paid big dollars to sign budding superstars such as "Dr. J" Julius Erving and scoring phenom Rick Barry. All of these strategies helped the ABA enjoy a loyal fan base. But because games were played in secondary markets like Pittsburgh, Louisville, and New Orleans, the national fan base was never large enough to generate a big television contract, and the league was unprofitable. The ABA did have one thing going for it that the AFL did not: basketball fans had become disenchanted with the NBA, and attendance was falling. In 1977, when the NBA agreed to absorb four ABA teams, it hoped that the infusion of the upbeat style embodied by Dr. J would change the league's fortunes. Indeed, Dr. J's popularity heralded a new era for basketball, based on stars rather than teams. The later success of the NBA and superstars like Magic Johnson, Larry Bird, Michael Jordan, and Kobe Bryant can be traced to the product differentiation strategy that embodied the short-lived ABA.

It is hard to fathom how a new sports league today could match even the modest success of the ABA. All the major sports leagues have blanketed the nation with teams. The NFL even has "minor league" teams in Europe. Free agency means that star players are sure to make at least as much money signing with major leagues as they could with any upstart league. And except for MLB, the leagues are constantly changing rules to assure a pleasing style of play. As a result, opportunities for favorable geographic or product differentiation by a new league are virtually nonexistent. Leagues have attempted to differentiate by time of year—notably the USFL and the XFL—but either because the product was poor or fans had moved on to other sports, these efforts failed.

Substitutes and Complements

Professional sports teams compete for entertainment dollars. Owners worry not only about the product on the field, but also the overall entertainment experience. One of the first owners to fully realize sports as entertainment was Tex Schramm, the legendary general manager of the Dallas Cowboys. In the early 1970s, Schramm hired professional models to cheer from the sidelines. The models were unaccustomed to the Dallas heat, however, and were quickly exhausted. In 1972, Schramm decided to create a squad of professional dancers. The Dallas Cowboy Cheerleaders first appeared in 1973, and the rest is history—there is even a movie about these athletic beauties. Today's professional sporting events feature skilled cheerleaders, musical performances, costumed mascots (most famously, the San Diego Chicken), and fan participation events during game breaks. Off-the-court entertainment is so important that during the depths of the post–Michael Jordan basketball era, the Chicago Bulls still sold out most games, thanks, in part, to the circus-like atmosphere at the United Center.

There are many complements to professional sports. The most successful sports league in the United States, the NFL, is helped by two important complements. One is television. The Super Bowl is the top-rated television show every year (that includes all programs, not just sports), and playoff games and Monday Night Football also have huge ratings. But football would not enjoy its phenomenal success without one other complement—gambling. Over $2 billion is bet legally on sports every year, mostly on the NFL through Las Vegas "sports books." This is just the tip of the iceberg; estimates of illegal sports betting (including gray market gambling through offshore Internet sites) exceed $100 billion, again mostly on the NFL. Millions of bets may be placed on each regular season NFL game and probably ten times that for the Super Bowl. With this many people betting so much money, it is no wonder that NFL games get huge television audiences, even when the home team is not playing.

Gambling poses a dilemma for professional sports. While gambling boosts fan interest, team owners fear that players will come under the influence of bookmakers and intentionally throw a game in exchange for a big payday. Fans might quickly lose interest. The 1919 "Black Sox" scandal, which resulted when eight Chicago White Sox baseball players were accused of taking bribes (seven of whom admitted to the fact), nearly took down the sport. It took the charismatic Babe Ruth and his prodigious bat to revive MLB's fortunes. More recently, Pete Rose, arguably one of the best ballplayers of all time, was banned from the Hall of Fame for gambling on baseball.

Supplier Power

We have discussed the most powerful suppliers, the players' unions, at length. Most players are trained in college, making undergraduate sports teams a critical supplier to professional sports. The National Collegiate Athletic Association (NCAA), which governs all undergraduate athletics, has been a benign supplier. At worst, it has pressured major league sports not to draft underclassmen, but it has never broached the topic of direct financial support from the major leagues.

Cities are another major supplier to sports teams. Most local politicians believe that local sports teams add significantly to their economies, despite research suggesting that the economic benefits are vastly overstated. Politicians are willing to use taxpayer dollars to subsidize new sports stadiums.[6] Such payments have precedent in American business—witness the millions of dollars in subsidies or tax breaks given to companies that build factories or relocate headquarters. The amounts spent by municipalities on sports stadiums are staggering, often reaching several hundred million dollars. This has changed during the recent economic downturn, as municipal finances have taken a big hit and voters have grown skeptical of the purported economic benefits from new stadiums. Sports team owners can no longer count on local governments to build their stadiums and must increasingly rely on corporate sponsorships or their own personal wealth.

Buyer Power

There are four major television networks and at least four major sports cable systems (ESPN, Comcast, Turner Broadcasting, and NBC Sports). They often compete head-to-head to obtain national broadcast rights for major sports. Most networks view professional sports as a loss leader and are willing to pay huge sums to get sports fans to associate the network's name with specific sports. (The "NFL on CBS" comes to mind.) Given that at any time of the year there are more networks than there are leagues in action, the upper hand in these negotiations will belong to the sports leagues. The same applies to negotiations over the right to broadcast games locally on television and radio.

Conclusion

Table 8.3 summarizes the five forces of professional sports. Loyal fans and league bylaws give sports teams the kind of product market differentiation and entry barriers that sellers of other goods and services envy. Teams set prices well above marginal costs, only to have the resulting profits bargained away by powerful unions. Buyer power cannot explain why many sports teams report operating losses. To explain this, we have to remember that many owners are not in the business to make money. Owner-hobbyists want to win, and spending an additional $10 million on a top free agent will not deter them. As long as the supply of billionaires keeps up, sports owners should continue to expect operating losses and capital gains.

TABLE 8.3
FIVE-FORCES ANALYSIS OF PROFESSIONAL SPORTS LEAGUES

Force	Threat to Profits
Internal rivalry	Low (output markets); high (input markets)
Entry	Low
Substitutes/complement	Low
Buyer power	Low
Supplier power	Low (except for players' unions)

Professional Search Firms

Many readers of this text will find themselves working at a professional services firm, perhaps in consulting, investment banking, accounting, or marketing. Competition in these sectors exhibits some common features, which are exemplified by professional search firms.

Market Definition

When businesses want to hire talented managers for corporate or midlevel jobs, they often outsource the search to independent professional search firms. Some professional search firms compete globally, helping large multinational firms fill senior management positions. Smaller clients usually confine their search nationally or regionally, and often retain smaller search firms with greater local knowledge and experience.

Most of the "production" of professional search firms is done by their search consultants. Search consultants usually begin their careers as employees; in time, they may become partners and enjoy a share of their firm's profits. A successful search consultant must know who is working where, what they are getting compensated, and what it will take to get them to switch employers. Search consultants are experts in judging corporate talent and learning about key personnel movements within an industry before Wall Street analysts or even the senior executives of the organization housing the individual. They must possess the persuasion skills required to convince talented performers to leave their current employer (and their current home, school district, and so forth) for the client organization. Search consultants must track compensation packages given to other job changers and have a sense of the "compensating differential"—the dollar value of the difference in the attractiveness of different jobs.

Internal Rivalry

Professional search is a $10 billion industry, and, like other professional services industries, it is highly fragmented. There are around 4,000 search firms, with an average of just 2.5 search consultants per firm. The top 10 search consulting firms have a combined market share of just 11 percent, and more than 80 percent of search firms collect less than $2 million annually in professional fees. Two of the largest firms in this industry are publicly traded firms—Heidrick & Struggles and Korn/Ferry International. The three most prominent private firms are Spencer Stuart, Russell Reynolds International, and the UK firm Egon Zehnder International.

Search firms set "prices" through a retainer policy. Firms receive one-third of the position's first-year salary (including any stock and other bonuses), and they often receive this fee regardless of whether the position is filled. Given the highly fragmented market structure, one might expect intense price competition, with search firms asking for a reduced retainer with the hope of gaining market share. But clients link price and quality, perhaps because price has an important incentive effect. In particular, clients may fear that a search firm working for a cut-rate retainer might devote less effort to the search.

Search firms are differentiated geographically and by industry. Larger firms like Korn/Ferry address the concerns of large international clients seeking to attract senior executives. These search firms have deep knowledge of what is happening in the executive suites of the world's largest businesses. Smaller search firms may specialize in specific industries or regions. For example Hazzard, Young and Attea specializes in helping U.S. public school boards find superintendents, while FGI serves global clients in the aerospace and transportation sectors and PSS focuses on search in India.

Entry

In a $10 billion business where a single successful placement can generate hundreds of thousands or even millions of dollars in revenue, there are clearly profits to be had in professional search. Given that anyone with a cell phone can develop contacts and call themselves a search consultant, it is not surprising that there are thousands of firms competing for their share of the pie. To some extent, competition in this industry resembles the monopolistic competition model described in Chapter 5. Recall that in a monopolistically competitive market, firms are differentiated but face entry costs. As a result, prices exceed marginal costs, yet entrants should not expect to turn a profit. Indeed, it can take a new search firm 18 months to establish relationships with employers and potential search targets. It is not enough to have a lengthy contact list. The firm must also have a demonstrated ability to match managers to employers. The resulting advantages of incumbency are especially large for executive-level search because the stakes are higher and the search firm may need to know about potential candidates around the world across a range of industries.

Substitutes and Complements

A client could use its in-house human resources department to fill senior job vacancies, but this is not likely to generate the best list of candidates. An in-house HR department would not know about eligible candidates at other firms, so it would have to advertise job availability and prescreen responding candidates. This process is likely to identify candidates who are unemployed or unhappy with their current employment position, not exactly what the company would want. In contrast, the search consultant relies on longstanding personal relationships to identify successful managers who might be lured to a new position; many of these managers are not actively seeking a new job when contacted by the search firm and would never learn of an HR department job posting.

Employers have two additional reasons to outsource search. Search consultants can provide the kind of discretion that the HR department could not: the fact that the firm is searching can be kept secret until appropriate candidates have been identified. This can also partially insulate the employer from internal or external challenges related to hiring decisions.

Management consulting firms already working with a client on another matter could be substitutes. Indeed, the industry developed out of such consulting efforts. (McKinsey starting doing executive search in 1957.) However, management consulting firms generally lack the specialized knowledge and focus of search firms. Other potential substitutes include specialist human resource firms, such as Manpower, and even some Internet-based employment listing firms, such as Monster.com. While these have the potential to compete against lower-level locally based searches, they as yet have not proven themselves to be viable substitutes for major executive search firms, largely because they deal with different pools of job candidates.

The globalization of the economy increases the frequency of contacts between potential clients, potential hires, and the search firm. This should make search even more efficient. However, as interconnectedness increases, it might be difficult for the largest search firms to maintain their advantages that were built on years of personal relationships in a less connected world.

Supplier Power

The "traditional" suppliers to the search consulting industry are individuals who choose to become search consultants. They pose a threat only to the extent that they can start up their own competing firms. This threat is minimal when it comes from new consultants who lack the contacts required for successful search. The threat is considerable when successful search consultants in incumbent firms strike out on their own or threaten to join a different firm. Star consultants can take with them their specialized knowledge of clients and potential hires, coupled with their track record of success. Search firms can minimize this threat through legal restrictions ("noncompete clauses"), but these are not binding in many places. Otherwise, firms may have to pay their stars a high enough wage to deter them from leaving, with the result that the stars end up with the lion's share of the profits.

We should also consider the pool of prospective prospects to be suppliers because search firms cannot meet their clients' needs without them. At any time, the best prospects may be speaking with several search firms. This may force the search firms to spend more time cultivating their prospects (for example, through additional phone calls and meetings), which drives up the cost of doing business.

Buyer Power

In general, buyers have power when they can lower the industry margins by demanding a higher level of service or lower prices. Because 85 percent of senior executive search fees are derived from repeat or referred business, larger employers that are likely to fill multiple positions can wield considerable power. Employers searching for CEOs have a lot of power because the CEO is likely to replace subordinates and will probably be partial to the same search firm. Powerful employers may not insist on lower retainers (see the earlier section, Internal Rivalry) but may instead ask for incentives for quality service, such as penalties for failure to identify candidates in a timely fashion or bonuses if the hire proves to be successful.

Conclusion

What kind of industry is this? There are thousands of small firms selling to sophisticated buyers who require specialized knowledge; low barriers to entry, especially by successful consultants in established firms, and a potential in-house substitute. It is no surprise that the vast majority of firms struggle to survive, even as a few large industry leaders sustain their success for decades.

How can a firm succeed? Entry and competition is a sort of trial-and-error process. Entrants are attracted by the prospect of charging high retainer fees. A few entrants will establish the personal connections required to land clients, and a few of these will have a series of successful placements. As a result, a small percentage of entrants will grow and enjoy sustained success, while most stay very small and remain at risk to exit. The successful firms must take care to keep their star consultants happy. At some point the stars will earn enough that they become a breakeven proposition for the firm. It is the profits generated by the up-and-comers, relying on established networks and reputations as they attempt to build their own, that allow search firms to prosper.

Table 8.4 summarizes how these forces affect industry profitably.

Table 8.4

Five-Forces Analysis of Search Consulting Industry

Force	Threat of Profits
Internal rivalry	Moderate
Entry	Moderate
Substitutes/Complements	Low
Buyer power	Low
Supplier power	Medium to high

CHAPTER SUMMARY

- An industry analysis provides an overview of the potential profitability of the average firm in an industry.

- A comprehensive analysis examines the five forces: internal rivalry, entry, substitutes, buyer power, and supplier power. The latter four operate independently and may also intensify internal rivalry.

- Internal rivalry is fierce if competition drives prices toward costs. This is more likely when there are many firms, products are perceived to be homogeneous, consumers are motivated and able to shop around, prices may be set secretly, sales orders are large and received infrequently, and the industry has excess capacity.

- The threat of entry is high if firms can easily enter an industry and capture market share from profitable incumbents while intensifying price competition.

- Substitutes also capture sales and intensify price rivalry.

- Buyers and suppliers exert power directly by renegotiating the terms of contracts to extract profits from profitable industries, and indirectly by shopping around for the best prices.

- The government can affect profitability and should be considered either as part of the five forces or as a separate force.

- Profits may be threatened by any or all of the five forces. Although it is useful to construct a "five-forces scorecard" on which the forces can be rated, the exercise of assessing the five forces is more important than the actual scores. Through this exercise, the analyst develops deep knowledge of key strategic issues affecting the industry in question.

- A sound five-forces analysis should be based on economic principles. The tools for analyzing internal rivalry, entry, and substitutes are derived from industrial organization and game theory, which are discussed in Chapters 5, 6, and 7. The tools for analyzing buyer and supplier power are derived from the economics of vertical relationships, which were discussed in Chapters 3 and 4.

QUESTIONS

1. It has been said that Porter's five-forces analysis turns antitrust law on its head. What do you think this means?

2. Comment on the following: All of wisdom contained in the five-forces framework is reflected in the economic identity:

$$\text{Profit} = (\text{Price} - \text{Average Cost}) \times \text{Quantity}$$

3. How does the magnitude of scale economies affect the intensity of each of the five forces?

4. How does capacity utilization affect the intensity of internal rivalry? The extent of entry barriers?

5. How does the magnitude of consumer switching costs affect the intensity of internal rivalry? Of entry?

6. How do exit barriers affect internal rivalry? Entry?

7. Rivalry among firms in an industry is typically stronger when which of the following is true about the underlying industry economics? (*Note:* It is possible that more than one—or none—of the answers to this question are correct. You must choose all correct answers to get full credit.)
   (a) Fixed costs of production are high.
   (b) There are two competitors in the industry.
   (c) Products are differentiated.
   (d) Production capacity in the industry is low relative to current demand.

8. Consider an industry whose demand fluctuates over time. Suppose that this industry faces high supplier power. Briefly state how this high supplier power will affect the variability of profits over time.

9. What does the concept of coopetition add to the five-forces approach to industry analysis?

10. Coopetition often requires firms to communicate openly. How is this different from collusion? How can antitrust enforcers distinguish between coopetition and collusion?

11. In the United States, the incomes of specialists such as heart surgeons can easily triple the incomes of primary care practitioners. Use the five forces to offer explanations for this disparity. Can you think of any other possible explanations?

APPENDIX: TEMPLATE FOR DOING A FIVE-FORCES ANALYSIS

FACTORS AFFECTING RIVALRY AMONG EXISTING COMPETITORS

To what extent does pricing rivalry or nonprice competition (e.g., advertising) erode the profitability of a typical firm in this industry?

	Characterization (Current)	Future Trend
Degree of seller concentration?		
Rate of industry growth?		
Significant cost differences among firms?		
Excess capacity?		
Cost structure of firms: sensitivity of costs to capacity utilization?		
Degree of product differentiation among sellers? Brand loyalty to existing sellers? Cross-price elasticities of demand among competitors in industry?		
Buyers' costs of switching from one competitor to another?		

	Characterization (Current)	Future Trend
Are prices and terms of sales transactions observable?		
Can firms adjust prices quickly?		
Large and/or infrequent sales orders?		
Use of "facilitating practices" (price leadership, advance announcement of price changes)?		
History of "cooperative" pricing?		
Strength of exit barriers?		
High industry price elasticity of demand?		

FACTORS AFFECTING THE THREAT OF ENTRY

To what extent does the threat or incidence of entry work to erode the profitability of a typical firm in this industry?

	Characterization (Current)	Future Trend
Significant economies of scale?		
Importance of reputation or established brand loyalties in purchase decision?		
Entrants' access to distribution channels?		
Entrants' access to raw materials?		
Entrants' access to technology/know-how?		
Entrants' access to favorable locations?		
Experience-based advantages of incumbents?		
Network externalities: demand-side advantages to incumbents from large installed base?		
Government protection of incumbents?		
Perceptions of entrants about expected retaliation of incumbents/reputations of incumbents for "toughness"?		

Factors Affecting or Reflecting Pressure from Substitute Products and Support from Complements

To what extent does competition from substitute products outside the industry erode the profitability of a typical firm in the industry?

	Characterization (Current)	Future Trend
Availability of close substitutes?		
Price-value characteristics of substitutes?		
Price elasticity of industry demand?		
Availability of close complements?		
Price-value characteristics of complements?		

Factors Affecting or Reflecting Power of Input Suppliers

To what extent do individual *suppliers have the ability to negotiate high input prices with typical firms in this industry? To what extent do input prices deviate from those that would prevail in a perfectly competitive input market in which input suppliers act as price takers?*

	Characterization (Current)	Future Trend
Is the supplier industry more concentrated than the industry it sells to?		
Do firms in industry purchase relatively small volumes relative to other customers of supplier? Is typical firm's purchase volume small relative to sales of typical supplier?		
Few substitutes for suppliers' input?		
Do firms in industry make relationship-specific investments to support transactions with specific suppliers?		
Do suppliers pose credible threat of forward integration into the product market?		
Are suppliers able to price-discriminate among prospective customers according to ability/ willingness to pay for input?		

Factors Affecting or Reflecting Power of Buyers

To what extent do individual *buyers have the ability to negotiate low purchase prices with typical firms in this industry? To what extent do purchase prices differ from those that would prevail in a market with a large number of fragmented buyers in which buyers act as price takers?*

	Characterization (Current)	Future Trend
Is buyers' industry more concentrated than the industry it purchases from?		
Do buyers purchase in large volumes? Does a buyer's purchase volume represent a large fraction of the typical seller's sales revenue?		
Can buyers find substitutes for industry's product?		
Do firms in industry make relationship-specific investments to support transactions with specific buyers?		
Is price elasticity of demand of buyer's product high or low?		
Do buyers pose credible threat of backward integration?		
Does product represent significant fraction of cost in buyer's business?		
Are prices in the market negotiated between buyers and sellers on each individual transaction, or do sellers post a "take-it-or-leave-it" price that applies to all transactions?		

ENDNOTES

[1]Community hospitals treat a variety of patients on a short-term basis. Another type of hospital not considered here is the psychiatric hospital.

[2]Benkard, L. "Learning and Forgetting: The Dynamics of Airplane Production," *American Economic Review*, September 2000.

[3]The Chicago Sky, a new team in the Women's NBA, does not play during the same time of the year.

[4]There are nuances in some sports, as in basketball where the worst teams participate in a "lottery" to decide which one gets the top pick. The Cleveland Cavaliers won the lottery in 2003 and selected LeBron James as the top pick, immediately rejuvenating a struggling franchise.

[5]The cities with overlapping franchises were New York and Los Angeles. By 1962, the Los Angeles franchise had moved to San Diego. In 1960, the NFL added a new franchise in Dallas, one of the original AFL cities. In 1963, the AFL Dallas franchise moved to Kansas City.

[6]The typical argument by politicians is that sports stadiums generate millions of dollars in ticket sales for the local economy. This ignores the fact that virtually all ticket buyers live in the community and would have spent their entertainment dollars on some other local activity had there been no sports. Moreover, many, if not most, athletes do not live in the community, so much of the ticket revenues flow out of the local market. This would not be the case for money spent on, say, restaurants or local theater.

PART THREE

STRATEGIC POSITION AND DYNAMICS

STRATEGIC POSITIONING FOR COMPETITIVE ADVANTAGE

9

$\mathbf{M}$ost industries feature a variety of firms pursuing their own unique strategies for success. Consider, for example, the variety of competitive strategies airlines have pursued since deregulation:

- American Airlines developed a nationwide route structure organized around the hub-and-spoke concept. It built traveler loyalty through its frequent-flier program, and it attempted to maximize revenue through its sophisticated computerized reservation system (known as SABRE) and its state-of-the-art yield management capabilities.

- Southwest Airlines eschews the hub-and-spoke concept, instead flying from one city to another in one or two short hops. Southwest provides point-to-point service between midsized cities that other carriers treat as feeders for their hubs. With less restrictive work rules than other major airlines, a highly motivated workforce, and a fleet that consists only of Boeing 737s to economize on maintenance and training, Southwest has average operating costs that are among the lowest in the industry. (Figure 9.1 shows unit costs, market shares, and profit margins for major U.S. airlines for 2010.)

- JetBlue Airways has outfitted its airplanes with leather seats, free television and radio programming from DIRECTV and XM Satellite. With much of its traffic originating from New York's JFK Airport, JetBlue has tried to convey an "edgy" urban "attitude" to appeal to tough, jaded New Yorkers. Within six months of its founding, JetBlue had turned a profit, and it remains among the most profitable U.S. airlines.

These examples illustrate several fundamentally different ways in which firms can position themselves to compete within the same industry. American attempts to differentiate its services from those of its competitors by offering an attractive frequent-flier program whose benefits are dramatically enhanced by American's vast domestic and international network. Southwest enjoys low costs and faces little to no competition in many of its origin–destination pairs. JetBlue targets a different customer segment than either American or Southwest, positioning itself to appeal to the tastes of younger fliers originating in its New York market.

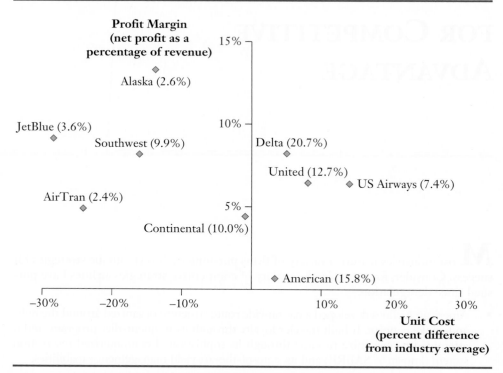

Unit costs are expressed as a percentage difference from the industry average.[1]

This chapter develops a conceptual framework for characterizing and analyzing a firm's strategic position within an industry. This framework employs simple economic concepts to identify conditions necessary for competitive advantage in a market. The chapter is organized in four sections. The first defines the concept of competitive advantage and argues that to achieve it a firm must create more value than its rivals. The ability to create value is shaped by how firms position themselves to compete in an industry. The second section discusses the economic and organizational logic of two broad alternative approaches to positioning: cost leadership and benefit leadership. The third section presents specific tools for diagnosing a firm's cost and benefit position in its market. The final section explores broad coverage versus focus strategies.

COMPETITIVE ADVANTAGE AND VALUE CREATION: CONCEPTUAL FOUNDATIONS

Competitive Advantage Defined

The five-forces framework presented in Chapter 8 is based on the idea that industry conditions are an important determinant of a firm's profitability. Profitability does not only vary across industries; it also varies within a particular industry, and in the

FIGURE 9.2

FRAMEWORK FOR COMPETITIVE ADVANTAGE

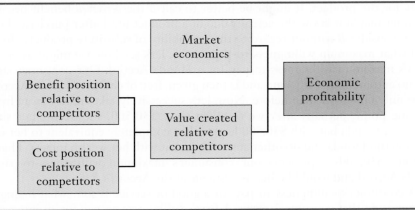

A firm's profitability depends jointly on the economics of its market and its success in creating more value than its competitors. The amount of value the firm creates compared to competitors depends on its cost and benefits position relative to competitors.

Introduction we described research evidence showing that intra-industry variability in profits is at least as large as inter-industry variability. When a firm earns a higher rate of economic profit than the average rate of economic profit of other firms competing within the same market, the firm has a *competitive advantage* in that market. (Careful application of this definition, of course, requires an economically sensible definition of the firm's market, a topic taken up in Chapter 5.) The main premise of this chapter is that firms achieve a competitive advantage by creating and delivering more economic value than their rivals and capture a portion of this value in the form of profits.

Figure 9.2 summarizes the framework that we develop in this chapter. According to this framework, a firm's economic profitability within a particular market depends on the economic attractiveness or unattractiveness of the market in which it competes (as summarized by a five-forces analysis) and on its competitive position in that market (i.e., whether it has a competitive advantage or disadvantage). Whether a firm has a competitive advantage or disadvantage depends on whether it is more or less successful than rivals at creating and delivering economic value. As we will see, a firm that can create and deliver more economic value than its competitors can simultaneously earn higher profits and offer higher net benefits to consumers than its competitors can.

Maximum Willingness-to-Pay and Consumer Surplus

Businesses that create more value than competitors will hold an advantaged position in the marketplace. To illustrate why, we need to define *value creation* and show how it relates to competitive advantage. Before defining value creation, we must first discuss maximum willingness-to-pay and consumer surplus.

Suppose that a particular software package is worth $150 to you. If its market price was $80, you would buy it. The purchase makes you better off because you have given up $80 to receive something more valuable—a software package that you feel is worth $150. The extent by which you are better off—in this case $150 − $80, or $70—is your *consumer surplus*.

More formally, let B denote a dollar measure of what one unit of a product is worth to a particular consumer, or equivalently, the consumer's maximum willingness-to-pay for the product. It might be better to call B the *perceived* benefit because the consumer may not know the actual value of a product until after purchase. For now, we will consider B without regard to the availability of substitute products. To understand what maximum willingness-to-pay means, let's see how we might assess a consumer's maximum willingness-to-pay for a Honda Accord. Our consumer starts off with no automobile of any kind and is then given, free of charge, a Honda Accord. She is certainly better off than before. Now, let's successively take money away from her. At some point, perhaps after we've taken away $30,500, she deems her situation (owning a Honda but with $30,500 less wealth) completely equivalent to her original situation (no Honda and no other automobile, but with her wealth intact). That dollar amount—$30,500—represents our consumer's maximum willingness-to-pay for a Honda Accord and would be her assessment of the Accord's B.

A consumer's willingness-to-pay for a good or service is somewhat intangible, as it depends on that consumer's tastes. A firm's willingness-to-pay for an input is easier to quantify because it is related to the impact of that input on the profitability of the firm, and profits are easier to measure than tastes. One way to measure a firm's willingness-to-pay is with *value-added analysis.* Consider, for example, a producer of soft drinks—say Cadbury Schweppes, the producer of 7-Up and Dr Pepper—that uses corn syrup sold by Archer Daniel's Midland (ADM) as a sweetener for its products. Cadbury Schweppes would like to determine the maximum amount it should be willing to pay for ADM's corn syrup. Suppose that Cadbury Schweppes's best available alternative to using corn syrup is to use sugar. As far as the end consumer of soft drinks is concerned, Cadbury Schweppes's choice of sugar or corn syrup is immaterial; the final product tastes exactly the same. Given this, the Cadbury Schweppes's maximum willingness-to-pay for ADM's corn syrup (i.e., the B for ADM's corn syrup) depends on the overall cost of production using corn syrup versus the cost using sugar.

The left-hand side of Figure 9.3 shows the economics of production when Cadbury Schweppes uses sugar to manufacture its soft drinks. In particular, when the cost of sugar is 3 euros per hundredweight, the "all-in" production cost using sugar (the sum of the costs of sugar, other materials, processing, and packaging) is 17 euros per hundredweight of soft drink. Cadbury Schweppes will prefer corn syrup provided that the "all-in" production costs are less than 17 euros. The right-hand side shows that by using corn syrup, Cadbury Schweppes incurs a somewhat higher processing cost and a somewhat higher cost of other materials, which limits the amount that Cadbury Schweppes would be willing to pay for corn syrup. Figure 9.3 shows that it would be willing to pay at most 2 euros per hundredweight. This is the *value added* of ADM's corn syrup and equals the price of corn syrup at which Cadbury Schweppes's "all-in" production cost using ADM's corn syrup is the same as its "all-in" production cost using sugar. If the price of ADM's corn syrup was any higher than 2 euros per hundredweight, Cadbury Schweppes would save money by switching to sugar as its sweetener.

From Maximum Willingness-to-Pay to Consumer Surplus

Recall that B represents the benefit that a consumer expects to derive from a product. If we let P denote the product's monetary price, the consumer surplus is the difference $B - P$. For example, if the price of the Honda Accord is $21,000, the consumer surplus of our hypothetical consumer would be $30,500 - $21,000 = $9,500. Suppose that

FIGURE 9.3

A SOFT-DRINK PRODUCER'S MAXIMUM WILLINGNESS-TO-PAY FOR CORN SYRUP

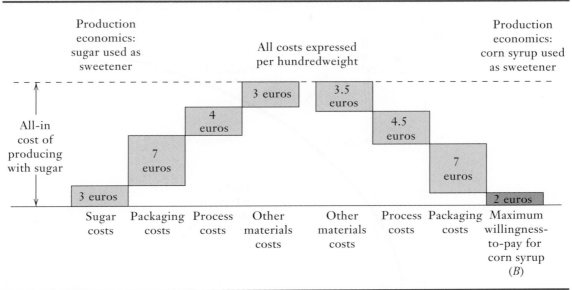

A soft-drink maker's maximum willingness-to-pay for corn syrup (i.e., its B) is represented by the height of the shaded bar at the far right. At this price of corn syrup, the soft-drink producer is just indifferent between producing a soft drink with corn syrup and producing a soft drink with the best available substitute for corn syrup, namely, sugar. If the price of corn syrup were any higher, the soft-drink maker would not purchase corn syrup and would use sugar instead.

the same consumer values a Nissan Leaf at $B = \$38,000$ and the price of the Leaf is $P = \$31,000$, creating a consumer surplus of \$7,000. This individual will purchase the Accord because it provides the higher surplus. This example suggests a simple model of consumer behavior: a consumer will purchase a product only if the product's consumer surplus is positive. Moreover, given a choice between two or more competing products, the consumer will purchase the one for which consumer surplus, $B - P$, is largest.

Whether its customers are firms or individuals, a seller must deliver consumer surplus to compete successfully. The value map in Figure 9.4 illustrates the competitive implications of consumer surplus. The vertical axis shows the monetary price P of the product. Each point in the value map corresponds to a particular price–quality combination. The solid upward-sloping line in Figure 9.4 is called an *indifference curve*.

For a given consumer, any price–quality combination along the indifference curve yields the same consumer surplus (i.e., has the same $B - P$). In Figure 9.4, products A and B offer the same $B - P$. A consumer choosing among products located along the indifference curve would thus be indifferent among the offerings. A product offering a price–quality combination located below a given indifference curve (e.g., product C) yields a higher consumer surplus than that yielded by products along the indifference curve. From the consumer's perspective, product C provides superior value to products A and B (and, as we will soon see, product D as well). A product offering a price–quality combination located above a given indifference curve (e.g., product D) yields a consumer surplus lower than that yielded by products

FIGURE 9.4
THE VALUE MAP

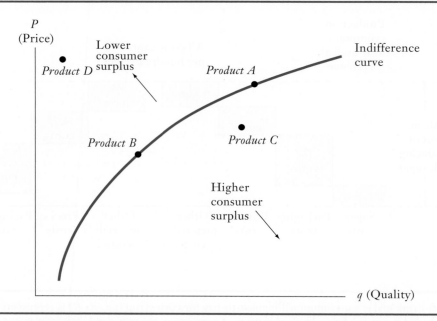

The value map illustrates the price–quality positions of firms in a market. The solid line is an indifference curve. It illustrates price–quality combinations that yield the same consumer surplus. Price–quality positions located below a given indifference curve yield a consumer surplus that is higher than that yielded by positions along the indifference curve. Price–quality positions located above an indifference curve yield consumer surplus that is lower than that yielded by positions along the indifference curve. When some products are positioned on a given indifference curve while others are positioned off the curve, consumers will flock to the firms providing the higher consumer surplus.

along the indifference curve. From the consumer's perspective, such products provide inferior value. From the consumer's perspective, product D provides inferior value to products A and B (and also C).

Competition among firms in a market can be thought of as a process whereby firms, through their prices and product attributes, submit consumer surplus "bids" to consumers. Consumers then choose the firm that offers the greatest amount of consumer surplus. A firm that offers a consumer less surplus than its rivals (e.g., the firm producing product D) will lose the fight for that consumer's business. When firms' price–quality positions line up along the same indifference curve—that is, when firms are offering a consumer the same amount of consumer surplus—we say that the firms have achieved *consumer surplus parity*. (In Figure 9.3, the firms selling products A and B have attained consumer surplus parity.) If firms achieve consumer surplus parity in a market in which consumers have identical preferences (i.e., the same indifference curves), no consumer within that market has an incentive to switch from one seller to another, and market shares will thus be stable. If all firms in the market have the same quality, then consumer surplus parity means that each firm charges the same price.

When a firm moves from a position of consumer surplus parity or consumer surplus advantage to one in which its consumer surplus is less than that of its competitors, its sales will slip and its market share will fall. This happened to Lexus and BMW in the early 2010s when its older designs lost share in the large sedan luxury segment to newer high-performance offerings by Audi, Jaguar, and Porsche.

Value-Created

Economic value is created when a producer combines inputs such as labor, capital, raw materials, and purchased components to make a product whose perceived benefit B exceeds the cost C incurred in making the product. The economic value created (or value-created, for short) is thus the difference between the perceived benefit and cost, or $B - C$, where B and C are expressed per unit of the final product.

Value-created must be divided between consumers and producers. Consumer surplus, $B - P$, represents the portion of the value-created that the consumer "captures." The seller receives the price P and uses it to pay for the inputs that are needed to manufacture the finished product. The producer's profit margin, $P - C$, represents the portion of the value-created that it captures. Adding together consumer surplus and the producer's profit gives us the value-created expressed as the sum of consumer surplus and profit:

$$\text{Value-Created} = \text{Consumer Surplus} + \text{Producer Surplus}$$
$$= (B - P) + (P - C)$$
$$= B - C$$

Figure 9.5 depicts value-created for a hypothetical producer of aluminum cans (e.g., a firm such as Crown, Cork and Seal). Start on the left side of the figure. The cost of producing 1,000 aluminum cans is $30 (i.e., $C = \$30$). The maximum willingness-to-pay

FIGURE 9.5
THE COMPONENTS OF VALUE-CREATED IN THE MARKET FOR ALUMINUM CANS

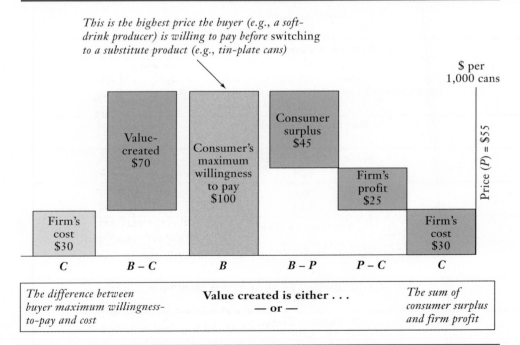

EXAMPLE 9.1   THE DIVISION OF THE VALUE-CREATED IN THE SALE OF BEER AT A BASEBALL GAME

Assigning numbers to the areas in Figure 9.5 is usually difficult because B is hard to measure. But when the product is sold under conditions of monopoly and no reasonable substitutes are available, B can be approximated by making some simplifying assumptions about the nature of the demand curve for the product. An example of a product sold under these circumstances is beer at a baseball game. Because a purchaser of beer would probably not regard soft drinks as a close substitute and because patrons are not allowed to bring in their own beer, the stadium concessionaire has as tight a monopoly on the market as one could imagine.

Here are some basic data on beer sold at Cincinnati Reds baseball games in the late 1980s. The price of a 20-ounce cup of beer was $2.50. The stadium concessionaire, Cincinnati Sports Service, paid the distributor $0.20 per cup for this beer; paid royalties to the city of Cincinnati of $0.24 per cup; paid royalties to

the Cincinnati Reds baseball team of $0.54 per cup; and paid an excise tax of $0.14 per cup. Its total costs were thus $1.12.[2]

If we assume that the demand curve for beer is linear, then a plausible estimate of consumer surplus that is consistent with the data above is $0.69 per 20-ounce cup of beer.[3] Table 9.1 shows the division of value in the sale of the beer using $0.69 per cup as an estimate of consumer surplus.

The brewer clearly captures only a small fraction of the value that is created.[4] By contrast, by controlling the concessionaire's access to the stadium and to the event, the city of Cincinnati and the Cincinnati Reds are able to capture a significant fraction of the value that is created. They can capture value because prospective concessionaires are willing to compete for the right to monopolize this market. As a result, the city and the Reds can extract a significant portion of the monopoly profit that would otherwise flow to the concessionaire.

TABLE 9.1

DIVISION OF VALUE IN THE SALE OF BEER AT RIVERFRONT STADIUM

Consumer Surplus $.69
Profit to Cincinnati Sports Service ?
· $1.38
Sports Service's Costs (labor, materials, insurance, etc.) ?
Profit to Cincinnati Reds $.54
Profit to City of Cincinnati $.24
Taxes $.14
Distributor's Profit
· ? · $.10
Distributor's Costs (exclusive of price paid to brewer) ?
Brewer's Profit $.30
Brewer's Costs $.07

for a buyer of aluminum cans, for example, a soft-drink bottler such as Coca-Cola Enterprises, is $100 per thousand (i.e., $B = \$100$). This represents the highest price the buyer is willing to pay for aluminum cans before switching to the best available alternative product, perhaps plastic containers. The difference between maximum willingness-to-pay and cost is the value-created, which in this case equals $70 (i.e., $B - C = \$70$). Working our way down the right side of the diagram, we see that value-created of $70 equals the sum of consumer surplus and producer profit. If the seller of aluminum cans charges a price of $55 (i.e., $P = \$55$), consumer surplus is $45 per thousand cans (i.e., $B - P = \$45$), while producer profit margin is $25 per thousand (i.e., $P - C = \$25$). The price P thus determines how much of the value-created sellers capture as profit and how much buyers capture as consumer surplus.

Value Creation and "Win–Win" Business Opportunities

No product can be viable without creating positive economic value. If $B - C$ was negative, there would be no price that consumers would be willing to pay for the product that would cover the cost of the resources that are sacrificed to make the product. Bubblegum-flavored soda, vacuum tubes, and video cassette recorders are products that at one time created positive value, but because of changes in tastes and technology, they no longer create enough benefits to consumers to justify their production.

By contrast, when $B - C$ is positive, a firm can profitably purchase inputs from suppliers, convert them into a finished product, and sell it to consumers. When $B > C$, it will always be possible for an entrepreneur to strike win–win deals with input suppliers and consumers, that is, deals that leave *all* parties better off than they would be if they did not deal with each other. In economics, win–win trade opportunities are called *gains from trade*. When $B > C$, clever entrepreneurs can exploit potential gains from trade.

Value Creation and Competitive Advantage

Although a positive $B - C$ is *necessary* for a product to be economically viable, just because a firm sells a product whose $B - C$ is positive is no guarantee that it will make a positive profit. In a market in which entry is easy and all firms create essentially the same economic value, competition between firms will dissipate profitability. Existing firms and new entrants will compete for consumers by bidding down their prices to the point at which all producers earn zero profit. In such markets, consumers capture all the economic value that the product creates.

It follows, then, that in order for a firm to earn positive profit in a competitive industry, the firm must create more economic value than its rivals. That is, the firm must generate a level of $B - C$ that its competitors cannot replicate. This simple but powerful insight follows from our earlier discussion of the competitive implications of consumer surplus. To see why, imagine that two sellers are competing for your business. The seller whose product characteristics and price provides you the greatest amount of consumer surplus will win your business. The most aggressive consumer surplus "bid" that either seller would be prepared to offer is the one at which its profit is equal to zero, which occurs when it offers a price P that equals its cost C. At such a bid, a firm would hand over all of the value it creates to you in the form of consumer surplus. The firm with the advantage in this competition is the one that has the highest $B - C$. This is because that firm will be able to win your patronage by offering you a slightly more favorable consumer surplus "bid" than the most aggressive bid its rival is prepared to offer, while retaining the extra value it creates in the form of profit.[5]

In one version of the above competitive scenario, all firms offer identical B. In this case, the "winning" firm must have lower C than its rivals. This reaffirms an idea introduced in Chapter 5, that successful firms in perfectly competitive industries must have lower costs than their rivals. This also holds true in concentrated markets when firms compete aggressively on the basis of price, such as in the Bertrand model also described in Chapter 5. The firm with the lowest cost can slightly undercut its rivals' prices, capture the entire market, and more than cover its production costs.

In markets with homogeneous products, the firm offering the highest $B - C$ captures the entire market. In most markets, different customers will make different trade-offs between price and the attributes that drive B, so that one firm might create a higher $B - C$ among one segment of consumers, while another firm may create a higher $B - C$ among other segments. We saw this, for example, in the personal computer industry in the late 1990s in which Gateway probably created more economic value in the SOHO (small office/home office) segment of the market, while Dell created more economic value in most of the rest of the market. As Figure 9.6 shows, both Dell and Gateway consistently outperformed industry peers during the latter half of the 1990s. We will discuss the implications of this market segmentation later in the chapter.

Analyzing Value Creation

Understanding how a firm's product creates economic value and whether it can continue to do so is a necessary first step in diagnosing a firm's potential for achieving a competitive advantage in its market. Diagnosing the sources of value creation requires

FIGURE 9.6
ECONOMIC PROFITABILITY OF PERSONAL COMPUTER MAKERS

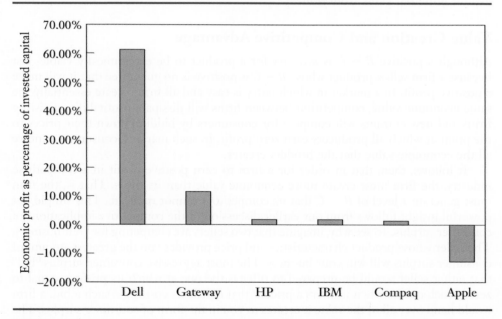

This figure shows average economic profits (expressed as a percentage of invested capital) of selected personal computer makers over the period 1995–1999.

Source: 2000 Stern Stewart Performance 1000 database.

an understanding of why the firm's business exists and what its underlying economics are. This, in turn, involves understanding what drives consumer benefits (e.g., how the firm's products serve consumer needs better than potential substitutes) and what drives costs (e.g., which costs are sensitive to production volume, or how costs change with cumulative experience).

Projecting the firm's prospects for creating value also involves critically evaluating how the fundamental economic foundations of the business are likely to evolve, an exercise that Richard Rumelt calls consonance analysis.[6] Perhaps the most basic of all

---

EXAMPLE 9.2 THE RISING PRICE TAG ON COMPETITIVE ADVANTAGE IN THE BEAUTIFUL GAME

One of the bases of competitive advantage is superior resources. As you may recall, resources are firm-specific assets that other firms cannot easily acquire. In football, each "firm" has the same value chain as those of its rivals, but within that value chain it can outperform its rivals by acquiring superior talent. With a few extremely wealthy individuals competing for the few top talents in the sport, prices were likely to rise, but few would have foreseen the heights to which the price tags on player transfers would rise.

For those not familiar with the sport, players who are under contract with one club need that club's agreement before being able to move to another club. In compensation, the club losing the player is paid a transfer fee. One of Spain's two top soccer clubs is Real Madrid. In the summer of 2009, Real's president, Florentino Perez, spent the equivalent of $225 million on two top players, buying Brazilian star Kaka from AC Milan for $94 million and then, just three days later, paying Manchester United $131 million for their star winger Cristiano Ronaldo. Observers of the sport suggested that Perez was likely to continue acquiring players; after all, the strategy had worked before.

In an interview with Spanish television (as quoted in a story from the *Los Angeles Times*) Perez stated that "the most expensive players are often the cheapest"[7] because what they bring in can be much greater than what they cost. Indeed, when Perez was Real Madrid president from 2000 to 2006 he acquired English star David Beckham, who alone brought in hundreds of millions through increased payments from sponsors and higher merchandise sales.

Perez has estimated that ticket sales, television right and merchandise sales already bring in $561 million a year to Real, and that number will likely rise with the addition of the new players. According to Simon Chadwick, director of the Center for the International Business of Sport at Coventry University in England, just the addition of Kaka and Ronaldo could mean an additional $175 million a year through foreign tours, sales of jerseys, improved television contracts, and other commercial ventures.[11]

However, having the players has to translate into winning and winning in a big way. Real lost both the Spanish Cup and the Champions League this season to its archrival FC Barcelona whose entire team payroll was less than what Perez spent on Kaka. And even with Beckham (along with French star Zidane and Brazilian star Ronaldo), Real Madrid did not win a trophy in the 2003-2006 seasons. Real Madrid's "brand" is built on a history of star power that has given it a competitive advantage in Spanish football.

is the question of whether changes in market demand or the conditions of technology are likely to threaten how the firm creates value. Although this point seems transparent, firms can easily overlook it when they are in the throes of month-to-month battles for market share with their immediate rivals. Evaluating future prospects is also difficult due to the sheer complexity of predicting the future and the risks involved in acting on such predictions.

The history of an industry may also dull managers to the prospects for change. Threats to a firm's ability to create value often come from outside its immediate group of rivals and may threaten not just the firm, but the whole industry. Honda's foray into motorcycles in the early 1960s occurred within segments that the dominant producers at the time—Harley-Davidson and British Triumph—had concluded were unprofitable. The revolution in mass merchandising created by Wal-Mart occurred in out-of-the-way locations that companies such as Kmart and Sears had rejected as viable locations for large discount stores. The music recording industry warily eyed Apple's iPod but was not fully upended until a start-up company called Napster offered users a way to easily (and, at the time, illegally) share music files over the Internet.

Value Creation and the Value Chain

Value is created as goods move along the vertical chain, which we first described in Chapter 3. The vertical chain is therefore sometimes referred to as the *value chain*.[8] The value chain depicts the firm as a collection of value-creating activities, such as production operations, marketing and sales, and logistics, as Figure 9.7 shows. Each activity in the value chain can potentially add to the benefit B that consumers get from

FIGURE 9.7
VALUE CHAIN

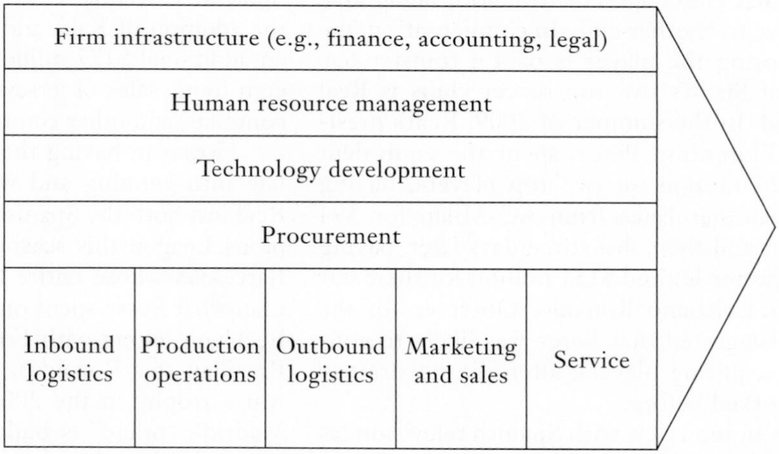

The value chain depicts the firm as a collection of value-creating activities. Porter distinguishes between five primary activities (inbound logistics, production operations, outbound logistics, marketing, and sales and service) and four support activities (firm infrastructure activities, such as finance and accounting, human resources management, technology development, and procurement).

the firm's product, and each can add to the cost C that the firm incurs to produce and sell the product. Of course, the forces that influence the benefits created and cost incurred vary significantly across activities.

In practice, it is often difficult to isolate the impact that an activity has on the value that the firm creates. To do so usually requires estimating the incremental perceived benefit that an activity creates and the incremental cost associated with it. However, when different stages produce finished or semifinished goods that can be valued using market prices, we can estimate the incremental value that distinctive parts of the value chain create by using value-added analysis, which we described earlier in this chapter.

Value Creation, Resources, and Capabilities

Broadly speaking, there are two ways in which a firm can create more economic value than the other firms in its industry. First, it can configure its value chain differently from competitors. For example, in the car-rental market in the United States, Enterprise's focus on the replacement-car segment has led it to operate with a fundamentally different value chain from the "Airport 7" (Hertz, Avis, National, Alamo, Budget, Dollar, and Thrifty), which are focused on the part of the market whose business originates at airports (primarily business and vacation travelers).[9] By optimizing its activities to serve renters seeking to replace their vehicles for possibly prolonged periods of time, Enterprise creates more economic value for this segment of customers than do the Airport 7 (see Example 9.3).

Alternatively, a firm can create superior economic value by configuring its value chain in essentially the same way as its rivals, but within that value chain, performing activities more effectively than rivals do. To do this, the firm must possess resources and capabilities that its competitors lack; otherwise, the competitors could immediately copy any strategy for creating superior value.

Resources are firm-specific assets, such as patents and trademarks, brand-name reputation, installed base, organizational culture, and workers with firm-specific expertise. The brand recognition that Coca-Cola enjoys worldwide is an example of an economically powerful resource. As a testament to the power of Coke's brand, the marketing consultancy InterBrand estimated that about half of Coca-Cola's market capitalization in 2010 was due to the value of the Coke brand name alone.[11] Unlike nonspecialized assets or factors of production, such as buildings, raw materials, or unskilled labor, resources cannot easily be duplicated or acquired by other firms in well-functioning markets. Resources can directly affect the ability of a firm to create more value than other firms. For example, a large installed base or an established reputation for quality may make the firm's B higher than its rivals. Resources also indirectly impact value creation because they are the basis of the firm's capabilities.

Capabilities are activities that a firm does especially well compared with other firms.[12] Capabilities might reside within particular business functions (e.g., Virgin Group's skills in brand promotion, American Airlines' capabilities in yield management, or Nine West's ability to manage its sourcing and procurement functions in the fashion shoe business). Alternatively, they may be linked to particular technologies or product designs (e.g., Facebook's web design and programming skills, Nan Ya Plastics' skills in working with polyester, or Honda's legendary skill in working with small internal-combustion engines and power trains).[13] Or they might reside in the firm's ability to manage linkages between elements of the value chain or coordinate activities across it (e.g., the Geisinger Clinic in central Pennsylvania is famous for its use of

---

EXAMPLE 9.3   CREATING VALUE: CADBURY IN INDIA

In 1824, a young entrepreneur opened a shop to sell coffee and tea in Birmingham, UK. Seeing an opportunity to market a beverage based on cocoa, he began to expand his product line. That entrepreneur was John Cadbury, and today, Cadbury controls about 70% of the world chocolate market.

According to the company's Vision into Action plan (for 2008–2011), Cadbury seeks to increase its market share by drawing on "untapped potential" with the goal of achieving its "vision of becoming the biggest and best confectionery company in the world." This is evident in the company's strategy in India.

With a population growing in both number and affluence, India has the purchasing power for consumer goods, and chocolate products have the advantage of being a relatively low-cost "luxury" good with the added advantage of novelty.

According to a *Wall Street Journal* article,[14] less than half of India's 1.1-billion population has ever tasted chocolate though "sweets" are generally popular and are associated with celebrations and given as gifts. Chocolate is catching on in India and Cadbury has the dominant share of a market (about 70%; Switzerland-based Nestlé has the second largest share at 25%) whose sales have seen an annual growth of 20% in the period 2006 through 2009. If Cadbury is looking for growth, then emerging markets such as India should figure prominently in its strategy.

Cadbury's sales strategy in India reaches across income divisions and geographic areas. It has increased its advertising and extended its reach to rural consumers, and has developed new products. For example, Cadbury Dairy Milk Shots are small sugar-shelled chocolate balls that are sold in fivegram packets costing two rupees (roughly equal to about .04 USD) or about a tenth of the average hourly wage for Indian workers.

But for a company concerned with profit margin, low prices are only possible with low costs. Cadbury has had to find ways to cut its costs in India. This has included reductions in the labor force and changes in production facilities. But the most significant challenge Cadbury has faced has to do with the cost of cocoa beans.

India is not a major producer of cocoa beans, and their import is subject to a 30 percent tariff. Cadbury's response? Help turn India into major cocoa producer by persuading the nation's farmers to change land use, planting cocoa instead of coconut (thus not leading to further deforestation). The Cadbury Cocoa Partnership was started in 2008 to assist local farmers in obtaining plants, free fertilizer (from the Indian government), and share expertise in cocoa cultivation.

As Indian cocoa bean production increases, there will be reduced shipping costs, but even more importantly, it would help to "derisk" cocoa[15] because the current sources of supply are countries (mostly in Africa) that are politically unstable. Cadbury India hopes that by 2015 it will no longer depend on imported beans.

True to the vision of its founder, Cadbury continues to seek and develop new opportunities and to grow and expand in new markets.

---

health information technology to reinvent how it delivers medical care across the spectrum from primary care through surgery and recovery.)

Whatever their basis, capabilities have several key common characteristics:

1. They are typically valuable across multiple products or markets.
2. They are embedded in what Richard Nelson and Sidney Winter call organizational routines—well-honed patterns of performing activities inside an organization.[16] This implies that capabilities can persist even though individuals leave the organization.
3. They are tacit; that is, they are difficult to reduce to simple algorithms or procedure guides.

EXAMPLE 9.4   MEASURING CAPABILITIES IN THE PHARMACEUTICAL INDUSTRY

Drawing on detailed quantitative and qualitative data from 10 major firms, Rebecca Henderson and Iain Cockburn attempted to measure resources and capabilities associated with new drug research in the pharmaceutical industry.[17] Although drug discovery is not the only skill that pharmaceutical firms must possess to compete effectively, it is extremely important. Henderson and Cockburn hypothesize that research productivity (measured as the number of patents obtained per research dollar invested) depends on three classes of factors: the composition of a firm's research portfolio; firm-specific scientific and medical know-how; and a firm's distinctive capabilities. The composition of the research portfolio is important because it is easier to achieve patentable discoveries in some areas than in others. For example, in the 20 years prior to Henderson and Cockburn's study, investments in cardiovascular drug discovery were consistently more productive than investments in cancer research. Firm-specific know-how is critical because modern drug research requires highly skilled scientists from disciplines such as biology, biochemistry, and physiology. Henderson and Cockburn use measures such as the firm's existing stock of patents as proxies for idiosyncratic firm know-how.

Henderson and Cockburn also hypothesize that two capabilities are likely to be especially significant in new drug research. The first is skill at encouraging and maintaining an extensive flow of scientific information from the external environment to the firm. In pharmaceuticals, much of the fundamental science that lays the groundwork for new discoveries is created outside the firm. A firm's ability to take advantage of this information is important for its success in making new drug discoveries. Henderson and Cockburn measure the extent of this capability through variables such as the firm's reliance on publication records in making promotion decisions, its proximity to major research universities, and

its involvement in joint research projects with major universities.

The second capability they focus on is skill at encouraging and maintaining flow of information across disciplinary boundaries inside the firm. Successful new drug discoveries require this type of integration. For example, the commercial development of HMG CoA reductase inhibitors (drugs that inhibit cholesterol synthesis in the liver) depended on path-breaking work at Merck on three disciplinary fronts: pharmacology, physiology, and biostatistics. Henderson and Cockburn measure this capability with variables such as the extent to which the research in the firm was coordinated through cross-disciplinary teams and giving one person authority to allocate resources for research. The team-based method would facilitate the flow of information across disciplines; the one-person approach would inhibit it.

Henderson and Cockburn's study indicates that differences in firms' capabilities explain much variability in firms' research productivity. For example, a firm that rewards research publications is about 40 percent more productive than one that does not. A firm that organizes by cross-disciplinary research teams is about 25 percent more productive than one that does not. Does this mean that a firm that switches to a team-based research organization will immediately increase its output of patents per dollar by 40 percent? Probably not. This and other measures Henderson and Cockburn used were proxies for deeper resource-creation or integrative capabilities. For example, a firm that rewards publications may have an advantage at recruiting the brightest scientists. A firm that organizes by teams may have a collegial atmosphere that encourages team-based organizations. A team-based organization inside a firm that lacks collegiality may generate far less research productivity. These observations go back to our earlier point. It is often far easier to identify distinctive capabilities once they exist than for management to create them.

Chapter 2 discussed the implication of point 1 for the horizontal and vertical boundaries of the firm. Points 2 and 3 have important implications for the sustainability of competitive advantages built on organizational capabilities and will be discussed more fully in Chapter 11.

STRATEGIC POSITIONING: COST ADVANTAGE AND BENEFIT ADVANTAGE

Generic Strategies

Competitive advantage cannot be reduced to a formula or an algorithm. Even if such formulas or algorithms could be concocted, describing them in a textbook such as this would make them valueless to firms because they would be accessible to everyone. Although there is no single formula for success, we can discern broad commonalities across industries in the different ways that firms position themselves to compete. For example, in sporting goods retailing, Sports Authority is a broad-based competitor, whereas Second Wind Fitness specializes in exercise equipment such as treadmills and weight benches. To take another example, Dell computer serves a wide array of customers, including business, government, and individual buyers, whereas Alienware specializes in high-end computers for hard-core gamers.

In the language of strategic management, Sports Authority and Dell on the one hand, and Second Wind Fitness and Alienware on the other, represent different types of *generic strategies*, a concept first introduced by Michael Porter.[18] A firm's generic strategy describes, in broad terms, how it positions itself to compete in the market it serves. Figure 9.8 illustrates Porter's generic strategies—benefit leadership, cost leadership, and focus—and briefly describes their economic logic.[19]

In the remainder of this chapter, we explore the economic logic of these generic strategies. We first consider the logic of positions based on cost leadership and benefit leadership. We then discuss the logic of focus strategies.

The Strategic Logic of Cost Leadership

A firm that follows a strategy of cost leadership creates more value (i.e., $B - C$) than its competitors by offering products that have a lower C than its rivals. This can happen in three qualitatively different ways. First, the cost leader can achieve *benefit parity* by making products with the same B but at a lower C than its rivals. The competitive advantage achieved by low-cost producers in commodity markets (e.g., Mittal Steel in the global steel industry) is an example of this. Second, the cost leader can achieve *benefit proximity*, which involves offering a B that is not much less than competitors. This could occur if the low-cost firm automates processes that are better performed by hand, hires fewer skilled workers, purchases less expensive components, or maintains lower standards of quality control. Yamaha's cost advantage over traditional piano producers, such as Steinway, is a good example of this. Finally, a cost leader may *offer a product that is qualitatively different from that of its rivals*. Firms can sometimes build a competitive advantage by redefining the product to yield substantial differences in benefits or costs relative to how the product is traditionally defined. For example, a formerly high-margin product may be redefined to allow for economies of scale in production and distribution while still providing benefits to consumers. The Timex watch and the 19-cent Bic crystal pen are well-known historical examples.

FIGURE 9.8
PORTER'S GENERIC STRATEGIES

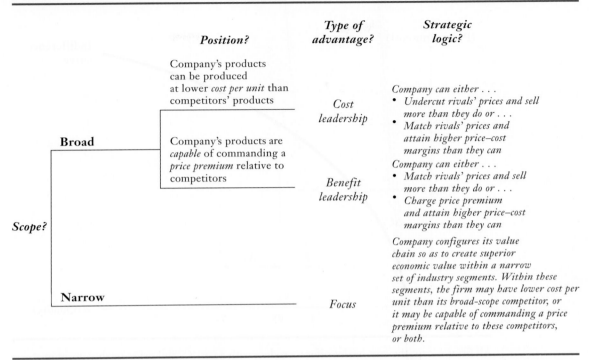

This figure depicts Michael Porter's generic strategies: benefit leadership, cost leadership, and focus. These strategies are distinguished by the breadth of a firm's product or customer scope and by whether the firm seeks competitive advantage by having the lowest costs in its industry or by offering products/services that deliver superior customer benefits.

Figure 9.9 illustrates the economic logic of cost leadership using a value map. For simplicity, let's consider an industry in which all firms except the cost leader offer a product with a cost C_E and price–quality position at point E. Through a combination of automation and cheaper components, suppose that the cost leader offers a product with a lower-quality level, q_F, but a substantially lower cost, C_F, resulting in a cost advantage of ΔC. Market shares in the industry will be stable when the cost leader and its higher-cost competitors attain consumer surplus parity. Consumer surplus parity is achieved when the cost leader operates at point F by charging a price P_F. From the figure, notice that $P_E - P_F < C_E - C_F$, or rearranging terms, $P_F - C_F > P_E - C_E$. Given consumer surplus parity between the cost leader and its higher-cost competitors, the cost leader achieves a higher profit margin. In essence, the leader's cost advantage gives it the ability to charge a price that is lower than that of its higher-cost, higher-quality rivals, while at the same time allowing it to "bank" some of its cost advantage in the form of a higher price–cost margin.

All firms except the cost leader offer a product with a cost C_E and price–quality position at point E. The cost leader offers a product with a lower-quality level, q_F, but a substantially lower cost, C_F, resulting in a cost advantage of ΔC. Consumer surplus

FIGURE 9.9

THE ECONOMIC LOGIC OF COST LEADERSHIP

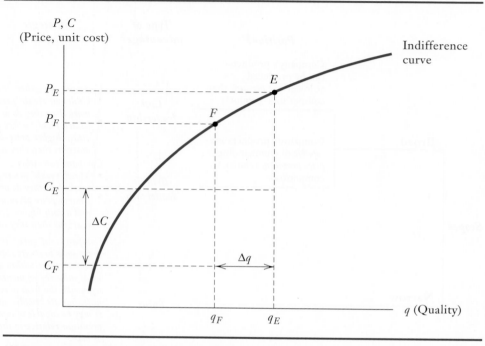

All firms except the cost leader offer a product with a cost C_E and price–quality position at point E. The cost leader offers a product with a lower-quality level, q_F, but a substantially lower cost, C_F, resulting in a cost advantage of ΔC. Consumer surplus parity is achieved when the cost leader operates at point F by charging a price P_F. At point F, $P_E - P_F < C_E - C_F$, or, rearranging terms, $P_F - C_F > P_E - C_E$. This tells us that despite its quality disadvantage, the cost leader achieves a higher profit margin than its higher-cost competitors.

parity is achieved when the cost leader operates at point F by charging a price P_F. At point F, $P_E - P_F < C_E - C_F$, or rearranging terms, $P_F - C_F > P_E - C_E$. This tells us that despite its quality disadvantage, the cost leader achieves a higher profit margin than its higher-cost competitors.

The Strategic Logic of Benefit Leadership

A firm that follows a strategy of benefit leadership creates more value (i.e., $B - C$) than its competitors by offering products that have a higher B than its rivals. This can happen in three qualitatively different ways. First, the benefit leader can achieve benefit parity by making products with the same C but at a higher B than its rivals. A good example is the Japanese automakers in the 1980s, whose family sedans (e.g., Honda Accord) were no more costly to produce than American-made models but offered superior performance and reliability. Second, the benefit leader might achieve cost proximity, which entails a C that is not too much higher than competitors. This characterizes the Japanese car makers today relative to their Korean competitors. Finally, a firm could offer substantially higher B and C, which arguably describes BMW's and Audi's compact sports sedans.

EXAMPLE 9.5 "HAUTE POT" CUISINE IN CHINA

"Hot pot" dining is very popular in China. A server brings a simmering metal pot of stock to the center of the table where it is placed over a heat source. While the hot pot is simmering, the server places the desired ingredients into the pot where they are cooked and served. For a long time, most Chinese consider hot pot restaurants to be a place where they could get a cheap meal. But low prices meant low-quality ingredients, shaky service, and a relatively uninviting ambience. All this changed in the 1990s when a small, private hot pot restaurant with only four tables opened in Sichuan province with a totally new idea about hot pot cuisine. Haidilao has since grown into one of China's top hot pot restaurants, noted for elevating the hot pot dining experience; it is almost possible to describe it as "haute pot."

Almost everything about Haidilao stands out from other hot pot chains. Although there is usually a wait for a table, the wait is orderly thanks to a video display of the wait list. While waiting, customers get free drinks and snacks and have access to computers with free Internet. Waiting customers can even get a free manicure and shoe shine! Once seated, everything needed to enjoy hot pot is close at hand: hot towels, aprons, hair bands for those with untied long hair, cleaning cloths for customers wearing glasses, even little plastic bags to wrap and protect cell phones that are placed next to the pot on the table. Hot pot ingredients are fresh and of high quality; the restaurants are clean. Servers offer to feed small children and even play with them in a separate recreational area. Customers finish the dinner with free and delicious desserts. Haidilao has also become the first restaurant that provides hot pot takeout. The takeout package includes a trash can, trash bags, and even the pot of stock, induction oven, and power strip that are needed for cooking at the table!

Yong Zhang, the president of Haidilao, takes pride in the customer service offered by his employees. The company has made a huge investment in training and retaining top staff. It also pays much better than other hot pot chains. While most workers of other restaurants can only afford living in a shabby basement, Haidilao's employees get nice apartments with air conditioning and Internet, free nanny services, and four free meals each day. The company also built a boarding school in its home city to assure managers a good education for their children. In exchange, employees are expected to work hard to maximize service. Performance evaluations are based on customer satisfaction rates, and a large portion of income is tied to bonuses and promotion.

Haidilao's stunningly good customer service has helped it deal with unexpected troubles. Customers are shocked by the passion and considerateness of Haidilao's staff and enjoy sharing their dining experience on the Internet. Here is a sampling of stories: "I had a little fight with my boyfriend during the dinner, and we soon got a bouquet and a hand-written card from Haidilao to wish us happy," "I complained a bit why there was no free ice cream as dessert, and three minutes later I got a free cone that the waitress ran to buy from the supermarket next door!" "We are served with a wrong dish, but at the end of the dinner, we get a huge pancake with 'we are sorry!'(Some customers wonder if Haidilao is responsible for posting some of these stories.)

Haidilao's strategy of benefit leadership has not translated into industry-leading profitability. Despite being one of the largest hot pot chains, the firm's profit margin is no better than the industry average. This is not surprising because much of Haidilao's strategy could be imitated by other firms. Even so, the company is opening 6 to 10 new branch restaurants every year, and some fans of the chain worry whether a bigger Haidilao can maintain the same level of care for every customer.

FIGURE 9.10
THE ECONOMIC LOGIC OF BENEFIT LEADERSHIP

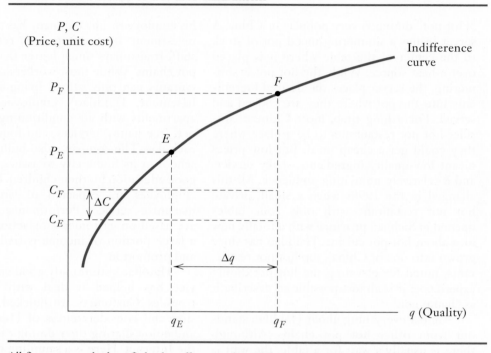

All firms except the benefit leader offer a product with a cost C_E and price–quality position at point E. The benefit leader offers a product with a higher-quality level, q_F, and in so doing, incurs a higher cost C_F, resulting in a cost disadvantage of ΔC. Consumer surplus parity is achieved when the cost leader operates at point F by charging a price P_F. At point F, $P_F - P_E > C_F - C_E$, or, rearranging terms, $P_F - C_F > P_E - C_E$. This tells us that despite its cost disadvantage, the benefit leader achieves a higher profit margin than its lower-benefit competitors.

Figure 9.10 illustrates the economic logic of benefit leadership using a value map. For simplicity, let's consider an industry in which all firms except the benefit leader offer a product with a cost C_E and price–quality position at point E. Suppose the benefit leader offers a product with a higher-quality level, q_F, and in so doing, incurs a somewhat higher cost C_F, resulting in a cost disadvantage of ΔC. Market shares in the industry will be stable when the benefit leader and its lower-quality competitors attain consumer surplus parity. Consumer surplus parity is achieved when the benefit leader operates at point F by charging a price P_F. From the figure, notice that $P_F - P_E > C_F - C_E$, or rearranging terms, $P_F - C_F > P_E - C_E$. Given consumer surplus parity between the benefit leader and its lower-quality competitors, the benefit leader achieves a higher profit margin. In essence, the leader's benefit advantage gives it the "wiggle room" to charge a price premium relative to its lower-benefit, lower-cost rivals without sacrificing market share.

Extracting Profits from Cost and Benefit Advantage

A firm that creates more value than its competitors would like to capture as much as possible of that value for itself in the form of profits. If consumers have identical preferences (i.e., the same value map applies to all consumers in the market), value extraction takes an especially stark form. When a firm increases its consumer surplus "bid" slightly above competitors, it captures the entire market. This leads to two clear recipes for retaining profits for a firm that creates more value than its competitors. Both involve making consumer surplus bids that the firm's rivals cannot match:

1. A cost leader that has benefit parity with its rivals can lower its price just below the unit cost of the firm with the next lowest unit cost. This makes it unprofitable for higher-cost competitors to respond with price cuts of their own and thus allows the firm to capture the entire market.

2. A benefit leader that has cost parity with its rivals can raise its price just below the sum of the following: (1) its unit cost, plus (2) the *additional benefit* ΔB creates relative to the competitor with the next highest B. To top this consumer surplus bid, a competitor would have to cut price below its unit cost, which would be unprofitable. At this price, then, the firm with the benefit advantage captures the entire market.

What happens if one firm is a cost leader and the other is a benefit leader? If consumers have identical preferences, then the firm that offers the higher $B - C$ can capture the entire market, by setting price at the point where the other firm cannot make a better consumer surplus bid and still cover its costs.

These extreme scenarios, in which one firm captures the entire market, result because consumers are assumed to have identical preferences. This would not happen in a market characterized by horizontal differentiation. As we discuss in Chapters 5 and 10, horizontal differentiation is likely to be strong when there are many product attributes that consumers weigh in assessing overall benefit B, and consumers disagree about the desirability of those attributes. In markets where there is horizontal differentiation, lowering price or boosting quality will attract some consumers, but others will not switch unless the differential in price or quality is large enough. In these markets, the price elasticity of demand an individual firm faces becomes a key determinant of a seller's ability to extract profits from its competitive advantage. Table 9.2 summarizes how the price elasticity of demand facing a firm influences the choice between two polar strategies for exploiting competitive advantage: a margin strategy and a share strategy.

Consider, first, a firm that has a cost advantage. When the firm's product has a low price elasticity of demand (i.e., when consumers are not very price-sensitive because of strong horizontal differentiation among competitors' products), even deep price cuts will not increase the firm's market share much. In this case, the optimal way for a firm to exploit its cost advantage is through a *margin strategy*: the firm maintains price parity with its competitors and profits from its cost advantage primarily through high price–cost margins rather than through higher market shares. By contrast, when the firm's product has a high price elasticity of demand (i.e., when consumers are price sensitive because horizontal differentiation is weak), modest price cuts can lead to significant increases in market share. In this case, the firm should exploit its cost advantage through a *share strategy*: the firm underprices its competitors to gain market share at their expense. In practice, the distinction between a margin strategy and a share strategy is one of degree and firms with cost advantages will often pursue mixed strategies: cutting price to gain share but also "banking" some of the cost advantage through higher margins.

Table 9.2 illustrates the notion that the logic governing the exploitation of a benefit advantage is analogous to that governing the exploitation of a cost advantage.

TABLE 9.2

EXPLOITING A COMPETITIVE ADVANTAGE THROUGH PRICING

		Type of Advantage	
		Cost Advantage (lower C than competitors)	Benefit Advantage (higher B than competitors)
Firm's Price Elasticity of Demand	**High price elasticity of demand** (weak horizontal differentiation)	• Modest *price cuts* gain lots of market share. • Exploit advantage through higher market share than competitors. • *Share strategy:* Underprice competitors to gain share.	• Modest *price hikes* lose lots of market share. • Exploit advantage through higher market share than competitors. • *Share strategy:* Maintain price parity with *competitors* (let benefit advantage drive share increases).
	Low price elasticity of demand (strong horizontal differentiation)	• Big *price cuts* gain little share. • Exploit advantage through higher profit margins. • *Margin strategy:* Maintain price parity with competitors (let lower costs drive higher margins).	• Big *price hikes* lose little share. • Exploit advantage through higher profit margins. • *Margin strategy:* Charge price premium relative to competitors.

When a firm has a benefit advantage in a market in which consumers are price sensitive, even a modest price hike could offset the firm's benefit advantage and nullify the increase in market share that the benefit advantage would otherwise lead to. In this case, the best way for the firm to exploit its benefit advantage is through a share strategy. A share strategy involves charging the same price as competitors and exploiting the firm's benefit advantage by capturing a higher market share than competitors. By contrast, when consumers are not price sensitive, large price hikes will not completely erode the market share gains that the firm's benefit advantage creates. The best way for the firm to exploit its benefit advantage is through a margin strategy: it charges a price premium relative to competitors (sacrificing some market share in the process), and it exploits its advantage mainly through higher profit margins.

The prospect of competitor reactions can alter the broad recommendations in Table 9.2. For instance, in markets with price-sensitive consumers, a share strategy of cutting price to exploit a cost advantage would be attractive if competitors' prices remained unchanged. However, it would probably be unattractive if the firm's competitors quickly matched the price cut because the net result will be lower margins with little or no net gain in the firm's market share. In this case, a margin strategy might well be a more attractive option.

Comparing Cost and Benefit Advantages

Under what circumstances is one source of advantage likely to be more profitable than the other? Though no definitive rules can be formulated, the underlying economics of the firm's product market and the current positions of firms in the industry can sometimes create conditions that are more hospitable to one kind of advantage versus another.

An advantage based on lower cost is likely to be more profitable than an advantage built on superior benefits when:

- The nature of the product limits opportunities for enhancing its perceived benefit B. This might be the case for commodity products, such as chemicals and paper. If so, then, more opportunities for creating additional value may come from lowering C rather than from increasing B. Still, we must bear in mind that the drivers of differentiation include far more than just the physical attributes of the product and that opportunities may exist for differentiation through better after-sale service, superior location, or more rapid delivery than competitors offer.

- Consumers are relatively price sensitive and will not pay much of a premium for enhanced product quality, performance, or image. This would occur when most consumers are much more price sensitive than quality sensitive. Graphically, this corresponds to the case in which consumer indifference curves are relatively flat, indicating that a consumer will not pay much more for enhanced quality. Opportunities for additional value creation are much more likely to arise through cost reductions than through benefit enhancements.

- The product is a search good. As detailed in Chapter 10, a *search good* is one whose objective quality attributes the typical buyer can assess prior to the point of purchase. Examples include commodity products as well as items such as stationery and office furniture. With search goods, the potential for differentiation lies largely in enhancing the product's observable features. But if buyers can discern among different offerings, so can competitors, which raises the risk that the enhancements will be imitated.

An advantage based on superior benefits is likely to be relatively more profitable than an advantage based on cost efficiency when:

- The typical consumer will pay a significant price premium for attributes that enhance B. This corresponds to the case in which the typical consumer's indifference curve is relatively steep. A firm that can differentiate its product by offering even a few additional features may command a significant price premium.

- Economies of scale or learning are significant, and firms are already exploiting them. In this case, opportunities for achieving a cost advantage over these larger firms are limited, and the best route toward value creation would be to offer a product that is especially well tailored to a particular niche of the market. Microbreweries, such as the Boston Beer Company, have attempted to build a competitive advantage in this way.

- The product is an experience good. An *experience good* is a product whose quality can be assessed only after the consumer has purchased it and used it for a while. Examples include automobiles, appliances, and consumer packaged goods. As we discuss in Chapter 10, consumers often judge experience goods on the basis of a firm's image, reputation, or credibility, which can be difficult for rivals to imitate or neutralize. In the early 2000s, Sony's strong reputation in consumer electronics helped it become a dominant player in the widescreen television market despite the fact that its LCD technology was inferior to the DLP technology offered by Samsung, a Korean firm with a weaker reputation at that time.

The points above should not be taken to imply that in any given industry there is one ideal strategic position toward which all firms should strive. More than anything else, a firm's ability to outperform its competitors arises from its ability to create and deliver a distinctive bundle of economic value. In markets in which consumers differ in their maximum willingness to pay or differ in how expensive it is for firms to access and serve them, a variety of powerful strategic positions can flourish at the same time. The U.S. mass-merchandising industry exhibits this point: Wal-Mart has thrived as the cost leader, while Target has successfully pursued a strategy of benefit leadership built on trendy merchandise and a bright, user-friendly shopping environment. In this and other industries, there is almost never one ideal strategic position.

"Stuck in the Middle"

Michael Porter coined the phrase *stuck in the middle* to describe a firm that pursues elements of cost leadership and benefit leadership at the same time and in the process achieves neither.[20] According to Porter, a firm that does not clearly choose between an emphasis on building a cost advantage or building a benefit advantage will typically be much less profitable than competitors that have clearly pursued a generic strategy of cost leadership or benefit leadership.

Firms end up stuck in the middle because they fail to make choices about how to compete, and as a result, their strategies lack clarity and coherence. Clear choices

---

EXAMPLE 9.6 STRATEGIC POSITIONING IN THE AIRLINE INDUSTRY: FOUR DECADES OF CHANGE

As we have discussed, the profitability of a firm's strategic position depends on underlying economic conditions. When these conditions change, a strategic position that, at one time, led to competitive advantage may no longer do so. The strategy followed by the "Big Three" U.S. airlines—American, United, and Delta— is an excellent illustration of this point.

For all the talk of upheaval in the airline industry, one remarkable fact is that all but one of the largest domestic carriers—American, Continental, United, USAir, Delta and Northwest— have been flying since the 1960s, either in their present incarnations or under an older name. (The one "new" carrier is Southwest Airlines.) Prior to deregulation of the airline industry in 1978, each of these trunk carriers was given a protected route corridor by the U.S. Civil Aeronautics Board (CAB). For example, United had protected transcontinental routes across the northern third of the nation, while American had protected routes across the southern east–west corridor. In exchange for obtaining

monopoly power over their routes, the airlines ceded pricing authority to the CAB.

The CAB kept prices very high, and while the airlines did engage in some forms of non-price competition on the routes served by more than one airline (most notably, competition over scheduling frequency and amenities), the airlines prospered under CAB regulation. The key threat to profitability came from powerful unions, which extracted handsome salary and work rule concessions in exchange for labor peace. This was not unusual—many protected monopolies "share the spoils" with strong unions. Even after deregulation, these costly labor agreements continued to bind, embedding costs into an airline's cost structure that were extremely difficult to reduce.

In a deregulated environment, an existing airline could no longer depend on protected monopoly status to assure profits. Carriers responded by adopting a strategy built around large hub-and-spoke systems. Delta had actually begun to build such a system with a hub in Atlanta prior to deregulation, while American and United quickly built systems based on multiple hub airports (Chicago and Dallas for American and Chicago and Denver for United).

Organizing a schedule around a hub-and-spoke system had clear advantages for a large airline. As described in Example 2.1, the hub-and-spoke model allowed a carrier to fill planes flying from feeder airports into a hub and refill them by flying from the hubs to destination cities. Full planes meant lower operating costs per revenue passenger mile, and protected incumbents from direct competition from new entrants (e.g., Peoples Express) with a point-to-point route structure. This advantage was especially strong in the battle for lucrative transcontinental traffic because point-to-point entrants typically lacked the jumbo jets required for nonstop transcontinental flights and did not have the hubs to facilitate one-stop flights.

Of course, hub-and-spoke operations involve significant trade-offs. A hub-and-spoke carrier requires a diverse fleet so that it can fly full airplanes over both short and long hauls between big and small cities. A diverse fleet means higher maintenance costs and less flexibility in utilizing airport gates. Flying through hubs also can result in lost baggage, delays that can cascade throughout the system, and missed connections. These disadvantages came on top of the already high labor costs that were a legacy of CAB regulation. Still, a large airline could shoulder these disadvantages as long as it kept its planes full. This was the strategic position of American, United, and Delta (and to a lesser extent, Continental, Northwest, and USAir as well). It made sense for a long time.

Southwest was the first airline to have great success using the point-to-point model. Owing to its legacy as an unregulated airline, Southwest enjoyed lower labor costs than the major carriers. With a fleet consisting entirely of Boeing 737s, it also enjoyed lower maintenance costs. It achieved consistent on-time performance by avoiding congested hub airports. And it carefully selected the markets it entered, restricting itself to city pairs that were underserved by the major carriers (thus avoiding destructive head-to-head competition with them), while at the same time having sufficient demand to fill its planes.

Over time, the advantages offered by the hub-and-spoke model over the point-to-point model have almost fully eroded, while the disadvantages continue to be significant. Simple population growth makes more city pairs large enough to support point-to-point flights. This takes money directly out of the big carriers' pockets and also makes it harder for them to keep flights full with traffic from the remaining spokes. "Fringe" airframe manufacturers Bombardier and Embraer have introduced small planes capable of nonstop transcontinental flight, removing yet another source of the major carriers' positioning advantage.

Given their inherent cost disadvantages, the hub-and-spoke carriers have learned that business as usual is not acceptable, and they have taken similar steps to respond to the changes that have undermined the economic power of their traditional competitive position. American, United, and Delta increasingly rely on international service, effectively exploiting the same benefits of hub-and-spoke operations that used to provide scale-based advantages in domestic service. In addition, they are working with their unions to eliminate cost and operational disadvantages. Even with all of these changes, the future of the major hub-and-spoke carriers in domestic air travel appears bleak. Every year, more and more passengers fly point to point via low-cost airlines built on the Southwest model. Unless one of the "points" is a hub, the hub-and-spoke carriers have no advantage serving that market.

Unable to secure competitive advantage, the major carriers are hoping to improve industry economics. Mergers and capacity reductions are contributing to steady fare increases. Increases in fuel costs have, for the moment, offset any resulting economic gains. But a smaller, less competitive marketplace may be just the ticket for this beleaguered industry.

about how to compete are critical because economically powerful strategic positions usually require trade-offs.[21] In the department store business, for example, shoppers at Neiman-Marcus expect fashionable, superior-quality merchandise, along with an upscale shopping experience. To satisfy this expectation, Neiman-Marcus must incur levels of merchandising, labor, and location rental costs that other department store retailers are not prepared to incur. At the other end of the spectrum, furniture retailer Ikea has made the conscious choice to sacrifice some elements of customer service (e.g., customers pick up, deliver, and assemble Ikea furniture themselves) in order to keep its costs low.

Despite Porter's admonition against being stuck in the middle, research suggests that firms can outperform their competitors even when pursuing both benefit leadership and cost leadership at the same time. For example, Danny Miller and Peter Friesen found that in consumer durables industries, firms that appeared to have achieved benefit advantages in their industries also tended to operate newer plants, had significantly better-than-average capacity utilization, and had direct costs per unit that were significantly lower than the industry average.[22] Firms that appeared to have achieved cost advantages also scored high on measures related to benefit superiority, such as product quality, and advertising and promotion expenses.

From a theoretical perspective, several factors might help firms to avoid the supposed trade-off between benefit and cost positions:

- A firm that offers high-quality products increases its market share, which then reduces average cost because of economies of scale or the experience curve. As a result, a firm might achieve both a high-quality and a low-cost position in the industry. Charles River Breeding Labs typified this situation in the 1970s with its germ-free technology for raising laboratory animals. The first to adopt germ-free barrier breeding technologies, Charles River Breeders became the quality leader, moved down the experience curve, and established a superior cost position relative to its nearest competitors.

- The rate at which accumulated experience reduces costs is often greater for higher-quality products than for lower-quality products. The reason is that production workers must exercise more care to produce a higher-quality product, which often leads to the discovery of bugs and defects that might be overlooked in a lower-quality product.

- Inefficiencies muddy the relationship between cost position and benefit position. The argument that high quality is correlated with high costs ignores the possibility that firms may be producing inefficiently—that is, that their C is higher than it needs to be given their B. If so, then at any point in time, in most industries one might observe firms that create less B and have higher C than their more efficient counterparts.

Despite these reservations, Porter's admonition to avoid being stuck in the middle is extremely important. It reminds us that trade-offs are fundamental in business decisions and that firms can rarely be excellent at everything. A belief that excellence can be attained on all dimensions can often lead to unfocused decision making and the pursuit of inconsistent actions that either have a limited impact in terms of lowering C or increasing B or cancel each other out entirely. It can also lead to uninspired imitation of rival firms' "best practices." Such a posture, at best, leads to competitive parity and, at worst, intensifies competition among a group of firms that end up looking alike. Kmart is a telling example of these points. Over the past two decades, Kmart has careened back and forth, at some points seeking to emulate Target's fashionability and trendiness (e.g., offering the Martha Stewart line on some merchandise), while at other points seeking to compete on price with Wal-Mart (e.g., its move to Every Day Low Pricing in 2001). But over no prolonged period of time has Kmart sustained a deep, consistent focus on achieving *either* superior customer benefits or superior cost efficiency relative to its key competitors. As a result, Kmart has attained neither.

DIAGNOSING COST AND BENEFIT DRIVERS

Cost and consumer benefits drive value creation. Understanding how a firm creates value and why it creates more or less value than its competitors often requires a diagnosis of cost and benefit drivers.

Cost Drivers

Cost drivers explain why average costs vary across firms. We can classify cost drivers into three broad categories, each of which has several subcategories:

- Cost drivers related to firm size, scope, and cumulative experience
- Cost drivers independent of firm size, scope, or cumulative experience
- Cost drivers related to organization of the transactions

Cost Drivers Related to Firm Size, Scope, and Cumulative Experience

Chapter 2 contains an extensive discussion of economies of scale, scope, and cumulative experience, so here we will just review the key ideas. A paramount source of economies of scale and scope is indivisible inputs. Indivisible inputs cannot be scaled down below a certain minimum size and thus give rise to fixed costs. As the volume or variety of output increases, these fixed costs get spread out, leading to lower per-unit costs of production. In the short run, fixed costs are often spread because of greater capacity utilization. In the long run, fixed costs are spread when it becomes economical for a firm to substitute a technology with high fixed costs but low variable costs for one with low fixed costs but high variable costs. Other important sources of economies of scale are: (1) the physical properties of processing units (i.e., the cube-square rule); (2) increases in the productivity of variable inputs as volume increases (e.g., because of greater specialization of labor); and (3) economies of inventory management. Cumulative experience can reduce average costs as firms move down the learning curve.

Cost Drivers Independent of Firm Size, Scope, or Cumulative Experience

These factors make one firm's unit costs different from a competitor's even if their sizes and cumulative experience are the same. An important cost driver independent of scale is input prices (e.g., wage rates, energy prices, and prices of components and raw materials). When firms in the same industry purchase their inputs in national markets, their input prices will be the same. But firms in the same industry often pay different prices for inputs. Differences in wage rates may be due to differences in the degree of unionization. Differences in wages, the price of energy, or the price of delivered materials can also be attributed to location differences among firms.

Economies of density refer to cost savings that arise with greater geographic density of customers. Economies of density can arise when a transportation network within a given geographic territory is utilized more intensively (e.g., when an airline's unit costs decline as more passengers are flown over a given route). They also arise when a geographically smaller territory generates the same volume of business as a geographically larger territory (e.g., when a beer distributor that operates in a densely populated urban area has lower unit costs than a distributor selling the same amount of beer in more sparsely populated suburbs). In both cases, the cost savings are due to an increase in density (e.g., passengers per mile, customers per square mile) rather than an increase in scope (e.g., number of routes served) or scale (e.g., volume of beer sold).

One firm may achieve lower average costs than its competitors because its production environment is less complex or more focused. A firm that uses the same factory to produce many different products may incur large costs associated with changing over machines and production lines to produce batches of the different products. It may also incur high administrative costs to track different work orders.

A firm may have lower average costs than its rivals because it has been able to realize production process efficiencies that its rivals have not achieved; that is, the firm uses fewer inputs than its competitors to produce a given amount of output, or its production technology uses lower-priced inputs than those utilized by rivals. This effect is often difficult to disentangle from the learning curve because the achievement of process efficiencies through learning-by-doing is at the heart of the learning curve.

One firm may also have lower average costs than its competitors because it avoids expenses that its rivals are incurring, such as advertising and sales expenses. These savings may translate into fewer customers, however.

Finally, a firm may have lower average costs than those of its rivals because of the effects of government policies. For obvious reasons, this factor affects international markets. For example, Japanese truck producers have long been at a disadvantage in selling trucks in the United States because of the steep import duty the U.S. government levies on foreign trucks.

Cost Drivers Related to Organization of the Transactions

Chapters 3 and 4 discussed how the vertical chain can influence production costs. Vertically integrated firms often have agency costs relative to firms that organize exchange through the market. An integrated firm's internal administrative systems, organizational structure, or compensation system may affect agency costs. For transactions in which the threat of holdup is significant, in which private information can be leaked, or coordination is complicated, a market firm may have higher administrative and production expenses than an integrated firm.

Agency costs often increase as the firm expands and gains more activities to coordinate internally or grows more diverse and thus creates greater conflicts in achieving coordination. The firm's agency efficiency relative to that of other firms can also deteriorate as its competitors adopt new and innovative internal organizations that solve the same coordination problems at lower cost.

Benefit Drivers

A firm creates a benefit advantage by offering a product that delivers larger perceived benefits to prospective buyers than competitors' products, that is, by offering a higher B. The perceived benefit, in turn, depends on the attributes that consumers value, as well as on those that lower the user and the transactions costs of the product. These attributes, or what we call benefit drivers, form the basis on which a firm can differentiate itself. Benefit drivers can include many things, and analyzing them in any particular case involves identifying who the firm's prospective buyers are, understanding how they might use the firm's product or service, and discovering which of their needs the firm's product satisfies.

Benefit drivers can be classified along five dimensions:

1. *Physical Characteristics of the Product Itself.* These drivers include factors such as product performance, quality, features, aesthetics, durability, and ease of installation and operation.
2. *The Quantity and Characteristics of the Services or Complementary Goods the Firm or Its Dealers Offer for Sale.* Key drivers here include postsale services, such as customer training or consulting, complementary products (e.g., spare parts) that the seller bundles with the product, product warranties or maintenance contracts, and the quality of repair or service capabilities.
3. *Characteristics Associated with the Sale or Delivery of the Good.* Specific benefit drivers include speed and timeliness of delivery, availability and favorability of credit terms, location of the seller, and the quality of presale technical advice.
4. *Characteristics That Shape Consumers' Perceptions or Expectations of the Product's Performance or Its Cost to Use.* Specific drivers include the product's reputation for performance, the seller's perceived staying power or financial stability (this would be important for industrial transactions in which the buyer anticipates an ongoing relationship with the seller), and the product's installed base (i.e., the number of consumers currently using the product; a large installed base would lead us to expect the costs of developing product know-how to be low).
5. *The Subjective Image of the Product.* Image is a convenient way of referring to the constellation of psychological rewards that the consumer receives from purchasing, owning, and consuming the product. Image is driven by the impact of advertising messages, packaging, or labeling, and by the prestige of the distributors or outlets that carry the products.

Methods for Estimating and Characterizing Costs and Perceived Benefits

Estimating Costs

Most firms invest considerable energy in measuring their own costs. Modern accounting tools such as activity-based costing (ABC) lend considerable precision to such calculations. Some firms are able to get good accounting data on their rivals; this is common in regulated markets like hospitals. In the absence of accounting data, firms can use *activity cost analysis* to make reasonably educated guesses about a firm's cost position *vis à vis* the competition.[23] When possible, activity cost analysis applies precise cost accounting data to each step in the vertical chain of production for all competing firms. Such detailed competitive intelligence is rarely available. More often, the analyst must rely on economics, rather than accounting, to compare costs across firms.

The economic approach to cost comparisons begins by identifying the key *cost drivers* in production. Cost drivers include obvious factors such as local labor market conditions and taxes, as well as subtle factors such as worker productivity and costs of regulatory compliance. We identified many other cost drivers in the previous chapter, when we discussed opportunities for achieving cost advantage.

The next step is to weigh how each competitor stacks up on each cost driver. Who pays the highest wages? Whose workers are most productive? Whether by crunching some data or relying on third-party research, it is sometimes possible to make fairly

TABLE 9.3
COST COMPARISON SCORECARD

Cost Driver	Importance (1 = high; 5 = low)	Firm's relative position (1 = most preferred position; 5 = least preferred position)	Cost Driver "Score" (Multiply columns 2 and 3)
Economies of scale			
Economies of scope			
Learning economies			
Capacity utilization			
Wages			
Labor efficiency (FTE per unit output)			
Materials purchasing costs			
Materials efficiency			
Others (specific to industry in question)			
			Overall Position =

precise estimates of the resulting cost differentials. For example, consider that labor costs account for about half of all hospital costs. If a particular hospital faces a soft local labor market and is able to pay 10 percent lower wages than hospitals in other communities, this will give it a 5 percent cost advantage. (Just multiply the wage difference by the share of total costs: $0.10 \times 0.50 = 0.05$.) Similar calculations can be performed for other cost drivers.

When it is not possible to make precise estimates of cost differences, one must rely on more qualitative approaches. Though less rigorous, they may still point to important cost differences across firms. Here are the steps:

1. List the industry's cost drivers. Table 9.3 provides a generic list. The last row is labeled "others," acknowledging that specific cost drivers will vary by firm and industry.
2. Rate the cost drivers on a 5-point scale according to their relative importance to total costs.[24] For example, if materials costs are a very small portion of total costs, then this should receive a rating of 1 (low importance). Fill the column in Table 9.3 labeled "Importance."
3. Rate each firm's relative position on each cost driver, again using a 5-point scale. A rating of 1 indicates that the firm has a preferred position (relatively low cost). Fill in the next column of Table 9.3.
4. Multiply the importance rating (column 1) by the relative position rating (column 2) and plug this cost driver "score" into the last column.
5. The firm's overall position is the sum of its cost driver scores.

Estimating Benefits

A product's perceived benefit is more difficult to estimate. Any approach to estimating and characterizing benefits has four components. First, the firm must measure the benefits provided to the consumer. Second, it must identify the relevant benefit drivers. Third, it must estimate the magnitude of the benefit. Fourth, it must identify the willingness of consumers to trade off one driver for another. A full analysis of the techniques for estimating benefits falls within the domain of demand estimation in economics and marketing research. Some of the most important techniques are discussed in the Appendix to this chapter.

STRATEGIC POSITIONING: BROAD COVERAGE VERSUS FOCUS STRATEGIES

The pursuit of cost leadership or benefit leadership relates to the broad issue of *how* the firm will create economic value. A second key positioning issue is *where* the firm will seek to create value. In particular, will a firm seek to create value across a broad scope of market segments, or will it focus on a narrow set of segments?

Segmenting an Industry

Nearly every industry can be broken down into smaller pieces known as segments. Figure 9.11 illustrates what Michael Porter terms an *industry segmentation matrix*. The industry segmentation matrix shows that any industry can be characterized by two

FIGURE 9.11
INDUSTRY SEGMENTATION MATRIX

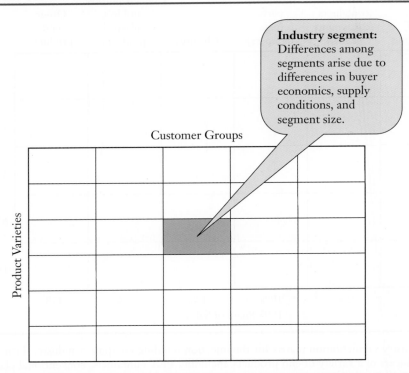

An industry segmentation matrix characterizes the industry along two dimensions: the variety of products that industry participants offer for sale and the different types of buyers that purchase those products.

Source: This figure is adapted from Hall, W. K., "Survival Strategies in a Hostile Environment." *Harvard Business Review*, September–October 1980, pp. 75–85.

dimensions: the varieties of products offered by firms that compete in the industry and the different types of customers that purchase those products. Each point of intersection between a particular buyer group and a particular product variety represents a potential segment. Differences among segments arise because of differences in customer economics (e.g., differences in willingness-to-pay or differences in willingness to trade off quality for price), supply conditions (e.g., costs of producing different product varieties), and segment size. Figure 9.12 shows an industry segmentation matrix for the injection molding equipment industry. This is the industry that makes the machines, molds, and ancillary equipment that are needed to produce molded plastic products such as polyethylene tetraphthalate (PET) containers.[25]

As a result of differences in customer economics, supply conditions, and size within a given industry, the structural attractiveness of segments—as characterized by a segment-level five-forces analysis—can differ greatly across segments. For example,

FIGURE 9.12

INDUSTRY SEGMENTATION MATRIX FOR THE INJECTION MOLDING EQUIPMENT INDUSTRY

Product Varieties	PET packaging	Conventional plastic food containers (e.g., yogurt cups)	Automobile parts (e.g., bumpers)	Closures	General-purpose molded plastic products	Other end products	1995 Share of Sales
Machines							25%
Hot runners							3%
Robotics							3%
Molds							67%
Value-added services							1%
1995 Share of Sales	4%	2%	19%	1%	57%	17%	

Customer Groups
Producers of . . .

The figure shows an industry segmentation matrix for the injection molding equipment industry. Firms in this industry sell to producers of a variety of end products, including PET containers, conventional plastic containers, and automobile parts. Industry participants manufacture a variety of different products including machines and molds. Some firms also offer value-added services related to the design of manufacturing facilities in which the equipment will be deployed.

Source: The data in this figure are drawn from "Husky Injection Molding Systems," Harvard Business School, Case 9-799-157.

in the steel fabrication industry, the fabrication of structural steel members (the cutting and welding of girders, beams, and so forth for use in construction projects) is a relatively unattractive segment since barriers to entry are relatively low. By contrast, the fabrication of metal plate products (e.g., the cutting and bending of steel pieces that are used to construct vats and tanks) has traditionally been more attractive because engineering know-how and product quality are important differentiators of firm success.

Broad Coverage Strategies

A broad coverage strategy seeks to serve all customer groups in the market by offering a full line of related products. For example, Gillette offers a full line of shaving products, including razors, shaving cream, and after-shave lotions. Frito-Lay also follows a broad coverage strategy, offering a full line of high-calorie and "light" snacks as well as condiments. Mexican retailer Controladora Comercial Mexicana (CCM) pursues a different kind of broad coverage strategy, with stores ranging in size from small bodegas (similar to American 7-11 stores) to hypermarts that rival the largest Wal-Mart stores. The economic logic behind a broad coverage strategy is the existence of economies of scope across product classes. These economies of scope might come from common production facilities or components, shared distribution channels, or marketing.

Focus Strategies

A firm with a focus strategy either offers a narrow set of product varieties or serves a narrow set of customers, or does both. Figure 9.13 uses industry segmentation matrices to illustrate a number of common focus strategies.

This figure illustrates three common focus strategies: customer specialization, product specialization, and geographic specialization. Under customer specialization, the firm offers an array of related products to a limited class of customers. Under product specialization, the firm produces a limited set of product varieties for a potentially wide class of customers. Under geographic specialization, the firm offers a variety of related products within a narrowly defined geographic market.

A firm that practices *customer specialization* offers an array of related products to a limited class of customers. An example would be a firm that produces and sells industrial process control systems and related devices, such as valves, flowmeters, and recording instruments, to a particular class of buyers such as petroleum refiners. The ability of a customer-specialized focuser to create extra economic value relative to a broad-coverage competitor rests on the extent to which broad-coverage competitors underserve or overserve the focuser's target customer group. For example, Microsoft's word processing software (Word) underserves the needs of authors who prepare technical manuscripts that include lots of mathematical symbols and expressions. These underserved customers created an opportunity for a focused software competitor, TCI Software Research, to offer a word processing product (Scientific Word) that is tailored to the needs of academic researchers who write technical manuscripts. In contrast, airlines such as United and American overserve leisure travelers who do not highly value frequent-flier programs, airport lounges, and other perks offered to business travelers. These perks drive up costs, allowing carriers like Southwest and JetBlue to target leisure travelers.

FIGURE 9.13
COMMON FOCUS STRATEGIES

Customer Specialization Focus

- Offer an array of product varieties to a limited class of customers.
- Cater to the particular needs of the customer group served.

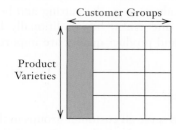

- **Examples:**
  - Enterprise in the rental car market
  - Neiman Marcus in apparel retailing

- **Product Specialization Focus**

  - Offer a limited set of products to an array of different customer groups.
  - Do an especially good job satisfying a subset of the needs of the customer groups being served.

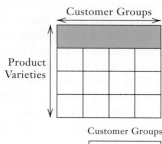

- **Examples:**
  - ZS in the management consulting industry
  - Boston Beer Company and other similar microbrewers

- **Geographic Specialization Focus**

  - Offer a variety of products and/or sell to a variety of customer groups within a narrow geography.

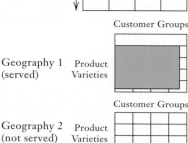

Geography 1 (served)

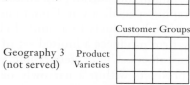

Geography 2 (not served)

Geography 3 (not served)

- **Examples:**
  - Pittsburgh Brewing Company
  - JetBlue in the airline industry

This figure illustrates three common focus strategies: customer specialization, product specialization, and geographic specialization. Under customer specialization, the firm offers an array of related products to a limited class of customers. Under product specialization, the firm produces a limited set of product varieties for a potentially wide class of customers. Under geographic specialization, the firm offers a variety of related products within a narrowly defined geographic market.

A second common basis of a focus strategy is *product specialization*. Here the firm produces a limited set of product varieties for a potentially wide set of customer groups. The specializer's goal is to do an especially good job satisfying a *subset* of the needs of the customer groups to whom it sells. A good example of a company with this sort of focus is the consulting firm ZS Associates. ZS serves an array of clients in a variety of different industries; however, its consulting work focuses primarily on sales force and marketing-related issues. This contrasts with the broad-based management consultancies with whom ZS competes (e.g., McKinsey and BCG), which consult on a broad range of operational and strategic issues faced by firms. The economic logic of product specialization focus rests on the ability of the focuser to exploit economies of scale or learning economies within the service or the product in which the focuser specializes.

A third common basis of a focus strategy is *geographic specialization*. Here the firm offers a variety of related products within a narrowly defined geographic market. Breweries such as Pittsburgh Brewing Company (brewer of Iron City beer) and Heileman's (brewer of Chicago favorite Old Style) rely on strong local brands, enhanced through promotional activities linked to local sports teams, to offset the economies of scale of national marketing enjoyed by Anheuser-Busch.

In addition to exploiting economies of scale or better serving underserved or overserved customers, focus strategies have another significant potential advantage: they can insulate the focusing firm from competition. In some segments, customer demand may only be large enough to allow just one or two firms to operate profitably. This implies that a firm may be far more profitable as a focused seller in a low-demand segment than as one of several competitors in high-demand segments. For example, Kubota has dominated the Japanese agricultural machinery market by producing lightweight, compact tractors that are especially well suited to small Japanese farms. Because that market is limited, Kubota faces little competition from U.S. giants such as Deere & Company, Case, and Caterpillar.

Chapter Summary

- A firm achieves a competitive advantage if it can earn higher rates of profitability than rival firms. A firm's profitability depends jointly on industry conditions and the amount of value the firm can create relative to its rivals.

- Consumer surplus is the difference between the perceived benefit B of a product and its monetary price P. A consumer will purchase a product only if its consumer surplus is positive. A consumer will purchase the product from a particular seller only if that seller offers a higher consumer surplus than rival sellers offer.

- A value map illustrates the competitive implications of consumer surplus. An indifference curve shows the price–quality combinations that yield the same level of consumer surplus.

- Value-created is the difference between the perceived benefit B and the unit cost C of the product. Equivalently, it is equal to the sum of consumer surplus and economic profit.

- To achieve a competitive advantage, a firm must create not only positive value, but also more value than rival firms. If it does so, it can outcompete other firms by offering a higher consumer surplus than rivals.

- The bases of competitive advantage are superior resources and organizational capabilities. Resources are firm-specific assets that other firms cannot easily acquire. Organizational capabilities refer to clusters of activities that the firm does especially well compared to rivals.

- There are three generic strategies: cost leadership, benefit leadership, and focus.

- A firm that follows a strategy of cost leadership seeks to achieve a cost advantage over rival firms by offering a product with a lower C for the same, or perhaps lower, B.

- A firm that follows a strategy of benefit leadership seeks to achieve a benefit advantage over rivals by offering products with a higher B for the same, or perhaps higher C.

- Building a competitive advantage based on superior cost position is likely to be attractive when there are unexploited opportunities for achieving scale, scope, or learning economies; the product's nature limits opportunities for enhancing its perceived benefit; consumers are relatively price sensitive and are unwilling to pay a premium for enhanced quality or performance; and the product is a search good rather than an experience good.

- Building a competitive advantage based on a superior benefit position is likely to be attractive when the typical consumer is willing to pay a significant price premium for attributes that enhance B; existing firms are already exploiting significant economies of scale or learning; and the product is an experience good rather than a search good.

- A firm is "stuck in the middle" when it pursues elements of a cost leadership strategy and a benefit leadership strategy at the same time, and in the process, fails to achieve either a cost advantage or a benefit advantage.

- Under a broad-coverage strategy, a firm offers a full line of related products to most or all customer groups in the market. Under a focus strategy, a firm either offers a narrow set of product varieties or serves a narrow set of customers, or does both.

- Focus strategies can often insulate a firm from competition. If the focuser's industry segment is small, it may face little competition and earn substantial returns.

QUESTIONS

1. A firm can outperform its rivals through cost leadership or benefit leadership, but not through price leadership. Explain.

2. This chapter describes the importance of $B - C$ in a competitive industry. Is $B - C$ equally important in other market structures?

3. How do economies of scale affect positioning?

4. How can the value chain help a firm identify its strategic position?

5. Two firms, Alpha and Beta, are competing in a market in which consumer preferences are identical. Alpha offers a product whose benefit B is equal to $75 per unit. Alpha's average cost C is equal to $60 per unit, while Beta's average cost is equal to $50 per unit.

   (a) Which firm's product provides the greatest value-created?
   (b) In an industry equilibrium in which the firms achieve consumer surplus parity, by what dollar amount will the profit margin, $P - C$, of the firm that creates the greatest amount of value exceed the profit margin of the firm that creates the smaller amount of value? Compare this amount to the difference between the value-created of each firm. What explains the relationship between the difference in profit margins and the difference in value-created between the two firms?

6. The following table summarizes information about U.S. pancake syrup products:

Brand	Average Consumer Willingness to Pay (Cents/Ounce)	Price (Cents/Ounce)	Average Costs (Cents/Ounce)
Hungry Jack	20	15	14
Aunt Jemima	21	19	17
Log Cabin	28	24	20
Mrs. Buttersworth	21	18	14

Assume the following apply to the time period relevant for the question:

- Demand remains stable.
- No new firms enter and no new products are introduced.
- No changes in advertising are made.
- Firms have constant returns to scale and input prices are constant.

(a) Given current prices, which brand do you expect to gain share in the next few months?

(b) Which brand can earn the highest profits in the longer run (assuming prices can be changed)?

7. Consider a market in which consumer indifference curves are relatively steep. Firms in the industry are pursuing two positioning strategies: some firms are producing a "basic" product that provides satisfactory performance; others are producing an enhanced product that provides performance superior to that of the basic product. Consumer surplus parity currently exists in the industry. Are the prices of the basic and the enhanced product likely to be significantly different or about the same? Why? How would the answer change if consumer indifference curves were relatively flat?

8. In the value-creation model presented in this chapter, it is implicitly assumed that all consumers get the identical value (e.g., identical B) from a given product. Do the main conclusions in this chapter change if consumer tastes differ, so that some get more value than others?

9. Identify one or more experience goods. Identify one or more search goods. How does the retailing of experience goods differ from the retailing of search goods? Do these differences help consumers?

10. Identify successful firms that offer good but not outstanding products at reasonable but not especially low prices. Do these firms disprove Porter's ideas about being "stuck in the middle?"

11. Recall from Chapter 2 Adam Smith's dictum, "The division of labor is limited by the extent of the market." How does market growth affect the viability of a focus (i.e., niche) strategy?

12. "Niche strategies are generally more profitable than "mass-market" strategies because they usually imply weaker price competition." Comment.

13. "Firms that seek a cost advantage should adopt a learning curve strategy; firms that seek to differentiate their products should not." Comment on both of these statements.

14. Suppose that two firms compete in a market where consumers have identical preferences. The benefits and costs of the two firms are B_1, C_1 and B_2, C_2, respectively, where $B_1 - C_1 > B_2 - C_2$. What price should firm 1 set so that it can capture the entire market and maximize profits?

15. Consumers often identify brand names with quality. Do you think branded products usually are of higher quality than generic products and therefore justify their higher prices? If so, why don't all generic product makers invest to establish a brand identity, thereby enabling them to raise price?

APPENDIX: METHODS FOR MEASURING A FIRM'S BENEFIT POSITION

Four approaches might be used to estimate a firm's benefit position relative to its competitors and the importance of benefit drivers. These methods require advanced statistical techniques, so we will only provide a brief description of each.

1. Reservation price method
2. Attribute-rating method
3. Hedonic pricing analysis
4. Conjoint analysis

RESERVATION PRICE METHOD

Because a consumer purchases a product if and only if $B - P > 0$, it follows that the perceived benefit B represents a consumer's reservation price—the maximum monetary price the consumer will pay for a unit of the product or service. One approach to estimating B, then, is simply to ask consumers the highest price they would pay. Marketing survey research that precedes the introduction of new products often includes such a question.

ATTRIBUTE-RATING METHOD

Attribute rating is a technique for estimating benefit drivers directly from survey responses and then calculating overall benefits on the basis of attribute scores. Target consumers are asked to rate products in terms of attributes. For example, for each attribute consumers might be given a fixed number of points to allocate among each product. Each attribute is then assigned an "importance weight," and relative perceived benefits are determined by calculating the weighted average of the product ratings. Weighted scores can be divided by costs to construct "B/C ratios." Recall that a firm's strategic position is determined by the amount of $B - C$ it generates versus its competitors. As long as products have cost and/or benefit proximity, the ranking of B/C ratios across firms will be similar (though not necessarily equal) to the rankings of $B - C$ differences. Thus, products with high B/C ratios will generally enjoy a superior strategic position to their lower B/C rivals.

HEDONIC PRICING ANALYSIS

Hedonic pricing uses data about actual consumer purchases to determine the value of particular product attributes. (The term *hedonic* comes from *hedonism* and is meant to convey the idea that the pleasure or happiness a consumer derives from a good depends on the attributes that the good embodies.) For example, consumers purchase automobiles according to a variety of attributes, including horsepower, interior room, and braking capabilities. By examining how automobile prices vary with different combinations of attributes, analysts can determine how much consumers are willing to pay for each individual attribute. Hedonic pricing has been used to identify the value of innovations in automobiles and computerized axial tomography, the value of spreadsheet compatibility, and the benefits of improving job safety.

Hedonic pricing requires multiple regression analysis to estimate the impact of product attributes on a product's price. The dependent variable in the regression is the product's price. The predictors are variables measuring the presence and extent of different product attributes. If you were studying the automobile market, hedonic pricing analysis could identify the extent to which a 1 percent increase in horsepower or chassis length, or the addition of side-impact air bags, translates into automobile prices. This analysis generates implicit "hedonic prices" for individual product attributes.

CONJOINT ANALYSIS

Hedonic pricing analysis uses market prices for existing combinations of product attributes. This is inadequate for studying the value of new features. To do this, market researchers use conjoint analysis. Like hedonic pricing, conjoint analysis estimates the relative benefits of different product attributes. Its principal value is in estimating these benefits for hypothetical combinations of attributes. Although conjoint analysis can take several different forms, consumers are usually asked to rank a product with different features at different prices. Researchers then use regression analysis to estimate the impact of price and product features on the rankings. From this, researchers can estimate the market value of different features.

Alternatively, consumers may be asked to state how much they are willing to pay for different combinations of features. Researchers then treat the responses as if they were actual market prices and use regression techniques to estimate the value of each attribute. This approach closely mirrors hedonic pricing, except that the prices and products are hypothetical.

ENDNOTES

[1]Source: Bureau of Transportation Statistics, U.S. Department of Transportation. Airline Financial Data and Airline Traffic Data. http://www.transtats.bts.gov/Data_Elements.aspx?Data=6, accessed July 21, 2011.

[2]The data for this example comes from "Sports and Suds: The Beer Business and the Sports World Have Brewed Up a Potent Partnership," *Sports Illustrated*, August 8, 1988, pp. 68–82.

[3]For interested readers, here is how this number was derived. Total (as opposed to per-unit) consumer surplus can be shown to equal the area under the demand curve above the price. For a linear demand curve given by the formula $P = a - bQ$ (where Q is total demand), this area is given by $0.5bQ^2$. Consumer surplus per unit is thus given by $0.5bQ^2 \div Q = 0.5bQ = 0.5P(bQ/P)$. But the term in parentheses is the reciprocal of the price elasticity of demand (i.e., $\eta = P/bQ$). Thus, per-unit consumer surplus is given by $0.5P/\eta$. To estimate η, we proceed as follows. The stadium concessionaire, Cincinnati Sports Service, pays the distributor $0.20 per 20-ounce cup of beer, pays royalties to the city of Cincinnati of $0.24 per cup, pays royalties to the Cincinnati Reds of $0.54 per cup, and an excise tax of $0.14 per cup. The concessionaire's marginal cost is thus at least $1.12 per cup of beer. If we assume that $2.50 is the profit-maximizing monopoly price, then the price elasticity of demand η at $2.50 must be at least 1.8 (we'll see why in just a moment). Using the preceding formula for per-unit consumer surplus, we conclude that the average consumer surplus for a 20-ounce cup of beer is no greater than $0.69. The reason that the price elasticity of demand must be at least 1.8 is as follows: from the Economics Primer, the optimal monopoly price is given by $(P - MC)/P = 1/\eta$. Thus, if $2.50 is the monopoly price, $(2.50 - MC)/2.50 = 1/\eta$. Since $MC = \$1.12$, straightforward algebra implies $\eta = 1.8$.

[4]Without knowing the production costs of Sports Service or the distributor, we cannot pin down the actual amount of value that is created through the vertical chain. Whatever it is, however, the brewer captures only a small portion of it.

[5]Here is a proof. Suppose firm 1 creates more value than firm 2, so that $B_1 - C_1 > B_2 - C_2$. The most aggressive bid firm 2 can offer is $P1^* = C2$, leaving you with consumer surplus of $B_2 - C_2$. Firm 1 can offer you a slightly more favorable bid than this by offering a price slightly lower than $P1^* = C2 + (B1 - B2)$. At this price, firm 1's profit is slightly less than $P1^* - C1$ which equals $C_2 + (B_1 - B_2) - C_1$. After rearranging terms, we can write this as $(B_1 - C_1) - (B_2 - C_2)$, which is positive. Thus, firm 1 can always profitably outbid firm 2 for your business.

[6]Rumelt, R., "The Evaluation of Business Strategy," in Glueck, W. F., *Business Policy and Strategic Management*, 3rd ed., New York, McGraw-Hill, 1980.

[7]The source for this quote and other information in the story is "Mad money dominates the world soccer scene," by Grahame L. Jones, the LA Times, June 17, 2009. Accessed on June 28, 2009 at http://www.latimes.com/sports/la-sp-soccer-commentary17-2009jun17,0,3882912.story

[8]The concept of the value chain was developed by Michael Porter. See Chapter 2 of *Competitive Advantage*, New York, Free Press, 1985.

[9]The term *Airport 7* was coined by Andrew Taylor, the current CEO of Enterprise, to describe the seven airport-based rental car firms. Actually, three pairs of the "Airport 7" operate under common ownership: Vanguard Rental owns both National and Alamo; Cendant Corporation owns both Avis and Budget; and Dollar Thrifty Automotive Group owns both Dollar and Thrifty.

[10]This example was developed by Jesus Syjuco and Li Liu, Kellogg School of Management, MBA class of 2002.

[11]"Bloomberg Business Week 100 Best Global Brands," http://www.businessweek.com/interactive_reports/best_global_brands_2009.html, accessed July 21, 2011.

[12]Other terms for this concept include distinctive competencies and core competencies.

[13]C. K. Prahalad and Gary Hamel emphasize this type of capability in their notion of "core competence." See "The Core Competence of the Corporation," *Harvard Business Review*, May–June 1990, pp. 79–91.

[14]"Cadbury Redefines Cheap Luxury: Marketing to India's Poor, Candy Maker Sells Small Bits for Pennies," by Sonya Misquitta (with contributions from Eric Bellman), Wall Street Journal, June 8, 2009 page B4. Online at http://online.wsj.com/article/SB124440401582092071.html

[15]"Cadbury sees India as regional cocoa hub" by Joe Leahy, Financial Times, June 1, 2009, p.13.

[16]Nelson, R. R., and S. G. Winter, *An Evolutionary Theory of Economic Change*, Cambridge, MA, Belknap, 1982.

[17]Henderson, R., and I. Cockburn, "Measuring Competence? Exploring Firm Effects in Pharmaceutical Research," *Strategic Management Journal*, 15, Winter 1994, pp. 63–84.

[18]Porter, Michael, *Competitive Strategy*, New York, Free Press, 1980.

[19]Porter uses the term *differentiation* to describe what we have called benefit leadership.

[20]See Chapter 2 of Porter, *Competitive Strategy*.

[21]Michael Porter makes this point most forcefully in his article, "What Is Strategy?," *Harvard Business Review*, November–December, 1996, pp. 61–78.

[22]Miller, D., and P. H. Friesen, "Porter's (1980) Generic Strategies and Quality: An Empirical Examination with American Data—Part I: Testing Porter," *Organization Studies*, 7, 1986, pp. 37–55.

[23]Thompson and Strickland's *Strategic Management* (Homewood, IL: Irwin Publishers) provides a nice example of activity cost analysis for the beer industry.

[24]Any point system will do.

This figure is adapted from Hall, W. K., "Survival Strategies in a Hostile Environment," *Harvard Business Review*, September–October 1980, pp. 75–85.

[25]See Chapter 7 of Porter, *Competitive Advantage*.

INFORMATION AND VALUE CREATION

10

C hapter 9 describes how firms can succeed by creating value for their customers by either decreasing costs or increasing perceived benefits. In this chapter we continue our examination of a benefit strategy. Roughly speaking, benefit enhancement comes in two varieties:

- Firms may enhance the benefit of their product for all consumers. This is known as *vertical differentiation*, a concept originally introduced in Chapter 5. BMWs and Fiats are vertically differentiated; all or virtually all consumers would prefer a BMW to a Fiat if price was not a factor.

- Firms may alter certain aspects of their product so that some consumers perceive that it offers more benefits, while others perceive that it offers less. This is known as *horizontal differentiation*. BMWs are horizontally differentiated from Lexus; BMWs appeal to drivers who prefer a sportier ride and can forgive the somewhat Spartan interior; Lexus is known for its luxurious ride and appointments but also offers above-average acceleration and handling.

Firms pursuing a benefit strategy may rely on both vertical and horizontal differentiation to outposition their rivals and fill product niches. But any discussion of benefit strategy must come to terms with a simple but powerful principle: a benefit strategy cannot succeed unless consumers know about the product's benefits. Informing consumers about a product's benefits is known as *disclosure* and is an essential component of any benefit strategy. Firms may disclose information about their own products, or disclosure may be performed by third-party *certifiers*.

Whoever discloses product information creates value for consumers, and potentially profits for themselves, by making it easier for consumers to solve the *shopping problem*, that is, to find the goods and services that best meet their needs.

This chapter begins by describing the various ways that consumers may solve the shopping problem.[1] We examine incentives for firms to disclose information about their own products and the alternative methods available to them. We then explore third-party disclosure by organizations and web sites such as Consumers Union (publisher of *Consumer Reports*) and HealthGrades.com. Most of the chapter is concerned with disclosure of vertically differentiated goods and services. The chapter concludes by considering disclosure in horizontally differentiated markets and explains how modern e-businesses such as Amazon, Facebook, and Netflix are transforming the shopping problem.

THE "SHOPPING PROBLEM"

The consumer's shopping problem is to find the seller offering the highest B − P (benefit minus price). The process of finding that seller is known as *search*. Consumers may search *sequentially*, learning about one seller at a time, or they may search *simultaneously*, learning about many products at once. Sequential search is characteristic of many consumer goods such as clothing and furniture. For these products, search is costly relative to B − P, usually because it involves considerable time and travel. A consumer who searches sequentially will often have a "threshold" B − P in mind and will buy from the first seller exceeding the threshold. Consumers who search sequentially do not always find the product offering the highest possible B − P because they may stop searching before then. Consumers may revise their threshold B − P during the course of sequential search if they learn that they were unrealistic about the level of B − P available in the market. This often occurs with clothing shopping, where consumers try on several outfits at different stores and then return to purchase from stores where they had previously searched.

In many cases the cost of search is relatively low compared to B − P and consumers will prefer to search simultaneously, gathering information about many products before deciding which one to purchase. Most prospective auto buyers and homeowners engage in simultaneous search. Because the Internet can greatly reduce search costs, many consumers have transitioned from sequential to simultaneous search for less costly goods such as athletic footwear, printers, and musical instruments. Simultaneous search assures consumers that they will find a product offering a high level of B − P. It also assures companies that those firms offering high B − P will enjoy a high market share. Using the terminology introduced in the Economics Primer, a reduction in search costs increases the elasticity of demand facing sellers.

It is not enough for consumers to seek out information about product attributes; they must also obtain, interpret, and understand the information. Products for which consumers can easily obtain the information required to compare alternatives are called *search goods*.[2] Gasoline is a quintessential example of a search good—rightly or wrongly, consumers believe that all gasolines are pretty much identical, and they usually purchase from the gas station posting the lowest price regardless of brand. There are two classes of goods whose benefits are more difficult to evaluate. First, consumers may not learn the full value of *experience goods* until after purchase. Most consumer products as well as nearly all personal services are experience goods. Second, consumers may never fully learn about *credence goods*, even after purchase. Table 10.1 summarizes the distinctions among search, experience, and credence goods and provides examples of each.

Whether shopping for search, experience, or credence goods, consumers value information. They want to know gasoline prices, learn about the fuel economy of automobiles, compare the on-time arrival rates of different airlines, and choose a primary care physician with good diagnostic skills. Sellers of search goods like gasoline can make it easy for consumers by prominently posting prices. Sellers of experience goods can help consumers by *voluntarily* disclosing quality (as opposed

TABLE 10.1
CHARACTERISTICS OF SEARCH, EXPERIENCE, AND CREDENCE GOODS

Type of Good	Characteristics	Examples
Search Good	Consumers can easily compare product characteristics. Search goods are often commodities, and consumers choose solely on the basis of price.	Gasoline, natural gas, copier and printer paper, batteries
Experience Good	Consumers cannot easily compare product characteristics and value information from others. Consumers do learn about quality after purchasing and using the product.	Automobiles, consumer electronics, restaurants, movies, hair salons
Credence Good	Consumers cannot easily evaluate quality even after purchasing and using the product.	Some auto repairs, medical services, and educational services

to relying on a third-party certifier to report the information). Toyota brags about the fuel economy of its Prius hybrid car. Southwest Airlines advertises its industry-leading on-time arrival rates. Physicians put their diplomas on their waiting room walls. Disclosing the quality of credence goods is difficult, if not impossible. Air travelers take it on faith that their planes are properly maintained for safety, and patients usually assume that their primary care physicians have made the right diagnoses.

Unraveling

One might expect all high-quality vertically differentiated sellers to follow the lead of Toyota and Southwest and voluntarily disclose their quality. A simple economic theory suggests that under the right conditions, even low-quality sellers will disclose. To illustrate the theory, consider 10 hospitals that have measured the cardiac surgery mortality rates of their own cardiovascular surgeons. Heart surgery patients (and their referring cardiologists) will prefer hospitals with lower mortality rates but may be unaware that there are differences among hospitals. If no hospitals disclose their quality, we can expect them to share patients fairly equally, with factors such as location playing a dominant role in admission patterns. The hospital with the lowest mortality rate will naturally wish to disclose in order to boost its share. Once the best hospital has disclosed, patients who do not go to that hospital will divide themselves among the remaining nine. By the same logic, the second best hospital will wish to disclose in order to separate from the pack, followed by the third best, the fourth best, and so forth. When the top eight hospitals have disclosed, the next to worst will also disclose so that it is not mistaken for the worst. Through this process of *unraveling*, patients learn the ranking of every hospital.

The theory of unraveling suggests that all firms, even the worst, will disclose their quality. This would leave no room for third-party certifiers, whose work would simply duplicate the voluntary disclosure. The reality is that voluntary disclosure is hardly universal and third-party certifiers play an important role in many markets. This is because theory requires several strong assumptions that are often violated in the real world. The theory requires sellers to cheaply and accurately assess their own quality and where they stand relative to other sellers; that is, the best sellers must know they are the best. If the best sellers are unaware of their superior product position, they may not set the unraveling in motion. The theory also assumes that consumers have reasonable beliefs about the distribution of quality. Otherwise, the best sellers may be reluctant to disclose unless everyone else does. For example, suppose that a hospital determines that its mortality rate for heart surgery is 1 percent—a very good rate. If patients believe that hospital mortality rates are usually much lower, then this hospital will be reluctant to disclose what ought to be considered good quality. Sellers may also be reluctant to disclose if they have not previously competed on quality. Calling attention to quality differences may increase consumer sensitivity to quality so that each seller ends up investing to improve its rankings. Unless sellers can pass these costs along through higher prices, they may earn lower profits than they did when consumers were unaware of quality differences.

Even when individual firms are reluctant to disclose, firms may collectively benefit if disclosure establishes consumer trust in the industry. In Chapter 1 we described how the Chicago Board of Trade established a system for grading and disclosing the quality of wheat in 1848. This facilitated the creation of futures markets by giving customers confidence about the quality of wheat they were committing to buy. The Joint Commission on the Accreditation of Healthcare Organizations (JCAHO) was formed 50 years ago by a consortium of health care providers in order to establish minimum quality standards for hospitals. Health insurers subsequently announced that they would only cover services provided at JCAHO accredited hospitals. In 1968, Hollywood film studios created the Classification and Rating Administration (CARA) to provide guidance to parents who may be concerned about the content of movies seen by their children. Disney Studios took advantage of the system by creating high-quality movies with a G-rating, securing a dominant position in a previously under-served niche.

The movie studios created CARA to ward off government censorship. Indeed, when industries fail to voluntarily disclose quality, governments sometimes step in. Government-mandated disclosure in the United States began with the 1906 Pure Food and Drug Act, which mandated federal inspection of meat products and forbade the sale of poisonous medications. The 1963 Amendments to the Food and Drug Act were a direct response to Thalidomide (a sleeping pill that, if taken by pregnant women, could cause horrible deformities in newborns) and several other drugs that had severe side effects. The 1963 FDA Amendments set the standard for research-driven drug review that has been adopted worldwide. There are many other examples of government-mandated quality disclosure, and we will mention just a few:

- The 1934 U.S. Securities and Exchange Act requires public companies to file unaudited financial statements quarterly and audited financial statements annually.

- The 1968 U.S. Truth in Lending Act requires clear disclosure of key terms and all costs associated with a lending contract. Similarly, the European Union, Russia, Turkey, and the Arab States that make up the Gulf Cooperation Council use the International Financial Reporting Standards for audited financial statements.

- The EU requires appliance retailers to display labels that rate products for energy consumption on a scale from A++ (best) to G (worst). In Japan, similar labels are required by local prefectures, while the U.S. Environmental Protection Agency issues "Energy Star" certification to ecofriendly appliances.

Governments can also establish minimum quality standards through *licensing*. In 1421, physicians petitioned the English Parliament to prohibit the practice of medicine by anyone lacking appropriate qualifications. In 1511, the parliament authorized bishops to regulate medicine, and in 1518 the College of Physicians was founded to license doctors in London. Six hundred years later, governments around the world require individuals to obtain licenses to practice medicine, law, architecture, acupuncture, hair coloring, and selling hot dogs from pushcarts. While licensing may set a quality floor, it also raises entry costs and protects incumbents from competition. For example, registered nurse anesthetists can perform nearly all of the same services as physician anesthesiologists. Even so, most nations restrict the ability of nurse anesthetists to practice without physician supervision and, as a result, they earn only a fraction of a physician anesthesiologist's income.

Alternatives to Disclosure

Consumers may be skeptical when a firm boasts of its quality—such talk is cheap. Firms can back up their words by offering a *warranty*, which is a promise to reimburse the consumer if the product fails. A warranty is a form of insurance, as the expected cost of honoring the warrantee is often included in the purchase price. Such insurance can be very valuable for big-ticket items such as automobiles, where repair costs could make a dent in a family's budget.

Of greater interest from the perspective of business strategy, warrantees also serve as a *signal* of quality. A signal is a message that conveys information about vertical positioning. A graduate from Harvard Law School may hold up her degree as a signal of quality. This is an effective signal because a third party (the law school) has certified the signaler through a rigorous screening process. Firms may attempt to signal their own quality through their public statements. But if other firms can utter the same claims, these signals may not be informative—consumers might not believe them. *A signal is informative only if it is more profitable for the high-quality firm to offer the signal.*[3] In other words, if a high-quality firm can afford to take some action that a low-quality firm could not, then consumers can infer that any firm taking such an action must be of high quality.

What does signaling have to do with warrantees? Consider two automobile manufacturers, Acme and Lemona. Acme makes a reliable car that rarely breaks down. Lemona's car is poorly designed, uses inferior components, and frequently breaks down. Acme expects to spend very little money honoring a five-year warranty. Lemona anticipates that honoring a five-year warranty would be very costly. Thus, the warranty fits the requirements of an informative signal: it is cheaper for Acme to offer the warranty than it is for Lemona. Taking our example to the real world, Hyundai made great strides penetrating a skeptical U.S. auto market when it offered an unprecedented 10-year new car warranty. Consumers liked the warranty for the peace of mind it offered (i.e., the warranty was a form of insurance). But many consumers correctly reasoned that Hyundai must make a durable car if it could afford to offer a 10-year warranty.

EXAMPLE 10.1   WARRANTEEING SURGERY

You can purchase just about anything with a warranty. We have come to expect warrantees for cars, appliances, and consumer electronics. There are clothing stores that guarantee customer satisfaction. Plumbers guarantee their work. Some colleges even guarantee that their students will get jobs! And lawyers who work on a contingency fee basis are effectively guaranteeing their work.

There is one sector of the economy where sellers rarely, if ever, guarantee their work—medicine. There are exceptions, of course. You can get a guarantee for Lasik eye surgery and sometimes for plastic surgery. But good luck trying to get your money back if your new hip doesn't allow you to walk or if your cancer therapy doesn't shrink your tumors.

Medical providers offer a number of reasons for why they do not guarantee their work. They immediately mention that all treatments have risks and some patients will not benefit even when the provider has done exemplary work. This does not preclude offering a warranty, however. Suppose that under the best of circumstances, a surgical procedure works 80 percent of the time. Instead of charging, say $8,000 for all patients, surgeons could charge $10,000 and offer a money-back guarantee in case the procedure fails. Perhaps a better reason not to offer a warranty is that it can be difficult to define failure. How much mobility must a hip replacement patient regain for the procedure to be deemed successful? How much must a tumor shrink? Medical providers may be concerned that patients will claim that the procedure "failed" in order to cash in on the warranty. Finally, there are some procedures such as hip replacement, where the outcome depends on the patient's effort to recover, which can complicate any effort to place blame on the provider.

By identifying the reasons not to offer warrantees, it is possible to identify specific ways in which warrantees might make sense. For example, eye surgeons could warrantee cataract surgery because success is easy to measure and, if the surgery is successful, patients would have no reason to demand a "replacement" procedure. Hospitals could offer a limited warranty on nearly all procedures, by offering free medical care if complications arise within a specified time frame. Again, patients would be unlikely to claim the warrantee unless they really did suffer from complications. The world-famous Geisinger Clinic in Danville, Pennsylvania, was perhaps the first medical provider to offer such a warrantee. Beginning in 2007, Geisinger offered to cover the costs of any complications occurring within 90 days of coronary bypass surgery. A few other hospitals have since followed suit.

By offering this warranty, Geisinger reassures patients who may be worried about ongoing medical expenses. Geisinger also signals its commitment to quality: if Geisinger did not have a low complication rate, it could not afford to enforce the warranty. And the warranty gives Geisinger an incentive to continue to improve quality. These improvements represent a win–win for Geisinger and its patients.

In 2011, the Center for Medicare and Medical Services (CMS) announced that it would withhold up to three percent of Medicare payments to hospitals with unacceptably high readmission rates. This is an important step towards full-blown warrantees in Medicare.

Firms can also promote product quality through branding. The term *branding* is derived from the practice of marking livestock that dates back as far as 2000 BC.[4] Product branding dates to the nineteenth century. Averill Paints secured the first U.S. trademark (an eagle) in 1870, while Bass and Company (the brewer) and Lyle's Golden Syrup both claim to be Europe's oldest brand, also in the late nineteenth century. Brands help consumers associate product names with product attributes. The Nike brand conjures up images of Michael Jordan winning basketball championships, while Budweiser is associated with parties and good times. These associations help sell products that are otherwise barely differentiated from their rivals. But in some cases, branding can also serve as an alternative to disclosure by signaling the quality of vertically differentiated products.

Recall that a signal is informative if it is more profitable for a high-quality seller to give the signal. If advertising is a signal of quality, it must be the case that high-quality firms stand to gain more from advertising. Let us once again consider the two manufacturers, Acme and Lemona. Suppose that the two companies have ignored the lessons from Chapter 2 and have made unrelated diversifications into laundry detergent. Acme manufactures AirFresh detergent while Lemona makes LikeIt Detergent. These are experience goods; consumers can determine if the detergent cleans effectively after using it. Now consider a consumer choosing between AirFresh and LikeIt. When choosing between the two products, the consumer may reason as follows:

> Advertising to promote a brand is costly. Acme is unlikely to recover its advertising expenses unless it sells a lot of AirFresh, and the only way that can happen is if it has a lot of satisfied customers making repeat purchases. It therefore stands to reason that Air-Fresh is a good cleaning detergent. On the other hand, Lemona has not advertised LikeIt at all. LikeIt could be a lousy product and Lemona could still make money, even if no one ever buys a second box. It is therefore much safer to buy AirFresh.

In other words, a high-quality seller of experience goods can afford to advertise, but a low-quality seller cannot. This is what makes advertising an effective signal. Because advertising is effective, sellers who advertise will attract more first-time purchasers. They can even charge higher prices, knowing that consumers will be suspicious of low-price competitors that do not advertise.

Most consumer goods manufacturers do not sell directly to consumers, finding it more efficient to distribute their products through independent retailers. Many of these retailers have their own brand reputations. Galleries Lafayette sells designer fashions; Fortnum and Mason's carries gourmet foods; and Best Buy sells state-of-the-art electronics. Consumers may infer product quality from the reputation of the retailer or from the brands that they carry. As described in Example 10.2, this creates a tension that has the potential to transform value creation, and value capture, in many product sectors.

Nonprofit Firms

Consumers are skeptical of the quality of experience goods and, especially, credence goods because managers and owners of firms that offer low quality while masquerading as high quality stand to prosper. But if managers and owners are unable to profit from their deception, incentives to skimp on quality would disappear. Perhaps the best way for owners to eliminate this incentive is to establish themselves as nonprofit firms. Under tax law in most nations, nonprofits are not permitted to use any revenues in excess of costs (nonprofits do not talk of "profits") to augment the compensation of owners and managers. Compensation may be tied to effort, training, and even to the accomplishment of specific goals, but not to excess returns.

Nonprofits are common in industries such as health care and education whose products may be described as credence goods. Consumers may gravitate to nonprofits in these industries precisely because they believe the nonprofit sellers will be less likely to skimp on quality.

EXAMPLE 10.2 THE EVOLUTION OF BRANDING IN APPLIANCE RETAILING

The first "modern" washing machines that used a drum to remove and wash away dirt were invented in the latter half of the nineteenth century. Maytag, the first famous washing machine brand, began in 1893, and Whirlpool produced the first electric motor-driven washers in 1911. The first washing machines were prone to break down and customers were naturally worried about servicing them. This helps explain why so many early appliance retailers began life as hardware stores: their proprietors possessed the kind of tinkering skills required to repair the finicky washers. In fact, repair service was so important that customers usually based their purchases more on the reputation of the local retailer than on the washer's brand.

Things changed slightly in 1927 when Sears introduced the first Kenmore washer. Like all of its product offerings, Sears outsourced production of the Kenmore, and companies like Whirlpool and GE often sold more products under the Kenmore name than under their own label. Like the local appliance stores, Sears banked on customers who valued service, and this required Sears to work very hard with local store owners to assure uniformity of service quality. The strategy worked, as Sears sold over one million Kenmore washers within 10 years. For the better part of the next 40 years, retailing of washing machines and other appliances followed the same model—customers either shopped at their local appliance store or shopped at Sears. These stores had legions of loyal customers who valued customer service. The stores charged accordingly and profited handsomely.

Appliance retailing today bears little resemblance to this model. Nowadays, consumers are more apt to purchase washers and other big-ticket appliances from "big-box" retailers like Wal-Mart, Target, Sears, Lowe's, and Home Depot. They buy consumer electronics from many of the same stores as well as Best Buy and Radio Shack. More and more consumers are shopping online from Amazon and other outlets. Few of these outlets provide any service, and price competition is intense. Profits depend on inventory management and low-cost sourcing; customer loyalty counts for very little.

To understand why this industry has undergone such fundamental change, it is helpful to consider when these changes began to occur. Sears's dominance as an appliance retailer began to slip in the 1960s. There were two important changes occurring at this time, both of which were out of Sears's control. First, the quality and durability of home appliances improved dramatically, so that machines needed fewer repairs. Second, Americans had fallen in love with their televisions, which allowed firms to create national brands at low cost. In particular, this allowed appliance manufacturers to create brand identities quite apart from Sears. These two changes came together in one of the most memorable advertising campaigns of all time, Maytag's "Loneliest Repairman in the World." Consumers were no longer concerned about the quality of their repair service. They could purchase a Maytag washer, or for that matter a GE or Whirlpool, confident that they were buying a quality product. The retailer was no longer adding any value.

And so it is that today's successful retailers offer little by way of service and their "brands" are far from imprimaturs of quality. Consider warehouse stores such as Costco and Sam's Club. These are little more than big impersonal boxes and offer no service to speak of. But the Maytag washers sold by Costco and Sam's Club work just as well as the Maytags sold by local appliance stores and probably come with lower price tags. The same is true for refrigerators sold by Lowe's and Home Depot hardware stores and Sony televisions sold over the Internet. Value creation today belongs to the most prized brands and the retailers who can put branded products in customers' hands at the lowest cost.

REPORT CARDS

Thus far, we have described a variety of ways that vertically differentiated firms can reassure consumers about product quality: disclosure, warrantees, and branding. When judging product quality, consumers do not have to rely on information provided by sellers and may instead draw on their own experiences and those of friends and family. Before there were brands and warrantees, this was the dominant way that consumers solved the shopping problem. One can imagine an eighteenth-century village square filled with townspeople debating where to get their horses shoed and how to find the best seamstress in town. Consumers still ask friends and family for recommendations; this is how many people find a primary care physician, a restaurant, or a hair stylist. Consumers also rely on trusted agents to assist with shopping. Primary care physicians help patients choose specialists and hospitals. Real estate agents help home buyers. Wine merchants recommend the best grand cru burgundies.

Independent firms have emerged in many markets to codify quality evaluation. In 1894, the National Board of Fire Underwriters established the Underwriters' Electrical Bureau (the predecessor to Underwriters Laboratories). The Underwriters' Bureau charged a fee for testing and reporting on the safety of fittings and electrical devices. Manufacturers willingly paid the fee because doing otherwise could be interpreted as an indication of poor quality. The Underwriters' Bureau report is an example of a *quality report card*—a grade that can be used to evaluate quality. The Underwriters' Bureau provided a simple pass/fail grade. Other report cards can have much finer gradations, as we will see. Thanks to the dramatic reduction in the cost of obtaining and analyzing information about product quality, firms that construct report cards have the potential to create enormous value for consumers and capture much of that value for themselves in the form of profits.

Report cards are ubiquitous. *Consumer Reports* publishes rankings for hundreds of consumer products. *Car and Driver* magazine publishes an annual list of the 10 best cars. The British magazine *Times Higher Education* ranks the world's 200 leading universities. Students rate professors on teacher evaluations. There are countless sources of rankings of U.S. hospital quality. If a report card is well constructed, high-quality sellers will stand a better than average chance of receiving a high ranking. Consumers may benefit from these rankings in three ways:

1. Consumers can more easily identify high-quality sellers.
2. Because consumers can identify high-quality sellers, the elasticity of demand with respect to quality increases. This gives sellers an incentive to improve quality.
3. Some consumers are willing to pay more for quality than others, and the highest quality sellers may lack the capacity to serve all consumers. Report cards can improve *sorting* by matching consumers who highly value quality to the best sellers.

Because of the policy importance of raising health care quality, considerable research has been done on the effectiveness of hospital report cards, and advocates can point to evidence of all three effects. Hospitals with good report card scores gain market share, and report card scores increase across the board after report cards are introduced. (There is some doubt about whether the latter reflects quality increases or "gaming," as explained in Example 10.5.) There is even evidence that surgical report cards facilitate sorting by steering the most complex cases to the best surgeons.[5]

Nearly all measures of quality are subject to random noise. One surgeon's patient may die, while another surgeon's patient lives for reasons that the surgeons cannot control. The Porsche tested by *Car and Driver* magazine may be the one lemon out of a thousand to roll off of the Stuttgart assembly line. When quality is measured with noise, the objectively best quality seller in a market may not receive the top ranking. Even so, the report card can still be valuable. As long as rankings are positively correlated with actual quality, consumers will still steer their business to higher ranking sellers, and sellers will gain customers by making further improvements to quality. But these benefits will be muted. Consumers may pay attention to other product attributes such as price and location if they are not sure about the accuracy of quality rankings, and sellers may invest less in quality if they are unsure whether the investment will translate into a higher market share.

Unfortunately, noise is not the only problem afflicting some report cards. Report cards that cover some aspects of performance but not others can encourage a problem known as *multitasking* (or what is commonly known as "teaching to the test"). And if a report card score depends on input from the customer, sellers may shun some business in order to boost their score. This is known as *selection*. Unless due care is taken with the construction of report cards, multitasking and selection can do more harm than good.

Multitasking: Teaching to the Test

Report cards usually measure some aspects of a product's performance but not others, perhaps focusing on metrics that "make sense" and that are easy to measure. The result can be report cards that do more harm than good. To understand the danger of the quick and dirty report card, we must introduce the concept of agency, which we describe in much more detail in Chapter 12. In an agency relationship, one party (the agent) is hired by another (the principal) to take actions or make decisions that affect the payoff to the principal. In the present context, we can think of the architect of the report card as the principal who hopes to improve the performance of the agent.

When designing a contract or a report card, the principal needs to be aware of the potential for *multitasking*. In layperson terms, multitasking means that someone is trying to do two or more things at once. In economics, the multitasking problem arises when efforts to promote improvements on one dimension of performance are confounded by changes in other dimensions of performance. This is sometimes known as *teaching to the test*. These efforts to promote improvement can involve direct financial incentives, such as when you pay your son to clean the bedroom and he spends less time cleaning up after himself in the kitchen. But they can also involve report cards. For example, if automobile report cards emphasize fuel economy, manufacturers might respond by making their cars lighter and thereby jeopardizing safety.

Bengt Holmstrom and Paul Milgrom explain that multitasking is a potential problem whenever two things occur simultaneously[6]:

- Incentive contracts or report cards are incomplete in the sense that they do not cover all relevant aspects of performance.

- The agent (or the son in the domestic example) has limited resources that must be allocated across tasks, where different tasks affect different aspects of performance.

Unfortunately, these two conditions are present for nearly all experience and credence goods. The result is that a contract or report card designed to boost some aspects of performance will necessarily affect other aspects of performance not covered by the contract or report card. Example 10.3 presents an example of multitasking in education.

EXAMPLE 10.3   TEACHERS TEACHING TO THE TEST[7]

Accountability is the new buzzword in American public school education. The most important example is the federal "No Child Left Behind" Act, one of the signature achievements of President George W. Bush. This Act requires all government-run schools to administer annual statewide standardized tests. Schools must demonstrate regular improvements in test scores or be subject to various forms of oversight and restructuring, including replacement of staff. Students at schools that fail to show improvement must be given the option to enroll elsewhere, taking enrollment-based funding with them to the new school.

Although most schools have demonstrated test score gains since No Child Left Behind was implemented, critics contend that the Act has caused teachers to emphasize performance on a single standardized test at the expense of broader and potentially more important skills. Although the jury is still out on the Act, research on similar laws that have been tried in various states is not encouraging. The evidence seems to show that America's public school teachers are very good at teaching to the test.

Texas was one of the first states to introduce accountability via standardized testing. In 1994, Texas introduced the Texas Assessment of Academic Skills (TAAS) program, which was designed to emphasize higher-order thinking skills. All students in grades 3–8 took the exam, and students had to pass an eleventh-grade-level exam to graduate from high school. The state held teachers and principals accountable for student performance by linking compensation and promotion to test scores. The TAAS program ended in 2003, when it was superseded by a new program tailored to meet the requirements of No Child Left Behind.

The TAAS program appeared to be an immediate success. Between 1994 and 1998, math and reading scores increased dramatically and the achievement gap between whites and minorities narrowed. However, other evidence suggests that the improvement on the high-stakes TAAS test may have masked more subtle changes in the curriculum. TAAS did not examine science, social studies, or art, and many schools suspended these classes for weeks so that students could have extra time preparing for the math questions on the TAAS. In some cases, social studies and art teachers spent significant time performing grammar drills, while math teachers drilled basic skills rather than teach higher-level concepts not covered by the TAAS. Some evidence of the impact of these curricular changes appears in test scores on a "low-stakes" test, the National Assessment of Educational Progress (NAEP), which was not linked to compensation. Overall NAEP scores did not dramatically improve, while the white-minority achievement gap on the NAEP actually increased. The latter may reflect concern on the part of teachers at predominantly minority schools that their students would have difficulty passing the TAAS.

Many other cities and states hold their schools accountable for student performance on just one or two high-stakes standardized tests. Studies of schools in Chicago and Florida confirm the research evidence from Texas. Students score much higher on the high-stakes test but show much smaller gains, if any, on low-stakes tests. These findings give comfort to both sides of the debate about using standardized tests for accountability. When schools are held accountable, administration and teachers respond. But accountability has unintended consequences. If we are testing math but not science, we had better be certain that we want our students to get better at math but not science.

Recent events in Georgia suggest that the unintended consequences of accountability can deteriorate from debatable changes in curriculum to something far worse. In July 2011, 178 teachers and principals at 44 Atlanta schools were found to be directly involved in cheating on the state's standardized test.

Bingxiao Wu provides an interesting example of "teaching to the test" by fertility clinics.[8] In the early 2000s, the U.S. Department of Health and Human Services (HHS; the principal) began publishing report cards on fertility clinics (the agents). Originally, HHS highlighted the percentage of treatments that resulted in a live birth, and after the report cards were published, the live birth scores improved significantly. But did this reflect improvements made through superior technology and training, or was something else going on? Clinics had another option for increasing their live birth score: they could implant multiple embryos, which also increases the chances of multiple live births. Sure enough, this is exactly what happened. A few years later, HHS revised the report card to highlight both the single live birth and multiple live birth scores. The multiple live birth rates fell significantly, while the single live birth rates increased above the baseline (pre report card) levels.

This example has two important features. First, HHS was able to include all relevant outcomes in its final report card. Wu's results suggest that including all relevant outcomes eliminates harmful teaching to the test. This is easy in the case of fertility clinics, where two measures are sufficient to capture almost everything that might matter to a patient. In its widely read automobile report cards, *Consumer Reports* presents dozens of dimensions of quality and probably omits many others that consumers might care about. In many situations, it is simply impractical to report all relevant outcomes. Consider a report card for the treatment of prostate cancer. Relevant outcomes include mortality, pain, incontinence, and impotence. It would be very costly and perhaps impossible to measure and report all of these outcomes.

A second important feature of fertility clinic report cards is that the steps initially taken by clinics to improve their scores on the reported live birth score (they implanted multiple embryos) harmed performance on the unreported multiple birth score. The results of multitasking do not always offset each other. Reporting prostate cancer mortality rates might cause doctors to improve their surgical technique (for example, through retraining). This might lead to reductions in all of the relevant outcomes, not just mortality. When constructing report cards, it is therefore useful to consider how the measured dimensions and unmeasured actions interact. Suppose that the principal cares about two dimensions of performance X and Y but can only measure and/or pay for X. We expect the agent to increase X. The agent will also increase Y if X and Y are *complements in production* and will decrease Y if they are *substitutes in production*. This is summarized in Table 10.2.

What to Measure

Most report cards contain several different quality measures. For example, the Times Higher Education ranking of world universities is a weighted average of five scores including teaching, international mix, and research. Other rankings of universities may include admission percentages and yields (percentage of admitted students who enroll), and still others may report student satisfaction, the size of the library, and the success

TABLE 10.2
DOES PAYING FOR X RESULT IN LESS OF Y?

	Pay for X and:
X and Y are complements	Get more of X and more of Y
X and Y are substitutes	Get more of X and less of Y

of the athletic program. To make sense of this dizzying array of report cards, we begin our discussion of quality measurement by providing a taxonomy of quality measures.

Health care sociologists have developed a taxonomy of health care quality measures. Donabedian divides quality measures into several categories.[9]

Outcome: This is what consumers ultimately care about. Most outcome measures tend to be specific to the good or service.

Process: Does the seller use accepted practices to produce the good or service? Process measures are useful if outcomes are hard to measure, there are concerns about multitasking, and good processes are known to lead to desirable outcomes. Process measures can promote multitasking by encouraging agents to invest in the reported processes but scale back on unreported processes.

Input: Is labor well trained? Does the seller use the latest manufacturing technologies? Input measures are useful if outcomes are hard to measure, there are concerns about multitasking, and good inputs are known to lead to desirable outcomes. Input measures can promote multitasking by encouraging agents to invest in the reported inputs but scale back on unreported inputs.

Table 10.3 gives examples of measures in each category for a range of goods and services. As seen in the table, process measures are more common for services than they are for products.

Consumers mostly care about outcomes. Most diners want to know if the food is good (an outcome measure), but only the most dedicated foodies pay much attention to the method of preparation (process) or how the kitchen staff is trained (input). Parents will tolerate most any curriculum (process) and teacher credentials (input) if their children get high test scores and gain admission to good colleges (outcomes). But

TABLE 10.3
EXAMPLES OF OUTCOME, PROCESS, AND INPUT MEASURES OF QUALITY

Industry	Outcome	Process	Input
Automobiles	Acceleration, braking, fuel economy, safety		
Smart Phones	Speed, network coverage		Operating system, number of available applications
Air Travel	On-time arrival rates; lost baggage		Pilot training, frequency of schedule, composition of the fleet
Restaurants	Customer satisfaction, hygiene	Method of food preparation	Training of kitchen staff, freshness and source of ingredients
Hair Salons	Customer satisfaction		Products used (e.g., Aveda)
Education	Test scores, college placement, income of graduates	Curriculum (e.g., number of Advanced Placement Classes)	Certification of teachers
Hospitals	Customer satisfaction, mortality, morbidity	Prescribe appropriate tests, procedures, and drugs	Staffing of hospitals, credentials of doctors, availability of latest technology

there are several reasons why it might make sense to report process and input measures of quality in addition to, or instead of, outcome measures:

- Outcome data may be unavailable. When ranking universities, it is essential to consider the quality of teaching. But it is difficult to develop an outcome-based measure of teaching quality. Instead, report cards like Times Higher Education rely on input measures such as faculty/student ratios and the PhD/bachelor's degree ratio (claiming that universities that award many doctorates have a more research-led teaching environment, which is assumed to enhance teaching).

- It may be difficult to obtain outcome measures for a large sample. This can cause statistical imprecision when there is measurement noise. For example, it is common to rank public schools based on the standardized test scores of graduating students. But there are typically fewer than 100 students in a given grade in a U.S. public school, so a school's ranking will have a big random component, based on which children were graduating that year, how they felt on the day of the test, and the specific questions appearing on that test. As a result, a high-quality school may have a low ranking due merely to random chance. In addition, a school near the top of the rankings might be statistically indistinguishable from a school at the bottom, making it difficult to base economic decisions on report card rankings.

- Noisy rankings often exhibit *mean reversion*. In general, firms with high scores will have more than their share of good luck; that is, the noisiness in the rankings has worked in their favor. Luck tends to even out (or it wouldn't be luck), so some high-scoring firms are likely to see their scores "revert to the mean" in subsequent rankings. For example, a public school may report high SAT scores because it happens to have an exceptional group of students that year. Next year, those unusually high scores are likely to be replaced by scores closer to the average. All organizations, be they schools or car makers, should avoid blowing their own horn when they receive unusually high report card scores. Nor should consumers be surprised when a seller's high ranking reverts to the mean.

- In some cases, differences in outcomes across sellers may reflect differences in the customers, rather than differences in seller quality. In health care, this is dealt with through *case mix* adjustment, which we describe in Example 10.5.

Given these problems, it may not be feasible or desirable to report outcomes. Certifiers should consider using process and input measures when the following conditions hold:

1. Process and input measures are positively linked to favorable outcomes. For example, research demonstrates that giving beta blocker drugs to heart attack patients improves their prospects for survival. Some health care report cards list the percentage of heart attack patients who have been prescribed beta blockers.
2. It is relatively inexpensive to measure process and inputs, and the same measures can be obtained from all firms. Data on beta blockers can be readily obtained from health care claims data.
3. Processes and inputs are not easily manipulated through multitasking. It takes virtually no time for a physician to prescribe beta blockers. It is unlikely that this takes away from other important tasks.

Although process and input measures can be useful, most certifiers focus on outcomes, which are, after all, what consumers ultimately care about. Outcome measures

EXAMPLE 10.4   CALORIE POSTING IN NEW YORK CITY RESTAURANTS

The United States is the most obese nation in the world. As of 2010, about one-third of U.S. adults were obese (with a body mass index over 30). On average, obesity reduces life expectancy by six to seven years and has been estimated to cost the U.S. economy at least $150 billion annually. Much of the blame goes to Americans' penchant for eating out, especially at fast-food restaurants where a burger, fries, and soft drink can easily top 1,000 calories and 40 grams of fat.

Many policy analysts believe that Americans would avoid Big Macs, fried chicken, and donuts if only they knew how unhealthy the food was.

In 2006, the New York City Board of Health approved a new rule mandating calorie posting by restaurants. Following several legal challenges, the law was implemented in mid-2008. Other cities and states would soon follow suit. New York City health inspectors verify the information and can fine restaurants up to $2,000 for noncompliance. Economists Bryan Bollinger and Philip Leslie have performed the first systematic study of whether such "calorie posting" affects American's food choices.[10] The results are perhaps slightly discouraging to those who hoped that a little bit of disclosure would help solve America's obesity epidemic.

Bollinger and Leslie obtained information on over 100 million transactions at all Starbucks coffee shops in New York City, Boston, and Philadelphia, over a 14-month period spanning the implementation of the law. (Boston and Philadelphia serve as controls for time trends that might affect menu choices.) Starbucks fans may be surprised that the economists did not study McDonald's or Kentucky Fried Chicken. Their decision to study Starbucks was partly pragmatic—they had a personal connection that provided the data. But Starbucks is not off the hook when it comes to filling out Americans' waistlines: a "grande" caffé mocha and muffin can easily top 750 calories. In fact, one might argue that consumers already know that a Big Mac and fried chicken have a lot of calories, but the high caloric content of a simple Starbucks snack might have come as a big surprise. Studying Starbucks offered another advantage: many patrons use a "Starbucks Card" that entitles them to special deals but also allows the economists to track the same customer's purchases over time.

Bollinger and Leslie obtained the following results:

- Mandatory calorie posting causes the average calories per transaction to decline by 6 percent, from 247 to 232 calories per transaction. The effect was long lasting; there was no evidence that, over time, consumers regressed to their old habits.

- Average beverage calories per transaction changed little, if at all; almost all of the calorie reduction came from reduced food purchases or substitution to lower calorie food items.

- Customers who averaged more than 250 calories prior to calorie posting (these would mainly be customers who made food purchases) decreased calories per transaction by 26 percent.

- Starbucks did not experience a statistically significant change in revenue overall. However, Starbucks stores located within 100 meters of a Dunkin' Donuts experienced a 3 percent increase in revenue. It could be that Dunkin' Donuts customers discovered that a seemingly innocuous poppy seed bagel with cream cheese contains 560 calories, more than any food product at Starbucks.

As a final note, Bollinger and Leslie conjecture that none of this would have occurred without mandatory disclosure. Starbucks would probably be unwilling to be the first to disclose, inasmuch as its relatively "healthy" offerings pack hundreds of calories and might cause customers to take their business elsewhere. And if Starbucks did not begin the unraveling process, it is doubtful that Dunkin' Donuts, McDonald's, and the like would voluntarily disclose.

usually vary by industry. Health care report cards list mortality rates. Automobile report cards detail acceleration and braking statistics as well as reliability. The state of New York reports the nutritional content of restaurant food, as discussed in Example 10.4. One outcome measure that cuts across industries is customer satisfaction, which simply indicates whether current and past customers like the good or service. This is what individuals learned from each other when they met in the town squares of yore. Amazon and other web sites are the modern equivalents of the town square, with the added benefit that they aggregate the opinions of hundreds of customers. Consumers can glean the Internet and other sources to obtain customer satisfaction ratings for automobiles, electronics, books, music, movies, restaurants, universities . . . nearly anything that is available for purchase.

Despite the ubiquity of customer satisfaction report cards, a prospective consumer who uses customer satisfaction ratings to compare sellers is necessarily relying on a noisy and possibly biased quality measure, for several reasons:

- Different customers may use different criteria to measure quality. One person may be satisfied with a restaurant because the food is fresh, while others may value flawless execution in the kitchen, attentive service, or an innovative wine list. As a result, different customers may generate different rankings.

- Customers have an incentive to exaggerate their ratings in order to influence the average score. For example, someone who liked but did not love the movie *The Hangover 2* might give the DVD an Amazon.com rating of five stars (out of five) so as to offset the low ratings given by most other reviewers, thereby helping to move the average higher.

- Customers may be reluctant to leave negative feedback. One study found that less than 1 percent of eBay buyers offer negative feedback.[11] Researchers have attributed the lack of negative feedback to desires to be "nice" and to fear of seller retaliation.[12] The desire to be nice is especially important when face-to-face purchases are required.

- Consumer feedback is unverifiable. As a result, individuals may offer feedback without having consumed the product. This invites sellers to leave favorable feedback of their own products while disparaging competitors, as is commonly alleged about reviews at Amazon, Angie's List (a web site that provides detailed customer feedback on local service providers), and other sites that do not make much effort to verify the veracity of the reviewer.

There are several ways to adjust consumer satisfaction scores to deal with many of these problems. Certifiers can report median rather than mean scores, thereby removing consumer incentives to exaggerate their scores. Certifiers can offer rewards to individuals whose ratings predict peer ratings.[13] Certifiers can also report scores on individual dimensions (e.g., Zagat's reports separate scores for a restaurant's food quality, ambience, and service) or provide a weighted average score that gives more weight to more important dimensions of quality. The weights can be derived using the regression and survey techniques discussed in the Appendix to Chapter 9.

Consumer satisfaction ratings may suffer from several other shortcomings. Response rates to voluntary surveys are notoriously low. For example, only about 10 percent of *Consumer Reports* subscribers respond to their annual survey. The result is *motivation bias*, whereby avid fans and disgruntled customers are disproportionately likely to turn in their surveys, leaving the average consumer unsure about how to interpret the results. In a similar vein, surveys of existing customers are susceptible to *survivor bias*, whereby those customers who did not like the product or service no longer use it and therefore are not surveyed. This is a problem for Amazon.com and similar ratings sites. Fans of specific authors and musicians tend to purchase their latest books and download their CDs and are also more likely to post rave reviews. A consumer who visits Amazon to learn about an unfamiliar author or musician will not see a representative set of reviews.

Customer demographics can also affect satisfaction ratings. For example, a study of patient satisfaction with mental health providers found that women and older patients tended to be more satisfied, even though the quality of care they received was objectively similar to the quality offered to younger, male patients.[14] Satisfaction can also vary with the customer's race, income, and education. As a result of these biases, firms that get good report card scores may not provide the best quality. Instead, they may simply be serving the "right customers"—those who tend to give higher scores as a matter of course. Not only does this add unwanted noise to report card rankings, it gives firms an incentive to judiciously choose their customers. In order to defeat these problems, the certifier should adjust the scores to account for differences in customer characteristics. Nowhere is the need to adjust quality ratings for customer characteristics more apparent than in health care, where report card scores that are not *risk adjusted* are worthless.

Risk Adjustment

Consider three surgeons, Doctors A, B, and C, performing the same hip replacement procedure on patients 1, 2, and 3. Patient 1 survives the surgery with no complications and six months later is able to do all normal daily activities such as climbing stairs and walking the dog. Patient 2 suffers a postoperative infection and, as a result, is never again able to climb stairs and walks with a pronounced limp. Patient 3's surgery is uneventful, but the patient also never fully regains mobility. It might be tempting to conclude that Doctor A did a better job than Doctors B and C, but this would be premature. Many factors besides the surgeon's skill determine outcomes. The anesthesiologist, nursing team, and physical therapist all play big roles, which is why it is important to consider the quality of the hospital and not just the individual surgeon.

Surgical outcomes also depend on the patient. Patient 1 may have been more persistent during weeks of painful rehabilitation. Patient 2 might have been older or frailer, while patient 3 lacked the financial resources to hire a caregiver after returning home from the hospital. Any of these factors may have contributed to patient 1's superior outcome, yet none should reflect badly on Doctors B and C.

In order to properly evaluate the quality of a medical provider, it is essential to perform *risk adjustment*. Risk adjustment is a statistical process in which raw outcome measures, such as a surgeon's average patient mortality rate, are adjusted for factors that are beyond the control of the seller.[15] Health care provider report cards that do not perform some form of risk adjustment can be extremely misleading. Bear in mind that the best medical providers often get the toughest cases. If report cards are not risk adjusted, the best providers can end up at the bottom of the rankings. Example 10.5 explains the risk adjustments used in one of the first and best hospital quality report cards—the New York State cardiac surgery report card.

Certifiers should perform risk adjustment whenever measured quality depends on the characteristics of the customer. This includes all quality reports based on customer satisfaction as well as report cards for services such as health care and education.

The certifier can follow the steps in Example 10.5, substituting the outcomes and risk adjusters that are appropriate for the industry in question. Unfortunately, most certifiers outside of health care do not perform any kind of risk adjustment, making it difficult to confidently identify the best quality sellers. For example, education metrics such as test scores and graduation rates may say more about student demographics than they do about teaching quality. Or consider the widely cited on-time arrival and lost baggage statistics for airlines. Southwest Airlines routinely outperforms other major U.S airlines on these dimensions of performance. Although many industry analysts cite this as evidence of Southwest's operational excellence, it more likely reflects Southwest's "point-to-point" route system, which is far easier to operate than the other carriers' "hub-and-spoke" systems. On any given origin/destination pair, Southwest may perform no better than other carriers. To take another example, one of the most widely cited metrics in consumer goods—the *Consumer Reports* automobile and appliance repair frequencies—may reflect how customers use different brands as much as the reliability of those brands. BMW drivers may accelerate hard and brake harder, while Lexus drivers may pamper their cars. Resulting differences in repair records may have little to do with actual build quality.

Presenting Report Card Results

The presentation of report card scores can have a big effect on their impact. For many years, General Motors collected enormous quantities of data on the quality of the health plans available to its enrollees. Beginning in 1996, GM provided this information to its employees in the form of easy to understand "diamond" ratings, as shown in Figure 10.1. Plans could receive up to three diamonds in each of six categories, including "Preventive Care" and "Access to Care." Employees responded by dropping from low scoring plans.[16] GM believed that the simplicity of the presentation was crucial to the success of the report card.

Another important feature of the GM report card was that it captured dozens of quality metrics using just six scores. GM did this by creating *composite scores*—scores that summarize the information in multiple measures. Other report cards that present composite scores include *U.S. News and World Reports'* rankings of universities and of hospitals as well as the World Health Organization's rankings of national health systems.

The simplest way to create a composite score is to sum up or average individual scores. This of course requires all of the individual component scores to be measured on the same numeric scale. For example, when computing a composite ranking of universities, one might use the following scoring procedure:

- Acceptance Rate Score = 100 − Acceptance Rate

- Yield Score = Yield

- High School GPA Score = (Average HS GPA/4) × 100

Composite score = (Acceptance Rate Score + Yield Score + High School GPA Score)/3

Using this formula, one can compute and compare composite scores for different universities. Table 10.4 gives an example.

The composite scores in Table 10.4 weight each component score equally. It is often appropriate to emphasize some scores more than others by computing a weighted average score. A student's grade point average is the weighted average of individual class grades, where the weights are the credit hours for each class. *U.S. News'*

FIGURE 10.1

COMPARING YOUR 1997 GM MEDICAL OPTIONS

The following table shows the rating of the HMO option(s) available in eight selected quality measures. The ratings are based on historical data and therefore may not necessarily represent the quality of care you will receive in the future. GM does not endorse or recommend any particular medical plan option. The medical plan you elect is your personal decision.

For a more complete description of the eight selected quality measures, see the *GM Medical Plan Guide*.

	NCQA Accredited?	Benchmark HMO?	Operational Performance	Preventive Care	Medical/ Surgical Care	Women's Health	Access to Care	Patient Satisfaction
0001 Basic Medical Plan	Information Currently Not Available							
0002 Enhanced Medical Plan	Information Currently Not Available							
PPO 2190 Blue Preferred Plus	Information Currently Not Available							
HMO 2103 Health Alliance Plan	Yes	No	▲▲▲	▲▲▲	▲▲▲	▲▲▲	▲▲▲	▲
HMO 2104 BCN Southeast Michigan	Yes	No	▲▲▲	▲	▲▲▲	▲	▲▲	▲
HMO 2106 SelectCare HMO	Yes	No	▲	▲	▲	▲	▲	▲▲
HMO 2109 OmniCare Health Plan	Yes	No	▲	ND	ND	▲	ND	▲▲▲
HMO 2119 Care Choices HMO	Yes	No	▲▲	▲▲▲	▲▲	▲▲▲	▲▲	▲▲▲

Key: ▲ = below expected performance ▲▲ = average performance ▲▲▲ = superior performance ND = no data was available from this plan

HMO and PPO options are based on the plan service area. Eligibility is determined by zip code. You may not be eligible for any or all options listed. You may be eligible for other options if you live near a state line. See your enrollment information for your available options.

Michigan – Detroit

TABLE 10.4
COMPOSITE REPORT SCORES FOR UNIVERSITIES

School	Acceptance Rate	Acceptance Rate Score	Yield	Yield Score	GPA	GPA Score	Composite Score
Eastern U.	30%	70	30%	30	3.2	80	60
Western U.	15%	85	50%	50	3.6	90	75
Southern U.	60%	40	40%	40	2.8	70	50
Northern U.	80%	20	40%	40	2.4	60	40

EXAMPLE 10.5   HOSPITAL REPORT CARDS

In 1999, the U.S. Institutes of Medicine published *To Err Is Human*, which reported that preventable medical errors caused as many as 100,000 deaths annually. In a subsequent study, *Crossing the Quality Chasm*, the Institutes of Medicine (IOM) identified several ways that providers can minimize errors, for example, by avoiding administering counterindicated medications.

In the previous year, health services researcher Robert Brook published an editorial in the *Journal of the American Medical Association*, in which he wrote:

> Thousands of studies . . . have shown that the level of quality care provided to the average person leaves a great deal to be desired and . . . the variation in quality of care by physician or by hospital is immense.[17]

The IOM told us that medical providers make mistakes and these mistakes can kill. Brook went further, telling us that some providers make more mistakes than others.

In most markets, sellers of substandard quality goods and services (i.e., sellers with low "B") must accept lower prices, lower quantities, or both. Health care experts have long suspected that this basic market mechanism is absent in medicine. Insurers have historically fixed prices for given services without regard to quality, with some arguing that when quality suffers, patients need more medical care and payments increase! Patients seem unable to compare quality, choosing their providers on the basis of bedside manner rather than on mortality rates. Who could blame them? Quantitative information about provider quality ranges from nonexistent to hard-to-find. In the past two decades, some policy makers, as well as some investor-owned enterprises, have sought to fill this information void.

In 1990, New York State introduced cardiac surgery report cards. The methods used by New York have been often copied, but New York has superior data, thanks to a requirement that hospitals submit detailed patient diagnostic information that can be used for "risk adjustment." Here is a summary of how New York constructs its report card; similar methods are used in virtually all other provider report cards.

1. Collect individual-level data, including the outcome (mortality) and clinical indicators that predict mortality.
2. Compute the average mortality rate for each provider's patients.
3. Use statistical models to predict how patient characteristics affect the probability of mortality.
4. Use the model from step (3) to predict mortality for each patient.
5. Use the predictions from step (4) to compute the average predicted mortality for each provider's patients. At the same time, compute the standard deviation of these predictions.
6. Compute the difference between the actual outcomes and predicted outcomes for every provider. The difference is each provider's *risk-adjusted quality*. Use the standard deviations to determine if differences in risk-adjusted quality are statistically meaningful.

Research shows that report cards like these have had several benefits. Demand has shifted toward higher ranked providers, overall quality seems to have increased, and there even seems to be better sorting of the sickest patients to the best providers. But researchers have also identified more nefarious market responses. Some hospitals may be gaming the system by reporting that their patients are very sick (a tactic known as upcoding) in order to improve their risk-adjusted score. Others may be shunning patients whose risk of dying (as perceived by the hospital) may be higher than the predicted risk (based on the model). For example, one study finds that hospitals have reduced surgical rates on Blacks and Hispanics, two groups with above-average mortality risk when compared with the predictions of the risk-adjustment models.

rankings of universities and hospitals are also weighted averages, where the weights are subjectively determined by the editor responsible for constructing the rankings.

Gaming Report Cards

In an ideal world, sellers will respond to the publication of report cards by making investments to improve their quality. But this can be difficult and expensive. Depending on how report cards are constructed, sellers can also boost their scores through careful manipulation of product attributes and judicious choice of customers. This helps the manipulative sellers, but does nothing to help consumers and can even be harmful.

Colleges and universities in the United States are acutely aware of their rankings in *U.S. News and World Reports*. Two key statistics used to construct these rankings are the acceptance rate and the yield. Colleges and universities can improve both by hiring top faculty, improving facilities, and even by having winning sports programs. But these are all costly and may not necessarily pay off in the rankings.

Universities have also found ways to game the rankings—taking steps that improve their rankings without changing anything tangible about their schools. For example, some universities have simplified the application process in order to encourage more applications. Because the number of admission slots usually remains fixed, these universities are able to reduce their acceptance rate. Northwestern University benefited from this strategy in 2007, when for the first time it accepted the "Common App," which allows applicants to use the same materials to apply to all participating schools. Applications to Northwestern immediately increased sharply, and the school was able to reduce its acceptance rate by several percentage points while still filling its freshman class. (In fairness to our employer, applications were already on the rise, but the move to the common app provided an extra jolt.) Schools will do surprising things to improve their yield rate. Schools ranked outside of the top 20, which are often considered "fallback" schools for students who apply to top places such as Harvard, Princeton, and Stanford, often reject applicants who are clearly qualified for admission to a better school. These rejections increase the yield because the students very likely would have turned down the fallback option.

To take another example from education, many states publish grade school report cards based on how students perform on standardized educational tests. But some states do not require every student to take these tests; for example, schools can exempt students with learning disabilities. David Figlio and Lawrence Getzler show that when Florida began testing students in 1996, some schools reclassified academically weak students as learning disabled in order to boost average test scores.[18] As described in Example 10.5, health economists have documented a variety of ways that providers have improved report card scores without improving the quality of care, possibly making things worse for patients.

These responses to report cards raise an important question: How can certifiers construct report cards that do more harm than good? The evidence that has emerged from education, health care, and elsewhere suggests the following:

1. In order to maximize the demand response, certifiers should report scores using simple graphics.
2. In addition to or instead of reporting many individual quality scores, certifiers should report simple composite scores.

3. To minimize multitasking, certifiers should measure quality at the most aggregated level possible. For example, instead of reporting cardiac surgery outcomes, they should report outcomes for patients with heart disease.
4. Certifiers should complement outcome measures with process and input measures.
5. When appropriate, report card scores should be risk adjusted.

THE CERTIFIER MARKET

Certifiers create value for consumers by helping them find the best sellers. Certifiers may be able to extract some of this value for themselves by charging for their services. Some firms, including Consumers' Union and Angie's List, receive most of their revenue from certification services. Other firms offer certification as a complement to their primary business. Newspapers and magazines publish movie reviews to sell subscriptions and increase advertising revenues. In a remarkable example of complements, Michelin Tires published the first *Michelin Guide* in 1900 to encourage drivers to tour France by car.

Nowadays, many e-businesses offer certification as a complement to their core business. Amazon provides user reviews of the books, DVDs, and the cornucopia of other goods and services that it sells. Amazon's web site is so convenient that few customers who find favorable reviews of a product at Amazon will search elsewhere for a better price. OpenTable.com allows diners to easily make reservations while offering extensive customer reviews. OpenTable does not charge diners for its services, and instead makes its money from restaurants, which pay a fee per reservation equal to about 1 percent of the dining bill. Amazon, OpenTable, and countless other web sites also make money by collecting and selling information about the habits of their users. This information can facilitate the matching of consumers and sellers, as we describe below.

Some certifiers succeed because their reviews are interesting to read, even if they are often highly idiosyncratic and do not always reflect mainstream tastes; film critics like Roger Ebert and Dave Kehr come to mind. Whether or not they are entertaining, most certifiers rely on a reputation for accuracy, as consumers will ignore those certifiers whose recommendations do not square with personal experience. Going hand-in-hand with accuracy, certifiers must also be unbiased. Unfortunately, bias can creep into certification, either intentionally or inadvertently.

Certification Bias

Certifiers depend on their reputations for neutrality, and the recommendation of a highly regarded certifier can cause consumers to reevaluate their own opinions about a seller, potentially changing the fortunes of a seller or even transforming an entire industry. Consider the following two examples. Japanese carmakers did not make major inroads into the U.S. market until the 1970s, when they garnered top ratings in *Consumer Reports*. Thanks to favorable reviews, Japanese automakers' combined market share in the United States rose from 3 percent in 1970 to 20 percent in 1980.[19] California table wines were considered cheap substitutes for French wine until California vintners swept the "best in category" awards at the Paris Wine Tasting of 1976, where 9 of the 11 judges in the blind tasting were French. Sales of California wines took off, as did prices.

Consumers may be concerned when business relationships create a potential conflict of interest between certifiers and the firms they certify. Conflicts of interest may arise in one of two ways. First, certifiers may require data from the firms they certify. Second, certifiers may be paid directly by the firms they certify. Often the two occur simultaneously. For example, audiophile magazines such as *Stereophile* or China's *Audio Technique* rarely issue negative product reviews. Many readers suspect that these magazines depend on audio manufacturers to provide products for testing and for advertisements and are therefore reluctant to bite the hands that feed them. One reason why *Consumer Reports* is so well respected is that it does not print outside advertising or accept free product samples.

Conflicts of interest are a great concern in the financial certification market. When a publicly traded company wishes to borrow money, it issues bonds. The U.S. Securities and Exchange Commission, the European Economic Commission, and other financial regulatory agencies require that all public bonds receive a rating from a certified agency. The three largest agencies certified to rate bonds issued by U.S. corporations are Moody's, Standard and Poors, and Fitch Ratings. Corporations that wish to issue bonds must choose one of these three agencies for certification. The chosen agency gets detailed information about the bond-issuing company, and the rating it issues determines the interest rate that the corporation must pay to bond buyers.

Prospective bond purchasers expect that bond ratings will be unbiased, but numerous studies indicate that conflicts of interest may compromise the bond-rating market. These concerns were heightened during the financial crisis of the late 2000s. Conflicts of interest may arise in bond markets because certifiers compete to be chosen by bond issuers. Bond issuers want the most favorable rating in order to hold down financing costs, and certifiers may be tempted to issue generous ratings in order to curry favor with sellers. Indeed, the presence of multiple certifiers may encourage a "race to the bottom," as certifiers use generous ratings to try to land bond-rating business.

Similar concerns about conflict of interest arise in the brokerage market. Investment banking firms such as Goldman Sachs make money by underwriting new stock issues, but they also sell investment advice. Research shows that "buy" recommendations made by analysts affiliated with underwriting firms tend to be overoptimistic compared with recommendations by independent analysts.[20] Moreover, overly optimistic analysts within underwriting firms tend to advance up the career ladder more rapidly. This research suggests that underwriters may curry the business of firms seeking to issue new stock by making optimistic forecasts. This is not necessarily bad for investors, provided they know about the conflict of interest and discount the forecasts accordingly.

Consumers should be skeptical of most certifiers, at least until they have proven to be neutral and accurate. But successful certifiers face a strategic dilemma: they can "cash in" on their reputation by investing less in accuracy or by taking "bribes" from sellers in return for biased reviews. Consider that after *Consumer Reports* admitted inaccuracies in recent tests of child safety seats, consumers chalked this up to a well-intentioned mistake and the magazine lost no subscribers. With so much good will behind it, the temptation for *Consumer Reports* to deliberately underinvest in accuracy, or to accept covert side payments in exchange for favorable reviews, must be great. To date, there is no reason to believe that *Consumer Reports* has succumbed to such temptation.

Consumer Reports is the dominant rater of automobiles and other consumer goods because consumers believe it is the most accurate and reliable rater. Competition among certifiers to be deemed the most accurate does not always lead them to issue unbiased reviews. A good example is provided by stock analysts. Investors delegate responsibility for picking stocks to analysts, who receive a commission based on the total amount invested. When deciding where to place their money, investors naturally prefer analysts who issue accurate forecasts. This gives analysts a strong incentive to do rigorous research. But career concerns—the desire for career advancement—may become paramount when an analyst's research leads to a contrarian view.

To understand how career concerns can weigh on an analyst's forecast, consider the dilemma facing a hypothetical analyst named Amit. Suppose that the majority of analysts believe that Google's stock price is going to increase, but Amit's diligent research leads to the opposite conclusion. (We will ignore for simplicity the possibility that Google's share price remains unchanged.) Amit must decide whether to issue a buy or sell order, after which the fate of Google's stock price will be known to all. Here are the four possible combinations of Amit's recommendations and stock price movements:

1. Issue a sell recommendation: Google's price falls.
2. Issue a sell recommendation: Google's price increases.
3. Issue a buy recommendation: Google's price falls.
4. Issue a buy recommendation: Google's price increases.

If Amit issues a sell recommendation and Google's share price falls, investors will believe that Amit's forecasts are more accurate than those of other analysts and they will give Amit more money to invest. But if Google's share increases, investors will question Amit's accuracy. Suppose instead that Amit ignores his research and follows the herd. Regardless of what happens to Google's share price, investors will believe that Amit is no more or less accurate than any other. In other words, Amit cannot lose by following the herd. When considering whether to follow convictions and pick against the majority opinion, Amit must assess whether the gains from correctly going against the grain exceed the losses if the majority proves to be correct. Research by Judith Chevalier and Glenn Ellison suggests that young analysts who go out on a limb are punished severely for their mistakes but are only moderately rewarded for their successes.[21] More experienced analysts, on the other hand, seem to be forgiven for daring blunders. As a result, young analysts are more conservative and follow the herd, while older analysts are more willing to go where their own research leads them.

Sometimes, certifiers may bias their findings in favor of buyers, particularly when the government requires certification before consumers may purchase a product. Tom Hubbard finds evidence of this in the auto emissions testing market.[22] All states require that car owners have their vehicles tested for smog emissions, and vehicle owners in some states have their choice of private testing stations. The testers receive a nice fee to conduct the tests. Hubbard observes that emissions testing is somewhat subjective, providing an opportunity for testers to bias their findings. Although car owners may prefer cleaner air, they also prefer not spending thousands of dollars on repairs to make sure that their cars are in compliance with emissions standards. Hubbard finds evidence that car owners seek out testing stations that issue favorable results, and, as a result, testing stations issue excessively favorable results as a way to lure customers.

MATCHMAKING

The certifier's role in vertically differentiated markets is fairly simple: establish and quantify the quality differences across products. Certification in horizontally differentiated markets is rather different. In these markets, consumers may disagree about product rankings, and a certifier who declares that a given seller is the best will be giving bad advice to many customers. For example, if you ask a Chicagoan to name the best restaurant, he or she might mention Alinea or L2O, both of which are in

Chicago and were awarded three Michelin stars. Ask the same question to someone in Copenhagen and he or she will probably brag that Noma was named the best restaurant in the world. As with beauty, the best restaurant is in the eye of the beholder.

There are many sources of horizontal differentiation, such as location. Diners will disagree about their favorite restaurants for many other reasons, based on preferences for different cuisines and ambience and how they feel about service. Such disagreements arise for virtually all horizontally differentiated goods and services, including entertainment, clothing, and automobiles. As long as consumers are not too strongly differentiated, vertical certification (i.e., "this seller is best") plays an important role because the certifier's favorite seller is likely to be among everybody's favorites. But certifiers can do more than offer a vertical ranking. With the right information, certifiers can match consumers to the horizontally differentiated firms that best meet their idiosyncratic needs. By using unprecedented amounts of information about consumer habits to refine this matching process, firms such as Google and Facebook have revolutionized how products are made and marketed.

Recall that when shopping for experience goods, consumers often rely on friends and family. This can be especially helpful for horizontally differentiated goods because consumers usually know something about their friends' tastes. This may explain why teenage children do not ask their parents for movie recommendations! Third-party certifiers of horizontally differentiated goods can fulfill the same role as trusted friends, by tailoring recommendations to the specific tastes of individual consumers. For example, consumers might read reviews by several movie and restaurant critics and gravitate toward those who share similar tastes.

When newspapers and magazines provided the bulk of movie and restaurant reviews, most individuals necessarily had access to only a few reviewers. This made it hard to find reviewers with the same tastes. This problem was not confined to artistic endeavors. Consumers might find it just as difficult to find someone with similar tastes for clothing or child care. And the shopping problem could be very difficult for medical patients needing specialized care because few if any friends and family have similar medical problems.[23]

The Internet is changing all this by making it possible for hundreds of millions of individuals to become certifiers, thereby allowing consumers to find a certifier with similar idiosyncratic preferences. For example, someone who enjoyed the *Lord of the Rings* movies can go to Amazon where he will find lists of movie recommendations by other fans of the fantasy trilogy. By allowing consumers to discuss and debate where to shop for personal services, clothing, food, and nearly everything else, the Internet is like the nineteenth-century town square on steroids. Chicago foodies no longer have to ask their neighbor if they have tried the new fusion restaurant; they can read dozens of reviews at opentable.com and decide which contributors to trust. Even better, their friends can provide instantaneous certification by tweeting reviews at Twitter.

When any Internet user can be a certifier, opportunities for biased certification multiply. Motivation bias and survivor bias remain problems. Market researchers compile lists of influential tweeters and offer them payments to try to influence their tweets. And authors sometimes conspire to increase downloads of their books on eReaders like Amazon's Kindle through "review swapping"—raving about each other's works. Netflix has taken the review-matching process one step further, as described in Example 10.6.

When Sellers Search for Buyers

We normally think of certification as a way to help buyers find sellers. But certification can also help sellers find buyers. In vertically differentiated goods markets, sellers include strong certification results in their marketing campaigns. For example, Jaguar

EXAMPLE 10.6 THE NETFLIX CHALLENGE

Fearful of a format war like the one between VHS and BetaMax home video systems, leading hardware makers joined Time Warner in 2005 to form the DVD Consortium. In March 1997, the DVD was born, and later that year, Marc Randolph and Reed Hastings founded Netflix, the first DVD-by-mail rental service. In April 1998, the Netflix web site went online, offering DVDs at $4 a rental (plus $2 postage). But the DVD format was still in its infancy, and Netflix was unknown outside of the community of early DVD adopters. At that time, Blockbuster Video was the 800-pound gorilla in movie rentals, and it relied on its vast store network, combined with purchasing and inventory economies, to maintain its dominance. Blockbuster did not view Netflix as a threat and was taking its time mulling over how to respond to the new disc format.

By 1999, the DVD had established itself as the most successful new consumer electronics technology in history, and Netflix's DVD library was second to none. In September 1999, Netflix launched a subscription plan, whereby renters could specify how many discs they would keep at any given time. When users returned a disc, Netflix would mail out the next one in the queue. By this time Blockbuster was stocking DVDs in most of its stores but was still uninterested in a DVD-by-mail model. This would prove to be a strategic blunder because the economics of DVDs all but wiped out Blockbuster's scale economies. Movie studios had set prices for DVDs far below those for video tapes, minimizing the importance of purchasing economies. And Netflix's regional warehousing provided lower inventory costs than could be achieved by Blockbuster's bricks and mortar stores.

Netflix did more than match Blockbuster's costs; it offered a service that Blockbuster could not match. Taking a lead from Amazon, Netflix provided users with movie ratings, based on input from other users. But Netflix went one step further. Using proprietary software called Cinematch, Netflix provided *individualized* ratings. Here is a gross simplification of how Cinematch worked. Suppose that Mark Shanley wanted to rent *The Dark Knight*, which he had never seen. Cinematch has already asked Shanley to rate other movies, and he has given five stars (the maximum) to *Blade Runner* and one star (the minimum) to *Transformers*. Cinematch scoured the ratings by other users, searching for users who have seen all three films. Cinematch might have found that the typical user who gave five stars to *Blade Runner* and one star to *Transformers* gave an average of 4.5 stars to *The Dark Knight*. Shanley's predicted rating for *The Dark Knight* is therefore 4.5 stars.

The Cinematch algorithm is, of course, much more complicated than this, and Netflix recommends that users rate hundreds of movies for its algorithm to give reliable predictions. Even when users have rated over a thousand movies, the Cinematch algorithm is far from perfect. Netflix used the statistic called the root-mean-square error (RMSE) to evaluate Cinematch. The RMSE is computed in steps:

- Compute the difference between the prediction and actual rating for each user and film.

- Square this difference and sum up the squares.

- Take the square root of the sum. Lower scores imply more accurate ratings.

Cinematch produced an RMSE of 0.9514, which implies that the typical prediction was off by a little less than one point. Netflix wanted to do better, and in 2006 it announced that it would award a $1 million prize to anyone who could improve upon the Cinematch RMSE by at least 10 percent. Within a week, a team had produced an algorithm that slightly outperformed Cinematch. But beating Cinematch by 10 percent proved to be a challenge. Finally, in July 2009, BellKor's Pragmatic Chaos and The Ensemble achieved virtually identical RMSE scores of 0.855 within a few days of each other. By preestablished rules, Netflix provided a second test and BellKor barely won. Netflix awarded BellKor the $1 million prize.

Netflix got a lot of publicity for this competition, but to Netflix this was a lot more than a game. The recommendation algorithm is serious business. At any time during the past decade, Blockbuster could have entered the DVD-by-mail business. Amazon could also have joined the fray. Netflix's inventory economies would have provided some protection. But streaming has rapidly overtaken DVD-by-mail. To sustain its advantage, Netflix has to offer something to consumers besides its large inventory of DVD discs. That something is personalized movie ratings. Users know that Netflix's film recommendations are very reliable. This reliability depends on three things:

1. Users who have to rate hundreds of films
2. Lots of other users who give similar ratings
3. An algorithm that generates accurate predictions

Netflix has all three; no one else does. Moreover, many Netflix users have been with the company for years, entering film ratings after every rental. These loyal users have high switching costs. Netflix is relying on this loyalty as it fends off video streaming services from Amazon, Apple, and others.

launched an expensive advertising campaign in 2009 after JD Powers ranked it first in reliability, helping it to overcome a bad reputation that had emerged, in part, from poor reliability ratings in *Consumer Reports*. It can be much more difficult for sellers of horizontally differentiated goods to reach out to buyers because this requires knowledge of individual customer tastes. Television facilitated some matching by allowing firms to place ads that reach a target market. For example, Chevrolet advertises pickup trucks during football games, while Mercedes promotes golf tournaments and Smuckers Jams sponsors figure skating. Cable television further subdivides the market and allows even more targeted marketing.

It goes without saying that horizontally differentiated sellers would like to know as much as possible about the spending habits of potential customers so as to most efficiently place their advertisements. While television and cable may allow for some targeting; the Internet goes one step further. At web sites such as Google and Facebook, every user click is compiled and catalogued. A user who spends time learning about hotels in Florence may soon receive pop-up ads, banner ads, and floating ads from Tuscan goldsmiths. (We know this because one of the textbook authors is still besieged by these ads!) Users who spend time at ikea.com may get ads from other furniture makers, electronics retailers, even real estate brokers. Moreover, advertisers only pay when users click through the message, forcing these web sites to constantly improve their ability to match buyers and sellers.

The revenue model for Google, Facebook, Craig's List (an online classified ad site), and countless other web sites that do not sell their own goods and services is similar to the revenue model for traditional television and newspapers. These firms make money by allowing sellers to get the attention of potential customers. Thanks to the Internet, sellers can more easily target their messages than ever before. This means not only that consumers are being bombarded with more sales messages than ever before, but also that these messages are more relevant to their idiosyncratic tastes.

As this business model evolves, the shopping problem may return to its roots. Before there was widespread branding and third-party certification, consumers relied on friends and family—the town square—to help evaluate experience goods. Consumers who are steered to sellers by Google or Craig's List will continue to value information about that seller's quality. Only now they will obtain that information from *virtual* town squares. But technology has its limits. Customer satisfaction remains only one dimension of quality, and online customer satisfaction ratings are not immune from the many biases discussed in this chapter.

CHAPTER SUMMARY

- Firms can differentiate their products and services vertically (offering additional benefits valued by all consumers) or horizontally (offering benefits valued by some but not all consumers).

- Firms can inform consumers about their products benefits by disclosing quality. Alternatively, third party certifiers can disclose firm quality.

- Consumers engage in search to find the products that best meet their needs. Search can be sequential or simultaneous.

- Products for which consumers can readily compare alternatives prior to purchase are called search goods. Consumers may not learn the value of experience goods until after purchase.

- Markets can unravel if high-quality sellers disclose their quality, leading all other firms to eventually disclose as well. When firms do not voluntarily disclose, government agencies may require them to disclose.

- Firms that wish to inform consumers about their quality have alternatives to disclosure. These alternatives include warrantees and branding.

- Third-party report cards can inform consumers about product quality when firms do not disclose. Report cards can be developed by independent firms and government agencies.

- Firms may respond to report cards by multitasking. They improve their performance on measured dimensions of quality while cutting back on unmeasured dimensions. This is sometimes referred to as "teaching to the test."

- Quality is multidimensional and quality metrics include the value of the product in use (in healthcare this is known as outcome quality), process (how the product was made), or inputs (the qualifications of those who made it). Customer satisfaction is a widely used quality metric but has many inherent drawbacks.

- Some quality metrics, such as healthcare report cards based on patient outcomes, must be risk adjusted. Otherwise, providers who take on the most difficult cases will obtain the lowest scores. Similar adjustments might be necessary for other professional services such as education.

- Report card scores should be presented in a simple, easy-to-digest fashion. Composites that combine many quality dimensions into a single score can be valuable.

- There are many ways that sellers can game report cards, improving their measured scores without changing actual quality or even reducing quality. Certifiers must design report cards to minimize opportunities for gaming.

- Certifiers may compete against one another. Certifiers must also take care to avoid issuing biased opinions. In some markets such as financial services, biases can help certifiers to prosper.

- In markets for horizontally differentiated goods, certifiers can match buyers to the sellers who best meet their idiosyncratic needs. The Internet allows sellers to obtain detailed information about consumer purchasing habits, facilitating close matching of products and customers.

QUESTIONS

1. Can a market be vertically differentiated and horizontally differentiated at the same time? If not, why not? If so, give some examples.

2. During the 1990s, a consortium of private health insurance firms began measuring their own quality. Within a few years, many of these insurers voluntarily disclosed their quality. Why do you believe this industry moved to create quality measures? Disclosure was more common in some states than in others. Why do you believe there was such geographic variation?

3. Which of the following meet the economic definition of an informative signal?
   (a) A man asks for a woman's hand in marriage and gives her a large diamond ring.
   (b) The same man takes his fiancée for a walk along the beach where he promises he will stop driving fast cars.
   (c) The same woman promises her employer that she will finish an important report before the wedding date.
   (d) The woman offers to accept a lower salary in exchange for a large bonus if she meets the completion deadline.

4. Advertising has been likened to offering a performance bond, where the seller must relinquish the bond if certain performance goals are not met. What is the link between advertising and bonding?

5. In the United States, most hospitals are nonprofit, but nearly all pharmaceutical firms are for-profit. Can you offer an explanation based on the consumer shopping problem?

6. When report cards are noisy, high-quality sellers can sometimes receive low rankings. Sellers complain that this is unfair. But is it necessarily bad for consumers?

7. Give examples of actions that are substitutes in production. Give examples of actions that are complements in production.

8. A former dean of the Kellogg School of Management used to warn faculty not to gloat about the school's #1 ranking in *Business Week*. Why do you suppose he issued this warning?

9. How might you perform a "risk adjustment" of *Consumer Reports'* automobile reliability ratings?

10. What strategies do college students employ in order to "game" their academic report cards? In light of this gaming, how can prospective employers and graduate schools determine the true academic performance of undergraduates?

11. Do teachers face a conflict of interest when "certifying" their students? What steps can schools and potential employers and graduate schools take to eliminate the problems created by these conflicts?

12. "There are huge economies of scale in the matchmaking market." Explain.

ENDNOTES

[1] Much of the material in this chapter is drawn from Dranove, D., and G. Jin, "Quality Disclosure and Certification: Theory and Practice," *Journal of Economic Literature* 48(4), 2010, pp. 935–963.

[2] The terms *search good* and *experience good* were introduced in Nelson, P., "Information and Consumer Behavior," *Journal of Political Economy*, 78(2), 1970, pp. 311–329.

[3]Spence, A. M., "Job Market Signaling," *Quarterly Journal of Economics*, 87(3), 1973, pp. 355–374.

[4] This information was obtained from Daye, D., and B., Van Auken, "History of Branding," http://www.brandingstrategyinsider.com/2006/08/history_of_bran.html, 2006. Searched December 15, 2008.

[5]Zhang, Y. "The Welfare Consequences of Patient Sorting," Northwestern University Doctoral Dissertation, 2011.

[6]Holmstrom, B., and P. Milgrom, "Multitask Principal-Agent Analyses: Incentive Contracts, Asset Ownership, and Job Design," *Journal of Law, Economics, and Organization*, 7, 1991, pp. 24–52.

[7]Parts of this example are drawn from Figlio, D., and S. Loeb, "School Accountability" in Hanushek, E., Machin, S., and L. Woessmann (eds.), *Handbook of the Economics of Education, Vol. 3*, 2011, Holland, Netherlands, Elsevier, 2011.

[8]Wu, B. "Information Presentation and Firm Incentives–Evidence from the ART (Assisted Reproductive Technology) Success Rate Reports, 2012, Northwestern University Unpublished Manuscript.

[9]Donabedian, A., "The Quality of Medical Care," *Science*, 200, 1978, pp. 856–864.

[10]Bollinger, B., and P. Leslie, "Calorie Posting in Chain Restaurants," Stanford University Working Paper, 2010.

[11]Resnick, P. and R. Zeckhauser, "Trust among Strangers in Internet Transactions: Empirical Analysis of eBay's Reputation System," in *The Economics of the Internet and E-Commerce*, M. Bayes (ed.), Amsterdam, Elsevier Science, 11, 2002, pp. 127–157.

[12]Dellarocus, C., "The Digitization of Word-of-Mouth: Promise and Challenges of Online Feedback Mechanisms," *Management Science*, 49(10), 2003, pp. 1407–1424.

[13]Miller, N., Resnick, P., and R. Zechhauser, "Eliciting Information Feedback: The Peer-Prediction Method," *Management Science*, 51(9) 2005, pp. 1359–1373.

[14]Simon, G., "Are Comparisons of Consumer Satisfaction Across Providers Biased by Non-Response or Casemix Differences?" *Psychiatric Services*, 60(1) 2009, pp. 67–73.

[15]For a thorough discussion of risk-adjustment methods in health care, see Iezzoni, L., *Risk Adjustment for Measuring Healthcare Outcomes*, 3rd edition, Chicago, Health Administration Press, 2003.

[16]Scanlon, D., Chernew, M., McLaughlin, C., and G. Solon, "The Impact of Health Plan Report Cards on Managed Care Enrollment," *Journal of Health Economics*, 21(1), 2002, pp. 19–41.

[17] See Brook, R., "Managed Care Is Not the Problem, Quality Is," *Journal of the American Medical Association*, 278, 1998, pp. 1612–1614. This example also cites Werner, R., and D. Asch, "The Unintended Consequences of Publicly Reporting Quality Information," *Journal of the American Medical Association*, 293(10), 2005, pp. 1239–1244.

[18]Figlio, D., and L. Getzler, "Accountability, Ability, and Disability: Gaming the System," in Gronberg, T., and D. Jansen (eds.), *Improving School Accountability (Advances in Applied Microeconomics, Volume 14)*, Emerald Group Publishing Limited, 2006, pp. 35–49.

[19]Train, K., and C. Winston, "Vehicle Choice Behavior and the Declining Market Share of U.S. Automakers," *International Auto Review*, 48(4), 2007, pp. 1469–1496.

[20]Michaely, R., and K. Womack, "Conflict of Interest and the Credibility of Underwriter Analyst Recommendations," *Review of Financial Studies*, 12, 1999, pp. 653–686.

[21]Chevalier, J., and G. Ellison, "Career Concerns of Mutual Fund Managers," *Quarterly Journal of Economics*, 114, 1999, pp. 389–342.

[22]Hubbard, T., "How Do Consumers Motivate Experts? Reputational Incentives in an Auto Repair Market," *Journal of Law and Economics*, 45(2), 2002, pp. 437–468.

[23]Satterthwaite, M. "Consumer Information, Equilibrium Industry Price, and the Number of Sellers," *Bell Journal of Economics*, 10(2), 1979, pp. 483–502.

SUSTAINING COMPETITIVE ADVANTAGE

11

$\mathbf{F}$ ederal Express created the overnight package delivery service in 1973, when it began service in 25 U.S. cities. For the better part of a decade, FedEx nearly monopolized the business, and the company's name became synonymous with overnight delivery. The success of FedEx caught the attention of UPS, the nation's leading "longer-than-overnight" package delivery service. In the early 1980s, UPS launched its own overnight service. Unfamiliar with what it took to deliver parcels overnight, UPS decided to learn from the market leader. UPS studied FedEx procedures for taking orders, scheduling, and delivering shipments. UPS even had its drivers follow FedEx trucks to learn their methods. By 1985, UPS was able to match FedEx's nationwide overnight service offerings and within a few years was also matching FedEx for reliability. UPS gradually won business from FedEx, and UPS now has nearly 35 percent of the total U.S. express-mail market, compared with nearly 50 percent for FedEx. Moreover, by taking advantage of the scale economies afforded by its existing fleet of delivery trucks, UPS could deliver overnight parcels at a lower cost than FedEx and enjoyed a substantially higher profit margin. FedEx responded by developing a ground delivery service of its own.

What happened to Federal Express has also happened to many other companies: competitive advantages that have taken years to build up are eroded by imitators who copy or improve the firm's formula for success or by innovators who neutralize the firm's advantage through new technologies, products, or ways of doing business. All this can destroy even the top firms. Yet, while competitive advantages for many firms are fleeting, other firms seem to sustain competitive advantages year after year. Coca-Cola in soft drinks, Tesco's in groceries and mass merchandising, and Nucor in steel have consistently outperformed their competitors.

This chapter explores the threats to sustained profits and how firms can guard against them. We also examine the long-run threat posed by innovation, which threatens the profitability of successful firms and entire industries, even as it allows a new generation of firms and industries to enjoy their own periods of sustained profitability.

MARKET STRUCTURE AND THREATS TO SUSTAINABILITY

In Chapter 5 we discussed how market structure affects industry performance in the short run. Market structure also affects the ability of firms to sustain long-run profitability.

Threats to Sustainability in Competitive and Monopolistically Competitive Markets

The theory of perfect competition is a logical starting point for our discussion of sustainability of competitive advantage. That theory—developed for industries with many sellers of homogeneous products and discussed in detail in the Economics Primer—has a fundamentally important implication: opportunities for earning profit based on favorable market conditions will quickly evaporate as new entrants flow into the market, increase the supply of output, and drive price down to the point where economic profits are zero (see Figure 11.1). If entry is free, then any firm lacking some advantage conferring superior B–C will earn zero profits.

The dynamic of competition can operate under more complex conditions than the textbook perfectly competitive market. Consider monopolistically competitive markets in which sellers are differentiated in distinct niches. Unlike perfect competition, a monopolistically competitive seller can raise its price without losing all its customers. In other words, it faces downward-sloping demand. Like any firm that faces downward-sloping demand, a monopolistically competitive seller will maximize profits by setting its price above its marginal cost. (See the Economics Primer for further discussion of this point.)

Even though a monopolistically competitive seller sets price above marginal cost, there is no guarantee that it will earn profits. The seller may be covering incremental costs, but it must also have sufficient sales volume to cover its fixed

---

FIGURE 11.1
THE PERFECTLY COMPETITIVE DYNAMIC

This figure depicts a market in which consumers have identical tastes, which are reflected by indifference curves, such as I_1, I_2, and I_3. The upward-sloping line is the efficiency frontier for this market. A price-quality position, such as (P_A, q_A), could not be sustained when there is free entry and costless imitation. An entrant could offer a lower price and higher quality (e.g., P_B, q_B) and steal the market from incumbent firms. The perfectly competitive equilibrium occurs at price-quality combination (P_Z, q_Z). At this point, economic profits are zero, and no other price-quality position simultaneously results in greater consumer surplus and higher profit.

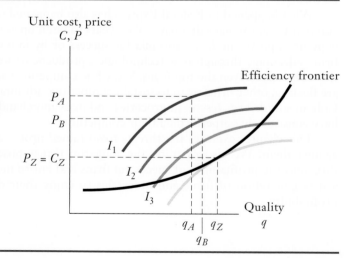

costs. If incumbent sellers are making profits, and there is free entry into the market, new firms will enter. By slightly differentiating themselves from incumbents, these entrants will find their own niches but will inevitably take some business from incumbents. Chapter 6 explained how entry will continue in this way until incremental profits just cover fixed costs. The fast-food market shows how entry by differentiated sellers (e.g., Taco Bell) ate into the profits of the successful incumbent (McDonald's). There are countless other examples across many industries.

Successful incumbents in both competitive and monopolistically competitive markets can do little to preserve profits unless they can deter entry. We discussed strategies for doing this in Chapter 6 and in the last part of Chapter 7, where we emphasized how incumbents can create endogenous sunk costs through branding and other strategies. Note that the conditions that tend to facilitate entry deterrence, such as high fixed costs and a dominant firm willing to enforce strategies such as limit pricing, tend to be absent in competitive and monopolistically competitive markets. Although competitive and monopolistically competitive markets do not tend to enjoy sustained periods of profits, individual firms within these markets can prosper by finding uniquely efficient production processes or product enhancements.

Threats to Sustainability under All Market Structures

Even in oligopolistic or monopolistic markets, where entry might be blockaded or deterred, a successful incumbent may not stay successful for long. Sometimes luck plays a role, as when success is due to factors that the incumbent cannot control, such as the weather or general business conditions. For example, the 2011 Japanese earthquake devastated the supply chain of Japanese car makers, allowing U.S. and Korean competitors to increase their market shares. Over time, parts suppliers returned to normal production and the Japanese car makers regained the share they had lost, and U.S. and Korean car makers lost the share they had gained. This is an example of how outlier performance can *regress to the mean*. The general point about regression to the mean is as follows. Whenever a firm does exceedingly well, one must consider whether it benefited from unusually good luck. Conversely, an underperforming firm might have had bad luck. Since good luck is unlikely to persist (or it would not have been luck), one should not always expect firms to repeat extreme performances, whether good or bad, for long.

Extremely good or bad performance may not always be the result of luck. (If it was, there would be little point in pursuing a business education!) As we discuss later in this chapter, firms may develop genuine advantages that are difficult for others to duplicate. Even this does not guarantee a sustainable flow of profits, however. Although the advantage may be inimitable, so that the firm is protected from the forces of rivalry and entry, the firm may not be protected from powerful buyers and suppliers. Chapter 8 described how powerful buyers and suppliers can use their bargaining leverage to extract profits from a thriving firm. By the same token, they will often give back some of their gains when the firm is struggling. This tends to even out the peaks and valleys in profits that might be experienced by firms that lack powerful buyers and suppliers.

A good example of where supplier power has threatened sustainability is Major League Baseball in the United States. As discussed in Chapter 8, Major League Baseball has enjoyed monopoly status thanks in part to economies of scale and an exemption from the U.S. antitrust laws. Even so, many team owners struggle to turn a profit. One reason is the powerful Major League Baseball Players' Association which, through litigation and a series of successful job actions in the 1970s and 1980s, earned full union rights and elevated the average annual salary of its players from $400,000 in 1987 to $3.3 million in 2011.

Evidence: The Persistence of Profitability

If the forces threatening sustainability were pervasive, economic profits in most industries would quickly converge to zero. By contrast, if there are impediments to the competitive dynamic (e.g., entry barriers discussed in Chapter 6 or barriers to imitation as we discuss later in this chapter), then profits would persist: firms earning above-average profits today continue to do so in the future, while today's low-profit firms remain low-profit firms in the future. What pattern of profit persistence do we actually observe?

The economist Dennis Mueller has done the most comprehensive study of profit persistence.[1] Though dated, the findings should resonate with today's managers. For a sample of 600 U.S. manufacturing firms for the years 1950–1972, Mueller used statistical techniques to measure profit persistence. Perhaps the easiest way to summarize Mueller's results is to imagine two groups of U.S. manufacturing firms. One group (the "high-profit" group) has an after-tax accounting return on assets (ROA)—that is, on average, 100 percent greater than the accounting ROA of the typical manufacturing firm. If the typical manufacturing firm had an ROA of 6 percent in 2012, the average ROA of the high-profit group would be 12 percent.[2] The other group (the "low-profit" group) has an average ROA of 0 percent. If profit follows the pattern in Mueller's sample, by 2015 (three years later), the high-profit group's average ROA would be about 8.6 percent, and by 2022 its average ROA would stabilize at about 7.8 percent. Similarly, by 2015 the low-profit group's average ROA would be about 4.4 percent, and by 2022 its average ROA would stabilize at about 4.9 percent. Thus, the profits of the two groups get closer over time but do not converge toward a common mean, as the theory of perfect competition would predict.

Mueller's results suggest that firms with abnormally high levels of profitability tend, on average, to decrease in profitability over time, while firms with abnormally low levels of profitability tend, on average, to experience increases in profitability over time. However, as Figure 11.2 illustrates, the profit rates of these two groups of firms do not converge to a common mean. Firms that start out with high profits converge, in the long run, to rates of profitability that are higher than the rates of profitability of firms that start out with low profits.

Mueller's work implies that market forces are a threat to profits, but only up to a point. Other forces appear to protect profitable firms. Michael Porter's five forces, summarized in Chapter 8, are an important class of such forces that mainly apply to entire industries. In this chapter we are concerned with a different class of forces: those that protect the competitive advantage of an individual firm and allow it to persistently outperform its industry. These forces are, at least in principle, distinct from Porter's five forces. A firm may prosper indefinitely in an otherwise unprofitable industry beset by intense pricing rivalry and low entry barriers (e.g., Southwest Airlines). The sources of its competitive advantage may be so difficult to understand or to imitate that its advantage over its competitors is secure for a long time.

FIGURE 11.2
The Persistence of Profitability in Mueller's Sample

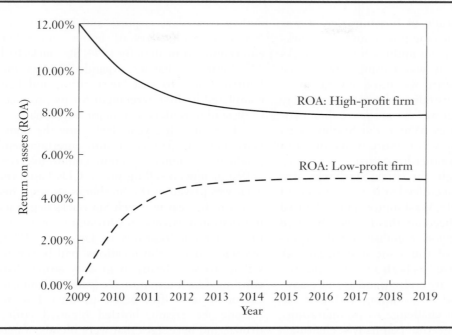

The high-profit group's average ROA starts out at 12 percent in 2009 and decreases over time, converging to slightly less than 8 percent. The low-profit group's average ROA starts at 0 percent in 2009 and increases over time, converging to about 4.9 percent. The profits of the two groups get closer over time but do not converge toward a common mean, as the theory of perfect competition would predict.

THE RESOURCE-BASED THEORY OF THE FIRM

Chapter 9 defined competitive advantage as the ability of a firm to outperform its industry, that is, to earn a higher rate of economic profit than the industry norm. To achieve a competitive advantage, a firm must create more value than its competitors. A firm's ability to create superior value, in turn, depends on its stock of resources (i.e., firm-specific assets and factors of production, such as patents, brand-name reputation, installed base, and human assets) and its distinctive capabilities (i.e., activities that the firm does better than competitors) that arise from using those resources.

Resources and capabilities alone do not ensure that a firm can sustain its advantage. A competitive advantage is sustainable when it persists despite efforts by competitors or potential entrants to duplicate or neutralize it.[3] For this to occur, there must be persistent asymmetries among the firms. Firms must possess different resources and capabilities, and it must be difficult for underperforming firms to obtain the resources and capabilities of the top performers. Resource heterogeneity is the cornerstone of an important framework in strategy: the *resource-based theory of the firm*.[4] This theory points out that if all firms in a market have the same stocks of resources and capabilities, no strategy for value creation is available to one firm that would not also be available to all other firms in the market. Any other firm could

EXAMPLE 11.1 LOSING FOCUS: STARBUCKS DOWN IN DOWN UNDER

After over a decade of boasting that it was opening a new location just about every workday, in 2008, the giant multinational Starbucks announced that it was closing stores. The company's downturn was most obvious in its operations in Australia, where the company announced that it was closing more than two-thirds of its stores. Where did Starbucks go wrong? And why was it more pronounced in Australia than in other locations?

Even though the first Starbucks was opened as a small coffee bar in Pike's Place (in the city of Seattle, Washington in the United States), it has become the frequently cited example of a mega-size multinational corporation (with all of the associated negatives). Starbucks sees itself as both a small coffee bar where beverages are crafted, and as an expanding international corporation, and that has presented a real challenge to its operations. In the words of the company's chairman, Howard Schultz, "The battle within the company is making sure growth doesn't dilute our culture."[5] And he should know.

The idea for Starbucks really started when Howard Schultz joined the company and, as director of retail operations and marketing, convinced the company to adopt the model of Italian espresso bars for the U.S. market. Ultimately, Schultz would start his own firm which would acquire Starbucks in 1987. At the time, the company operated out of 17 locations in the United States and Canada.[6]

By 1992, there were 165 locations, and Starbucks went public, selling shares for the first time on the NASDAQ (an American stock exchange; the letters stand for National Association of Securities Dealers Automated Quotations). In the span of five years, Starbucks had developed its mail order business and had entered into agreements with other retail outlets. These agreements included the sale of its roasted coffee beans at the up-scale department store Nordstrom's and the sale of its brewed coffees and other products in outlets located at airports and in Barnes & Noble stores (sellers of books and other entertainment media). By 1994, Starbucks had 425 locations, having expanded across the United States to east coast cities, and had completed its first agreement for its products to be sold in outlets in a major hotel chain.

The following year, 1995, saw the company make its first move into entertainment products (designed to complement its core coffee products) selling music CDs based on what was played in the Starbucks stores. This was also the year in which Starbucks began its international expansion (through a joint venture) to open locations in Japan. By 1998, Starbucks had 1,886 locations, had begun to sell its roasted beans in grocery stores, had continued its international expansion, and had extended its coffee-based product line to include ice cream, bottled blended coffee drinks, and beverages that were blends of teas and fruit juices.

In 2000 Howard Schultz stepped down as CEO and not long after the company started to lose sales and revenues. An observer might be tempted to attribute this to the company's expansion into both other products and other markets, or to the dilution of its high status brand through increased accessibility. But more fundamentally, the company changed the way it produced its core product. Instead of a barista manually drawing a shot of espresso, semiautomatic machines were introduced. While this increased productivity by decreasing the amount of time involved, and also provided more consistent quality, it took away from what customers had come to expect as the "Starbucks experience."

By July 2008, Starbucks was closing stores and Schultz was back as CEO, vowing to refocus the company's attention on the coffee. In a memo to company executives he warned that the introduction of hot foods and a reduction in the grinding of the coffee had resulted in the loss of what Shultz he called "perhaps the most powerful nonverbal signal we had in our stores," the aroma of coffee.[7]

The more severe retrenchment in Australia was because the Starbucks's business model of introducing "European-style" coffee and coffee drinking experiences did not work in that market. Australia already had a "cafe culture" in place before Starbucks arrived. According to Associate Professor Nick Wailes, expert in strategic management in the Faculty of Economics and Business at the University of Sydney, failing to understand that culture meant that Starbucks became "an example of the big corporate machine it originally tried to differentiate itself from." Schultz has recognized that Australia presents unique challenges but believes that the company can transform their operations in a way that will lead to future success.[8]

immediately replicate a strategy that confers advantage. To be sustainable, a competitive advantage must be underpinned by resources and capabilities that are *scarce* and *imperfectly mobile*.

It should be readily apparent why resources must be scarce to sustain a competitive advantage. But scarcity is not itself a guarantee of sustainability. When value-creating resources are scarce, firms will bid against one another to acquire them. The additional economic profit that results from owning the resource is transferred to the original owner. We will discuss this point in more detail later in the chapter.

Imperfect Mobility and Cospecialization

A firm that possesses a scarce resource can sustain its advantage if that resource is *imperfectly mobile*. This means that the resource cannot "sell itself" to the highest bidder. A valuable piece of real estate whose owner can sell to the highest bidder is an imperfectly mobile asset from the landlord's perspective and a perfectly mobile asset to a prospective tenant. When that real estate is sold or rented, the landlord and not the tenant will enjoy most, if not all, of the profits. One might think that the tenant can prosper if the land unexpectedly becomes even more valuable, say through gentrification of the neighborhood. Had such improvement been anticipated, however, the old landlord would have factored it into the selling price and reaped the profits.

Talented employees who can sell their labor services to the highest bidders are another example of mobile resources. "Superstar" lawyers and free agent athletes are good examples, and these professionals usually reap most of the benefits of their productivity. Firms can limit labor mobility through long-term contracts or "noncompete clauses." Highly productive workers are usually aware of the value they bring to organizations, however, and can negotiate higher wages in advance of signing such contracts.

Fortunately for firms, many resources are imperfectly mobile. Some resources are inherently nontradable. These include the know-how an organization has acquired through cumulative experience, or a firm's reputation for toughness in its competition with rivals. Some resources may be *cospecialized*—that is, they are more valuable when used together than when separated. For example, Lufthansa's gates and landing slots at Frankfort Airport are probably far more valuable to it than they are to a potential bidder for those slots because of Lufthansa's hub operation in Frankfort. Employees in productive work teams are also cospecialized to the extent that their collective output exceeds what they could do if they worked independently or in other teams. Although a productive team of workers could conceivably agree to sell its services to another firm, such coordination is in practice rather difficult, especially if some of the workers have personal ties to the local market.

Isolating Mechanisms

Scarcity and immobility of critical resources and capabilities are necessary for a competitive advantage to be sustainable, but they are not sufficient. A firm that has built a competitive advantage from a set of scarce and immobile resources may find that advantage undermined if other firms can develop their own stocks of resources and capabilities that duplicate or neutralize the source of the firm's advantage. For example, Xerox's advantage in the plain-paper copier market in the 1970s was built, in part, on superior servicing capabilities backed by a network of dealers who provided on-site service calls. Canon successfully challenged Xerox in the small-copier market by building highly reliable machines that rarely broke down and did not have to be serviced as often as Xerox's. Canon's superior product neutralized Xerox's advantage and reduced the value of Xerox's servicing capabilities and its dealer network.

Richard Rumelt coined the term *isolating mechanisms* to refer to the economic forces that limit the extent to which a competitive advantage can be duplicated or neutralized through the resource-creation activities of other firms.[9] Isolating mechanisms thus protect the competitive advantages of firms that have enough luck or foresight to have acquired them. Isolating mechanisms are to a firm what an entry barrier is to an industry: Just as an entry barrier impedes new entrants from coming into an industry and competing away profits from incumbent firms, isolating mechanisms prevent other firms from competing away the extra profit that a firm earns from its competitive advantage.

There are different kinds of isolating mechanisms, and different authors classify them in different ways.[10] We divide them into two distinct groups:

1. *Impediments to Imitation.* These isolating mechanisms impede existing firms and potential entrants from duplicating the resources and capabilities that form the basis of the firm's advantage. For example, many firms compete in the golf equipment market, but few have been able to match Callaway's distinctive capabilities in designing innovative golf clubs and golf balls. Clearly, impediments prevent competitors from copying the strengths of this successful firm. One tangible indicator of how hard it is to imitate Callaway's capabilities in golf club design is the number of firms that try to make counterfeit versions of Callaway clubs, rather than offer their own designs. In March 2004, for example, Callaway seized 27,000 club heads from a company, Newport Golf, that was accused of counterfeiting Callaway clubs. Callaway continues to police counterfeit activity worldwide.
2. *Early-Mover Advantages.* Once a firm acquires a competitive advantage, these isolating mechanisms increase the economic power of that advantage over time. Cisco Systems, for example, dominates the market for products such as routers and switches, which link together LANs (local area networks). Its success in this business helped establish its Cisco Internetwork Operating System (Cisco IOS) software—now in its fifteenth version—as an industry standard. This, in turn, had a feedback effect that benefited Cisco's entire line of networking products.

Figure 11.3 illustrates the distinction between these two classes of isolating mechanisms. In Figure 11.3a, all firms in an industry initially occupy the same competitive position. A *shock* then propels firm G into a position of competitive advantage over other firms in the market. "Shock" here refers to fundamental changes that lead

EXAMPLE 11.2 AMERICAN VERSUS NORTHWEST IN YIELD MANAGEMENT

An example of resource mobility arose in a lawsuit involving American Airlines and Northwest Airlines. The case centered on an allegation that Northwest Airlines stole valuable information related to American's yield management capabilities.

Yield management refers to a set of practices designed to maximize an airline's yield—the dollars of revenue it collects per seat-mile it flies. Yield management techniques combine mathematical optimization models with forecasting techniques to help an airline determine fares, fix the number of seats it should sell in various fare categories, and adjust its inventory of seats in response to the changes in demand conditions. American Airlines has the most sophisticated yield management capabilities in the airline industry. At the time of the lawsuit in the early 1990s, American's system was thought to have added $300 million to American's annual revenues.

By contrast, Northwest's yield management capabilities were below average. In the late 1980s, it hired a consultant to devise a mathematical model to underpin a new system. But management soon became skeptical of the consultant's efforts. The system the consultant devised was estimated to cost $30 million, but its success was uncertain. In 1990, Northwest fired the consultant.

Northwest then tried to purchase a yield management system from American. However, in return for the system, American demanded Northwest's operating right to fly between Chicago and Tokyo, a route whose market value was estimated at between $300 million and $500 million. Northwest refused to trade.

Instead, in the fall of 1990, Northwest hired John Garel, the chief of the yield management department at American. Garel then tried to lure American's best yield managers to Northwest. Out of the 38 new yield management employees hired by Northwest in 1990, 17 came from American, often with generous raises of 50 to 100 percent.

Along with hiring many of American's yield managers, Northwest also managed to acquire a diskette containing American's "spill" tables, which are a key part of mathematical models used to plan the acquisition of new aircraft. Northwest had tried to purchase the spill tables along with American's yield management system in 1990. American alleged that one of its former employees recruited by Northwest copied the diskette. Northwest also obtained internal American documents on how to improve a yield management system. One of the documents was entitled "Seminar on Demand Forecasting," which Northwest used to vastly improve its system called AIMS. American alleged that its system contains five critical techniques, all of which Northwest copied. One Northwest yield manager characterized the revision as "a heart transplant of the AIMS system."

In 1993, American sued Northwest in federal court. It sought to bar Northwest from using its revised yield management system and $50 million in damages. American also brought a suit against KLM, the Dutch airline that is Northwest's international marketing partner. According to American, Northwest passed along the internal American documents to KLM.

This example illustrates that the resources that are the basis of competitive advantage can be highly mobile. This is especially true when those resources are talented individuals, but is also true when the resource is information, a technique, or a formula that can be written down and copied. It is also noteworthy that Northwest was unable to capture all of the extra value that it hoped to obtain by hiring the American yield managers. Some of it had to be shared with these individuals by paying them higher salaries. This highlights a general point about competitive markets. When a scarce resource is fully mobile and is as valuable to one firm as to another, the extra profit that the firms can earn from the resource will be competed away as they bid against one another to acquire it.

FIGURE 11.3

IMPEDIMENTS TO IMITATION AND EARLY-MOVER ADVANTAGES

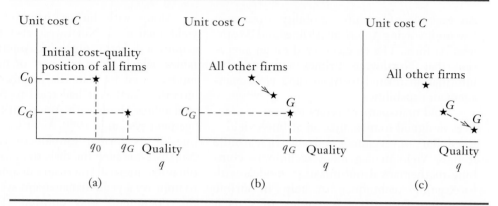

(a) The initial cost-quality position of all firms in the markets is (C_0, q_0). Following a shock, firm G achieves a competitive advantage based on higher quality and lower cost. (b) Impediments to imitation: As time passes, G's competitors may be able to reduce costs and increase quality, but they cannot duplicate G's superior cost-quality position. (c) The dynamics of an early-mover advantage: As time passes, G's cost and quality advantage over competing firms grows more pronounced.

to major shifts of competitive positions in a market. Examples of shocks are proprietary process or product innovations, discoveries of new sources of consumer value or market segments, shifts in demand or tastes, or changes in regulatory policy that enable firms to significantly shift their strategic position in a business. Isolating mechanisms that impede imitation prevent other firms from fully replicating G's advantage. This is shown in Figure 11.3b as the inability of other firms to match G's. Early-mover advantages work somewhat differently. Because G was the first firm to benefit from a shock, it can eventually widen its competitive advantage over other firms in the market. This is shown in Figure 11.3c. Just to reiterate, Figure 11.3a depicts the initial shock, Figure 11.3b depicts the effect of isolating mechanisms, and Figure 11.3c depicts the effect of an early-mover advantage.

If shocks are infrequent and isolating mechanisms are powerful, a firm's competitive advantage will be long-lived. Firms whose competitive advantages are protected by isolating mechanisms, Rumelt argues, may be able to take their strategies as given for a long time, while still earning higher returns than existing competitors (or new entrants that might come into the business). The companion insight is that consistently high profitability does not necessarily mean that a firm is well managed. As Rumelt notes, "even fools can churn out good results (for a while)."[11]

In the next two sections, we discuss impediments to imitation and early-mover advantages in greater detail.

IMPEDIMENTS TO IMITATION

In this section, we discuss four impediments to imitation:

1. Legal restrictions
2. Superior access to inputs or customers

3. Market size and scale economies
4. Intangible barriers to imitating a firm's distinctive capabilities: causal ambiguity, dependence on historical circumstances, and social complexity

Legal Restrictions

Legal restrictions, such as patents, copyrights, and trademarks, as well as governmental control over entry into markets, through licensing, certification, or quotas on operating rights, can be powerful impediments to imitation. Jeffrey Williams points out that patent-protected products as a group have yielded higher returns on investment than any single industry in the United States.[12]

Patents, copyrights, trademarks, and operating rights can be bought and sold. For example, Google's 2011 acquisition of Motorola Mobility was widely viewed as an effort to obtain Motorola's 21,000 active and pending patents, prompting many analysts to ask why Google did not purchase the patents rather than the entire company. Though scarce, these assets may be highly mobile. As discussed earlier in this chapter, asset mobility implies that a firm that tries to secure a competitive advantage by purchase of a patent or an operating right may have to pay a steep price to get it. If so, the purchase of the asset will be a breakeven proposition unless the buyer can deploy it in ways that other prospective purchasers cannot. This requires superior information about how to best utilize the asset or the possession of scarce complementary resources to enhance the value of the asset. Google paid $12.5 billion for Motorola Mobility but believes that the acquisition can create value because Motorola Mobility's patents complement Google's Android operating system.

We encountered this issue in Chapter 2 in our discussion of acquisition programs by diversifying firms. Target firms are mobile assets—their owners may sell them to the highest bidder. The evidence shows that acquirers generally lose money unless there are complementarities between the business units of the acquiring and target firms. (In Chapter 2, we used the term *relatedness* to describe such complementarities.) Otherwise, the owners of the target firm reap all the profits from the acquisition. Google believes that the Motorola deal passes the relatedness test.

The owner of a mobile asset may be better off selling it to another firm. For example, many universities sell the patents obtained by faculty members, realizing that it makes sense for other firms to commercialize these inventions. Likewise, Motorola Mobility's patents may be more valuable when employed by Google. These examples illustrate a key point about patents and other operating rights: once a patent or operating right is secured, its exclusivity gives it sustainable value. Whoever holds that asset holds its value. But maximizing that value is ultimately a make-or-buy decision, whose resolution rests on the principles developed in Chapter 3.

Superior Access to Inputs or Customers

A firm that can obtain high-quality or high-productivity inputs, such as raw materials or information, on more favorable terms than its competitors will be able to sustain cost and quality advantages that competitors cannot imitate. Firms often achieve favorable access to inputs by controlling the sources of supply through ownership or long-term exclusive contracts. For example, International Nickel dominated the nickel industry for three-quarters of a century by controlling the highest-grade deposits of nickel, which were concentrated in western Canada. Topps monopolized the

EXAMPLE 11.3 COLA WARS IN VENEZUELA

The longstanding international success of Coca-Cola and Pepsi shows that a powerful brand name can confer a sustainable advantage. In recent years, there have been few credible challengers to the two leading cola makers. The reason has only partly to do with taste—many consumers believe that other colas, such as RC Cola, taste just as good as Coke or Pepsi. But competitors lack Coke and Pepsi's brand images and would need to spend huge sums in advertisements to achieve it. The owner of one potential competitor even risked his life to boost his cola's brand image. Richard Branson twice attempted to fly around the world in a hot-air balloon emblazoned with the Virgin Cola logo.

While Coca-Cola and Pepsi have remarkable international brand recognition, they do not share international markets equally. For example, Coca-Cola has long been the dominant cola throughout South America. The lone exception was Venezuela, where Pepsi held an 80 percent share of the $400 million cola market until August 1996. That is when Coca-Cola struck a deal to buy half of Venezuela's largest soft-drink bottler, Hit de Venezuela, from the Cisneros Group. The bottler, which changed its name to Coca-Cola y Hit, immediately switched operations to Coca-Cola, and 4,000 Pepsi trucks became Coke trucks. As might be expected, Coke had to pay dearly for this change—an estimated $500 million for a 50 percent stake in Hit. Economic theory suggests that Coca-Cola should not have profited from this deal. After all, the source of monopoly power in this market belonged to the Cisneros Group rather than cola makers. Coca-Cola officials claimed that the benefits from the Venezuelan acquisition would accrue in the long run. A Venezuelan director stated, "We'll do whatever we have to win this market. We

don't think about today. We think about ten years from now.[13]

Whether Coca-Cola overpaid to gain market share became moot in May 1997 when Panamco, an independent Coke bottler headquartered in Mexico, paid $1.1 billion to acquire Coca-Cola y Hit. Coca-Cola appears to have made out handsomely from these deals: it profited from the purchase and subsequent sale of Hit de Venezuela, and it still has a dominant market share in Venezuela.

Coca-Cola might have wrested control of the Venezuelan market from Pepsi, but Pepsi still possessed valuable assets in Venezuela: Pepsi's brand image and taste. (Many Venezuelans apparently prefer Pepsi's sweeter taste.) Months after Coca-Cola's takeover of the market, Venezuelans continued to express a decided preference for Pepsi—if they could find it in the stores. To exploit its assets, Pepsi formed a joint venture—known as Sorpresa—with Polar, Venezuela's largest brewer. The joint venture had fewer bottling plants in Venezuela than Coca-Cola had, but its plants were larger and were believed to be more efficient than Coke's. This enabled Pepsi to compete aggressively on price with Coke, and by the end of the 1990s, it was able to rebuild its market share to 38 percent.

Cisneros Group, Polar, and Coke were the clear winners of this competitive battle. Although Pepsi was able to recover partially from its drastic drop in market share in 1996, on balance, it has probably been a loser. One other loser: any other soft-drink maker that contemplated entry into the Venezuelan market. As a combined force, Coke and Pepsi were stronger in 1998 than they were before August 1996. As always seems to happen, Coca-Cola and Pepsi might bloody themselves in the cola wars, but in doing so they gain protection from outside threats.

market for baseball cards in the United States by signing every professional baseball player to a long-term contract giving Topps the exclusive right to market the player's picture on baseball cards sold with gum or candy. This network of long-term contracts, which was declared illegal in the early 1980s, blocked access by other firms to an essential input in card production—the player's picture.

The flip side of superior access to inputs is superior access to customers. A firm that secures access to the best distribution channels or the most productive retail locations will outcompete its rivals for customers. A manufacturer could prevent access to retail distribution channels by insisting on exclusive dealing clauses, whereby a retailer agrees to sell only the products that manufacturer makes. Before World War II, most American automobile producers had exclusive dealing arrangements with their franchised dealers, and according to Lawrence White, this raised the barriers to entering the automobile business.[14] Most of these clauses were voluntarily dropped in the early 1950s, following antitrust decisions that seemed to threaten the Big Three's ability to maintain their exclusive dealing arrangements. Some observers speculate that the termination of these exclusive dealing requirements made it easier for Japanese manufacturers to penetrate the American market in the 1970s and 1980s.[15]

Just as patents and trademarks can be bought and sold, so too can locations or contracts that give the firm control of scarce inputs or distribution channels. Thus, superior access to inputs or customers can confer sustained competitive advantage only if the firm can secure access at "below-market" prices or if the firm has unique resources or capabilities that enable it to create more value from the inputs and customers it acquires. For example, suppose that a certain site in South Australia is widely known to contain a high-quality supply of uranium and the owners of the site have elected to put it up for auction. At auction, the price of that land would be bid up until the economic profits were transferred to the original owner, and the profitability of the firm that purchases the land would be no higher than the profitability of the losing bidders.

The corollary of this logic is that control of scarce inputs or distribution channels allows a firm to earn economic profits in excess of its competitors only if it acquired control of the input supply when other firms or individuals failed to recognize its value or could not exploit it. Continuing our example, the firm that buys the South Australia uranium site can profit only if it has some unique knowledge of the value of the site, or some unique ability to extract uranium from that site. Either might occur if the firm is already mining an adjacent site. In that case, it could buy the land at a price that just exceeds what other firms thought it was worth, and use its unique position to create value in excess of the winning bid.

The Winner's Curse

Firms that lack a unique advantage expose themselves to the possibility of a *winner's curse*, in which the winning bidder ends up worse off than the losers. Returning one more time to the example of the uranium mine, all of the bidding firms would have first engaged in research to estimate its value. Suppose that there are no mines adjacent to the South Australia uranium site, so that the value of the site is largely independent of which firm wins the bid. This is an excellent example of a *common value* auction. Oil tracts, loose diamonds, and treasury bills, among many other commodities, are also sold in common value auctions. Although the uranium site is worth the same amount regardless of which firm wins the bidding, the firms' estimates of the value of the site might vary widely, depending on how each firm performs its geological studies. Some firms will have optimistic estimates, some pessimistic, and some will come pretty close to estimating the actual value. Because these firms are likely to be highly experienced at valuing mining sites, we might expect the average bid to be a pretty good predictor of the mine's actual value. But the firm that submits the highest bid and wins this common value auction will usually be the one that has the highest estimate of its value. This means that *the winning bidder tends to be overoptimistic*, which implies that if it bid anywhere close to its estimate, it will have probably paid too much.

If firms are to make money in a common value auction, they must anticipate that winning bidders tend to be overoptimistic and they must shade their bids accordingly.[16] By bidding below their estimates, firms can be sure that when they do win an auction, their winning bid is realistic. Firms often convince themselves that they have a unique advantage that justifies a higher bid. But other firms may also have their own unique advantages, which can lead to a different kind of winner's curse—the winning bidder thought too highly of its own uniqueness. The bottom line is that it is difficult to prosper by purchasing someone else's scarce asset.

Market Size and Scale Economies

Imitation may also be deterred when minimum efficient scale is large relative to market demand and one firm has secured a large share of the market. We have already discussed this situation in Chapters 2 and 6, where we described how economies of scale can limit the number of firms that can "fit" in a market. Scale economies can also discourage a smaller firm already in the market from seeking to grow larger to replicate the scale-based cost advantage of a firm that has obtained a large market share. Figure 11.4 illustrates the logic of this isolating mechanism. Two firms, one large and one small, produce a homoge-

FIGURE 11.4
ECONOMIES OF SCALE AND MARKET SIZE AS AN IMPEDIMENT TO IMITATION

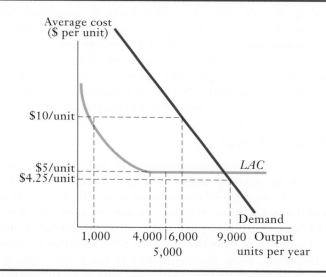

A large firm and a small firm are currently competing in a market in which the product cannot be effectively differentiated. The downward-sloping straight line is the market demand curve. Production technology is characterized by economies of scale, with the long-run average cost function (*LAC*) declining until the minimum efficient scale of 4,000 units per year is reached. The large firm currently has a capacity of 5,000 units per year, while the small firm has a capacity of 1,000 per year. If the small firm attempted to expand capacity to 4,000 units, and both firms produced at full capacity, the market price would fall to $4.25. At this price, the small firm would be unable to cover the costs of its investment in the new plant. Thus, although the small firm could theoretically imitate the source of the large firm's cost advantage, it would be undesirable to do so.

neous product and face the same long-run average cost function. The large firm's volume of 5,000 units per year exceeds minimum efficient scale (MES), which is 4,000 units in the figure; the small firm's volume—1,000 units per year—is less than MES. If the small firm invested in additional capacity and expanded output to MES to lower its average cost, the market price would fall below the minimum of long-run average cost ($5 in the figure). The small firm would thus be unable to earn an adequate rate of return on its investment in its new plant. Thus, although a small firm may theoretically imitate the source of a larger firm's competitive advantage, it may nevertheless be unprofitable for it to do so.

Scale-based barriers to imitation and entry are likely to be especially powerful in markets for specialized products or services where demand is just large enough to support one large firm. This has been the case, for example, in the market for hot sauce, which has been monopolized by McIlhenny (producer of Tabasco sauce) for over a century. But a scale-based advantage can be sustainable only if demand does not grow too large; otherwise, the growth in demand will attract additional entry or induce smaller competitors to expand, allowing them to benefit from economies of scale. This happened in the market for personal computers, as Dell and Gateway expanded in a growing market in the late 1990s and virtually matched the scale advantages held by industry leaders Compaq and Hewlett-Packard. This led to intensified price competition, with the result that Compaq and Hewlett-Packard profits from personal computers failed to keep pace with the growth of the market.

Intangible Barriers to Imitation

Legal restrictions and superior access to customers or scarce inputs are tangible barriers to imitation. But barriers to imitation may also be intangible, especially when the basis of the firm's advantage is distinctive organizational capabilities. We can identify these conceptually distinct intangible barriers to imitation:

- Causal ambiguity

- Dependence on historical circumstances

- Social complexity

Causal Ambiguity

Richard Rumelt uses the term *causal ambiguity* for situations in which the causes of a firm's ability to create more value than its competitors are obscure and only imperfectly understood.[17] Causal ambiguity is a consequence of the fact that a firm's distinctive capabilities typically involve tacit knowledge. That is, capabilities are difficult to articulate as an algorithm, formula, or set of rules. Swinging a golf club in a way to hit the ball with long-range accuracy is an example of tacit knowledge: one could conceivably learn how to do it with enough practice, but it would be difficult to describe how a person should do it. Much of the know-how and collective wisdom inside an organization is of this sort. Tacit capabilities are typically developed through trial and error and refined through practice and experience; rarely are they written down or codified in procedures manuals. As a result, the firm's managers may not even be able to describe persuasively what they do better than their rivals. For this reason, causal ambiguity not only may be a powerful impediment to imitation by other firms, but it also may be an important source of diseconomies of scale. For example, David Teece has pointed out that causal ambiguity might prevent the firm from translating the operational success it achieves in one of its plants to another.[18]

Just as superior firms may be unable to describe what they do especially well, ordinary firms may mistakenly believe they have superior skills. Their inability to articulate their strengths may be chalked up to causal ambiguity. Absent evidence of superior skills (e.g., cost data, market research, competitive benchmarks relative to other firms, financial measures, or comments of knowledgeable observers, such as securities analysts), managers should never assume that they are more capable than competitors.

Dependence on Historical Circumstances

Competitors might also be unable to replicate the distinctive capabilities underlying a firm's competitive advantage because the distinctiveness of these capabilities is partly bound up with the history of the firm. A firm's history of strategic action comprises its unique experiences in adapting to the business environment. These experiences can make the firm uniquely capable of pursuing its own strategy and incapable of imitating the strategies of competitors. For example, in the 1960s and 1970s, Southwest Airlines was constrained by U.S. regulatory policy to operate out of secondary airports in the unregulated (and thus highly price competitive) intrastate market in Texas. The operational efficiencies and the pattern of labor relations it developed in response to these conditions may be difficult for other airlines, such as American and United, to imitate. Neither of these large carriers would be comfortable with Southwest's smaller scale of operation and historically constrained route structure.

Historical dependence implies that a firm's strategy may be viable for only a limited time. To use another airline example, People's Express prospered in the period immediately after deregulation through a low-price strategy based on lower labor costs. This strategy was viable, however, only as long as the major carriers were burdened by high labor costs from their union contracts. In time, these costs were reduced as more labor contracts were renegotiated. This, in turn, made it difficult for People's Express to sustain its advantage.

Social Complexity

A firm's advantage may also be imperfectly imitable because it stems from socially complex processes. Socially complex phenomena include the interpersonal relations of managers in a firm and the relationship between the firm's managers and those of its suppliers and customers. Social complexity is distinct from causal ambiguity. For example, every one of Toyota's competitors may understand that an important contributor to Toyota's success is the trust that exists between it and its component suppliers. But it is difficult to create such trust, however desirable it may be.

The dependence of competitive advantage on causal ambiguity, history, and social complexity implies that major organizational change runs the risk of neglecting these factors and thus harming the firm's position. If the sources of advantage are complex and difficult to articulate, they will also be hard to consciously redesign. This may be why organizational changes, such as reengineering, are often more successful in new or "greenfield" plants than in existing ones.

EARLY-MOVER ADVANTAGES

This section discusses four distinctive isolating mechanisms that fall under the heading of early-mover advantages:

1. Learning curve
2. Reputation and buyer uncertainty

3. Buyer switching costs
4. Network effects

Learning Curve

We discuss the economies of the learning curve at length in Chapter 2. A firm that has sold higher volumes of output than its competitors in earlier periods will move farther down the learning curve and achieve lower unit costs than its rivals. Firms with the greatest cumulative experience can thus profitably "underbid" rivals for business, further increasing their cumulative volume and enhancing their cost advantage.

Reputation and Buyer Uncertainty

In the sale of experience goods—goods whose quality cannot be assessed before they are purchased and used—a firm's reputation for quality can give it a significant early-mover advantage. Consumers who have had a positive experience with a firm's brand will be reluctant to switch to competing brands if there is a chance that the competing products will not work. Buyer uncertainty coupled with reputational effects can make a firm's brand name a powerful isolating mechanism. Once the firm's reputation has been created, the firm will have an advantage competing for new customers, increasing the number of customers who have had successful trials and thus further strengthening its reputation. And newcomers who wish to steal share from the incumbent will set a lower price in order to offer consumers an attractive "B–C" proposition.

Buyer Switching Costs

For some products, buyers incur substantial costs when they switch to another supplier. Switching costs can arise when buyers develop brand-specific know-how that is not fully transferable to substitute brands. For example, a consumer who develops extensive knowledge in using applications developed for the iPhone would have to reinvest in the development of new know-how upon switching to a smart phone that uses Google's Android operating system. Switching costs also arise when the seller develops specific know-how about the buyer that other sellers cannot quickly replicate or provides customized after-sale services to buyers. For example, a client of a commercial bank whose managers have developed extensive knowledge of the client's business would face a switching cost if it changed banks.

Sellers can design their products and services to increase switching costs in several ways. Sellers can offer coupons or "frequent-customer" points that tie discounts or special offerings to the completion of a series of transactions. Everyone is familiar with airline frequent-flier programs. Restaurants, car washes, and even law firms are among many other businesses that use similar programs to encourage customer loyalty. Manufacturers can offer warranties that become void if the product is serviced at an unauthorized dealer. Consumers will thereby tend to patronize authorized dealers, who usually charge higher fees and share the resulting profits with the manufacturer. Automakers and consumer electronics firms have imposed such requirements. However, in the late 1990s the U.S. Supreme Court overturned certain provisions of

EXAMPLE 11.4   BUILDING BLOCKS OF SUSTAINABLE ADVANTAGE

Denmark's Lego Group possesses one of the world's most famous brands. Founded in 1932, Lego Group sells over $1 billion of its iconic toy building blocks annually. Lego also sells children's clothing and computer games and operates four theme parks in Europe and California. But Lego blocks could not be simpler to produce, and there are no trade secrets to prevent someone else from figuring out how to make them. It is somewhat of a wonder, then, why Lego has been so successful for so long. It is not for want of potential competition. Mega Bloks of Montreal has been fighting an uphill battle against Lego since the early 1990s, and even smaller firms like Best-Lock of British Columbia are hoping to join the fray.

At first blush, it seems that Lego is protected from competition by switching costs—a child with a collection of Lego blocks cannot easily incorporate Mega Bloks into the same play set. This is true, provided that Mega Bloks does not duplicate Lego's sizes and colors. Given the relatively primitive technology, it is no surprise that Lego's true source of sustained advantage has been its patents and trademarks. Lego's patents provided virtual blanket protection against imitation. But the last of the patents expired in 1978. Trademark protection lasts far longer than patent protection (75 years versus 20 years), and Lego now relies on the former to ward off entrants.

The first threat to Lego came from giant Tyco Industries, which attempted to introduce its own line of bricks in the United States in the 1980s. Lego sued to stop Tyco, arguing that the Lego brick design deserved trademark protection due to their unique "look and feel." Tyco ultimately prevailed, but by that time Tyco's toy division had been acquired by Mattel, which decided not to enter the building block market. Unfortunately for Lego, Mega Bloks was waiting in the wings.

Mega Bloks already had a toe hold in the market, selling jumbo bricks targeting infants and toddlers. In 1991, Mega Bloks began selling Lego-sized blocks that were compatible with original Legos. Lego sued to stop Mega Bloks, again citing trademark protection. Over the next decade, Lego lost nearly every one of its legal challenges to Mega Bloks. To make matters worse, German courts struck down the "Lego Doctrine" that effectively banned competition in Germany. As Mega Bloks and smaller firms gained share, they also put downward pressure on prices. By 2002, Lego was losing money and had to lay off one-third of its Danish workforce, even as Mega Bloks posted modest profits.

But Lego had already taken steps to undo the damage. In 2001, the company hired outsider Jorgan Vig Knudstorp to be the new head of strategy. Knudstorp spent two years learning the business, and in 2004 Lego implemented his turnaround plan. The key to Knudstorp's strategy is an emphasis on theme product lines, such as Lego Star Wars Bionicles, Lego City, and Lego Architecture. These lines carry on the Lego tradition of demand complementarities—a child with one Bionicle will want another to join in a Bionicle battle. More importantly, the theme lines enjoy trademark protection; Mega Bloks can manufacture generic Lego-sized building blocks, but that is where the competition ends.

Sales of theme lines are up, and they are selling at premium prices. Despite the global economic downturn, Lego has enjoyed several years of steady and sometimes spectacular profit growth.

warranties for Kodak cameras, limiting the effectiveness of warrantees as a source of switching costs.

Finally, sellers can offer a bundle of complementary products that fit together in a product line. Once customers have purchased one product, they will naturally seek out others in the same line. Example 11.4 offers a quintessential example that will be familiar to any parent or child—Legos.

Network Effects

Consumers often place higher value on a product if other consumers also use it. When this occurs, the product is said to display *network effects* or *network externalities*. In some networks, such as telephone and social media networks, consumers are physically linked. The network effect arises because consumers can communicate with other users in the network. These are known as *actual networks*. The more users in the actual network, the greater the opportunities for communication, and the greater the value of the network.

In *virtual networks*, consumers are not physically linked. The network effect arises from the use of complementary goods. Computer operating systems, video gaming (e.g., Sony Playstation), and smart phones are all examples of virtual networks. As the number of consumers in a virtual network increases, the demand for complementary goods increases. This increases the supply of the complementary goods, which in turn enhances the value of the network. This is evidenced by the vast selection of programs to run on IBM-based personal computers, games to play on the Playstation, and applications to download to Apple's iPhone and iPad. Remarkably, consumers in virtual networks never need to communicate with each other to enjoy the network effects. As long as their collective purchasing power encourages the supply of complementary products, each individual consumer benefits from the network.

In markets with network effects, the first firm that establishes a large installed base of customers has a decided advantage. New customers will observe the size of the network and gravitate toward the same firm. In this way, network effects offer a prime opportunity for first-mover advantage, provided the first mover can develop an installed base.

Networks and Standards

Many networks evolve around standards. Microsoft's Windows 7 operating system is a direct descendant of its original MS-DOS standard introduced in 1982 for use with IBM personal computers and quickly adopted by makers of PC "clones." Sony's Blu-ray technology for high-definition home theater emerged after a brief format war waged against Toshiba's HD-DVD format. The persistence of standards makes standard-setting a potentially powerful source of sustainable competitive advantage and raises two key issues. First, should firms in fledgling markets attempt to establish a standard, thereby competing "for the market," or should they share in a common standard, thereby competing "in the market"? Second, what does it take to topple a standard?

Competing "For the Market" versus "In the Market"

A firm must consider several factors when deciding whether to compete "for the market" or "in the market."

- The oligopoly theory presented in Chapter 5 shows that, on average, it is better to be a monopolist half the time than a duopolist all the time. This means that if all other factors are equal, a firm will earn higher expected profits by trying to achieve monopoly status for its own standard (competing for the market) than by settling for a share of the market with a common standard (competing in the market).

- When two or more firms compete for the market, the winner is often the firm that establishes the largest installed base of customers, thereby enhancing the value of the network and attracting even more customers. Competition to grow the installed base can be very costly, however, as firms invest heavily in advertising, pay steep fees to encourage production by complementary product manufacturers, and offer deep discounts to lure early adopters. When the prospects for a costly standards battle loom large, the firms might be better off agreeing to a common standard.

- To win a standards war, it is critical to attract early adopters. Sellers need to tailor their products to the tastes of early adopters while hoping that mainstream consumers will be sufficiently attracted by these products to jump into the market themselves.

- When complementary products are extremely important, a standards war may deter manufacturers of the complements from entering the market until a standard has emerged. This can destroy the value of all the competing standards and stifle the growth of the entire industry.

- By the same token, the manufacturers of the complementary products will favor the standard that provides them with the greatest share of the value added. Thus, to win a standards battle, a firm must take care of the other firms in its value net.

Many of these factors came into play in the battle between Sony and Toshiba for dominance of the high-definition home theater market. Both invested heavily in their proprietary formats, hoping to secure monopoly position. Sony enjoyed a huge advantage in installed base by incorporating Blu-ray technology into its Playstation gaming consoles. The two technologies coexisted for several years in the mid-2000s; during this time there was only a trickle of software available for either platform. Eventually, Toshiba realized that it could not outlast Sony and announced that it would stop producing new HD-DVD hardware. Almost immediately, movie studios ramped up production of Blu-ray movies.

Knocking off a Dominant Standard

It is not easy to knock off a dominant standard. The installed base of the incumbent gives it a decided advantage in any battle. The rival standard can succeed, however, especially in markets with virtual networks. There are two keys to success. First, the rival must offer superior quality, or new options for using the product, that would appeal to a large segment of current users. Second, the rival must be able to tap into complementary goods markets.

Both keys to success were available to Sony and Toshiba as they attempted to replace the dominant DVD standard. Growing sales of big-screen plasma and LCD televisions meant that there were millions of homeowners able to exploit the superior resolution of high-definition discs. And the movie studios were anxious to jump-start software sales, much as DVD did for them a decade earlier. Sony may have won the format battle yet lost the war; during the time it took for Blu-ray to emerge victorious, consumers had already started experimenting with and enjoying direct streaming over the Internet.

Early-Mover Disadvantages

Some firms pioneer a new technology or product but fail to become the market leader. Royal Crown in diet cola and EMI with computerized axial tomography (the CT scanner) are notable examples. This suggests that it is not inevitable that early movers will achieve sustainable competitive advantage in their industries.

Early movers may fail to achieve a competitive advantage because they lack the complementary assets needed to commercialize the product. This happened to EMI Ltd., a British music and electronics company perhaps best known for signing the

Beatles to a record contract in the early 1960s. EMI lacked the production and marketing know-how to successfully commercialize the CT scanner developed in its R&D laboratory, and it sold this business to GE in the late 1970s. Early movers may also fail to establish a competitive advantage because they bet on the wrong technologies or products. Wang Laboratories bet that the "office of the future" would be organized around networks of dedicated word processors. Given the uncertainty about demand or technology that exists when an early mover enters a market, these bets may be good ones; that is, the expected present value of profits exceeds the cost of entering the market. But an inherent property of decision making under uncertainty is that good decisions do not always translate into good outcomes. In the 1970s, Wang could not have known that the personal computer would destroy the market for dedicated word processors.

IMPERFECT IMITABILITY AND INDUSTRY EQUILIBRIUM

Steven Lippman and Richard Rumelt point out that when there is imperfect imitability, firms in an otherwise perfectly competitive market may be able to sustain positive economic profits over long periods, but some firms will earn below-average profits and indeed may appear to be making negative economic profits.[19] These arguments can be illustrated with a simple numerical example. Consider an industry in which firms produce undifferentiated products but have different production costs. Average variable cost (AVC) and marginal cost (MC) are constant up to a capacity of 1 million units per year. We assume that this level of capacity is small relative to the overall size of the market, so the industry can accommodate many firms producing at capacity. The most efficient firms in this industry can achieve an AVC of $1 per unit. There are many potential entrants into this market, but because imitation is imperfect, not all of them can emulate those that achieve the low-cost position in the market. (See Figure 11.5.)

The problem that each entrant faces is that, before entry, it does not know what its costs will be. Accordingly, before entering the market, a prospective competitor believes that there is a 20 percent probability that its AVC will take on each of five values: $1, $3, $5, $7, or $9. Suppose, finally, that a firm must incur the cost of

FIGURE 11.5
AVERAGE VARIABLE AND MARGINAL COST FUNCTIONS WITH IMPERFECT IMITABILITY

The figure shows the different average variable cost functions (AVC) that a firm might have if it enters this market. Since AVC is constant up to the capacity of 1 million units per year, the AVC function coincides with the marginal cost (MC) function. The firm's AVC can take on one of five values— $1, $3, $5, $7, or $9—each with equal (i.e., 20 percent) probability. The equilibrium price in this market is $6 per unit. At this price, each firm's expected economic profit is zero.

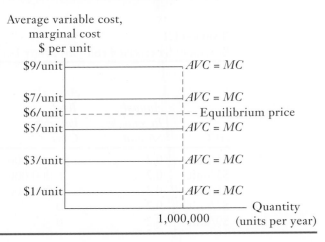

building a factory if it comes into the industry. This factory costs $36 million to build and (for simplicity) never depreciates and cannot be converted to another use. Investors expect a return of 5 percent on their capital, so the annualized cost of the factory is $0.05 \times \$36,000,000 = \$1,800,000$, or $1.8 per unit of capacity.

What will the equilibrium price be? In equilibrium, firms in the market will have positive operating profits while a potential entrant's expected operating profit will be equal to or below the cost of entry. In this example, the price that makes a prospective entrant just indifferent between entering and not entering is $6.[20] At that price, firms that enter and learn that their *AVC* is $7 or $9 will immediately exit. Firms with an *AVC* of $1, $3, or $5 will produce up to capacity and earn a per-unit operating profit of $5, $3, and $1, respectively.

A potential entrant's expected operating profit per unit of capacity, when the price is $6, is thus:

$$(0.2 \times 5) + (0.2 \times 3) + (0.2 \times 1) + (0.2 \times 0) = \$1.8$$

This expected operating profit equals the entry costs of $1.8 per unit, so a price of $6 leaves potential entrants just indifferent between entering or not. Put another way, at a price of $6, each firm's expected rate of return on its invested capital (ROIC) is equal to its cost of capital of 5 percent. This is illustrated in Table 11.1.

The example illustrates the distinction between *ex ante* and *ex post* economic profitability. Before entering (i.e., *ex ante*), each firm's expected economic profit is zero; that is, each firm expects to earn its 5 percent cost of capital (see Table 11.1). After entering (i.e., *ex post*), a firm's economic profit may be positive or negative; that is, a firm may earn more or less than the competitive return of 5 percent. This yields a fundamental insight: to assess the profit opportunities available in a particular business, managers should not just focus on the performance of the most successful firms (i.e., those firms that are still in the business). In the preceding example, the average ROIC of active producers is $(13.89 + 8.33 + 2.78)/3 = 8.33$ percent, yet *ex ante* profitability is just 5 percent. The reason for this is that a simple average of the profitability of active firms ignores unsuccessful firms that have lost money and exited the industry.

This example offers another fundamental insight about profitability. If one takes an "*ex ante*" perspective and entry is free, then it is impossible to have positive expected profits without unique resources and capabilities. Before entering the market, firms in this example all have the same expected profits. The same can be said more generally about entrepreneurs before they sink investments into their new business ideas. Unless they

TABLE 11.1
SUMMARY STATISTICS FOR IMPERFECT IMITABILITY EXAMPLE

AVC	Annual Revenue @ $6/unit	Annual Total Variable Costs	Annual Operating Profit	Annual Operating Profit	ROIC (annual operating profit/$36 million)
$1/unit	0.2	$6,000,000	$1,000,000	$5,000,000	13.89%
$3/unit	0.2	6,000,000	3,000,000	3,000,000	8.3
$5/unit	0.2	6,000,000	5,000,000	1,000,000	2.78
$7/unit	0.2	0	0	0	0
$9/unit	0.2	0	0	0	0

possess unique resources and capabilities, they will be competing against others for the same potential profit. Competition intensifies until there are no profits to be had. This occurred when the dot-com bubble of the 1990s sobered overly optimistic investors. A few of the firms from that era survived, but most did not. Likewise, some investors made a bundle, but most did not. Health information technology is supposed to be the "next big thing," so it too is attracting hundreds of start-up businesses and the expected profits of a start-up are close to zero. The same story has been retold in countless markets. To reiterate, competition eliminates overall industry profits, even though some firms prosper and a handful reap fortunes.

CREATING ADVANTAGE AND CREATIVE DESTRUCTION

Before firms can sustain advantage they must create it. Simply put, firms create advantage by exploiting opportunities that other firms either ignore or cannot exploit. Seizing such opportunities is the essence of entrepreneurship, which is often seen as synonymous with discovery and innovation. But, as Joseph Schumpeter has stated, entrepreneurship is also the ability to act on the opportunity that innovations and discoveries create:

> To undertake such new things is difficult and constitutes a distinct economic function, first, because they lie outside the routine tasks that everybody understands and secondly because the environment resists in many ways that vary, according to social conditions, from simple refusal either to finance or to buy a new thing, to physical attack on the person who tries to produce it. To act with confidence beyond the range of familiar beacons and to overcome that resistance requires aptitudes that are present in only a small fraction of the population and define the entrepreneurial type as well as the entrepreneurial function. This function does not essentially consist in either inventing anything or otherwise creating the conditions which the enterprise exploits. It consists in getting things done.[21]

Schumpeter believed that innovation causes most markets to evolve in a characteristic pattern. Any market has periods of comparative quiet, when firms that have developed superior products, technologies, or organizational capabilities earn positive economic profits. These quiet periods are punctuated by fundamental "shocks" or "discontinuities" that destroy old sources of advantage and replace them with new ones. The entrepreneurs who exploit these shocks achieve positive profits during the next period of comparative quiet. Schumpeter called this evolutionary process *creative destruction*.

Schumpeter's research was largely concerned about the long-run performance of the economy, and he criticized economists who focused exclusively on the outcomes of price competition when promoting the benefits of free markets. What really counted was not price competition, but competition between new products, new technologies, and new sources of organization.

> This kind of competition is as much more effective than the other as a bombardment is in comparison with forcing a door, and so much more important that it becomes a matter of comparative indifference whether [price] competition in the ordinary sense functions more or less properly; the powerful lever that in the long run expands output and brings down prices is in any case made of other stuff.[22]

Disruptive Technologies

There is no end to the list of new technologies that "creatively destroyed" established markets and their dominant firms—quartz watches, cellular communication, and computer flash memory are just a few examples. In the parlance of Chapter 9, these technologies succeeded because they had higher $B-C$ than did their predecessors. In the popular book, *The Innovator's Dilemma*, Clay Christensen identified a special class of products that offer much higher $B-C$ than their predecessors, but do so not through incremental improvements but with entirely new technologies that drastically lower C.[23] In the spirit of Schumpeter, Christensen calls these *disruptive technologies*. Examples include computer workstations (replacing more powerful mainframes), ink jet printers (replacing higher visual-resolution laser printers), electronic mail (replacing more personal "snail mail" and the telephone), and downloadable MP3 recordings (replacing higher audio-resolution compact discs). Not all low C technologies are disruptive. Backers of the Segway human transporter thought for a brief moment that it would replace the automobile for urban commuting. Most commuters thought the B was too low, and so the Segway was relegated to niche status.

The concept of the innovator's dilemma raises a fundamental question about sustainability: Are large firms doomed to be less innovative than smaller rivals? Economists have identified four factors that weigh on this question: (1) the productivity effect, (2) the sunk cost effect, (3) the replacement effect, and (4) the efficiency effect.

The Productivity Effect

Suppose that a large firm and five small firms all pursue the same research objective. The first firm to succeed obtains a patent and enjoys sustained profits. To make for a level playing field, suppose that the total size of the research effort of the small firms equals the total research effort of the large firm. Will the large firm win the race? The answer depends in part on whether the large firm will be more productive at research, or what we call the *productivity effect*.

The large firm may have the advantage of scope economies. For example, a large pharmaceutical company could maintain a biostatistics department that services all of its research activities. But these scope economies can be defeated by the sheer statistical power of the innovative process. In this example, innovation is a winner-take-all activity rewarded by a patent. Economists call this type of competition *patent racing*. Statistical analysis shows that if there are no scope economies, then the winner of the patent race is most likely to be one of the five small firms each pursuing an independent research agenda. This is because the large firm may not explore all possible research directions, which handicaps its effort to be the first innovator. The large firm could counter this by dividing its efforts among five smaller internal research labs. But this tactic only works if the internal labs are truly independent. If lab managers are influenced by a common corporate research philosophy, or if they mimic each other's strategies, then the research efforts will be correlated and one of the five independent firms will be more likely to win the race.

The incentive and bureaucratic effects of vertically integrated firms also weigh on large firms seeking to motivate internal research labs. It is very difficult for large firms to provide a financial incentive for innovation that rivals the potential rewards earned by the innovative entrepreneur. Countering this, Jeremy Stein observes that investors in R&D firms often have little direct understanding of the underlying science and cannot easily evaluate research progress.[24] However, this may work to the benefit of the firms because the investors do not meddle in research decisions. The managers of small R&D firms are usually also their founders. This may work against the firms because the managers/founders might overstate the success of ongoing research rather than see the plug pulled on their projects and, therefore, on their firms. In contrast, allocation of R&D in large firms is conducted by scientists (often with the title of vice president for research). They oversee the funding of numerous projects. If one project is faltering, they can reallocate funds to another without fear of losing their jobs. In this way, larger firms may do a better job of allocating research dollars.

The Sunk Cost Effect

The *sunk cost effect* has to do with the asymmetry between a firm that has already made a commitment to a particular technology or product concept and one that is planning such a commitment. The sunk cost effect arises because a firm that has already committed to a particular technology has invested in resources and organizational capabilities that are likely to be specific to that technology and are thus less valuable if the firm switches to another technology. For an established firm, the costs associated with these investments are sunk and thus should be ignored when the firm considers whether to switch to a new technology. Ignoring these sunk costs creates an inertia that favors sticking with the current technology. By contrast, a firm that has not yet committed to a technology can compare the costs of all of the alternative technologies under consideration and is thus not biased in favor of one technology over another.

The Replacement Effect

Who stands to gain more from an innovation: a profit-maximizing monopolist or a new entrant? The Nobel Prize–winning economist Kenneth Arrow considered the incentives for adopting a process innovation that would lower the average variable costs of production.[25] The innovation is drastic: once it is adopted, producers using the older technology will not be viable competitors. Arrow compared two different scenarios: (1) the opportunity to develop the innovation is available to a firm that currently monopolizes the market using the old technology, and (2) the opportunity to develop the innovation is available to a potential entrant who, if it adopts the innovation, will become the monopolist. Under which scenario, Arrow asked, is the willingness-to-pay to develop the innovation greatest?

Arrow concluded that assuming equal innovative capabilities, an entrant would be willing to spend more than the monopolist to develop the cost-reducing innovation. The intuition behind Arrow's insight is this: a successful innovation for a new entrant leads to it becoming a low cost monopolist; a successful innovation by the established firm maintains its monopoly, albeit at lower cost. So the entrant gets the full benefit of being a low cost monopolist while the incumbent monopolist gets the partial benefit of increasing its monopoly profits further. Thus, the entrant has greater incentive to innovate. Put another way, through innovation an entrant can replace the monopolist, but the monopolist can only replace itself. For this reason, this phenomenon is called the *replacement effect*.[26]

The Efficiency Effect

If an incumbent monopolist anticipates that potential entrants may also have an opportunity to develop the innovation, then the efficiency effect comes into play. To understand the *efficiency effect*, compare the following: (1) the loss in profits when a monopolist becomes one of two competitors in a duopoly, and (2) the profits of a duopolist. Most oligopoly models, including the Cournot model discussed in Chapter 5, suggest that (1) is larger than (2). In other words, a monopolist usually has more to lose from another firm's entry than that firm has to gain from entering the market. The reason is that the entrant not only takes business from the monopolist, but also tends to drive down prices. The efficiency effect makes an incumbent monopolist's incentive to innovate stronger than that of a potential entrant.

In the competition between established firms and potential entrants to develop new innovations, the productivity effect, sunk cost effect, replacement effect, and efficiency effect will operate simultaneously. Which effect dominates depends on the specific conditions of the innovation competition. For example, the replacement and sunk cost effects may dominate if the chance that smaller competitors or potential entrants will develop the innovation is low. Then, the main effect of the innovation for the established firm will be to cannibalize current profits and reduce the value of established resources and organizational capabilities associated with the current technology. By contrast, the efficiency effect may dominate when the monopolist's failure to develop the innovation means that new entrants almost certainly will. In this case, a key benefit of the innovation to the established firm is to stave off the deterioration of profit that comes from additional competition from firms that may develop a cost or benefit advantage over it if they successfully innovate.

Disruption versus the Resource-Based Theory of the Firm

There are countless examples of industries in which seemingly dominant firms are replaced by newcomers, who, in turn, eventually cede the market to yet another generation of innovators. For example, there was a time when the assets possessed by Wang and Digital Equipment created enormous value and thus generated enormous profits for their shareholders. These assets were eventually supplanted by new assets owned by Intel and Microsoft. Eventually, Apple and Google created a newer set of assets—let's call them "cloud computing capabilities"—that have begun to supplant Intel and Microsoft. Some might contend that Wang and DEC, and more recently Intel and Microsoft, made strategic blunders by failing to out-innovate their rivals. As the previous suggestion indicates, there is no guarantee that incumbents will win the race to develop disruptive technologies, and it is unfair to say that incumbents have blundered when disruption occurs. This is like saying that Ken Jennings, champion of the television game show *Jeopardy*, blundered when he lost to Watson the computer.

INNOVATION AND THE MARKET FOR IDEAS

David Teece has observed that a new firm's ability to prosper from its inventions depends on the presence of a "market for ideas"—a place in which the firm can sell its ideas for full value.[27] Teece identifies two elements of the commercialization environment that affect the market for ideas: (1) the technology is not easily expropriated by others, and (2) specialized assets, such as manufacturing or marketing capabilities, must be used in conjunction with the innovative product. The first point is obvious: if a technology is not well protected by patents, the innovator can hardly expect to enjoy significant returns. Consider the fate of Robert Kearns, who invented the intermittent windshield wiper in the early 1960s. He showed the technology to Ford, which rejected a licensing agreement with Kearns, only to introduce its own intermittent wiper soon thereafter. It was not until the 1990s that Kearns was able to uphold his patent in court. An important takeaway is that secrecy is not enough to protect innovators—at some point they must divulge some of their ideas to trading partners. Without good patent protection, they are immediately at risk for expropriation.

EXAMPLE 11.5 ONE CAN NEVER BE TOO THIN: INNOVATION IN TV SETS

In July of 2009, Korea's LG Electronics and Japan's Hitachi Ltd. announced that they had agreed to settle patent infringement lawsuits and countersuits between the two firms and were formulating cross-licensing agreements on technologies used in making, among other things, plasma TVs. In some ways, this was just more evidence of the decreasing value of that TV technology.

Earlier the same month, two manufacturers, Pioneer Corp. and Vizio, Inc., had announced that they would no longer produce plasma TVs because of a shift in consumer preferences to the newer technology used in LCD (liquid crystal display) TV sets. This was an about-face from previous years when plasma TVs were considered superior in terms of picture quality and viewing angles.

Put quite simply, the LCD technology had caught up with and even surpassed plasmas in some aspects. Consumers were attracted by higher contrast, larger screens, and more detailed images. LCDs were less bulky and used less energy. But there was more to come.

A major breakthrough was made by using light-emitting diodes (LED) in the backlighting system of the set. By replacing the old fluorescent tube backlighting with the LEDs, it allowed manufacturers to reduce the depth or thickness of the TV set by about 75%. It also makes the sets more energy efficient.

In January of 2009, Korea-based Samsung announced at the Consumer Electronics Show in Las Vegas that it had produced a new TV that was even thinner than one of its own earlier models (which, when introduced, was the thinnest of all its competitors). The model was so thin that skeptics wondered if the TV tuner were actually inside or whether there would have to be a separate "box" outside the screen.

In March of the same year Samsung introduced the market to its complete line of ultra-thins, which included a 55-inch screen model with a depth of only 30.5 millimeters (about 1.2 inches). In just a matter of months, LG bested Samsung, introducing a 55-inch screen model of its own with a thickness of just 24.8 millimeters (about 0.98 inches).

Clearly, this innovation is driven by profit seeking. The price of LCD TVs has fallen and sales have been hurt because of the economic downturn. Changing product design is a tried-and-true way to reinvigorate a market and "thinness" is an obviously measurable and easily understandable characteristic of a TV set. Consumers who want to have the latest gadgets, or those influenced by style gurus and still have money to spend will want to have these TVs. According to an article in the *Wall Street Journal*, although ultrathin TVs are likely to account for less than 1% of the overall TV market, which translates to sales of about 200 million units this year, it does show the direction in which TV design is headed, and for the moment, it still does yield sizable price and profit premiums for manufacturers.[28]

Over time, TV sets are likely to get thinner and thinner. Sony Corp. already has a TV that uses organic LEDs (called OLEDs) which eliminates the need for backlighting and can therefore be only 3 millimeters thick (that's less than one-eighth of an inch). The problem is that the set costs $2,500 and only has an eleven-inch screen.

But not all manufacturers are following the lead of Samsung and LG. According to Scott Ramirez, vice president of TV marketing at Toshiba America Consumer Products, the company does not believe that thinness matters to people enough for them to be willing to pay a premium price. In the company's view, their thicker sets allow for important differences in picture quality, which is ultimately what most consumers care most about. As Ramirez puts it, "No one is complaining about their sets being 3 or 4 inches thick."[29]

Moreover, manufacturers are not abandoning plasma TVs either. Indeed, Samsung has indicated that it will continue to manufacture plasma sets and will work for further improvements in their offerings, particularly since plasma technology is cheaper to manufacture than LCD for large screens. These cost savings have been reflected in significantly lower retail prices for plasma TVs and allowed Samsung to continue to be a strong seller at the low end of the market too.

Teece's second point is more subtle. Innovative products must be produced and marketed. If many firms have the required expertise in production and marketing, they will compete for the rights to the innovation, leaving most of the profits for the innovator. This is yet another example of the *ex ante zero* profit constraint we have discussed earlier in this chapter and another illustration of rent-seeking behavior that we described in Chapter 7. If the required expertise is scarce, the innovator can no longer sell to the highest bidder. The balance of power shifts away from the innovator and toward the established firm that will produce and market the product. Consider that when Nintendo dominated the video game market, game developers had no choice but to accept Nintendo's terms for new software. Nintendo no longer commands such power, and software developers such as Blizzard Entertainment and UbiSoft have gained the upper hand in negotiating rights fees.

EVOLUTIONARY ECONOMICS AND DYNAMIC CAPABILITIES

The theories of innovation we discussed in the previous section are rooted in the tradition of neoclassical microeconomics. In these theories, firms choose the level of innovative activity that maximizes profits. Evolutionary economics, most commonly identified with Richard Nelson and Sidney Winter, offers a perspective on innovative activity that differs from the microeconomic perspective.[30] According to evolutionary economics, firms do not directly choose innovative activities to maximize profits. Instead, key decisions concerning innovation result from organizational routines: well-practiced patterns of activity inside the firm. To understand innovation, it is necessary to understand how routines develop and evolve.

A firm's routines include methods of production, hiring procedures, and policies for determining advertising expenditure. Firms do not change their routines often because getting members of an organization to alter what has worked well in the past is an "unnatural" act. As Schumpeter stressed, however, firms that stick to producing a given set of products in a particular way may not survive. A firm needs to search continuously to improve its routines. The ability of a firm to maintain and adapt the capabilities that are the basis of its competitive advantage is what David Teece, Gary Pisano, and Amy Shuen have referred to as its *dynamic capabilities*.[31] Firms with limited dynamic capabilities fail to nurture and adapt the sources of their advantage over time, and other firms eventually supplant them. Firms with strong dynamic capabilities adapt their resources and capabilities over time and take advantage of new market opportunities to create new sources of competitive advantage.

For several reasons, a firm's dynamic capabilities are inherently limited. First, learning is typically incremental rather than pathbreaking. That is, when a firm searches to improve its operations, it is nearly impossible for the firm to ignore what it has done in the past, and it is difficult for the firm to conceptualize new routines that are fundamentally different from its old ones. Thus, the search for new sources of competitive advantage is *path dependent*—it depends on the path the firm has taken in the past to get where it is now. Even small path dependencies can have important competitive consequences. A firm that has developed significant commitments to a particular way of doing business may find it hard to adapt to seemingly minor changes in technology.

The presence of complementary assets—firm-specific assets that are valuable only in connection with a particular product, technology, or way of doing business—can enhance or impede a firm's dynamic capabilities. The development of new products or capabilities or the opening of new markets can either enhance or destroy the value of complementary assets. Microsoft's installed base in the old MS-DOS ("Microsoft disk operating system") was a valuable complementary asset when it developed Windows in the late 1980s. By contrast, the development of the basic oxygen furnace in the steel industry reduced the value of American steel firms' existing capabilities in the open hearth process. A proposed change in an organizational routine that undermines the value of a complementary asset can give rise to the sunk cost effect discussed earlier, thereby reducing the likelihood that a firm will adopt the change.

"Windows of opportunity" can also impede the development of dynamic capabilities. Early in a product's development, its design is typically fluid, manufacturing routines have not been developed, and capital is generally nonproduct specific. Firms can still experiment with competing product designs or ways of organizing production. However, as time passes, a narrow set of designs or product specifications often emerge as dominant. At this point, network externalities and learning curve effects take over, and it no longer becomes attractive for firms to compete with established market leaders. This variant of the sunk cost effect implies that firms that do not adapt their existing capabilities or commit themselves to new markets when these uncertain windows of opportunity exist may find themselves eventually locked out from the market or competing at a significant disadvantage with early movers.

THE ENVIRONMENT

In *The Competitive Advantage of Nations*, Michael Porter argues that competitive advantage originates in the local environment in which the firm is based.[32] Despite the ability of modern firms to transcend local markets, competitive advantage in particular industries is often strongly concentrated in one or two locations: the world's most successful producers of high-voltage electrical distribution equipment are in Sweden; the best producers of equipment for tunneling are Swiss; the most successful producers of large diesel trucks are American; and the leading microwave firms are Japanese.

Porter views competition as an evolutionary process. Firms initially gain competitive advantages by altering the basis of competition. They win not just by recognizing new markets or technologies but by moving aggressively to exploit them. They sustain their advantages by investing to improve existing sources of advantage and to create new ones. A firm's home nation plays a critical role in shaping managers' perceptions about the opportunities that can be exploited; in supporting the accumulation of valuable resources and capabilities; and in creating pressures on the firm to innovate, invest, and improve.

Porter identifies four attributes in a firm's home market (which he collectively refers to as the "diamond") that promote or impede a firm's ability to achieve competitive advantage in global markets:

1. Factor conditions
2. Demand conditions
3. Related supplier or support industries
4. Strategy, structure, and rivalry

Factor Conditions

Factor conditions describe a nation's position with regard to factors of production (e.g., human resources, infrastructure) that are necessary to compete in a particular industry. Because general-purpose factors of production are often available locally or can be purchased in global markets, the most important factors of production are highly specialized to the needs of particular industries. For example, since the 1950s, Japan has had one of the highest numbers of engineering graduates per capita. This, according to Porter, has had much more to do with its success in such industries as automobiles and consumer electronics than the low wages of its production workers.

Demand Conditions

These conditions include the size, growth, and character of home demand for the firm's product. Sophisticated home customers or unique local conditions stimulate firms to enhance the quality of their products and to innovate. For example, in air conditioners, Japanese firms such as Panasonic are known for producing small, quiet, energy-efficient window units. These product characteristics are critical in Japan, where air conditioning is important (summers are hot and humid), but large, noisy units would be unacceptable because houses are small and packed closely together, and electricity is expensive.

Related Supplier or Support Industries

Firms that operate in a home market that has a strong base of internationally competitive supplier or support industries will be favorably positioned to achieve competitive advantage in global markets. Although many inputs are mobile, and thus firms do not need geographic proximity to make exchanges, exchanging key inputs, such as scarce production know-how, does require geographic proximity. Companies with skillful home-based suppliers can be early beneficiaries of newly generated production know-how and may be able to shape innovation in supplying firms. For example, Italian shoe manufacturers have established close working relationships with leather producers that allow the shoe manufacturers to learn quickly about new textures and colors. Leather producers, in turn, learn about emerging fashion trends from the shoe manufacturers, which helps leather producers to plan new products.

Strategy, Structure, and Rivalry

The final environmental determinant of competitive advantage, according to Porter, is the context for competition in the firm's home market. This includes local management practices, organizational structure, corporate governance, and the nature of local capital markets. For example, in Germany and Switzerland, most shares in publicly traded firms are held by institutional investors who do not trade frequently, and capital gains are exempt from taxation. As a result, day-to-day movements in share price are not significant, which, according to Porter, creates a stronger propensity for companies in these industries to invest in research and innovation than is true of their counterparts in the United States and Britain.

Rivalry in the home market is another important part of the competitive context. According to Porter, local rivalry affects the rate of innovation in a market far more than foreign rivalry does. Although local rivalry may hold down profitability in local markets, firms that survive vigorous local competition are often more

EXAMPLE 11.6 THE RISE OF THE SWISS WATCH INDUSTRY[33]

In the eighteenth century, Britain was the largest producer of watches in the world. British master craftsmen produced nearly 200,000 watches per year by 1800, or roughly half the world's supply. Britain's dominance was the result of several factors. First, watchmakers employed laborers in the British countryside, at a considerably lower wage than laborers in London would demand. Second, the watchmakers benefited from the division of labor. In an eight-mile stretch from Prescot to Liverpool in northwest England, one could find cottages of springmakers, wheel cutters, dialmakers, and other specialists. Large local demand helped make this specialization possible. During the 1700s, Britain accounted for half the worldwide demand for watches. Finally, a key raw material, crucible steel, was manufactured by a British monopoly. Foreign manufacturers elsewhere did not learn how to make crucible steel until 1800.

The confluence of specialized, low-cost workers, high local demand, and access to a crucial input gave the British advantages that no other watchmakers could match. In the mid- to late 1700s, British watches were considered the finest in the world and commanded a premium price. But British watchmakers could not keep up with world demand. They began importing watches made elsewhere and reselling them as their own. Watchmakers in Geneva benefited from this policy.

Geneva had been a center of watchmaking ever since Protestant refugees arrived from France in the mid-1500s. By the mid-1700s, Geneva was second only to Britain in watchmaking. Many of today's most prestigious brands, including Constantin Vacheron (formerly Abraham Vacheron) and Patek Philippe (formerly Czapek and Philippe), began during this period.

The Geneva watchmakers differed from their British counterparts in one key respect. The British did not have to market their product—they made high-quality watches and waited for customers to come to them. Geneva watchmakers could not match the reputations of their British counterparts and so had to become merchants as well as artisans. To keep costs down, they outsourced much of the production to workers in the nearby French and Italian Alps, at labor costs well below those in England. They also developed new markets for watches. They marketed themselves in areas such as Italy, where few people wore watches. Some watchmakers devoted themselves to niche markets, such as that for extremely thin watches. Others targeted cost-conscious buyers. As David Landes has written, "The Swiss made watches to please their customers. The British made watches to please themselves."

In the nineteenth century, British watchmakers suffered. Wars drained the British economy and dried up local demand for watches. Ill equipped to market their watches overseas, domestic watch producers in Britain nearly disappeared. At the same time, the Swiss enjoyed growing sales and the benefits of the division of labor. The Swiss also gained access to crucible steel, which by then was available outside of Britain. In addition, desperate British watchmakers exported uncased movements and parts, helping the Swiss match British quality. By the middle of the nineteenth century, Swiss watchmakers were dominant. They made watches at all levels of quality, at costs below those achievable anywhere else. They tailored new product to consumer tastes. The Swiss dominated the watch industry until the mid-twentieth century, when the Japanese used cheap quartz movements to achieve unprecedented accuracy at remarkably low costs.

efficient and innovative than are international rivals that emerge from softer local conditions. The airline industry is a good example. The U.S. domestic airline industry is far more price competitive than the international industry, where entry is restricted and many flag carriers receive state subsidies. Coming out of the intensely competitive U.S. industry, U.S. airlines (such as American and United) that fly international routes are far more cost efficient than many of the international airlines they compete with and rely on profits from international routes to offset losses domestically.

CHAPTER SUMMARY

- Under the dynamic of perfect competition, no competitive advantage will be sustainable, and the persistence of profitability over time should be weak, because most firms' profits will converge to the competitive level.

- Evidence suggests that the profits of high-profit firms decline over time, while those of low-profit firms rise over time. However, the profits of these groups do not converge to a common mean. This lack of convergence cannot be ascribed to differences in risk between high-profit and low-profit firms. More likely, it reflects impediments to the operation of the dynamic of perfect competition.

- The resource-based theory of the firm emphasizes asymmetries in the resources and capabilities of firms in the same business as the basis for sustainable competitive advantage. Resources and capabilities must be scarce and immobile—not tradable on well-functioning markets—to serve as the basis of sustainable advantage.

- Competitive advantages must also be protected by isolating mechanisms to be sustainable. An isolating mechanism prevents competitors from duplicating or neutralizing the source of the firm's competitive advantage. Isolating mechanisms fall into two broad classes: barriers to imitation and early-mover advantages.

- Specific barriers to imitation are: legal restrictions, such as patents or copyrights, that impede imitation; superior access to scarce inputs or customers; economies of scale coupled with limited market size; and intangible barriers to imitation, including causal ambiguity, dependence on historical circumstances, and social complexity.

- Sources of early-mover advantages include: the learning curve, brand-name reputation when buyers are uncertain about product quality, and consumer switching costs. Early-mover advantages are also possible in markets with network effects.

- Creative destruction is the process whereby old sources of competitive advantage are destroyed and replaced with new ones. Economist Joseph Schumpeter wrote that the essence of entrepreneurship is the exploitation of the "shocks" or "discontinuities" that destroy existing sources of advantage.

- A dominant established firm's incentive to innovate may be weaker than that of a smaller firm or a potential entrant. The sunk cost and the replacement effect weaken the established firm's incentive to innovate. The efficiency effect, by contrast, strengthens the dominant firm's incentive to innovate as compared with a potential entrant's incentive.

- Evolutionary economics sees the firm's decisions as determined by routines—well-practiced patterns of activity inside the firm—rather than profit maximization. Firms typically need to engage in continuous search for ways to improve their existing routines.

- Dynamic capabilities are a firm's ability to maintain the bases of its competitive advantage.

● Michael Porter argues that competitive advantage originates in a firm's local environment. He identifies four attributes in a firm's home market that promote or impede its ability to achieve competitive advantage in global markets: factor conditions; demand conditions; related supplier or support industries; and strategy, structure, and rivalry.

QUESTIONS

1. "An analysis of sustainability is similar to a five-forces analysis." Comment.
2. How do economies of scale affect sustainability?
3. Coke and Pepsi have sustained their market dominance for nearly a century. General Motors and Ford were hard hit by competition and never fully recovered. What is different about the product/market situations in these two cases that affects sustainability?
4. Provide an example of a firm that has cospecialized assets. Has the firm prospered from them? Why or why not?
5. Mercury is a hypothetical store that sells athletic shoes, particularly shoes for runners. Mercury is distinctive in the training of its sales staff. The store has a variety of diagnostic tools, including weight distribution analysis and slow-motion replay, and the staff are trained to use those tools to help customers figure out exactly which shoe will be best for them. Mercury also carries a wide assortment of shoes from the full range of athletic shoemakers, some of which are otherwise-hard-to-find models. Although Mercury is an independent store, it is part of a buying cooperative that enables it to obtain its shoes from suppliers at volume discount prices that would otherwise be available only to large chains. Mercury sponsors a variety of races in its greater metropolitan area, the largest of which is a high-profile annual marathon.

   Of the following list of Mercury's activities, which **two** have the greatest potential for cospecialization?

   (a) Diagnostic skills of staff
   (b) Buying cooperative membership
   (c) Broad product assortment
   (d) Race sponsorship
6. Which of the following circumstances are likely to create early-mover advantages?

   (a) Maxwell House introduces the first freeze-dried coffee.
   (b) A consortium of U.S. firms introduce the first high-definition television.
   (c) SmithKline introduces Tagamet, the first effective medical treatment for ulcers.
   (d) Wal-Mart opens a store in Nome, Alaska.
7. In light of the winner's curse, must winning bidders in auctions necessarily "lose" in the sense of paying more than the item is worth? What steps can bidders take to prosper in auctions?
8. Two incompatible high-resolution audio formats, Super Audio CD (SACD) and DVD Audio (DVDA), were introduced in 2000. Both offered surround-sound music at a quality that approaches the original studio master recordings from which they are made. Both formats could be added to new DVD players for an

additional $25 to $250 per format, depending on the quality. SACD was originally supported by Sony. While Sony has abandoned the format, it has since won
support from numerous classical music and jazz labels that sell in small numbers
to "audiophiles." DVDA has been abandoned by its backers. Why do you think
high-resolution audio remained a niche product?

9. Consider an industry in which firms can expect to sell 1,000 units annually at a
market price of P. Before firms enter, they do not know their production costs
with certainty. Instead, they believe that unit costs can be $2, $4, $6, or $8 with
equal probability. Annualized sunk production costs are $1,500—firms cannot
recover this expense should they choose to exit. What is the equilibrium price at
which firms are indifferent about entering? What is the average profit of firms
that are producing? (*Hint:* Firms will produce as long as the price equals or
exceeds unit production costs.)

10. Is the extent of creative destruction likely to differ across industries? Can the risk
of creative destruction be incorporated into a five-forces analysis of an industry?

11. Is patent racing a zero-sum game? A negative sum-game? Explain.

12. What are a firm's dynamic capabilities? To what extent can managers create or
"manage into existence" a firm's dynamic capabilities?

13. "Industrial or antitrust policies that result in the creation of domestic monopolies
rarely result in global competitive advantage." Comment.

14. IQ, Inc., currently monopolizes the market for a certain type of microprocessor, the 666. The present value of the stream of monopoly profits from this
design is thought to be $500 million. Enginola (which is currently in a com-
pletely different segment of the microprocessor market from this one) and IQ
are contemplating spending money to develop a superior design that will make
the 666 completely obsolete. Whoever develops the design first gets the entire
market. The present value of the stream of monopoly profit from the superior
design is expected to be $150 million greater than the present value of the
profit from the 666.

Success in developing the design is not certain, but the probability of a firm's
success is directly linked to the amount of money it spends on the project
(more spending on this project, greater probability of success). Moreover, the
productivity of Enginola's spending on this project and IQ's spending is exactly
the same: Starting from any given level of spending, an additional $1 spent
by Enginola has exactly the same impact on its probability of winning. The
following table illustrates this. It shows the probability of winning the race if
each firm's spending equals 0, $100 million, and $200 million. The first number represents Enginola's probability of winning the race, the second is IQ's
probability of winning, and the third is the probability that neither succeeds.
Note: This is not a payoff table.

	IQ's Spending		
Enginola's Spending	*0*	*$100 million*	*$200 million*
0	(0,0,1)	(0,.6,.4)	(0,.8,.2)
$100 million	(6,0,.4)	(4,.4,.2)	(3,.6,.1)
$200 million	(8,0,.2)	(6,.3,.1)	(5,.5,0)

Assuming that

(i) each firm makes its spending decision simultaneously and noncooperatively;

(ii) each seeks to maximize its expected profit; and

(iii) neither firm faces any financial constraints,

which company, if any, has the greater incentive to spend money to win this "R&D race"? Of the effects discussed in the chapter (productivity effect, sunk cost effect, replacement effect, efficiency effect), which are shaping the incentives to innovate in this example?

ENDNOTES

[1]Mueller, D. C., "The Persistence of Profits Above the Norm," *Economica*, 44, 1997, pp. 369–380. See also Mueller, D. C., *Profits in the Long Run*, Cambridge, Cambridge University Press, 1986.

[2]Our characterization of these patterns of profit persistence is based on the results in Table 2.2 of Mueller's book, *Profits in the Long Run*. Mueller's study is far more elaborate than we have described here. He uses regression analysis to estimate equations that give persistence patterns for each of the 600 firms in his sample. Our grouping of firms into two groups is done to illustrate the main results.

[3]This definition is adapted from Barney, J., "Firm Resources and Sustained Competitive Advantage," *Journal of Management*, 17, 1991, pp. 99–120.

[4]Presentations of this theory can be found in numerous publications, including Barney, J., "Firm Resources and Sustained Competitive Advantage," *Journal of Management*, 17, 1991, pp. 99–120; Peteraf, M. A., "The Cornerstones of Competitive Advantage: A Resource-Based View," *Strategic Management Journal*, 14, 1993, pp. 179–191; and Dierickx, I., and K. Cool, "Asset Stock Accumulation and Sustainability of Competitive Advantage," *Management Science*, 35, 1989, pp. 1504–1511. The pioneering work underlying the resource-based theory is Penrose, E. T., *The Theory of the Growth of the Firm*, Oxford, Blackwell, 1959.

[5]"The Big Gulp at Starbucks," by Barbara Kiviat, Time, 12/10/2006, online at http://www.time.com/time/magazine/article/0,9171,1568488,00.html. Retrieved on June 19, 2009.

[6]Data on number of locations and other operational changes are from the Starbucks website at http://www.starbucks.com/aboutus/timeline.asp

[7]"Starbucks alters its daily grind," reported by Julie Jargon for the Wall Street Journal, 6/17/2009, on line at http://articles.moneycentral.msn.com/Investing/Extra/starbucks-altersits-daily-grind.aspx. Accessed on June 19, 2009.

[8]"Starbucks: What went wrong?" by Daniel Palmer, Australian Food News, July 31, 2008, online at http://www.ausfoodnews.com.au/2008/07/31/starbucks-what-went-wrong.html. Accessed June 19, 2009.

[9]Rumelt, R. P., "Towards a Strategic Theory of the Firm," in Lamb, R. (ed.), *Competitive Strategic Management*, Englewood Cliffs, NJ, Prentice-Hall, 1984, pp. 556–570.

[10]See, for example, Chapter 5 of Ghemawat, P., *Commitment: The Dynamic of Strategy*, New York, Free Press, 1991, or Yao, D., "Beyond the Reach of the Invisible Hand," *Strategic Management Journal*, 9, 1988, pp. 59–70.

[11]Quotation from p. 359 in Rumelt, R. P., "Towards a Strategic Theory of the Firm," in Lamb, R. (ed.), *Competitive Strategic Management*, Englewood Cliffs, NJ, Prentice-Hall, 1984, pp. 566–570.

[12]Williams, J., "How Sustainable Is Your Advantage?" *California Management Review*, 34, 1992, pp. 1–23.

[13]Quoted in Beard, D., "The Champ Returns," *Fort Lauderdale Sun Sentinal*, December 1, 1996, p. 1G.

[14]White, L., "The Automobile Industry," in Adams, W. (ed.), *The Structure of American Industry*, 6th ed., New York, Macmillan, 1982.

[15]See, for example, Scherer, F. M., and D. Ross, *Industrial Market Structure and Economic Performance*, 3d ed., Boston, Houghton Mifflin, 1990, pp. 563–564.

[16]For further discussion of the winner's curse and the difficulties of finding an optimal bidding strategy, see Thaler, R., "Anomalies: The Winner's Curse," *Journal of Economic Perspectives*, 2(1), 1988, pp. 191–202.

[17]Rumelt, R. P., "Towards a Strategic Theory of the Firm," in Lamb, R. (ed.), *Competitive Strategic Management*, Englewood Cliffs, NJ, Prentice-Hall, 1984, pp. 556–570. See also Reed, R., and R. J. DeFillipi, "Causal Ambiguity, Barriers to Imitation and Sustainable Competitive Advantage," *Academy of Management Review*, 15, 1990, pp. 88–102.

[18]Teece, D., "Applying Concepts of Economic Analysis to Strategic Management," in Harold Pennings and Associates (eds.), *Organizational Strategy and Change*, San Francisco, Jossey-Bass, 1985.

[19]Lippman, S. A., and R. P. Rumelt, "Uncertain Imitability: An Analysis of Interfirm Differences in Efficiency under Competition," *Bell Journal of Economics*, 13, Autumn 1982, pp. 418–438.

[20]We calculated the equilibrium price through trial and error. A systematic method exists for calculating the equilibrium price in this market, but its discussion would add little to the economic insights that this example generates.

[21]Schumpeter, J., *Capitalism, Socialism, and Democracy*, New York, Harper & Row, 1942, p. 132.

[22]Ibid., pp. 84–85.

[23]Christensen, C., *The Innovator's Dilemma*, New York, Harper Business, 2000.

[24]Stein, J., "Internal Capital Markets and the Competition for Corporate Resources," *Journal of Finance*, 52(1997), pp. 111–133.

[25]Arrow, K., "Economics Welfare and the Allocation of Resources for Inventions," in Nelson, R. (ed.), *The Rate and Direction of Inventive Activity*, Princeton, NJ, Princeton University Press, 1962.

[26]This term was coined by Jean Tirole. Tirole discusses the replacement effect in his book, *The Theory of Industrial Organization*, Cambridge, MA, MIT Press, 1988.

[27]Teece, D., 1986, "Profiting from Technological Innovation: Implications for Integration, Collaboration, Licensing, and Public Policy," *Research Policy*, 15, pp. 285–305.

[28]"LG Electronics Debuts Ultrathin Television," by Evan Ramstad, *The Wall Street Journal*, June 26, 2009. Accessed online at http://online.wsj.com/article_email/SB124595473000755293-lMyQjAxMDI5NDI1NjkyNTYOWj.html

[29]As quoted in "TV makers hope thin is in for newest sets" by Barbara Ortutay (with contributions from Peter Svensson), The Associated Press, accessed July 6, 2009 at http://www.google.com/hostednews/ap/article/ALeqM5gxHUmKgHabSuc3D4Fh GDEkCAO MawD9992GA00

[30]Nelson, R. R., and S. G. Winter, *An Evolutionary Theory of Economic Change*, Cambridge, MA, Belknap Press, 1982.

[31]Teece, D. J., G. Pisano, and A. Shuen, "Dynamic Capabilities and Strategic Management," University of California at Berkeley, *Strategic Management Journal*, 18, August 1997, pp. 509–534. See also Teece, D. J., R. Rumelt, G. Dosi, and S. Winter, "Understanding Corporate Coherence: Theory and Evidence," *Journal of Economic Behavior and Organization*, 23, 1994, pp. 1–30 for related ideas.

[32]Porter, M., *The Competitive Advantage of Nations*, New York, Free Press, 1998.

[33]This example is drawn from Landes, David, *Revolution in Time*, Cambridge, MA, Belknap Press, 1983.

PART FOUR

INTERNAL ORGANIZATION

PERFORMANCE MEASUREMENT AND INCENTIVES

12

$\mathbf{A}$s CEO of investment bank Merrill Lynch, Stan O'Neal transformed the firm. After taking the helm in 2003, O'Neal changed the firm's top management team, shook up the staid corporate culture, and drove the firm to take more risk in search of higher returns. According to the *Wall Street Journal*, "Whenever Goldman Sachs Group Inc. would report quarterly profits in recent years, the pain would be felt nearby, at the downtown headquarters of Merrill Lynch & Co. There, Merrill Chief Executive Stan O'Neal would grill his executives about why, for instance, Goldman was showing faster growth in bond-trading profits. 'It got to the point where you didn't want to be in the office' on Goldman earnings days, one former Merrill executive recalls."[1]

O'Neal's emphasis on *relative performance* helped change mindsets. Employees who knew their bonuses depended on outperforming Goldman investigated new ways to grow their business. Many began selling credit default obligations (CDOs), financial instruments that obligated Merrill Lynch to pay investors if certain businesses defaulted on their debt. Merrill Lynch grew rapidly and O'Neal was hailed as a visionary, until the financial crisis put Merrill Lynch at risk of taking huge losses on its CDO contracts. O'Neal was ousted by his board, and Bank of America purchased the assets of the financially distressed Merrill Lynch in 2009.

O'Neal's tribulations raise key issues for any firm. A firm's central office may set strategy, but its employees must implement it. How should the firm measure the performance of its employees? How should it use those performance measures to reward employees for actions that advance the firm's strategy? Are there risks associated with tying rewards to specific performance measures? In this chapter we address these questions in detail. We start by considering the economics of performance measurement. If the firm can devise performance measures that allow it to reward exactly the activities it wants its employees to pursue, linking pay to performance can lead to increased profits. It can, however, be difficult to devise good measures of an employee's job performance, and managers must be able to distinguish good and bad measures of performance. We then consider the various ways that firms reward employee performance.

THE PRINCIPAL–AGENT RELATIONSHIP

A *principal–agent relationship* or *agency relationship* occurs when one party (the agent) is hired by another (the principal) to take actions or make decisions that affect the payoff to the principal.[2] As one example, consider the relation between a public firm's shareholders (the "principal") and its chief executive officer (CEO) (their agent). The CEO's job description usually includes strategic planning, hiring operating officers, and managing the organization. If the CEO manages and plans effectively, the firm's share price will rise and shareholders will be paid larger dividends. If the CEO does a poor job running the firm, the return to shareholders will suffer.

The principal–agent framework is broadly applicable. All of a firm's employees can be thought of as agents of the firm's owners, since they all take actions or make decisions that might impact the payoff to the owners. The principal–agent framework can also be used to think about relationships between firms, between professionals and their clients, or even outside of the business world entirely. Advertising agencies act as agents for consumer product companies, doctors act as agents for their patients, and elected officials are expected to act as agents on behalf of voters.

Difficulties in agency relationships can arise when two conditions are met: (1) The objectives of principal and agent are different, and (2) the actions taken by the agent or the information possessed by the agent are hard to observe. We discuss each condition in turn.

The typical principal would like to maximize the difference between the value it receives as a result of the agent's actions and any payment it makes to the agent. If the agent had the same objective, we would say that the goals of the principal and agent were aligned. But the agent does not directly care about the value generated for the principal; the agent cares about the value it generates for itself. Their interests are normally not aligned. Legal scholar Adolf Berle and economist Gardiner Means were among the first to describe the differences in objectives in the shareholder–CEO agency relationship.[3] One important objective of a firm's shareholders, they wrote, is to "earn the maximum profit compatible with a reasonable degree of risk." The objectives of management are often harder to discern. Managers may wish to maximize their personal wealth even if shareholders do not benefit. Managers may wish to limit their personal risk, avoiding risky strategic initiatives that shareholders view as "reasonable." Managers may wish to boost their prospects for another job, and could therefore take actions that pump up the firm's short-run performance even if shareholders are harmed in the long run. Finally, managers could simply be averse to excessive effort—putting in a series of 80-hour weeks doing strategic planning is, after all, very hard work.

Differences in objectives are not by themselves sufficient to lead to problems in agency relationships. If actions and information are easily observable, then the principal can write a complete contract with the agent that aligns their interests. We discussed complete contracts in Chapter 3, where we identified several reasons why it is difficult to write them. In particular, contracting can be hindered by *hidden action* or *hidden information*, things known to the agent but not to the principal. When the principal and agent have different objectives, and the agent can take hidden actions or has hidden information, agency problems can arise.

Combating Agency Problems

One way to mitigate hidden action and hidden information problems is to expend resources watching employees or gathering information that employees use to make

EXAMPLE 12.1 DIFFERENCES IN OBJECTIVES IN AGENCY RELATIONSHIPS: YAHOO! AND ENGLISH FRUIT

Differences in objectives in agency relationships can take many forms, and principals must be prepared to think quite broadly about how an agent's objectives might differ from theirs. Two examples help illustrate this point.

On February 1, 2008, the Internet portal firm Yahoo! received a takeover bid from software giant Microsoft. A corporate takeover occurs when a firm or an individual (Microsoft, in this case) offers to buy all shares in a "target firm" (such as Yahoo!) and thus take control of the target. Negotiations between the two firms led to a revised bid in May of 2008, with Microsoft CEO Steve Balmer reportedly offering $33 per share. Yahoo! CEO Jerry Yang refused, and insisted that the firm was worth at least $37 per share. The firm remained independent as of May 2012.

There are at least three potential explanations for Yang's decision to turn down Microsoft's offer. First, it could be the case that Yang believed the firm was worth more than Microsoft's offer. If, as an independent entity, the firm could generate dividend payments to shareholders with a net present value of more than $33 per share, then accepting Microsoft's offer would not be in the shareholders' interest. Note, however, that the firm was trading at a mere $19 per share prior to Microsoft's February bid, so stock market participants appeared to think that Yahoo's value as an independent entity was considerably less than Microsoft's offer.

A second possibility is that Yang was working hard on the shareholders' behalf to try to maximize the purchase price from Microsoft. If Microsoft's maximum willingness to pay for Yahoo! was $40, then Yang could merely be trying to drive a hard bargain. If he was eventually able to get Microsoft to increase its offer, then shareholders would benefit.

A third possibility, however, is that Yang had different preferences than shareholders regarding Yahoo!'s independence. Shareholders generally might not care whether Yahoo! is an independent entity; instead, they just want to maximize the return on their investment. On the other hand, Yang, who founded Yahoo! in 1994 with fellow Stanford engineering grad student Dave Filo, might value the firm's continued independence for its own sake. Some simple arithmetic will help draw out the implications of this preference. Suppose Yang, who directly and indirectly owned around 50 million Yahoo! shares as of early 2008, believed that Yahoo! could achieve a stock price of $30 as an independent entity. Then, rejecting Microsoft's $33 offer costs Yang $3 * 50 million = $150 million. If Yang (whose holdings in Yahoo! were worth around a billion dollars) was willing to give up $150 million in order to keep the firm he founded independent, then his preferences may have differed from those of the firm's shareholders, and an agency problem may have exist. Some shareholders did seem to be unhappy with Yang; in August of 2008, more than one-third of the firm's shareholders voted not to reappoint him to the firm's board.

A second example of differences in objectives in agency relationships comes from a field experiment conducted by economists Oriana Bandiera, Iwan Barankay, and Imran Rasul.[4] Bandiera and colleagues visited a fruit farm in England and worked with management to try to improve the efficiency of the firm's fruit-picking operation. Field workers at the farm were paid "piece rates"—that is, they received a set rate per piece of fruit (or pound of fruit) they picked. Using statistical analysis, the researchers found that worker productivity varied in systematic ways depending on the supervisor to whom the worker was assigned. Worker productivity was highest when the worker and supervisor had a "social connection," as measured by shared country of origin, shared living quarters, or similar duration of employment at the farm. (Workers at this farm were hired on seasonal contracts and came from eight nations in eastern Europe.)

What can explain this odd pattern? Bandiera and colleagues suggest that supervisors' social connections led to favoritism. That is, supervisors may simply like some workers more than others and may therefore have a preference for helping some workers more than others, so that the favored workers can earn more money through piece rates. Note that this preference likely differs markedly from that of the fruit farm. The principal (the fruit farm) does not care which of its fruit pickers earns the highest pay, while the agent (the supervisor) does. Interestingly, favoritism seems to have stopped (and overall fruitpicking efficiency rose) after the firm tied supervisor pay to worker productivity. This suggests that favoritism was not leading supervisors to allocate their efforts in the most efficient manner.

decisions. For example, one important role of corporate boards of directors is to monitor the decisions of the firm's CEO. Directors are usually themselves current and former top executives at other firms, which can make them skillful monitors of other CEOs. Directors meet regularly and often spend time talking to a firm's employees, suppliers, and customers. They review financial statements, reports, and investment decisions, and they frequently vote to approve or disapprove major decisions made by the CEO, such as undertaking a large acquisition.

While monitoring can help firms resolve problems of hidden action and information, it does have some significant limitations. First, it is often imperfect. While most members of corporate boards are business experts with years of experience, they typically do not spend more than about 25 days per year on company business. Given the complexity of many large, modern organizations, it is difficult to imagine that directors could digest all information that is relevant for CEO decision making. Second, hiring monitors can be quite costly. Members of corporate boards are paid large retainers (frequently in excess of $250,000 annually). Similarly, general counsels at large corporations earn salaries that can approach a million dollars per year. Even in lower level jobs where managers who monitor employees earn a fraction of the salary paid to a director, such as assembly lines, call centers, and retail sales, these costs can be substantial. Third, hiring a monitor often introduces another layer to the agency relationship. Adding a board of directors may help solve agency conflicts between the shareholders and the CEO, but shareholders may then have to worry about agency conflicts between themselves and the directors.

When principals cannot adequately monitor their agents' actions, or find it excessively costly to do so, they may prefer to tie pay directly to performance.

PERFORMANCE-BASED INCENTIVES

Using pay-for-performance incentives can mitigate agency conflicts by aligning the interests of the agent and the principal. To do this, the principal links the agent's pay (or, more generally, the value the agent receives) to the payoff the principal receives from the agent's action. The agent earns more when the principal does well and less when the principal does badly, and so is more willing to take actions that benefit the principal.

Performance-based incentives are everywhere. Salespeople at department stores like Nordstrom and Galleries Lafayette receive commissions equal to approximately 5 percent of their customers' purchases. Brand managers at consumer goods firms like Kraft or Maruchan typically receive year-end bonuses that are linked to the profit generated by their brands. Most publicly traded firms grant stock and stock options to chief executive officers, thereby linking CEO wealth to the return that shareholders earn. Firms can also offer nonmonetary rewards—"employee of the month" parking, vacations for top sales agents, and "status" rewards such as plaques and special mention at company events.

The best way to explain the properties of performance-based incentives is with a simple economic model of how a hypothetical employee may respond to such incentives. We will use this model to consider more complex aspects of incentives, so pay careful attention to the notation. Consider a firm that hires an employee to perform a sales function. Let the employee's effort level be represented by e. Think of units of effort as "hours during which the employee puts forth *high* effort." We make this distinction because the principal may be able to observe the number of hours that the employee works, but is unlikely to observe the number of hours during which the employee puts forth high effort. Thus, e represents a hidden action and cannot be included in a contract.

Now suppose that the employee is willing to put forth some high effort regardless of compensation, but will exert extra effort only if compensated in some way. One way to represent this is to write the employee's cost of exerting effort level e in monetary terms. Specifically, let the cost of exerting effort level e be given by the following formula, which is also depicted in Figure 12.1:

$$c(e) = \begin{cases} 0 & \text{if } e \leq 40 \\ 1/2(e - 40)^2 & \text{if } e > 40 \end{cases}$$

The interpretation of this function is as follows. The employee is willing to increase effort from e_0 to e_1 if and only if the additional compensation (whether monetary or nonmonetary) is at least $c(e_1) - c(e_0)$. The flat region on the curve in Figure 12.1 indicates that the employee is willing to put in up to 40 units of effort for no extra compensation. However, the employee is willing to exert additional effort beyond 40 units only if compensated for doing so. The cost function is convex, indicating that extra effort becomes more and more costly as the employee's effort level increases.

Now consider an employee who puts in 40 units of effort and is considering putting in one additional unit of effort. According to the preceding formula, the effort costs the employee $c(41) - c(40) = \$0.50$. Suppose that each unit of effort generates \$100 in extra sales to the principal. Thus, sales = \$100e. Hence, one additional unit

FIGURE 12.1
A CONVEX COST OF EFFORT FUNCTION

This employee is willing to exert up to 40 units of effort without being compensated for doing so. The employee is willing to increase effort from e_0 to e_1 only if compensation will increase by $c(e_1) - c(e_0)$ as a result. The marginal cost of effort increases as the employee works harder.

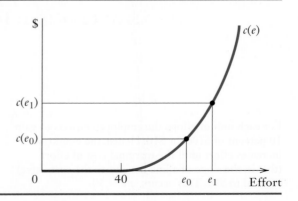

of effort generates a net surplus of $99.50 for the two parties—the $100 in extra sales captured by the firm less the $0.50 in effort cost borne by the employee. How can the firm get the employee to make the extra effort? If effort were observable, the firm could simply offer to pay the employee an additional $0.50 for the extra unit of effort. As noted earlier, it might not be possible for the firm to observe whether the employee is putting in extra effort, so this offer is not feasible.

Let us consider some compensation schemes that are feasible. Suppose that the firm pays the employee a straight salary that matches the market wage, which we assume is $1,000 per week. The employee's payoff net of effort costs is $1,000 − c(e). Given that pay does not depend on sales, the employee in this case is unwilling to put in more than 40 units of effort. Phrased another way, if the employee has nothing to gain from extra effort, then no extra effort should be expected. The employee's 40 units of effort result in $4,000 in sales, while the wage paid is $1,000. The firm earns $3,000 in profits.

Suppose instead that the firm offers a salary of $1,000 per week, but adds a 10 percent commission on sales. Given that each unit of effort produces an extra $100 of sales, we can write the employee's payoff as

$$\$1{,}000 + 0.10(100e) - c(e)$$

The employee will increase effort until the marginal benefit of effort is equal to the marginal cost. As shown in Figure 12.2, the marginal benefit of effort to the employee is always 10 percent of $100, or $10—each unit of effort translates into another $10 in commission. The marginal cost of effort is the slope of the effort curve. The convex shape of this curve implies that it becomes more and more costly for the employee to exert additional effort. A bit of calculus shows that the employee is best off choosing $e = 50$; at any effort beyond this, the marginal cost of effort exceeds the marginal

FIGURE 12.2
THE EMPLOYEE INCREASES EFFORT UNTIL THE MARGINAL BENEFIT OF EFFORT IS EQUAL TO THE MARGINAL COST

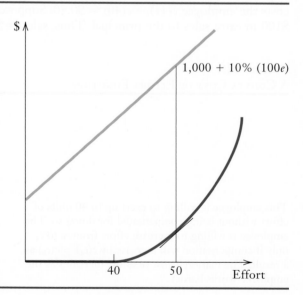

For each unit of effort, the employee expects to gain 10 percent of $100, or $10. Hence, the employee increases effort until the marginal cost of effort (that is, the slope of a line tangent to the cost curve) is equal to $10. This occurs at $e = 50$.

benefit.[5] When $e = 50$, we can calculate the following: total sales are $5,000, the employee's commission is $500, and total cash compensation is $1,500. The employee's compensation, net of effort costs, is $1,500 - 0.5(50 - 40)^2 = $1,450, and the firm realizes profits of $5,000 - $1,500 = $3,500. Compared with straight salary plan, we see that the increase in wages paid by the firm under the salary-plus-commission plan is more than offset by the increase in the employee's productivity. Both the firm and its employee are better off.

The firm may be able to achieve even higher profits by slightly adjusting the salary-plus-commission plan. Under the current plan, the employee has net compensation of $1,450, which is $450 more than the market wage. The employee should therefore be willing to accept a contract that offers up to $450 less than the current plan; put another way, the employee should agree to a plan that pays at least $550 plus 10 percent commission. The employee would still put in 50 hours of extra effort and would earn $1,000 in net compensation, just enough to prefer this job to another one at $1,000. The firm would see its profits increase from $3,500 to $3,950.

This example illustrates several key points about performance-based incentives:

1. The slope of the relationship between pay and performance, rather than the absolute pay level, provides incentives for effort. As Figures 12.2 and 12.3 illustrate, raising the employee's salary (say, from $900 to $1,000) does not change the cost-benefit trade-off determining the employee's effort choice.
2. The firm earns a higher profit when it offers the salary-plus-commission job than with a fixed salary job.
3. The firm can do even better if it sets a higher commission rate. In fact, the firm's profit-maximizing commission rate is 100 percent! (That is, the worker keeps all the sales revenues.) Why? The firm would like to maximize total value, which is the difference between total revenues and worker costs. This occurs if the worker

FIGURE 12.3
THE FIRM CAN OFFER A LOWER SALARY WITHOUT CHANGING INCENTIVES FOR EFFORT

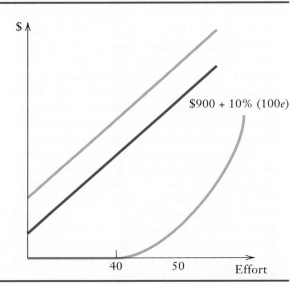

$900 + 10% (100e)

If the firm offers a salary of $900, the employee still selects effort by making a cost-benefit comparison. Since neither the marginal benefit of effort nor the marginal cost is affected, the employee's effort choice is unchanged.

EXAMPLE 12.2 PERFORMANCE-BASED INCENTIVES: THE ZAMBIA PERFORMANCE-BASED INCENTIVES PILOT STUDY

The Republic of Zambia is a country in Southern Africa surrounded by the Democratic Republic of the Congo, Tanzania, Malawi, Mozambique, Zimbabwe, Botswana, Namibia and Angola. Like its neighbors, Zambia is a developing country facing many challenges and primary among them is providing healthcare to its people. Through the 1990s, many such nations undertook healthcare reform projects, most of which decentralized the provision of services.

As part of its reforms in that period, the Zambian government instituted a program through which 10% of the fees collected by a health facility would be returned to that facility and divided among its staff as a bonus. The government hoped that this would encourage more healthcare providers to work in the public sector and would, at least in part, compensate for the low salaries in that sector. But the monetary amount of the bonus was too small to provide the needed incentive.

In 2005, the Zambian Central Board of Health (CBOH) commissioned a pilot study of performance-based incentives. The study, authored by Rebecca Furth, was conducted by Initiatives Inc. through the Quality Assurance Project (QAP) which is funded by the U.S. Agency for International Development (USAID). QAP serves developing countries eligible for USAID assistance, USAID Missions and Bureaus, and other agencies and nongovernmental organizations that cooperate with USAID, and offers technical assistance in the management of quality assurance and workforce development in healthcare, helping to develop feasible, affordable approaches to comprehensive change in health service delivery.[6]

In the report on the study, Furth suggests that the greatest challenge posed for such programs in developing countries is the need to establish effective performance management systems, for without this component, performance incentives will not be effective. Staff will not feel the benefits of the incentive if they think that the expectations regarding their performance are uncertain or if there are perceived elements of unfairness.

The Zambia Performance-based Incentives Pilot Study was based on performance management systems existing in the health care system, notably the team structure already in place. Over a period of 12 months in the same province, the pilot study tested the "bonus" system of financial incentives (the 10% of fees) in one district against non-monetary awards (trophies) in another. In both cases, the awards went to teams, rather than to individuals, and it was up to the teams to decide how an award would be shared. Interviews with involved staff were used to assess the effect of each incentive program on motivation.

As reported by Furth, the results varied significantly between the two districts. Staff that received the trophies felt "motivated and encouraged" by the award, with managers indicating that the process helped them in staff management. In the district where the monetary bonus system was used, staff were "frustrated with and suspicious of the process,"[7] and, perhaps not surprisingly, staff motivation was unchanged.

It should be noted that there was a significant difference in the size of the two districts, which may have translated into differences in strength of leadership and so affected the outcome of the study. As Furth notes, "the study findings confirmed other work on performance incentives that stresses the importance of strong leadership and performance management systems as requisites for successful performance-based incentives programs." Moreover, the study found that performance-based awards worked best when staff was not burdened with having to collect additional data on new indicators of performance.[8]

What is perhaps most interesting about this study is the effect that small rewards such as trophies can have. Indeed, Furth points out that "non-financial awards were as motivating, if not more motivating, for staff than financial awards and did not generate as much conflict, suspicion, or frustration."[17] Thus, the recommendation of the researchers was that the non-monetary awards should continue to be piloted until there was more familiarity and comfort with performance monitoring.

chooses effort so that additional sales revenue from extra effort exactly equals the marginal cost. But a worker equates the additional sales revenue *multiplied by the commission rate*, to marginal cost. Total value is therefore maximized if the commission rate is 100 percent. In our example, if the firm offers a 100 percent commission, the employee will exert 140 units of effort, yielding sales of $14,000 at an effort cost of $5,000. Since the commission equals total sales, the firm can require the worker *to pay the firm $8,000* and still make the employee's total pay-off (commission less effort costs less payment to the firm) equal $1,000.[9] The firm makes a profit of $8,000, which is the best the firm can do with any contract offer. Commission rates approaching 100 percent and "negative" salaries are observed in practice; franchising (which we discussed in Chapter 4) is a good example where the agent (the franchisee) pays a fixed fee to the principal (the franchiser) and keeps most of the revenues.

4. Performance-based pay can help resolve hidden information problems as well. Suppose, for example, that the salesperson receives better information than the firm regarding a hot sales prospect. Clearly, it is in the firm's interest to have the salesperson spend relatively more time with clients who are somewhat likely to buy and less time with those who are unlikely to buy. When paid a fixed salary, the salesperson has little reason to quickly move on from clients who are unlikely to buy. A salesperson paid on commission, however, will have an incentive to make effective use of information about the likelihood of making a sale.

PROBLEMS WITH PERFORMANCE-BASED INCENTIVES

Using high-powered incentives such as large commission rates invites two potentially big problems. The first arises if the performance measure is affected by random factors that are beyond the employee's control and therefore subjects the employee to unwanted risk. The second arises if the measure fails to capture all aspects of desired performance. Employees might focus attention on the measured aspects of performance at the expense of other aspects that may be equally or more important for profitability.

To understand how random factors in performance measures affect the cost of providing incentives to employees, we take a short detour to examine individuals' preferences over risky outcomes.

Preferences over Risky Outcomes

Consider a freshly minted MBA graduate who is presented with two job opportunities. The jobs are identical in every way except compensation is "safe" in the first job and "risky" in the second. At the safe job, the employer will pay the graduate $100,000 at the end of the first year of employment. At the risky job, the employer will flip a coin at the end of the first year. If the coin comes up heads (which happens with probability one-half), the employer will pay $40,000. If it comes up tails, the employer will pay $160,000. Note that the expected values of the two jobs are identical—$100,000. Putting yourself in the shoes of this graduate, which job would you prefer?

Most people would prefer the safe job because most people are *risk averse*.[10] A risk-averse person prefers a safe outcome to a risky outcome with the same expected value. People are risk averse because they tend to have diminishing marginal utility for wealth. This would imply that the inherent value of the "stuff" they can purchase from earnings between $40,000 and $100,000 is more than the inherent value of the "stuff"

TABLE 12.1
AN MBA GRADUATE'S PREFERENCES OVER JOBS

Safe Job Pays	Risky Job Pays	Graduate's Preference
$100,000	$40,000 with probability ½ $160,000 with probability ½	Safe job
$99,000	$40,000 with probability ½ $160,000 with probability ½	Safe job
$90,000	$40,000 with probability ½ $160,000 with probability ½	Safe job
$80,000	$40,000 with probability ½ $160,000 with probability ½	Indifference
$70,000	$40,000 with probability ½ $160,000 with probability ½	Risky job

they can purchase from earnings between $100,000 and $160,000. An income of $40,000 puts a family at about 200 percent of the poverty line, forced to avoid all of life's luxuries. Moving from $40,000 to $100,000 allows the family to live in a modest home, buy some new clothes, take a decent vacation, and drive a new family sedan. Most families would welcome even these modest luxuries. Moving up to $160,000 buys a bigger home, fancier clothes, an overseas vacation, and maybe even a luxury car. Faced with these prospects, risk-averse individuals would not give up a certain income for $100,000 for a gamble that nets them $100,000 on average, but puts them at risk for a much lower standard of living.

The same MBA graduate would definitely prefer the risky job if the safe job paid only $40,000, as there would be no downside to the risky job. There must be some salary between $40,000 and $100,000 at which the graduate is indifferent between the two jobs. To locate this indifference point, consider reducing the payment associated with the safe job in $10,000 increments. As shown in the first row of Table 12.1, the safe job is preferred to the risky job when the safe job offers the same expected value. Suppose that the graduate would prefer the risky job when the safe job pays $70,000, but prefers the safe job at a salary of $90,000. Suppose that the indifference point between the safe job and the risky job occurs when the safe job pays $80,000.

We define $80,000 to be this decision maker's *certainty equivalent* for this risk. It is the certain amount that makes the decision maker indifferent between taking the risk and taking the certain payment. Put another way, the certainty equivalent is the smallest certain amount the decision maker would be willing to accept in exchange for the risky payoff. We define the difference between the expected value of a risk and the decision maker's certainty equivalent as the decision maker's *risk premium*. In this case, the expected value of the risk is $100,000, while the graduate's certainty equivalent is $80,000. Hence, the risk premium is $20,000. The risk premium can be thought of as the cost to the decision maker of having to bear the risk of an uncertain outcome.

The notions of certainty equivalent and risk premium have three key properties:

1. Different decision makers will have different certainty equivalents for the same risk. Ask *yourself* what safe wage (i.e., what certainty equivalent) makes you indifferent between the safe job and the risky job. If you reached a higher certainty equivalent than did our graduate, you are less risk averse than our graduate. If you reached a smaller certainty equivalent, you are more risk averse.

2. For a given decision maker, the certainty equivalent is lower (and the risk premium higher) when the *spread* or *variability* in payments is greater. Consider an even riskier job that pays either $180,000 or $20,000. Because of risk aversion, this job is less attractive than the one offering either $160,000 or $40,000. Hence, the riskier job has a lower certainty equivalent and thus a higher risk premium.

3. In choosing between two risky outcomes, a decision maker will select the one with the higher certainty equivalent.

Risk Sharing

Risk-averse individuals can often make themselves better off by *sharing* their risks. To illustrate this principle, consider two risk-averse homeowners. Each owns a wooden frame house worth $200,000, and each faces the possibility that the house may be destroyed by fire. Suppose the probability that a house burns down in a given year is 10 percent. If a house burns down, the entire value is lost, and the homeowner will have to pay $200,000 to rebuild. Hence, a homeowner's rebuilding costs will be

Home burns down: Cost = $200,000 with probability = 0.10

Home does not burn down: Cost = $0 with probability = 0.90

A homeowner's expected rebuilding cost is $20,000, but the uncertainty makes the house a risky asset.

Suppose that the first homeowner approaches the second and makes the following contract offer: if either home burns down, the two homeowners will share the cost evenly. We will assume that the events under which the houses burn down are independent, so that the probability that *both* burn down is $(0.10)^2 = 0.01$.

Each homeowner now faces the following "gamble":

Both homes burn down: Cost = $200,000 with probability = 0.01

One home burns down: Cost = $100,000 with probability = 0.18

Neither home burns down: Cost = $0 with probability = 0.81

Each homeowner's expected rebuilding cost is therefore:

$$(0.01 \times \$200,000) + (0.18 \times \$100,000) + (0.81 \times \$0) = \$20,000$$

In other words, each homeowner faces the same expected cost whether or not the second homeowner accepts the offer from the first. Note, however, that the probability of the *worst* outcome (that is, incurring rebuilding costs of $200,000) has fallen from 0.10 to 0.01. Similarly, the probability of the best outcome (incurring $0 costs) has fallen from 0.90 to 0.81. While this contract does not change expected rebuilding costs, it does reduce the *variability* in these costs by making the extreme worst and best outcomes less likely. Being risk averse, the second homeowner will gladly accept the offer. By sharing their risks, the two homeowners reduce the variability in their payoffs and both are made better off.

Some of the earliest insurance companies were organized on precisely this principle. The great Fire of London in 1666 destroyed property worth £10 million, a figure estimated to be around one-quarter of the total gross domestic product of England at the time. In its aftermath, Londoners searched for ways to protect their wealth against these risks. In 1696, a total of 100 subscribers joined together to form the Amicable Contributorship, a mutual insurance organization whose subscribers pledged their personal wealth to rebuild the homes of other subscribers in the event of damage by fire. Although most modern insurance firms do not rely on the personal wealth of a group of subscribers to pay claims (with Lloyd's of London being a notable exception), the principle of risk sharing nonetheless continues to underlie the demand for insurance of all forms. Furthermore, the insurance industry is only one of a number of modern institutions that facilitate the sharing of risks. Financial markets serve a similar purpose. In an initial public offering, an entrepreneur sells ownership shares, which are an uncertain claim on the firm's future cash flows, to investors in exchange for a certain, upfront payment. This transaction shifts risk from the entrepreneur to the investor.

An immediate corollary to the logic of risk sharing is the following. If one party is risk averse and another is risk neutral, the efficient allocation of risk places *all* risk with the risk-neutral party and gives a certain payoff to the risk-averse party. The reason is that the risk-neutral party values the gamble at its expected value, but the risk-averse party values it at a certainty equivalent that is less than the expected value. The risk-neutral party can offer the risk-averse party an amount of money somewhere between the expected value and the risk-averse party's certainty equivalent, and both will be better off by accepting this transaction.

Risk and Incentives

We are now ready to incorporate our discussions of risk aversion and risk sharing into the theory of incentives. As noted earlier, the main costs of basing pay on measures of performance stem directly from difficulties in measurement. For example, measured performance depends *in part* on the agent's actions, but it also depends on random factors that are beyond the agent's control. Tying pay more closely to observed performance therefore links the agent's pay to these random factors. A risk-averse agent dislikes random variations in pay, and the principal must compensate the agent for the cost of bearing this risk.

To illustrate, we adapt an agency model developed by Bengt Holstrom and Paul Milgrom.[11] Consider a firm that selects a commission rate α for a salesperson working in a retail store. We assume that the salesperson is risk averse. We also assume that the firm is risk neutral. This is reasonable because a firm has many salespeople and is likely not greatly concerned about variation coming from the sales of any one salesperson. Also, if the firm's stock is publicly traded, its shareholders can easily diversify any risk that is idiosyncratic to the firm.

It stands to reason that a salesperson who works harder will generate more sales. But the dollar value of goods sold by a salesperson will also depend on a number of factors beyond the salesperson's control. The local economy may suffer a downturn. The store's buyers may bet on the wrong merchandise to stock in the store. In a given week, the salesperson may also be unlucky; perhaps an unexpectedly large fraction of the customers are "just looking." Building on a previous agency model supposes that sales depend on both effort, e, and a random variable, $\tilde{\varepsilon}$:

$$\text{Sales} = \$100e + \tilde{\varepsilon}$$

Let $\tilde{\varepsilon}$ be a random variable with expected value zero and variance σ^2. A positive realization of $\tilde{\varepsilon}$ causes the employee's sales to be higher than they otherwise would have been. This can be interpreted as resulting from a good local economy, a favorable selection of merchandise, or just good luck. Conversely, a negative realization of $\tilde{\varepsilon}$ means that sales are unexpectedly low.

Suppose that our salesperson is risk averse and has certainty equivalent for an uncertain wage outcome of

$$E(\text{Wage}) - [1/2 \times \rho \text{Var}(\text{Wage})]$$

where $E(\text{Wage})$ is the expected value of the wage payment and $\text{Var}(\text{Wage})$ is the variance of the wage payment.[12] The parameter ρ, known as the coefficient of absolute risk aversion, is indicative of how risk averse the employee is. Larger values of ρ imply greater risk aversion, since as ρ increases the employee applies a greater discount to the uncertain wage due to its variability. Following our earlier agency example, the employee's cost of effort is 0 up to 40 units of effort and $1/2 \times (e - 40)^2$ thereafter, and the employee's next-best job opportunity offers a certainty equivalent of $1,000, net of effort costs.

Suppose that the firm pays its sales force a fixed salary F per week and a commission of α on sales. For an effort level e and random variable realization $\tilde{\varepsilon}$, the employee's actual pay will therefore be $F + \alpha(100e + \tilde{\varepsilon})$. Given that the random variable $\tilde{\varepsilon}$ has an expected value of zero, the employee's expected pay is $F + \alpha(100e)$, while the variance is $\alpha^2\sigma^2$. Hence, the employee's certainty equivalent minus effort costs is

$$F + \alpha(100e) - \frac{1}{2}(e - 40)^2 - \frac{1}{2}\rho\alpha^2\sigma^2$$

This expression consists of the employee's base salary (F), the expected commission ($\alpha 100e$), less costs from effort ($(1/2)(e - 40)^2$) and the cost of bearing risk ($-(1/2)\rho\alpha^2\sigma^2$). If the firm hopes to attract the employee to this job, this amount must be greater than $1,000. If the firm asks the employee to bear more risk or exert more effort, it must compensate by offering a higher base salary and/or commission rate. This corresponds to the intuitive notion that people are willing to take jobs that are risky or difficult only if they are well compensated for doing so.

The employee gets a marginal benefit of 100α for each additional unit of effort expended. The employee incurs a marginal cost of exerting additional effort equal to $(e - 40)$. Equating the two, we find that the employee will exert $40 + 100\alpha$ units of effort.[13] As in the earlier agency example, effort increases with the commission rate. However, it is no longer optimal for the firm to set $\alpha = 100$ percent (i.e., "sell" the business to the employee). This is because any increase in α will increase the employee's cost of bearing risk, which the firm must offset by offering a higher base salary.

The mathematical analysis can be summarized as follows. As the firm ties pay more closely to performance, it provides stronger incentives. This leads to more effort and, hence, more revenue. However, since the performance measure is subject to random factors, tying pay more closely to measured performance also increases the variability of the employee's compensation. This makes the job less attractive to the employee and means that the firm has to pay higher overall wages in order to attract the employee. This leads to higher costs for the firm. The optimal strength of incentives is determined by a balancing of these two forces.

We can compute how the firm's profit changes when it offers various compensation plans. For concreteness, we assume that the employee's coefficient of absolute risk aversion, ρ, is equal to 3 and that the variance of sales, σ^2, is 10,000.[14] Suppose first that the firm offers a job without commissions. Since this job motivates no extra effort and places no risk on the employee, the firm can pay a salary of $1,000. As shown in Table 12.2, the employee will put in 40 units of effort, and the firm's expected profit will be $3,000.

TABLE 12.2
THE TRADEOFF BETWEEN RISK AND INCENTIVES

Commission Rate	Effort Level	Effort Costs	Risk Premium	Expected Commission	Salary	Revenue	Profit
0%	40	0	0	0	$1,000	$4,000	$3,000
10	50	50	150	500	700	5,000	3,800
20	60	200	600	1,200	600	6,000	4,200
25	65	312.5	937.5	1,625	625	6,500	4,250
30	70	450	1,350	2,100	700	7,000	4,200

If the firm offers a commission rate of $\alpha = 10$ percent, the employee will put in 50 units of effort (leading to effort costs of $50) and earn expected commissions of $500. Because the pay now depends on output, which, in turn, is affected by random factors beyond the employee's control, the employee is subject to risk. The employee discounts the value of the job because of this risk, applying a risk premium of $150. The firm must ensure that the certainty equivalent minus effort costs is greater than or equal to $1,000. Thus, in order to overcome the increased risk and effort costs, the firm must offer a fixed salary F of $700. The firm's total expected wage bill goes up to $1,200, which is just enough to compensate for the increased risk and effort costs associated with the commission-based job. Here, the increase in expected productivity ($5,000, compared to $4,000 for the salary-only job) more than compensates for the increase in expected wages. Thus, the firm's expected profit is higher if it offers the commission-based job than if it offers the salary-only job.

Filling in the remaining rows of Table 12.2, we see that further increases in the commission rate have similar effects. As the firm increases α, the employee exerts more effort but bears more risk. The extra effort leads to additional revenue for the firm, but the extra risk leads to a larger risk premium and thus to higher expected wages. The optimal commission rate is determined by a trade-off between these benefits and costs. In our example, the firm's profit-maximizing choice of α is 25 percent.

To summarize this analysis, we have shown that if a firm wants to tie pay to a performance measure that is affected by random factors, the firm must compensate employees for the resulting increase in the variability of their pay. In determining how closely to tie pay to performance, the firm must weigh the costs of imposing risk onto risk-averse employees against the benefits of providing additional incentives. There is, therefore, a trade-off between risk and incentives.

Firms rarely have detailed information regarding employees' risk preferences ρ and effort costs c. Therefore, they cannot solve precisely for an optimal commission rate as we have done here. However, our model does yield a number of insights into the factors that favor the use of incentives. Without going into the mathematical details, the model shows that stronger incentives are called for if:

• The employee is less risk averse.

• The variance of measured performance is lower.

• The employee's marginal cost of effort is lower.

• The marginal return to effort is higher.

EXAMPLE 12.3   PAY AND PERFORMANCE AT YAKIMA VALLEY ORCHARDS

The state of Washington is well known for its apples. East of the Cascade Mountains, dry air and plentiful groundwater make for perfect apple-growing conditions. In 2006, the state shipped more than 92 million boxes of apples to buyers worldwide. Apple-growing is a labor-intensive process. Trees must be pruned (usually in the off-season), harvested (when apples are ripe, usually in early fall), and thinned. Apple tree thinning is done in the middle of the growing season. Small, imperfect apples are removed from the tree so that the tree's resources will be focused on the better part of the crop.

Yakima Valley Orchards (YVO) is a large orchard operation in Central Washington state. The farm covers 800 acres and grows a variety of fruits including apples, cherries, and pears. Prior to 2006, YVO used hourly wages, usually around $10, to pay its tree-thinning employees. During July 2006, the firm began experimenting with a variety of new methods of paying employees. One such plan involved a form of piece rate. Piece-rate compensation systems offer employees a fixed payment for each unit of output they produce. YVO's plan was to leave some of its employees on the hourly pay but shift others to a system in which pay depends on the number of trees thinned.

YVO's goal in experimenting was to find ways to boost employee productivity. According to a study by Lan Shi, it seems that this objective was been achieved.[15] Analyzing detailed information on individual-level tree-thinning productivity, Shi finds that workers thinned, on average, around 80 trees per hour when paid hourly wages. After the switch to piece rates, this figure jumped around 50 percent, to 125 trees per hour.

An often-stated concern about piece-rate-based compensation systems has to do with the quality of worker effort. If the firm rewards output directly, what is to stop workers from cutting corners in order to increase production? YVO solves this problem by auditing the number of apples on the ground under a thinned tree. Workers who speed their work by leaving too many apples on a tree are sent back to finish the job before being paid.

Another issue with piece rates is their association with "sweatshops." During the rapid industrialization of the United States in the late 1800s, many workers were employed in cramped, dirty, and unsafe factories, working piece-rate jobs that paid barely enough for subsistence. Given this history, many people associate piece rates with worker exploitation. Changing from fixed-wage to piece-rate pay need not, however, make employees worse off. As long as the increase in worker productivity is sufficiently large, the firm will be more than happy to compensate the worker for the risk and effort costs he or she incurs by having pay tied to performance. YVO's is experience bears this point out. As part of the farm's experiment, one group of workers was kept on hourly wages, while the other was put on piece rates. The "hourly" group was not told about the piece-rate experiment. The two worker groups set out from different ends of the orchard, meeting near the middle at lunchtime. Upon hearing about the piece-rate system, some hourly workers asked to be put on piece rates. These workers were told about the experiment and were informed that all workers would be on piece rates soon.

A final issue with piece rates has to do with setting the rate itself. Before implementing the plan, the firm did not know how much the piece rate would increase worker productivity. If the firm sets a low piece rate and worker productivity does not improve much, then it is possible that overall worker pay may fall as a result of the change. This would likely lead to costly employee turnover. If the firm sets a high piece rate and productivity rises a lot, then overall pay may rise "too much." This latter possibility seems to have occurred at YVO. Productivity increased so much that average hourly wages—computed as the per-tree piece rate times the average number of trees thinned per hour—rose to nearly $18, an 80 percent raise for each worker. A firm that guesses wrong on implementing a piece rate may then face worker resistance if it tries to reduce piece rates.

The model also shows that a firm's profits are higher when there is less random variability in measured performance. When there is less variability, the firm can reduce its wage costs by paying a smaller risk premium for a given strength of incentives; it can also increase its revenues by using stronger incentives. Firms can reduce the risk that employees are exposed to by selecting performance measures that are subject to as little randomness as possible and investing in reducing the randomness in available measures.

PERFORMANCE MEASURES THAT FAIL TO REFLECT ALL DESIRED ACTIONS

In the retail sales model developed earlier, the performance measure (sales) is a reasonably complete summary indicator of the various aspects of job performance. In other jobs, however, the available measures may not cover all aspects of job performance. Use of pay-for-performance incentives in this case will cause employees to focus on aspects of performance that are reflected in the measure and to neglect aspects that are not reflected in the measure. In Chapter 10 we called this multitasking.

A well-known example of multitasking is commonly called "teaching to the test." We will use primary school teaching to illustrate the problem.[16] Let's think about dividing the various activities of teachers into two types: (1) activities that develop students' test-taking skills and (2) activities that enhance students' higher-order thinking skills. For skills like multiplication, reading comprehension, and spelling, it is easy to devise a standardized test to measure students' progress. However, it is considerably more difficult to design a tool that assesses whether a student can reason effectively or think creatively. Hence, while both of these teaching activities build students' ability to think, only the first can be measured effectively.

If teachers are rewarded on the basis of their students' test scores, then they will devote more time to teaching test-related skills like multiplication. So far, so good. But if teachers have increasing costs of effort, when they devote more time to teaching multiplication, the marginal cost of making an effort to teach reasoning skills will increase. As a result, they will devote less time to the latter. If compensation is not at all tied to reasoning skills, then teachers will devote 100 percent of their effort to teaching test-taking skills. This reasoning is an application of the multitask principle developed in Chapter 10, which states that when allocating effort among a variety of tasks, employees will tend to exert more effort toward the tasks that are rewarded.

Our conclusion—that in the presence of test-based incentives teachers will allocate *all* effort toward test-taking skills—is clearly subject to a number of caveats.[17] Most seriously, perhaps, we have ignored the fact that teachers self-select into their profession. A person who becomes a teacher is likely one who cares directly about student achievement. Such nonpecuniary benefits from student progress offer a counterweight to the pecuniary incentives derived from bonuses. Nevertheless, it is clear that the use of such test-based incentives will shift teachers' effort choices in the direction of test-taking skills at the potential expense of reasoning skills.

A performance measure will sometimes reward activities that the firm *does not* want the employee to undertake. Consider the case of Lantech, a small manufacturer of packaging equipment based in Louisville, Kentucky.[18] Hoping to increase productivity, the firm implemented employee bonuses based on the profits recorded by each of the firm's five manufacturing divisions. The employees quickly discovered, however, that there is more than one way to increase a division's profits. Increasing productivity is one, but fighting to have overhead charges allocated to other divisions is another. Disagreements over such charges grew heated, and much of top management's time was consumed in mediating these disputes. Some divisions also began engaging in "channel stuffing"—a practice in which orders from other parts of the company were rushed to be filled at the end of each month. This allowed the division filling the order to recognize the revenue from this sale (and thus increase profits), but it led to problems with excess inventory. Internal strife became so severe that the firm eventually elected to discontinue the division-based bonuses and instead make profit-sharing payments based on the performance of the entire firm.

A manager designing pay plans should identify the activities an employee can undertake to improve measured performance and then ask how well this set of activities overlaps with those the firm would like the employee to pursue. Are there activities important to the firm that are not reflected in measured performance? Are there activities that improve measured performance that the firm does not want employees to pursue? The larger these sets of activities, the lower the efficacy of pay-for-performance based on the measure in question.

Organizations may respond to this problem in a number of ways. First, they may elect not to use any pay-for-performance incentives. If the performance measures are of poor quality, the firm may be better off paying fixed salaries and instructing employees in how to allocate their efforts toward various activities. While this approach does not motivate employees to exert extra effort on the job, it has the virtue of not motivating them to ignore tasks that are important but difficult to measure. Most U.S. public schools offer little or no compensation based on teacher performance. The problems of identifying good performance measures may be so severe that the best outcome may be to rely on teachers' inherent concern for students' educational progress.

Firms may also deal with limitations in measurement through careful job design. Grouping tasks according to ease of measurement can mitigate the multitasking problem. Suppose, for example, that activities A and B are easy to measure but activities C and D are hard to measure. If, on one hand, tasks A and C are assigned to one employee and B and D are assigned to another, the firm faces the multitask problems identified earlier. If, on the other hand, the firm assigns tasks A and B to one employee and C and D to the other, it can provide strong incentives for tasks A and B without pulling focus away from C and D.

Finally, firms can augment explicit incentive contracts with direct monitoring and subjective performance evaluation. Recalling the Lantech example, it may be difficult to base an explicit contract on whether a manager is fighting "too hard" to allocate overhead to another division. But it may be relatively easy for a CEO or other top manager to subjectively assess whether this is going on. If such assessments can be incorporated into the determination of overall compensation, subjective evaluations of performance can mitigate the problems we have described. Critics of U.S. public schools contend that the tenure system and rigid pay and promotion criteria limit the ability of school administrators to reward teachers based on subjective evaluations.

SELECTING PERFORMANCE MEASURES: MANAGING TRADE-OFFS BETWEEN COSTS

The foregoing discussion identifies three features of a good performance measure:

- A performance measure that is less affected by random factors will allow the firm to tie pay closely to performance without introducing much variability into the employee's pay.

TABLE 12.3
JOBS WITH VARYING EASE OF PERFORMANCE MEASUREMENT

Job for Which Performance Is Relatively Easy to Measure	Job for Which Performance Is Relatively Difficult to Measure
Harvesting grapes	Vintner
Bicycle messenger	Flight attendant
Pharmaceutical sales representative	Pharmaceutical research scientist
Manager of advertising campaign	Manager of customer service center

- A measure that reflects all the activities the firm wants undertaken will allow the firm to use strong incentives without pulling the employee's attention away from important tasks.

- A performance measure that cannot be improved by actions the firm *does not* want undertaken will allow the firm to offer strong incentives without also motivating counterproductive actions.

Unfortunately, performance measures meeting all three of these criteria are rare. In Table 12.3, we highlight a selection of jobs for which performance is relatively easy to measure, and compare this to another selection for which performance is relatively more difficult to measure. In Table 12.4, we list performance measures that might be used for various jobs, and identify some problems associated with each.

A firm's search for the best performance measure involves trade-offs among the costs identified earlier. Consider the question of whether to use "absolute" or "relative" measures of an employee's performance. A relative measure is constructed by comparing one employee's performance to another's. If the sources of randomness affecting the two employees' individual performance exhibit a positive correlation, basing each employee's pay on the *difference* between the individual performance measures will shield employees from risk.[19] Hence, a firm using relative performance measures may be able to pay a smaller risk premium and therefore use stronger incentives. But relative measures can exacerbate multitask problems. Consider the possibility that one employee might be able to take actions that *reduce* the productivity of another employee. Clearly, the firm does not want to encourage this activity; however, relative performance evaluation directly rewards it. In determining whether to use relative rather than absolute performance measures, firms must weigh the possible reductions in risk against potential increases in the incentive to undertake counterproductive actions.

In a well-known application of this idea, the fictional real estate salesmen in the play *Glengarry Glen Ross* were compensated based on relative performance. Their boss announced that the first prize in a sales contest was a Cadillac El Dorado. Second prize was a set of steak knives. Third prize was "you're fired." This scheme was excessively harsh, but it did reward hard work and ability and shielded the salesmen from correlated risks (such as macroeconomic fluctuations). It also led one salesman to do something entirely counterproductive—he stole the list of promising leads.

Similar considerations enter into the choice between narrow or broad performance measures. An example of a narrow measure might be the number of pieces of output produced by an individual employee. A broad measure might be the accounting profits of the plant where the employee works. The broad measure has the advantage of rewarding the employee for helping coworkers or for making suggestions that

TABLE 12.4
PERFORMANCE MEASURES OF VARYING QUALITY FOR DIFFERENT JOBS

Job Description	Performance Measure	Discussion
Baseball pitcher	Number of games won	Depends on how team's batters perform when pitcher is pitching; this measure is therefore affected by random factors beyond the pitcher's control.
	Opponents' batting average	May motivate pitcher to pitch too cautiously. Pitcher would rather issue a walk (which does not count against batting average) than possibly surrender a hit.
	Earned run average	Less noisy than number of wins, and motivates pitcher to take any action that will prevent other team from scoring runs.
Police officer	Crime rate on beat	Crime rates vary considerably by neighborhood; this measure therefore depends on factors beyond the police officer's control.
	Number of arrests	Officer can make an arrest only if a crime has been committed; this measure therefore limits incentive to prevent crimes from being committed.
	Change in crime rate	Less noisy than the level of crime, and motivates officer to take actions that reduce crime even if no arrest results.
Local TV news producer	Profits of station	Profits depend crucially on the quality of network programming shown on the station; this measure may therefore be noisy.
	Number of journalism awards won	May motivate producer to overspend on high-profile stories.
	Share of viewing audience retained when news comes on	Motivates actions that retain the potential audience; less noisy than profits.

improve the plant's overall efficiency. However, the broad measure is also likely to be subject to more random factors. The broad measure depends on the actions of many workers and many sources of randomness; hence, linking an individual employee's pay to this measure exposes that employee to considerable risk. A firm may therefore find it very costly (in terms of employee risk premiums) to use high-powered incentives based on broad measures. In determining whether to use the broad measure or the narrow one, the firm must weigh the benefit associated with "help" activities and extra suggestions against the cost of weaker incentives for individual effort. The firm

EXAMPLE 12.4 HERDING, RPE AND THE 2007–2008 CREDIT CRISIS

One of the clearest examples of how random factors can affect measured performance comes from the very top of most organizations. Pay for top executives like chief executive officers, chief operating officers, and chief financial officers is frequently tied directly to the price of the firm's stock through grants of equity or equity-based instruments such as stock options.

The theory of financial markets suggests that the price of a firm's stock will move up or down for a variety of reasons. Share prices are clearly affected by any news bearing directly on the firm's future cash flow, but they are also affected by overall movements in the market. For example, during the late 1990s a major bull market pulled all U.S. share prices up by 25 percent or more annually. Even mediocre firms saw great gains in their share prices over this period. Similarly, the declining stock market during 2001 to 2002 saw nearly all firms' share prices fall—even those of firms with good operating performance over the period. As a result, some analysts believe that a better performance measure might be the firm's performance relative to competitors or market indices.

Jeff Zwiebel argues that while relative performance evaluation has some benefits, substantial costs are present as well.[20] Zwiebel notes that relative performance evaluation could encourage "herding." Herding is a phenomenon whereby individuals ignore their own information about the best course of action and instead simply do what everyone else is doing.

Zwiebel's argument is this: Suppose a manager is likely to be fired when her firm's performance is poor relative to industry rivals but will keep her job otherwise. Suppose also that the manager faces the following strategic choice: she can "follow the herd" by making strategic choices that are similar to those made by competitors, or she can adopt a new, promising, but untested strategy. Following the herd means the manager's performance is unlikely to be much different from that of rivals, and so she is unlikely to be fired. The contrarian strategy has a higher expected payoff than the herd strategy, but its newness means that there is at least some chance it will fail. If the contrarian strategy fails, the firm's performance will lag the industry, and the manager will be fired. Under these conditions, the manager may well stick with the herd, even if she knows the potential returns to the contrarian strategy are high. As we noted at the start of this chapter, Merrill Lynch CEO O'Neal seems to have been comparing his firm's trading performance to that of rivals. One reason for his insistence on matching Goldman may have been that his continued job security depended on achieving earnings similar to Goldman's. Could this form of relative performance evaluation have led to herding on Wall Street? It is difficult to say for sure, but it is clearly the case that many, many financial institutions were actively involved in financing risky subprime mortgages. As housing prices rose through the late 1990s and early 2000s, mortgage default rates stayed low and these risky investments paid off handsomely. Any firm choosing not to play this risky game would show poor relative performance. Managers of such firms might begin to feel the heat from shareholders, as Zwiebel suggests.

Any manager with the contrarian strategy—taking, say, a short position in the subprime mortgage securities, betting that default rates will rise—would have incurred losses through the 2000 to 2006 period. But this strategy would have earned huge profits as house prices fell and the subprime mortgage market imploded in 2007. Would a contrarian manager have kept her job long enough to earn those profits? Or would the poor relative performance between 2000 and 2006 have led to that manager's firing?

could incorporate both narrow and broad measures into an employee's compensation, paying attention to how the relative weights on the two measures will affect the employee's on-the-job decisions.

Whatever measures are used in explicit incentive contracts, it is almost always the case that direct monitoring and subjective evaluation are used in tandem with the explicit contract. The role of such monitoring is often to offset the risk and multitask problems associated with the performance measures in the explicit contract. Since monitoring consumes valuable managerial resources, firms should also consider how the choice of performance measures will affect what activities will need to be directly monitored. If it is easy for the firm to monitor actions taken by one employee that are intended to reduce the performance of another, this favors the use of relative measures. If, on the other hand, it is easy for the firm to gain information regarding the common random factors affecting employees' performance, these random factors can be filtered through monitoring without relying on relative comparisons.

DO PAY-FOR-PERFORMANCE INCENTIVES WORK?

There is considerable evidence that employees consider the effects on their compensation when making decisions.[21] One series of studies examined simple jobs for which measures of on-the-job performance are easily available. As discussed in Example 12.3, Lan Shi documented large increases in productivity after Yakima Valley Orchards implemented a piece-rate-based compensation system. Harry Parsch and Bruce Shearer conducted a similar analysis using payroll records from a tree-planting firm in British Columbia. They estimate that tree planters were 22.6 percent more productive when paid on a piece-rate basis as compared to a fixed wage.[22]

It is somewhat more difficult to assess whether the use of incentive compensation increases productivity in complex jobs. Researchers have instead offered evidence suggesting that pay-for-performance incentives improve performance *along measured dimensions*. Martin Gaynor, James Rebitzer, and Lowell Taylor, for example, have studied incentives for physicians in an HMO network.[23] Under the HMO's contract, a physician's pay increased by 10 cents for every $1.00 reduction in medical expenditures. Implementation of this contract led to a reduction in medical expenditures of 5 percent, and linking pay to measures of quality led to improvements along these quality dimensions. Health care quality is difficult to measure, however, and it is possible that the cost reductions and improvements in measured quality came at the expense of lower quality on unmeasured dimensions. In fact, it is relatively easy to find examples in which pay-for-performance compensation plans have destructive effects. For example, an Australian study found that employees help each other less and exert more individual effort when individual-based promotion incentives are strong.[24] This and many other studies like it illustrate why it is difficult for firms to know whether they should use high-powered pay-for-performance incentives, especially when jobs are complex.

IMPLICIT INCENTIVE CONTRACTS

Jobs in which pay is tied to performance through some predetermined formula are the exception rather than the rule. For many jobs, such formulaic compensation would be counterproductive, for the reasons we explain above. This is why firms often rely on implicit incentive contracts, in which workers expect to be rewarded for their productive efforts, even if evaluations are subjective and no explicit rewards are written down. The primary advantage of implicit incentive contracts is the range of performance measures that can be incorporated. In an explicit pay-for-performance contract, pay is tied to a measure through a predetermined formula. This measure must be verifiable in case there is a dispute between the firm and the worker and the contract must be enforced by a third party such as a judge or an arbitrator. No such restrictions apply to implicit measures.

Many aspects of performance are verifiable, including the earnings of an investment bank, the number of patients seen by a physician, or the dollar value of goods sold by a salesperson. But other aspects of performance may be hard to measure or may invite counterproductive actions. Consider a firm that wants its employees to share knowledge. How would it measure "knowledge sharing?" If it based compensation on the number of written reports, this could motivate employees to write trivial reports. Ideally, firms would like to write incentive contracts that reward employees for sharing valuable information, but a third party would probably find it difficult to measure value. Hence, any explicit contract based on whether the employee shares valuable information will not be enforceable.

A supervisor, on the other hand, might easily determine whether an employee is sharing valuable information and the supervisor's assessment could be incorporated into an implicit incentive contract. A firm may announce to employees, "Your bonus, raise, or promotion depends in part on whether your supervisor believes your information-sharing efforts were good, satisfactory, or poor." As long as the firm and its employees have a similar understanding about what constitutes valuable information, such an approach can improve on explicit contracts. E-Land, a South Korean fashion retailer, provides an example. While suffering through a severe business slump in late 1998, the firm began asking its employees to post useful information on its Intranet. The quality of these tidbits, collected on an employee's "knowledge résumé," figures prominently in promotion and bonus decisions.[25] The firm credits this practice with large increases in productivity. Its revenues increased by 21 percent in 2001, and it has remained a market leader.

By definition, implicit contracts are not enforceable by third parties. So what keeps the firm from simply claiming that the employee's information-sharing efforts were poor and from pocketing the funds earmarked for bonuses or raises? A firm that reneges on its current promises may find that its employees expect it to renege on future promises. If so, employees may be unwilling to exert extra effort in the future. Thus, a firm that reneges on its promises will profit in the short term, but its damaged reputation will cost it in the longer term. A firm using implicit contracts must reassure employees that it will act in accordance with those contracts. The firm should verify that performance standards are applied consistently and should communicate clearly with employees in the event that economic conditions preclude the payment of promised bonuses or raises.

Subjective Performance Evaluation

Firms implement subjective performance evaluation in a variety of ways. Some perform *360-degree peer reviews*, in which an employee's supervisor, coworkers, and subordinates are all asked to provide information regarding that employee's performance. Others use *management by objective systems* whereby an employee and a supervisor work together to construct a set of goals for the employee. At the end of some specified period, the two meet to review the employee's performance on those goals.

The supervisor will consider whether the goals were reached but can also take into account other factors that may have made them unexpectedly easy or difficult to attain. Still other firms implement *merit rating systems*, in which employees are given numerical scores. Often these systems give supervisors a fixed pool of points to be allocated among employees. In all these systems, subjective opinions complement or replace objective performance measures.

There are three costs to incorporating subjective performance assessments. First, supervisors may find it personally unpleasant to reward some employees but not others and may give all their subordinates an average (or even above-average) grade. This effect, known as *ratings compression*, weakens incentives. Some firms use forced rankings systems, in which evaluators are required to grade employees on a curve. Sun Microsystems, for example, requires supervisors to rate 20 percent of employees as superior, 70 percent as Sun standard, and 10 percent as underperforming.[26] Firms using forced rankings must be careful to apply evaluation criteria fairly. Since 1999, Microsoft, Ford Motor Company, and Conoco, among others, have been sued by employees who have alleged that poor evaluations reflect supervisors' biases rather than their own performance.

Second, subjective assessments of performance are subject to influence activity, which we described in Chapter 3. Subordinates may attempt to affect their evaluations by establishing good personal relationships with supervisors, perhaps spending too much time developing them. Chris Congdon, a computer support specialist at Ford, says that he was able to increase his ranking by regularly e-mailing computing-related news articles to all members of his department. This, he claims, increased his visibility to supervisors, even though the articles were of little value to computer users.[27] Employees may also excessively promote their own pet projects while lobbying against, or even worse, hiding information from other employees who have their own projects.

Finally, subjective measures may be noisy, just as objective measures are. This introduces unwanted variation in compensation, with the requisite costly risk premium. As with objective measures, implementation of subjective measures requires a deft balancing of benefits and costs.

Promotion Tournaments

Subjective evaluations are often crucial to promotion decisions. Firms usually do not state promotion criteria as part of an explicit contract. Instead, there is a general understanding between the firm and its employees as to what sorts of actions will lead to promotion. As Edward Lazear and Sherwin Rosen have pointed out, promotion-based incentives often take the form of a *promotion tournament*.[28] A set of employees competes to win a promotion, and the "prize" is usually a substantial increase in compensation.

Consider the case of a bank that employs two senior loan officers, one of whom will be promoted to vice president. If the duties of a vice president are somewhat similar to those of a senior loan officer, it may be sensible for the bank to promote the loan officer who turns in the best performance in that job. Suppose that the salary paid to senior loan officers is w. As part of the promotion, the winning loan officer receives a raise that increases salary to w^*. The losing loan officer remains with the firm as a loan officer but receives no raise. Hence, the prize that accompanies the promotion is the wage differential $w^* - w$. Each loan officer can increase the likelihood of promotion by increasing effort. The marginal benefit of effort is the increased probability of winning the promotion multiplied by the reward $w^* - w$. Each loan officer will equate this to the marginal cost.[29]

The firm can encourage the loan officers to work harder by increasing the size of the prize w^*. It should simultaneously reduce w. To see why it should adjust both, note that a potential employee will consider both w and w^* when choosing where to work. Increasing w^* gives the senior loan officers more incentive to work hard. It also makes the senior loan officer's job more attractive (since the promotion prospects attached to this job are more attractive) and means that the firm can reduce w somewhat and still hire senior loan officers.

If there are more than two loan officers competing for promotion, the bank can maintain the same incentives for effort simply by increasing the size of the prize. To illustrate this point, consider the effect of adding a third senior loan officer to the tournament. This presumably reduces the likelihood that the first officer will win, as the officer must outperform *both* loan officer 2 *and* loan officer 3 to earn the promotion. The firm can offset this reduction in officer 1's marginal benefit of effort by increasing w^* or reducing w, thus making winning more valuable.

If there are successive rounds of promotion tournaments, the wage differentials between levels must increase in order to maintain the same incentives for effort.[30] Consider adding another round to the bank promotion tournament. Suppose that a senior loan officer promoted to vice president eventually participates in another tournament that may result in promotion to chief executive officer. A senior loan officer who is not promoted to vice president cannot subsequently become CEO. Accordingly, part of the prize associated with being promoted to vice president is the right to compete for the CEO position. Senior loan officers therefore anticipate two potential prizes (promotion to VP and eventually to CEO), and this may motivate them to work extra hard. If the firm wants to motivate the same extra-effort level from vice presidents (who have only to look forward to becoming CEO), the CEO/vice president wage differential must be larger than the vice president/senior loan officer wage differential.

In deciding whether to use tournaments to provide incentives, a firm must consider the extent to which these factors apply to its specific situation. Advantages of using tournaments for incentives include the following:

- Tournaments circumvent the problem of supervisors who are unwilling to make sharp distinctions among employees. A promotion is an indivisible reward, the difference between the payoffs received by top and bottom performers is necessarily large, and incentives to be a top performer are strong. These factors necessarily counteract compression in subjective evaluations.

- Tournaments are a form of relative performance evaluation. Because only the relative ranking of competitors affects who gets the prize, any common random factors that affect performance are netted out.

Potential disadvantages of tournaments include the following:

- The individual who is best at performing a lower-level job may not be the right choice for a higher-level job. This may be especially likely if the lower- and higher-level jobs require markedly different skill sets.

- Relative performance evaluation rewards employees for taking actions that hamper the performance of other employees. Hence, firms need to consider whether such actions can be monitored and discouraged before implementing tournament-based incentives.

EXAMPLE 12.5   QUITTERS NEVER WIN[31]

Faced with a skilled rival, do you stand up to the challenge or concede defeat? Proponents argue that internal competition—pitting worker against worker for tenure, promotion, and rewards—leads to increased effort. Common intuition suggests that rivalry may encourage competitors to "step up their game." But is it the case that harnessing the power of competition always bolsters effort and performance? Recent research by Jennifer Brown suggests that this may not always be the case. In fact, the presence of a superstar in a tournament can lead to worse performance from other competitors. Tournaments—where rewards are based only on the relative performance of those vying for the prize—are found in many contexts. For example, firms reward the top salesperson; contracts are awarded to firms with the best technological innovation; and corporate vice presidents compete to become company president. The benefits of tournaments depend critically on the degree of heterogeneity in competitors' underlying ability.

Professional golf offers a real-world laboratory in which to examine the effect of a superstar on his competitors. Participants are professionals and the stakes are significant. Most importantly, for many years, professional golf had an undisputed superstar: Tiger Woods.

As in most tournament settings, effort on the PGA Tour is not costless. Before events, effort is about physical and mental preparation. During competition, a player may exercise extra care in considering his target, the conditions, and his club choice. The opportunity cost of effort is also substantial: a popular player may collect well over $100,000 for attending a corporate outing.

In her work, Brown uses rich course, prize, weather, and television viewership data to isolate the impact of Woods on the performance of other competitors. The data include scores for every PGA Tour event from 1999 to 2010. In her work, she asks: How does a player perform when Woods is in a tournament compared to that player's performance in the same event when Woods is not in the field? She finds that, on average, PGA golfers' first-round scores are approximately 0.2 stroke worse when Woods participates, relative to when Woods is absent. The overall superstar effect for tournament scores is 0.8 stroke. The magnitude of the adverse effect appears particularly large when Woods is playing well and disappears when Woods is struggling. She finds no evidence that the reduced performance is due to the intensity of media attention or the adoption of risky strategies.

It is useful to know not only that incentives are adversely affected by the presence of a superstar, but also the economic magnitude of the effect. To address this question, Brown asks: What if any single player were able to overcome his own adverse performance by exerting costly effort? Results suggest that an average ranked golfer would have earned $28,000 more between 1999 and 2006 by playing one stroke better in the presence of the superstar. The simulations provide compelling evidence that, while the adverse performance effect is strikingly large, individual players may simply say: Why should I exert more costly effort when the marginal payoff in the presence of a superstar is low?

The implications of the adverse superstar effect extend beyond the PGA Tour and, in principle, require firms to be cautious in using "best athlete" hiring policies when competition is a key driver of incentives. For example, sales managers should be aware of the consequences of introducing a superstar team member, and law firms should consider the impact of a superstar associate on the cohort's overall performance. Understanding the superstar effect is a step toward learning how to structure situations where competition exists between workers of very heterogeneous abilities.

A study by George Baker, Michael Gibbs, and Bengt Holmstrom confirms the link between promotions and wage growth.[32] They obtained confidential personnel records from a large U.S. firm and found that employees received substantial increases in pay (5 to 7 percent, depending on level) when they were promoted. They also report that firms use promotion tournaments in conjunction with objective and subjective merit-based raises within job ranks. Other researchers have studied intrafirm wage differentials for evidence of tournament effects. Brian Main, Charles O'Reilly, and James Wade, for example, found that wage differentials increase with rank, as predicted by the theory.[33] They also found that the difference in salary between CEOs and vice presidents is larger in firms that have more VPs, also as predicted by the theory. Tor Eriksson obtained similar findings using a broad sample of 2,600 executives at 210 Danish firms between 1992 and 1995.[34]

EFFICIENCY WAGES AND THE THREAT OF TERMINATION

Firms can also motivate workers by threatening to fire them. Like tournaments, firing is usually based on implicit criteria. Firms fire workers whose performance is "unsatisfactory," where the meaning of this term is usually understood by both parties but not carefully defined. To study termination-based incentives, we sketch a simple model in which an employee must decide whether to work hard. Suppose that the cost to the employee of working hard is \$50 but that if the employee works hard, the probability of being retained is 1. If the employee does not work hard, the firm will detect this lack of effort with probability p, where $p < 1$. If this happens, the firm will fire the worker.

The employee earns wage w from this job. The next best opportunity for a fired employee is a job that pays w^{**}.[35] In deciding whether to work hard, the employee compares the net payoff from working hard to the net payoff from shirking (that is, choosing not to work hard). Working hard guarantees a payoff of:

$$w - \$50$$

Shirking leads to one of two possible outcomes. With probability $1 - p$, the employee keeps the job and earns w. With probability p, the employee is detected, fired, and earns w^{**}. The expected payoff from shirking is thus:

$$pw^{**} + (1 - p)w$$

The employee will choose to work hard if

$$w - \$50 > pw^{**} + (1 - p)w$$

or, equivalently, if

$$p(w - w^{**}) > \$50$$

This last inequality has a highly intuitive interpretation. The variable p is the probability of being fired if the employee shirks, and $w - w^{**}$ is the cost associated with being fired. Hence, $p(w - w^{**})$ is the expected cost of shirking, whereas \$50 is the cost of working hard. The inequality states that the employee will work hard if the expected cost of shirking is greater than the cost of working hard.

As one might expect, the firm can more easily motivate hard work if it detects shirking more often. That is, if p is higher, the expected cost of shirking is higher, and this tips the employee's cost/benefit trade-off in the direction of hard work. However, this model also identifies a second way for the firm to affect the employee's actions. Firms can increase the expected cost of shirking by *raising the employee's wage, w*. That is, by making the job more valuable, the firm can motivate an employee to take actions (such as working hard) to avoid losing the job.

Carl Shapiro and Joseph Stiglitz refer to a wage that is high enough to motivate effort as an *efficiency wage*.[36] They use this idea to explain how having a pool of unemployed workers in a labor market serves to provide incentives for those who are employed. If, on the one hand, all firms offer a wage *w* and fired workers can easily find new employment at this wage, then being fired involves no loss to the worker and hence has no incentive effects. If, on the other hand, being fired means taking a less attractive job (or even worse, a long and costly spell of unemployment), the prospect of being caught shirking provides an incentive to work hard.

It is not difficult to find cases of firms paying what appear to be above-market wages. In one well-known example, on January 5, 1914, the Ford Motor Company announced an increase in workers' wages from $2.30 per day to $5. The "Five-Dollar Day," as it became known, was introduced in tandem with adoption of the eight-hour workday and an increase in the number of work shifts from two to three. Henry Ford told reporters that his plan was "neither charity nor wages, but profit sharing and efficiency engineering."[37] According to Ford's later statements, the firm found that the change in wage policy improved both the discipline and efficiency of its workforce. Ford workers did not dare risk their jobs—there were no alternatives anywhere near as attractive. Efficiency wage theory may also explain why some firms offer attractive nonwage benefits. For example, firms that appear on lists such as *Fortune* magazine's "Top 100 Companies to Work For" offer employee-friendly policies that encourage workers to do what they can to retain their jobs, lest they end up at one of the "Worst Companies to Work For."

INCENTIVES IN TEAMS

Firms often find that the most effective means of production involves asking a group of employees to work together. Leading Indian car market Mahindra & Mahindra used teams to design its first global sports utility vehicle, the Scorpio. The firm split a 120-person development staff into 19 cross-functional teams combining marketing and engineering professionals. Each team tried to find ways of meeting marketing aims while keeping manufacturing costs low. Team leaders were made accountable for guaranteeing that targets were met. Mahindra & Mahindra credits this approach with keeping design costs under control; the firm claims that it spent just 6 billion rupees ($120 million) to design the Scorpio, compared to the 17 billion rupees rival Tata Engineering spent on the Indica passenger car. Examples such as this have become common throughout the world in recent years.

Achieving the full benefits of team production requires rewarding individuals for the performance of the team. Mahindra & Mahindra could have attempted to separately identify each team member's contribution toward the final Scorpio design, rewarding engineers for design improvements and marketing executives for improving the Scorpio's market appeal. This approach might have caused individuals to work at cross purposes. A marketing executive might have proposed a product feature that increased manufacturing costs. The design engineers, whose pay depended on holding down costs, would have balked and might even have exaggerated the impact on costs in order to block the proposal. An engineer might have found a way to cut costs but make the car seem more generic. The marketers would have objected and might have exaggerated the marketing impact. When performance is measured at the individual level, there is little incentive for the employees to combine their knowledge to make the decision that is best overall. Measuring performance by the overall profits generated by the new product eliminates this problem and motivates all parties to work together.

In order to realize this important benefit, firms must develop ways to combat the costs of team-based performance measures. To illustrate these costs, consider a design engineer working as part of a six-person team to design part of a new automobile. Suppose that all team members are evaluated on whether their design meets marketing objectives and cost targets. The team will split a bonus of $10,000 if the targets are met, but it will receive no additional compensation if targets are not met.

Suppose that the engineer believes that redesigning a vehicle part will reduce manufacturing costs substantially and therefore will increase the likelihood of meeting design targets from 40 to 70 percent. Although the idea seems promising, it will take considerable time and effort for the engineer to work out all the details. Will the engineer be willing to incur the cost, in terms of time and effort, necessary to fully develop this idea? If the engineer develops the idea, the likelihood of the team's success in meeting targets goes up by 30 percentage points, which means that the expected bonus paid to the team increases by $3,000. From the team's perspective, the idea should be pursued as long as the cost is less than $3,000. (From the firm's perspective, the idea should be pursued as long as the cost is less than $10,000.) But the engineer will split the team's bonus and only stands to gain $500. So the engineer will work on the idea as long as the expected cost is less than $500. The engineer's incentives and the team's incentives are not the same.

We can think about this problem more generally. Consider any actions with the following two properties:

1. Total benefit to team from action > total cost of action
2. Total cost of action > $(1/n)$ × total benefit to team from action

Actions with property (1) are value-creating actions in that the total benefit is greater than the total cost. However, since the individual undertaking the action compares this cost to the *personal benefit*, actions with property (2) may not be undertaken. The mismatch between the total benefit to the team and the personal benefit to the individual team member means that the individuals may not take actions that maximize overall welfare.

This effect is known as the *free-rider problem*, although this name may be something of a misnomer. The phrase suggests that one team member may elect not to work and instead try to get a "free ride" on the efforts of teammates. The problem is even worse than the phrase suggests, however, since it affects not just one but *every* team member, because everyone has an incentive to free ride on the group.

While our example makes use of a bonus based on a verifiable performance measure, free-rider problems are present even if team performance is an input into a subjective performance evaluation system. Suppose that a marketing executive's compensation depends on a supervisor's subjective assessment of the quality of the marketer's joint work with the design engineer. The design engineer's efforts will affect the performance evaluations of both employees. In making an effort choice, however, the design engineer may fail to account for the impact on the marketer's compensation.

The free-rider problem can be exacerbated by multitasking. Suppose, for example, that a design engineer pursues two tasks. The first is a solo project in which the engineer works to design parts for a new vehicle without input from marketing. The second is the team-based project described earlier. The design engineer receives the full benefit if the solo project succeeds but shares the benefit associated with the second task with team members. The engineer will naturally devote more effort to the solo project.

There is considerable evidence of free-riding in professional partnerships. Partnership arrangements are common in law, accounting, medicine, and consulting. Such firms typically pool the profits generated by each partner's activities and divide this pool according to some predetermined sharing rule. Some firms divide the pool equally (so that each partner receives share $1/n$ of the total), while others award larger shares to partners who are more productive or more senior. Regardless of the particular sharing rule, some fraction of the profit generated by an individual is captured by the other partners. This means that the personal benefit from effort is always lower than the total benefit, raising the possibility that partners will provide too little effort. Martin Gaynor and Mark Pauly demonstrated this effect in their study of medical practices. They found that increases in the size of partnerships led to reductions in individual productivity.[38] Similarly, a study of law firms by Arleen Leibowitz and Robert Tollison revealed that larger firms were less able to contain costs than smaller ones.[39]

Firms can mitigate the free-rider problem in a number of ways. First, they can keep teams small. Second, firms can allow employees to work together for long periods. Repeated interaction allows team members to make their current actions depend on what other members have done in the past. Thus, if one member fails to contribute to the team's goals today, others can punish the miscreant in the future, through peer pressure, social isolation, or simply a refusal to help that individual. This is analogous to the "tit-for-tat" solution to harmful competition discussed in Chapter 7.

The firm will reap the benefits of repeated interactions if team members can identify the free riders and do something about it. Mark Knez and Duncan Simester illustrated this point in their study of team-based incentives at Continental Airlines.[40] In 1995, the airline offered each hourly worker a $65 bonus for every month in which it ranked among the top five in the industry in on-time arrivals. Although this scheme would appear to suffer from severe free-rider problems, Knez and Simester found that Continental's on-time arrival rates increased at airports where the system was implemented. They argued that an important aspect of Continental's success was the division of the firm's employees into autonomous work groups at each airport location. Members of these groups could easily observe one another's actions. Sources of delay were quickly discovered, and employees were motivated to offer help in clearing the bottlenecks. Workers publicly challenged underperforming team members and sometimes reported them to management. These benefits could not have been achieved had employees been unable to observe one another's actions.

Firms can promote repeated interactions by keeping teams together for a long time. However, it can be difficult for firms to discern the individual abilities of members of stable teams. The success of a team could be due to the high ability of any one member, and as long as the team stays together, there is no way for the firm to figure out which member that is. By varying team assignments, the firm can better determine which employees are most productive.

EXAMPLE 12.6   TEAMS AND COMMUNICATION IN STEEL MILLS[41]

As the final step in production, sheet steel is subjected to various processes on what is called a finishing line. Typically, coils of sheet steel weighing up to 12 tons are unrolled at the line's entry point. A finishing line processes the unfinished steel by cleaning, heating, stretching, softening, or coating it. At the end of the line, the treated steel is coiled again for shipment to customers.

Jon Gant, Casey Ichniowski, and Kathryn Shaw argue that steel finishing lines offer an especially useful place to study the impact of team-based incentives on productivity. The production methods used on finishing lines do not vary significantly from one firm to another. This process is extremely capital intensive, so a line's profitability depends crucially on the amount of time it is operating correctly. If a line is shut down for repairs, or if it is producing defective steel that cannot be sold to customers, the firm's bottom line suffers. Hence, the key task for operators, maintenance workers, and managers is to identify and solve problems as quickly as possible.

Lines also make markedly different choices with regard to their human resource management policies. Gant and colleagues place lines in two categories: involvement-oriented and control-oriented. Involvement-oriented (IO) lines tend to have broadly defined jobs, work teams, screening of potential employees, incentive pay based on output quality, and skills training. Control-oriented (CO) lines have adopted few of the policies characteristic of IO lines; they run their processes with limited worker–manager communication and less worker involvement.

The authors visited a number of finishing lines and conducted surveys of all employees. They found that the levels of intra-crew communication were dramatically higher at IO lines than at CO lines. In IO line crews, the average crew member communicated regarding operational issues with 70 to 80 percent of other crew members. At CO lines, these figures were much lower, averaging less than 20 percent.

The IO lines' higher levels of communication meant that crew members were able to share information and identify problems more quickly. As an example of how this increased communication might help, Gant and colleagues described a CO line where sheets of steel were shifting from side to side as they passed through the equipment. This caused sheets to crumple at the edges, leading to a high rate of defective output. A team of engineers and managers was created to fix the problem but was unable to identify the cause for some time. The problem was finally resolved after an hourly worker noticed a piece of equipment that appeared to be in the wrong location. By chance, this employee mentioned the problem to others, and a fix was immediately found. The authors argue that regular communication among all employees working on the line would have led to speedier resolution of the problem.

Gant and colleagues attribute the increased communication at IO lines to the broader job design and the output-based incentives. Broader jobs and frequent job rotation mean that employees have a wider perspective on the line's operations. Incentives based on team output give a strong incentive to combine knowledge and communicate to solve problems. Increased communication, it appears, does translate into higher productivity; IO lines have longer operating times and higher yields (that is, lower rates of defects) than CO lines.

CHAPTER SUMMARY

- Agency problems arise when (1) a principal hires an agent to take actions that affect the payoff to the principal, (2) the agent's interests differ from those of the principal, and (3) there is hidden action or hidden information.

- Agency problems can be addressed by direct monitoring of the agent's actions or information. Monitoring is typically imperfect and expensive, and, if the monitor is an agent as well, results in adding a layer of agency to the organization.

- Performance-based incentives—where the agent is paid more when the payoff to the principal is high—work by aligning the interests of principal and agent.

- If a performance measure is affected by random factors, linking pay more closely to performance places more risk on an employee. Since employees are risk averse, they dislike jobs that involve risky pay, and the firm must compensate the employee for bearing this risk. This means that there is a trade-off between risk and incentives.

- Performance measures may fail to reflect activities that the firm wants the employee to pursue while rewarding activities that the firm does not want the employee to pursue. According to the multitask principle, stronger incentives will cause employees to focus more on activities that are measured at the expense of activities that are not measured.

- Selecting from among performance measures often involves trading off these costs against each other.

- For many jobs, firms can improve on explicit incentive contracts by using implicit incentive contracts. This is true when the available verifiable performance measures are noisy, reward activities that the firm does not want employees to pursue, or fail to reward activities that the firm does want employees to pursue.

- Implicit incentive contracts allow firms to make use of performance measures that cannot be verified by external enforcement mechanisms such as judges or arbitrators. A firm that fails to follow through on promises made as part of an implicit contract will lose its reputation as a good employer, and employees will not respond to future incentives based on implicit contracts.

- Often firms use supervisors' subjective assessments of employees' actions as performance measures in implicit contracts. If supervisors find it difficult to make sharp distinctions among employees, all employees might end up with similar evaluations. This weakens incentives to be a top performer.

- Strong incentives can be provided through the use of promotion tournaments. The strength of incentives provided by tournaments depends on the size of the prize—that is, on the difference between the wages earned by the tournament's winner and losers.

- Firms can also provide incentives by threatening to fire underperforming employees. The strength of these incentives depends on the value of the job to employees. Firms that pay efficiency wages make their jobs more valuable to employees and thus increase incentives for effort.

- Firms can motivate employees to work together by using team-based performance measures. Such measures can suffer from free-rider problems, however. Firms can combat free-rider problems by keeping teams small, allowing employees to work together repeatedly, and making sure employees working together can observe one another's actions.

QUESTIONS

1. Using your own experience, if possible, identify three types of hidden information that could affect an agency relationship. Identify three forms of hidden action as well.

2. In the United States, lawyers in negligence cases are usually paid a contingency fee equal to roughly 30 percent of the total award. Lawyers in other types of cases are often paid on an hourly basis. Discuss the merits and drawbacks of each from the perspective of the client (i.e., the principal).

3. Suppose that you were granted a "risky job" of the type examined in this chapter. The job pays $40,000 with probability 1/2 and $160,000 with probability ½. What is your certainty equivalent for this risky payoff? To answer this question, compare this risky job to a safe job that pays $100,000 for sure. Then reduce the value of the safe job in $1,000 increments until you are indifferent between the safe job and the risky job. What is your certainty equivalent for a job paying $10,000 or $190,000, each with equal probability?

4. In the United States, lawyers in negligence cases are usually paid a contingency fee equal to roughly 30 percent of the total award. Lawyers in other types of cases are often paid on an hourly basis. Discuss the merits and drawbacks of each from the perspective of the client (i.e., the principal).

5. Suppose that a firm offers a divisional manager a linear pay-for-performance contract based on the revenues of the division the manager leads. The manager's pay includes a fixed yearly salary F and a fraction of the division's revenue α that is paid to the manager. Suppose that the demand for this type of divisional manager increases, meaning that the firm has to increase this manager's pay in order to retain her. Should the firm do this by increasing the salary F, the commission α, or both? Explain.

6. Regulated firms, such as electric utilities, typically have limited discretion over the prices they charge. Regulators set prices to guarantee a fixed return to the firm's owners after gathering information about operating costs. Studies of executive pay practices have consistently shown that the compensation of utility CEOs is significantly less sensitive to the firm's performance than that of nonutility CEOs. Explain why, using the trade-off between risk and incentives.

7. Firms often use quotas as part of compensation contracts for salespeople. A quota-based contract may stipulate, for example, that the salesperson will receive a $10,000 bonus if yearly sales are $1 million or more, and no bonus otherwise. Identify actions a firm probably does not want pursued that the employee will be motivated to pursue under such a contract.

8. While in principle it is feasible for business schools to write explicit pay-for-performance contracts with professors, this is rarely done. Identify the drawbacks of the following performance measures for this job:

   • Number of research articles published

   • Students' ratings of professors' courses

   • Dollar value of research grants won

   • Starting salaries of students after graduation

9. Suppose that Minot Farm Equipment Corporation employs two salespeople. Each covers an exclusive territory; one is assigned to North Dakota and the other

to South Dakota. These two neighboring states have similar agricultural economies and are affected by the same weather patterns. Durham Tractor Company also employs two salespeople. One works in North Carolina, while the other is assigned to Oregon. Farm products and methods vary considerably across these two states. Each firm uses the dollar value of annual sales as a performance measure for salespeople. Which of the firms do you think would benefit most from basing pay on its salespeople's relative performance? Why?

10. Consider a potential employee who values wages but also values the opportunity to pursue non–work-related activities. (You may think of these activities as relating to family obligations, such as child care.) Suppose that other jobs available to this employee pay $100 per day but require him to work at the company's facility, effectively eliminating his ability to pursue nonwork activities. Ignore "effort" for the purposes of this problem and assume that the only agency problem pertains to how the employee allocates his time. Suppose that if the employee allocates all of his time in a day to "work," he creates $150 worth of value (gross of wages) for the firm. The employee may also have access to two forms of "nonwork" activities: (1) a high-value nonwork activity (think of unexpected child-care needs) and (2) a low-value nonwork activity (think of leisure—playing video games or watching TV). The employee values the ability to complete the high-value nonwork activity at $200 and the ability to complete the low-value nonwork activity at $50.

(a) Suppose first that the low-value nonwork activity does not exist and that the high-value nonwork activity exists with probability 0.10. (Interpretation: There is a 10 percent chance that the employee will need to perform an important child-care duty each day.) Suppose that your firm is considering offering this employee a telecommuting job. Assume here that if the employee telecommutes and the high-value activity arises, he spends all his time on this activity and creates no value for the firm that day. If the high-value nonwork activity does not arise, he spends all his time working on behalf of the firm. What daily wage should you offer? What will your profits be? Is your firm better off than if it offered the employee a nontelecommuting job? Why?

(b) Suppose now that the low-value nonwork activity does exist. Unlike the high-value activity (which only arises with some probability), the low-value activity is always present. Suppose also that the firm cannot pay this employee based on individual performance because the available performance measures are of insufficient quality. Suppose that your firm offers the telecommuting job you described in part (a). According to the multitask principle, how will the employee spend his time? Are your profits higher offering the telecommuting job or the nontelecommuting job?

(c) Next suppose that the firm does have access to a good measure of individual performance. It can make pay contingent on whether the employee works on the firm's activity. Which job (telecommuting or nontelecommuting) and compensation arrangement (fixed or fixed plus some variable dependent on output) will maximize the firm's profits? Comment on the types of jobs in which one might expect to see firms offering telecommuting.

11. Giganticorp, a large conglomerate, has just acquired Nimble, Inc., a small manufacturing concern. Putting yourself in the shoes of Nimble's employees, what concerns do you have about the implicit incentive contracts that governed your relationship with Nimble before the merger? Now place yourself in the position

of Giganticorp's merger integration team. How might concern about implicit contracts affect your dealings with Nimble's employees?

12. Oil companies such as British Petroleum and Royal Dutch Shell sell gasoline through their own branded gas stations. In some cases, these companies own their gas stations; in others, the stations are owned by local franchises. How might the following factors affect the choice of corporate versus local ownership?

(a) The gas station also does a lot of automotive repairs.

(b) The gas station is located on an interstate highway.

(c) The gas station has a large convenience store.

ENDNOTES

[1] "O'Neal Out as Merrill Reels from Loss; Startled Board Ditches a Famously Aloof CEO," *The Wall Street Journal*, October 29, 2007.

[2] Principal–agent relationships have long been a subject of study for economists. See, for example, Jensen, M., and W. Meckling, "Theory of the Firm: Managerial Behavior, Agency Costs and Ownership Structure," *Journal of Financial Economics*, 3, 1976, pp. 305–360, or Holmstrom, B., "Moral Hazard and Observability," *Bell Journal of Economics*, 4, 1979, pp. 4–29.

[3] Berle, A., and G. Means, *The Modern Corporation and Private Property*, New York, Macmillan, 1932.

[4] I. Barankay, Q. Bandiera, and I. Rasul, "Social Connections and Incentives in the Workplace: Evidence from Personnel Data," *Econometrica*, 77(4), 2009, pp. 1047–1094.

[5] To derive this, we differentiate the employee's objective with respect to e and find the value of e at which the resulting quantity is equal to zero. This yields $10 = e - 40$, or $e = 50$.

[6] The information for this story comes from Furth R. 2006. Zambia Pilot Study of Performance-based Incentives. Operations Research Results. Published for the U.S. Agency for International Development Agency (USAID) by the Quality Assurance Project (QAP). Accessed June 30, 2009 on the web at http://www.qaproject.org/news/PDFs/ZambiaPerformancePilotStudyInitiatives.pdf

[7] Ibid.

[8] Ibid.

[9] Here, we have calculated the employee's commission payment ($14,000) less effort costs $(1/2\,(100)^2 = \$5,000)$ as equal to $9,000. Hence, even if the employee is required to pay the firm $8,000 in order to take the job, the employee will be indifferent between this job and other jobs available in this labor market.

[10] If you think you prefer the risky job, consider the following thought experiment. Suppose that you and a friend each take the safe job. You can easily convert these two safe jobs into two risky jobs by betting $60,000 on a coin flip at the end of the year. Would you be willing to do this? Note that it would be easy for people to inject randomness into their wealth in this way, but we rarely observe anyone doing so. This suggests that most people do indeed dislike large random fluctuations in their wealth.

[11] See Holmstrom, B., and P. Milgrom, "Aggregation and Linearity in the Provision of Intertemporal Incentives," *Econometrica*, 55, 1987, pp. 308–328, and Holmstrom, B., and P. Milgrom, "Multitask Principal–Agent Analyses: Incentive Contracts, Asset Ownership and Job Design," *Journal of Law, Economics and Organization*, 7, 1991, pp. 524–552.

[12] This specification of the employee's certainty equivalent is useful for expositional purposes, but it does oversimplify preferences somewhat. In particular, the specification ignores the possibility that an individual may become less risk averse as he or she becomes wealthier.

[13]The marginal cost of effort is the first derivative (or slope) of the cost function with respect to e. The cost function is $\frac{1}{2}(e - 40)^2$, which has derivative $(e - 40)$. To find the value of e for which marginal benefit to marginal cost, we have $100\alpha = e - 40$, which yields $e = 40 + 100\alpha$.

[14]Note that if the variance of sales is 10,000, the standard deviation of sales is 100.

[15]Shi, L., "Productivity Effect of Piece Rate Contracts: Evidence from Two Small Field Experiments," Working Paper, University of Washington, 2007.

[16]This example is discussed in Holmstrom and Milgrom, "Multitask Principal–Agent Analyses."

[17]Note, however, that teaching to the test does happen in practice. According to *Catalyst*, an independent publication assessing public school reform in Chicago, some schools have "narrowed their curriculum in the pursuit of (standardized test) gains. At one South Side elementary school, the principal told her faculty to cut science, social studies, and writing from the curriculum and 'just prepare for the test,' an eighth grade teacher reports." See "Accountability Impact Both Positive, Negative," *Catalyst: Voices of Chicago School Reform*, October 2000.

[18]See "Incentive Pay Can Be Crippling," *Fortune*, November 13, 1995.

[19]To illustrate, consider a setting in which two salespeople's individual performance measures depend on their effort, their individual luck, and the condition of the local economy. Suppose that employee A's individual performance is $e_A + \varepsilon_{A1} + \varepsilon_2$, where ε_{A1} is a random variable representing individual luck and ε_2 is a random variable representing the condition of the local economy. Suppose similarly that employee B's individual performance is $e_B + \varepsilon_{B1} + \varepsilon_2$, and that ε_{A1} and ε_{B1} are independent. In this case, the total variation in employee A's performance is $\varepsilon_{A1} + \varepsilon_2$. This is positively correlated with the variation in employee B's performance because ε_2 affects both. If the firm uses the *difference* between the employees' individual output as a performance measure, employee A's pay will depend on $e_A - e_B + \varepsilon_{A1} - \varepsilon_{B1}$. If the variance of ε_2 is large relative to that of ε_{A1} and ε_{B1}, this relative measure exposes employees to less risk than does the absolute measure.

[20]Zwiebel, J., "Corporate Conservatism and Relative Compensation," *Journal of Political Economy*, 103, 1995, pp. 1–25.

[21]This discussion draws from a survey article written by Candice Prendergast. See "The Provision of Incentives in Firms," *Journal of Economic Literature*, 37, 1999, pp. 7–63.

[22]Parsch, H., and B. Shearer, "Piece Rates, Fixed Wages, and Incentive Effects: Statistical Evidence from Payroll Records," *International Economic Review*, 41, 2002, pp. 59–92.

[23]Gaynor, M., J. Rebitzer, and L. Taylor, "Physician Incentives in Health Maintenance Organizations," *Journal of Political Economy*, 2004, pp. 915–932.

[24]Drago, R., and G. Garvey, "Incentives for Helping on the Job: Theory and Evidence," *Journal of Labor Economics*, 16, 1998, pp. 1–25.

[25]"Knowledge Management Sweeping Korea's Corporate Landscape," *Korea Herald*, June 22, 2002.

[26]"Rank and File Attrition Isn't Working, So Best-to-Worst Grading is Gaining," *Time*, June 18, 2001.

[27]"More Firms Cut Workers Ranked at Bottom to Make Way for Talent," *USA Today*, May 30, 2001.

[28]Lazear, E., and S. Rosen, "Rank Order Tournaments as Optimal Labor Contracts," *Journal of Political Economy*, 89, 1981, pp. 841–864.

[29]Our discussion here omits a subtle aspect of tournament theory. Because it is the best loan officer who earns the promotion, the probability that loan officer 1 will win the tournament depends not just on his own effort but also on that of the second loan officer. Officer 1's optimal effort choice therefore may depend on the effort choice made by officer 2. The simultaneous choice of efforts by competitors in a tournament is conceptually similar to the simultaneous choice of quantities by Cournot duopolists. Lazear and Rosen derived

reaction functions for tournament competitors and solved for the Nash equilibrium of this game.

[30]Rosen, S., "Prizes and Incentives in Elimination Tournaments," *American Economic Review*, 76, 1986, pp. 921–939.

[31]This example is based on Brown, J., *Journal of Political Economy*, forthcoming. We thank Professor Brown for writing the example.

[32]Baker, G., M. Gibbs, and B. Holmstrom, "The Wage Policy of a Firm," *Quarterly Journal of Economics*, 109, 1994, pp. 921–956.

[33]Main, B., C. O'Reilly, and J. Wade, "Top Executive Pay: Tournament or Teamwork? *Journal of Labor Economics*, 11, 1993, pp. 606–628.

[34]Eriksson, T., "Executive Compensation and Tournament Theory: Empirical Tests on Danish Data," *Journal of Labor Economics*, 17, 1999, pp. 262–280.

[35]The wages w and w^{**} in this model can be interpreted rather broadly. The wage w, for instance, can be viewed as the net present value of the employee's future employment prospects conditional on retaining her current job today. The wage w^{**} can be interpreted as the net present value of future employment prospects conditional on being fired from the current job. Many factors could cause w^{**} to be less than w; firing may result in a long and costly period of unemployment, a black mark on a résumé, or a lower-paying next job.

[36]Shapiro, C., and J. Stiglitz, "Equilibrium Unemployment as a Discipline Device," *American Economic Review*, 74, 1984, pp. 433–444.

[37]Quoted in Allan Nevins, *Ford: the Times, the Man, the Company*, New York, Charles Scribner's Sons, 1954. See also Raff, D., and L. Summers, "Did Henry Ford Pay Efficiency Wages?" *Journal of Labor Economics*, 5, 1987, pp. 57–86.

[38]Gaynor, M., and M. Pauly, "Compensation and Productive Efficiency in Partnerships: Evidence from Medical Group Practice," *Journal of Political Economy*, 98, 1990, pp. 544–573.

[39]Leibowitz, A., and R. Tollison, "Free Riding, Shirking, and Team Production in Legal Partnerships," *Economic Inquiry*, 18, 1980, pp. 380–394.

[40]Knez, M., and D. Simester, "Firm-wide Incentives and Mutual Monitoring at Continental Airlines," *Journal of Labor Economics*, 19, 2001, pp. 743–772.

[41]This example is drawn from Gant, J., C. Ichniowski, and K. Shaw, "Working Smarter by Working Together: Connective Capital in the Workplace," Working Paper, Stanford University, 2003.

STRATEGY AND STRUCTURE   13

U ntil the early 1980s, the Pepsi-Cola Company comprised three divisions that reported to corporate headquarters. Pepsi USA created marketing campaigns—the famous "Pepsi Challenge" was its brainchild. The Pepsi Bottling Group (PBG) bottled and distributed the product in local markets in which Pepsi chose not to use independent bottlers. PBG was also responsible for local marketing campaigns. The Fountain Beverage Division (FBD) sold to other distributors besides bottlers, including fast-food outlets, restaurants, bars, and stadiums. While this structure had much to recommend it, it also created problems. It made it difficult for Pepsi to negotiate with regional and national retailers, such as Piggly Wiggly and Wal-Mart. Pepsi USA and PBG often ran competing (and sometimes conflicting) promotional campaigns that required ongoing rather than exceptional coordination. Employee backgrounds, characteristics, and compensation also varied across divisions, with workers in PBG and FBD resenting the high salaries and high profiles of the Pepsi USA employees.

To resolve these problems, Pepsi reorganized its beverage operations in 1988. Pepsi USA, PBG, and FBD ceased to exist. Sales and account management responsibilities were decentralized among four geographic regions and handled more locally. Decisions about national marketing campaigns, finance, human resources, and corporate operations, including trucking and company-owned bottlers, were centralized at headquarters and handled nationally. But this reorganization did not solve Pepsi's coordination problems for long. Negotiations with national accounts often had to pass through several layers of management before a final decision could be reached, resulting in the loss of important accounts, notably Burger King. Conflicts between national and local promotional campaigns continued to arise. So in 1992, Pepsi reorganized again. This time, marketing and sales campaigns were further centralized, and responsibility for a given retail outlet was delegated to a single salesperson.

Throughout these two reorganizations, Pepsi enjoyed popular products, a motivated workforce, strong stock price performance, and a benign competitive environment. Even so, the firm's top managers believed that these favorable factors could not guarantee continued success and that to remain profitable, Pepsi needed to reorganize to better deploy its capabilities and resources in pursuit of its strategies.

This attention to organization increased when Pepsi fundamentally altered its strategy through M&A and international expansion. Since these reorganizations, Pepsi significantly expanded by acquiring Tropicana in 1998 and merging with Quaker Oats in 2001. In 2010, PepsiCo acquired its two largest bottlers—Pepsi

Bottling Group and PepsiAmericas—which strengthened the company's beverage business in North America and Europe and largely consolidated bottling operations within a single unit. In 2011, PepsiCo completed its largest-ever transaction outside of the United States with the acquisition of Wimm-Bill-Dann, the largest manufacturer of dairy products in Russia. As a result of these strategic changes, Pepsi's corporate structure is now fundamentally different and comprised of four business units organized on the basis of global geography: PepsiCo Americas Beverages (PAB), PepsiCo Americas Foods (PAF), PepsiCo Europe, and PepsiCo Asia, Middle East, & Africa (AMEA).

Changing corporate structure is costly. Pepsi pays seven-figure fees to consultants who design and implement organization change. Work flows are disrupted. Teams are split apart and reformed. Throughout the restructurings, Pepsi's technology, product mix, and market position remain largely unchanged. Pepsi would not have engaged in so many restructurings if it did not believe that these factors alone are insufficient for explaining firm performance. Research supports this view. For example, Richard Caves and David Barton found that firms in the same industry, with similar technologies and labor forces, often have substantially different levels of productivity.[1] While some of the reasons for differences in performance are idiosyncratic and do not lend themselves to general principles (e.g., the role of Steve Jobs in attracting talent to Apple Computer and spurring the development of his "digital hub" strategy), others can be generalized. We have previously discussed, for example, the importance of appropriately applying resources and capabilities to the competitive environment. In this chapter, we consider *organizational structure*.

Organizational structure describes the arrangements, both formal and informal, by which a firm divides up its critical tasks, specifies how its managers and employees make decisions, and establishes routines and information flows to support continuing operations. Structure also defines the nature of agency problems within the firm—who has authority for which decisions and who controls flows of information. Structure can even determine whether workers' goals are aligned with each other, with management, and with owners.

Does it matter how a firm is organized? Are some structures better than others? We argue that the way a firm organizes matters for its success in implementing its strategic choices. These choices do not implement themselves, and the activities necessary to collect information, circulate it to the appropriate people, bring people together to make decisions, and then follow up on how decisions are carried out are costly to coordinate. The right structure will enable managers to link a firm's resources and capabilities with the opportunities that managers perceive in their business environment more easily and effectively than alternatives. This implies that an optimal structure permits the firm to create the most value, thereby making the ability to organize in pursuit of strategic goals a critical capability for a firm.

In his classic set of case studies of the growth of such large corporations as General Motors and Sears, *Strategy and Structure*, Alfred Chandler made essentially the same argument. He observed that the founding top managers of large industrial and mass distribution firms structured their firms to best allow them to pursue their chosen business strategy—or, simply put, that *structure follows strategy*.[2] We will return to this crucial idea near the end of the chapter.

The growth of the Internet, the spread of globalization, the continuing deskilling and computerization of entire occupations, changing workforce demographics, and other factors have led some observers to question whether organizational structure has the same importance for firms that it once did, such as in the high-growth period for American corporations after World War II. Traditional divisional structures that were once the hallmark of large corporations are being scaled back and even dropped in favor of either more complex matrix structures or less elaborate and more flexible "hybrid" structures. Formerly critical parts of large firms have been shut down, spun off as separate businesses, or sold off to other firms. The large corporate actors of today are often loose alliance networks or business groups rather than integrated formal organizations. Although some skepticism is certainly reasonable regarding the persistence of a given set of structural choices, we remain convinced of the more general importance of structure—that firms must organize (and reorganize) so as to maintain the linkages between their evolving resources and capabilities and the changing contexts in which they must be put to work.

AN INTRODUCTION TO STRUCTURE

Before further developing the link between strategy and structure, it is helpful to introduce some basic concepts and describe the major kinds of organizational structures.

Individuals, Teams, and Hierarchies

Large complex organizations often grow out of small ones that are initially organized on a few simple principles. These provide a starting point for how complex structures might develop both by illustrating some basic organizing principles and by serving as building blocks for more complex structures.

Simple tasks performed by a small group of people can be structured in several ways:

- *Individually.* The members of the work group are organized and paid based on individual actions and outcomes, with little interaction among team members. The group is really an assemblage of individuals performing a set of tasks. This is the same whether a group is composed of personnel search advisers, each working with separate clients, or temporary workers stuffing envelopes for a firm as part of one of its mailing campaigns. This approach to organizing will be important whenever individuals can contribute significantly to the success or failure of the firm by their individual efforts. Examples can be found in how trading activities have come to be organized at large financial services and energy firms. The success of traders drove the rapid growth of such large financial firms as Bear Stearns or Goldman Sachs and of energy firms such as Enron or Dynergy following industry deregulation. When traders suffer poor performance, whether due to poor judgment, bad luck, or fraud, the results for firms organized around them can be devastating, as in the trading-related scandals at UBS in 2011, Societe Generale in 2008, and Barings in 1995. The scandal at Barings is illustrative. Barings was the oldest merchant bank in London when it failed after being in business for 233 years, due to the activities of "rogue trader" Nick Leeson, who tried to cover up losses of over $1.3 billion from futures and derivatives trades.

- *Self-Managed Teams.* A collection of individuals work together to set and pursue common objectives. The team's results depend on how team members work together, share information, and coordinate their actions. Examples of situations where teams would be employed include management consultants serving a corporate client or a construction team working on a complex installation project. Team performance determines team rewards, though the team may choose to divide the rewards unevenly, based on individual contributions to the overall outcome. Teams are especially important for complex development projects where it is unlikely that any one individual would possess the experience and skills necessary to bring the project to completion under a tight deadline. Steve Jobs was famous for assembling and driving such teams to develop new products at Apple, often placing these teams in competition with other groups in the firm. This was the case for the initial development and launch of the first Mac computer in 1984, as well as for Apple's string of successful product launches after Jobs's return to leadership of the firm in 1997.

- *Hierarchy of Authority.* In any group that grows in size or complexity, members will confront the need to coordinate with one another in order to carry out basic tasks. While it is tempting to rely on notions of entrepreneurship and individual initiative as the solution to a business's problems, as small firms achieve success and grow, they quickly become much more complicated and require more organizing efforts just to maintain a given level of performance. The more that the attention of group members is focused on coordination and order maintenance, the less it will be focused on their basic tasks and performance. Hierarchy of authority is common in nearly all complex organizations and is introduced into a team when one member of the group specializes in monitoring and coordinating the work of the other group members, including resolving disputes in the group. In a business school, for example, there is usually an associate dean drawn from the faculty who has ultimate responsibility for course scheduling. Left to their own devices, individual professors would probably produce a schedule that was nightmarish for students and wasteful of facilities that could be utilized more fully by scheduling across a week, even during times that are less convenient for senior professors. The use of hierarchy increases as firms become larger, owing to the increase in the volume and diversity of activities that accompany increases in firm size. Hierarchy can also be introduced into smaller organizations, if the need for coordination is coupled with strong needs for individual accountability. For example, most police agencies in the United States are fairly small (less than 50 members), and yet most employ well-articulated command hierarchies, due to the need for police accountability in their interactions with citizens.

Most firms, even small ones, combine these simple arrangements in some way. An employee may do some tasks individually and others in a team. The extent to which an authority relationship enters into small-group arrangements also varies among firms, with some resembling a collection of independent workers, a common situation in professional service firms. At the other extreme, some firms may employ varying degrees of hierarchy, chain of command, and related formal controls. A work group may organize some activities around individuals and others around the group, while a supervisor may monitor the activities and outputs of both groups and individuals.

The appropriateness of each way of organizing tasks in small groups varies according to circumstances. Treating the workers as self-managing individuals is most appropriate when their tasks do not require coordination, for example, in a social service agency in which staff members interact with clients on a case-by-case basis and where coordination is restricted by privacy regulations and considerations. When coordination is necessary, say because the work involves design attributes or relationship-specific investments, as discussed in Chapter 3, then organizing by teams or hierarchy is more appropriate.

Group self-management is more appropriate than a hierarchy when work outcomes benefit from frequent group interaction and group incentives (such as from information sharing or from increased motivation and group support) and when the costs of group coordination do not detract from other group outcomes. Organizing by self-managing groups, however, makes it difficult to monitor and control individual outputs and align individual incentives with the activities of the larger firm, whose goals can come into conflict with those of the group. Armen Alchian and Harold Demsetz raise these issues about groups and hierarchies in explaining why firms exist.[3] Beyond a certain size, group self-management becomes too costly, and some form of hierarchy is necessary to maintain and evaluate the group as well as reduce agency problems that occur when individuals try to influence firm decisions for their private benefit.

For examples of these tensions, consider investment banks. Although these banks may organize their front-office selling and trading on an individual basis, it would be less appropriate to organize middle-office activities, such as risk management, or back-office activities, such as order execution, on an individual basis, since these necessarily focus on firm performance with scant opportunities for individual incentives. Moreover, if these activities became subject to competition among groups for key resources, the overall effect for the firm and its reputation could be very negative, such as when trading partners come to doubt the firm's ability to fulfill its obligations in clearing transactions. How much control is introduced depends on the extent of agency problems and the time and effort needed to control them. These comprise the influence costs that we also discussed in Chapter 3.

Although nearly everyone is familiar with these issues in organizing small firms or work groups, this level of organizing is seldom of strategic importance in larger firms, especially when compared to the investments these firms make to achieve large scale or serve extended markets. In small firms, these simpler structures can be readily changed, but can also affect relatively small numbers of individuals at a given time. Of much greater importance are the organizational schemes used in larger firms that affect considerable numbers of people and govern the allocation of significant organizational assets. These are *complex hierarchies*, which involve organizing large numbers of groups within extensive and potentially overlapping schemes. These are discussed in more detail below.

Complex Hierarchy

Large firms require *complex hierarchies*—that is, the structure of the firm involves multiple groups and multiple levels of groupings. Complex hierarchy arises from the need not just to organize individuals into groups, but to organize groups into larger groups. This process quickly becomes complicated and involves two related problems:

1. *Departmentalization*, or partitioning of workers into subgroups
2. *Coordination of activities* within and between subgroups to attain the firm's objectives

Most organization designs combine solutions to departmentalization and coordination problems under the specific conditions a firm faces.[4]

Departmentalization

Departmentalization involves the partition of the organization into different groups and sets of groups. It may occur along several dimensions: tasks (or functions), inputs, outputs, geography, and time of work. Given that multiple dimensions are at work, this process involves two related steps. First, the dimensions that are relevant to a given firm need to be identified. Should products or functions be used as an organizing dimension? What about geography or customers? Second, along with identifying the dimensions, it is also necessary to specify the relationships between chosen dimensions. Which coordination problems need to be handled first? Which problems are best handled at a more general level within a firm, after more basic issues of coordination have been considered? It is the need to choose organizing dimensions as well as relationships among those dimensions that makes organization design difficult in large firms.

At its most basic level, departmentalization represents the choices of managers regarding the appropriate division of labor in the firm. Samples of departments organized around common tasks or functions include accounting, marketing, and production. Other grouping schemes can focus on criteria related to the firm's inputs and outputs. Examples of these schemes include the Pepsi Bottling Group and Fountain Beverage Division that we discussed earlier.

To illustrate how grouping schemes can differ internationally, consider Jaipur Rugs, in 2008 the largest manufacturer and exporter of Indian hand-knotted rugs, with 2008 revenue of $21.1 million and compound annual growth of over 30 percent. The firm offers a wide range of products, operates in a complex production environment, and must organize the activities of 7 family members, 300 full-time employees, and 40,000 contractors, of whom 28,000 are weavers, with the remainder involved in other aspects of the firm's complex supply chain. The business had traditionally been organized as an association of separate legal entities tied together by family. With rapid growth, the firm has had to change from a partnership into a corporation to coordinate its activities through investments in information technology. It has also reorganized into a unified hierarchy focusing on key functions of marketing, finance, operations, supply chain, design and development, and human resources and information technology.[5]

Departments and divisions can also be organized around locations, such as with regional sales offices or service centers. There can even be time-based groupings that would reflect different priorities in organizational activities at different times of the week or some other cycle of activities. This is illustrated by 24-hour call centers, whose employees deal with the customer service issues of people in different parts of the world, depending on the shifts they work. While outsourcing customer service activities to these centers has been popular with many U.S. consumer products firms, large retail banks, such as Citigroup or Chase, have been the leaders. These centers have largely been located in India, but by early 2011 the Philippines had taken a narrow lead, with 350,000 call center employees versus 330,000 in India. The reasons for the change appear to be that U.S. customers have fewer problems with the accents of Filipinos and employers there have fewer problems recruiting workers for night-shift positions.

Deciding how to organize tasks within a firm reflects the choices of managers regarding what activities are to be done and their relative importance. These reflect key elements of the firm's strategy, including who its core customers are and which of its activities will be the most critical for its success. Thus, departmentalization is also associated with the choice of a firm's boundaries. For example, diversification into new businesses will be reflected in an expansion in the set of a corporation's divisions, departments, and other groups. A decision to outsource a significant function will lead to a contraction of a firm's structure; this removes the individuals and activities associated with that function from the organization, placing it outside the firm's boundaries. We discussed decisions about the firm's boundaries in earlier chapters, and the results of boundary choices will be apparent in the contours of a firm's structure.

In general, when selecting organizing dimensions, managers should consider economies of scale and scope, transactions costs, and agency costs. A firm should combine workers or teams into a department when their activities involve economies of scale or scope. For example, if a multiproduct firm can achieve significant scale economies in research and development, then an organizational structure that included a companywide research department would be more efficient than dispersing R&D personnel throughout a number of independent product groups. This would be the case for research into core technologies that clearly influence most of the firm's products. The classic example of this would be the 3M Corporation, with its longstanding skills in adhesive chemistry. However, there may also be situations in which research is most valuable when it focuses on production processes or on how the firm's products are best employed by customers. This would suggest the wisdom of organizing R&D on the basis of divisions or distinct customer business areas. An example of a firm with such an approach to R&D would be Crown Holdings (formerly Crown Cork and Seal) which shifted its research in a mature business (metal cans) to help its customers best employ Crown's products to advantage in their own production processes.

While it is easy to recommend that managers organize around available scale or scope economies, in practice this is often difficult to do, since in any given situation, there may be potential economies both within units and between units, such that the "best" structural choice is not apparent in advance. For an example of this, consider Apple's success in coming to dominate the digital music business through the combination of its iPod and its iTunes Store. A natural question that observers asked while this domination was taking place was what Sony would do about it. Sony was the firm that launched portable music players with its Walkman, owned a substantial record company, and was one of the few firms that could compete with Apple in producing stylish electronics for consumers. Yet Sony failed and Apple transformed the industry.

A possible reason for this outcome is organizational. Apple's triumph came from combining its iPod device with its rights management regime. This is what convinced the major record companies and artists to agree to sell their works on iTunes. This success involved a merging of hardware and content that was the key to the product. Although Sony possessed significant hardware and content, it was not organized to combine them effectively. Instead, it was organized into distinct divisions, each with its own responsibilities and profit objectives. This allowed Sony to capitalize on the economies specific to hardware or to content, but not the synergies between them. When Sony attempted to imitate Apple, this arrangement created a conflict that limited cooperation and allowed Apple, which was not organized into divisions, to find a solution that worked.[6]

Finally, the choice of an organizing dimension has implications for agency costs, such as we discussed in Chapter 12. For example, measuring the performance of a firm's functional departments, such as finance and purchasing, can be difficult because it is difficult to identify tangible outcomes directly related to profitability. Moreover, because of the weak linkage with overall firm performance, individuals in these departments are likely to think of their performance in terms of functional excellence rather than overall firm success. This makes it hard to evaluate and reward department managers, which further increases agency costs inside the firm.

Coordination and Control

Once groups have been identified and organized, the interrelated problems of coordination and control arise. *Coordination* involves the flow of information to facilitate subunit decisions that are consistent with each other and with organizational objectives. *Control* involves the location of decision-making and rule-making authority within a hierarchy. Coordination and control choices can affect both efficiency and agency costs. They influence efficiency because decision makers need access to low-cost, accurate, and timely information, while assuring that the firm takes full advantage of economies of scale and scope in production. For example, poor coordination between the Pepsi Bottling Group and Pepsi USA resulted in technical inefficiencies when the two divisions failed to economize on marketing and sales efforts. This suggests that decision rights should be allocated so that individuals with the best and most timely information are empowered to make decisions, provided of course that the decision maker's goals are aligned with those of the firm.

Coordination and control also affect agency costs because structures designed for similar tasks may differ in the opportunities they offer managers to pursue personal or unit objectives that are inconsistent with the firm's objectives. By allocating formal decision rights throughout a hierarchy, a firm's managers designate a legitimate basis of authority that they perceive will best support overall firm objectives. In the next chapter, we will discuss formal authority and its relationship to other bases of power and influence.

By addressing coordination and control issues, organization structure provides a focus for *accountability*—aligning individual and group tasks with those of the firm and aligning incentives so that individuals and groups will consistently work in the same direction. Structure also needs to be capable of adjusting to changes in both the firm's capabilities and its business environment. These shifting and potentially conflicting demands comprise what Robert Simons calls the "creative tensions" that are part of organization design.[7]

Two examples of these tensions illustrate the need for firms to adapt their structures to align with their strategic needs. First, consider the situation faced by a relatively focused firm with divisions in mature high-volume businesses. A divisional structure coupled with a control system stressing sales volume and production efficiency may be an optimal structure for such a firm. However, if that firm decided to diversify and acquire smaller firms in high-growth innovative businesses, the structure would be far from optimal. This structure would penalize managers at the newly acquired divisions because their businesses could not match the volume and cost performance of established divisions. A new structure and set of performance metrics would be needed to adapt to the firm's change in strategy and capabilities. David Garvin and Lynne Levesque discuss this as a problem of organizing for *corporate entrepreneurship* and cite IBM and Ashland Oil as examples of firms that crafted hybrid organization designs to accommodate the developmental needs of new subsidiaries as well as their needs for eventual incorporation into the corporation's broader organization.[8]

Firms facing a changeable business environment that necessitates a change in strategy would also benefit from adaptability. For example, consider the Lincoln Electric Company, a manufacturer of welding equipment headquartered in Cleveland. Lincoln had a long record of success serving U.S. customers with a complex structure and control system that made heavy use of piece-rate incentives. When the evolution of its industry required that the firm expand into international markets in the late 1980s, however, its initial efforts met with less success. Lincoln Electric was unable to replicate its complex structure and systems in international settings, such as Indonesia, China, or India. Even small changes in structure and systems required to do business overseas seemed to harm performance. It was only after the turn of the millennium, following years of trial and error, that Lincoln learned how to more effectively adapt to its new markets.[9]

Approaches to Coordination

There are two alternative approaches for developing coordination within firms.[10] The first emphasizes *autonomy* or *self-containment*, whereas the second emphasizes strong *lateral relations*. When firms organize using autonomous work units, unit managers control information about operating decisions. Operating information remains within the units, and unit managers provide summary financial and accounting data, including profit data when available, to headquarters. But the flow of information *across units* is minimal. Firms that are organized this way are more likely to employ corporate strategies featuring mergers and acquisitions, since units that are organized autonomously are easier to both append to a current structure or to detach from that structure and transfer to the control of an acquirer.

A common approach to self-containment is to organize into separate product groups, each of which contains the basic business functions of manufacturing and sales and could plausibly exist by itself in the marketplace (as a spinoff). These autonomous groups, often called *profit centers*, are controlled on the basis of a target profit goal. Managers in autonomous groups are rewarded for meeting or exceeding a profit goal and punished for failing to meet it. Managers in autonomous divisions may have limited interactions with their counterparts in other units. Diversified firms, such as Procter & Gamble and Johnson & Johnson, make frequent use of profit centers. As discussed in Chapter 2, there is considerable research evidence questioning whether such diversification is profitable. After all, if individual profit centers are fully autonomous, there is little to be gained by joining under a single corporate umbrella. When groups focus on other performance measures besides profit, such as cost, revenue, or investment goals, they are called *responsibility centers*. Research programs at pharmaceutical companies often make use of responsibility centers and base their performance judgments on such criteria of research productivity as patents and research publications.

The alternative to self-contained groupings is the development of lateral relations across units. Lateral relations make sense when realizing economies of scale or scope requires close coordination among work groups. Lateral relations can be informal, such as with *ad hoc* or temporary teams or liaisons, or they can be formalized within the firm's structure. An example of a formal attempt to foster lateral relations is the *matrix organization*, in which employees are subject to two or more sets of managers at once. This occurs, for example, when an engineer reports both to a research and development department and a project office, or when a salesperson reports both to the head of sales for a particular product and to a regional manager. We discuss matrix organizations in more detail in the next section.

A firm's authority is often described in terms of *centralization* or *decentralization*. As more decisions are made by senior managers, the firm is said to be more centralized regarding those decisions. Since 2000, centralization decisions have been associated with efforts by corporations to adjust to harsher industry conditions and generally declining demand. An example of this can be seen in the 2008 announcement that the European aerospace firm EADS was considering an extensive restructuring that would consolidate the firm's five divisions into three. Conversely, as more decisions

EXAMPLE 13.1   ABB's Matrix Organization[12]

Asea Brown Boveri (ABB) is a large global producer of heavy capital equipment, such as turbine generators and railway engines. It was formed in 1988 when ASEA of Sweden merged with Brown Boveri of Switzerland. Soon after the merger, ABB's senior management concluded that to be more responsive to customer needs in different parts of the world, ABB's organization would have to be decentralized and made flexible to local conditions. ABB was thus reorganized. The reorganization resulted in a matrix structure in which ABB's 1,300 local business units (e.g., its railway engine division in Norway) were organized along two dimensions: products and geography. On the product dimension, ABB created 65 business areas (BAs), each responsible for one of ABB's product lines. On the geography dimension, ABB created countrywide organizations. At the intersection of a matrix were local business units, each responsible for a particular product line within a particular country. The head of each local unit was subject to "dual reporting." That is, the manager for a particular product line in a given country would report to both the worldwide business area manager for that product line and to the head of the countrywide organization for that country.

Some of the immediate successes that arose from ABB's restructuring were reductions in manufacturing costs through rationalizing production operations and improving new product development through better targeting of R&D funding. The BAs organized themselves according to a "lead center"

concept. Under this concept, for each product line, one location was chosen to provide worldwide product leadership and support. All R&D and process improvement efforts were concentrated in this location, from which successful strategies were transferred to other locations. Each lead center became the single source for the collective knowledge within each of ABB's product lines.

ABB's matrix structure also encouraged healthy competition among the various geographic units that made up a BA. The units that provided the most efficient manufacturing facilities were retained to cater to the BA's worldwide requirements. These plants were then expanded to achieve global-scale production levels, thereby giving them scale efficiencies. This helped the company become the leader in almost all the product groups in which it competed. Inefficient plants were shut down or sold. ABB encountered one serious problem with its matrix structure, however. Because the structure essentially requires multiple reporting, important decisions had to be taken by multimember teams from all over the world. This slowed down decision making. To overcome this, ABB embarked on an ambitious internal mail and information system based on Lotus Notes. This system allowed managers to freely communicate, exchange files and data, and thus make decisions more quickly. With over 70,000 users around the world, ABB's Lotus Notes network became a backbone for reporting and decision making within the organization.

are made at lower levels, the firm becomes more decentralized regarding those decisions. Decentralization is frequently associated with diversification, so that as the variety of a firm's businesses increases, decision making will naturally devolve to the firm's divisions. An example of such a decentralized firm would be Johnson & Johnson, a diversified corporation with significant businesses in consumer products, pharmaceuticals, and medical devices.

Firms are often referred to as either centralized or decentralized, but the situation in most firms is more complicated because they are often centralized on some dimensions and decentralized on others. Because a firm delegates operating authority to division managers (decentralization) does not mean that senior managers have given up their authority. Rather, they have likely retained authority to review division performance and make decisions that influence the career advancement of division managers (centralization).

The balance between centralization and decentralization is to some degree self-correcting. This is apparent in the idea of *span of control*, which refers to the number of individuals who directly report to a manager. The larger the number of individuals reporting to a manager, the wider is that manager's span of control (and vice versa).

Debates among management practitioners and scholars regarding the optimal span of control have not reached lasting conclusions. Changes in expectations regarding how many reports one should have differ by the type of work being managed and the sector involved. It is generally recognized that with a broader span of control individuals need to be managed differently than with a narrow span of control. When the span of control increases, managers have more reports to oversee and less time to intensively review any particular staffer. Managers must therefore narrow their focus on results and pay less attention to the processes by which those results are obtained or else standardize critical processes. Control over operations in apparently centralized organizations is thus decentralized to lower level managers, even while the review of these managers remains with more senior managers. Firms like Sears pioneered this approach to management with their focus on store management in the era of postwar growth. More diversified firms, such as GE under Jack Welch, developed it further. This approach is less common in areas with narrower spans of control, such as professional service businesses and R&D groups.[11]

TYPES OF ORGANIZATIONAL STRUCTURES

There are four basic structures for large organizations.[13]

1. The unitary *functional* structure (often called the U-form)
2. The *multidivisional* structure (often called the M-form)
3. The *matrix* structure
4. The *network* structure

Functional Structure (U-form)

Figure 13.1 represents the unitary functional structure or U-form. The term *unitary functional* refers to the fact that in this structure a single unit is responsible for each basic business function (e.g., finance, marketing, production, purchasing) within the firm. The Jaipur Rug Company structure discussed earlier is an example of this structure. A division of labor that allows for specialization of basic business tasks characterizes this structure. As a firm grows, new tasks can be added or existing departments can be subdivided without jeopardizing the logic of the structure. The component groups or units in the functional structure are called *departments*. Because of this division of labor, departments are dependent on direction from central headquarters and probably could not exist outside of the firm except as contract vendors. Individuals grouped within departments share similar backgrounds, norms of behaviors, goals, and performance standards. This promotes performance within the department but makes coordination with other departments difficult. Firms organized this way tend to centralize their strategic decision making.

FIGURE 13.1

SAMPLE CHART OF A FUNCTIONAL ORGANIZATIONAL STRUCTURE

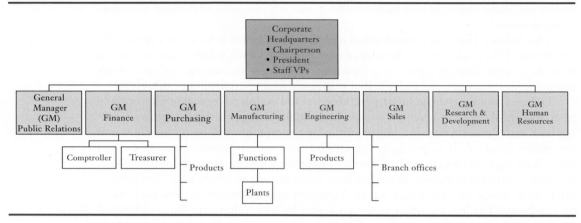

Functional structures developed as firms grew bigger and more specialized in the nineteenth century. These structures are suited to relatively stable conditions in which operational efficiency is valued. Even so, large firms were slow to adopt these structures. The early growth of large firms that we discussed in Chapter 1 was characterized by loose combinations of formerly independent firms, often still run by founders. These failed to coordinate leadership and generally did not combine work groups performing similar tasks into departments. Rather, they resembled alliances of equals. (U.S. Steel looked this way when it became the first billion-dollar firm in 1901.)

Functional organization in large firms became widely adopted once managers realized that firms that were organized this way could outperform competitors that were not. The widespread adoption of the functional structure among large firms occurred during the first merger wave that took place in the 1890s. In addition, older firms, such as Standard Oil and the Union Pacific Railroad, were also further rationalized around this time. A similar rationalization took place recently among European firms with the increased likelihood of European economic integration.

Multidivisional Structure (M-form)

Figure 13.2 shows the divisional (often called M-form or multidivisional) structure. It encompasses a set of autonomous divisions led by a headquarters office and assisted by a corporate staff that provides information about the internal and external business environment. Rather than organizing by function or by task, a multidivisional structure starts with an interrelated group of subunits (called a division) as the building block. The subunits that comprise a division could be functionally organized departments but could also be other divisions, which in turn are composed of departments. Divisions can be organized in multiple ways, such as by product line or the degree of business relatedness, by geography, or by customer. The classic example of a firm with such a structure is General Motors, where the divisional structure emerged during the 1920s. Indeed, the multidivisional structure is sometimes referred to as the "General Motors" model.

Oliver Williamson, who identified the distinction between M- and U-forms, argues that the M-form develops in response to problems of inefficiency and agency

FIGURE 13.2
SAMPLE CHART OF A MULTIDIVISIONAL STRUCTURE

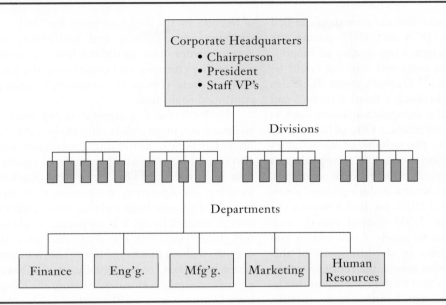

that arise in U-form firms as they increase in size and complexity. Relative to a functional structure, the M-form improves efficiency through a division of labor between strategic and operating decisions. Division managers focus on operational issues, while strategic decisions are left to top managers and corporate staff. The M-form reduces agency problems by fostering an internal capital market, in which division managers compete for discretionary corporate funds on the basis of results. Corporate staff, using strategic controls, promotes corporate goals by monitoring division performance and advising managers on how to align their activities with corporate goals. A strong corporate staff is important for the M-form, and its absence leads to a weaker *holding company* form that generates less value.

M-form structures help to address problems of coordination across large distances that are common in large and newly diversified firms. As firms diversify across geographic markets, they have to coordinate different functional areas within each market. For example, geographically diversified firms, such as McGaw Cellular Communications or Waste Management, run what amount to autonomous businesses in each of their geographic markets. A structure organized along these lines allows these firms to coordinate production, distribution, and sales within their different markets, each of which may face unique competitive conditions.

The divisional structure solves another problem of large organizations: the desire to reduce agency costs by closely linking individual pay to performance. Operating authority is generally decentralized to division managers, who are held accountable for divisional performance. A simple example of this occurs in retailing. In a chain of retailers, such as Sainsbury, Kohls, or Printemps Department Stores, each store is, in effect, its own division, with profits calculated on a store-by-store basis. This provides top managers with a simple measure of store performance that can then be used to evaluate and reward store managers based on their results.

EXAMPLE 13.2 ORGANIZATIONAL STRUCTURE AT AT&T

Robert Garnet examined the growth of the Bell System between 1876 and 1909, during the early years of the firm when neither its monopoly status nor its corporate survival could be taken for granted.[14] Garnet's study illustrates the relationship between a firm's structure and its environmental contingencies factors, such as size and market turbulence. One of his conclusions was that as the volume of its activities increased, the firm needed to reorganize to meet the increased informational demands. AT&T faced this situation during these years. Between 1885 and 1920, the Bell System went from fewer than 2,000 central offices with 25,000 employees to nearly 6,000 offices and 240,000 employees. In the aftermath of this growth, Bell needed substantial reorganization.

Garnet also came to the conclusion that as AT&T's environment became more volatile, for example, because of increased competition, it needed to reorganize to promote rapid processing of information. AT&T faced increased competition during its early period. Its initial patents expired in 1894, after which new competitors entered local markets. The changes made by AT&T in its organization structure are consistent with the need for firms to organize in a manner consistent with environmental pressures. When the firm was first consolidated around 1880, it was a loose affiliation of Bell Company interests and licenses, held together not by formal structure, but by the terms of licenses and by partial equity ownership

of licenses by the Bell Company. By 1884, this structure was obsolete and inefficient, and attempts were made to tighten leases, improve accounting controls, and consolidate the firm. Despite these efforts, the company's earnings continued to decline.

By 1890, the first significant organization structure was proposed, largely along territorial lines. Corporate accounting procedures were also revised in 1891. Another major reorganization occurred at AT&T in 1909, this time focusing on operating companies that were organized on state lines and that were subject to overall control by AT&T corporate headquarters. Each operating company was internally organized along functional lines. This reorganization occurred, coincidentally, at the lowest ebb of corporate performance before the Kingsbury Commitment, a 1913 agreement between AT&T and the U.S. Department of Justice that secured the firm's dominant market position in exchange for a commitment to allow competitors to interconnect with the AT&T system. AT&T corporate headquarters was also reorganized along functional lines in 1912. These reorganizations are consistent with a contingency view. The functional structure improved the operating companies' ability to handle the increased volume of operations that developed during this period. The new headquarters structure fostered a division of labor between operating companies and headquarters and allowed the firm to expand as the Bell system grew.

As we discussed in Chapter 12, having better performance measures means that pay-for-performance contracts will be more effective at motivating managerial effort and reducing agency costs. The divisional structure clearly measures how much the performance of each division contributes to overall corporate success: divisional profits and losses. In contrast, functional structures tend to focus on operational efficiency rather than profitability because it is more difficult to attribute profits to functional divisions.

Matrix Structure

Figure 13.3 illustrates the matrix structure: The firm is organized along multiple dimensions at once (usually two). Any particular combination of dimensions may be used. For example, matrix structures can include product groups and functional

FIGURE 13.3
A MATRIX ORGANIZATION STRUCTURE WITH PROJECT AND FUNCTION DIMENSIONS

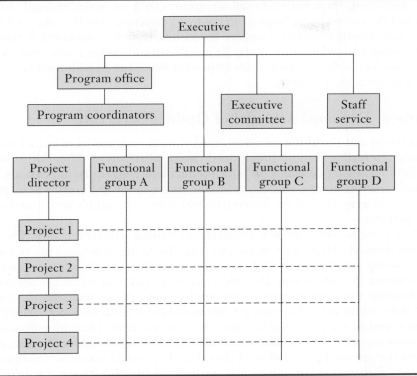

Source: Adapted from McCann and Galbraith, 1980.

departments, or two different types of divisions (such as geographic and client divisions). Individuals working at the intersections of the matrix (usually middle managers) report information to two hierarchies and have two bosses. For example, the Pepsi matrix that was created in the late 1980s was organized along geographic and functional lines. The Northeast regional manufacturing manager simultaneously reported to the Northeast regional general manager and a national senior vice president for manufacturing. Although a matrix structure may extend throughout the entire firm, in practice it is costly to do so and some levels of the firm are often organized into a matrix while others are not. Thus, Pepsi's national marketing group remained outside of the matrix.

A matrix is valuable when economies of scale or scope or agency considerations provide a compelling rationale for organizing along more than one dimension simultaneously or when some important issues, such as regulatory or environmental issues, are not well addressed by the firm's principal organizing approach. For example, Pepsi believed that national coordination of manufacturing helped achieve scale economies in production, justifying organization along functional lines, while regional coordination increased Pepsi's effectiveness in negotiating with large purchasers, justifying organization along geographic lines.

Managers often struggle to meet conflicting demands within the matrix, so the presence of multiple dimensions of scale economies is not sufficient to justify the structure. A matrix is most suitable when the demands of competing dimensions are roughly equivalent and difficult to address sequentially. If one dimension was clearly more important, then the preferred structure would be multidivisional, with the dominant dimension being "higher" in the firm's structure than the other and receiving greater priority from top managers. If decisions regarding structural demands can be addressed sequentially, then it may be possible to address big issues early on and at a high position in the hierarchy. Less important issues can be addressed later on and further down in the hierarchy.

Matrix or Division? A Model of Optimal Structure

David Baron and David Besanko developed an economic model of shared incentive authority to further explore the optimal choice of structure. They focus on firms that face organizing demands on both product and geographic dimensions.[15] The optimal structure to use emerges from the interplay of spillovers within product lines and geographies and the interrelationships among multiple activities that local units perform.

Baron and Besanko see two considerations driving structural choice. The first is whether demand-enhancing activities, such as advertising or product promotion, and cost-reducing activities, such as downsizing or production rationalization, are profit complements or substitutes. Demand-enhancing and cost-reducing activities are complements when an increase in the level of one activity increases the marginal profitability of the other. For example, this would occur when managers redesign their products and in the process also reduce their defect rates. Demand-enhancing and cost-reducing activities are substitutes when an increase in the level of one activity reduces the marginal profitability of the other. This would occur, for example, when managers allocate scarce resources (e.g., managerial attention) to some activities, such as new business development, at the expense of others, such as control.

The second consideration driving a choice is whether spillovers of know-how are positively or negatively correlated. Spillovers refer to the transfer of knowledge within the firm that occurs when a given activity is performed. The spillovers that are available to a firm in a given situation depend on the firm's capabilities at that time. Spillovers in two activities are positively correlated if they both primarily benefit a single dimension. This would occur if the introduction of a new product in one market helps the firm produce or sell the product in other markets. They are negatively correlated if spillovers from some activity positively benefit one dimension (e.g., products) but reduce benefits on another dimension (e.g., geography).

The problem for top managers in a decentralized multiproduct and multilocation firm is to shape incentives for local managers so that they perform appropriately on product and geographic dimensions. Doing this counteracts the free-rider problem that arises when local managers fail to internalize the benefits that their activities generate for the rest of the firm. The choice of an appropriate organization design can shape local managers' incentives to perform optimally.

Baron and Besanko identify the conditions in which a matrix is never optimal and those conditions in which it can be optimal. A matrix will never be optimal when spillovers are positively correlated and activities are profit complements. When activities are profit complements but spillovers are negatively correlated, a matrix can be optimal if spillovers do not disproportionately favor one dimension over another. If activities are profit substitutes and spillovers are positively correlated, then a matrix can be optimal if the activities are strong substitutes. Otherwise, a product or geographic structure is optimal. Finally, if spillovers are negatively correlated and activities are profit substitutes, a matrix will be optimal if spillovers are strongly product-specific in one activity and strongly specific to geography in the other activity.

To see if (and how) real global firms acted on these considerations of their model, Baron and Besanko looked at how Citibank reorganized as it adopted a global approach to its business that required a balance between product and local market demands.[16] They examined the formation of the Global Relationship Bank (GRB) in 1994 and the creation of the Global Markets unit in 1997 to bridge between the GRB and Emerging Market units within Citibank. They concluded that Citibank's reorganizations were consistent with a need to balance customer and geographic orientations within a global framework.

Network Structure

Recall from Chapters 3 and 4 that the value chain can be arranged along a continuum from full integration to arms-length. We observed that when organizing the value chain, it is important to think about the relationships among the individual components. Firms need to be flexible, "making" some components themselves while "buying" others from the market. The *network structure* (see Figure 13.4) places a similar emphasis on the relationships among workers and the benefits of flexibility. Workers, either singly or in combination, can contribute to multiple organizational tasks and can be reconfigured and recombined as the tasks of the organization change.

Gary Hamel describes a network structure in operation at the Morning Star Company in California. Morning Star is a privately held company that is the largest tomato processor in the world, with 400 full-time employees, $700 million in annual sales, and an annual share of 25 to 30 percent of the tomatoes processed in the United States each year. Morning Star has a well-articulated company mission, some procedural rules of order, but no formal bosses, no titles or formal job descriptions, and peer-based compensation. Each individual's tasks, responsibilities, and obligations to other workers are negotiated in discussions between the employees involved and summarized in a Colleague Letter of Understanding (CLOU). The network that arises out of the dyadic relationships summarized in the CLOUs is what constitutes the firm's structure. There are occasional disputes among colleagues, which if not settled informally can be subject to peer review for resolution with a possible appeal to the firm's owner. There are 23 separate business units with the firm, each with its own profit and loss responsibility. These business units also manage their buyer-supplier relationships with each other by negotiating binding agreements with each other, similar to the process for developing CLOUs.[17]

At a more aggregated level of analysis, networks develop from the patterned relationships of units that may or may not be part of a single integrated organization. Networks of small autonomous firms can even approximate the behavior of larger firms, earning them the name "virtual firms." This can occur as networks grow out of dyadic business-to-business relationships among firms or as part of a larger consortium effort, such as with the original Airbus consortium.[18]

Network structures and their component work groups can be organized into cross-cutting teams on the basis of task, geography, customer, or other bases. However these structures are formally organized, the actual relationships between work groups are frequently governed more by the often-changing requirements of common tasks than by the formal lines of authority.[19] A network is preferable to other structures when the substantial coordination costs of employing it are compensated for by technical efficiency, innovation, or cooperation. The Japanese *keiretsu* structure discussed in Chapter 4 is a type of network in which informal ties between members also facilitate coordination and reduce agency problems. The same could be said for most Asian business group structures in which nominally independent autonomous firms could be incorporated into a network structure through such means as bilateral contracts, board interlocks, and patterns of cross-ownership among members of the larger business group.[20]

The interrelationships among firms in the biotechnology industry provide an example of network structures that facilitate information flows. Such flows are necessary because these technologies have applications in such diverse areas as seeds, pharmaceuticals, and beer. Observers have seen these networks as a principal reason for the industry's historically high level of new product development. This setting provides an example of an alliance network in which separate firms can act collectively through a combination of informal relationships, bilateral contracts, and more complex joint venture agreements.[21]

Network structures become more popular as their organizational costs decline. The spread of the Internet has provided an infrastructure with which networks can form and continue operating at a much lower cost than was the case for more traditional relationship-based infrastructures or for more dedicated but less flexible coordination schemes such as Electronic Data Interchange. In this sense, networks have always been possible modes of organizing but have been too costly to rely on in most environments. There are exceptions, of course. For example, the world diamond industry has long been characterized by extensive informal networks that routinely handle large amounts of expensive product, relying almost solely on interpersonal trust. Those informal networks have also rested on the more formal contractual networks of the world diamond cartel maintained by DeBeers in conjunction with its suppliers and buyers.[22]

"Modular organization," an alternative to network structure, involves relatively self-contained organizational units tied together through a technology standard. Network externalities, described in Chapter 11, provide opportunities for modularity. For example, consider the individuals and firms that work closely with Apple to develop applications ("Apps") for the iPhone and the iPad. These are largely independent contractors who produce their products for Apple as they wish, provided that they meet Apple's rigid technical specifications. This permits Apple to outsource the development of software applications and capitalize on their innovative capabilities while at the same time maintaining the controls over their products that would traditionally be expected to require inclusion within a firm's authority system. Boeing has also moved into modular design and manufacturing with its highly publicized 787 Dreamliner, most of whose component systems are outsourced to contractors while Boeing serves as the designer and ultimate assembler of this complex aircraft. This proved to be a challenge, as we discussed in Example 3.4.

Although modular organization limits some opportunities for scope economies, it also helps networks to grow by fostering modification of the network through the addition or subtraction of subunits without significant disruption to existing relationships. Modularity also facilitates adaptation to technological change by diffusing R&D among many firms, each of which is free to pursue its own avenues for innovation. The long-term relationships established by the firms in a modular organization allow them to adapt to changes in the unifying technology. The overall effect of modularity is to increase the possibilities for cooperative action in networks by reducing search, monitoring, and control costs without significantly increasing the transactions costs of interactions.

Why Are There So Few Structural Types?

The preceding discussion suggests a relatively small number of structural types from which a would-be organization designer might choose. At first glance, this might seem strange. Given the size and complexity of large firms, one might suspect that there could be a large number of design variables and many ways to organize. Yet this does not seem to happen. While there are a huge variety of firms and numerous organizing criteria, it also seems that, once industry particularities are taken into account, the range of organizational types employed in real firms is fairly constrained. One reason for the limited range of types might be imitation. As large, successful, and visible firms reach solutions regarding how they should organize, other firms may see what they do and what results they achieve and then imitate them. Indeed, as we have already mentioned, it was not uncommon after World War II to hear about the "General Motors" model of multidivisional organization as a norm to which other firms aspired. This explanation may have some value, but it is still hard to see how a small number of firms are so widely imitated across industries as to justify a small set of general types. Nor is it clear how pathbreaking firms identify these types in the first place.

John Roberts suggests that the reasons for the limited range of structural types may be more fundamental.[23] Although a large number of design variables are available, choices from among these variables are not independent. Structural variables and related change activities are interdependent and thus may share *complementarities*, such that choosing more of one design variable increases the returns to choosing others. For example, organizing to pursue a product differentiation strategy based on product quality will be associated with lower volume performance, specialized staffing, frequent product redesign, and higher prices. Design variables may also be interdependent as *substitutes*, such that doing more of some activities reduces the value from doing more of others.

The ways in which design variables are interdependent determines the structural types that emerge. Complementarities among choice variables will result in a set of variables having a greater overall value for a firm than could be obtained from changing particular variables in isolation. It could even mean that changes in any one design variable might fail to contribute to firm performance and could even detract from it. This suggests that organization design choices will tend to cluster together and that a "mix and match" approach will prove infeasible. If this is so, it suggests that intermediate positions between structural types will not promote effectiveness and may actually reduce it, relative to a choice of one clear type or another.

STRUCTURE—ENVIRONMENT COHERENCE

Discussing organizational structure in the context of a firm's strategy implies that some sort of optimal structure is identifiable and appropriate for the firm. That is indeed a presumption of much of what consultants and academics have contributed to this topic. But what does it mean for a structure to be optimal for a firm? Is it that an optimal structure will help a firm to make good decisions and to make them efficiently, with the least amount of time and effort relative to the quality of the decisions?

Making quality decisions efficiently does seem like a good idea. But what is a "quality" decision when discussing firms and their strategies? In this context, "quality" involves the requirement that decisions be effective in terms of the business and market conditions that the firm is facing. It would be hard to call a structure optimal if it led the firm to efficiently make decisions that did not fit well with the demands of competitors, consumers, or regulators.

Knowing that a structure is coherent is a first step toward solving the organizational design problem. It is also necessary for managers to determine whether a given structure is appropriate for them. A coherent structure will destroy rather than create value if it fails to enable the firm to apply its resources and capabilities to opportunities within its business environment. Thus, the optimal organizational structure for a firm depends on the environmental circumstances it faces.

A functional structure may work well for a manufacturer of supercomputers, such as Cray, but would probably work poorly for a large bank, such as JP Morgan Chase or Citigroup. This is because the banks face a much more complex business environment than Cray. Cray's customers include large technology firms, businesses in sectors requiring extensive use of data, government agencies, and research universities. Cray and its customers know each other, and while the business environment has its own threats and opportunities, these are likely to be fairly predictable and understandable to all the participants in the industry. These are conditions in which a functional structure can work well.

The environment faced by large banks, on the contrary, is much more complex in terms of products, customers, and regulatory burdens than that faced by Cray. They operate on a global scale in multiple national markets. Even the technological needs of Chase or Citi are significant, as both have spent heavily in building their infrastructures. In addition, the volatility of their businesses is often high and, as the 2008 financial crisis demonstrated, also unpredictable. These are conditions in which large banks will face competing and often conflicting demands for organizing that cannot be easily handled within a traditional hierarchy. This is why these firms have frequently employed more complex organization structures, such as a matrix.

Contingency-based research examines how environmental characteristics may be associated with structural characteristics of firms without considering the product market choices that a firm might make. The idea is that any firm working in such an environment must adapt its structure to address environmental demands. This work has focused on two sets of environmental factors that may influence the relative efficiency of different structures: (1) technology and task interdependence and (2) information processing.

Technology and Task Interdependence

Technology generally refers to the base of scientific knowledge underlying what a firm does, as well as the general state of know-how behind the application of scientific knowledge to specific products and services. While many firms invest in their own R&D to enhance their competitive positioning, most must take their technology as exogenous, at least in the short term. The characteristics of a firm's knowledge base will influence the structural type that it adopts. A firm employing a well-known and mature technology will organize differently from a firm working with a rapidly evolving and less well-known technology. The former is better off adopting a hierarchical structure conducive to more stable, standardized, and higher volume production. The latter may prefer a decentralized structure that offers flexibility and responsiveness to change.

As the firm's technology changes, its structure will also need to change to accommodate new coordination needs. For example, suppose that a firm's technology changes to permit increased production volume and more routine handling of raw materials. This firm might need to create a new division with purchasing responsibilities in order to accommodate the increased volume of activities. This idea is not confined to technology-driven changes in strategy. To take another example, a firm that expands internationally may need to set up a government affairs department that coordinates all regulatory related activities. As an example, Giulio Bottazzi and his colleagues document the interaction of these technological and regulatory factors and their implications for firms in their study of the evolution of the global pharmaceutical industry.[24]

James Thompson argues that technology determines the degree of *task interdependence*—the extent to which two or more positions depend on each other to do their own work.[25] Thompson defines three modes of task interdependence: reciprocal, sequential, and pooled. *Reciprocal interdependence* exists when two or more workers or work groups depend on each other to do their work. Apple's hardware and software development teams display reciprocal interdependence. *Sequential interdependence* exists between two or more workers, positions, or groups when one depends on the outcomes of the others, but not vice versa. The regulatory affairs and sales divisions of a pharmaceutical company display sequential interdependence. Messaging by sales depends on regulatory oversight on product labeling. Finally, *pooled interdependence* exists when two or more positions are not directly dependent on each other but are associated through their independent contributions to the success of the firm. For example, the success of Disney's Pixar animated motion picture division is largely independent of the success of Disney's ESPN sports network. This distinction suggests that organization design processes successively group individuals to coordinate their activities and utilize their shared resources. Positions and tasks that are reciprocally interdependent should be grouped together first, since they are the most costly to coordinate. Less costly to coordinate are positions that are sequentially dependent, such as positions at different points of the value chain. Finally, positions that lack a direct interdependence and are related solely in terms of a common affiliation with a firm are the least costly to coordinate.

As technology changes, so may the basis for competition in an industry by changing the industry's core assets.[26] This in turn will alter task interdependence within firms and thus suggest possible changes in what an appropriate structure is for affected firms. Advances in computers and telecommunications weaken reciprocal and sequential interdependence among many positions and reduce the costs of coordinating activities among individuals and groups within the firm or with partners in other firms. Sharing data in the Internet "cloud," engineers and product specialists located on different continents can coordinate the design of a new product even while few managers of such a team ever meet face to face. With such technology, a small investment research firm based in Zurich can provide analysis to subscribers in Tokyo, while the firm's marketing agent resides in London and its publicist in New York. Neither of these arrangements would have been possible 20 years ago. This reduction in coordination costs reduces the need for team members to be in the same part of the firm's formal organization or even to be part of the same firm. (We also note that virtual firms appear to suffer from diseconomies of scale if they attempt to grow too large, since relationships among members become complex and costly to coordinate above a small number of individuals.)

EXAMPLE 13.3   STEVE JOBS AND STRUCTURE AT APPLE[27]

A persistent issue regarding organization structure is the relationship between structure and the dominant charismatic leaders that often seem to dominate larger firms. Structures are frequently treated as substitutes for dominant leaders, with the idea that the success of the firm should not be dependent on any single person, who could leave to go elsewhere, become ill, run afoul of some accident, or behave irresponsibly.

A famous example of this tension between structure and corporate leadership concerned Alfred Sloan, the leader behind the growth of General Motors as a force in the world economy. Sloan's volume of memoirs, *My Years at General Motors*, is arguably the most influential business book of the twentieth century. In it, Sloan outlines the structures and systems that he pioneered at GM, including the multidivisional form, which has served as a model for all large U.S. manufacturing firms. What is relevant to our discussion here is that Sloan wrote his classic in response to a book about GM by Peter Drucker (*The Concept of the Corporation*), which Sloan regarded as too focused on matters of individual personalities and styles—even though Sloan himself was, by all accounts, a dominant and highly influential leader.

With this in mind, consider Steve Jobs, the brilliant, charismatic, and reclusive leader at Apple at its inception and since soon after his return to the firm in 1997. Jobs was the acknowledged force behind the rebirth of Apple and its turnaround from near failure to perhaps the most successful technology company in the world, with over $65 billion in revenues and over $14 billion of profits. Apple employs over 60,000 people worldwide, and some claim it has more cash than the U.S. government. Jobs was the force behind the introduction of the iPod, the iPhone, and the iPad, which together are critical components of his "Digital Hub" concept that transformed a variety of industries and society more broadly.

What organization structure did Steve Jobs use in running Apple? This is a reasonable question to ask, since the firm is very large, so it is unlikely that it could be run informally without a structure. However, Steve Jobs and his firm have also been notoriously secretive and release little information about corporate structure—or much else internal. In his biography of Jobs, Walter Isaacson recounts that Jobs initially was pushed out of his position at Apple during a divisional reorganization by John Sculley after losing a leadership battle. This suggests that Jobs would not have favored a divisional structure. But which structure would he have favored?

In May 2011, Adam Lashinsky published a story in *Fortune* detailing how things worked "Inside Apple." In the story, he presented a circular organization chart, with Jobs at the center. In an inner ring, there were 15 direct reports in total—9 members of an executive team and an additional 6 vice presidents who reported directly to Jobs. An additional ring of 31 vice presidents reported to the inner ring but not to Jobs directly. Lashinsky calls this "an unconventional org chart for an unconventional organization."

Assuming that Lashinsky is correct about this structure, what is one to make of it? Is Apple centralized or decentralized? Are there too many direct reports? Did Jobs have problems delegating? At one level, the structure does seem to support the dominance of Steve Jobs in the Apple organization, which is not surprising. It is clear that his personality set the tone for the culture of the firm, that his drive influenced everyone around him to high levels of achievement, and that his authority within Apple was unquestioned. So at the level of product development and strategic direction, Apple is clearly centralized.

But consider the large number of direct reports to Jobs. Each of these represents numerous major projects and commitments by Apple, all of which involve the efforts of multiple project teams worldwide. After Jobs's return to Apple, its success rate on major projects was high and the culture of the firm, spurred on by Jobs's personality, emphasized attention to detail and perfectionism in follow-through.

Given Apple's structure and what we clearly know about its projects and their results, it is doubtful that Steve Jobs was guilty of micromanaging. He would not have had the time to do so effectively, given all of his other responsibilities. While he may have wanted to micromanage projects—though that is not clear—Apple's structure ensured that while he maintained control over the direction of the firm, he needed to delegate on implementation. Lashinsky also makes clear that Jobs had a clear inner circle with which he was comfortable. This need to delegate is also a potential explanation for Jobs's famous tirades over Apple's few mistakes: he was frustrated that he had to delegate but that the project had not worked out as planned.

Efficient Information Processing

Jay Galbraith argues that organizations should be designed to facilitate information processing.[28] Work groups can normally operate independently and manage themselves by work rules that become increasingly routine with more experience. Administrative hierarchy develops to handle "exceptions"—decisions that cannot be easily made using standard organizational routines. Successively higher levels of organization are needed to handle more difficult exceptions. Decisions at the top of an organization are presumably the most difficult and least routine of all—that is, they are strategic decisions. The test of a structure is its ability to efficiently process routine information flows while ensuring that the exceptional situations are attended to by those with the most appropriate knowledge and the requisite authority for action.

Galbraith's account suggests that structural change occurs in response to changes in the amount, complexity, or speed of information processing that a firm must undertake. As work groups are forced to process more information or act more quickly, existing routines become strained, and some adjustment, either in additional supervision or some cross-cutting team arrangement, is needed. For example, marketing decisions that are routine in industries with stable demand, high entry barriers, and a few well-known domestic competitors become less routine as markets globalize or changes in technology destroy entry barriers. Examples include the response of Kodak and Polaroid to the advent of digital photography and strong Asian competitors. In a similar manner, the entire frame of reference of U.S. automakers was shaken by the nearly simultaneous attack on the U.S. market by low-end Asian competitors as well as high-quality luxury entrants from both Asia and Europe. Pricing and promotion decisions now require keeping track of foreign competitors and monitoring demand in increasingly segmented markets. These changes can overwhelm standard operating procedures and require increased hierarchical oversight.

Luis Garicano models the influence of information processing on organization design and achieves a result consistent with Galbraith.[29] He describes a *knowledge hierarchy* in which firms—usually thought of as professional services firms in law, consulting, and so forth—encounter problems that differ according to their difficulty and the frequency. Workers can acquire and communicate knowledge about solutions to problems. Garicano finds that an optimal organization design involves dividing workers into production workers and "problems solvers" who specialize in dealing with more difficult and/or infrequent problems. So in a law firm, less skilled attorneys tackle routine problems such as filing legal documents while passing along to their senior partners the more challenging tasks. Garicano finds that a decrease in the cost of acquiring or transmitting knowledge increases the average span of control of the "problem solvers" and reduces the number of organizational levels.

Arthur Stinchcombe emphasizes the role of organizational structure in promoting more efficient *information retrieval*.[30] Firms should be structured to facilitate the efficient retrieval of information in the varied conditions they face on a regular basis. For example, a pharmaceutical firm might want an independent R&D department capable of rapid interaction with medical school faculty, an important source of new product development. Different levels of structure can deal with different informational needs. Information about labor costs or consumer demand may be highly local. If local work groups control these factors, they will have the proper incentives to

---

EXAMPLE 13.4 STRATEGY, STRUCTURE, AND THE ATTEMPTED MERGER BETWEEN THE UNIVERSITY OF CHICAGO HOSPITAL AND MICHAEL REESE HOSPITAL

The idea that strategy follows structure has implications for mergers between firms that have pursued different strategies. In melding two such organizations together, issues relating to the control of assets and resources frequently arise. As we saw earlier, the allocation of rights of control of assets is a key determinant of how efficiently a vertical chain or a partnership of two organizations performs. Inside an organization, structure determines the basic rights to control the firm's assets. Thus, organizational structure can critically affect the success of a merger.

The attempted merger between the University of Chicago Hospital and the Michael Reese Hospital provides an example in which the control of assets and resources was a key issue in the attempted integration of the two organizations. The University of Chicago Hospital is on the campus of a leading research university, which led the hospital to pursue a strategy based on a reputation for providing state-of-the-art medicine. Indeed, advertisements for the hospital celebrated the research accomplishments of its medical staff. Consistent with this strategy, most physicians had faculty appointments in the university's medical school, and faculty were evaluated on the basis of their research. Physician salaries were based more on their academic standing than on the patient revenues they brought to the hospital.

The University of Chicago Hospital's nearest competitor on the city's south side was the Michael Reese Hospital. This hospital also had a long history of quality care, with special emphases on community service and close relationships between medical staff and patients. The medical staff was organized according to a traditional scheme—staff members were identified by clinical areas but billed patients for their services independently of the hospital's billings. In other words, physicians were rewarded exclusively for providing patient care.

The two hospitals sought to merge in 1985. The merger would allow them to consolidate and reallocate some services and possibly avoid price and nonprice competition in their shared markets. Anticipating a potential conflict between medical staffs over resources and authority to set policy, the two hospitals attempted to negotiate an organizational structure before they merged. As it turned out, they could not develop an agreeable structure to manage their surgical departments as an integrated unit. University physicians refused to be evaluated on the basis of clinical care, while Reese physicians refused to be thought of as research faculty. Unable to coordinate this vital area and fearful that economies in surgery would not be realized, the hospitals called off the merger.

gather information. Dealing with federal regulations, however, should be the responsibility of a work group with a broader scope. Stinchcombe also argues that firms should internalize activities (rather than rely on market coordination) when the information from those activities is of critical importance. Firms need to be "where the news breaks, whenever it breaks," since rapid information processing facilitates effective adjustments and environmental changes.

An example of Stinchcombe's arguments can be seen in the Spanish firm Inditex, whose Zara subsidiary is a major competitor in the global fashion business. The key to Zara's success was a forward integration to own its stores and place them in critical locations in its important markets. This enables Zara to obtain critical and timely information on which of its products are selling, which are not, and how customer tastes are apparent to store managers. With this information, Zara has developed processes for linking design, manufacturing, and retail so that it can bring new products to market quickly and without excessive advertising. This allows Zara to succeed relative to its competitors through quicker inventory turnaround, reduced discounting, and better use of its working capital.[31]

Bruce Kogut and Udo Zander make a similar argument for the superiority of organizational structure in processing information relative to market alternatives.[32] They focus on knowledge sharing and the multinational structure, which can be thought of as a variant of the multidivisional structure whose units cross national boundaries. They argue that this structure is superior at transferring specific types of knowledge across national boundaries rather than as a means of internalizing transactions in the face of market failure, although such failures play a role in firm boundaries. They argue that this structure is especially valuable for transferring tacit knowledge—knowledge that is complex and difficult to codify and teach. Kogut and Zander support these arguments with survey data on a sample of global innovations by Swedish firms.

STRUCTURE FOLLOWS STRATEGY

Throughout this chapter we have emphasized that the choice of structure depends on environmental factors such as market conditions, technology, and information. These factors may have conflicting implications for structure. A firm that relies on the personal relationships between sales personnel and clients may benefit from a decentralized structure. The same firm may enjoy substantial scope economies, which favors centralization or a matrix structure. When facing conflicting environmental factors, the firm should focus on those factors that are critical to its strategic success. If the firm is dependent on maintaining benefits leadership based on close relationships to customers, then it should favor decentralization. If the firm is pursuing cost leadership based on scope economies, centralization is preferred. If both strategic goals are important, the firm may attempt to overcome the complexity of the matrix structure.

The famed business historian Alfred Chandler first articulated how firms' strategic choices influence their subsequent choices of structure in his book *Strategy and Structure*.[33] Based on case studies of firms such as DuPont, General Motors, Standard Oil of New Jersey (which has become ExxonMobil), and Sears, Chandler concludes that changes in organization structure are driven by changes in strategy, which, in turn, are associated with changes in the external conditions firms face. In short, Chandler's thesis is that *structure follows strategy*.

Chandler developed this thesis by careful study of evolving markets. In the late nineteenth century, developments in the technological and market infrastructures (which we describe in Chapter 1) created opportunities for achieving unprecedented economies of scale and scope in such industries as tobacco, chemicals, light and heavy machinery, and meatpacking. Firms such as American Tobacco, DuPont, McCormick Harvesting Machine Company (which became International Harvester), and Swift responded by investing in large-scale production facilities and internalizing activities, such as sales and distribution, that independent companies had previously performed for them. They also invested in the development of managerial hierarchies. The first structure typically employed by these early hierarchical firms was the U-form. This was an appropriate structure because it permitted a specialized division of labor that facilitated economies of scale in manufacturing, marketing, and distribution.

The firms that were the first in their industries to invest in large-scale production facilities and develop managerial hierarchies expanded rapidly and often dominated their industries. But most of the early growth of these firms was within a single line of business or occurred within a single market. Shortly after 1900, however, this began to change. Such firms as Singer and International Harvester aggressively expanded overseas. Indeed, by 1914, the largest commercial enterprises in Russia were Singer and International Harvester. Others, such as DuPont and Procter & Gamble, diversified their product lines. This shift in strategy revealed shortcomings in the U-form. According to Chandler, the attempt by the top management of the newly diversified firms to monitor functional departments in the U-form structure led to administrative overload. Managers needed to find a way to delegate decision-making authority, and this motivated them to experiment with alternative organizational structures.

The multidivisional structure, or M-form, that emerged after 1920 was a response to the limitations of the U-form in larger diversified firms. The M-form removed top managers from involvement in the operational details of departments, allowing them to specialize in strategic decisions and long-range planning with the support of a professional staff. Division managers monitored the operational activities of the functional departments that reported to them. Top managers were comfortable delegating decision making to division managers because it was straightforward to instill proper incentives. Divisions were run as profit centers, and division managers were rewarded on the basis of division profit-and-loss statements.

Although corporate structures have evolved since the days of the M-form, the principle that structure follows strategy still applies. The network structure developed in SAP AG, a German firm that is one of the world's largest software producers and the leading producer of real-time, integrated applications software for client/server computing, provides an example of this principle. Its founders have been intent on SAP remaining largely a product development firm with a flat organization structure. To do this, SAP managers decided not to expand into related but different lines of business, such as training and implementation consulting, even though meeting customer needs during implementation would be critical for growth. To accomplish its growth objectives, SAP has developed a network organization of partners, who perform 80 to 90 percent of the consulting implementation business generated by SAP products. Partners range from major consulting firms, such as Accenture and CSC Index, to hardware manufacturers, such as IBM, HP, and Sun Microsystems, to software and chip manufacturers, such as Oracle, Microsoft, and Intel. Relationship managers for these partnerships play an important role in SAP's corporate structure.

EXAMPLE 13.5   SAMSUNG: CONTINUING TO REINVENT A CORPORATION[34]

Major environmental shifts often force firms to reassess strategies and restructure their organizations. The Samsung business group provides an example of how to continually reinvent a corporation facing the hostile market forces that Asian firms have increasingly endured in recent decades. Samsung was founded in 1938 as a general trading store, exporting fruit and dried fish to Japanese-occupied Manchuria. By 1995, it had become the largest South Korean business group, or *chaebol*, at $54 billion in sales. Today, Samsung Group remains the largest business combination in the country, with 2010 sales of over $227 billion and over 315,000 employees worldwide. The group operates globally in such diverse industries as aerospace, chemicals, and finance. This is in addition to Samsung's longstanding presence as one of the world's largest maker of semiconductors and as a force in the production of cell phones, TVs, LCD flat panels, and the like.

Samsung's rise to prominence was based on strong support from the Korean government, inexpensive labor, and an authoritarian culture. As a result, Samsung's strategy from the 1960s until the mid-1980s was based on using cheap labor to produce lower-quality products at low prices. By also producing large volumes, Samsung reaped economies of scale and thus captured comfortable margins, which also enabled it to enter a variety of businesses with great success.

In the late 1980s, however, a combination of factors impaired Samsung's historical sources of competitive advantage and caused its managers to reevaluate strategies that had brought the company such success for over two decades. South Korean wages began to rise, and workers began to unionize and strike, causing labor instability. Samsung does not have unions because it pays high wages. Even so, the general labor climate became less friendly. The value of the South Korean currency, the won, had also appreciated, making South Korean exports more expensive. In addition, increased global competition further eroded Samsung's competitive positioning.

In response, Chairman Lee Kun-Hee has launched a sweeping remake of Samsung's culture, including a restructuring of operations. Lee has radically decentralized decision making and encouraged individuality in a company that was known for its rigid hierarchy and subservience to authority. Managers who are not able to assume such responsibility are fired. To encourage individuality, Lee has initiated training programs and other innovative techniques. For instance, each year Samsung sends 400 managers abroad, fully subsidized, for 12 months to do whatever they want. The only requirement is that when they return, they must show proficiency in the host country's language and culture. In addition to reinventing Samsung's culture, Lee has consolidated groups in related businesses and specialized in more capital- and technology-intensive industries. Samsung has also tried to shift from being a low-quality, low-cost producer to producing higher-quality goods, competing on an equal basis with leading American, Japanese, and European firms.

This shift in culture and operations forced Samsung to be at the leading edge in innovation and productivity. The firm traditionally adopted its technology from more advanced firms, but Lee instituted massive R&D spending to make Samsung more self-sufficient. Furthermore, Lee has automated plants and even moved some plants to Mexico to save labor costs. Samsung has transformed itself in response to major changes in both global markets and South Korea. The group has actively borrowed the "best practices" of foreign and domestic firms and continues its investment programs today. By 2004, it was the second most profitable firm in the world after Toyota. Even during the global financial crisis, Samsung has maintained its profits, surpassing other Asian electronics manufacturers and comparing favorably to industry leaders such as Intel.

Strategy, Structure, and the Multinational Firm

The idea that structure follows strategy applies to firms that compete internationally. As multidivisional firms grow, they are more likely to expand their operations overseas. These firms often create "international divisions" to manage their foreign activities. As foreign business grows, however, this structure increasingly fails to coordinate foreign

---

EXAMPLE 13.6   MULTINATIONAL FIRMS: STRATEGY AND INFRASTRUCTURE?[35]

As large multinational firms expand, they face the issue of what to do when their strategies require them to move into nations and markets that are not characterized by the degree of infrastructure development they are used to in their home markets. In Chapter 1, we discussed the importance of infrastructure in considerable detail and suggested that its absence would impair the operations of large firms and impede national economic development. This suggests that large firms would be reluctant to move their operations into markets lacking the infrastructure support that their strategies presume.

While the need for an acceptable infrastructure remains important for firms, multinational firms are increasingly reexamining their options for entry into markets that lack aspects of infrastructure that are taken for granted in developed markets. Tarun Khanna and Krishna Palepu examine the strategies of firms that have succeeded in emerging markets—which are defined as markets with incomplete but potentially usable infrastructures. Their conclusion is that it is possible for firms to craft successful strategies in their markets by including limited investments in infrastructure as part of their strategic implementation plan. They view this as a process of identifying and filling "institutional voids," and they devote considerable attention to developing substitutes for some institutional feature that is missing or in a weakened state in a given market.

To see how this works, consider Microsoft's experience in China. An institutional void that they encountered was that the government placed excessive burdens on foreign direct investment relative to the restrictions on domestic firms. In response to this problem, Microsoft formed a partnership with a local software firm that reduced its financial burdens. A second void that Microsoft identified

was that the supplier network was weak in terms of the quality of suppliers and the contractual protections that were available to foreign firms. This was addressed by investments in building a supplier network to facilitate future collaboration. A third void was the lack of credit for consumers that would restrict their ability to purchase Microsoft products. This had to be addressed by experimenting with alternative payment systems to allow demand to be accessed, such as a subscription system or alternative product versions that were affordable and usable on cell phones. A final institutional void involved intellectual property issues that have been common in China since the beginnings of economic liberalization. These issues could only be addressed incrementally, such as through workshops, lobbying, and support for reform policies.

Khanna and Palepu's ideas are related to C. K. Prahalad's research on how firms can compete in "Bottom of the Pyramid" markets, where it is necessary to develop new product options, new distribution channels, and new financing arrangements to reach potentially enormous markets of individuals with reduced but usable purchasing power. They apply to larger developing markets, such as Brazil, Russia, India, or China (the so-called BRIC markets) as well as to smaller developing markets. Both of these lines of research challenge traditional strategy assumptions that infrastructure is exogenous to the firm's strategic considerations and expand the investments that firms might consider in implementing their strategic decisions. Once infrastructure decisions become relevant to the strategic decisions of large firms, it is appropriate to consider them by the same strategy-structure logics used elsewhere in this chapter.

operations that, in effect, duplicate the activities of the domestic firm in multiple foreign markets. This leads to reorganization into multinational structures, which are characterized by separate divisions for different countries (or regions, if national markets were sufficiently similar or if the volume of business in a given area was small). Growing multinational firms soon face further pressures for coordination across countries and specialization within countries, especially firms with technologies that permit substantial scale and scope economies. This leads to the creation of global strategies that view the world as the firm's market. These firms reorganize to promote scale and scope economies in global production and distribution. The global appliance firm Electrolux provides an example of this sort of global strategy. It began as a Swedish firm and grew to achieve scale and scope economies along with the growth of European economic integration following the Second World War.

Gradually, multinational firms develop structures that are appropriate for their increased levels of international activity. This occurs when corporate managers learn to balance responsiveness to local conditions with centralization to achieve global economies. This represents what some call a transnational strategy and is associated with flexible organizations that combine matrix and network structures in ways that permit a great variety of organizational designs. Recent research has focused on the variety of structures that can emerge within internally differentiated multinational firms. A parallel interest of this work has been in the processes used to manage corporate activities in transnational contexts. This supports the idea of corporate management as focusing on the evolving interactions among business units and groups worldwide, rather than on their particular product market strategies that we inherited as legacies of previous strategies.

Multinational firms today not only outsource their manufacturing to lower cost areas, but they also increasingly locate their critical corporate functions wherever in the world it is best to do so. R&D functions, for example, may be located overseas, in order to be closer to production facilities and thus be more effective in developing process innovations. R&D could also be located overseas to better access local talent pools or to build connections with local scientific networks. Moving critical functions overseas is sometimes called offshoring to distinguish it from outsourcing, since it is the firm's own employees who are relocated to critical locations and the relocation is not primarily motivated by a desire to access cheap labor sources.

CHAPTER SUMMARY

● Organizational structure concerns the arrangements, both formal and informal, by which a firm divides up its critical tasks, specifies how its managers and employees make decisions, and establishes routines and information flows to support operations so as to link opportunities in the environment with its resources and capabilities.

● Organization design typically involves two steps. First, simple tasks performed by simple work groups need to be organized. Second, work groups and their activities must be linked together into complex hierarchies.

● Simple tasks performed by small work groups can be structured in three ways: (1) individually—members of the work group are treated as if they were independent and receive incentives based on individual actions and outcomes; (2) self-managed teams—a collection of individuals, each member of which works with others to set and pursue common objectives, with individuals rewarded, in part, on the basis of group performance; and (3) hierarchy of authority—one member of the group monitors and coordinates the work of the other members.

● Large firms often require complex hierarchies, by which is meant a structure that involves multiple groups and multiple levels of groupings. Complex hierarchy arises when there is a need to organize simple work groups together into larger groups.

● The allocation of authority within the firm is typically considered in terms of centralization versus decentralization. As decisions are made at higher levels within a firm's hierarchy, the firm is said to be more centralized regarding those decisions. Conversely, as certain decisions are made at lower levels, the firm is more decentralized regarding those decisions.

● Four basic types of structure for large organizations can be identified: (1) the unitary functional structure (often called the U-form); (2) the multidivisional structure (often called the M-form); (3) the matrix structure; and (4) the network structure.

● The functional structure, or U-form, allows a specialization of labor to gain economies of scale in manufacturing, marketing, and distribution.

● The multidivisional structure, or M-form, creates a division of labor between top managers and division managers. Top managers specialize in strategic decisions and long-range planning. Division managers monitor the operational activities of functional departments and are rewarded on the basis of overall divisional performance.

● Matrix structures involve overlapping hierarchies and are necessary in situations where there are conflicting decision demands and severe constraints on managerial resources.

● Network structure focuses on individuals rather than on positions and is the most flexible of the structural types. Recent developments in networking technologies and modular product designs have greatly expanded the potential applications of network organizations.

● Many plausible contingencies may affect a firm's structure at any given time. Those factors addressed by the firm's strategy will be the most important in determining an appropriate structural choice for the firm. In other words, structure follows strategy.

● The thesis that structure follows strategy has been applied to firms that compete internationally. Multinationals have discovered the need to balance responsiveness to local conditions with centralization to achieve global economies. This is the transnational strategy, and it is becoming associated with flexible organizations that combine matrix and network structures.

QUESTIONS

1. A team of six individuals must fold, stuff, seal, and stamp 250 preaddressed envelopes. Offer some suggestions for organizing this team. Would your suggestions differ if the team was responsible for processing 2,500 envelopes? For assembling 250 personal computers? Why would you change your recommendations?

2. Consider a firm whose competitive advantage is built almost entirely on its ability to achieve economies of scale in producing small electric motors that are used by the firm to make hair dryers, fans, vacuum cleaners, and food processors. Should this firm be organized on a multidivisional basis by product (hair dryer

division, food processor division, etc.) or should it be organized functionally (marketing, manufacturing, finance, etc.)?

3. What types of structures would a firm consider if it was greatly expanding its global operations? What types of organizing problems would it be most likely to encounter?

4. In the 1980s, Sears acquired several financial services firms, including Allstate Insurance and Dean Witter Brokerage Services. Sears kept these businesses as largely autonomous divisions. By 1994, the strategy had failed and Sears had divested all of its financial services holdings. Bearing in mind the dictum that structure follows strategy, identify the strategy that Sears had in mind when it acquired these businesses, and recommend a structure that might have led to better results.

5. Matrix organizations first sprang up in businesses that worked on scientific and engineering projects for narrow customer groups. Examples include Fluor, which built oil refineries in Saudi Arabia, and TRW, which supplied aerospace equipment to NASA. What do you suppose the dimensions of the matrix would be in such firms? Why would these companies develop such a complex structure?

6. It is sometimes argued that a matrix organization can serve as a mechanism for achieving *strategic fit*—the achievements of synergies across related business units resulting in a combined performance that is greater than units could achieve if they operated independently. Explain how a matrix organization could result in the achievement of strategic fit.

7. Is is possible to organize too much or too little to meet the needs of the environment? This would be a case of *strategic misfit*. How would you know if a misfit has occurred? Think of an example of misfit caused by an inappropriate organization design. Explain how a firm's structure could systematically increase its costs and place it at a strategic disadvantage.

8. While Internet entrepreneurs worked hard to get their venture to the point of a successful initial public offering (IPO), many discovered that their organizational issues changed and became more daunting after the IPO than before it, when they were just working to accommodate rapid growth. Explain why "going public" might put such a stress on a small firm's structure.

9. The "#1 or #2; Fix, Sell, or Close" rule was one of the most memorable aspects of Jack Welch's corporate strategy at GE. (Business units needed to achieve a #1 or #2 market share; if not, they had to fix, sell, or close the unit.) In the 1990s, however, this rule was changed to focus on smaller (10 to 15 percent) market-share requirements but a requirement that business unit managers demonstrate significant growth potential. What impact did this change in corporate strategy have on the organizational design of business units?

10. Many of the most pressing organizational issues attracting public attention today seem to concern government agencies, especially those with responsibilities for preventing man-made disasters and attacks or responding to natural ones, such as hurricanes. How do the organizational design issues facing large firms compare with those facing rapid-response public agencies such as FEMA or the EPA?

11. While most managers might agree that firms should organize appropriately for their environmental conditions, they might easily differ on what environmental conditions were facing a firm and what an appropriate response to those conditions might entail. Explain the role of the manager in developing a fit with the firm's environment.

12. The Lincoln Electric Company is a longtime maker of welding equipment in Cleveland, Ohio, whose industry performance has been legendary. Its operations have focused around its well-known piece-rate incentive system, which permits it to gain significantly greater utilization of its capital assets than competitors, with a resulting competitive advantage on costs. In the mid-1990s, however, Lincoln experienced some difficulties in establishing new facilities outside of the United States and ended up modifying its organizational system when it opened facilities in Asia. What factors might contribute to the difficulties that even a well-managed firm might face in transferring its management and production systems to international locations?

ENDNOTES

[1]Caves, R., and D. Barton, *Efficiency in U.S. Manufacturing Industries*, Cambridge, MA, MIT Press, 1990, pp. 1–3.

[2]Chandler, A. D., *Strategy and Structure*, Cambridge, MA, MIT Press, 1962.

[3]Alchian, A., and H. Demsetz, "Production, Information Costs, and Economic Organization," *American Economic Review*, 62, 1972, pp. 777–795.

[4]The classic statement of these two problems is in March, J., and H. Simon, *Organizations*, New York, Wiley, 1958, pp. 22–27. For a review of research on these problems, see McCann, J., and J. R. Galbraith, "Interdepartmental Relations," in Nystrom, P. C., and W. H. Starbuck, *Handbook of Organizational Design*, rd. 2, New York, Oxford University Press, 1981, pp. 60–84.

[5]Prahalad, C. K. *The Fortune at the Bottom of the Pyramid*, Upper Saddle River, NJ, Wharton School Publishing, 2010, pp. 175–206.

[6]Isaacson, W., *Steve Jobs*, New York, Simon & Schuster, 2011, pp. 407–408.

[7]Simons, R., *Levers of Organization Design: How Managers Use Accountability Systems for Greater Performance and Commitment*, Boston, Harvard Business School Press, 2007, pp. 7–13.

[8]Garvin, D. A., and L. C. Levesque, "Meeting the Challenge of Corporate Entrepreneurship," *Harvard Business Review*, 84(10), 2006, pp. 102–112.

[9]Siegel, J., *Lincoln Electric*, HBS Case #9-707-445 (rev. August 25, 2008); Bartlett, C., and J. O'Connell, *Lincoln Electric: Venturing Abroad*, HBS Case #9-398-095.

[10]This distinction is taken from information processing approaches to organization design. For a review, see McCann and Galbraith (1981). A similar distinction between informational decentralization and informational consolidation is sometimes made in economic analyses of organization structure. See Baron, D., and D. Besanko, "Information, Control, and Organizational Structure," *Journal of Economics and Management Strategy*, 1, Summer 1992, pp. 237–276.

[11]Hindle, T., *The Economist Guide to Management Ideas and Gurus*, London, Profile Books, 2008, pp. 169–170.

[12]We would like to thank Suresh Krishna for developing this example.

[13]The network structure described in the first section is an alternative that relies on external contracting relationships.

[14]Garnet, R. W., *The Telephone Enterprise: The Evolution of the Bell System's Horizontal Structure, 1876–1909*, Baltimore, MD, Johns Hopkins University Press, 1985.

[15]Baron, D. P., and D. Besanko, "Shared Incentive Authority and the Organization of the Firm," unpublished mimeo, Northwestern University, Department of Management and Strategy, July 1997.

[16]Baron, D. P., and D. Besanko, "Strategy, Organization, and Incentives: Global Banking at Citicorp," unpublished mimeo, Northwestern University, Department of Management and Strategy, April 1998.

[17]Hamel, G., "First, Let's Fire All the Managers," *Harvard Business Review*, December 2011, pp. 48–60.

[18]Anderson, J. C., Hakansson, H., and Jan Johanson, "Dyadic Business Relationships within a Business Network," *Journal of Marketing*, 58(4), 1994, pp. 1–15.

[19]For an extended discussion of the network organization, see Baker, W. E., "The Network Organization in Theory and Practice," in Nohria, N., and R. G. Eccles, *Networks and Organizations*, Boston, Harvard Business School Press, 1992, pp. 397–429.

[20]Kali, R., and J. Sarkar, "Diversification, Propping and Monitoring: Business Groups, Firm Performance, and the Indian Economic Transition," Indira Gandhi Institute of Development Research, Mumbai Working Papers -WP-2005-006, November 2005.

[21]For studies of interfirm networks that focus on European network examples, see Rank, C., Rank, O., and A. Wald, "Integrated versus Core-Periphery Structures in Regional Biotechnology Networks," *European Management Journal*, 24(1), February 2006, pp. 73–85. For studies of Japanese and biotechnology examples, see Nohria, N., and R. G. Eccles (eds.), *Networks and Organizations*, Boston, Harvard Business School Press, 1992, pp. 309–394.

[22]Richman, Barak D., "Community Enforcement of Informal Contracts: Jewish Diamond Merchants in New York," *Harvard Law School John M. Olin Center for Law, Economics and Business Discussion Paper Series*. Paper 384 (2002). http://lsr.nellco.org/harvard_olin/384.

[23]Roberts, J., *The Modern Firm: Organizational Design for Performance and Growth*. Oxford, Oxford University Press, 2004, pp. 32–67.

[24]Bottazzi, G., Dosi, G., Lippi, M., Pammolli, F., and M. Riccaboni, "Innovation and Corporate Growth in the Evolution of the Drug Industry," *International Journal of Industrial Organization*, 19(7), July 2001, pp. 1161–1187.

[25]Thompson, J. D., *Organizations in Action*, New York, McGraw-Hill, 1967.

[26]McGahan, A. M., *How Industries Evolve*, Boston, Harvard Business School Press, 2004.

[27]This example was developed from materials in Isaacson, W., *Steve Jobs*, New York: Simon & Schuster, 2011, and Lashinsky, A., "Inside Apple," *Fortune*, May 23, 2011.

[28]Galbraith, J. R., and R. K. Kazanjian, *Strategy Implementation: The Role of Structure and Process*, 2d ed., St. Paul, MN, West Publishing, 1986.

[29]Garicano, L., "Hierarchies and the Organization of Knowledge in Production," *Journal of Political Economy*, October 2000.

[30]Stinchcombe, A. L., *Information and Organizations*, Berkeley, University of California Press, 1990.

[31]Badia, E., *Zara and Her Sisters: The Story of the World's Largest Clothing Retailer*, New York, Palgrave Macmillan, 2009.

[32]Kogut, B., and U. Zander, "Knowledge of the Firm and the Evolutionary Theory of the Modern Corporation," *Journal of International Business Studies*, 1993, pp. 625–645.

[33]Chandler, *Strategy and Structure*.

[34]This example draws from multiple sources, including: Khanna, T., Song, J. Y., and K. M. Lee, "The Paradox of Samsung's Rise," *Harvard Business Review*, 89(7–8), 2011, pp. 142–147; "Samsung's Radical Shakeup," *Business Week*, February 28, 1994, pp. 74–76; Samsung: Korea's Great Hope of High Tech," *Business Week*, February 3, 1992, pp. 44–45; "Good to Be Big; Better to Be Good," *The Economist*, August 18, 1990, pp. 7–10; and "Samsung: South Korea Marches to Its Own Drummer," *Forbes*, May 16, 1988, pp. 84–89.

[35]This example is based on material from Khanna, T., and K. G. Palepu, *Winning in Emerging Markets: A Road Map for Strategy and Execution*, Boston, Harvard Business Press, 2010.

14 ENVIRONMENT, POWER, AND CULTURE

Throughout the book, we have offered economic tools to managers seeking to be responsive to their environments. For example, Chapters 3 and 4 detail the economic factors affecting the decision to outsource, while Chapters 5 and 7 provide competitive models for firms considering whether to expand capacity in new technologies. In this chapter, we examine several aspects of managerial decision making that are not traditionally included in economic analyses. In particular, we examine the social context of firm behavior—the nonmarket, noncontractual relationships and activities that are essential to business.

Some academics view social context as distinct from economic behavior and potentially in conflict with economic principles. Others note that contextual factors such as power and culture are largely consistent with economic principles but that their details are complex and specific to the conditions faced by decision makers. It is doubtful that the tensions inherent in studying how individuals pursue their aims within a complex social context will ever be resolved, but as Kenneth Arrow suggests, it is important to understand the role of government and nongovernmental organizations, as well as broad social institutions, both visible and invisible, in permitting economic action to take place within a broader society.[1] In this chapter, we observe that the social context of business forms the foundation for economic transactions by providing managers with the order and predictability needed for ongoing business activity.

THE SOCIAL CONTEXT OF FIRM BEHAVIOR

Regulation is the most visible example of a firm's social context. Even in a *laissez-faire* economy, some government regulation is required to secure property rights, enforce contracts, and assure the smooth functioning of markets. There are myriad other ways that the government intervenes in business. There are laws governing labor relations and financial transactions. Governments penalize polluters. Antitrust laws limit business combinations and other practices that might restrict competition. The 2010 Patient Protection and Affordable Care Act (PPACA) gives the U.S. government an unprecedented ability to intervene in nearly all aspects of the nation's health care system, including health insurance, the organization of health care delivery, and medical research and development. Governments in other nations have even greater latitude in regulating health care markets.

Firms comply with regulations to avoid penalties, but compliance also gives firms a recognized legitimacy and a right to compete. For example, the U.S. Food and Drug Act of 1906 and, especially, the 1962 Kefauver-Harris Amendments to the FDA Act, assure American consumers about the quality of brand-name prescription drugs. With FDA approval in hand (and with similar approval from the European Medicines Agency, the Japanese Ministry of Health and Welfare, and their counterparts around the world), drug companies have a ready market for their costly new medicines. Some industries achieve similar benefits though self-regulation. For example, appliance makers can obtain a seal of approval from the Underwriters' Laboratory, certifying the safety of their products. On the other hand, efforts by cellular telephone companies to establish standard billing practices have failed to placate many consumers.

The behaviors of firms facing similar market situations may be circumscribed within narrow bounds even in the absence of government and self-regulation. Firms in the same market situation will likely operate within a set of shared general understandings and values regarding customers, competitors, products, and other aspects of a business, which necessarily leads to similar conclusions about how to produce and sell their products. This need not imply collusion or even lockstep consistency. While managers may agree on the facts concerning demand, competition, and so forth, they can differ sharply on how to perform those tasks to best satisfy consumer needs and generate profits. They may choose to compete for different market segments, offer different sets of products and services, and bring different capabilities and skills in their approaches. These differences are critical for effective competition.

Shared understandings may stem from a common history, such as when managers all grow up in a similar location or social context. In some businesses, such as restaurants and hotels, there may be a set of competitors from particular ethnic backgrounds whose entrepreneurial networks have chosen to specialize in some businesses over others. For example, among U.S. immigrants, those from the Philippines are much more likely to work as nurses than their overall proportion of the population would suggest, while those from Vietnam are much more likely to be working as hairdressers. Shared understandings may stem from common regulatory and technological constraints. Managers facing common constraints may develop common assumptions and sets of "best practices" to address those constraints.

Disagreements about what are thought to be consensual matters in an industry may signal the emergence of new opportunities for competitive advantage. For example, the growth of practices associated with mortgage securitization in the early 1980s led to significant changes in lending practices that violated long-held industry assumptions.[2] Technological or regulatory changes can also stimulate a reexamination of shared assumptions about industry competition. For example, the use of joint ventures and strategic alliances as modes of corporate growth has increased markedly since the early 1990s as a result of both technological changes and the relaxation of U.S. antitrust enforcement policies regarding joint ventures and alliances.[3]

While shared understandings can persist in industries for long periods of time, they also can change quickly and dramatically. The changes that occurred across the Middle East and North Africa in 2011 that have come to be known as the "Arab Spring" have roots in regional economies just as they have in regional politics. Of special importance has been the development, much of it prior to 2011, of beliefs, values, and behavioral norms of an emergent Muslim middle class that is strongly supportive of the development of thriving market economies. The implications of this emergent business culture are unclear, and managers are attempting to identify which of their former assumptions about doing business remain relevant and which have been replaced by new assumptions and new rules.[4] Similar events followed the fall of communism in Eastern Europe and the former Soviet Union after 1989. This also entailed changes from Cold War habits in entire patterns of doing business, managing government relations, and developing new market opportunities. The effects of these changes are still being sorted out in the region today.[5]

The norms of business practice vary widely across industries. Formal contracting is common in many industries such as aerospace and biotechnology. But there are many examples of established business practices that do not involve contracts. Business practice norms can develop around such areas as pricing, customer service, product design, research or advertising expenditures, dispute resolution, merger and acquisition activity, and restructuring. These norms reflect the habits or "ways of doing business" that develop in an industry and are taken for granted until times of industry change. Although these norms seldom have any formal status, they often are important to industry participants and, once established, change slowly. Here are just a few examples of noncontractual business norms. In the diamond trade, large transactions often occur on the basis of a handshake. In higher education, universities generally do not recruit each other's faculty after May 1, so as to permit each school to schedule the next year's classes. Dealers for a particular automobile manufacturer will trade cars when a customer in one town wants a particular car that the dealer in another town has in the showroom.

These noncontractual norms result from the social context in which businesses operate. Social context includes both the context in which firms act and the context in which managers make decisions. This permits a distinction between *external* and *internal* contexts. External context concerns not only the business environment in which the firm operates, which we have discussed in detail throughout this book, but also the legal, regulatory, political, and cultural environment in which the firm acts. Internal context concerns the political and cultural environment within a firm that affects how managers and employees behave. Of course, the behavior of managers and employees is also formally determined by its authority system. This was already discussed in Chapter 13 in terms of organizational structure. Below, we consider internal context first and complete the chapter by considering external context.

INTERNAL CONTEXT

The *internal context* of the firm describes the formal and informal mechanisms that guide the actions of managers and workers as they act as agents for the firm. Individuals link their activities and rewards to those of the groups to which they belong, and ultimately to the firm. Individual performance thus ultimately determines firm performance, although this requires coordination with other individuals and groups along the way. Environmental uncertainty, along with complex goal and reward structures, makes it likely that workers will have conflicting views about what goals to pursue and how and when to pursue them. Regardless of a firm's formal incentive and authority structure, individuals are unlikely to put their own personal goals and career interests in abeyance while working for a firm. As we discussed in Chapter 12, an individual's self-interest can work to the detriment of the firm. When individuals rise to top management positions, it is increasingly likely that their personal goals become aligned with those of the firm, however, which decreases the chance for serious agency problems. Even so, the interests of owners and managers almost never coincide.

One would think that controls could be designed to integrate individual behaviors into unified organizational action. As we have observed in Chapters 12 and 13, however, this is difficult. The goals pursued by different actors may be grossly divergent and not amenable to compromise. Managers may need to coordinate among themselves over matters that may be much more important to some of them than to others. The firm can address the resulting agency problems using an array of incentives, such as pay for performance or efficiency wages, but these tools often have limited effectiveness. Finally, because of the limitations of formal structures and controls, many activities within and between organizations must occur outside of their boundaries. Managers from different units may need to cooperate but are not required to do so. In such situations of goal conflict, differential motivation, and incomplete authority, formal controls are inadequate, and cost-effective contracts are hard to fashion. As a result, *power* and *culture* become important as alternative means for accomplishing goals.

POWER

Because "power" and related terms like "influence" or "authority" are so widely used, the meanings associated with them are often confusing. We take *power* to be an individual actor's ability to accomplish his or her goals by using resources obtained through *noncontractual exchange relationships*. By this we mean exchanges of goods, services, or promises on terms that take place outside of traditional economic markets and that are not enforceable in court. For example, someone in need of emergency assistance may receive help from an individual and have little to offer that particular individual in return immediately. The individual providing assistance may never have need of reciprocation in kind. Nevertheless, there may still be an implied promise that the favor would be returned if needed. The terms of the agreement are not specified, since it is not known in advance when or how the favor can be best returned. A failure to provide future assistance when requested would not give cause to legal action either, because there was no contract. Still, one can consider such an arrangement as an exchange whose obligations many people would fulfill out of a felt need to reciprocate. There are, of course, limits to these obligations. For example, it is unlikely that many would agree to provide assistance that was illegal, put one's employment at risk, or entailed significant extended commitments.

Power is different from *authority*, which stems from the explicit contractual decision-making and dispute-resolution rights that a firm (or another source) grants to an individual. A manager exercises power by redirecting the activities of other actors away from their immediate goals and toward accomplishing the manager's own goals. Others follow, not because they are contractually or morally obligated to do so, but because they perceive it is in their best interest to do so. In this sense, power is the ability to get things done in the absence of contracts. *Influence*, a related term, refers to the use of power in a given situation by an individual. The influence a person has over others is thus an effect of his or her broader power.

Power exists at many levels in a firm. Individual managers, such as the CEO, may be powerful relative to others on the management team. It is also common to discuss the power of units or subgroups of an organization. In universities, academic departments continually vie with each other for budgetary resources and view their success in obtaining such resources as evidence of their power, which stems from their popularity with students, the research productivity of their faculty, or their success in securing government and foundation grants. Firms also exercise power in their product markets, factor markets (such as for raw materials or labor), or in relations with suppliers, competitors, or other actors in the firm's environment. For example, Disney's Pixar Animation Studios may obtain a more favorable distribution of a new animated film than would a rival studio. It would also have power in negotiations with toy companies seeking to develop products based on Pixar characters.

The Sources of Power

Power is often exerted in an economic market, as when a firm with a patent for a popular new drug uses its market power to set a high price–cost margin. Not surprisingly, this is often referred to as *pricing power*. Our interest here is in power that cannot be exerted in the market; that is, power that cannot be easily priced. Individuals attain this power when they possess resources that others value but are not readily bought and sold in a market. This includes the power to control the allocation of resources within firms or other administrative domains, where internal markets for such resources are virtually nonexistent, often by design.

One way to look at sources of power is in terms of *power bases*—by which we mean attributes of the individual that convey resources that help an individual gain power. Power can stem from an individual's position within a hierarchy. This is known as *legitimate power* or *formal power*. An individual who possesses formal power has reason to expect compliance, at least on those matters that are of moderate or little importance to others. Chester Barnard uses the term *zone of indifference* to define the set of issues over which the powerful individual with formal authority usually prevails. For example, an individual hired to teach classes at a professional school would be unlikely to question the right of a superior to assign the individual to teach particular classes at particular times. The employee, however, would cease being indifferent to the actions of the superior if they went beyond expectations for what the job entailed, such as by scheduling the individual to teach on holidays or on Saturday nights. The employee would also likely take issue with demands that were not related to the general nature of the work that was agreed to at the time of employment—for example, if the new instructor was assigned to bring coffee and doughnuts for the other instructors. Because this view of compliance involves managers acting within agreed-on boundaries, it is sometimes discussed in terms of a "psychological contract" with employees.[6]

Power can also stem from an ability to grant rewards or administer punishments, or from the possession of specialized knowledge valued by other actors. In academic and research bureaucracies, examples of individuals possessing this power are the key editors of top journals, such as the *Journal of the American Medical Association*, or the grants officers of major funding agencies, such as the National Institutes of Health. The decisions of these individuals can make or break careers, and as a result, these individuals wield considerable power in their professions.

Power can be based on one's position in a social order, due to status, image, or reputation. For example, an individual with a well-known history of winning in prior conflicts will have reputation-based power that could lead potential adversaries to comply with future demands. This last type of power is rooted not only in individuals and their attributes, but also in the relationships that develop among individuals as they participate in networks of tasks, exchange, or information sharing. For example, the successes of ascendant executives in a business community are regularly announced by corporate press releases, reported on by the business press, and enshrined in various listings of "up and coming" executives by the business press and local institutions. Reputations may also be put at risk by significant or poorly timed failures. An example of this is seen in the ups and downs of the career and reputation of Jon Corzine, from his leadership of Goldman Sachs, to his election to the U.S. Senate in 2000, to his election as governor of New Jersey in 2005, to his leadership of the failed firm MF Global in 2011.

Relational views of power are often based on *social exchange*. Social exchange is a transfer between two or more parties of resources, or rights to control resources, that occurs outside of a market.[7] Power arises in future social exchanges as a result of persistent inequalities in past social exchanges. To illustrate how power might arise out of social exchanges, suppose that Amy and Beth are exchange partners. If an acceptable exchange occurs between them, their transaction is complete. Suppose, however, that they cannot complete an exchange in a mutually acceptable manner, and as a result, Amy provides more of value to Beth than Beth can provide to Amy. In effect, Beth "owes" Amy the deficit of the exchange. Unless it is explicitly considered as such, this is not a formal debt, and Amy cannot sue Beth to recover the deficit. If Beth's deficit to Amy increases over successive exchanges, Beth is said to be increasingly dependent on Amy. Conversely, Amy is said to have power over Beth to the extent that Beth is dependent on Amy. The dependence of Beth on Amy would be mitigated to the extent that Amy depends on Beth for some other matter or in some other set of exchanges.

Such a pattern could develop in the workplace if a junior employee asked a senior colleague for advice on some matter that is unimportant to the senior. How does the junior repay the senior colleague for providing assistance? Sometimes deference and respect from the recipient might suffice. When deference and respect do not suffice, it might lead to inappropriate demands on the junior or to the estrangement of the senior colleague or even the creation of an enemy. That is why such informal exchanges are constrained in many organizational settings. Informal exchanges can pose significant costs to the firm if they become too involved, time consuming, or distracting. It is even possible that individuals will arrange personally favorable exchanges that detract from the work of the firm. (This would be an example of influence activities that we described in Chapter 3.) As a result, in settings where such exchanges are often necessary, firms may promote strong norms among employees that both encourage cooperative exchanges across the organization and impose sanctions for individuals who refuse requests for assistance. Firms often supplement these norms with individual incentives, knowledge databases (for example, the collected work product of professional colleagues that others could consult), and increased formal training, development, and recognition for consultants who excel at both knowledge generation and knowledge sharing.[8]

In an economic exchange, contracts and the rule of law dictate the transfer of resources and dollars between trading partners. Voluntary exchanges resulting from power relationships seem harder to explain. Why would Beth choose to become dependent on Amy and presumably commit future resources to Amy's discretion? Why would Amy provide resources in the present in return for the uncertain future obligations of Beth? After all, despite Beth's "debt," Amy cannot use formal means, such as the courts, to force compensation from Beth. Several explanations come to mind. An individual actor choosing a dependence relation may lack a better alternative. The resources controlled by the other actor may be important, with no clear substitutes or alternative sources. Finally, it just may be too costly to write a formal contract. This is the *resource dependence* view of power, expressed by Jeffrey Pfeffer. Individuals and firms seek to gain power by reducing their dependence on other actors, while increasing the dependence of others on them. This is

EXAMPLE 14.1 THE SOURCES OF PRESIDENTIAL POWER[12]

One of the most famous studies of the bases of power was *Presidential Power*, Richard Neustadt's 1960 examination of how Franklin Roosevelt, Harry Truman, and Dwight Eisenhower dealt with power and influence during their administrations. The book was widely read at the beginning of the Kennedy administration and has remained important to sitting presidents, their staffs, and policy analysts.

The important issue for Neustadt is the conflict between the image of the president as powerful and the reality of the presidency as institutionally weak. Presidential power does not consist of the president taking direct action on some front, such as Truman's recall of General Douglas MacArthur or his seizure of the steel mills in 1952, or Eisenhower's decision to send troops to Little Rock, Arkansas, in 1957 to assist in desegregation. These command decisions were more exceptions than typical uses of power. Nor did any of them solve the president's policy problems. Instead, they used up scarce presidential power and, at best, allowed the president and others involved in the situation more time to search for a lasting solution. Neustadt suggests that decisions made by command or fiat are more likely to be evidence of a lack of power than of its effective use. In a given situation, however, there may have been no other choice than to command. For example, whatever problems Truman encountered in recalling MacArthur, the cost of not recalling him and thus allowing civilian authority to be flouted would probably have been higher.

Presidential power is the ability to influence the people who make and implement government policies. It has three sources. The first is the bargaining advantage that comes with the office that enables the president to persuade others to work in his interest—the formal powers and authority of the president. The second source is professional reputation, which comprises the expectations of professional politicians, bureaucrats, and others in the political community regarding the president's power and his willingness to use it. This is related to the ability to control the votes of Congress on key issues. Once the president loses control of a majority in Congress, he cannot guarantee that his programs will be enacted and will lose power as a result. A third source of presidential power is his prestige among the public, specifically how the political community assesses his support among different constituencies and the consequences that failure to support the president will have for politicians.

Although the political situations facing the president of the United States are different from those facing the CEOs of large firms, Neustadt's three sources are consistent with those discussed earlier. The formal powers of the job, whether stemming from the Constitution, laws, or customs, along with the institutional routines that have grown up around it, provide a basis for incumbent power, a basis that can be used well or poorly. Professional reputation in a firm refers to how observers expect the powerholder to act in a given situation, based on their accumulated experience with the powerholder. Finally, prestige for politicians is analogous to control over critical resources. For the president and professional politicians, that resource is public sentiment, which translates into votes.

Looking back to 1990, in light of the six presidents who had served since *Presidential Power* was first published, Neustadt saw little reason to change his fundamental conclusions. For example, the experience of Nixon and Watergate, on the one hand, and Johnson and Vietnam, on the other, showed the importance of credibility and perceived legitimacy for both public prestige and professional reputation. Similarly, although Neustadt still emphasizes the importance of political skills for the president, the experiences of Johnson and Nixon also emphasize the relevance of individual temperament for success in office. The president needs to be patient enough to tolerate a complex political system that rarely allows him to successfully implement major policy initiatives immediately. Neustadt still sees political skills and experience as crucial for success in office. (The presidency is no place for amateurs.) Political skills and experience, however, though necessary to success in the presidency, are not sufficient. Both Nixon and Johnson were highly experienced in elective office and possessed formidable political skills, yet their sense of power led both of them to support policies that ultimately dissipated their power and impaired their effectiveness.

In 2010, Neustadt's book was 50 years old and outlived its author, who died in 2003. Nev- ertheless, it remained the sixth most assigned book in college courses on the U.S. presidency in American colleges and universities. In an essay on the book's influence for the *Chronicle of Higher Education*, Michael Nelson notes that the crises plaguing American presidents since 1990, including the wars in Iraq and Afghani- stan, along with the financial crisis of 2008 and the recession that followed it, have shown how the decision-making issues raised in *Presidential Power* are still appropriate today and are likely to remain so for the foreseeable future.

---

analogous to the efforts by firms to avoid supplier power by securing multiple sup- ply channels and to achieve market power by selling to customers who have few alternatives.[9]

Resource dependence helps explain why firms voluntarily choose to become dependent, but not why individuals willingly give up resources today in exchange for an uncertain future response. One explanation is that, on the merits of the exchange itself, it may prove beneficial to Amy to trust Beth. Once trust has been established by repeated interactions, similar exchanges will seem less risky. Conversely, Amy may value what she expects Beth to provide so highly that Amy is willing to tolerate the chance that Beth will not reciprocate. The willingness of an actor to provide resources in exchange for unspecified future consideration may also be based on more gener- ally held norms of reciprocity that are part of the broader culture.[10]

Along with the idea that actors will work to reduce their dependence on others, the resource dependence view also states that individuals who control critical resources will be the ones who accumulate power. Those who help the firm cope with problems that pose major threats will come to exercise the most power. Examples also can be seen where members of critical occupational or professional groups gain control (petroleum engineers in oil companies), where individuals with links to key regulators or stakeholders gain control (lawyers in regulated businesses), or where individuals with unique and valuable skills gain control (surgeons in hospitals).[11]

Structural Views of Power

A firm's structure, or some broader structure within which an actor operates, may also serve as a source of power. Those who occupy certain critical locations within that structure have more power. Often the most powerful individuals in a firm occupy multiple key positions. For example, an individual who serves as both chair- man and CEO of a firm likely has more power than if that individual occupied only one of the two top positions. Indeed, firms sometimes separate these top positions to reduce the structural power of its top manager. This is happening more fre- quently since the financial crisis of 2008 and allows boards of directors to restruc- ture relations with their top managers. An example of this restructuring occurred in December 2011, when Avon Products announced that it would separate these two roles and find a replacement for Andrea Jung as CEO while maintaining Jung in the chairman's role.[13]

There are other types of structure-derived power that are less direct but potentially as important for the firm. As we saw in Chapter 13, structure involves information networks within firms and networks of social relationships that develop among the firm's employees, customers, suppliers, and other stakeholders. These networks can both support and impede the power of their participants. Having a prominent position within important informal networks in firms can give an individual holding that position a degree of power that enhances his or her formal authority and makes it easier to influence organizational outcomes. Individuals in minor or marginal positions in networks will likely find their power limited relative to those holding more central positions.

Ronald Burt provides an explanation of how structural power can be conferred by network positions in his theory of structural holes.[14] *Structural holes* are relationships in social networks in which one actor is the critical link between individuals or entire groups. To associate with each other, these individuals or groups must go through the actor who spans the structural hole. The individual who can "span the hole" uses control of information or resource flows as a source of power. If representatives of the two separate groups can interact regularly, they may eliminate their dependence on the focal individual, thereby eliminating his or her structural power.

Burt uses the term *tertius gaudens* (happy third) strategy to describe how structural holes create opportunities for individuals to obtain power. The *tertius* is the "third who benefits," and the strategy involves spanning a structural hole and bargaining with the parties on either side for the most favorable terms. The "third" may be a go-between in a trading relationship, such as a real estate broker. Alternatively, the "third" may possess a scarce resource required by two or more parties, such as a manager who must divide limited time among several subordinates.

The potential for those spanning structural holes to accumulate power can prompt concerns among other members of the network. One way to address this is to reconfigure networks to reduce the number of structural holes. Depending on the costs of forging redundant or duplicate connections, this may be infeasible. It may pay to have specialized network actors, even if they could abuse their positions. Another way to limit abuses by specialized network actors is by developing regulations and norms governing them. Roberto Fernandez and Roger Gould made this finding in their study of the influence of five types of brokerage positions on national health policy.[15] By "brokerage position," they mean a position in a social network that connects otherwise unconnected pairs of actors. Fernandez and Gould identify a "paradox of power" in which brokers had to appear neutral to influence decision processes. This suggests that key network positions might augment one's power as long as the positions are not also used to pursue personal interests.

Do Successful Organizations Need Powerful Managers?

Unless employee relationships can be completely governed by incentive contracts, a manager must possess some power in order to be successful. But the presence of a powerful manager does not guarantee success. A major purpose of corporate governance is to rein in the power of senior management. In the presence of agency costs arising from hidden actions, hidden information, and related problems, a powerful manager may divert information and resources toward personal goals. However, a powerful manager is necessary in order to reduce the agency costs to the firm that

EXAMPLE 14.2 POWER AND POOR PERFORMANCE: THE CASE OF THE 1957 MERCURY[16]

Although power may be useful in getting things done, it can also be dysfunctional if it helps the wrong programs to be accomplished—that is, if it is used to circumvent the checks and balances that are necessary to evaluate the market feasibility and cost effectiveness of any effort. An example of this occurred with the development of the 1957 Mercury. Called the "Turnpike Cruiser" by Ford managers and a "steel cartoon" by its critics, the model was introduced to great fanfare but failed to make good on its high costs and lofty sales projections. Overall, Ford lost an estimated $369 on every 1957 Mercury it sold, and the car proved a harbinger of even greater problems that came with the now-infamous Edsel. In his group history of the careers of the "Whiz Kids" at Ford, John Byrne provides an example of the functions and dysfunctions of power in the career of the Whiz Kid responsible for the new Mercury, Francis "Jack" Reith.

Reith had a number of power bases from which to push the development of the new Mercury. First, he was a dynamic and almost charismatic leader, who drove his subordinates but inspired considerable admiration in the process. He was also highly intelligent and effective at persuading others to follow his direction. Reith had accumulated a considerable track record since he joined Ford in 1946. Most recently, he had received credit for the successful turnaround and sale of Ford's subsidiary in France. On the basis of this success, Reith enjoyed the support of his superiors, Lewis Crusoe and Henry Ford II. He also gained standing from his association with the Whiz Kids, who had nearly all distinguished themselves at Ford and who were clearly recognized as a group as well as individually. Finally, Reith had position power, in that he was promoted to the head of the Mercury division once his 1957 plan had been approved.

Reith saw the 1957 Mercury as part of a larger plan by which Ford could contend with General Motors for leadership in automobiles through a major expansion of an existing make (Mercury) and the introduction of an entirely new one (the Edsel). Reith's boss, Lewis Crusoe, promised him his support (and the top job) at Mercury, if the plan could be approved by the board of directors. In preparing for that board meeting, Reith used all of his bases of power effectively.

Reith was perhaps too effective. There were doubts about the initiative in several quarters. The plan promised too much (a 54 percent sales increase). It required a larger expansion of the dealer network than Ford had ever anticipated. The projected expenses of the project were staggering and, in effect, required a large increase in market share to justify the project. As one executive remembered, "the numbers were totally unrealistic. They had to be. It was the only way to justify the plan" (Byrne, p. 225). The estimated price for the project was equal to the company's total profit before taxes the previous year ($485 million).

These doubts were not raised, however, because Reith's colleagues, whose job it was to ask difficult questions about projects, failed to do so in this case out of deference to their friend. When questions were raised, Reith and Crusoe jointly overpowered the opposition. Much of this persuasion was based on fear, intimidation, and concern for the career consequences of resistance. The norm for rational project analysis that the Whiz Kids had introduced to Ford was forgotten in the process of securing project approval. The failure of the car, which ended Reith's career at Ford, was due in part to the flawed decision processes described above that allowed Reith to push through his initiative at the expense of critical analysis. Reith and his managers, however, also failed to pay attention to market research, which indicated increased consumer interest in safety and decreased interest in the stylistic flourishes that characterized the car. Instead, the 1957 Mercury was based on managerial intuitions about consumer preferences for stylish cars rather than on data. The car also suffered from numerous quality and safety problems. In making this error, however, Reith was not alone. The year 1957 was a strong one for the Volkswagen, a small, simple car that focused on economy. It was also the first year in which consumers' interest in automobile safety and quality increased. Many managers in Detroit missed this shift in the market, which would lead to further problems for the industry in the 1960s and 1970s and beyond.

stem from the actions of those at lower levels in the organization. Whether giving a manager power has positive or negative effects also depends on the stability of the firm's environment. In a relatively stable environment, power arrangements within the firm can evolve and adjust, until an arrangement results that seems to work. This is analogous to Chandler's idea that structure follows strategy, which we discussed in the prior chapter. However, in an environment that is undergoing significant changes, prior power arrangements may prove ineffective and the power previously granted to managers may end up impeding the efforts of the firm to adapt to environmental changes. Overall, power is a two-edged sword whose effects can be positive or negative for firms. We expect that the accumulation of power will be helpful or harmful according to the following conditions:

Accumulation of power is helpful when

1. There are high agency costs in coordinating managers and lower-level workers.
2. The firm's environment is relatively stable.

Accumulation of power is harmful when

1. There are high agency costs in coordinating among levels of upper management.
2. The firm's environment is relatively unstable.

In situations where neither condition holds—for example, when there are high agency costs in coordinating managers and lower-level workers and the firm's environment is unstable—then the allocation of power will prove much more difficult to accomplish effectively.

The Decision to Allocate Formal Power to Individuals

Thus far, our discussion has skirted two interrelated issues. First, when should the firm grant formal authority to individuals who already wield great power by virtue of their control over key resources? Second, who should exercise that authority and discretion? The simple answer to the first question is that firms should internalize decisions when fiat and administrative discretion are efficient ways of settling disputes. We covered this idea when we discussed corporate governance in Chapter 4. Problems with corporate oversight are also discussed in Chapter 12. If formal power is to be used effectively, its holders should be informed about the policies they will need to approve and the disputes they will need to resolve. This expert knowledge forms an important basis for authority, and power has been recognized since the earliest writings on bureaucratic organizations.[17]

This does not imply that knowledge and power are perfectly correlated. In some settings (e.g., research laboratories), it would be inefficient to make the most knowledgeable individual the manager, since that individual would be most useful to the firm as a generator of knowledge or new products rather than as a resolver of disputes. An outsider who joins the top management of a firm may bring considerable knowledge of functional areas, but may lack detailed local knowledge of the new firm and the specific businesses the firm pursues.

A second basis for allocating authority concerns the need to ensure that managerial motivations and interests are productively aligned with the goals of the firms

---

EXAMPLE 14.3 POWER IN THE BOARDROOM: WHY LET CEOs CHOOSE DIRECTORS?

According to the *Economist* magazine, CEO pay in the United States has risen more than ten times as fast as average worker wages since the 1970s. Many observers have wondered whether this increase in pay was justified by changes in the labor market for CEOs, or whether pay increases stem from some other, less benign cause.

Graef Crystal, a onetime compensation consultant turned pay critic, argues for the latter. His book, *In Search of Excess*, asserts that CEOs control the pay-setting process through their control of compensation consultants. Consultants, ostensibly hired by the board to give directors some sense of "appropriate" pay levels for the CEO, artificially boost these figures in order to please the CEO and increase his pay. Consultants do this, Crystal claims, because it is the CEO, not the board, who determines whether that consultant is hired again by the firm in the following year. And why do directors allow the CEO to get away with this? Crystal argues it occurs because of the vital role that CEOs play in selecting the board members in the first place.[20]

Kevin Hallock offers evidence that board "interlocks" do seem to affect CEO pay.[21] If an employee of firm A sits on firm B's board, and vice versa, then the boards of the two firms are said to be interlocked. Board interlocks are associated with higher-than-normal CEO pay. One possible explanation for this result is that a quid pro quo exists. Acting in his role as firm B director, the firm A CEO allows the firm B CEO to be overpaid, and the firm B CEO responds in kind. Given the possibility for such collusive behavior, though, one wonders why CEOs are allowed so much influence in determining the composition of their boards. A director's role, after all, is to monitor the CEO—wouldn't shareholders prefer independent monitors?

Benjamin Hermalin and Michael Weisbach suggest a potential answer that centers on managerial power.[22] Power, in their context, comes from scarcity. Consider a CEO with a track record of great success. Given the CEO's record, it is unlikely that the firm's best alternative CEO is nearly as good. That is, the CEO the firm would hire if the current CEO were to leave probably would not be able to run the firm as well as the current CEO. Examples of powerful CEOs—in the sense that the alternative CEO is unlikely to be as good—might include Steve Jobs of Apple (before his death in 2011) and Warren Buffett of Berkshire Hathaway. Powerful CEOs can use the threat of departure to bargain with the board over what they want. And what might they want? Higher pay, of course, but also control over the board of directors.

Hermalin and Weisbach's power-based analysis fits with a number of key facts about CEOs and boards. First, "independent" directors—those with no ties to the CEO—are more likely to be added to boards if the firm's performance has recently been poor. Second, board independence tends to decline the longer a CEO has held the position. Third, the probability that a CEO will be fired after poor performance is greater when there are more independent directors. Their insights also suggest that Hallock's findings—that board interlocks are associated with higher pay—might not reflect a causal relationship. That is, it might not be the case that interlocks cause high pay; instead, both high pay and interlocks might just be symptoms of managerial power.

they serve. In Chapter 3 we described how powerful trading partners can hold up a firm; the same analysis applies to powerful individuals within the firm. Suppose that a firm has made relationship-specific investments with a manager and that the firm cannot enforce a contract that would spell out all of that manager's responsibilities. In this situation, the firm is dependent on the manager and the manager can pursue selfish objectives without fear of retaliation. An example of this could occur in diversified firms when managers of unrelated divisions are not subject to sufficiently powerful incentives and as a result engage in excessive rent-seeking behaviors at the expense of the overall firm. Gertner, Powers, and Scharfstein study the pre- and post-spinoff behavior of such divisions and find evidence consistent with such a conclusion.[18]

If those who wield power in the firm are also necessary for the effective control and allocation of its critical resources, then the firm is also potentially vulnerable to their departure. This threat implies that firms should invest in and allocate power to those individuals who are more likely to stay with the firm. A firm can take several steps to assure that powerful managers do not leave. They can offer stocks or stock options that do not vest for several years. Alternatively, they can structure compensation as a tournament (see Chapter 12) and emphasize internal promotion. They can invest in supportive work conditions that will increase the manager's productivity. They might even consider whether the individuals have a family or other obligations that might tie them to the local community. Julio Rotemberg argues that firms may actually prefer to give decision makers power rather than higher wages as a way of reducing turnover. Power may be thought of as a firm-specific asset—the decision maker may get better pay elsewhere but might not achieve comparable levels of power and influence.[19]

CULTURE

When making decisions, individuals are guided by explicit and implicit rewards. Contracts form the foundation for explicit rewards. Power provides a way for individuals to understand and implement implicit rewards. Culture offers yet another alternative. A firm's *culture* is a set of values, beliefs, and norms of behavior shared by its members that influences employee preferences and behaviors. It also involves the special mindsets, routines, and codes that shape how members view each other and the firm. It thus sets the context in which relations among members develop, and it provides the basis for implicit contracts between them.[23] Culture represents the behavioral guideposts and evaluative criteria in a firm that are not spelled out by contract but still constrain and inform the firm's managers and employees in their decisions. As David Kreps explains, "culture gives hierarchical inferiors an idea *ex ante* how the firm will 'react' to circumstances as they arise—in a very strong sense, it gives identity to the organization."[24]

The behavioral guideposts and "identity" instilled by culture create a set of norms for managers and workers to follow. These norms can both hinder and help the firm. The existence of norms may constrain the freedom of management to make decisions. For example, managers accustomed to unit autonomy and individual accountability may find it difficult to cooperate with other managers on activities that require cooperation and joint action. They may also have difficulties with the exercise of centralized authority by corporate managers. An example of this is Bertelsmann, A.G., a multidivisional German media firm with global scope that since 1998 has been developing a corporate culture of shared values and partnership, even while promoting divisional decentralization and entrepreneurship. The presence of strong corporate norms, such as for individual or group accountability, may also aid managers, provided that the norms support the firm's strategies. For example, the famous piece-rate system used by the Lincoln Electric Company is dependent for its success on supportive norms for individual achievement and accountability, coupled with strong supervision by management and appropriate organizational policies.

This interlocking of culture, structures, practices, and people provides an example of the multidimensional nature of organization design and its influence on performance. John Roberts develops these links further in terms of a PARC, referring to *p*eople interacting with organizational *a*rchitecture, *r*outines, and *c*ulture.[25] As we mentioned in the last chapter, these links, once established, may make it very difficult to replicate some of the firm's practices in other settings where the culture and history supporting the practices are different. This is especially the case in international operations, for which the cultural contexts can vary widely for a given activity.

Part of the problem that culture poses for managers is that it is difficult to manage prospectively. While a supportive culture can develop over time around a given set of activities, it has proven very difficult to engineer such cultural support by design and according to a schedule. Such efforts are vulnerable to problems of unintended consequences that create more costs than benefits. Examples of this were apparent in well-publicized efforts to reform the "quality of work life" in the United States in the 1970s and 1980s. In these efforts, shop-floor activities were changed to permit greater opportunities for worker interaction on the job and thus build up a more supportive culture. These efforts were frustrated, however, when the multiple goals of these projects conflicted with each other, such as when workers used their newly obtained flexibility to go home earlier rather than attend skill classes or interact with their managers, their unions, or their coworkers. The result was that while workers were pleased with the chance to pursue their personal and family interests, this did not translate into a more supportive workplace culture, since the workers were not around as much to interact. Other efforts in these directions have attempted to build on employee stock ownership plans (ESOPs) and related programs to link the objectives of individual employees with the broader goals of the firm. These programs are popular with a wide range of firms, including such large firms as Cargill and Wal-Mart. While the adoption of these plans is associated with firm performance, the causality is unclear and there is considerable disagreement among managers and scholars as to whether these plans are effective, why they are effective, and how much cultural elements have to do with their realized results.[26]

Jay Barney identifies the conditions under which culture can be a source of sustained competitive advantage.[27] First, something about the firm's culture and values must be linked to the value the firm creates for customers. We will say a lot more about this issue in a moment. A culture that creates value can be analyzed much like any other resource or capability. The culture must also be particular to the firm. If the culture is common to most firms in the market, so that it reflects the influence of the national or regional culture, then it is unlikely to lead to a relative competitive advantage, since most of the firm's competitors will share the same cultural attributes. This changes, of course, if a firm with a distinctive national or regional culture that supports performance diversifies internationally and begins competing with foreign firms, whose cultures are not as supportive. The experience of Japanese automakers entering the U.S. market provides an example of this, and the success of firms like Honda has often been attributed to the cultural attributes of Japanese firms.

More recent examples of foreign entry into the U.S. market, such as by Indian and Chinese firms, have not been linked to cultural issues as was the case with Japanese firms. Neither China nor India is associated with homogenous cultures as Japan was when its businesses expanded globally. Both China and India display considerable cultural diversity within their borders, and to the extent that Indian or Chinese firms reflect national cultural attributes, it is not generally associated with high firm performance, innovation, or other performance attributes. As a result, entry efforts have been more concerned with maintaining the cultural identity of the acquired firm so that the acquirer can learn from the acquisition, retain talent in the acquired firm, and promote a corporate culture of diversity. Hindalco's 2007 acquisition of Novelis, an Atlanta-based global producer of rolled aluminum products, provides an example of this, as the Indian firm attempted to manage both the organizational and cultural integration of the firms, along with the more typical financial and operational combinations that are necessary with such mergers.[28]

If aspects of a firm's culture are easy to imitate, other firms will begin to do so, which will soon nullify any advantage for the firm where the culture first developed. A firm's culture can be hard to imitate, however, because it is likely to rest on tacit factors that are not easily described and that represent the accumulated history of the firm much better than does a simple description. The complexity that makes a culture difficult for others to imitate also makes it difficult for managers to modify the culture of their own firms to significantly improve performance. Firms like Lincoln Electric, for example, have experienced troubles in opening new plants and attempting to replicate their own system, which suggests that competitors will have an even harder time. This difficulty in reproducing one's culture globally is not unique to U.S. firms. Very few firms are "born global." For example, Essel Propack, an Indian manufacturer of laminated and plastic tubes with plants in a dozen countries and $300 million in annual sales, had to partner with its global customers, such as P&G, in order to launch a global diversification program.[29]

Barney even suggests a trade-off between the degree to which a culture is manipulable and the amount of sustained value that a firm can obtain from it. A culture that is manipulable is not likely to be linked to the fundamental resource commitments of the firm that form the basis for sustained competitive advantage. Rather, it is more likely to be common to several firms, more easily imitable, and hence less valuable.

Culture creates value for firms in two ways. First, culture can complement formal control systems and reduce monitoring costs. Second, it shapes the preferences of individuals toward a common set of goals. This reduces negotiation and bargaining costs and fosters cooperation that would be difficult to achieve through more explicit means.

Culture Complements Formal Controls

Chapter 12 described the classic economic approach to the problem of agency: the firm relies on incentives to control employees' activities. As explained in Chapter 13, organization structure facilitates the monitoring required to evaluate and reward employees by determining information flows. Culture complements these formal controls on the basis of the employee's attachment to the firm rather than on the basis of incentives and monitoring. Individuals who value belonging to the culture will align their goals and behaviors to those of the firm. Culture has the potential to be more efficient than formal control systems because a thriving culture requires little in the way of monitoring or tangible rewards.

EXAMPLE 14.4   CORPORATE CULTURE AND INERTIA AT ICI[30]

Andrew Pettigrew provides an example of how cultural inertia can stymie organizational adaptation in his case studies of Imperial Chemical Industries (ICI), the leading British chemical manufacturer. In 1973, ICI was the largest manufacturing firm in Great Britain. It had possessed a strong and homogeneous culture for the nearly 50 years it had existed. Sales growth in 1972 was strong in chemicals, at twice the national growth rate for manufacturing. ICI had also been successful at new product development, with half of its 1972 sales coming from products that had not been on the market in 1957.

Strong threats to ICI's continued success developed in its business environment in the 1970s. These threats included overcapacity in its core businesses, threats of both inflation and recession in the British domestic economy, and import threats from Europe and North America. These pressures substantially affected ICI's profitability in 1980, when its profit totals and profitability ratios were halved. Several years of consistently poor performance followed. In the five years between 1977 and 1982, ICI cut its domestic workforce by nearly one-third.

For years, individuals within top management had been recommending changes in the structure and governance system of ICI to allow it to better adapt to changed economic and political conditions. These calls for change went back at least to 1967, when they were raised by a single individual during a board election and ignored. A board committee on the need for reorganization had been set up in 1973 and issued a report calling for extensive organizational changes within ICI. The report encountered extreme political opposition from the start and, in the words of an executive director, "sank at the first shot." ICI did not adopt these calls for reorganization and strategic change until 1983, when the firm had already experienced several years of poor performance.

Pettigrew's analysis of this history highlights the culture of conservatism and the "smoothing" of problems that dominated ICI at this time. These aspects of its culture were functional during prosperous and stable times, but were dysfunctional during environmental shifts. Individuals who had benefited from the prior success of the firm were able to block initiatives, while external stimuli that could move management to action, such as poor performance, were not forthcoming until 1980. As management and board members changed during the 1970s, however, the culture also changed, so that management became more receptive to new ideas. Despite the best efforts of individuals who saw the need for change, the culture constrained the firm and kept its managers from deciding on change until serious conditions were present. The culture of ICI, which had benefited the firm during its first 50 years, kept it from adapting in the late 1970s.

As an example of how culture complements more formal processes, consider the information-sharing needs in major global consulting firms, such as McKinsey. Consulting firms create value for clients through their stock of expertise, high-quality professional staff, and proprietary intellectual assets. The continued success of these firms and the development of new business opportunities thus depend on the continued maintenance, replenishment, and upgrading of knowledge and skill. This is not easy, however, because at any time the great bulk of a consulting firm's professional staff is serving clients in situations that are heavily context dependent and specific to those clients. Successful consulting firms use these specific projects not as drains on knowledge, but as opportunities to generate new knowledge. That is, consultants learn from their colleagues. Given the complexity of these firms' operations, any single formal database approach to knowledge management will be inadequate. Firms incorporate knowledge management issues into how they design their firm structures and how they organize the positions and careers of their consultants. Many firms use a variety of matrix structures, often involving three or more dimensions, to reflect client, disciplinary, and even geographic areas of emphasis.

Consulting firms complement these structural approaches through culture, training, and periodic review. For example, McKinsey consultants are given incentives to both generate and distribute knowledge; consultants are rewarded for the number of position papers accepted into their internal system and the number of times these papers are accessed within the systems. Furthermore, McKinsey consultants are encouraged to actively respond to requests for assistance from other teams throughout the firm, with an expectation that requests for assistance receive quality and timely responses. This knowledge sharing is part of the firm's culture, and assistance is provided to projects when requested and where possible from those in a position to help anywhere in the world.[31]

Communication norms are important parts of knowledge management not only for management consulting firms but also for firms whose activities are distributed geographically and for whom knowledge sharing is critical to the accomplishment of the firm's mission—what Catherine Cramton calls "the mutual knowledge problem." These include software development firms, investment banks, or other professional service firms with national and international clients, as are common in law, real estate, or public relations.[32]

Culture Facilitates Cooperation and Reduces Bargaining Costs

Gary Miller argues that culture mitigates the detrimental effects of power dynamics within firms by creating "mutually reinforcing" norms.[33] These norms permit mutually beneficial cooperative activities to emerge that would not be likely among self-interested actors outside the organization. Miller builds on the work of David Kreps, who examines the problems of securing cooperative outcomes in repeated games. Both Miller and Kreps are interested in the implications of a result called the *folk theorem*.

The folk theorem concerns the possibilities for achieving an equilibrium result in repeated play of games, such as the prisoners' dilemma (discussed in earlier chapters). Its general result is that multiple equilibria are possible in infinitely repeated games. Some can be conflictual, combining expectations of opportunistic behavior with threats of strong retaliation if the other player responds inappropriately. The folk theorem implies that it may not be possible to arrive with certainty at a cooperative organizational arrangement—cooperation is only one of many possible arrangements. Even if cooperation was possible, the costs of reaching it, in terms of the bargaining costs involved in choosing one arrangement over others, are likely to be high.

Miller argues that attempts to solve organization problems through contracts, incentives, and formal controls will entail large influence costs, as the individuals involved expend much time and effort to arrive at an organizational solution that provides them with the greatest benefits. To the time and effort involved in finding an organizational solution must be added the further costs of organizing that result from conditions in the firm that posed problems of asset specificity or that raise the costs of monitoring and measurement for any solution that is reached. The problem with hierarchical organization is that, although it mitigates transactions costs associated with market coordination of economic activity, it creates dilemmas of its own that can be significant, depending on the technology and business environment of the firm.

For example, just because a supplier to a firm has been internalized through backwards vertical integration does not mean that problems involved in working with the supplier have gone away. Managers in the new subsidiary can still withhold information from managers in other units, fail to fulfill commitments, and take advantage of the commitments made by other units. The ways in which the parent firm addresses these issues can be more or less effective, but it is unlikely that internal management and governance arrangements will be sufficiently complete to eliminate these problems in firms possessing any significant degree of complexity. Miller's point is that these dilemmas cannot be resolved by recourse to formal governance mechanisms or by increased controls over employees. He argues that any hierarchical organization will have serious principal–agent problems built into its structure.

Most real organizations arrive at some acceptable organizational arrangements, despite these problems. They do so by supplementing formal structures and controls with informal norms and social conventions, which provide a focus for actors around which a consensus can form. This set of norms and conventions is the organization's culture. Echoing David Kreps, Miller states that corporate culture is "the means by which a principle [of group decision making] is communicated to hierarchical inferiors." It says "how things are done and how they are meant to be done" in the firm. Miller argues that a firm's culture resolves these problems if its norms stress cooperation and not conflict. A cooperative culture modifies individual expectations and preferences and allows actors to expect cooperation from others. These mutually reinforcing values and norms allow firms to reach solutions to agency problems that would not be possible in markets.

Miller also recognizes the difficulties managers encounter in intentionally influencing a firm's culture. On the one hand, managers can exercise leadership that fosters cooperation rather than conflict among employees. On the other hand, a cooperative culture is also likely to be fragile, so that attempts to modify it to gain advantage could backfire and result in employees becoming more uncooperative. Cultivating and using power and influence may be more feasible for managers than cultivating culture, even though a cooperative culture may be more desirable.

Culture, Inertia, and Performance

The values of a firm's culture must be consonant with the values required by its strategic choices. Poor fit between culture and strategy can develop for several reasons. For example, start-up high-tech companies often have a culture that rewards creativity and risk taking. But initial success and resulting growth can increase formality and bureaucracy and discourage further innovation. One example of this is Clay Christensen's Innovator's Dilemma, which we described in Chapter 11. According to the Innovator's Dilemma, the success and subsequent commitments of firms pursuing a given technology become resistant to change in the face of disruptive technologies.

Conversely, a cultural misfit could occur when a firm's culture stresses routines, efficiency, and stability, while the firm's environment changes in ways requiring innovative, entrepreneurial, and flexible responses. This requires the firm to shift from a cost-based strategy to one of differentiation. An example of this situation can be seen with the firm of James Hardie, the world leader in the manufacture of fiber cement products for construction sectors. The firm has over $1.2 billion in annual sales and serves markets in the United States, Canada, Europe, Australia, New Zealand, and the Philippines. The firm's current strategy and culture are based on significant research and development in high levels of product differentiation. The strategy developed out of a corporate crisis in the 1980s when the firm's product lines were asbestos based and significant product liabilities became apparent. The firm was forced to innovate out of its traditional product lines and into new ones. This in turn required a significant shift in strategy and a consequent change in the corporate culture.

Cultural conflicts can also occur if a firm pursuing a given strategy acquires or merges with a firm committed to a different strategy. This is the well-known "culture clash" problem of merger integration.[34] This problem does not always arise right away, because communications and social interactions tend to remain focused within pre-merger boundaries up to three years post-merger.[35] These interactions are likely to increase where there are task interdependencies among the merging business units. Ironically, such interdependencies may present the best opportunities for achieving scale economies or avoiding coordination and holdup problems, even as they present the greatest opportunities for culture clashes. The persistence of cultural patterns within business units also appears to follow in reverse with spinoffs; a business unit can retain the culture of its former parent firm for many years. This appears to be especially the case if the former parent firm maintains an ownership stake or board membership on the unit that was spun off.[36]

When the environment changes and firms must adapt to survive, a culture that was once a source of competitive advantage can impair performance. In an unfavorable environment, an unmanageable culture can become a barrier to change. Executives with long tenure may have learned their jobs during prosperous times and thus be poorly equipped to handle change. Internal politics, if not controlled, may allow powerful managers to block change. The terms of managers and directors, the rules by which they are chosen, and the procedures by which they operate may be designed conservatively to frustrate rather than permit change, such as through the use of staggered terms of office on the board of directors.

A Word of Caution about Culture

It is conventional wisdom that a good corporate culture is essential for good performance. Indeed, culture and performance are often correlated. Just ask any professional sports team. A winning team always seems to display more camaraderie and energy than a losing team. But correlation does not imply causality, and it may be that success breeds a thriving culture rather than the other way around. To take an example that is more pertinent to business strategy, consider the case of one-time corporate icon IBM. Until it experienced problems in the late 1980s, IBM was thought to have a strong culture of customer service, employee development, and demanding professional standards. However, IBM's history of persistently high earnings and market leadership, as well as its strong competitive practices, may have also provided sufficient resources to foster an environment in which a strong culture could develop. It is unclear whether IBM's culture caused its high performance or vice versa. Whether a good culture is essential for good performance versus whether the two are merely correlates remains largely unresolved.

EXTERNAL CONTEXT, INSTITUTIONS, AND STRATEGIES

Once managers transact with stakeholders outside of the firm, their formal authority can no longer be used to resolve disputes. Many business-to-business relationships are governed by contracts. Many other relationships between trading partners, and nearly all relationships among competitors, are guided by the "invisible hand" of the market. Market-based interactions often are less freewheeling than one might expect. All firms are subject to regulatory oversight for environmental concerns, employment activities, new product development and testing, and potential anticompetitive interactions with competitors. Firms are subject to persistent power and dependence relationships with their trading partners. Managers at competing firms often acknowledge valuable industry norms and traditions, resulting in resistance to change on such matters as the adoption of new technologies and changes in work practices. The behavior of top managers in an industry sometimes appears oriented more toward winning peer approval and respect for themselves and their firms than toward maximizing shareholder wealth.

Sociologists study these aspects of firm behavior by focusing on *institutions*, which are relatively stable organizational arrangements, often possessing a distinct identity within the broader social context, that help bring order to sets of economic transactions. Institutions can involve the formal regulation of firms, whether by government agencies or other nongovernmental regulatory organizations. They can also be less formal and involve ongoing power–dependence relationships between firms that come to be taken for granted. Finally, similar to how we discussed a firm's culture earlier in this chapter, institutional arrangements may embody general patterns of values, beliefs, and behavioral norms that motivate and stabilize affected firms.[37]

Firms not only react to the demands of the external environment; firms sometimes influence their external environment to their advantage. Large and successful firms such as Google, Hyundai, and Tata may be able to influence regulation, drive industry innovation, discipline their buyers and suppliers, and even modify industry culture on their own terms. Smaller firms, often in conjunction with competitors and media organizations, may jointly lobby regulators and cooperate with government agencies to bring about favorable regulatory or environmental changes or oppose the actions of strong competitors. In many U.S. communities, for example, local retailers have successfully lobbied their legislators to block the expansion of Wal-Mart and other superstores.

Institutions and Regulation

Government regulation imposes rules on firms and enforces them by imposing penalties for noncompliance. A variety of quasi-public and professional groups, such as professional and trade associations, may also set rules for membership. When those professional groups have public legitimacy, these rules are as binding as government regulations. For example, health insurers will not reimburse hospitals unless they are accredited by the private Joint Commission on the Accreditation of Healthcare Organizations (JCAHO). The coercive side of rules and regulations must generally be minor, however, since rules based largely on the threat of force are unlikely to be widely accepted and valued, and monitoring and enforcement are costly. Indeed, JCAHO accreditation requirements are fairly unrestrictive, and few hospitals are ever put on "probation," let alone lose accreditation. Regulations must also be seen as legitimate to be effective. They constitute the "rules of the game" that provide a common basis for all participants in an industry.[38]

Regulatory activity has a huge influence on the strategic behavior of firms. The Sherman and Clayton Acts in the United States, and similar laws in the Treaty on the Functioning of the European Union, limit the size and scope of firms. There are laws governing how firms share information and whether they can "steal" information, for example, by hiring key employees from competitors. Interlocking corporate directorships are generally illegal in the United States and Europe but allowed in Asia. Tax regulations can alter the course of whole sets of corporate activities, ranging from charitable donations to the securing of advice on corporate control transactions. In certain industries, such as commercial aviation, regulations of the U.S. Department of Homeland Security have greatly increased the costs of doing business for all competitors while eliminating the competitive value of some capabilities (rapid gate turnaround) that some airlines, such as Southwest, had developed since the industry was deregulated in 1978.

Regulation imposes costs on firms. These include the direct costs of compliance, the increased business costs due to noncompliance (for example, the costs of borrowing with a poor rating from a rating agency), the costs of strategic options that must be forgone because of regulations, the higher prices for goods that consumers pay, along with other potential distortions to a market that may result from the imperfections of a given regulatory regime. If a firm, often jointly with others, pursues what David Baron calls a "nonmarket" strategy that attempts to shape legislation through lobbying, then the costs of such a strategy must also be considered.[39] Such a strategy can be very successful, at least for a time, but it is also expensive and risky.

Some firms can gain a strategic advantage from regulation. Patents grant inventors up to 20 years exclusivity in which they may enjoy monopoly profits. Licensure laws restrict entry into professions. Governments subsidize some technologies while imposing regulatory costs on others. For example, farmers in the United States benefit from rules requiring ethanol in gasoline, while natural gas developers face steep environmental hurdles. These rules can be explained by simple political economy. Powerful incumbents may find that government regulators are receptive to their campaign contributions, while potential entrants are unable to assure the same level of support. Industry-specific regulatory agencies may actually protect incumbents and come to associate with their economic interests. In times of significant change, however, such as from technological innovations or increased global competition, protective regulations are more likely to impede the ability of incumbents to adapt. The strategic implications of regulations for firms are complicated by the fact that regulatory organizations are seldom neutral third parties but instead are pursuing their own strategies, using their regulatory power to do so.

Interfirm Resource Dependence Relationships

Firms develop relationships with other firms and organizations in their environment, whether competitors, buyers, suppliers, complementors, or nonbusiness organizations. Just as individuals can develop power/dependence relationships with other individuals, firms can develop power/dependence relationships with other firms. Asymmetries in information, resources, capabilities, and other factors often characterize these relationships and lead to the development of these relationships. For example, an importing firm can become dependent on its supplier, especially if the imported goods are of critical importance and not otherwise available.

The concept of power/dependence relationships between firms is closely related to the holdup problem that we discussed in Chapter 3, and the solutions are similar as well. Firms can reduce their dependence on trading partners through vertical integration, long-term contracting, or joint ventures and alliances. Several studies have documented such effects. Jeffrey Pfeffer documented how asymmetric power relations between buyers and sellers were associated with the motivation for vertical mergers.

Menachem Brenner and Zur Shapira found that asymmetric trading was positively associated with vertical mergers, while mutual trading was inversely associated. Sydney Finkelstein replicated Pfeffer's study, but only weakly, showing that, although resource dependence contributes to our understanding of vertical mergers, it is not the principal explanation.[40]

The discussion thus far centers on bilateral power/dependence relationships. In some situations, many firms become dependent on a key player in the vertical chain. For example, in developing economies, a shortage of capital along with profound market imperfections may discourage foreign investment. In these situations, we often see the emergence of business groups centered on either a trading family with a strong name or a large financial institution. These groups serve as intermediary structures between governments and markets, and are common in Japan, Korea, India, and other Asian nations. More recently, multinational firms have adopted approaches similar to those of business groups in their strategies for emerging markets. Tarun Khanna and Krishna Palepu develop this approach in terms of institutional voids, by which they refer to the absence of important market intermediaries that provide market participants with the requisite information, contract enforcement, and related services needed to consummate their transactions.[41] Strategies in these markets require firms, either individually or collectively, to address institutional voids, in effect doing some of the work expected of government in providing infrastructure, such as assuming an intermediary role in a market. Failing this, firms in emerging markets need to determine how to adapt their business models to work around institutional voids and ensure that they can do business effectively. If adaptations are not possible, then firms must either postpone their entry to these markets or consider exiting them if they are already competing there.

Important industry resources can be tangible, such as money and raw materials, or intangible, such as status and reputation. A firm with a strong and positive reputation or high status can more easily establish a presence with customers, negotiate with suppliers, and secure cooperation within the vertical chain. Smaller and less established firms will want to associate with high-status firms to benefit from their superior standing and higher status. This interaction can provide a basis for associations among firms. For example, Joel Podolny studied the groupings that arose among investment banks around the issuance of new securities, based on evidence from "tombstone" announcements for a sample of financial transactions.[42] Tombstone notices are plain advertisements printed in black and white that inform investors of the date when a security issue will become available, how many securities are being offered in the issue, and the names of the underwriters that have undersigned the securities. The Securities and Exchange Commission regulates what information can be included in these announcements. The lead firms in an issue, along with other participating high-status firms, are listed prominently on these notices, and the placement of names on them is a matter of negotiation for the principal firms. The additional firms participating in an issue are listed on the announcement below the lead firms. The role of a bank in a given deal, and its compensation from the deal, were associated with its position in the status ordering suggested by the announcement.

There are many ways that a firm's reputation can suffer. A product may fail or be recalled for safety reasons, such as Merck's Vioxx drug. Disasters, both natural and man-made, can strike, such as Hurricane Katrina or the 2010 BP Deepwater Horizon oil spill in the Gulf of Mexico. While Hurricane Katrina clearly damaged the reputations of New Orleans and FEMA and BP is a clear loser from the spill, firms such as Wal-Mart, Home Depot, and Lowe's actually saw their reputations enhanced as a result of Katrina. This is because they could use their local knowledge about supply chains and infrastructure to provide emergency relief and reopen stores ahead of FEMA. Subsequent FEMA planning has come to include these retailers. Firms could also become tainted by the involvement of top managers in major scandals, such as the 2011 scandal over phone hacking and bribery involving the now defunct *News of the World* and other media businesses owned by News Corporation and its controversial owner, Rupert Murdoch.[43]

EXAMPLE 14.5 SETTING THE STANDARDS FOR ESG

Companies all around the globe have felt increasing pressure to assess and report on the environmental, social, and governance (ESG) impacts of their businesses. Investors have demanded more disclosure of firm performance in these areas (referred to as "sustainability reporting"), more standardization of measurements of performance, and more evidence that ESG concerns are integrated with corporate strategy. For investors it's a matter of evaluating the risks associated with their portfolios. For companies that develop data sources and measurement tools, it is a big business with lots of competition.

When the Norwegian government pension fund added an "extra layer of ESG information" to its investment criteria[44] it chose to have data supplied by Zurich-based ECOFACT, a global consulting firm with expertise in translating "non-traditional risks into relevant analyses and practical strategies for business."[45] Using a variety of media sources to identify companies that may be facing issues related to the environment, government regulation, or their workforce, ECOFACT provides a kind of early warning signal on impending risks. Charlotte Mansson of ECOFACT said, "We find it's very important to look at the live picture—quite often you will find a discrepancy between a nice CSR [corporate social responsibility] report and what's going on on [sic] the ground" Mansson added, "Our clients want to know if there are any environmental, social or reputational risks attached to the companies they invest in."[46]

Peter Ohnemus, chief executive of rival firm Asset4 (also based in Switzerland), emphasizes that the strength of his firm's analysis is in the framework it provides so that investors can make better comparisons, and therefore make better decisions, particularly important after the global financial crisis of 2008. According to Ohnemus, after the crisis, "people are saying they need standardization. [sic]"[47]

ESG data has become easier to obtain, as CSR reporting has become more common. Firms have found increased transparency is needed in order to attract investors. According to the 2009 International Survey of Corporate Responsibility Reporting from KPMG (another Swiss consulting firm which also provides audit and tax services), more than half of Global Fortune 250 corporations issue performance reports.

These firms are just a few of the hundreds of signatories to the United Nations Principles for Responsible Investment (UNPRI). Put forward in April of 2006 by then UN Secretary General Kofi Annan, they are "a framework for achieving better long-term investment returns, and more sustainable markets" and "a path for integrating environmental, social and governance criteria into investment analysis and ownership practices." If implemented, he stated," they have tremendous potential to more closely align investment practices with the goals of the United Nations, thereby contributing to a more stable and inclusive global economy."[48]

The six principles of the UNPRI are:

1. We will incorporate ESG issues into investment analysis and decision-making processes.

2. We will be active owners and incorporate ESG issues into our ownership policies and practices.
3. We will seek appropriate disclosure on ESG issues by the entities in which we invest.
4. We will promote acceptance and implementation of the Principles within the investment industry.
5. We will work together to enhance our effectiveness in implementing the Principles.
6. We will each report on our activities and progress towards implementing the Principles.

Estimates are that anywhere from $12 to $15 trillion of assets (somewhere near 15% of monies in global capital markets) are being managed by institutions that have signed the UNPRI.

Individual countries have stepped up their efforts as well. The government of the UK passed a revision of the Companies Act and the Accounts Modernization Directive which mandates ESG reporting by corporations, and the U.S. Securities and Exchange Commission (SEC) requires firms to disclose their environmental impacts, although social impacts have not yet been addressed; this is also true of most corporations in Asian countries.

Investors looking for growth opportunities have increasingly looked to emerging markets and this has led to increased ESG disclosure by corporations in those markets. According to a report issued by the independent research organization EIRIS better ESG disclosure would likely result in increased investment. As reported by SocialFunds.com, EIRIS found that "An impressive 70% of respondents reported that lack of good ESG disclosure hampered their efforts to increase their investments in emerging markets."[49]

The report indicated that Brazil is ahead of other emerging-market nations in increasing ESG disclosure. Investors surveyed attributed this to the ability of the Brazilian government to create a more transparent economy. This is linked to the presence of local ESG investment research activity in Brazil, which provides vital information to potential investors from the developed world.[50]

For the firms that provide investors with the data and the analysis, the challenge is to continue to innovate in formulating benchmarks that will be reliable indicators of performance.

Industry Logics: Beliefs, Values, and Behavioral Norms

As firms in an industry or sector interact over time, they tend to develop shared conceptions about the nature of the business, how they serve customer needs, the most effective ways to conduct their operations, and other matters. The extent to which these common beliefs develop will be influenced by the stability of the industry's environment and its relationships to other industries. Sectors with long and fairly continuous histories (for example, higher education) will develop stronger sets of common beliefs than sectors subject to continual regulatory and technological change or constant combination with other sectors (for example, entertainment). Out of these common beliefs come common ideas and practices regarding what managers should do, how changes should occur, how business should be transacted, and what types of innovations are worthwhile. These interrelated beliefs, values, material practices, and norms of behavior that exist in an industry at any given time are referred to as *industry logics.*

Paradoxically, to the extent that they are commonly held in stable contexts, industry logics have relatively little strategic importance since they concern what firms take for granted. If most firms share a common logic, then that logic does not provide a basis for competition advantage among the firms but is more of an implied requirement for reaching consensus performance expectations. Competitive advantage must come on some other dimension. Given the dynamic nature of markets, it is common for some firms not to share the industry logic. Fairly continual changes, even if small, in competitive dynamics, technologies, and regulations can lead to situations in which competitors see alternative logics as plausible. Alternative logics can also stem from the entry of foreign firms into an industry or the experience of an industry incumbent in a foreign market. There may be strategic advantage to be had in such situations, and the innovators and entrepreneurs present in many industries are those that are pursuing alternative logics.

In start-up industries, all of the logics are alternative logics, at least until a dominant logic is established. This was the case with the rise of various Internet-related industries in the late 1990s. Michael Lewis's account of serial entrepreneur Jim Clark captures this perfectly when he notes that Clark's strategy was to compete in a new industry aggressively until Microsoft showed up, after which time he would exit the industry, suggesting that Microsoft was going to impose a new dominant logic on the industry that the start-ups would not be able to match.[51]

At some point, the alternative logics may prove themselves to be successful and may even lead their adherents to aspire to industry dominance. If that shift in logic occurs, then other competitors may view it as necessary to adopt the new logic or risk being left behind. This is akin to the processes by which structural and process innovations diffuse through industries. For example, as M-form structures proved their efficiency for large industrial firms, they diffused throughout affected industries, neutralizing the competitive advantage in adopting the structure but making all firms adopters more efficient.

Changes in industry logics can stem from changes in industry regulations or conditions that force incumbents to dramatically alter their routines and develop new logics. The subprime mortgage lending business, and the related securitization of the resultant mortgages into more complex financial products such as leveraged buyout deals (LBOs) and collateralized debt obligations (CDOs), provides a good example of the rush to adopt new industry logics. When these products were originally introduced into the market, they were seen as a fringe product that respectable institutions would not sell. This attitude changed rapidly as the market for these products developed. Large and well-established institutions, such as Citigroup, came to compete aggressively by initiating these securities to distribute to structured security markets rather than initiating them to hold, as had been traditional industry practice. In November 2007, Citigroup's CEO Chuck Prince stepped down at a special board meeting in response to Citi's continuing billion dollar write-downs of assets as a result of losses in the escalating financial crisis that was engulfing the U.S. financial industry. Earlier that year, Prince had given an interview to the *Financial Times* in which he was asked about the large risks that were increasingly attached to these products. He responded with a quote that has become legendary:

"When the music stops, in terms of liquidity, things will be complicated.
But as long as the music is playing, you've got to get up and dance. We're still dancing."

Prince's clear implication was that Citigroup had to compete like everyone else, even though there was some awareness that the bubble was not sustainable and would prove damaging to his bank.[52]

Individuals attempting to develop their businesses in contexts that are strongly linked to broader societal currents of thought must balance needs for technical efficiency and professional management in their plans with pressures for institutional legitimacy that push them toward conformity with prevailing ways of doing business. Heather Haveman and Hayagreeva Rao came to this conclusion after studying the evolution of the thrift industry in California.[53] They examined the different forms of these early savings institutions, forerunners of S&Ls, that developed from the end of the nineteenth century through 1920, along with the parallel development of the institutional logics for thrifts. They found that these institutions developed in part as a result of experimentation and technical problem solving. They also developed under the influence of more macro pressures of large population growth and the development of values of bureaucracy and voluntary effort associated with Progressivism, in opposition to the less formal and more collective values characterizing early thrift plans.

It is sometimes unclear whether industry logics drive change in firm practices or whether they result from changes in practices. Put another way, the belief system in an industry can be a by-product of industry economics, or it can shape the industry economics. On the one hand, as industry participants experiment with new products and services, some prove more successful than others and come to be adopted. Once adopted, common beliefs develop around recognition of the benefits of the new products and services. At the same time, the industry or the broader society may have longstanding beliefs regarding such matters as the importance of research and development, opposition to government intervention, the value of individual initiatives, the fostering of family values, and the need for public education. The stronger these beliefs, the more possible it is that they may constrain experimentation in an industry or influence judgments made about products and services.

Chapter Summary

- Firms act within a broader social context that constrains how their strategic decisions are made and implemented. Culture and power relations within a firm comprise its internal social context, which influences how its managers make and implement decisions. The external social context of the firm includes its regulatory environment, its resource-dependence relationships, and its institutional domain.

- Power refers to an individual actor's ability to accomplish his or her goals by means of resources obtained through noncontractual exchange relationships. Particular positions within the firm permit the control of resources, information, and access and thus give their incumbents power and influence.

- Concentrating power within the firm can be helpful when there are high agency costs between managers and lower-level workers and when the firm's environment is stable. It is harmful when there are high agency costs between levels of upper management and when the firm's environment is unstable.

- Culture is a set of collectively held values, beliefs, and norms of behavior among members of a firm that influences individual employee preferences and behaviors on the job. It frees them from the need to renegotiate their tasks, reduces their costs of making decisions, and permits more specialization of effort.

- Culture controls the activities of employees on the basis of their attachment to the firm, rather than on the basis of individual incentives and monitoring. It mitigates power dynamics by creating "mutually reinforcing" norms that permit the emergence of mutually beneficial activities that would not be likely in the marketplace.

- When a firm's strategy "fits" with the demands of its environment, then its culture supports the direction of the firm and its policies, making it more efficient. When the environment changes, however, and requires firms to adapt to changes, culture is more likely to be inertial and lead to maladaptive firm behavior.

- Firm behavior in the external environment is governed by rules and regulations that are supported by accepted behavioral norms as well as more formal sanctions. Regulations provide a common basis for action by all participants in an industry or a sector.

- Regulation imposes costs on firms, including the direct costs of compliance, the indirect costs of forgone activities, and the costs of influencing regulators. Regulations may also strategically advantage regulated firms, by restricting entry and allowing incumbents to enjoy greater scale and reduced price competition.

- Firms develop power dependence relationships in their environment that are characterized by asymmetries in information, resources, capabilities, and other factors.

- Firms enter into cooperative relationships through long-term contracts, mergers and acquisitions, or strategic alliances and joint ventures, to manage these dependence relationships with other organizations and reduce environmental uncertainty.

- Analogous to corporate culture, the institutional environment of firms also involves shared beliefs about the world, shared values about what is important, and norms about appropriate and inappropriate behaviors. These interrelated beliefs, values, material practices, and norms of behavior that exist in an industry at any given time are referred to as institutional logics.

- It is sometimes possible to link changes in industry logics to specific external stimuli. In other industries, however, changes in industry logics occur as a result of multiple stimuli, without a clear external cause, and still significantly influence firms.

QUESTIONS

1. How does the resource-dependence view of power differ from the market-imperfections perspective of transactions-costs economics?

2. When might it not be reasonable to remedy a power differential with a critical buyer or supplier?

3. Power often accrues to individuals who are very effective in their jobs or to firms that enjoy sustained high performance. If this is so, how is power different from basic competence, efficiency, or performance?

4. Major professional schools are highly competitive, and most applicants do not get past the admissions process. That makes admissions a critical gatekeeper function for these schools. Given that, why don't admissions officers enjoy higher status and power among the faculty and staff of professional schools?

5. How might a favorable location in the interpersonal networks within a firm help an individual acquire and maintain additional bases of power?

6. How would you go about identifying the powerful people within your organization? What indicators would you look for? From what types of problems would these indicators suffer?

7. All firms operate within an institutional environment of some kind. How do the common beliefs, values, and norms of behavior that characterize the institutional environment affect the ability of firms to pursue sustainable strategies? Are institutional influences always constraining or can they ever promote competition and innovation?

8. Discuss the idea of structural holes in the context of competitive strategy. How can you link network advantage to value creation and competitive advantage for firms enjoying favorable positions?

9. While every firm has a culture, not all cultures are relevant for a decision maker or analyst. Under what conditions is it important to pay attention to culture? When is it less important to analyze the influence of culture?

10. Why is firm growth often antithetical to the maintenance of a stable corporate culture?

11. How can powerful individuals influence a firm's culture? Do "superstar" CEOs really exert the influence on firms that is claimed for them in the popular business press? How much does the leader matter in a firm with a long history and a strong corporate culture?

12. "The more manageable a firm's culture is, the less valuable it will be for the firm." Agree or disagree—and explain.

13. Visitors to China are sometimes puzzled by the combination of a very strong central government and a very competitive economic system. What is the connection between the strength of government agencies and the type of market activities that develop within that regulatory context?

ENDNOTES

[1] Arrow, K. J., *The Limits of Organization*, New York, Norton, 1974, pp. 25–26.

[2] Cohan, W., *House of Cards: A Tale of Hubris and Wretched Excess on Wall Street*, New York, Anchor Books, 2010, Chapter 18; Morris, C. R., *The Trillion Dollar Meltdown*, New York, Public Affairs, 2008.

[3] Piraino, T. A., "Reconciling Competition and Cooperation: A New Antitrust Stand for Joint Ventures," *William & Mary Law Review*, 871, 1993–1994, p. 35.

[4]Nasr, Vali, *Forces of Fortune: The Rise of the New Muslim Middle Class and What It Will Mean for the World*, New York, Free Press, 2009.

[5]Bjornskov, C., and N. Potrafke, "Politics and Privatization in Central and Eastern Europe: A Panel Data Analysis," *Economics of Transition*, 19(2), April 2011, pp. 201–230.

[6]Barnard, C., *The Functions of the Executive*, Cambridge, MA, Harvard University Press, 1938, pp. 167–171; Zhao, H., Wayne, S. J., Glibkowski, B. C., and J. Bravo, "The Impact of Psychological Contract Breach on Work-Related Outcomes: A Meta-Analysis," *Personnel Psychology*, 60(3), 2007, pp. 647–680.

[7]For the principles of social exchange, see Coleman, J. S., *Foundations of Social Theory*, Cambridge, MA, Belknap, 1990, Chapter 2.

[8]Bartlett, C. A., "McKinsey & Co., Managing Knowledge and Learning." HBS Case (396357), January 20, 2000.

[9]Pfeffer, J., *Managing with Power: Politics and Influence in Organizations*, Boston, Harvard Business School Press, 1992; Pfeffer, J., *Power in Organizations*, Marshfield, MA, Pitman, 1981.

[10]Gouldner, A. W., "*The Norm of Reciprocity*: A Preliminary Statement," *American Sociological Review*, 25, 1960, pp. 161–178.

[11]This is a variant of resource dependence referred to as the *strategic contingencies view* of power. See Hickson, D. J., Hinings, C. R., Lee, C. A., Schneck, R. E. and J. M. Pennings, "A Strategic Contingencies Theory of Intraorganizational Power," *Administrative Science Quarterly*, 16, 1971, pp. 216–229.

[12]The material for this example is taken from Neustadt's 1990 revision. See Neustadt, R. E., *Presidential Power and the Modern Presidents*, New York, Free Press, 1990. Also see Nelson, M., "Neustadt's 'Presidential Power' at 50," *Chronicle of Higher Education*, March 28, 2010.

[13]On the general point, see Lublin, J. S., "Chairman-CEO Split Gains Allies: Corporate Leaders Push for Firms to Improve Oversight by Separating Roles," *The Wall Street Journal*, March 30, 2009, http://online.wsj.com/article/SB123816562313557465.html. For the Avon announcement, see Boyle, M., "Avon to See New CEO, Separating Top Role with Jung as Chairman," *San Francisco Chronicle*, December 14, 2011.

[14]Burt, R. S., *Structural Holes: The Social Structure of Competition*, Cambridge, MA, Harvard University Press, 1992.

[15]Fernandez, R. M., and Gould, R. V., "A Dilemma of State Power: Brokerage and Influence in the National Health Policy Domain," *American Journal of Sociology*, 99, May 1994, pp. 1455–1491.

[16]This example was developed from material in Byrne, J. A., *The Whiz Kids*, New York, Currency Doubleday, 1993. The Whiz Kids were a group of academics and operations analysts, including Reith, Charles Thorton, Robert McNamara, and Arjay Miller, who distinguished themselves in operations analysis for the Army Air Force in World War II and later joined the management of Ford as a group in early 1946. Most rose to senior positions within Ford, and two, McNamara and Miller, rose to its presidency.

[17]Weber, M., *Economy and Society*, Vol. 1, Berkeley, University of California Press, 1978, pp. 212–226.

[18]Gertner, R., Powers, E., and D. Scharfstein, "Learning about Internal Capital Markets from Corporate Spin-offs," *Journal of Finance*, 57(6), December 2002, pp. 2479–2506.

[19]Rotemberg, J. J., "Power in Profit-Maximizing Organizations," *Journal of Economics and Management Strategy*, 2, 1993, pp. 165–198.

[20]Crystal, G., *In Search of Excess*, New York, Norton, 1991.

[21]Hallock, K., "Reciprocally Interlocking Boards of Directors and Executive Compensation," *Journal of Financial and Quantitative Analysis*, 32, 1997, pp. 331–341.

[22]Hermalin, B., and M. Weisbach, "Endogenously Chosen Boards of Directors and Their Monitoring of the CEO," *American Economic Review*, 88, 1998, pp. 96–118.

[23]Roberts, J., *The Modern Firm*. Oxford, Oxford University Press, 2004, p. 18.

[24]Kreps, D. M., "Corporate Culture and Economic Theory," in Alt, J., and K. Shepsle (eds.), *Perspectives on Positive Political Economy*, Cambridge, UK, Cambridge University, 1990.

[25]Roberts, *The Modern Firm*, pp. 41–44, 260–262.

[26]Feder, B. J. "The Little Project That Couldn't: Others Learn from a Failed Test in Worker Democracy," *The New York Times*, February 21, 1998; on ESOPs, see Kruse, D., Freeman, R., Blasi, J., Buchele, R., and A. Scharf, "Motivating Employee-Owners in ESOP Firms: Human Resource Policies and Company Performance," NBER Working Paper #10177, December 2003.

[27]Barney, J. B., "Organizational Culture: Can It Be a Source of Sustained Competitive Advantage?" *Academy of Management Review*, 11, 1986, pp. 656–665.

[28]Kumar, N., *India's Global Powerhouses*. Boston, Harvard Business Press, 2009, pp. 114–118.

[29]Kumar, *India's Global Powerhouses*, pp. 95–106.

[30]This example was developed from the following sources: Pettigrew, A. M., *The Awakening Giant: Continuity and Change at ICI*, Oxford, UK, Blackwell, 1985, Chapter 10, pp. 376–437; Pettigrew, A. M., "Examining Change in the Long-Term Context of Culture and Politics," Chapter 11 in Johannes M. Pennings and Associates, *Organizational Strategy and Change*, San Francisco, Jossey-Bass, 1985, pp. 269–318.

[31]Bartlett, C. A., "McKinsey & Co., Managing Knowledge and Learning." HBS Case (396357), January 20, 2000.

[32]Cramton, C. D., "The Mutual Knowledge Problem and Its Consequences for Dispersed Collaboration," *Organization Science*, 12(3), May–June 2001, pp. 346–371; Ghosh, T., Yates, J., and W. Orlikowski, "Using Communication Norms for Coordination: Evidence from a Distributed Team." *Proceedings of the International Conference on Information Systems*, 2004.

[33]Miller, G. J., *The Political Economy of Hierarchy*, Cambridge, UK, Cambridge University Press, 1992, Chapter 10; Kreps, D. M., *A Course in Microeconomic Theory*, Princeton, NJ, Princeton University Press, 1990, Chapter 14.

[34]For a discussion of cultural clash issues in acquisitions, see Haspeslagh, P. C., and D. B. Jemison, *Managing Acquisitions: Creating Value Through Corporate Renewal*, New York, Free Press, 1991. For a general discussion of these conflicting sets of values, see March, J. G., "Exploration and Exploitation in Organizational Learning," *Organizational Science*, 2, 1991, pp. 71–87.

[35]Allatta, J. T., and H. Singh, "Evolving Communication Patterns in Response to an Acquisition Event." *Strategic Management Journal*, 32(10), October 2011, pp. 1099–1118.

[36]Semadeni, M., and A. A. Cannella, "Examining the Performance Effects of Post Spin-Off Links to Parent Firms: Should the Apron Strings Be Cut?" *Strategic Management Journal*, 32(10), October 201, pp. 1083–1098.

[37]Scott, W. R., *Institutions and Organizations*, 2d ed., Thousand Oaks, CA, Sage, 2001.

[38]North, D. C., *Institutions, Institutional Change, and Economic Performance*, Cambridge, UK, Cambridge University Press, 1990.

[39]Baron, D. P., *Business and Its Environment*, 3d ed., New York, Prentice-Hall, 2000.

[40]Pfeffer, J., "Merger as a Response to Organizational Interdependence," *Administrative Science Quarterly*, 17, 1972, pp. 382–394; Brenner, M., and Z. Shapira, "Environmental Uncertainty as Determining Merger Activity," Chapter 3 in W. Goldberg (ed.), *Mergers*, New York, Nichols Publishing, 1983, pp. 51–65; Finkelstein, S., "Interindustry Merger Patterns and Resource Dependence: A Replication and Extension of Pfeffer (1972)," *Strategic Management Journal*, 18, 1997, pp. 787–810.

[41]Khanna, T., and K. G. Palepu, *Winning in Emerging Markets*, Boston, Harvard Business Press, 2010, pp. 13–50.

[42]Podolny, J., "A Status-based Model of Market Competition," *American Journal of Sociology*, 98, 1993, pp. 829–872.

[43]On Hurricane Katrina, see U.S. Government, National Commission on the DP Deepwater Horizon Oil Spill and Offshore Drilling. Report to the President. January 2011; Huffman, M. "Real Katrina Hero? Wal-Mart, Study Says," ConsumerAffairs.com, http://articles.moneycentral.msn.com/Insurance/InsureYourHome/RealKatrinaHeroWalMartStudySays.aspx. On the News Corporation scandal, see Sandle, P., "Quick Guide to the News Corp Hacking Scandal," *Reuters*, July 21. 2011.

[44]"Innovation key to staying ahead of ESG game," by Sophia Green, Financial Times, Monday July 6, 2009, p. 9.

[45]See the company website at http://www.ecofact.com/aboutus.htm

[46]Green, op.cit.

[47]Ibid.

[48]As quoted on http://www.hsbc.com/1/2/sustainability/reports/the-un-principles-forresponsible-investment-unpri

[49]"Investors Call for Improved ESG Disclosure by Companies in Emerging Markets," by Robert Kropp, Social Investment News, July 8, 2009. Accessed at http://www.socialfunds.com/news/article.cgi/2732.html

[50]Ibid.

[51]Lewis, M., *The New New Thing: A Silicon Valley Story*, New York, Penguin, 2001.

[52]Michiyo, N., and D. Wighton, "Citigroup Chief Stays Bullish on Buy-outs," *The Financial Times*, July 9, 2007. For an analysis of the more general change in financial industry logic, see Shivdasani, A., and Y. Wang, "Did Structured Credit Fuel the LBO Boom," Working Paper, Kenan-Flagler School. April 23, 2009.

[53]Haveman, H. A., and H. Rao, "Institutional and Organizational Coevolution in the Thrift Industry," *American Journal of Sociology*, 102, 1997, pp. 1606–1628.

GLOSSARY

360-degree peer review A review that occurs when an employee's supervisor, coworkers, and subordinates are all asked to provide information regarding that employee's performance

accommodated entry Entry is accommodated if structural entry barriers are low, and either (a) entry-deterring strategies will be ineffective, or (b) the cost to the incumbent of trying to deter entry exceeds the benefits it could gain from keeping the entrant out

activity-cost analysis A method of assigning costs that views the firm as a set of value-creating activities and then assigns costs accordingly. Templates such as Porter's value chain or the McKinsey Business System Framework can be used to identify the relevant activities for this analysis

agency costs Costs associated with slack effort by employees and the costs of administrative controls designed to deter slack effort

agency efficiency Agency efficiency refers to the extent to which the exchange of goods and services in the vertical chain has been organized to minimize coordination, agency, and transactions costs

agency theory A theory that examines the use of financial incentives to motivate workers

agent One to whom responsibility has been delegated

arm's-length market transaction A market transaction in which autonomous parties exchange goods or services with no formal agreement that the relationship will continue in the future

assignment problem Assurance that the right people do the right jobs with minimal duplication of effort

asymmetry requirement A requirement for entry barriers to be present. The incumbent must have incurred sunk costs that the entrant has not

attribute-rating method Technique for estimating benefit drivers directly from survey responses and then calculating overall benefits on the basis of attribute scores

autonomous work units Business units in which the unit managers control information about operating decisions, and in which the flow of information between units is minimal

backward integration An organizational arrangement in which a downstream firm owns the assets of an upstream firm, so that the downstream firm has control over both operating decisions

barriers to entry Factors that allow incumbent firms to earn positive economic profits by making it unprofitable for newcomers to enter the industry

benefit advantage One of the major strategies to achieve a competitive advantage. When pursuing a benefit advantage, firms seek to attain a higher perceived benefit while maintaining a cost that is comparable to competitors

benefit drivers Attributes of a product that form the basis on which a firm can differentiate itself, including: the physical characteristics of the product the quality and characteristics of the services or complementary goods the firm or its dealers offer for sale; characteristics associated with the sale or delivery of the good; characteristics that shape consumers' perceptions or expectations of the product's performance or its cost in use; and the subjective image of the product

blockaded entry A condition where the incumbent need not undertake any entry-deterring strategies to deter entry

bounded rationality Limits on the capacity of individuals to process information, deal with complexity, and pursue rational aims

broad coverage strategy A targeting strategy that is aimed at serving all segments in the market by offering a full line of related products

bundling A situation that occurs when a combination of goods or services is sold for less than what it would cost to buy the same items separately

buyer power The ability of individual customers to negotiate purchase prices that extract profits from sellers

capabilities Clusters of activities that a firm does especially well in comparison with other firms

causal ambiguity A term coined by Richard Rumelt to refer to situations in which the causes of a firm's ability to create more value than its competitors are obscure and only imperfectly understood

certainty equivalent (of a gamble) Payment which must be offered to a risk-averse individual to willingly accept the gamble

certification bias Any of a number of factors that may cause certifiers to issue biased quality ratings

certifiers Individuals or firms that certify the quality of products and services

Chaebol South Korean firms doing business through a complex web of institutional linkages, often with family connections

competitive advantage The ability of a firm to outperform its industry, that is, to earn a higher rate of profit than the industry norm

complementarities Synergies among organizational practices, whereby one practice is more effective when others are in place

complete contracts Stipulate each party's responsibilities and rights for each and every contingency that could conceivably arise during the transaction

complex hierarchy Involves multiple groups and multiple levels of groupings. Complex hierarchy arises from the need not just to organize individuals into groups, but to organize groups into larger groups

composite scores Aggregation of several individual scores into a single score. Composite scores often represent weighted averages of individual components

conjoint analysis A set of statistical tools used by market researchers to estimate the relative benefits of different product attributes

constant returns to scale Indicates that average costs remain unchanged with respect to output

consumer surplus The perceived benefit of a product per unit consumed minus the product's monetary price

contestable market A situation in which the threat of entry limits a monopolist's ability to raise prices

control The location of decision-making rights and rule-making authority within a hierarchy

cooperative pricing Refers to situations in which firms are able to sustain prices in excess of those that would arise in a noncooperative single-shot price or quantity-setting game

coordination The flow of information within an organization to facilitate subunit decisions that are consistent with each other and with organizational objectives

corporate culture A set of collectively held values, beliefs, and norms of behavior among members of a firm that influences individual employee preferences and behaviors

corporate governance The mechanism through which corporations and their managers are controlled by shareholders

cospecialized assets Assets that are more valuable when used together than when separated

cost advantage One of the major strategies to achieve a competitive advantage. When pursuing a cost advantage, firms seek to attain lower costs while maintaining a perceived benefit that is comparable to competitors

cost drivers The basic economic forces that cause costs to vary across different organizations

cost of capital The rate of return just sufficient to induce investors to provide financial capital to the firm

creative destruction When quiet periods in markets are punctuated by fundamental "shocks" or "discontinuities" that destroy old sources of advantage and replace them with new ones

credence goods Goods whose quality is difficult to ascertain even after purchase and use

cross-price elasticity of demand Given two products x and y, the cross-price elasticity of demand measures the percentage change in demand for good y that results from a 1 percent change in the price of good x

cube-square rule As one increases the volume of a vessel (e.g., a tank or a pipe) by a given proportion, the surface area increases by less than this proportion. A source of scale economies

customer specialization A targeting strategy in which the firm offers a variety of related products to a particular class of consumers

delegation Determination of which decisions will be made by individuals higher up in the corporate hierarchy and which will be left to individuals at lower levels

departmentalization The division of an organization into formal groupings

design attributes Attributes of a production process that need to relate to each other in a precise fashion

deterred entry Occurs when an incumbent can keep an entrant out by employing an entry-deterring strategy

differentiation advantage   One of the major strategies to achieve competitive advantage. When pursuing a differentiation advantage, firms seek to offer a higher perceived benefit while maintaining costs that are comparable to competitors

direct competitor   When firms are direct competitors, the strategic choices of one directly affect the performance of the other

direct labor costs   The costs of labor that are physically traceable to the production of the finished goods

direct materials costs   The costs of all materials and components that can be physically traced to the finished goods

disclosure   The process of revealing information about product quality

diseconomies of scale   Indicates that average costs increase as output increases

disruptive technologies   Class of technologies that has higher B-C than their predecessors, but does so primarily through a combination of lower B and much lower C

division of labor   Refers to the specialization of productive activities, such as when a financial analyst specializes in startup biotech companies

dominant strategy   A strategy that is the best decision for the firm, no matter what decision its competitor makes

dynamic capabilities   Ability of a firm to maintain and adapt the capabilities that are the basis of its competitive advantage

dynamic efficiency   The achievement of long-term growth and technological improvement

early-mover advantages   Once a firm acquires a competitive advantage, the early-mover advantage increases the economic power of that advantage over time. Sources of early-mover advantages include: the learning curve, brand name reputation buyer uncertainty about product quality, and consumer switching costs

economic profit   A concept that represents the difference between the profits earned by investing resources in a particular activity, and the profits that could have been earned by investing the same resources in the most lucrative alternative activity

economies of scale   Indicates that average costs decrease as output increases

economies of scope   Cost savings that the firm achieves as it increases the variety of activities it performs, such as the variety of goods it produces

efficiency effect   Refers to the fact that the benefit to a firm from being a monopolist as compared with being one of two competitors in a duopoly is greater than the benefit to a firm from being a duopolist as compared with not being in the industry at all

efficiency wage   A wage payment made to an agent that exceeds his opportunity cost of working. The extra payment is made to discourage the agent from shirking

endogenous sunk costs   Sunk investments by incumbents that create barriers to entry

exclusive dealing   A practice whereby a retailer agrees to sell only the products made by one manufacturer

experience good   A product whose quality can be assessed only after the consumer has used it for a while

explicit incentive contract   Incentive contract that can be enforced by an outside third party such as a judge or an arbitrator

five-forces analysis   A method, developed by Michael Porter, which systematically and comprehensively applies economic tools to analyze an industry in depth. The five forces are internal rivalry, entry, substitute and complement products, supplier power, and buyer power

fixed costs   Costs that must be expended regardless of total output

focal point   A strategy so compelling that it would be natural for a firm to expect all others to adopt it

focus strategy   A targeting strategy that concentrates either on offering a single product or serving a single market segment or both

folk theorem   An idea that concerns the possibilities for achieving an equilibrium result in repeated play of games, such as the prisoner's dilemma. Its general result is that many Nash equilibria are possible in infinitely repeated games

forward integration   An organization arrangement in which an upstream firm owns the assets of a downstream firm, so that the upstream firm has control over both operating decisions

franchising   A business format franchise agreement allows one firm (referred to as the franchisee) to use the trade name and business plan of another firm (the franchisor) for a specified period of time

free-rider problem   Problem that affects teams. Because every team member receives only a fraction of the total benefit from his actions, every team member will elect not to undertake actions that would be in the best interests of the entire team

fundamental transformation   A situation that occurs after parties invest in relationship-specific assets, when their relationship changes from a "large numbers" to a "small numbers" bargaining situation

game theory   The branch of economics concerned with the analysis of optimal decision making when all decision makers are presumed to be rational, and each is attempting to anticipate the likely actions and reactions of its competitors

geographic specialization   A targeting strategy in which the firm offers a variety of related products within a narrowly defined geographic market

grim trigger strategy   A strategy that relies on the threat of an infinite price war to keep firms from undercutting their competitors' prices

hedonic pricing   Uses data about actual consumer purchases to determine the value of particular product attributes

Herfindahl index   The sum of the squared market shares of all the firms in a market

hidden action   Situations in which aspects of the agent's action that are important to the principal cannot be observed

hidden information   Situations in which aspects of the productive environment that are important to the principal cannot be observed

hierarchy of authority   An organizational arrangement in which one member of a group specializes in monitoring and coordinating the work of the other members

holdup problem   A problem that arises when a party in a contractual relationship exploits the other party's vulnerability due to relationship-specific assets. For example, a seller might attempt to exploit a buyer who is dependent on the seller by claiming that production costs have risen and demanding that the price be renegotiated upward

horizontal differentiation   Differences between products that increase perceived benefit for some consumers but decrease it for others

human capital theory   A theory, developed by Gary Becker, which suggests that workers might accept very low wages early in their careers if they receive on-the-job training that enhances their productivity and job opportunities later on

implicit incentive contract   Contract based on information that cannot be observed by courts or arbitrators

indifference curve   The set of price-quality combinations that yields the same consumer surplus to an individual

indirect competitor   When firms are indirect competitors, the strategic choices of one also affect the performance of the other, but only through the strategic choices of a third firm

indirect labor costs   Salaries of production workers whose efforts usually are not directly traceable to the finished good, including personnel, quality-control workers, and inspectors

influence costs   A concept, developed by Paul Milgrom and John Roberts, that denotes the costs of activities aimed at influencing the distribution of benefits inside an organization

informative signal   A signal is informative only if it is more profitable for the high-quality firm to offer the signal

innovator's dilemma   A problem that arises when innovative investments by incumbents cannibalize their successful business model while failure to innovate may invite entry

institutional logics   Interrelated beliefs, values, material practices, and norms of behavior that exist in an industry at any given time

internal capital markets   Used to describe how firms allocate financial and human resources to internal divisions and departments

internal rivalry   Competition for share by firms within a market

isolating mechanisms   A term coined by Richard Rumelt that refers to economic forces that limit the extent to which a competitive advantage can be duplicated or neutralized through the resource-creation activities of other firms

joint venture   A particular type of strategic alliance in which two or more firms create, and jointly own, a new independent organization

keiretsu   Japanese firms doing business through a complex web of institutional linkages

key success factors   The skills and assets a firm must possess to achieve profitability in a given market

learning curve   An idea that refers to the cost advantages that flow from accumulating experience and know-how

legitimate power   Formal authority one receives by occupying a high-ranking position

limit pricing   The practice whereby an incumbent firm can discourage entry by charging a low price before entry occurs

M-form   *See multidivisional structure*

macrodynamics   The evolution of overall market structure

make-or-buy decision   The decision of a firm whether to perform an upstream, downstream, or professional supporting activity itself or to purchase it from an independent firm

management by objective system System whereby an employee and a supervisor work together to construct a set of goals for the employee

manufacturing overhead All the costs associated with manufacturing other than direct labor and indirect materials

marginal cost Refers to the rate of change of total cost with respect to output

margin strategy Strategy by which a firm maintains price parity with its competitors and profits from its benefit or cost advantage primarily through high price-cost margins, rather than through a higher market share

market definition The process of identifying the market or markets in which a firm competes

market for corporate control An idea, first proposed by Henry Manne, which states that control of corporations is a valuable asset that exists independently of economies of scale and scope. If this is so, then a market for this control exists and operates such that the main purpose of a merger is to replace one management team with another

market segment A group of consumers within a broader market who possess a common set of characteristics

market structure The number and size distribution of the firms in a market

matrix organization An organizational form in which employees are subject to two or more sets of managers at once

mean reversion *See regression to the mean*

merchant coordinators Independent firms that specialize in linking suppliers, manufacturers, and retailers

merit rating system A system whereby employees are given numerical performance evaluation scores

microdynamics Unfolding of competition, over time, among a small number of firms

minimum efficient scale The smallest level of output at which economies of scale are exhausted

misread problem A problem that occurs when a firm either mistakenly believes a competitor is charging one price when it is really charging another or when it misunderstands the reasons for a competitor's pricing decision

monopolistic competition A theory of competition for markets in which there are many sellers and each seller is slightly differentiated from the rest

monopsonist A firm that faces little or no competition in one of its input markets

most favored customer clause A provision in a sales contract that promises a buyer that it will pay the lowest price the seller charges

multidivisional structure An organizational form that is comprised of a set of autonomous divisions led by a corporate headquarters office, assisted by a corporate staff that provides information about the internal and external business environment. Rather than organizing by function or by task, a multidivisional structure organizes by product line, related business units, or customer type

multitask principle Principle stating that when allocating effort among a variety of tasks, employees will tend to exert more effort toward those tasks that are rewarded

N-firm concentration ratio The combined market share of the N largest firms in a market

Nash equilibrium Indicates an outcome of a game where each player is doing the best it can, given the strategies of all of the other players

net present value (of an investment) The present value of the cash flows the investment generates minus the cost of the investment

network externality Refers to a situation where, when additional consumers join a "network" of users, they create a positive external benefit for consumers who are already part of the network

network structure An organizational form in which work groups may be organized by function, geography, or customer base, but where relationships between work groups are governed more by often-changing implicit and explicit requirements of common tasks than by the formal lines of authority that characterize other structures

niche strategy A targeting strategy in which the firm produces a single product for a single market segment

numbers-equivalent The number of equal-sized firms that can generate a given Herfindahl index in a market. The numbers-equivalent is also equivalent to the reciprocal of the Herfindahl index

oligopoly A market in which the actions of individual firms materially affect industry price levels

opportunity cost A concept which states that the economic cost of deploying resources in a particular activity is the value of the best foregone alternative use of those resources

option value The expected net present value that arises when a firm leaves itself with options that allow it to better tailor its decision making to the underlying circumstances it faces

organizational structure Describes how a firm uses a division of labor to organize tasks, specify how its staff performs tasks, and facilitate internal and external information flows. Structure also defines the nature of agency problems within the firm

overserve   A broad-coverage competitor overserves a customer group when it offers costly product attributes that customers in that group do not especially value

own-price elasticity of demand   The percentage change in a firm's sales that results from a 1 percent change in its own price

patent race   A term used to characterize the battle between firms to innovate first

path-dependence   A process shows path-dependence if past circumstances could exclude certain actions or outcomes future

pay-for-performance   Contract by which the value of the compensation depends on the measured performance of the employee

perceived benefit   The perceived gross benefit of a product minus the user cost of the product, purchasing costs, and transactions costs

percentage contribution margin   The ratio of profit per unit to revenue per unit on additional units sold

perfectly contestable market   A market in which a monopolist cannot raise price above competitive levels because of concern over possible entry

performance measure   Piece of information on which an incentive contract (explicit or implicit) can be based

performance standard   The output that a hard-working agent can be expected to produce

perpetuity   A level cash flow received each year forever

piece-rate contract   A contract that pays a fee for each unit of output

pooled interdependence   Exists when two or more positions are not directly dependent on each other, but are associated through their independent contributions to the success of the firm

predatory act   Entry-deterring strategies that work by reducing the profitability of rivals

predatory pricing   The practice of setting a price with the objective of driving new entrants or existing firms out of business

price elasticity of demand   The percentage change in quantity demanded brought about by a 1 percent change in price

principal   One who delegates responsibility to another, known as the agent

private information   A firm's *private information* is information that no one else knows. It may pertain to production know-how, product design, or consumer information

product performance characteristics   A product's performance characteristics describe what it does for consumers. Though highly subjective, listing product performance characteristics often clarifies whether products are substitutes

product specialization   A targeting strategy in which the firm concentrates on producing a single type of product for a variety of market segments

productivity effect   Used to evaluate the potential advantages of incumbency in the innovative process; assesses whether the incumbent is more productive at research

profit center   Autonomous groups within a firm whose managers are rewarded on the basis of a target profit goal

promotion tournament   Situation in which a set of employees competes to win a promotion

quality report card   A grade or list of grades used to compare quality to evaluate quality

quasi-rent   An amount equal to the difference between (a) the revenue a seller would actually receive if its deal with a buyer were consummated according to the original terms of the implicit or explicit contract, and (b) the revenue the seller must receive to be induced not to exit the relationship after it has made its relationship-specific investments

real option   A real option exists when a decision maker has the opportunity to tailor a decision to information that will be received in the future

regression analysis   A statistical technique for estimating how one or more factors affect some variable of interest

regression to the mean   A process shows regression to the mean if its shocks are not persistent over time

related acquisition   A purchase of one firm by another, where both firms are active in similar lines of business

relationship-specific asset   An investment made to support a given transaction

rent   An amount equal to the difference between the revenue a seller receives in a transaction and the minimum amount it must receive to make it worthwhile for it to enter into a relationship with the buyer

rent-seeking behavior   Costly activities intended to increase the chances of landing available profits

replacement effect   A phenomenon whereby, despite equal innovative capabilities, an entrant is willing to spend more to develop an innovation. The reasoning behind this phenomenon is that through innovation the entrant can potentially replace the monopolist in the industry; however, the monopolist can only "replace" itself

reservation price   The maximum monetary price the consumer is willing to pay for a unit of a product or service

residual rights of control   All rights of control that are not explicitly stipulated in a contract

resource dependence (view of power)   Theory in which individuals and firms seek to gain power by reducing their dependence on other actors, while increasing the dependence of other actors on them

resource-based theory of the firm   A framework used in strategy based on resource heterogeneity. It posits that for a competitive advantage to be sustainable, it must be underpinned by resource capabilities that are scarce and imperfectly mobile, which means that well-functioning markets for the resources and capabilities do not or cannot exist

resources   Firm-specific assets such as patents and trademarks, brand-name reputation, installed base, and organizational culture. Resources can directly affect the ability of a firm to create more value than other firms, and can also indirectly impact value-creation because they serve as the basis of the firm's capabilities

responsibility center   A self-contained group that focuses on other performance measures besides profit, such as cost, revenue, or investment goals

risk adjustment   The process of adjusting report card scores to account for differences across sellers in the products or services sold. Risk adjustment is often used in hospital and physician report cards

risk averse   Describes an agent who prefers a sure thing to a gamble of equal expected value

risk neutral   Describes an agent who is indifferent between a sure thing and a gamble of equal expected value

risk premium   An extra payment above and beyond the expected outcome of a gamble which must be offered to a risk-averse individual to willingly accept the gamble

risk-sharing contract   A contract that guarantees an agent some payment, but provides enough incentive so that the agent does not shirk

search goods   Goods whose quality is relatively easy to evaluate before purchase

selection   In the context of report cards, a process whereby sellers may practice selection by choosing not to sell to certain customers in order to boost their report card score

self-managed team   A collection of individuals, each member of which works with others to set and pursue some common set of objectives

sequential search   A search that occurs when consumers learn about the attributes of products one at a time. Consumers usually incur an additional cost with each additional search

share strategy   Strategy by which a firm exploits its benefit or cost advantage through a higher market share rather than through high price-cost margins

shirking   A practice that occurs when managers and workers knowingly do not act in the best interests of their employer

shopping problem   The problem faced by consumers attempting to determine the quality of a good or service

short run   The period of time in which the firm cannot alter key choices of interest (such as price or capacity)

SIC code   Standard Industrial Classification (SIC), as defined by the U.S. Bureau of the Census. SIC codes identify products and services by a seven-digit identifier, with each digit representing a finer degree of classification

signal   A message that conveys information about vertical positioning

simultaneous search   A search that occurs when consumers simultaneously learn about the attributes of several products

social exchange   A transfer between two or more parties of resources, or rights to control resources, that occurs outside the terms of a market context

soft commitment   A commitment made by a firm such that, no matter what its competitors do, the firm will behave less aggressively than if it had not made the commitment. Thus, in a Cournot game a soft commitment will cause the firm to produce relatively less output, while in a Bertrand game a soft commitment will induce the firm to charge a higher price than if it had not made the commitment

SSNIP criterion   According to the DOJ, an analyst has identified all of the competitors of a given firm if a merger among those firms would facilitate a *small but significant nontransitory increase in price*

stakeholders   Shareholders, employees, and others with a stake in the firm

static efficiency   The optimal allocation of society's resources at a given point in time

strategic alliance   An agreement between two or more firms to collaborate on a project or to share information or productive resources

strategic commitments   Decisions that have long-term impacts and that are difficult to reverse

strategic complements   Two or more products whose reaction functions are upward sloping with respect to the actions taken by one another

strategic intent   An idea, developed by Gary Hamel and C. K. Prahalad, describing fundamental focus of a firm's strategy that commits it well beyond its current resource profile

strategic substitutes   Two or more products whose reaction functions are downward sloping with respect to the actions taken by one another

structural hole   A relationship in a social network in which one actor is the critical link between individuals or entire groups. The presence of a structural hole allows the individual who can span the hole to use the control of information or resource flows to his or her own advantage

structure (of a market)   The number and characteristics of the firms that compete within a market

stuck in the middle   The idea—argued by Michael Porter—that firms which attempt to pursue both a cost advantage and differentiation advantage simultaneously will be ineffective, providing both a lower perceived benefit to consumers than those firms that pursued a differentiation advantage and incurring higher costs than those that pursued a cost advantage

subgame perfect Nash equilibrium   An outcome of a game where each player chooses an optimal action at each stage in the game that it might conceivably reach and believes that all other players will behave in the same way

sunk cost effect   A phenomenon whereby a profit-maximizing firm sticks with its current technology or product concept even though the profit-maximizing decision for a firm starting from scratch would be to choose a different technology or product concept

sunk costs   Costs that have already been incurred and cannot be recovered

supplier power   The ability of input suppliers to negotiate prices that extract profits from their customers

sustainable competitive advantage   A competitive advantage that persists despite efforts by competitors or potential entrants to duplicate or neutralize it

switching costs   Refers to costs incurred by buyers when they switch to a different supplier

tactical decisions   Decisions that are easily reversed and where impact persists only in the short run

tapered integration   A mixture of vertical integration and market exchange in which a manufacturer produces some quantity of an input itself and purchases the remaining portion from independent firms

targeting   Refers to the selection of segments that the firm will serve and the development of a product line strategy in light of those segments

task interdependence   Extent to which two or more positions depend on each other to do their own work

teaching to the test   Effort to improve the measured aspects of performance, possibly at the expense of unmeasured aspects. See also *multitask principle*

technical efficiency   The degree to which a firm produces as much as it can from a given combination of inputs. A broader interpretation is that technical efficiency indicates whether the firm is using the least-cost production process

termination-based incentives   Implicit contract in which incentives come from the threat by the employer to fire the employee if some easily measurable aspect of performance is below a preset standard

tertius gaudens   Providing a valued relationship between two unconnected parties (actors or groups of actors). The tertius is the "third who benefits," and the strategy involves spanning a structural hole and bargaining with the parties on either side for the most favorable terms

throughput   The movement of inputs and outputs through a production process

tit-for-tat strategy   A policy in which a firm is prepared to match whatever change in strategy a competitor makes

total cost function   Represents the relationship between total cost and output, assuming that the firm produces in the most efficient manner possible given its current technological capabilities

total quality management   A management philosophy which teaches that firms can lower their costs and maintain or increase quality by improving the efficiency of their production processes

tough commitment   A commitment made by a firm such that, no matter what its competitors do, the firm will behave more aggressively than if it had not made the commitment. Thus, in a Cournot game a tough commitment will cause the firm to produce relatively more output, while in a Bertrand game a tough commitment will induce the firm to charge a lower price than if it had not made the commitment

tournament   Competition among workers to outperform one another to earn rewards and move up the hierarchy of the firm. Arises when individuals are ranked relative to one another and when the hardest-working and most able workers are promoted

transactions costs   A concept, developed by Ronald Coase, which denotes the costs to using the market—such as costs of organizing and transacting exchanges—which can be eliminated by using the firm

U-form   *See unitary functional structure*

umbrella branding   The practice of offering a broad product line under a single brand name. A source of scope economies

underserve   A broad-coverage competitor underserves a customer group when it offers insufficient levels of product attributes that customers in the target set especially value

uniform delivered pricing   A single delivered price that a seller quotes for all buyers and in which the seller absorbs any freight charges itself

uniform FOB pricing   A price that a seller quotes for pickup at the seller's loading dock, and the buyer absorbs the freight charges for shipping from the seller's plant to the buyer's plant

unitary functional structure   An organizational form in which there is a single department responsible for each of the basic business functions within the firm. This structure is characterized by a division of labor that allows for specialization of the basic tasks that a business performs. Each department depends on direction from central headquarters and probably could not exist autonomously outside the firm except as contract vendors to a firm that independently secures the other functions

unraveling   A market process in which high-quality sellers disclose their quality, followed by medium-quality sellers, and so forth, until all sellers have disclosed

unrelated acquisition   A purchase of one firm by another, where the two firms are active in different lines of business

value-added analysis   The process of using market prices of finished and semifinished goods to estimate the incremental value-created by distinctive parts of the value chain

value chain   A concept, developed by Michael Porter, which describes the activities within firms and across firms that add value along the way to the ultimate transacted good or service

value-created   The difference between the value that resides in a finished good and the value that is sacrificed to produce the finished good

value net   The firm's "value net" which includes suppliers, distributors, and competitors whose interactions can enhance total industry profits, and the profits of each member of the net

variable costs   Costs, such as direct labor and commissions to salespeople, which increase as output increases

vertical chain   The process that begins with the acquisition of raw materials and ends with the distribution and sale of finished goods

vertical differentiation   Distinction of a product that makes it better than the products of competitors

vertically integrated firm   A hierarchical firm that performs many of the steps in the vertical chain itself

warranty   A promise to reimburse the consumer if a product fails

winner's curse   The firm that wins the bidding war for an input may be overly optimistic about its value. Unless it accounts for the possibility of overoptimism, the winning bidder may end up overpaying for the asset

zone of indifference   The set of issues over which a powerful individual usually prevails

Name Index

Abdelhak, Sherif, 142
Adams, W., 60n.13, 225n.10, 397n.11
Alchian, A., 441, 468n.3
Aldrich, L., 195n.13
Allatta, J. T., 499n.35
Alt, J., 130n.11, 499n.24
Amaran, M., 256n.12
Ambrose, S. E., 59n.8
Amihud, Y., 89, 97n.23
Anderson, E., 144, 161n.8
Anderson, J. C., 469n.18
Andrews, K., 1, 8n.2
Armour, Philip, 44
Armstrong, M., 130n.6
Arnold, Tom, 235
Aronson, Micky, 277
Arrow, K. J., 387, 398n.22, 470, 497n.1
Asch, D., 362n.17
Attia, Peter, 106
Auerbach, A., 161n.14
Avery, C., 89, 97n.21
Axelrod, R., 238, 256n.20

Bacon, N. T., 194n.12
Badia, E., 469n.31
Bain, J. S., 199, 224n.4, 224n.5, 225n.11
Baker, G., 426, 435n.29
Baker, W. E., 469n.19
Balmer, Steve, 403
Bandiera, O., 403, 434n.4
Barankay, I., 403, 434n.4
Barnard, C., 474, 498n.6
Barney, J. B., 397n.3, 397n.4, 483, 484, 499n.27
Baron, D. P., 452–453, 468n.10, 468n.15, 468n.16, 490, 499n.39
Barry, Rick, 278

Bartlett, C., 468n.9
Bartlett, C. A., 498n.8, 499n.31
Barton, D., 438, 468n.1
Baruch, Lev, 89
Baumgardner, J., 70, 96n.4
Baumol, W. J., 219, 225n.22
Bayes, M., 362n.11
Bazerman, M., 88, 97n.19
Beard, D., 397n.10
Becker, G., 106, 130n.9
Benkard, C. L., 97n.12
Benkard, Lanier, 80, 272, 288n.2
Berle, A., 402, 434n.3
Bertrand, J., 185, 195n.17, 196
Bertrand, M., 152, 161n.16
Besanko, D., 252, 257n.36, 452, 453, 468n.10, 468n.15, 468n.16
Bettis, R. A., 84, 97n.15
Bird, Larry, 279
Bjornskov, C., 498n.5
Blair, J., 248, 257n.32
Blasi, J., 499n.26
Bollinger, B., 347, 362n.10
Borenstein, S., 219, 225n.23
Bottazzi, G., 457, 469n.24
Botticelli, 59
Boyle, M., 498n.13
Brandenburger, Adam, 258, 259, 264–266
Branson, Richard, 374
Bravo, J., 498n.6
Brenner, M., 491, 499n.40
Bresnahan, T., 191, 195n.22
Brodie, John, 278
Brook, R., 352, 362n.17
Brown, Jennifer, 425, 436n.32
Bryant, Kobe, 279
Buchele, R., 499n.26
Buffett, Warren, 481

Bulow, J., 256n.5, 256n.8
Burrows, John, 41–43, 58
Burt, R. S., 478, 498n.14
Bush, George W., 343
Butkus, Dick, 278
Byrne, J. A., 479, 498n.16

Cannella, A. A., 499n.36
Capps, C., 167, 194n.2
Case, Stephen, 98
Caves, R., 438, 468n.1
Chamberlin, E. H., 177, 194n.10, 236, 256n.16
Chandler, A. D., 1, 8n.1, 49, 60n.10, 438, 461, 462, 468n.2, 469n.33, 480
Chandler, A. D., Jr., 60n.12
Chase, Andrew, 181
Chernew, M., 362n.16
Cherry, Andrew, 256n.19
Chevalier, J. C., 89, 97n.21, 356, 362n.21
Chizen, Bruce, 105
Christensen, C., 251, 386, 398n.20, 487
Christensen, Clayton M., 257n.34
Clark, Jim, 494
Coase, R., 118, 130n.21
Cochran, T. C., 59n.4, 59n.5
Cockburn, I., 307, 332n.14
Cohan, A., 497n.2
Coleman, J. S., 498n.7
Collins, J. C., 3, 8n.7
Congdon, Chris, 423
Constantinides, G. M., 97n.17
Cook, Wendell, 113, 130n.16
Cool, K., 397n.4
Cortada, J. W., 60n.12
Cortés, Hernán, 227

511

Subject Index

517

Kimberly Clark
KindyROO
Kirin
KLM
Kmart
Koc Holding
Kodak
Kohlberg Kravis
    Roberts
Kohls
Kolon Industries
Korn/Ferry
    International
Kraft
Kroger
Kubota

L2O
Land Rover
Lantech
Le Mosaiste
Lego Group
Leo Burnett
Lexicon
Lexus
LG
Lidl
Lincoln Electric
    Company
Little Sheep
Lloyd's of London
Loblaw
Lockheed
Lombard Sporting
    Goods
Lowes
Lufthansa
Lyle's Golden Syrup

Mahindra & Mahindra
Major League Baseball
Malt-O-Meal
Manchester United
Marlboro

Marmon Group
Martha Stewart
Maruchan
Mason's
Matsushita
Mattel
Maytag
McCormick
McCormick Harvesting
    Machine Company
McDonald's
McGraw Cellular
    Communications
MCI
McIlhenny
McKinsey & Company
Mega Bloks
Mercedes
Merck
Mercy Health Center
Merrill Lynch &
    Company
Metro
MF Global
MGM
Miami Heat
Michael Reese Hospital
Michelin Tires
Micron
Microsoft
Millenium
    Pharmaceuticals
Mitsubishi
Mitsui
Mittal Steel
Moody's
Morning Star Company
Motorola
MSNBC
MTV
Mylan Laboratories Inc
MySpace

Nabisco

Nan Ya Plastics
Napster
National
National Basketball
    Association
National Beef
National Board of Fire
    Underwriters
National Collegiate
    Athletic Association
National Football
    League
National Hockey
    League
Navistar
NEC Lenovo Japan
    Group
Neiman-Marcus
Netflix
New Jersey Nets
New York Jets
New York Knicks
New York Rangers
Newport Golf
News Corporation
Nike
Nine West
Nintendo
    Entertainment
    Systems
Nokia
Noma
Nordstrom
North Star
Northland Cranberries
Northwest Airlines
Northwestern
    Memorial Hospital
Novelis
Nucor
Nueva Rumasa

Oakland Raiders
Ocean Spray
OPEC

Open Table
Oppo Digital
Oracle
Orange
Orion
Panamco
Peapod
Peerless Industries
People's Express
Pepsi Bottling Group
Pepsi-Cola Company
PepsiAmericas
PepsiCo Asia, Middle
    East & Africa
PepsiCo Europe
Peugeot
Pfizer
Philadelphia Phillies
Philip Morris
Piggly Wiggly
Pittsburgh Brewing
    Company
Pixar Animation
    Studios
Pizza Hut
Polaroid
Porsche
POSCO
Power Barge
    Corporation
Pratt & Whitney
Pret-a-Manger
Printemps Department
    Stores
Procter & Gamble
Prudential
PSS

Qantas
Quaker Oats
Quanjude
Quiznos
Qwest